# LITERARY THEMES
## *for Students*

# LITERARY THEMES
## for Students

**Examining Diverse Literature to Understand and Compare Universal Themes**

## THE AMERICAN DREAM

### VOLUME 2

*Anne Marie Hacht, Editor*

*Foreword by Margaret Brantley*

GALE
CENGAGE Learning

Detroit • New York • San Francisco • New Haven, Conn • Waterville, Maine • London

## Literary Themes for Students: The American Dream

**Project Editor**
Anne Marie Hacht

**Editorial**
Ira Mark Milne

**Rights Acquisition and Management**
Robbie Mc Cord, Lista Person, Kelly Quin, Andrew Specht

**Manufacturing**
Rita Wimberley

**Imaging**
Lezlie Light and Robyn Young

**Product Design**
Pamela A. E. Galbreath and Jennifer Wahi

**Vendor Administration**
Civie Green

**Product Manager**
Meggin Condino

For permission to use material from this product, submit your request via Web at http://www.gale-edit.com/permissions, or you may download our Permissions Request form and submit your request by fax or mail to:

*Permissions Department*
Gale
27500 Drake Rd.
Farmington Hills, MI 48331-3535
Permissions Hotline:
248-699-8006 or 800-877-4253, ext. 8006
Fax: 248-699-8074 or 800-762-4058

Since this page cannot legibly accommodate all copyright notices, the acknowledgments constitute an extension of the copyright notice.

While every effort has been made to ensure the reliability of the information presented in this publication, Gale, Cengage Learning does not guarantee the accuracy of the data contained herein. Gale accepts no payment for listing; and inclusion in the publication of any organization, agency, institution, publication, service, or individual does not imply endorsement of the editors or publisher. Errors brought to the attention of the publisher and verified to the satisfaction of the publisher will be corrected in future editions.

### LIBRARY OF CONGRESS CATALOGING-IN-PUBLICATION DATA

Literary themes for students : the American dream : examining diverse literature to understand and compare universal themes / Anne Marie Hacht, editor ; foreword by Margaret Brantley.
    p. cm. – (Literary themes for students)
Includes bibliographical references and index.
ISBN-13: 978-1-4144-0433-2 (set : alk. paper)
ISBN-10: 1-4144-0433-6 (set : alk. paper)
ISBN-13: 978-1-4144-0285-7 (vol. 1 : alk. paper)
ISBN-10: 1-4144-0285-6 (vol. 1 : alk. paper)
[etc.]
    1. American literature–History and criticism. 2. American literature–Themes, motives.
3. National characteristics, American in literature. I. Hacht, Anne Marie.
    PS169.N35L58 2007
    810.9'358–dc22
                                              2007005602

**ISBN-13:**
978-1-4144-0433-2 (set)
978-1-4144-0285-7 (vol. 1)
978-1-4144-0286-4 (vol. 2)

**ISBN-10:**
1-144-0433-6 (set)
1-4144-0285-6 (vol. 1)
1-4144-0286-4 (vol. 2)

This title is also available as an e-book.
ISBN-13: 978-1-4144-2931-1
ISBN-10: 1-4144-2931-2
Contact your Gale sales representative for ordering information.

Printed in the United States of America
2 3 4 5 6 7 14 13 12 11 10 09 08

# *Table of Contents*

*Volume 1*

# *Foreword*

Each volume of *Literary Themes for Students* brings together dozens of renowned works of literature that share a specific theme. The theme for this volume of *Literary Themes for Students* is The American dream.

The settlement of the New World brought strange, exciting experiences and ideas for the people who were destined to call it "home." Unfamiliar civilizations, animals, plants, climates, and landscape became familiar quickly enough, but new ideas and ideals are still the hallmark of the New World, even six centuries after the first Europeans lay claim to it. Those ideas—of a new home, new opportunities, new freedoms, and a new life—are at the heart of the American dream. While the concept of the American dream is well known at home and around the world, the definition may be as varied as the individuals who attempt to define it. As the literature shows, all who pursue the American dream have aspirations; what they aspire to spans the breadth of human experiences.

If it is human nature to hope, dream, and progress, what, then makes the American dream peculiar to the United States? The promise of opportunity, equality, and dignity, in a land that rewards hard work and respects the individual give the dream its shape; the array of stories of triumph and success from people of every background give the American dream its power. The literature of the American dream serves to shape,

chronicle, and examine Americans' aspirations, both as persons and as a people. It is not one thing to all people, although that they aspire is one thing those people have in common. The difficulty of defining the dream is part of its strength and beauty. Walt Whitman captures the feeling of that vague yet vast power in his seminal poem, "Song of Myself":

> The past and present wilt—I have fill'd
>     them, emptied them,
> And proceed to fill my next fold of the
>     future.
>
> Listener up there! what have you to confide
>     to me?
> Look in my face while I snuff the sidle of
>     evening,
> (Talk honestly, no one else hears you, and I
>     stay only a minute longer.)
>
> Do I contradict myself?
> Very well then I contradict myself,
> (I am large, I contain multitudes.)
>
> *(Whitman, Walt, "Song of Myself," Leaves of Grass, Signet Classics, 1980, pp. 49–96; originally published in 1892.)*

Some of the selections in *Literary Themes for Students* are chronicles of the experiences of different Americans. Alvar Núñez Cabeza de Vaca's *Chronicle of the Narváez Expedition* introduced the New World and its possibilities to Europeans in the mid-1500s. His descriptions of the land's natural wealth inspired others to explore, settle, and make new lives as the first American dreamers. Native Americans, people all but exterminated by the Europeans who followed Cabeza de Vaca, found little voice for their experience with the American dream until the twentieth century, when chronicles like *Black Elk Speaks* (1932) emerged speak for those so long voiceless. Laura Ingalls Wilder's *Little House on the Prairie* (1935) tells of life as a white pioneer in the nineteenth century. Henry Roth's *Call it Sleep* (1934), was published about the same time as Black Elk's and Wilder's stories, and offers a third, completely different, perspective. While a work of fiction, Roth's novel is based on the author's own experiences as a young Jewish immigrant to New York in the early twentieth century and captures the feeling of the experience for a large segment of American dreamers.

Such chronicles are but a small part of the literature of the American dream. Literature has given the dream form, and continues to refine, reshape, and refresh it. Nonfiction, like John Winthrop's 1630 address "A Model of Christian Charity," Thomas Paine's revolutionary "Common Sense," Benjamin Franklin's *Autobiography,* and the Declaration of Independence helped the fledgling country establish its ideals and identity. Later nonfiction, like Emerson's "Self-Reliance" (1841) and President Kennedy's 1961 inaugural speech refreshed established ideals of the American dream and even introduced new tenets into the philosophy of Americanism. Fiction and poetry have also shaped the American dream for many, creating new examples and expressions of the individual pursuit of happiness. Whitman's "Song of Myself" written after the Civil War, boldly celebrates the individual— every individual—in a wholly original American style and voice. Jack Kerouac's masterpiece of modern disillusionment, *On the Road* (1957) served as the model for generations of Americans seeking their own version of the dream.

Perhaps literature's most important role is to examine ideologies as they exist in the world, expose their flaws, and explore higher ideals that might yet be reached. Writers may question society's values, as do Henry James in "Daisy Miller" (1878) and F. Scott Fitzgerald in *The Great Gatsby* (1925). The tone of a call for a national change in course may range from mocking, as with Stephen Colbert's 2006 speech at the White House Correspondents' Association Dinner, to outrage, as with John Steinbeck's *The Grapes of Wrath* (1939). Langston Hughes's *Montage of a Dream Deferred* (1951), Tomás Rivera 's . . . *And the Earth Did Not Devour Him* (1971), N. Scott Momaday's *House Made of Dawn* (1968), and Marie Lee's *Finding My Voice* (1992) bring the hopes and struggles well known within some American subcultures to the broad awareness of Americans in general. The works that prompt self-examination may be gentle and slightly melancholy, such as Robert Frost's "Mending Wall" (1915) and Thornton Wilder's *Our Town* (1938). Some writers try to shock their readers out of complacency with darker takes on the human condition, such as Arthur Miller in *Death of a Salesman* (1949) and John Updike in *Rabbit, Run* (1960).

The works explored in this volume represent the gamut of genres, tones, and reactions, but all prompt readers to re-examine their notion of the American dream. *Literary Themes for Students* cannot take the place of experiencing firsthand the books it presents. This overview of the topics, points-of-view, and critical interpretations is meant to guide readers who want to explore more on their own. By celebrating the variability and mutability of the American dream, it encourages all individuals—not just Americans—to define the dream for them selves, pursue their own goals, and aspire to creating a better life.

*Margaret Brantley*
*Brantley is a literature critic and a literary reference editor.*

# Introduction

## Purpose of the Book

The purpose of *Literary Themes for Students* *(LTfS)* is to provide readers with an overview of literary works that explore a specific theme. The volumes analyze poetry, plays, short stories, novels, and works of nonfiction that address the theme in some capacity, and the reader discovers how that theme has been treated in literature at different times in history and across diverse cultures. Volumes Five and Six, *Literary Themes: The American Dream in Literature*, include "classic" political and historical texts, as well as more contemporary accounts of race and prejudice and works by minority, international, and female writers.

These volumes begin with an overview essay that introduces the theme of race and prejudice in literature. This essay is followed by fourteen sub-essays, which break these themes down further into subthemes that correspond to recurring ideas in the literature of the American dream. Sub-essays examine particular titles that exemplify the subthemes and by treating them the volume can thus track how that subtheme has developed over time.

Each work is discussed in a separate entry. These entries include an introduction to the work and the work's author; a plot summary, to help readers understand the action and story of the work; an analysis of themes that relate to the subject of the American dream, to provide readers with a multifaceted look at the complexity of the aspirations, obstacles, and inspirations of American dreamers; and a section on important historical and cultural events that shaped the author and the work, as well as events in the real world (from the time of the author or another time in history) that affect the plot or characters in the work.

Additionally, readers are presented with a critical overview discussing how the work was initially received by critics and how the work is presently viewed. Accompanying the critical overview is an excerpt from a previously published critical essay discussing the work's relation to the theme of race and prejudice. For further analysis and enjoyment, an extended list of media adaptations is also included, as well as a list of poems, short stories, novels, plays, and works of nonfiction that further address the theme of race and prejudice, and thus students are encouraged to continue their study of this theme.

## Selection Criteria

The titles of each volume of *LTfS* were selected by surveying numerous sources on teaching literature and analyzing course curricula for a number of school districts. Our advisory board provided input, as did educators in various areas.

## *How Each Entry is Organized*

Each chapter focuses on the ways in which an entry relates to the theme of the American dream. Each entry heading includes the author's name, the title of the work being discussed, and the year it was published. The following sections are included in the discussion of each entry:

**Introduction:** a brief overview of the work being discussed. It provides information about the work's first appearance, any controversies surrounding its publication, its literary reputation, and general details about the work's connection to the theme of the American dream.

**Plot Summary:** a description of the events that occur in the work. For poems, some additional insight into the context and interpretation of the poem—and discussion of symbols and elements—is provided. The plot summary is broken down by subheadings, usually organized by chapter, section, or stanza.

**Themes:** a discussion of how the work approaches the issue of the American dream through various themes. Each theme is addressed under a separate subheading. Several of the major recurring themes are discussed at more length in individual sub-essays.

**Historical and Cultural Context:** a discussion of the historical and cultural events that appear in the work or that affected the writer while the work was being written. This can include large-scale events such as wars, social movements, and political decisions, as well as smaller-scale events such as cultural trends and literary movements. If the work is set during a different time period from that in which the author wrote it, historical and cultural events from both periods are included.

**Critical Overview:** a discussion of the work's general critical reputation, including how it was initially received by reviewers, critics, and the general public. Any controversy surrounding the work is treated in this section. For older works, this section also includes information on the ways that views of the work have changed over time.

**Criticism:** a previously published critical essay discussing how the work addresses the issues of race and/or prejudice. When no appropriate criticism could be found, *LTfS* commissioned essays that deal specifically with the work and are written for student audiences.

**Sources:** an alphabetical list of sources used in compiling the entry, including bibliographic information.

In addition, each entry includes the following sidebars, set apart from the rest of the text:

**Author Biography Sidebar:** a brief biography of the author, including how he or she was affected by or led to write about the American dream.

**Media Adaptations:** a list of film, television, and/or stage adaptations, audio versions, and other forms of media related to the work. Source information is included.

## *Other Features*

*LTfS* includes "We Contain Multitudes: The Literature of the American Dream" by Mo Brantley, a writer and editor of language arts reference books. This is a foreword about how the literature of the American dream can help contemporary readers appreciate the history, the varieties, the vagaries, and the universality of the many forms the American dream may take.

Each entry may have several illustrations, including photos of the author, depictions of key elements of the plot, stills from film adaptations, and/or historical photos of the people, places, or events discussed in the entry.

Fourteen sub-essays discuss various focuses of the literature of the American dream: in different time periods, including the colonial era, the nineteenth century, the twentieth century, and the modern day; for different populations of Americans, including African Americans; Asian Americans, Native Americans, Hispanic Americans; American Immigrants; as it relates to certain specific experiences, such as among frontiersmen, Southerners, feminists, foreigners and expatriates, and public figures. Each sub-essay addresses approximately a dozen works that deal directly with the subtheme, and discusses how treatment of that theme has changed over time.

A Media Adaptation list compiles more than seventy films, plays, television series, and other media that deal with the subject of the American dream. The adaptations are organized by subtheme for easy access.

The *What Do I Read Next?* section provides over one hundred plays, short stories, poems, novels, and nonfiction works on the subject of the American dream. These works are also organized by subtheme.

An overview essay on the theme of the American dream in literature discusses how the American dream represents many things to many people. It goes on to argue that its pervasive allure and power come from the capacity for it to encompass so many aspirations. Discussion of key poems, plays, short stories, novels, and nonfiction works reflect the continuing evolution of the American dream.

### *Citing Literary Themes for Students*

When writing papers, students who quote directly from any volume of *Literary Themes for Students* may use the following general formats. These examples are based on MLA style. Teachers may request that students adhere to a different style, so the following examples should be adapted as needed.

When citing text from *LTfS* that is not attributed to a particular author (i.e., from the Themes or Historical Context sections), the following format should be used in the bibliography section:

> *"O Pioneers!." Literary Themes for Students.* Ed. TK. Vol. TK. Detroit: Thomson Gale, 2007. TK–TK.

When quoting a journal or newspaper essay that is reprinted in a volume of *LTfS*, the following format may be used:

> Heddendorf, David, "Rabbit Reread," in the *Southern Review*, Vol. 36, No. 3, Summer 2000, pp. 641–47; excerpted and reprinted in *Literary Themes for Students*, Vol. TK, ed. TK (Detroit: Thomson Gale, 2007), pp. TK–TK.

When quoting material reprinted from a book that appears in a volume of *LTfS*, the following form may be used:

> Schubnell, Matthias, *N. Scott Momaday: The Cultural and Literary Background*, University of Oklahoma Press, 1985, pp. 101–39; excerpted and reprinted in *Literary Themes for Students*, Vol. TK, ed. TK (Detroit: Thomson Gale, 2007), pp. TK–TK.

### *We Welcome Your Suggestions*

The editorial staff of *LTfS* welcomes your comments, ideas, and suggestions. Readers who wish to suggest themes and works for future volumes, or who have any other suggestions, are cordially invited to contact the editor. You may do so via email at ForStudentsEditors@gale.cengage.com or via mail at:

Editor, *Literary Themes for Students*
Gale
27500 Drake Road
Farmington Hills, MI 48331-3535

# Acknowledgments

**COPYRIGHTED EXCERPTS IN *LTSAD*, VOL-UMES 1-2, WERE REPRODUCED FROM THE FOLLOWING PERIODICALS:**

*American Drama*, v. 2, fall, 1992. Copyright (c) 1992 American Drama Institute. Reproduced by permission.—*American Heritage*, v. 47, July-August, 1996. Copyright 1996 American Heritage, A Division of Forbes, Inc. Reproduced by permission of American Heritage.—*American Transcendental Quarterly*, v. 19, September, 2005. Copyright (c) 2005 by The University of Rhode Island. Reproduced by permission.—*Atlantic Monthly*, v. 289, February, 2002 for "Sheer Data" by Benjamin Schwarz. Reproduced by permission of the author.—*Children's Literature*, v. 24, 1996. Copyright (c) 1996 by Yale University. All rights reserved. Reproduced by permission.—*College Literature*, v. 20, October, 1993. Copyright (c) 1993 by West Chester University. Reproduced by permission.—*CRITIQUE: Studies in Contemporary Fiction*, v. 47, fall, 2005. Copyright (c) 2005 by Helen Dwight Reid Educational Foundation. Reproduced with permission of the Helen Dwight Reid Educational Foundation, published by Heldref Publications, 1319 18th Street, NW, Washington, DC 20036-1802.—*Cross Currents*, v. 43, fall, 1993. Copyright 1993 by Cross Currents, Inc. Reproduced by permission.—*Early American Literature*, v. 35, fall, 2000. Copyright (c) 2000 by the University of North Carolina Press. Used by permission.—*FindLaw's Writ*, May 9, 2006. Copyright (c) 2006 FindLaw, a Thomson business. This column originally appeared On FindLaw.com. Reproduced by permission.—*Kenyon Review*, summer-fall, 2002 for "Deadpan Huck" by Sacvan Bercovitch. Copyright 2002 Kenyon College. All rights reserved. Reproduced by permission of the author.—*The Massachusetts Review*, v. 14, autumn, 1973. Copyright (c) 1974 by The Massachusetts Review, Inc. Reproduced by permission.—*MELUS*, v. 8, fall, 1981; v. 27, winter, 2002. Copyright MELUS: The Society for the Study of Multi-Ethnic Literature of the United States, 1981, 2002. Both reproduced by permission.—*Modern Fiction Studies*, v. 49, fall, 2003. Copyright (c) 2003 by Purdue Research Foundation, West Lafayette, IN 47907. All rights reserved. Reproduced by permission of The Johns Hopkins University.—*The New York Review of Books*, v. 38, October 10, 1991. Copyright (c) 1991 by NYREV, Inc. Reprinted with permission from The New York Review of Books.—*Philosophy and Literature*, v. 21, 1997. Copyright (c) 1997 The Johns Hopkins University Press. Reproduced by permission.—*Prologue*, v. 22, spring, 1990 for "The Stylistic Artistry of 'The Declaration of Independence'" by Stephen E. Lucas. (c) 1989 Stephen E. Lucas. Reproduced by permission of the author.—*Southern Review*, v. 36, summer, 2000 for "Rabbit Reread" by David Heddendorf. Copyright (c) 2000 by Louisiana State University. Reproduced by permission of the author.—*Southwest*

*Review*, v. 48, autumn, 1963. Copyright (c) 1963 Southern Methodist University. All rights reserved. Reproduced by permission.—*Studia Anglica Posnaniensia*, v. 41, 2005. Copyright 2005 Adam Mickiewicz University Press. Reproduced by permission.—*Studies in Short Fiction*, v. 25, fall, 1988. Copyright (c) 1988 by North Texas State University. Reproduced by permission.— *Studies in the Novel*, v. 23, spring, 1991. Copyright (c) 1991 by North Texas State University. Reproduced by permission.—*Texas Studies in Literature and Language*, v. 43, summer, 2001 for "Peasant Dreams: Reading 'On the Road'" by Mark Richardson. Copyright (c) 2001 by the University of Texas Press. Reproduced by permission of the publisher and the author.

## COPYRIGHTED EXCERPTS IN *LTSAD*, VOLUMES 1-2, WERE REPRODUCED FROM THE FOLLOWING BOOKS:

Brown, John Mason. From *Dramatis Personae: A Retrospective Show*. Viking Press, 1963. Copyright 1929, 1930, 1934, 1938, 1940, 1944, 1946, 1948-1955 inclusive, (c) 1957, 1958, 1962, 1963, renewed 1991 by John Mason Brown. Used by permission of Viking Penguin, a division of Penguin Group (USA) Inc.—Conder, John J. From *Naturalism in American Fiction: The Classic Phase*. University Press of Kentucky, 1984. Copyright (c) 1984 by The University Press of Kentucky. Reproduced by permission of The University Press of Kentucky.—Couser, G. Thomas. From *Altered Egos: Authority in American Autobiography*. Oxford University Press, 1989. Copyright (c) 1989 by Oxford University Press, Inc. All rights reserved. Reproduced by permission of Oxford University Press, Inc.—Goldstein, Malcolm. From *The Art of Thornton Wilder*. University of Nebraska Press, 1965. Copyright (c) 1965 by the University of Nebraska Press. (c) renewed 1993 by the University of Nebraska Press. All rights reserved. Reproduced by permission of the University of Nebraska Press.—Kennedy, Rick. From "Building a City on a Hill," in *Events that Changed America Through the Seventeenth Century*. Edited by John Findling and Frank Thackeray. Greenwood Press, 2000. Copyright (c) 2000 by John E. Findling and Frank W. Thackeray. All rights reserved. Reproduced by permission of Greenwood Publishing Group, Inc., Westport, CT.—The Massachusetts Review, v. 14, autumn, 1973. Copyright (c) 1974 by The Massachusetts Review, Inc. Reproduced by permission.— Schubnell, Matthias. From *N. Scott Momaday: The Cultural and Literary Background*. University of Oklahoma Press, 1985. Copyright (c) 1985 University of Oklahoma Press. Reproduced by permission.—Singal, Daniel Joseph. From *William Faulkner: The Making of a Modernist*. University of North Carolina Press, 1997. Copyright (c) 1997 by the University of North Carolina Press. All rights reserved. Used by permission of the publisher.—Sloane, David E. E. From *Sister Carrie: Theodore Dreiser's Sociological Tragedy*. Twayne Publishers, 1992. Copyright (c) 1992 by Twayne Publishers. All rights reserved. Reproduced by permission of Thomson Gale.—Weisbuch, Robert. From *New Essays on Daisy Miller and The Turn of the Screw*. Cambridge University Press, 1993. Copyright (c) 1993 Cambridge University Press. Reprinted with the permission of Cambridge University Press.

# National Advisory Board

# Contributors

**Margaret Brantley:** Brantley is a literature critic and a literary reference editor. Foreword.

**Ann Guidry:** Guidry is a freelance writer and editor with a B.A. in English from the University of Texas. Major Work on the *Autobiography of Benjamin Franklin*, *The Grapes of Wrath*, John F. Kennedy's Inaugural Speech, *O Pioneers!*, *Rabbit, Run*, and "Song of Myself," as well as the essays "The Colonial American Dream," "The American Dream in the Nineteenth Century," "The Immigrant American Dream," "The American Political Dream," and "The Southern American Dream."

**Jonathan Lampley:** Lampley is a doctoral candidate in English at Middle Tennessee State University and is a freelance writer. Major work on the Declaration of Independence and the White House Correspondents' Association Dinner 2006 Speech, as well as the essay "The American Dream Today."

**Michelle Lee:** Lee has been a freelance writer and editor for the past 15 years, and is working toward a Ph.D. in English literature at the University of Texas. Major Work on *The Big Money*, *The Great Gatsby*, "Mending Wall," and *Our Town*, as well as the essays "The American Dream," "The American Dream Abroad," "The American Feminist Dream," "The Asian American Dream," and "The Frontier American Dream."

**Ray Mescallado:** Mescallado holds a master's degree in English and is a freelance writer. Major Work on *Sister Carrie*

**Annette Petrusso:** Petrusso is a freelance writer and editor with a B.A. in history from the University of Michigan and an M.A. in screenwriting from The University of Texas at Austin. Major work on *Absalom, Absalom!*, *Adventures of Huckleberry Finn*, ... *And the Earth Did Not Devour Him Autobiography of My Dead Brother*, *Cane*, *Chronicle of the Narváez Expedition*, *Daisy Miller*, *Death of a Salesman*, "Elbow Room," *Finding My Voice*, *House Made of Dawn*, *Little House on the Prairie*, *Main Street*, and "My Kinsman, Major Molineux.

**Laura Baker Shearer:** Shearer holds a Ph.D. in American literature and works as an English professor and freelance writer. Major work on "Common Sense" and "Self-Reliance."

**Greg Wilson** Wilson is a freelance literature and popular culture writer. Major work on *Black Elk Speaks*, *Call It Sleep*, *Lonesome Dove*, "A Model of Christian Charity," *Montage of a Dream Deferred*, and *On the Road*, as well as the essays "The African American Dream," "The American Dream in the Twentieth Century," "The Hispanic American Dream," and "The Native American Dream."

# Literary Chronology

**1485:** Alvar Núñez Cabeza de Vaca is born between 1485 and 1492, probably in Jerez de la Frontera, Spain.

**1555:** Cabeza de Vaca's *Chronicle of the Narváez Expedition* is published.

**1559:** Cabeza de Vaca dies in 1559 or 1560 in Spain.

**1588:** John Winthrop is born on January 12 in Suffolk, England.

**1630:** Winthrop's "A Model of Christian Charity," is published.

**1649:** Winthrop dies on March 26.

**1706:** Benjamin Franklin is born on January 17 in Boston, Massachusetts.

**1737:** Thomas Paine is born in England.

**1743:** Thomas Jefferson is born on April 13 in Virginia.

**1776:** Paine's *Common Sense* is published.

**1776:** Jefferson's *The Declaration of Independence* is adopted on July 4.

**1790:** Franklin dies on April 17 in Philadelphia, Pennsylvania.

**1803:** Ralph Waldo Emerson is born on May 25 in Massachusetts.

**1804:** Nathaniel Hawthorne is born on July 4 in Salem, Massachusetts.

**1809:** Paine dies in June in New York City, New York.

**1819:** Walt Whitman is born on May 31 in West Hills, New York.

**1826:** Jefferson dies on July 4.

**1832:** Hawthorne's "My Kinsman, Major Molineux" is published.

**1835:** Samuel Langhorne Clemens (Mark Twain) is born on November 30 in Florida, Missouri.

**1841:** Emerson's "Self-Reliance" is published.

**1843:** Henry James is born on April 15 in New York City, New York.

**1864:** Hawthorne dies on May 19 from cancer.

**1867:** Laura Ingalls Wilder is born on February 7 in Pepin, Wisconsin.

**1871:** Herman Theodore Dreiser is born on August 27 in Terre Haute, Indiana.

**1873:** Willa Sibert Cather is born on December 7 in Back Creek Valley, Virginia.

**1874:** Robert Lee Frost is born on March 26 in San Francisco, California.

**1878:** James's *Daisy Miller* is published.

**1882:** Emerson dies on April 27.

**1885:** Twain's *Adventures of Huckleberry Finn* is published.

**1885:** Harry Sinclair Lewis is born on February 7 in Sauk Centre, Minnesota.

**1886:** Franklin's *The Autobiography of Benjamin Franklin* is published.

**1891:** John Gneisenau Neihardt is born on January 8 near Sharpsburg, Illinois.

**1892:** Whitman's "Song of Myself" is published.

**1892:** Whitman dies on March 26 in Camden, New Jersey.

**1894:** Nathan Eugene Pinchback (Jean) Toomer is born on December 26 in Washington, D.C.

**1896:** John Dos Passos is born on January 14 in Chicago, Illinois.

**1896:** Francis (F.) Scott Fitzgerald is born on September 4 in St. Paul, Minnesota.

**1897:** William Faulkner is born on September 25 in New Albany, Mississippi.

**1897:** Thornton Wilder is born on April 17 in Madison, Wisconsin.

**1900:** Dreiser's *Sister Carrie* is published.

**1902:** John Ernst Steinbeck is born on February 27 in Salinas, California.

**1902:** James Langston Hughes is born on February 1 in Joplin, Missouri.

**1906:** Herschel (Henry) Roth is born on February 8 in Tysmenica, Galicia, Austria-Hungary (now part of the Ukraine).

**1910:** Twain dies of heart disease on April 21 in Redding, Connecticut.

**1913:** Cather's *O Pioneers!* is published.

**1915:** Frost's "Mending Wall" is published.

**1915:** Arthur Miller is born on October 17 in New York City, New York.

**1916:** James dies on February 28 of edema following a series of strokes in London, England.

**1917:** John Fitzgerald Kennedy is born on May 29 in Brookline, Massachusetts.

**1920:** Lewis's *Main Street* is published.

**1922:** Jean-Louis Lebris de Kerouac (Jack Kerouac) is born on March 12 in Lowell, Massachusetts.

**1923:** Toomer's *Cane* is published.

**1925:** Fitzgerald's *The Great Gatsby* is published.

**1932:** John Hoyer Updike is born on March 18 in Shillington, Pennsylvania.

**1932:** Neihardt's *Black Elk Speaks* is published.

**1934:** Roth's *Call It Sleep* is published.

**1934:** Navarre Scott Mammedaty (N. Scott Momaday) is born on February 27 in Lawton, Oklahoma.

**1935:** Tomás Rivera is born December 22 in Crystal City, Texas.

**1935:** Wilder's *Little House on the Prairie* is published.

**1936:** Faulkner's *Absalom, Absalom!* is published.

**1936:** Dos Passos's *The Big Money* is published.

**1936:** Larry McMurtry is born on June 3 in Wichita Falls, Texas.

**1937:** Walter Milton Myers (Walter Dean Myers) is born on August 12 in Martinsburg, West Virginia.

**1937:** Wilder dies on February 10 in Mansfield, Missouri.

**1938:** Wilder's *Our Town* is published.

**1939:** Steinbeck's *The Grapes of Wrath* is published.

**1940:** Fitzgerald dies on December 21 of a heart attack in Hollywood, California.

**1943:** James Alan McPherson is born on September 16 in Savannah, Georgia.

**1945:** Dreiser dies on December 28 of a heart attack in Los Angeles, California.

**1947:** Cather dies on April 24 of a cerebral hemorrhage in New York, New York.

**1949:** Miller's *Death of a Salesman* is published.

**1951:** Lewis dies of a heart attack on January 10 near Rome, Italy.

**1951:** Hughes's *Montage of a Dream Deferred* is published.

**1957:** Kerouac's *On the Road* is published.

**1960:** Updike's *Rabbit, Run* is published.

**1961:** Kennedy delivers his inaugural address on January 20.

**1962:** Faulkner dies on July 6 in Byhalia, Mississippi.

**1963:** Kennedy is assassinated on November 22 in Dallas, Texas.

**1963:** Frost dies on January 29 in Boston, Massachusetts.

**1964:** Marie G. Lee is born on April 25 in Hibbing, Minnesota.

**1964:** Stephen Colbert is born on May 13 in Charleston, South Carolina.

**1967:** Toomer dies on March 30 in Doylestown, Pennsylvania.

**1967:** Hughes dies on May 22 of congestive heart failure in New York, New York.

**1968:** Steinbeck dies on December 20 of heart disease in New York City, New York.

**1968:** Momaday's *House Made of Dawn* is published.

**1969:** Kerouac dies of cirrhosis of the liver and internal bleeding on October 21 in St. Petersburg, Florida .

**1970:** Dos Passos dies on September 28 in Baltimore, Maryland.

**1971:** Rivera's *. . . And the Earth Did Not Devour Him* is published.

**1973:** Neihardt dies on November 24 in Columbia, Missouri.

**1975:** Wilder dies of a heart attack on December 7 in Hamden, Connecticut.

**1977:** McPherson's "Elbow Room" is published.

**1984:** Rivera dies on May 16 in Fontana, California.

**1985:** McMurtry's *Lonesome Dove* is published.

**1992:** Lee's *Finding My Voice* is published.

**1995:** Roth dies on October 13.

**2005:** Miller dies on February 10 of heart failure in Roxbury Connecticut.

**2005:** *Autobiography of My Dead Brother* is published.

**2006:** Colbert delivers his speech at the White House Correspondents' Association Dinner on April 29.

# *Lonesome Dove*

**LARRY McMURTRY**

**1985**

Larry McMurtry's Pulitzer Prize–winning *Lonesome Dove* (1985) is a gritty novel of the American West. However, the author does not attempt to glamorize the events and people of his novel in the way many figures of the American West have reached almost mythic proportions in the American consciousness. Instead, McMurtry offers a realistic portrait of life in the American West during the last half of the nineteenth century.

The book centers on two old men, Gus McRae and Woodrow Call, former Texas Rangers who have settled down in the Texas border town of Lonesome Dove. They run the Hat Creek Cattle Company, and they spend much of their time reclaiming ponies stolen by Mexican thieves and selling them to cowboys or settlers passing through the area. Call, in a fit of dissatisfaction over their dull lifestyle, decides that the Hat Creek outfit is going to gather a cattle herd and drive it north to Montana. The journey turns out to be perilous and filled with diversions, but the men ultimately reach their goal. Along the way, they and the other characters they meet are forced to carefully consider what is most important in their lives.

Although not strictly a historical novel, *Lonesome Dove* depicts important places of the American West such as Dodge City and Ogallala with accurate and evocative details. It also provides historical context for the characters, noting that the rapidly developing nation, with advancing transportation technology and dwindling

# BIOGRAPHY

## LARRY MCMURTRY

Larry McMurtry was born on June 3, 1936, in Wichita Falls, Texas, and grew up on a ranch just south of Wichita Falls near a town called Archer City. After attending North Texas State University and Rice University, McMurtry wrote his first novel, *Horseman, Pass By* (1961), which depicts life on a Texas cattle ranch in the years following World War II. The novel was adapted into the acclaimed movie *Hud* (1963) starring Paul Newman.

Although McMurtry has written dozens of critically and commercially successful novels, he remains best known for a handful of novels that have been adapted into films: *The Last Picture Show* (1966); *Terms of Endearment* (1975); *Texasville* ( 1987); *The Evening Star* (1992); and especially *Lonesome Dove* (1985), which began as

a film screenplay by McMurtry, was transformed into a best-selling novel, and was eventually adapted into an award-winning television miniseries. McMurtry has written three follow-up novels in the Lonesome Dove series, two of them prequels to *Lonesome Dove* and one a sequel: *Dead Man's Walk* (1995), *Comanche Moon* (1997), and *Streets of Laredo* (1993). All three have been adapted into television miniseries.

Although continuing to write novels, McMurtry has also gained fame as a screenwriter. He wrote the television miniseries *Johnson County War* in 2002, and he co-wrote the screenplay for the acclaimed film *Brokeback Mountain* (2005), for which he received a Golden Globe and an Academy Award for Best Adapted Screenplay.

---

American Indian populations, is losing its need for men with a frontier spirit like Gus and Call.

Although *Lonesome Dove* achieved enormous success for a Western novel, even earning McMurtry a Pulitzer Prize for fiction in 1986, an even larger audience is familiar with the story thanks to its adaptation as a television miniseries in 1989. The world of the Old West may be far removed from modern American life, but it represents a core component of the national identity. When it comes to the American dream, the cowboy is a symbol of freedom and opportunity as vast as the Texas plains.

## PLOT SUMMARY

### Part 1
### Chapters 1–12

*Lonesome Dove* begins in the title town, a backwater Texas settlement near the Mexican border. There, Augustus "Gus" McRae and Woodrow Call, both former Texas Rangers, run the Hat Creek Cattle Company, selling cattle and horses to ranchers and cattle drivers heading north. Their outfit consists of several other men: Bolivar, their Mexican cook; Pea Eye, their dim but dependable

ranch hand; Newt, a boy whose prostitute mother died when he was just six, and who is approaching adulthood under the care of Gus and Call; and Deets, a black man who can track and guide better than anyone else in the area.

The other town notables include Lorena Wood, a quiet prostitute who works out of the Dry Bean, the local saloon, and whom Gus visits regularly; Xavier Wanz, the French owner of the Dry Bean; and Lippy, the large-lipped piano player and barkeep who works for Xavier.

A cattleman named Dish Boggett enters town, in between jobs and looking for love from Lorena. Gus, on friendly terms with Dish, loans him some money to enjoy Lorena's company and lets the man sleep on their back porch afterward. Before he leaves, Call offers him a job with them. First, Call plans to head south into Mexico and acquire some horses from one of their longtime foes, a Mexican horse thief named Pedro Flores; second, and to nearly everyone's surprise, Call wants to get some cattle together and drive them north.

This plan is solidified when an old friend of the two, Jake Spoon, arrives in town. Jake is fleeing from the law in Fort Smith, Arkansas, where he accidentally shot the mayor dead. Jake offers the

*Larry McMurtry* © *Jerry Bauer*

men tantalizing descriptions of Montana, a land farther north than anyone had ever considered driving cattle. Although Gus remains unsure, Call decides that Montana is their destination.

The group secures some horses from Mexico and have the good fortune to avoid an encounter with the dangerous Pedro Flores. They soon discover that nearly forty of the horses belong to a cattle rancher named Wilbarger. The man gratefully takes back his stolen horses, and when he hears about the group's plan to drive cattle to Montana, he cautions them to reconsider: "Too far, too cold, full of bears and I don't know about the Indians. They may be beat but I wouldn't count on it." In addition to securing horses in Mexico, the group acquires two lost Irishmen, Allen and Sean O'Brien, who are unaccustomed to the land. They bring the O'Briens back with them, and make the inexperienced men a part of their new cattle driving team.

### Chapters 13–25

Jake Spoon meets Lorena and woos her with promises of taking her to San Francisco. Suddenly devoted to Jake, Lorena gives up her career as a prostitute—much to the dismay of

the residents of Lonesome Dove, because she was the only one in town. When Xavier learns that Lorena is going to leave Lonesome Dove, he breaks down and professes his love for her. He offers to take her away to Galveston if she agrees to stay with him. She refuses.

Meanwhile, Call rounds up men for the cattle drive. He hires four local boys, all much in need of good experience. Two are brothers from the Spettle household, and two are from the Rainey household. He also hires a man named Jasper Fant who has recently come to town looking for work. At around the same time, Call and Gus discover that their old nemesis Pedro Flores has died. This explains why the horses were so easy to steal back, and Call sees this as yet another sign that the Hat Creek outfit should move on from Lonesome Dove.

Jake tries to back out of the cattle drive, and he attempts to convince Lorena that the two of them would be better off just going to San Antonio. Lorena, having had a bad experience in San Antonio before, has no intention of going back. They decide that Jake and Lorena will accompany the cattle drive at least partway, keeping a separate camp so the working men are not distracted by Lorena. Just before they depart, Lippy includes himself in the cattle drive team, seeing no future left in Lonesome Dove. Gus allows him to join, knowing they will need all the hands they can get.

Finally, the cattle drive starts north with roughly twenty-six hundred cattle, one hundred horses, and two pigs that Gus refuses to leave behind.

### Part 2
### Chapters 26–35

In Fort Smith, Arkansas, sheriff July Johnson is left to deal with the aftermath of Jake Spoon's accidental killing of Ben Johnson weeks before. Ben Johnson was not only the mayor of Fort Smith, but also July's older brother, as well as the town dentist. Ben's wife Peach wants July to bring Jake Spoon to justice for the killing. July's new wife Elmira, however, does not want him riding off to Texas over an accidental shooting. July wavers between the two viewpoints, and he spends weeks sick enough with jaundice that he cannot travel anyway. When he finally recovers, he decides that his duties as a sheriff must come first. Taking Elmira's twelve-year-old son Joe with him as she requests, July rides for Texas and leaves his deputy, Roscoe Brown, in charge of keeping the town's peace.

Even before July leaves, Elmira begins to reconsider her life as a wife and mother. In truth, she longs only for the company of a man named Dee Boot, a former lover—and Joe's father—who has gone north. Secretly pregnant with July's baby, Elmira leaves the town of Fort Smith on a whiskey boat bound upriver. When Peach discovers what has happened, deputy Roscoe is given a new responsibility: to find July and tell him his wife has run off. Reluctantly, Roscoe, an inexperienced traveler, rides off for Texas.

After the Hat Creek outfit reaches the Nueces River, tragedy strikes: One of the Irishmen, Sean O'Brien, happens upon a nest of water moccasins as he crosses the river on horseback. He is bitten several times and dies quickly. All the men are stunned at the freak accident, but his brother and Newt—who had grown especially close to the young man—are hit the hardest.

## Chapters 36–43

July's wife Elmira rides north on a whiskey boat filled with buffalo hunters. For the most part they do not bother her, but the largest and roughest-looking one, Big Zwey, takes an interest in her. Although he does not talk to her, he protects her from the other men when they make untoward advances.

As Roscoe heads west to find July, he encounters a blunt woman named Louisa who has been thrice widowed and runs a farm on her own. He helps her pull a stump, and he stays for a dinner of corn bread when she offers. She quickly suggests that Roscoe marry her and stay at her farm, his main attributes being that he is quiet and skinny: "If you don't last, you'll be easy to bury." When Roscoe rejects her proposal, she attempts to sway him with sex. In the morning, although Roscoe is tempted to stay, he knows he must first find July.

Near San Antonio, the Hat Creek outfit experiences another surprising accident: Bolivar, asleep on the mule wagon, accidentally fires his ten-gauge rifle and sends the mules running off a creek bank. Although Bolivar is knocked clear of the wagon when the gun goes off, Lippy is almost drowned in the creek and the wagon is wrecked. Bolivar decides to quit the cattle drive to return south to his seldom-seen wife and family in Mexico. Call and Gus ride into San Antonio to

buy a new cart, but they fail to find a replacement cook.

With the help of some soldiers, Roscoe finally finds his way into Texas. He stops at a cabin for the night, where an old skunk trader lives with a young woman he claims is "bought and paid for." The old man warns Roscoe to stay away from her, and though Roscoe hears the man abusing her during the night, he heeds the warning.

After he leaves the next morning, Roscoe inadvertently rides into a wasp nest and gets stung several times. While tending to his wounds, he notices that the girl from the cabin has followed him. She tells him that her name is Janey, and she says that she is running away from the cruel old skunk trader. Although Roscoe is hesitant to take her along, she immediately proves her worth by helping treat his wasp stings and by catching food for them to eat. Roscoe agrees to take her, if only to find a better place for her to live.

## Chapters 44–58

North of San Antonio, Call and Gus make plans to hire a cook in Austin. Before they get there, though, Gus makes a detour to a place near the Guadalupe River that he calls "Clara's orchard." Clara, Gus's former love who married a horse trader and settled in Nebraska, is at least part of the reason he has decided to make the trip north. He holds out hope that he might find her a widow, ready to resume their life together, and if so, he is ready to stop short of Montana and settle down. Gus confesses to Call that the happiest times of his life were not spent with either of his two previous wives, but with Clara at that spot near the Guadalupe.

Gus and Call discover that Jake has gone into town and left Lorena alone in her secondary camp. Gus agrees to stay with her until Jake returns. A Comanchero Indian named Blue Duck rides into their camp and warns Gus to stay south of the Canadian River. Gus tells Lorena that Blue Duck is an infamous killer and thief whom Gus and Call had never been able to catch during their days as Texas Rangers. Gus sends Deets to track Blue Duck, and because Lorena refuses to come to the cattlemen's camp, he sends Newt to watch over her for the time being. The camp's new cook, Po Campo, arrives and introduces the men to new foods such as fried grasshoppers. Blue Duck creates a stampede to distract Newt long enough to snatch Lorena and disappear across the plains before the men notice. Gus sets off to find Lorena and bring her back.

July Johnson and Joe reach Fort Worth in their search for Jake Spoon, and July is surprised to find a letter waiting for him at the post office. The letter, from his sister-in-law Peach, tells him that Elmira has run off and Roscoe is on his way to find him. July is also surprised to learn that Joe's father Dee Boot is still alive—Elmira had said that Joe's father died of smallpox—and that Elmira has probably gone looking for him in Dodge City. July and Joe head back east to find Roscoe before starting north in search of Elmira.

July and Joe come across Roscoe just in time to rescue him from two thieves. Roscoe and Janey follow July back into Fort Worth. July pays a woman to board Janey for two months, but Janey insists on staying with the group even after they try to leave her behind.

Elmira gets off the whiskey boat and decides to stay with Big Zwey, who promises to take her to Ogallala by wagon. He brings along another buffalo hunter named Luke, whom Elmira does not entirely trust.

Blue Duck sells Lorena to both a violent group of Kiowas and a pair of buffalo hunters, all of whom rape her when the mood strikes them. Blue Duck wins the girl back by gambling with both groups of men. Then he offers to give the girl to them as a gift if they agree to kill Gus, who Blue Duck knows is coming. They accept the offer.

Gus encounters the attackers, killing one of the Kiowas and seriously wounding one of the buffalo hunters. He also encounters July, Roscoe, Joe, and Janey, and the group makes camp while Gus and July head off to reclaim Lorena. Gus kills the captors efficiently, and when he finds that Blue Duck is not present, he warns July to return to camp quickly. When July arrives back at camp, he discovers that Blue Duck has already slaughtered Roscoe, Joe, and Janey. July is determined to find Blue Duck and bring him to justice, but Gus tells him that he would not be able to catch him. He also tells July to not be consumed by a need for vengeance. "'Don't be trying to give back pain for pain,' he said. 'You can't get even measures in business like this. You best go find your wife.'" July leaves for Dodge City.

## Chapters 59–74

The Hat Creek outfit continues north with the herd, past the Red River. Most of the men give up hope that Gus is still alive, because he has been away for so long. As the group approaches the Canadian River, they endure a terrible lightning storm that kills thirteen cattle and one of the Spettle brothers. On the other side of the Canadian, they are relieved to find Gus and Lorena, who have been provisioned thanks to a chance encounter with the cattle rancher Wilbarger, who is also moving a herd north. Lorena, traumatized from her ordeal, insists on staying only in Gus's company.

Jake, having left the Hat Creek outfit after Lorena's abduction, spends some time gambling in Fort Worth, in the frequent company of a sharp-tongued prostitute named Sally; when she is killed trying to escape from jail after a minor altercation, Jake takes her stashed savings and heads to Dallas. There he joins with the Suggs brothers and their buddy Frog Lip, a group of murdering thieves that makes Jake uneasy. Still, he accompanies the men as they head toward Kansas.

Elmira, on the wagon trip to Ogallala with Big Zwey and Luke, finds herself fighting off Luke's unwanted advances night after night. She chases him off at gunpoint, but he returns days later and tries to force himself on her once again. This time Zwey grabs him and smashes his head into the iron spokes of the wagon wheel. Luke survives but takes weeks to recover.

In a town called Doan's Store, Jake flirts with a young woman in a wagon who turns out to be married. The husband returns and cracks Jake on the head with the butt of his rifle, and Jake responds by shooting and killing him. Jake convinces himself that he had no choice but to shoot. He and the Suggs brothers head north, where the Suggs boys and Frog Lip rob a family of German farmers and destroy their sod house.

At the Hat Creek outfit, Newt's favorite horse, Mouse, is killed by yet another freak accident. The horse is gored in the abdomen by a small cow with sharp horns during a routine cattle maneuver. Lorena decides she would like to marry Gus, even though she knows he is eager to reconnect with his old love Clara when they reach Ogallala.

The Suggs brothers and Jake, on their way to Dodge City, encounter cattle rancher Wilbarger and two of his men. The Suggses wound Wilbarger and kill the two others in a move to steal the men's horses, but their buddy Frog Lip is killed in the altercation. The Suggses continue their spree by killing two settlers on a whim, then hanging the bodies and burning them. Jake makes plans to break free of the murderous bunch at the next opportunity.

The Hat Creek outfit happens upon the wounded Wilbarger, who reveals his attackers. Deets can tell by their tracks that Jake, with his unique pacing horse, is with them. Gus, Call, Deets, and Pea Eye catch the thieves and see them hanged for their crimes. They also hang their old friend Jake, who futilely asserts his innocence to Gus. "Ride with an outlaw, die with him," Gus explains, though Jake is already familiar with the code. Before Jake dies, he gives his prize horse to Newt.

## Part 3
### Chapters 75–89

Elmira, Zwey, and Luke stop at the home of Clara Allen, Gus's old love, on their way to Ogallala. Clara runs a horse trading business with her husband, Bob, who has recently been badly injured by a horse kick. Bob still breathes on his own, and eats with assistance, but otherwise seems very near death. While stopped at the house Elmira learns that Dee Boot is indeed in Ogallala. However, she is too weak to make the trip, and that night, thanks to the help of Clara's hired hand Cholo, Elmira gives birth to a baby boy. To Clara's surprise, Elmira shows no interest in the baby at all: "It was July's and she didn't want to have anything to do with anything of July's." Elmira, Zwey, and Luke head off for Ogallala without notice, leaving the baby in Clara's care.

In Ogallala, Elmira discovers that Dee Boot is in jail, waiting to be hanged for killing a boy. Still weak and ill from the birth, Elmira faints and must be taken to the town doctor. When she regains her senses, she discovers that Dee Boot has already been hanged. She also learns that Zwey has stayed by her side throughout her illness.

By chance, July stops at Clara's home on his way to Ogallala. When Clara discovers his identity, she tells him the baby she cares for is actually his child. July visits the still-recovering Elmira in Ogallala, hoping to make a life together with her and their new son. After his first visit, though, Elmira leaves town with Zwey and heads east into Sioux territory. Although July wants to go after her, Clara convinces him to stay on with her as a hired hand and care for his son. July later hears that a woman and a buffalo hunter have been killed by the Sioux, somewhere out east.

Gus, Call, Newt, and Lorena travel to Clara's while the rest of the Hat Creek outfit spend time in Ogallala. Although Lorena is at first jealous of this woman who still holds Gus's heart, she soon comes to like both Clara and her two daughters, Betsey and Sally. Clara convinces Lorena to stay on with them instead of risking her life in Montana. Clara also talks to Gus about Call and Newt: She can tell, though no one talks about such matters, that Newt is almost certainly Call's son. Call has never mentioned it to the boy, and Clara thinks it is time he did. Before they leave, Clara gives Newt one of her finest horses.

Back with the herd, Gus and Call are disappointed to discover that the next body of water is eighty miles away—too far to drive the herd without risking that many will die of thirst. The crew takes the chance, weathering a sandstorm and struggling for days to reach Salt Creek. They are surprised to discover that almost all the cattle have survived.

### Chapters 90–102

On Salt Creek, twelve of the outfit's horses are stolen by Indians. Call, Deets, and Gus track the Indians to a pitiful camp, where they discover that the starving Indians are using the horses for food. Though they do not intend to hurt the Indians, a frightened young warrior spears Deets as he tries to help an Indian child. Call and Gus both shoot the warrior, but they are too late to save Deets. The men bury Deets, and Call carves an inscription on a plaque to mark the grave site.

The Hat Creek outfit finally reaches Montana, and every man is impressed by its beauty. Call asks Gus and Pea Eye to go on ahead and determine the best place to make their home. While scouting, the two men are attacked by Indians, and Gus is shot through the leg with an arrow. They find safety in a cave along the riverbank, and Gus sends Pea Eye to get help. Pea Eye manages to walk all the way back to camp. Gus, not content to wait for death, starts off with a makeshift crutch and encounters a trader named Hugh Auld. Hugh lets Gus borrow his horse to ride into Miles City and see a doctor about his worsening leg.

The doctor takes Gus's left leg, but when Gus refuses to give up his right leg as well, he condemns himself to death. Call reaches Gus

*HE KNEW THE COUNTRY HE KNEW, AND HE HAD NEVER BEEN LOST IN IT, BUT THE COUNTRY HE KNEW STOPPED AT THE ARKANSAS RIVER. HE HAD KNOWN MEN TO SPEAK OF THE YELLOWSTONE AS IF IT WERE THE BOUNDARY OF THE WORLD; EVEN KIT CARSON, WHOM HE HAD MET TWICE, HAD NOT TALKED OF WHAT LAY NORTH OF IT."*

before he dies, and Gus requests that Call bury him in the place he calls Clara's orchard, near the Guadalupe River—three thousand miles away. Call reluctantly agrees.

After the cattle ranch is established and Newt learns how to negotiate sales and trades, Call puts him in charge of the outfit. Some of the older men object but see that Newt has Call's favor. Call even gives the boy his prize horse before he departs for Texas to bury Gus. On the way to Texas, he learns that Blue Duck has been apprehended and is scheduled to be hanged in Santa Rosa. Call makes a detour to witness the event. Before Blue Duck can be hanged, he takes his fate in his own hands and dives from a third-story courthouse window, taking the man who caught him—Deputy Decker—with him.

After Call fulfills his duty to Gus and buries him in Clara's orchard, Call continues on down to Lonesome Dove, just to see the town once again. He finds Bolivar still there, but the town seems otherwise lifeless. Not long after Call left, he learns, Xavier Wanz, the owner of the Dry Bean saloon, locked himself in Lorena's old room and burned the place to the ground with himself inside it.

## THEMES

### Freedom and Exploration

At the heart of *Lonesome Dove* is the theme of restlessness, which manifests itself as a desire for freedom and exploration. At the beginning of the novel, the men of the Hat Creek outfit live a dull, predictable existence in south Texas; Call, in most ways the leader of the group, seems to

desire something different from the pattern of life they have fallen into. It is he who first suggests that the group drive a herd of cattle north, though Jake Spoon later convinces him that Montana is the best destination. Similarly, Lorena seems to simply be biding her time in Lonesome Dove, waiting for a genuine opportunity to head west.

July Johnson's wife Elmira is another character who seems intent on never settling down. After she marries July, which is done more for her son Joe's sake than anything else, she runs off on a whiskey boat in search of her first love. In fact, nearly all of the characters in *Lonesome Dove* make a journey across the Great Plains at some point, though each does it for a different reason. Each character seems to be searching for the fulfillment of a dream. Some die during the journey, while others find their dreams and settle down in places like Nebraska and Montana.

Call, the catalyst for the cattle drive and in the end the central figure of the novel, ultimately returns to the exact point where he started: Lonesome Dove. Unlike the other characters, he does not seem to know what he is searching for. As Gus tells him before they start on the cattle drive, "I hope it makes you happy. If it don't, I give up. Driving all these skinny cattle all that way is a funny way to maintain an interest in life, if you ask me."

The novel also emphasizes the freedom the characters have to simply pull up stakes and move at will. In the book, the entire population of the West seems to be adrift, pressing northward and westward, exploring new areas. Gus notes that the American mindset is in fact the opposite of the Indian perspective when it comes to the land: "To them it's precious because it's old. To us it's exciting because it's new."

### Heroism

Heroism is an important part of the American view of the Old West, and it is a fundamental theme of *Lonesome Dove*. Many of the men and women in the novel are depicted as heroes for their actions. This is especially true of Gus and Call, though most of their heroic actions have taken place long before the start of the novel. Everywhere they travel, their reputations as Texas Rangers precede them. In turn, the two men expect and in some cases demand respect. This is seen in the Buckhorn bar in Fort Worth, where Gus breaks a bartender's nose after the man insults him and Call. Afterward, Gus takes down a photograph from the bar that shows the two men from their Texas Ranger days.

Gus's greatest display of heroism in *Lonesome Dove* occurs when he single-handedly rescues Lorena from a violent group of Kiowas and buffalo hunters after Blue Duck has abducted her. By contrast, Jake Spoon is shown to be a coward when he leaves the Hat Creek outfit after Lorena's abduction to go play cards in Fort Worth instead of trying to save her.

For many characters in the book, heroism is simply a matter of doing what one believes is the right thing to do. Clara adopts Elmira's child for this reason, expecting nothing but the child's love and company in return. Although they are in the middle of a cattle drive, Gus, Call, and their men track down Jake and the murderous Suggs brothers simply because they know someone must, out of respect for Wilbarger and to keep the men from hurting any more innocent people.

## HISTORICAL OVERVIEW

### *The Texas Rangers*
The Texas Ranger Division was a law enforcement agency first formed by Stephen F. Austin in 1823 to protect settlers from attack by Mexican bandits. The Texas Rangers were officially created as a government organization in 1835 and served as an important defense force between the formation of the independent Republic of Texas and its official annexation by the United States in 1845.

During the Mexican-American War (1846–1848), when Mexico attempted to reclaim Texas from the United States, companies of Texas Rangers fought alongside American soldiers at many decisive battles such as Cerro Gordo and the Siege of Veracruz. They came to be referred to by many Mexicans as *Los Diablos Tejanos* (The Texas Devils).

After the Mexican-American War, the Texas Ranger Division was all but disbanded since the U.S. Army now had jurisdiction over the state. In the 1850s, however, the Texas Ranger Division was called back into action to help clear the region of hostile Comanche Indians and protect against Mexican attackers. It was in the 1870s that the Texas Ranger Division developed the mythic reputation by which it is still known.

During this time, the Texas Rangers captured infamous criminals such as gunfighter John Wesley Hardin and helped subdue the Kiowa and Apache tribes. Though some of their methods were controversial—for example, they sometimes executed criminals without a trial—they were well regarded throughout the United States for their swift and effective brand of justice.

In the early decades of the twentieth century, the brutal methods of the Texas Rangers were called into question by the Texas Legislature, and the organization underwent changes aimed at better regulating the behavior of its agents. In 1935, the Texas Ranger Division became part of the Texas Department of Public Safety, which it remains to this day. Unique among state law enforcement agencies, the Texas Ranger Division is currently protected by a Texas government statute that states that it cannot be abolished.

### *Cattle Driving in the Old West*
Although the era of the cattle drive in the United States covers a fairly short time frame, the idea of cowboys driving herds of cattle north across the Great Plains has become a permanent part of the American identity.

Cattle were first introduced to the Americas by early Spanish explorers. The open, unfenced grasslands of Texas proved to be an ideal location for cattle, and they thrived. Territorial disputes drove many of the original Mexican settlers out of the region, but to a large extent their herds remained. By the end of the Civil War, the vast plains of Texas had become home to millions of untended and unbranded—and therefore unclaimed—cattle.

With a great demand for beef on the East Coast and new railroads in Kansas, enterprising cowboys began rounding up the unbranded Texas cattle and forming herds to take north for rail transport. Several trails were established for driving the cattle, including the Chisholm Trail from north Texas to Abilene and the Goodnight–Loving Trail from west Texas to Denver. Teams of cattle drivers would move each herd at around ten miles per day, with trips to Kansas or Denver often taking several months to complete.

As railroads expanded to the north and south across the Great Plains, the cattle drive became a largely unnecessary task. By the close of the nineteenth century, the practice had all but vanished. However, the image of the cattle drive continues to define the persona of the American cowboy to people around the world.

## CRITICAL OVERVIEW

When *Lonesome Dove* was published in 1985, Larry McMurtry was already well established as a best-selling novelist of both Western and contemporary novels such as *Horseman, Pass By* (1961) and *Terms of Endearment* (1975). With *Lonesome Dove*, McMurtry had a rare creation: a genre Western that was both a popular and critical success.

Nicholas Lemann, writing for the *New York Times Book Review*, reports that "everything about the book feels true." Lemann credits this to the author's "refusal to glorify the West," but paradoxically notes, "These are real people, and they are still larger than life." Lemann also credits McMurtry with being "a first-rate novelist." Walter Clemons, in a review for *Newsweek*, applauds, "The whole book moves with joyous energy." He also claims that the book "shows, early on, just about every symptom of American Epic except pretentiousness." R. Z. Sheppard, writing for *Time*, also calls the novel an epic and calls attention to the author's "outsize talent for descriptive narrative."

In his review for the *New York Times*, Christopher Lehmann-Haupt argues that while some of the book's elements are old-hat, the novel constitutes a fresh look at Western genre conventions. "There's hardly a frame in this story that you couldn't splice from the memory of Westerns past," he states, but also states that the author "has a way of diverting the progress of his clichés in odd and interesting ways." Referring to the art on the book's dust jacket, he concludes, "By the time you get finished reading it, that jacket painting almost seems to be moving." Whitney Balliett, writing for the *New Yorker*, offers a less enthusiastic assessment of the novel, noting that it "never quite gets free of the glutinous pace McMurtry sets in the opening pages." Still, she concedes that the author "skirts the worst clichés of Western writing." Another complaint logged by Balliett: "The book needs an endpaper map. McMurtry is as vague about place as he is about time, and it would have helped us across the Great Plains."

# MEDIA ADAPTATIONS

*Lonesome Dove* was adapted as a four-hour television miniseries in 1989 and aired on CBS. It stars Robert Duvall as McCrae and Tommy Lee Jones as Call, and included such notable stars as Danny Glover, Diane Lane, Robert Urich, Rick Schroder, and Anjelica Huston. It won the Golden Globe award in 1989 for best miniseries and actor (Duvall), and it won acting nominations for Jones and Huston. It also won seven Emmy awards and was nominated for twelve others. It is available from Lions Gate on a two-DVD set.

In addition to its critical and popular success, *Lonesome Dove* went on to win the 1986 Pulitzer Prize for fiction. In addition, a filmed adaptation of the novel was created for television in 1989; the miniseries, which stars Robert Duvall as Gus and Tommy Lee Jones as Call, is widely considered to be among the greatest Westerns ever put to film. In turn, the miniseries inspired many viewers to read the original novel, creating a new generation of McMurtry enthusiasts.

## CRITICISM

### John Miller-Purrenhage

*In the following excerpt, Miller-Purrenhage argues that the message of* Lonesome Dove, *despite the conventions of the Western genre, is a statement against the possibility of any novel truly capturing the spirit and "story" of more than a sliver of the American experience.*

The epigraph to Larry McMurtry's 1985 novel *Lonesome Dove* is symptomatic of the intriguing interpretive challenges that this book offers. McMurtry follows the dedication page with a quotation from T. K. Whipple's *Study Out the Land*:

*Anjelica Huston and Robert Duvall in a scene from the movie* Lonesome Dove, *1988* CBS Photo Archive/Getty Images

All America lies at the end of the wilderness road, and our past is not a dead past, but still lives in us. Our forefathers had civilization inside themselves, the wild outside. We live in the civilization they created, but within us the wilderness still lingers. What they dreamed, we live, and what they lived, we dream.

Right away, McMurtry wants us to know that his novel concerns America writ large. He indicates that his individuals, groups, and families stand in for the nation, or at least a certain conception of the nation. In a way, this move is too predictable to be as bold as the opening "All America" might imply. After all, readers of westerns may be familiar with the status of those works in American culture as the repositories of the myth of the frontier, one of "our" oldest origin myths. Therefore, they may expect that any novel set in the west, especially the "Old West" of the late-nineteenth century, will somehow be "about" America. An academic reader might think of Richard Slotkin's work on how frontier narratives, including western

novels and films, have reflected and helped shape the nation's consciousness.

However, someone reading with a more critical eye—someone skeptical that the McMurtry who wrote the bitter *Horseman, Pass By* could be writing a typical western or someone familiar with minority discourse analysis—will ask the contentious, but nonetheless pertinent, question, "Who is this 'we'?" Does this "we" include Native Americans, for example, or even women, or anyone else who might be considered outside the borders of this "civilization"? McMurtry does not accept Whipple's statement at face value and expects his readers to find it troubling. Given *Lonesome Dove*'s depiction of multiple groups and families that disintegrate rather than cohere, I would argue that McMurtry's theme is the failure of any sort of "we" to hold together; thus, he criticizes the possibility of any novel, western or otherwise, narrating a coherent version of the nation.

In *Lonesome Dove*, McMurtry shares the concerns of minority writers such as Rudolfo Anaya and Leslie Silko who question the narration of the nation. Homi Bhabha writes that "minority discourse [. . .] contests genealogies of 'origin' that lead to claims for cultural supremacy and historical priority. Minority discourse acknowledges the status of national culture—and the people—as a contentious, performative space." A critical genealogy of America should not only examine the challenges posed by minority discourse but also analyze the performance of cultural supremacy implied by Bhabha's words. Although some characters in *Lonesome Dove* may appeal to a superior culture (at least Call believes he is superior), and the Hat Creek outfit certainly thinks of itself as attaining a symbolic "historical priority" by driving the first cattle into Montana, McMurtry uses the failure of groups and families to cohere to reveal fault lines in the national myth of origins that is the western.

I seek to show how one well-known white western writer has used icon and genre to destabilize the meaning of words like "us" and "them" when used to describe the people of the United States; read in the context of nonwhite writing from the American West, McMurtry's work contributes to the rewriting of our nation's narrative of itself. I argue that we cannot use *Lonesome Dove*—or, given its lessons, any other western story—as support for reading the larger narrative of the conquest of the United States as the country's myth of origins. I read the disruption of genealogy in *Lonesome Dove*—its embodiment of the pointlessness and even the impossibility of maintaining or tracing family, national, or ethnic ties—as a purposeful disruption of the nation's ability to narrate a coherent story of itself.

The introduction of the Hat Creek outfit in chapter 1 presents many of the vexing problems of the epigraph, problems I take to signify McMurtry's interest in troubling group identity formation. Gus McCrae is a former Texas Ranger, now largely retired, who served Texas most of his adult life. Yet, when McMurtry introduces him, the state of his birth is mentioned first and placed in the context of how inhospitable the Lonesome Dove sun can be: "a hell for pigs and Tennesseans." After describing Gus as the half-owner of the cattle company, McMurtry further cements Gus's birthplace as determinative of his identity when Gus calls Dillard Brawley "a fellow Tennessean." Gus's claim of kinship ("fellow")

with another man based on state of birth makes it seem that he would prefer to think of himself as a Tennessean. When he drinks, his pleasant feelings are "foggy and cool as a morning in the Tennessee hills." The characterization of Gus as a Tennessean makes a reader wonder how long one needs to live in Texas to become a Texan, or how much service to the state one must perform to become "naturalized." Additionally, McMurtry presents Gus as someone for whom origins—even those based simply on state of birth—matter to the exclusion of experiences. Readers will find little in the book to explain what a Tennessean is or how one acts, but will find Gus as Texan as anyone.

McMurtry depicts the setting in racist and nationalist terms, adding to the troubling difficulty of becoming naturalized, more like a native of the place. All Lonesome Dove citizens know the border between Texas and Mexico demarcates national identity; moreover, they evidently are prepared to police that identity in case of threat. When Gus considers shooting a snake, he reconsiders because of the potential effect on the community: "Everybody in town would hear it and conclude either that the Comanches were down from the plains or the Mexicans up from the river," and if they were drunk or unhappy, "they would probably run out into the street and shoot a Mexican or two." Although Gus remains a Tennessean, the more obvious markers of race allow him to be included among the (white) citizens of the town, who can tell (simplistically speaking) who does not belong.

A story about Dillard Brawley, the "one white barber in Lonesome Dove," also establishes racial and national borders: Brawley is shot by an unhappy *vaquero*, whom he was trying to help; the subsequent amputation of his leg causes him to lose his voice, then his customers, who "in time [. . .] drifted off to the Mexican barber." Presumably, they have previously gone to Brawley under the presumption that the Anglo barber is superior to the Mexican one, or that it is proper for Anglos to patronize other Anglos. McMurtry finishes the episode with a telling joke that establishes Call as intolerant but, more important, sets up further racial divisions: "Call even used the Mexican, and Call didn't trust Mexicans or barbers." We must infer a stereotype of Mexicans as untrustworthy as the necessary anchor of this joke that also takes in barbers.

Racial and national characteristics clearly form a large part of identity for Call and other characters.

Bolivar, the Mexican cook (who, unlike the Mexican barber, at least is humanized with a name) offers a final example of the shaky ground on which McMurtry establishes the cohesion of his Hat Creek outfit. McMurtry establishes Bol as a cantankerous former bandit whose rude, loud ringing of the dinner bell at the ranch, causes Gus to quip, "I figure he's calling bandits." Like the joke about the Mexican barber, this one depends for its humor on the character of Bol himself; were he not actually a former bandit, it would make no sense. While joking, Gus establishes the possibility of Bol's treachery (as in the case of the barber) and describes his old gang in derogatory racial terms that compound the quality of slipperiness or trickery: "Why, you remember that greasy bunch he had."

Yet, as so often is the case with stereotyping, the joke reveals more about Gus and the outfit than it does about Bolivar. If the story of the town's unified reaction to invading Comanches or Mexicans introduces a form of group cohesion, that cohesion does not always hold. In *Lonesome Dove*, the international border is permeable: With Mexicans raiding north and white Americans raiding south, and each group ignoring the laws of both countries. The identity established by Gus, Call, and the groups they represent (Lonesome Dove, Hat Creek, the Rangers, Texas) must be called into question when the former lawmen break the law so frequently and as a matter of course. Gus goes so far as to base Bolivar's presence and utility at the ranch on his questionable ethics: "In the business we're in, it don't hurt to know a few horse thieves, as long as they're Mexicans." The foreign identity of the horse thieves enables the relationship to work. Far from being innocent of Bol's previous lawlessness, they profit by it, using the convenience of the nearby border to hide not only from the laws of their own country, but also from their consciences. The lawmen in *Lonesome Dove* are far more slippery or "greasy" than any Mexican bandits. Their lawlessness calls into question their identity, and if famous Texas Rangers do not exemplify the values of the "civilization" they fought to protect, how can anyone?

One treasured American story about its national character involves the naturalization of citizens from all over the world—anyone can become American (even if there are many stipulations on that identity based on color, religion, time spent in the country, and so forth). But in *Lonesome Dove*, Gus is not even a naturalized Texan; in his mind, he remains a Tennessean. In a further troubling episode from the early, establishing chapters of the novel, McMurtry's characters reveal restrictive ideas of how one becomes American. No matter that Gus may cross the nation's borders to engage in activity his nation forbids, he is a stickler for origins when it comes to establishing national identity. When Bolivar wants to show his independence, he comments that "General Lee freed the slaves," thus launching Gus's strange comments on nationality. First, Gus corrects Bol (skipping over the fact that Bol has compared himself to a freed slave, despite Gus's attempts to "master" him, but figuratively making himself an American, subject to such emancipation). Pea Eye tries to point out how the emancipation didn't apply to Bol: "He just freed Americans"; that comment shows that Pea Eye sees Deets and other freed slaves as Americans. Pea Eye sees Mexicans as needing freedom, but as ineligible for it as non-Americans. The dominance of Anglos over Mexicans in Texas since the Treaty of Guadalupe Hidalgo is implicit here, but the men's confusion over how a historical act might affect or be affected by nationality gives one little faith in the clarity of national identities or the standards that determine them.

Gus snorts, "Who Abe Lincoln freed was a bunch of Africans, no more American than Call here." Call defends himself: "I'm as American as the next," a claim Gus disputes on the basis of Call's birth in Scotland. Apparently, in his view, being born in Tennessee or Scotland or descended from those who were born in Africa prevents one from ever obtaining another identity. To Gus, one's origin determines one's fate. Gus makes that remark half-jokingly, but because most jokes in the book anchor themselves to some stereotype, I think it accurate to call these Gus's actual thoughts. Gus does not analyze how the migration of populations might affect issues of nationality, thus ignoring a major factor in North and South American history. Although he is generally sympathetic to Deets and Call, if not to Bolivar, Gus's comments constitute in-group snobbery, a fetishizing of origins that allows no change or escape. He effectively narrates a story about a United States whose citizens are defined by their birth and whose borders are permanently closed to outsiders. As he did with the too-bold-and-romantic-to-be-true epigraph about a "we" who dream of a homogeneous past, McMurtry makes Gus's arguments boldly ridiculous. Gus's arguments are analogous to Call's stature as a legendary Texas Ranger, bold and imposing beyond their true measure.

Given these fractious negotiations, we must hesitate to treat the Hat Creek Outfit's adventures as an "American" story, as both the definition of American and the cohesiveness of the outfit are unsettled.

**Source:** John Miller-Purrenhage, "'Kin to Nobody': the Disruption of Genealogy in Larry McMurtry's *Lonesome Dove*," in *CRITIQUE: Studies in Contemporary Fiction*, Vol. 47, No. 1, Fall 2005, pp. 73–90.

## SOURCES

Balliett, Whitney, Review of *Lonesome Dove*, in the *New Yorker*, Vol. 61, November 11, 1985, p. 153; reprinted in *The Book Review Digest (Eighty-First Annual Cumulation)*, edited by Martha T. Mooney, The H. W. Wilson Company, 1986, p. 1064.

Clemons, Walter, Review of *Lonesome Dove*, in *Newsweek*, Vol. 105, June 3, 1985, p. 74; reprinted in *The Book Review Digest (Eighty-First Annual Cumulation)*, edited by Martha T. Mooney, The H. W. Wilson Company, 1986, p. 1064.

Lehmann-Haupt, Christopher, Review of *Lonesome Dove*, in the *New York Times*, June 3, 1985, Section C, p. 20.

Lemann, Nicholas, Review of *Lonesome Dove*, in the *New York Times Book Review*, June 9, 1985, p. 7; reprinted in *The Book Review Digest (Eighty-First Annual Cumulation)*, edited by Martha T. Mooney, The H. W. Wilson Company, 1986, p. 1064.

McMurtry, Larry, *Lonesome Dove*, Pocket Books, 1986.

Sheppard, R. Z., Review of *Lonesome Dove*, in *Time*, Vol. 125, June 10, 1985, p. 79; reprinted in *The Book Review Digest (Eighty-First Annual Cumulation)*, edited by Martha T. Mooney, The H. W. Wilson Company, 1986, p. 1064.

# *Main Street*

## SINCLAIR LEWIS

## 1920

Sinclair Lewis's *Main Street* (1920) was the first best-selling American novel of the century, selling almost 300,000 copies in its first year of publication and nearly 100,000 in the second year. When it was published, a reviewer in the *Nation* wrote, "*Main Street* would add to the power and distinction of the contemporary literature of any country." The novel brought Lewis fame and glory, making up for his past literary disappointments and establishing him as a serious force among his vaunted literary generation.

*Main Street* follows the life of idealistic Carol Milford from the time she is a student at Blodgett College in 1906, focusing on the period from 1912 to 1920 and her life in the fictional Gopher Prairie, Minnesota. The novel depicts the town as smug, conformist, and intolerant of the free-thinking, and it challenges established ideas about life in small-town America as well as marriage, gender roles, and early feminist thought. Carol is idealistic from the start, considering "creation of a beautiful town" a career option. While working as a librarian in St. Paul, Minnesota, Carol meets and marries Dr. Will Kennicott, a middle-aged doctor from Gopher Prairie. When Carol moves there, the relatively sophisticated new wife finds life in the town dull and the people complacent. She tries to change and enlighten the city, to no avail.

Throughout *Main Street*, Carol's life has some high points as she tries to maintain her

# BIOGRAPHY

## SINCLAIR LEWIS

Sinclair Lewis was born Harry Sinclair Lewis on February 7, 1885, in Sauk Centre, Minnesota. His experiences there provided some of the inspiration for his masterpiece, *Main Street*. Sauk Centre was a small town similar to the fictional Gopher Prairie, and Lewis was the son of a doctor there. A misfit in Sauk Centre, Lewis left the small town after high school to attend Yale. After graduating in 1908, he worked for newspapers and magazines for several years. He also wrote four unsuccessful novels beginning with *Our Mr. Wrenn* in 1914, but these books had little in common with his better-known works. He and his first wife, Grace, had their only child, Wells, in 1917.

*Main Street* (1920) was Lewis's fifth novel and a literary smash that established him as a successful author worldwide. He followed it with more social satire and criticism, starting with *Babbitt* (1922), his masterwork satire about business, and *Arrowsmith* (1925), a novel about an upright doctor dealing with a commercialized, petty world. Lewis refused the Pulitzer Prize for the latter. After *Elmer Gentry* (1927) and *Dodsworth* (1929), Lewis was awarded the Nobel Prize for literature in 1930. He and his second wife, the celebrated journalist Dorothy Thompson, also had their son, Michael, that year. While he continued to publish a number of novels in the 1930s and 1940s, they were undistinguished. He and Dorothy divorced in 1942, and his son Wells died fighting in France in World War II in 1944. Traveling in Europe the last years of his life, he died of an alcoholism-related heart attack on January 10, 1951, near Rome.

---

idealism while members of community regularly show their ignorance and limited worldview. She gives birth to a beloved son named Hugh and has strong relationships with some people that many townsfolk would not consider socializing with, such as Bea and Miles. However, many of Gopher Prairie's residents regard her as a snob and do not take her as a friend. Even her husband resents her attempts to share culture with him and her constant criticisms of the town. Though Will has heroic qualities as a doctor, he also shares some of the town's prejudices and cannot always appreciate his wife's enthusiasm. Several times she wonders if she is in love with another man, most seriously with Erik Valborg, a tailor's assistant.

Near the novel's end, Carol temporarily separates from her husband and takes Hugh to Washington, D.C., where she finds a job in a government office at the end of World War I. There, she finally enjoys a long-desired freedom to find herself and to escape the stifling life in Gopher Prairie. While Carol finds life in the nation's capital more stimulating, a visit from Will more than a year later helps her decide to return to Gopher Prairie. As she matures, she comes to consider the place home, although she does not give up her idealism entirely.

Critics note that *Main Street* is filled with accurate details of small-town life. They especially praised Lewis for capturing language, including slang of the area and the dialect of recent immigrants. Contradictions abound in many characters, giving them depth, which reviewers appreciated. They also gave kudos for the story of Carol's struggles to define herself and the seething indictment of small-town life, where sensitivity is unappreciated, if not disdained or even scorned.

Lewis based the novel on his own experiences growing up a sensitive loner in the small town of Sauk Centre, Minnesota. Those in Sauk Centre, who had never really understood young Lewis and did not take him seriously as an author early on, resented what he wrote in the 1920s. Ivy Hidebrand, an amateur historian from Sauk Centre, told Michael Dobbs of the *Washington Post* in 1988, "They almost burned Sinclair in effigy here when the book appeared. They felt rather cosmopolitan, and they thought he had held them up to ridicule." Years later, the community embraced their native son, who was buried there in 1951. A street was named for him, and Lewis-centered tourist attractions sprung up, including an annual Sinclair Lewis Day.

Lewis felt *Main Street* would be a turning point in his writing career, devoting more energy to it than anything else he had yet written. According to Martin Light in *The Quixotic Vision of Sinclair Lewis*, before the novel was published, Lewis wrote, "I believe that it will be the real beginning of my writing. No book and no number of short stories I've ever done have meant a quarter of what this does to me." This sentiment was confirmed by scholars such as Stuart P. Sherman, who writes in *The Significance of Sinclair Lewis*,

> In its exhibition of the interwoven lives of the community, it has the authority, the intimacy, the many-sided insights, . . . which are possible only, one is tempted to say, to one who packs into his book the most vital experience and observation of a lifetime.

*Sinclair Lewis* The Library of Congress

## PLOT SUMMARY

### Chapter 1

*Main Street* opens with the introduction of Carol Milford, an idealistic college senior at Blodgett College, where her classmates think she is smaller than she seems, "a fragile child who must be cloaked with understanding kindness." A sociology class inspires her to want to improve a prairie town as a teacher, though she later decides to become a librarian. Carol goes to Chicago for further training, then spends three years working at a library in St. Paul.

### Chapter 2

In St. Paul, the culture-loving Carol meets Dr. Will Kennicott, a somewhat older general practitioner in the small town of Gopher Prairie, Minnesota, at the house of an acquaintance. He courts her, shows her pictures of his home, and wants her to come to Gopher Prairie to improve the town, saying, "I'll admit we aren't any too darn artistic. . . . But go to it! Make us change!"

### Chapters 3–4

Carol and Will have married, but on the train to Gopher Prairie, she starts to have doubts and wonders if she has made a mistake. Once there, she is overwhelmed by the simple, friendly townspeople who come to meet their train. She finds comfort in Will but is unsure about much else.

Carol comes to hate Will's house. She walks around Gopher Prairie and finds the town smaller than she expected. At the same time, Bea Sorenson, another young woman newly arrived in town, is also taking her first look around. Having come to escape the dullness of country life, Bea finds Gopher Prairie exciting and cosmopolitan. Will takes Carol to a party given by the Clarks, where she makes several small gaffes in conversation with her conservative neighbors.

### Chapters 5–7

Going hunting with Will, Carol tries to convince herself she is content. She starts to connect with others and sees some good aspects of her new community, and she hires Bea to be her maid. She befriends Vida Sherwin, a schoolteacher, with whom she enjoys conversation about culture. She also meets Guy Pollock, a cultured bachelor lawyer in town.

Carol is unhappy that Will does not give her an allowance and will not work out a system with her to cover the household expenses. They have a party, which Carol tries to make it different than the other, very similar gatherings she has gone to in Gopher Prairie. Her party shocks some of the attendees, but Will is supportive.

Her first winter in Gopher Prairie, Carol organizes fun outdoor activities such as ice skating and skiing, but she cannot get anyone to do such things twice. She grows bored and tired of pushing people. Yet she decides again to reform the community, in part by becoming part of it. She joins the Jolly Seventeen, a social club for the leading young married women in Gopher Prairie. At her first meeting, the ladies are shocked when they learn how generously Carol pays her maid. She also has a disagreement with the town librarian over whether the librarian's role is to encourage reading or to preserve books. Vida does her best to diffuse the tension.

## Chapters 8–10
Vida calls on her at her home. Carol confides in her, and she finds that Vida also wants to improve the town. Vida also informs Carol why the town is critical of her, including different complaints that she is affected, a show-off, frivolous, patronizing, flip, eccentric, and impious. When Will returns later, he also explains that some merchants are offended that she seems to find their stores lacking.

Because of the criticism, Carol becomes uncomfortable when she goes into town. She sees derision everywhere goes, whether real or not. Her fears are not unfounded as she learns that people in the community have been talking about her. She also questions her marriage and whether she made a mistake, but also finds comfort in her husband. Carol only confides her fears to Vida and considers Bea her closest companion.

Lonely when Will is away treating a patient, Carol takes a walk around town and runs into Miles Bjornstam, the town handyman. They connect as they share critiques of Gopher Prairie. After Will returns, the town seems friendlier to Carol. She starts her reform with her husband by reading poetry to him, which does not impress him.

## Chapter 11
Carol goes to her first meeting of the Thanatopsis, a weekly women's study club Vida has encouraged her to attend. It is supposed to be a leading group in Gopher Prairie, and Carol hopes to use it to improve the community. Once there, she is proud that she fits in but is

tense and uncertain. She is voted in as a member and again finds pride in being a resident of Gopher Prairie.

Carol looks around the town and wants to stop thinking about how to improve everything, but she cannot help herself. She makes plans for how to make the community more physically pleasing and again decides to use Thanatopsis to put these changes into action, as many of the women are married to the city's leading men.

When she tries to push reform to members of the group, it does not go as well as she expected. Carol asks the richest man in town, Mr. Dawson, to support town renovations, but he turns her down. Miles, to Carol's surprise, agrees with him. At another Thanatopsis meeting, Carol wants them to help the poor with programs that offer self-help. They turn her down. Recognizing defeat, Carol thinks, "Had she actually believed that she could plant a seed of liberalism in the blank wall of mediocrity?"

## Chapter 12
That summer, she goes on medical calls in the country with her husband and is content with the outdoor, rural life with Will. In the fall, she starts a literary salon with Vida and Guy, but they only manage to meet once. She also enjoys visiting some longtime locals, the Perrys, and reading about Gopher Prairie's past. The Perrys and their attitudes ultimately disappoint her.

## Chapter 13
Carol tries to call on the Perrys again, but they are not home. Instead, she visits with Guy Pollock and shares her idea that Gopher Prairie needs to be improved. Carol asks him why he remains there, and he explains that he suffers from "Village Virus" and tells her how things work in small communities like this one: "Gopher Prairie isn't particularly bad. It's like all villages in all countries."

## Chapter 14
Walking home, Carol considers whether she is in love with Guy, but she decides she is fond of her husband. When she returns home, she asks Will about issues raised by Guy about rival doctors and dentists. They end up having a serious fight about their clashing values and the town. Will tries to point out things she has not yet learned about the residents of the town, himself included: "If you think for one moment I want

to be stuck in this burg all my life, and not have a chance to travel and see different points of interest and all that, then you simply don't get me."

## Chapter 15

In December, Carol sees Will's many virtues and falls back in love with her husband. In the middle of the night, he has to leave to operate on a German woman, and one Sunday cares for a man with a deep cut on his leg. Carol sees and appreciates what he does as a doctor. To keep herself busy, she thinks of surprises and other amusements. One day, she puts together a treat for her husband and takes it to his office. Seeing his waiting room is somewhat shabby, she does a little redecoration that Will only appreciates when completed.

One day, Carol rides with Will as he visits his patients the Erdstroms. While there, a call comes that his services are urgently needed at Adolph Morgenroth's farm because he has crushed his arm in a farm accident. Carol has to help with the operation to remove his arm by delivering the anesthetic. Though she becomes ill, she greatly admires Will.

## Chapter 16

Around Christmas, Carol continues to try to understand her husband. After the couple goes to the movies one night, Carol becomes sarcastic about the content on their way home. They argue, and Will tells her that he thought she had gotten over her high-minded ideas. When he is asleep, she ponders her situation. She thinks about how she reads and plays piano less and has given up her ideas for local improvements: "I'm not trying to 'reform the town' now.... I'm trying to save my soul."

Her problems weigh on her heavily and she tries to work them out with the help of Vida and Guy. Carol realizes that she has been projecting ideas about Guy that are not true; he is really of Gopher Prairie. "Carol saw that he was a stranger. She saw that he had never been anything but a frame on which she had hung shining garments." Vowing to press on, Carol is happy when Miles comes to the house to build a range. She becomes a little jealous when Miles shows interest in Bea.

## Chapters 17–18

On a sleigh ride with other leading citizens, Carol suggests they form a drama club and put on a play. Carol is selected to be president of the group. With Will, she goes to Minneapolis to see a show, explore, and have fun. They go to a drama school to view some productions, which leave Will somewhat confused.

For the community production, Carol wants to do something artistic, but she is appalled that even Vida does not share her sentiments. The committee votes to perform *The Girl from Kankakee*, though Carol is a dissenting vote. As director and actor with a small role, she comes to hate the play. The production does not go well, and Carol cannot get the group to commit to putting on another play.

## Chapters 19–20

Bea leaves the Kennicott's employ when she marries Miles. Carol plans the wedding. She replaces Bea with Oscarina, who proves to be as competent and nearly as close a companion to Carol as Bea.

Carol spends a two-year term on the library board, a position to which she is appointed. She tries to offer ideas for improvement, but her suggestions are ignored. She finds another outlet in Chautauqua, a traveling education and entertainment group that spends a week in Gopher Prairie. While she attends the lectures, she finds it is not what she expected, except in its critique of Gopher Prairie. Soon after the Great War begins, she learns she is pregnant.

Though Carol is sick through her pregnancy, she is happy when her son Hugh is born. His birth temporarily lessens her desire to leave Gopher Prairie. She focuses much of her attention on Hugh for the first two years of his life, and she stops criticizing and aspiring as much for that time period.

Her domestic bliss is tempered by a visit by Will's uncle and aunt, Whittier N. Smail and his wife Bessie. They irritate Carol when they stay with the family, arriving before Hugh's birth and staying for three weeks. They are critical of nearly everything she does and have what she considers ridiculous ideas. They buy a home and business in Gopher Prairie.

Carol finds relief in the Jolly Seventeen. She is part of the community now and realizes her place within it. She is sometimes embarrassed to take Hugh to Bea's to visit her friend and former maid's family, which now includes a son named Olaf.

## Chapters 21–22

It is revealed that Will had flirted with Vida before marrying Carol, and that Vida had developed feelings for him. Vida thought she was going to marry him before he brought Carol to Gopher Prairie.

When Carol arrived in the community, Vida felt an odd connection to her. While Vida liked Carol the first year she lived in Gopher Prairie, she resents her reform ideas, as Vida has worked to similar ends for much longer. Vida grew more indignant about Carol after Hugh's birth, because she believes Carol is not fulfilled enough by Hugh. Vida soon becomes involved with Raymie Wutherspoon, whom she marries.

Carol reflects on changes in married Vida. Still lonely, Carol buys and borrows many books to read. She sees the sameness in American small towns, and she shares this opinion with Vida. Carol soon becomes re-obsessed with cultural reform. Vida chides her for giving up and not really seeing her plans through, while Vida has worked with a group and gotten a new school building constructed. Carol becomes more active but not yet satisfied.

## Chapter 23

The United States enters the Great War, and Vida's husband joins the military. Though Will wants to sign up as well, he stays to be the town's doctor. Two months after the United States joins the war, Percy Bresnahan, a former resident of Gopher Prairie, visits. He is a friend of Will's and now the rich president of Velvet Motor Company in Boston. Unlike everyone else in town, Carol is not initially impressed with him. They talk about why she dislikes Gopher Prairie, and she tells him how dull it really is. Percy tells her, "My humble (not too humble!) opinion is that you like to be different. You like to think you're peculiar," though she is like many other women elsewhere. By the end of the visit, she feels young again because of his flirtations.

## Chapter 24

That summer, Carol observes more about Will as the couple stays in town instead of moving to a summer cabin. She has little to say to him and their marriage becomes distant. She idealizes Percy and wonders what he would be like as a husband. After an argument with Will, Carol moves to her own room. Her domestic situation worsens when Oscarina leaves and Carol has

problems finding a replacement, much to the delight of the gossips. She often does the housework herself. Will wants to get a new house, but the couple disagrees on what should be included and the plans are soon dropped.

Carol is desperate to go on vacation but it does not happen, in part because of Will's work commitment. They take a day trip to a nearby town like Gopher Prairie, but this excursion does not help refresh Carol. She tries to get her husband and their companions to do something different, such as riding a merry-go-round, but she cannot get anyone to join her.

## Chapter 25

The narrative shifts to Will's point of view. He broods about Carol, whom he calls Carrie, and resents that she has been trying to change him for all these years. He feels like an outsider in his own home. Though he regrets it, Will begins having an affair with Mrs. Dyer. The Kennicotts' neighbor Mrs. Bogart gossips to Carol, implying that Will might be doing something he should not, but Carol dismisses what she says.

## Chapter 26

Carol spends a lot of time walking through town with Hugh. She often takes him to Miles and Bea's home to play with Olaf, though Will disapproves. Carol thinks of the couple as better friends than the Jolly Seventeen and others in town. Miles tells her that he is a pariah in town. He is proven right when Bea and Olaf become sick with typhoid, and no one else in town really cares until it is too late. Though Carol helps take care of them, they both die. A neighbor remarks to Carol at the funeral: "I don't waste any sympathy on that man of hers. Everybody says he drank too much, and treated his family awful, and that's how they got sick."

## Chapters 27–29

Miles leaves Gopher Prairie. Carol finds a new friend in Mrs. Flickerbaugh, an attorney's wife who shares Carol's disdain for the town. Erik Valborg, a tailor's apprentice, is a new young man in Gopher Prairie. Carol meets him and finds he is a kindred spirit. As their friendship develops, she learns that he wants to be a clothing designer back East. Carol also becomes friends with the new teacher in town, Fern Mullins. Carol, Erik, and Fern talk about organizing another play.

Carol and Erik's friendship grows deeper as they talk together. She learns about his background and tells him that she does not belong in Gopher Prairie. She is embarrassed to be seen with him in town and is uncomfortable with how personal he gets when he flirts with her. Prejudice grows in the town against Erik. Carol feels affection and interest, as well as shame because of his lower social class. She is unhappy in her marriage to Will, and she realizes that she might be falling in love with Erik. People tease her about liking him.

## Chapter 30

On a picnic with the Dyers, Cy Bogart, and Fern, Carol and Erik go off in a boat for some time by themselves and talk until dark, which causes more gossip. Thrilled by his attention and potential, she decides she wants to leave Gopher Prairie:

> It was not Erik to whom she must escape, but universal and joyous youth, in class-rooms, in studios, in offices, in meetings to protest against Things in General.... But universal and joyous youth rather resembled Erik.

She is jealous when she sees him at a Baptist church supper paying attention to Myrtle Cass. He insists he is only trying to forget that he really wants: Carol. Carol asks Will to go away with her or if she can go somewhere by herself. Will assures her they will go on vacation when the war ends. The dullness of her life makes Carol feel pushed toward Erik.

As Erik becomes more accepted by some of the citizens of Gopher Prairie, he wants to stay, learn about the wheat business, and give up dreams of living in the East. At home, she is conflicted by what she feels for Erik.

## Chapter 31

Erik shows up at the Kennicott home one night when Will is away on a call. Carol worries about gossip, but she tells him that she wants him but that they can be just friends. Rumors abound in town about Carol and Erik, Vida reports to her one day. Vida also tells her that she was once interested in Will. Aunt Bessie tries to imply to Carol that Will is having an affair. Carol feels that everyone is watching and that everyone knows her thoughts.

## Chapter 32

A scandal involving Fern embroils the town, fueled by Mrs. Bogart. Bogart's son Cy, a high school-aged bully, drove Fern, a young teacher at the high school, to a country barn dance. Cy got drunk and had to be driven home by Fern, where his mother found him sick on the porch. He said it was Fern's fault. Mrs. Bogart also implied that Fern and Cy had gotten physically intimate. Mrs. Bogart has been repeating her story all around town, including to the school board. Carol hates that Fern is being gossiped about and condemned for an error of her youth, merely wanting so much to have fun that she would go to a party unchaperoned. She also worries that Fern might be being attacked because of her lower social status, something that prevented such harshness in the gossip about Carol and Erik.

Carol visits Fern and hears her side of the story. Cy stole liquor from a man's pocket at the dance and got drunk. He kissed her and tried to do more. Fern had to drive his car to get them home. Carol tries to help Fern by talking to the school board president but he tells her that the members favor Mrs. Bogart. Fern is forced to resign and leave town. She finds it nearly impossible to find another teaching job.

## Chapter 33

Though Carol has not been seeing Erik much, she is sure that she loves him. When Will is gone another time, Erik shows up again and asks her to meet in the country to walk and talk. They hold hands and Erik tells her that he likes her. Driving home, Will comes upon them and tells them to get into the car. He is nice to Erik but ignores Carol. When they get home, Will tells her that he has heard the gossip and she must stop. They argue. Though Carol wants to believe that Erik will support her, Will tells her that Erik probably will not be a success, that he will never act on his dreams. Carol kisses him and promises to avoid Erik.

Soon after, Erik leaves for Minneapolis. Carol and Will make love. A week later, Erik's father shows up at the Kennicott door. He demands to know where his son is because he wants him to return to the family farm. Carol is upset by the incident. When Will comes home, she tells him she wants to go to California. They plan to leave in a few weeks and arrange for Hugh to be cared for by his aunt and uncle while they are away.

## Chapters 34–35

The couple travels for three and a half months in the West. Will participates in many activities that Carol likes. They come home to a sleet storm. While Will is happy to be back, Carol wonders why she should stay. Though she is happy to see Hugh, nothing has changed and she wants to leave. The town undergoes an economic boom and attracts new people, and hires James Blausser, a land speculator, to take charge of a campaign to boost the town's image. While he and others push the town to be bigger, Carol is doubtful and hates the town's new ego.

## Chapters 36–38

Will does not understand why Carol has doubts. He wants her to be supportive because she wanted the town changed. They argue over a nearby sheriff preventing a political meeting. Carol says she is leaving, perhaps for a year or forever, and she is taking Hugh with her. They continue to argue for a month, with Will focused on duty and Carol on freedom. Carol takes Hugh to Washington, D.C., to work in a government office at the end of the war. She finds the office is as full of cliques and gossip as Gopher Prairie, but she feels more whole. Carol enjoys the mystery of the city and does some work with suffragettes. This experience bolsters her low opinion about Gopher Prairie.

Carol stays in D.C. for a year, and she grows tired of life there. She runs into the Haydocks on the street and learns that Blausser is gone. Seeing people from Gopher Prairie makes her realize that she is homesick. When she has been gone thirteen months, Will comes to visit. Though he stays in a hotel, they tour the capital together. Carol sees him in a new light, especially as he tries to please her.

One night, he tells her he wants her to come home, but it has to be her choice. He also tells her that he has been unfaithful. Before he leaves, Will asks her to go on vacation in the South with him to have fun. During the trip, Will also promises to make her happy and to leave the town more often. When she returns to D.C., Carol asks the advice of a leader in the suffragette movement. Carol decides to go back a few months later. She does not hate Gopher Prairie any more and now sees it as home.

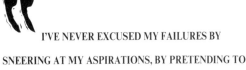

I'VE NEVER EXCUSED MY FAILURES BY SNEERING AT MY ASPIRATIONS, BY PRETENDING TO HAVE GONE BEYOND THEM. I DO NOT ADMIT THAT MAIN STREET IS AS BEAUTIFUL AS IT SHOULD BE! I DO NOT ADMIT THAT GOPHER PRAIRIE IS GREATER OR MORE GENEROUS THAN EUROPE! I DO NOT ADMIT THAT DISH-WASHING IS ENOUGH TO SATISFY ALL WOMEN!"

## Chapter 39

When Carol returns home, she realizes some people had missed her. She finds more balance in her life. While Mrs. Dyer resents her return, Carol is able to see those who annoyed her in a new light. She has another baby, a girl, and learns to shoot a gun. Carol still has her own ideas and problems with the community, but they are more tempered. She tells Will, "I may not have fought the good fight, but I have kept the faith."

# THEMES

## Limitations of Small-Town America

One of the primary themes in Lewis's satire is the limitations of American small towns in early twentieth-century America. As the country became more urban and industrial, Americans tended to feel nostalgic about the way things used to be. Never finding happiness in small-town life himself, Lewis skewers that idealism in *Main Street*. Through the eyes of Carol, who comes to Gopher Prairie as an outsider, Lewis shows how small-minded, petty, simple, gossipy, cliquey, prejudiced, insular, and set in their ways the inhabitants of such communities can be. While Lewis points out that there are some good points to these places—such as the stability of many relationships and a generally unhurried rhythm of life—he generally depicts them as limiting and dull.

Gopher Prairie is a town socially divided. Those who are prosperous spend time with their social and economic peers. They reject anyone who is different, such as Miles Bjornstam, who has some radical ideas. Social lines are rarely crossed, something that angers Miles as Bea and Olaf near death from typhoid. As Carol nurses them, Vida, Mrs. Dyer, and Mrs. Zitterel, the Baptist pastor's wife, come to the door of the Bjornstam home with grapes, books, and magazines, offering to do something. Miles answers, but sends the women away angrily, telling them,

> You're too late.... Bea's always kind of hoped that you folks would come see her. She wanted to have a chance and be friends. She used to sit waiting for somebody to knock.... Oh, you ain't worth [cursing].

Though even Carol is aware of social strata and sometimes embarrassed to be friends with Miles and Bea, she usually acts the way she wants and ends up flouting such social barriers. She generally likes those considered different, such as Erik Valborg, a tailor's apprentice who dresses fashionably. Many in Gopher Prairie consider his attire feminine, so they dub him "Elizabeth" and shun him without knowing him when he first moves there. Leading citizens ruin the first tennis exhibition he organizes in chapter 29 by agreeing to be there and then holding it at another location without telling him and those who committed to play there.

While Erik's situation improves somewhat over time, his relationship with Carol is the topic of much gossip in Gopher Prairie. Many in the community thrive on gossiping about each other, including the Kennicotts' neighbor, Mrs. Bogart. Carol grows paranoid on several occasions that the town is talking about her and judging her, feelings that often turn out to be true. Gossip is also the medium for accusing others: Several people imply that Will is having an affair, but Carol does not believe it. Will, indeed, is involved with Mrs. Dyer.

Throughout the novel, Carol tries to get those in the community to change, or at least to try new things, but her efforts generally fail. She cannot get them to go sledding or ice skating more than once, and the initial production of the drama club is the only production. She tries to push enlightenment on those who do not want it, including her husband, because the inhabitants are not interested in changing their ways. The residents believe they are living the right way and do not want to be told otherwise. Carol is a square peg in the round hole of Gopher Prairie.

She ultimately comes to consider it her home, but not because she changes it—in the end, it changes her.

### Searching for Self and Personal Growth

Though it is the birthright of every American to dream, to grow, and to pursue happiness, the actual achievement of happiness is much more elusive. Much of *Main Street* is devoted to Carol's search for herself in her life. She never knows quite who she is or who she wants to be, but she is on a quest for personal growth and happiness. Because she often cannot find acceptable answers in her own life, Carol tries to change those around her, including her husband and the town. She pushes herself as well and is not afraid to act outside of acceptable societal norms in her actions and friendships if she believes it is the right thing to do.

From the beginning, Carol questions who she wants to be and continually looks for something new. While a college student at Blodgett, "By turns she hoped to discover that she had an unusual voice, a talent for the piano, the ability to act, to write, to manage organizations. Always she was disappointed, but always she effervesced anew." Carol acts the same way when it comes time to choose a career as a senior, vacillating between teaching, law, nursing, social work, and screenwriting, before finally settling on becoming a librarian as a way of affecting lives. Improving a prairie village becomes her secondary career, but something she also takes rather seriously in her musings.

After marrying Dr. Will Kennicott, Carol is rarely content with her marriage and her life in Gopher Prairie. She looks down on many of the residents for who they are and for their actions, typified by the mundane parties she and Will attend. During the first one he takes her to at the Clarks' in chapter 4, she hears the townspeople's amusing anecdotes. The narrator reveals, "During the winter Carol was to hear Dave Dyer's hen-catching impersonation seven times, 'An Old Sweetheart of Mine' nine times, the Jewish story and the funeral oration twice." Carol finds such repetition intolerable and often suggests something new in part because she craves culture, but also as a means of shaking up the community.

Over the years, Carol grows less content with Gopher Prairie and her husband. While she loves her son and becomes close to Bea and

Miles, Carol regularly tries to figure out what she wants looks to find someone new to make her life more interesting. She wonders if she is in love with Guy Pollock after he flirts with her, and she has the same feelings about Percy Bresnahan when he comes to town. Carol's relationship with Erik Valborg comes closest to a romantic entanglement. She sees him as a fellow sensitive artistic type with boundless potential, until her husband confronts her about the situation and offers a much more plausible, pessimistic vision of Erik's future.

After moving to Gopher Prairie, Carol asks her husband on a number of occasions if they can go on vacation or get away for a while. She is desperate to escape her life there. Save for the one time they go to a town just like Gopher Prairie, Will puts her off until Carol and Erik become the subject of rumors. When Will confronts Carol about Erik, he also finally agrees to take a trip with her, an extended three-and-a-half month vacation in the West. This trip brings some closeness back to their marriage, but it does not solve Carol's problems.

She and Will continue to fight until she tells him she is leaving Gopher Prairie for some time and taking Hugh with her. She tells Will, "I have a right to my own life." While the office in Washington, D.C., proves to be full of people who are just as petty as the citizens of Gopher Prairie, Carol also loves the city and its many complexities. Though she returns to Gopher Prairie of her own volition and is more content with her life, Carol justifies herself, telling Will, "I've never excused my failures by sneering at my aspirations, by pretending to have gone beyond them.... I have kept the faith."

## HISTORICAL OVERVIEW

### Reform

In early twentieth-century America, the concept of reform could be found nation-wide, especially in the tumultuous first two decades of the century when the progressive era was at a peak. Reform groups tried to shape government policies through organizations such as the American Bar Association, the National American Woman Suffrage Association, and the Association for the Study of Negro Life and History. While each group pushed its own issues, there was an overall movement toward demanding reform of the education and legal systems, social justice, and urban environments.

Reformers challenged the established power structures in the United States, especially in social welfare and morality. The most widely accepted goals of the progressives were threefold: opposition of the abuse of power, social institution reform, and better and more widespread use of emerging scientific efficiencies and cooperation. Many members of the newly emerging middle class, including doctors, teachers, and lawyers, pushed such ideas of reform for the betterment of American society.

Both the working and upper classes also had reforming goals. The working class, especially in urban America, wanted government-enforced safety improvements in the workplace and better housing and health care, among other reforms. Upper-class reformers wanted to use the principals of efficiency as used in business in organizing how schools, hospitals, and other social institutions operated.

Upper-class women took reform action through groups like the Women's Christian Temperance Union and the Young Women's Christian Association. Such groups were key to the passage of the Eighteenth Amendment to the U.S. Constitution. Implemented in 1920, the amendment prohibited the production, sale, and transportation of alcohol, beginning the era of Prohibition in the United States.

### Women's Rights

Another key area of the early twentieth-century progressive movement was in the area of women's rights. At the time, white males dominated American society. Women could not vote and had fewer legal rights than men. Before 1910, women's quest to break out of the home and into social and welfare activities, receive college educations, and hold jobs was called the "woman movement." Their agenda was often pushed through women's clubs that could help better society and encourage the government to improve regulation of the labor of children and women, and to improve education and housing reform, among other issues. After 1910, the term "feminist" came into widespread use. Feminists wanted women to come together and call for an end to discrimination based on gender. They believed women should hold jobs, be on equal terms with men sexually, and have access to contraception.

One area in which women achieved victory was the suffrage movement. Though the suffrage movement began in the 1890s with elite women who believed educated women such as themselves should be given the right to vote, feminists believed that all women, including lower-class workers, should have the right to vote because all women contributed to the betterment of American society. By 1912, nine western states allowed women to vote in state and local elections. The suffrage movement gained public notice through the activities of the National American Woman Suffrage Association and other groups, as well as women's participation in the war effort during World War I. The Nineteenth Amendment, which gave women the right to vote nationally, was ratified in 1920.

### Population Shifts in America

The American population was shifting geographically in the early twentieth century. More and more Americans were moving to cities with a population greater than 2,500. In 1890, about 35 percent of Americans lived in such cities. By 1920, that number increased to over 51 percent. This marked the first time that a majority of Americans lived in urban environments. The trend continued through the 1920s as six million Americans left the farm for cities both large and small, close by and far away. Many Midwesterners, especially young single people, moved to regional centers or to California. Suburbs around major cites such as Chicago, Cleveland, Los Angeles, and Detroit grew rapidly through the 1920s. The expansion of car ownership allowed workers to move to the suburbs. Despite the expansion of urban environments, small towns were still regarded in an idealistic light as the center of innocence and simplicity, though many intellectuals believed such places did not allow for much personal growth.

### CRITICAL OVERVIEW

When Lewis published *Main Street* in 1920, it was a literary bombshell. Over the years, the novel has remained a classic work of American literature. Since it was published, it has been seen as the archetype of early twentieth-century society in small-town America. Early critics recognized the book's merits while debating its flaws. Stanton A. Coblentz of the *Bookman* writes in an early review of *Main Street*,

Life in Gopher Prairie, small and changeless and perpetually narrow, is made photographically real; yet while the author writes with the most minute and unerring sense of detail, he peers beneath the surface with a keenness that is more than photographic.

Other early critics bristled at Lewis's satire and depiction of small-town people as shallow and dull. This concept was shocking in its time as American small towns were nearly always depicted as good and their residents as moral, hard-working, and neighborly. While some early critics took issue with the way he composed his characters, believing they were more types than fully drawn characters, others saw them as uniquely American and representative of humanity.

The plot or lack thereof also was the center of critical debate. While also noting how representative the book is of all small towns in America, the critic in the *New York Times Book Review* observes, "There is practically no plot yet the book is absorbing. It is so much like life itself, so extraordinarily real. These people are actual folk, and there was never better dialogue written than their revealing talk."

This was not the only critic to praise Lewis's keen ear for natural speech. The critic in the *Nation* in 1920 comments, "his dialogue, which he uses very freely, is brilliant. The exactness of this dialogue is a literary achievement of a very high order. . . . it is living talk."

Reviewers who did not like the book felt that *Main Street* was unfair to small cities and those people who lived in them, some charging that it amounted to libel. A number of critics believed that the characters and their actions were often inconsistent. Even today, some critics believe the novel is too long, despite the fact that Lewis cut 20,000 words before it was originally published. Some also believed that the story was too small for the novel's length. In 1922, Americanus, writing in the *Spectator* (U.K.), claims, "*Main Street* was too much a mere collection of material, a cataloguing of facts. There was almost nothing there beyond those things which made us acquainted with the milieu, which let us see, hear, smell and feel it."

Over the years, Carol and her point of view became the subject of critical and scholarly attention. She was often compared to the primary character in Gustav Flaubert's *Madame Bovary*, and other impractical female dreamers.

# MEDIA ADAPTATIONS

*Main Street* was released as an unabridged audiobook in 1996; Barbara Caruso narrates the story and voices the characters in this nineteen-hour recording. It is available on audio cassette or for download from Penguin Audio.

Writing in *The Quixotic Vision of Sinclair Lewis* (1975), Martin Light argues,

> I think that we are better informed about *Main Street*—and better able to assess it—if we see it as an account of a quixotic figure—idealistic, disillusioned, of limited vision, yet a challenge to the community.... She is more honest and more deceived than anyone around her, and thereby both more trapped and more alive.

In the early 1990s, *Main Street* was inducted into the Library of America. This is a collection of books that reflects the best of the best in American fiction and nonfiction. By the mid-1990s critics like James E. Person Jr. of the *Washington Times* claims that since the book was published, "The very words 'Main Street' became a byword in American culture."

## CRITICISM

### Benjamin Schwarz

*In the following excerpt, Lingeman reviews the Lewis biography* Rebel from Main Street *and asserts that* Main Street *was Lewis's biggest accomplishment but that the masterpiece reveals many of his shortcomings as a writer.*

Lewis can be rightly appreciated only by concentrating on his anomalous book *Main Street*, the story of a slightly pretentious new bride's frustrating combat with the petty society of Gopher Prairie, a small Minnesota town (modeled after Lewis's home town of Sauk Centre), and with her stodgy and self-satisfied husband. It evoked the directionless struggle of

thousands of Americans (especially women in the hinterland, hundreds of whom were convinced that Lewis was writing about them) to live what the protagonist, Carol Kennicott, calls "a more conscious life." Published when, for the first time in the nation's history, more people were living in cities than in the country, the book was in part a satire exposing the idiocy of rural life, so it also resonated with urban sophisticates and with those—like Carol—who aspired to be such. To be sure, Hamlin Garland (*Main-Travelled Roads*, 1891, *Rose of Dutcher's Coolly*, 1895) and other novelists had earlier described village life as narrow and dreary, but *Main Street* was the right book at the right time, and as Lewisohn wrote, "Perhaps no novel since '*Uncle Tom's Cabin*' had struck so deep over so wide a surface of the national life." The novel is remembered for its sociological significance and as the epitome of what the critic Carl Van Doren called "the revolt from the village." But today's reader, expecting a satirical indictment, is struck—just as Mencken, Forster, and other astute critics at the time were struck—by the novel's sympathy and nuance.

With a fresh and vigorous photographic method, Lewis introduced readers to Main Street as Carol, just arrived from St. Paul, saw it—building by building, detail by detail. Slowly and relentlessly Lewis focused: on the food-stained tablecloths in the hotel dining room, on the drugstore's greasy marble soda-fountain counter, on the "pictures of coy fat prostitutes" in the tobacco shop. But while the reader is sharing Carol's dismay at the dingy, haphazard ugliness of the town, Lewis reveals the view of another newcomer, Bea Sorenson, who, bored with farm life, has come to Gopher Prairie in hopes of finding work as a hired gift. Carol, looking through the flyspecked windows of the hotel, sees only rickety chairs and Cuspidors, but Bea thrills to "the swell traveling man" she spies there, to the "lovely marble" soda fountain, and to all the stores—"one just for tobacco alone." And then, in what Lewis has already established as a four-block downtown, "the roar of the city began to frighten her." The reader knows that Carol's is the more discerning vision, but also that she sneers too easily and that her view of Main Street—and Lewis's—isn't the only perspective.

What impressed most readers was the ceaseless, precise detail ("The amount of sheer data in it is amazing," the young F. Scott Fitzgerald,

*American suffragettes marching in the Wake Up America parade in New York 1917* Topical Press Agency/Getty Images

who was but briefly infatuated with Lewis's writing, exclaimed in a fan letter). Lewis had captured and catalogued middle-class provincial life—its speech, its houses, its gadgets, its caste marks, its stultifying social rounds. But more important, he had captured the vague stirrings—stymied because they cannot be articulated—of the slightly better than average. By eschewing a main character who would show up the subjects of his satire with clever retorts and sparkling wit, Lewis avoided the trap that ensnares most writers of satirical protest, who use their protagonists to take potshots at buffoons. In fact, though he drew her sympathetically, Lewis made Carol a difficult and shallow young woman, frustrated because she's smart enough to be discontent with her life and her surroundings but not smart enough, as he later wrote, to have "any clearly defined vision of what she really wants to do or be"—a situation far more common (and moving) than that of the heroically protesting artist or genius.

Above all, Lewis apprehended what Mencken called—in the most penetrating and witty assessment of Lewis's artistry yet written—"the essential tragedy of American life, and if not the tragedy, then at least the sardonic farce; ... the great strangeness that lies between husband and wife." Lewis empathized with Carol's feeling of entrapment in her marriage to the obtuse and cloddish Will, and also with Will's decent but constricted code ("Do your work, care for your family ... venerate the flag") and his "pathetic inability to comprehend the turmoil that goes on within her" (a limitation wrenching to both parties). Lewis's great achievement, Mencken recognized, was not to take sides in the resultant conflict, not "to turn the thing into a mere harangue against one or the other."

Above all, he is too intelligent to take the side of Carol, as nine novelists out of ten would have done. He sees clearly what is too often not seen—that her superior culture is, after all, chiefly bogus—that the oafish Kennicott, in more ways than one, is actually better than she is ... Her dream of converting a Minnesota prairie town into a sort of Long Island suburb, with overtones of Greenwich Village and the Harvard campus, is quite as absurd as his dream of converting it into a second Minneapolis, with overtones of Gary, Ind., and Paterson, N.J.

Extravagant claims cannot be made for the novel. Lewis's grasp of the moral distinctions and ambiguities of the human condition at the heart of great fiction was unsteady in *Main Street*, as is evident when the novel is compared with the one that beat it for the 1921 Pulitzer Prize—Edith Wharton's *The Age of Innocence*. Nevertheless, the novel was and remains an astonishing accomplishment, and Lewis, then thirty-five, seemed to be a first-rate—perhaps had the makings of a great—novelist.

**Source:** Benjamin Schwarz, "Sheer Data," in *Atlantic Monthly*, Vol. 289, No. 2, February 2002, pp. 98–101.

## Nan Bauer Maglin

*In the following excerpt, Maglin examines the development of Carol over the course of the novel and how the desperation she experiences is symptomatic of the limited opportunities afforded women at that time.*

Although in *The Job* Sinclair Lewis writes of a woman who succeeds in achieving a type of independence, three years later when he writes *Main Street* he depicts a woman who is wholly trapped into a dependent existence as a wife and mother in a small midwestern town. In a sense, it is Sinclair Lewis's *Diary of a Mad Housewife*. Certainly, the book is an examination of the limitations of life and culture, 1906–1920, in a small town—the aspect of the book on which most critics have tended to concentrate. However, the issue of the stultifying effects of marriage upon women in this era is at least equally prominent and has significance for big cities and small towns alike.

Carol is pictured as a rebellious young woman of the Middle West. She has no ties, having lost her parents as a child. First she goes to Blodgett College and then to library school in Chicago. She is a restless woman, interested in causes and clubs. She consciously rejects a life of housekeeping and dishwashing because she wants to be active in the world and not sequestered in the home.

Rather abruptly, after three years of working as a librarian in St. Paul, Carol marries Dr. Will Kennicott of Gopher Prairie. She marries him because "she is slightly weary of her employment and sees no glory ahead." She does see glory ahead in an alliance with a doctor semi; as the wife of a doctor, she can dedicate herself to uplifting the town. In addition, Dr. Kennicott, who is twelve years older than Carol, provides her with "a shelter from the perplexing world."

The rest of the novel details Carol's disillusionment with marriage and its jobs: housekeeper, husband-tender, childbearer. This disillusionment begins the moment she arrives in Gopher Prairie, her new home. She suddenly feels Will Kennicott to be a stranger to her and a distasteful one at that. She realizes he is coarse, drab, and unimaginative. However, she is not ready to heed her momentary intuition that in order to preserve her sanity and her identity "she would have to wrench loose from this man and flee." Worse than her repulsion for her husband is her realization that the myths of marriage are only myths:

> Why do these stories lie so? They always make the bride's homecoming a bower of roses. Complete trust in noble spouse. Lies about marriage. I'm *not* changed. And this town—O my God! I can't go through with it. This junk-heap!

She is disappointed to learn that she is still Carol Kennicott; marriage has caused no magical transformation.

After this first traumatic day, with Will "escaped to the world of men's affairs," Carol tries to adjust herself to her new life. She tries to take pride in being a housewife. Nevertheless, depite her real efforts to be happy in her new role, she can see herself only as a servant and her home as a prison. Significantly, Carol Kennicott's life in *Main Street* struck a chord of recognition in many women. Sinclair Lewis received numerous letters from women who saw Carol's prison as their own.

Nevertheless Lewis appears to understand that, given the limited alternatives open to women in that era, many women viewed marriage as a blessed haven. Vida Sherwin, for one, at thirty-nine, after years of teaching school, is literally esctatic over her own wedding. She "was hungry for housework, for the most pottering detail of it. She had no maid, nor wanted one. She cooked, baked, swept, washed supper-cloths, with the triumph of a chemist in a new laboratory. To her the hearth was veritably the altar."

Carol, though, sees very limited alternatives for herself: "have children; start her career of reforming; or become so definitely a part of the town that she would be fulfilled by the activities of church and study-club and bridge parties." A fourth option, employment, is taboo for a married woman, especially a doctor's wife in a small town. Carol tries all three of the options which are open to her.

She first fears and postpones pregnancy, seeing a baby, quite realistically, as the final lock on her prison. Yet she desires something to commit herself to. And so she has a baby. Hugh, her son, becomes simultaneously her reason for living and her jailer. Carol also works frenetically "reforming" the town and organizing women's clubs. But finding none of these activities satisfying, in desperation, she finally goes beyond the accepted alternatives for respectable married women. She begins but

never consummates an affair. In the end, a combination of fear and the realization that another man is not her answer serve to restrain her.

Carol is growing emotionally more desperate as the novel progresses. She swings between the extremes of love and hate toward her husband and home; she rebukes herself for her feelings of dissatisfaction; she feels isolated and friendless; she reverts to childlike behavior and girllike fears; she longs for a father-protector; she rages; she is immobilized; she dreams of escape; she succumbs to the ghostlike performance of her routines. She edges close to hysteria and insanity. At thirty she begins to fantasize about killing people with carving knives. She thrashes around for something or someone to flee to—a room, a male, her fantasies. She has sleepless nights envisioning Will firt married to another woman, then imprisoned, then dead. She goes deeper and deeper into a depressed and desperate state.

If *The Job* describes the emotional frustration of the working woman, *Main Street* details the same condition in the middle-class housewife. Like those of the 1950s described by Betty Friedan in *The Feminine Mystique*, the middle-class housewife of the years around World War I faced an over-abundance of spare time, feelings of inadequacy, boredom, and uselessness.

Carol takes her son and moves to Washington, D.C., working for the Bureau of War Risk Insurance. She finds a "home, her own place and her own people" among militant suffragists who "when they were not being mobbed or arrested, took dancing lessons or went picnicking up the Chesapeake Canal or talked about the politics of the American Federation of Labor."

After one year passes, Will Kennicott visits Carol. Although he wants her to return to Gopher Prairie, he does not pressure her. Carol, somewhat confused, consults the "generalissima of suffrage" as to her predicament. The suffrage leader says she is giving Carol the advice she would give to any woman who came to her:

> I'm thinking of thousands of women who come to Washington and New York and Chicago every year, dissatisfied at home and seeking a sign in the heavens—women of all sorts, from timid mothers of fifty in cotton gloves, to girls just out of Vassar who organize strikes in their own father's factories!

She tells Carol that if she is not willing to give up everything, including her son, she should return home and work for feminism there. She says:

you can keep on looking at one thing after another in your home and church and bank, and ask why it is, and who first laid down the law that it had to be that way.

It is unclear whether Sinclair Lewis is reflecting or merely mocking conditions in the feminist movement. The advice the "generalissima" gives is obviously unrealistic for Carol (though politically the movement needs extension). She tells Carol to go back home, back to the original source of her oppression, and be a radical in isolation from the movement—unless she is willing to give up her son, even though she has been doing well enough with him for over a year.

So, Carol returns to Gopher Prairie, Main Street, and her husband. She is pregnant with a second child and, at first, pregnant with commitment to bring feminism to the hinterland. Her baby girl is born and her commitment slowly dies as the demands of the storm-windows, the hunting trip, and all the petty details of life on Main Street take precedence.

**Source:** Nan Bauer Maglin, "Women in Three Sinclair Lewis Novels," in *Modern Critical Views: Sinclair Lewis*, edited by Harold Bloom, Chelsea House, 1987, pp.103–18.

## SOURCES

Americanus, "Georgie from Main Street," in the *Spectator* (U.K.), Vol. 129, No. 4929, December 16, 1922, pp. 928–29.

Coblentz, Stanton A., "A Shelf of Recent Books: 'Main Street'," in the *Bookman*, Vol. LII, No. 5, January 1921, pp. 357–58.

Dobbs, Michael, "Feelings Are Down on Novelist's 'Main Street'," in *The Washington Post*, September 3, 1988, p. A12.

"The Epic of Dulness [sic]," in the *Nation*, Vol. CXI, No. 2888, November 10, 1920, pp. 536–37.

Lewis, Sinclair, *Main Street*, Harcourt, Brace, 1920, reprint, Signet Classic, 1998.

Light, Martin, "*Main Street*," in *The Quixotic Vision of Sinclair Lewis*, Purdue University Press, 1975, pp. 60–72.

Person, James E., Jr., "Sinclair Lewis' Best Decade," in the *Washington Times*, June 23, 1996, p. B8.

Review of *Main Street*, in the *New York Times Book Review*, November 14, 1920, p. 18.

Sherman, Stuart P., *The Significance of Sinclair Lewis*, Harcourt Brace Jovanovich, 1922.

"Time Line," *Sinclair Lewis & His Life*, www.english.ilstu.edu/separry/sinclairlewis/timeline.html (November 4, 2006).

# Mending Wall

## ROBERT FROST

### 1915

"Mending Wall" (1915) is Robert Frost's tribute to one man's notion of being a good neighbor, even as that notion is the opposite of his own. It is the opening poem in Robert Frost's second collection of poetry, *North of Boston* (1915). Homesick for America, Frost wrote "Mending Wall" while living in England with his wife and four children before World War I. Napoleon Guay had been Frost's neighbor in New Hampshire a few years earlier and inspired the poem, "Mending Wall." Apparently, French-Canadian Guay made an impression on Frost by often repeating the phrase, "Good fences make good neighbors," during the routine repairs on the wall between their farms.

The idea of "good fences" is one of personal boundaries, evoking the American pioneer mentality of staking a claim and taking ownership. With this poem, Frost questions that version of the American dream and hints at another version. After becoming a well-known poet, Frost was eager to reclaim his own space in New Hampshire; "Mending Wall" illustrates the personal and natural freedoms, as well as limitations, of a rural existence. The poem questions the necessity of a wall, like questioning the wisdom of perpetuating an old habit. In America, a land of vast frontier, do we need walls to maintain relationships with others? This question becomes even more interesting in light of Frost's later position as American "goodwill ambassador" to South America, and later to

# BIOGRAPHY

**ROBERT FROST**

Born Robert Lee Frost in San Francisco on March 26, 1874, Frost began writing poetry in high school. He married his co-valedictorian, Elinor White, in 1895, after dropping out of Dartmouth College. While trying to establish a career as a poet, Frost worked as a newspaper editor, cobbler, and farmer, and even attended Harvard for a time. Those years were lean for Frost and his family, but in 1906, he took a job as a teacher, which supported him as he composed most of the poems in his first book, *A Boy's Will.* After a stint living in England and a second book of poetry, *North of Boston* (1915), which contained "Mending Wall," Frost returned to America where he received critical acclaim for his poetry and four Pulitzer Prizes between 1922 and 1942.

During his career, Frost published over thirty-three volumes of poetry and acquired more than forty honorary degrees from universities and colleges, including the University of Michigan, Oxford, and Cambridge. Among his best-known works are "Stopping by Woods on a Snowy Evening," "The Road Not Taken," "Dedication" (which he composed for President Kennedy's inauguration), and "The Gift Outright" (which he recited at Kennedy's inauguration). Frost died in Boston on January 29, 1963.

the Soviet Union during President Kennedy's administration. In light of his interest in the dilemma of borders in "Mending Wall," it is fitting that he would reach across them to foster positive relations with other people and cultures.

Some scholars consider Frost as a nature poet in the manner of Ralph Waldo Emerson and William Wordsworth or an Imagist in the school of Ezra Pound; however, Frost did not classify himself that way. His poems deal with nature in an everyday, human fashion and are written in the language of ordinary speech. This colloquial tone is relevant for looking at Frost's

poems in the context of the American dream: His poetry speaks to the common man with simple, yet evocative images. Frost is easy to approach, not esoteric or verbose, using words that allow the reader to connect with tangible objects and authentic emotion. He uses no pretense, as shown by this straightforward line from "Mending Wall": "We keep the wall between us as we go." His popularity and resonance with common Americans earned him the nickname America's Poet. He writes of home, of "yelping dogs," apple trees, and rough fingers. His poems recall a simpler, idealized time of prosperity and fertility.

As America's Poet, Frost received a multitude of awards and distinctions, including four Pulitzer Prizes. Though popular with the public, Frost did not participate in the modernistic, free-verse experiments of his fellow poets. He preferred to convey his thematic messages through meter, rhyme, and form. The U.S. Senate passed a resolution dedicated to Frost on his seventy-fifth birthday, declaring that "His poems have helped to guide American thought and humor and wisdom, setting forth to our minds a reliable representation of ourselves and of all men."

## PLOT SUMMARY

Before analyzing the narrative of "Mending Wall," it is important to look at the structure and language. The poem is not divided into stanzas and its forty-five lines make one solid verse narrated in first-person voice. The speech is colloquial, filled with the natural stops and pauses found in everyday conversation. In addition, Frost uses contractions to emphasize the vernacular rhythms, such as in the first line, "Something there is that doesn't love a wall," and in line 32, "Before I'd built a wall I'd ask to know." By this same token, Frost keeps his syllables short and simple for easy comprehension, as in line 31, "Where there are cows? But here there are no cows."

Since "Mending Wall" is not broken into sections, the meaning of the poem can be best seen through groupings of lines that comprise sentences or complete ideas. Lines 1–4 open the poem and establish the core image: a wall being up-ended by a "frozen-ground-swell." Nature, it seems, does not "love a wall" and "spills the upper boulders in the sun." This upheaval

*Robert Frost* © *Corbis*

creates "gaps" in the wall large enough for two people to walk through side by side. With this last image comes the possibility of men aligning themselves against nature, an idea that will be up-ended by the end of the poem, much like the stones themselves. Transcendentalism also comes into play with these first few lines, as nature takes on a mysterious divine role with the introductory word, "Something." Frost does not explicitly identify nature as the culprit causing the upheaval, but instead uses a word evoking a powerful unknown, rather like a deity. The "Something" also has judgment, as well as emotion to act on that judgment: It "doesn't love a wall," and in feeling that way, "sends the frozen-ground-swell" to break the wall. Frost makes the reader question: Why does this "Something" not want the wall?

Lines 5–9 frame the next sentence, though the sentence actually ends in the middle of line 9. Men have also upset these stone walls, in their pursuit of the hunt. In their overzealous charge, "they have not left one stone on a stone." The hunters come with the season, as does the eruption of the earth and rock. But the narrator acknowledges that even the hunters do not make as much damage as the earth. Again, Frost gives nature an all-powerful role in this situation, suggesting that man must be aware of what nature can accomplish.

The next few lines announce that the crumbling rock wall is a regular occurrence; the gaps form when the narrator is not present: "No one has seen them made or heard them made, / But at spring-mending time we find them there." The "we" suggests another person is sharing the narrator's experience; it is the entrance of the narrator's neighbor, who plays a key role in the poem's central conflict. The "we find" also establishes a connection between the narrator and the neighbor; while the poem chronicles their aloof relationship, this small phrase unites them in this experience, showing that they could be on the same side of the wall, so to speak, if they desired.

Lines 12–14 offer further details about the seasonal routine the narrator and his neighbor perform. The narrator tells his neighbor about the gaps in the wall and eventually they "meet to walk the line" and repair the damage. They will not allow the wall between them to disintegrate, as if a boundary must be maintained, both physically and personally. However, Frost does give the sense, particularly with the repetition in lines 14 and 15, that the narrator might regret the wall, saying: "[We] set the wall between us once again. / We keep the wall between us as we go." The emphasis on the wall "between us" shows the narrator's awareness of the wall, which helps foreshadow his uncertainty about the structure later in the poem.

Lines 15–19 begin to describe the action shared by the narrator and his neighbor. Both stay on their side of the wall and replace "the boulders that have fallen." Because of their varying size and shape as indicated by the line, "some are loaves and some so nearly balls," the narrator jokes that he and his neighbor "use a spell to make them balance: / 'Stay where you are until our backs are turned!'"

In line 20, the narrator mentions the difficulty in the hard work by describing how they "wear [their] fingers rough" replacing the stones. Yet in the next two lines, he refers to the annual process as an "out-door game," each man "on a side." The tone is playful, and although the narrator knows it is futile, he performs the ritual of rebuilding the wall every year. For the first time, the narrator indicates that the neighbor wants the wall more than the narrator does. In line 23, the narrator questions the barrier's purpose, as it only separates the narrator's apple orchard and the neighbor's pines, neither of which poses any threat of trespassing. But as shown in line 25, a natural boundary is not enough for the neighbor. But with the narrator's reference to himself and his neighbor in metaphors of nature, Frost suggests the narrator's awareness of their connection to nature, hinting at the question: Why do two natural entities need a wall between them?

The narrator's rumination over his neighbor's obsession with the stone wall continues in the next lines. "Good fences make good neighbours," his neighbor always says when the narrator tries to point out that his apples will never "eat the cones under his pines." However, the narrator still does not completely understand his neighbor's philosophy and wonders what would happen if he asked his neighbor why fences "make good neighbours." Line 28 also points to the narrator's connection to nature: "Spring is the mischief in me," he says. Spring does not make mischief in him or inspire him to mischief, but is mischief. As with the line "I am apple orchard," Frost shows that man is nature.

The narrator could understand if they both owned cows, because cows would obviously stray into each other's pastures. But, as the narrator says in line 31, "here there are no cows." Next, he wonders if the wall is appropriate at all:

> Before I built a wall I'd ask to know
> What I was walling in or walling out,
> And to whom I was like to give offence.
> Something there is that doesn't love a wall,
> That wants it down.

In line 36, the narrator is tempted to joke with the neighbor and say that "Elves" were creating the gaps in the wall. But instead of joking, he would really like to know why his neighbor feels so strongly that the wall is necessary, even when nature clearly feels that it is not.

The turn in the poem comes with the second half of line 38, as well as lines 39 and 40: "I see him there / Bringing a stone grasped firmly by the top / In each hand, like an old-stone savage armed." Every year, when the narrator encounters his neighbor, he sees him as a throwback to another age. Suddenly, he sees the stone wall as a manifestation of a generations-old tradition: The neighbor is no longer simply his neighbor,

HE IS ALL PINE AND I AM APPLE ORCHARD.

MY APPLE TREES WILL NEVER GET ACROSS

AND EAT THE CONES UNDER HIS PINES, I TELL HIM.

HE ONLY SAYS, "GOOD FENCES MAKE GOOD

NEIGHBOURS."

but a man doing what men have always done in protecting their property. His neighbor "will not go behind his father's saying," as stated in line 43; in other words, he will never let his father, or generations of men in his family, down. The narrator also sees his neighbor as fighting nature, despite being part of nature, "old-stone," himself.

The poem ends with the narrator's impression of his neighbor:

> He moves in darkness as it seems to me,
> Not of woods only and the shade of trees.
> He will not go behind his father's saying,
> And he likes having thought of it so well
> He says again, "Good fences make good
>     neighbours."

The narrator feels that the neighbor's insistence on maintaining this barrier, clinging to whatever urge or habit that motivates it, is unenlightened.

## THEMES

### *Property*

The American dream of property ownership undergirds many other aspects of the American dream, including control, privacy, and wealth. In a country where people may own their own land (rather than living at the pleasure of the sovereign or state), property-owning citizens are more secure. To own property means that the owner controls the use of the property, may benefit from the property, may sell the property, and may exclude others from the property. The last of these basic property rights is the one being exercised by the neighbor in "Mending Wall." Knowing that they have a place to call home frees landowners from the basic human worry of having a place to sleep, allowing them to focus on progress, or wealth, or whatever other pursuit they think may bring them happiness. Property also represents a legacy, one that future generations may inherit and use as the foundation of their future American dream.

The seventeenth-century English philosopher John Locke believed that it was the natural order of the world that men should own land:

> As a man had a right to all he could employ his labour upon, so he had no temptation to labour for more than he could make use of. This left no room for controversy about the title, nor for incroachment on the right of others; what portion a man carved to himself, was easily seen; and it was useless, as well as dishonest, to carve himself too much, or take more than he needed. (Section 51 of *Two Treatises of Government*, 1689)

> Man being born, as has been proved, with a title to perfect freedom, and an uncontrolled enjoyment of all the rights and privileges of the law of nature, equally with any other man, or number of men in the world, hath by nature a power, not only to preserve his property, that is, his life, liberty and estate, against the injuries and attempts of other men. (Section 87 of *Two Treatises of Government*, 1689)

Locke's ideas of men's right to "life, liberty, and estate" appear in the *American Declaration of Independence* as the "inalienable Rights, ... Life, Liberty, and the pursuit of Happiness." Adam Smith, the eighteenth-century economist and philosopher, lays the groundwork for modern capitalism in *Inquiry into the Nature and Causes of the Wealth of Nations* (1776). He builds on Locke's philosophy and explains that the ownership of capital resources, and the motivation to best apply those resources to make a profit, is the engine that drives capitalism.

## Privacy

The American right to privacy is among the most basic and precious of freedoms, and is prescribed and protected by the Fourth Amendment:

> The right of the people to be secure in their persons, houses, papers, and effects, against unreasonable searches and seizures, shall not be violated, and no Warrants shall issue, but upon probable cause, supported by Oath or affirmation, and particularly describing the place to be searched, and the persons or things to be seized.

To possess that privacy and use it however one desires is another tenet of the American dream. People argue about whether privacy fosters trust or suspicion and whether it helps or hinders intimacy, but no one seems to question the desire for privacy as an innate human impulse. Though the narrator of "Mending Wall" questions the need for a physical wall to separate him from his neighbor, he also recognizes that his neighbor puts up personal, figurative walls between them. He and his neighbor are not on the same side: "He is all pine and I am apple orchard." The narrator represents bounty, harvest, fruit, things to share. He wonders "to whom [he] was like to give offence." Obviously, he does not feel the same way as his neighbor with "a stone grasped firmly by the top / In each hand, like an old-stone savage armed." His neighbor feels the need to maintain not only the actual wall of rock, but also the wall preventing intimacy. "He moves in darkness," the narrator says, acknowledging that his neighbor does not reveal or expose much about himself. The form of this poem reflects its ironic message: It is not broken into stanzas but rather is one solid block, reflecting the neighbor's walls.

## Community

Although "Mending Wall" begins with a brotherly image of two men walking "abreast" through a gap in the stone fence, the poem ultimately encapsulates the story of two neighbors who "set the wall between [them] once again" and "keep the wall between [them] as [they] go." The narrator calls the rebuilding a "kind of out-door game," but more aptly, the mending of fences symbolizes a tenuous keeping of the peace. The image of the men "meet[ing] to walk the line" evokes an allusion to war, of eyeing the enemy from opposite sides of the fence. The image also refers to "toeing the line," or following the rules, not straying from what is right and wrong. If the two men allow the fence between them to fall into disrepair, would they turn into "old-stone savage[s] armed"? The third to the last line, "He will not go behind his father's saying," shows that this rebuilding has probably been continuing for generations, and by keeping the peace, the apple orchards and pines have thrived; one has not overtaken the other. Good fences have made, and will continue to make, good neighbors.

Though the walls in Frost's poem function as a distinct and questionable barrier between the speaker of the poem and his neighbor, they also offer an opportunity for the men to evaluate, or even "mend," their relationship. These walls in need of "mending" indicate an existing, yet fractured, relationship, and each season, when the crumbling walls require attention and

*A rock fence in Rhode Island* © *Peter Finger/Corbis*

care, the narrator wonders whether replacing the stones will leave his relationship with his neighbor in ruins or if leaving the fallen stones will actually repair their strained and impersonal connection. This inner conflict is shown when the narrator says, "Before I'd built a wall I'd ask to know / What I was walling in or walling out." In other words, the narrator questions the purpose of the wall: In rebuilding, was he walling out a true, intimate relationship with another human, and at the same time, making sure his personal property and identity was protected? S. L. Dragland, in his January 1967 review of Frost's poem published in the *Explicator*, suggests "the walls defin[e] the difference between individual and collective modes of thought and existence." If the walls were not re-established, would the narrator and his neighbor begin to form a closer community of sorts as they learned to understand and accept one another? Or would they grow more antagonistic toward each other as their individual space became invaded? In any case, the recurring situation of "mending" these walls presents an open door for the narrator and his neighbor as each year they are faced with the chance to patch their friendship and not their fences.

## Nature

In his 1836 essay *Nature*, Ralph Waldo Emerson wrote this:

> Nature, in the common sense, refers to essences unchanged by man; space, the air, the river, the leaf. Art is applied to the mixture of his will with the same things, as in a house, a canal, a statue, a picture. But his operations taken together are so insignificant, a little chipping, baking, patching, and washing, that in an impression so grand as that of the world on the human mind, they do not vary the result.

With this, Emerson established American Transcendental philosophy, and the idea that humans are a part of nature, not above it. "Mending Wall" illustrates the idea that in drawing boundaries between each other, our property, and our lives, we gain a false sense of well-being. Nature is unpredictable, as alluded to in the first two lines, "Something there is that doesn't love a wall, / That sends the frozen-ground-swell under it," yet humans want to believe they can control, claim, and tame nature. The narrator of the poem realizes that no matter how many times he and his neighbor rebuild the wall year after year, the gaps return at "spring mending-time"; the men are forever losing nature's battle. They "wear [their] fingers rough with handling" the stones and rely on a magic "spell" in hopes that the stones will stay in place. But each spring, after nature has run her course once again, the men must repair the "gaps where even two can pass abreast."

### Tradition

"Mending Wall" provides a snapshot of rural life "North of Boston" at the turn of the twentieth century. The second line of the poem immediately describes a thaw after the hard winter "frozen-ground-swell" and inspires an image of a cold countryside lined with crumbling stone walls. In addition to the narrator and his neighbor, this rural landscape belongs to "hunters" and their "yelping dogs," but while the narrator and his neighbor live their lives on separate sides of the boundary, hunters have the freedom to knock down stones to encourage "the rabbit out of hiding." The hunters seem a natural part of this rural landscape, arriving on the scene according to season like the apple trees and pine. The narrator expects them, but obviously cannot control their actions. This poem provokes questions about the nature of change: Despite the crumbling stones that must be annually repaired, rural life remains the same. The narrator knows the cause of the "fallen boulders" and accepts his yearly task. Ultimately, he wonders why he and his neighbor need a wall to separate them and whether the wall is holding things in or out, but he does not move to change the situation. When "spring-mending time" rolls around, he follows through with habit; routine seems comforting, rather like the closing two lines of the poem that refer to his neighbor's tradition: "And he likes having thought of [his father's saying] so well / He says again, 'Good fences make good neighbours.'"

## HISTORICAL OVERVIEW

### The History of the "Good Fences" Proverb

Robert Frost did not invent the proverb, "Good fences make good neighbours" with his poem "Mending Wall." The saying began long before the poem was published, in communities all around the world. According to Wolfgang Meider in an article in *Folklore*, translations include "There must be a fence between good neighbours" in Norwegian; "Between neighbours' gardens a fence is good" in German; "Build a fence even between intimate friends" in Japanese; "Love your neighbour, but do not throw down the dividing wall" in Hindi; and "Love your neighbour, but put up a fence" in Russian. The phrase even relates back to a late medieval Latin proverb, "Bonum est erigere dumos cum vicinis," or "It is good to erect hedges with the neighbours."

In April 1754, Benjamin Franklin told the readers of his *Poor Richard's Almanack* to "Love thy Neighbour; yet don't pull down your Hedge," marking the proverb's influence in the United States. However, Reverend Ezekiel Rogers of Rowley, Massachusetts, might be the first to note the saying in the New World, with his advice to Governor John Winthrop on June 30, 1640: "Touching the buisinesse of the Bounds, which we [have] now in agitation; I [have] thought, that a good fence helpeth to keepe peace betweene neighbours; but let [us] take heede that we make not a high stone wall, to keepe [us] from meeting." Rogers agrees that having boundaries "keepe[s] peace betweene neighbours," but believes the wall should not completely close off one man to another.

### The Stone Walls of New England

The central image in "Mending Wall" is a typical stone wall criss-crossing farmland in New England. According to the Stone Wall Initiative, a group dedicated to preserving the walls in New England much like "classical ruins," early American farmers constructed most of the walls with stones that erupted from the ground after thousands of years. When the colonists began farming America, the soil began to change. The loss of the organic mulch and topsoil, not to mention colder winters, acted as a catalyst in forcing the stones out of the soil. As stones churned up into fields and pastures, farmers desperately needed them removed. As in "Mending Wall," farmers usually hauled them away by hand, and because the weight of the stones did not allow easy transportation, the stones were dumped along the nearest fence line. Now, stone walls represent the early rural American dream and recall a time when stones marked a man's property, a man's worth, and a man's future.

## A New America

The stone wall of Frost's poem acts as a nostalgic marker, one that suggests the days of claiming one's territory and living off the land are coming to an end. With the dawn of the twentieth century, new frontiers were characterized by industry, machines, and new technology. Urban centers and lifestyles beckoned, and farmers soon found it difficult to maintain their pioneering way of life. A man could not build a solid future for himself behind stone walls. The "frozen-ground-swell" was pushing up the stones just as it was pushing up the farmer. Traditions of father and country were eschewed for urban dreams. Darkness was settling upon the "old-stone savage" as he desperately tried to rebuild the walls around his heritage and identity.

## Imagist Poetry

Robert Frost is called one of the "pioneers" of the Imagist Poetry movement, though Frost himself has denied that credit, as well as his contribution to that particular genre of poetry. However, Amy Lowell, in her article, "On Imagism," in *Tendencies in Modern American Poetry*, claims otherwise. She defines Imagist poetry with six key "rules," which include "us[ing] the language of common speech, [and] employ[ing] always the exact word, not the nearly-exact, nor the merely decorative word"; "present[ing] an image . . . [that] render[s] particulars exactly"; and "produc[ing] poetry that is hard and clear, never blurred nor indefinite." Frost's "Mending Wall" adheres to those rules, as well as to Lowell's others. His colloquial speech, strong imagery, and precise, straight-forward style make this poem Imagist without a doubt, as illustrated in this group of lines: "I see him there / Bringing a stone grasped firmly by the top / In each hand, like an old-stone savage armed." Imagists, Lowell says, present images, rather than represent images. Essentially, instead of using metaphors or other overblown language to convey an image, Imagists describe the image clearly and purposefully, as shown through this no-nonsense image of stacking the stones in "Mending Wall": "We wear our fingers rough with handling them." The rules of Imagist poetry, Lowell notes, "boil down into . . . [s]implicity and directness of speech; subtlety and beauty of rhythms; individualistic freedom of idea; clearness and vividness of presentation; and concentration." Other famous Imagist poets include Lowell herself, H. D. (Hilda Doolittle), and Ezra Pound, who began the movement in London around 1912.

## Nature Poetry

In 1836, Ralph Waldo Emerson wrote *Nature*, an essay establishing the Transcendental belief in nature as the divine, a divine accessible, understandable, and knowable to humans, if they remain aware. Because of Frost's keen poetic relationship to the natural world, particularly with regard to the way humans connect to nature, he is often classified with Emerson, William Wordsworth, and Henry Thoreau as a nature, or Transcendental, poet. "Mending Wall" certainly deals with man's connection to nature as both narrator and neighbor struggle to battle the "frozen-ground-swell" that "spills the upper boulders in the sun." However, as the men face nature's intervention, Frost reminds the reader that the narrator and his neighbor not only fight with nature but also are a part of nature with the line: "He is all pine and I am apple orchard." By that token, if man is aware of his surroundings, if he becomes one with those surroundings, without constantly rebuilding walls between himself and his neighbor, perhaps he might grow closer to the divine. With "Mending Wall," Frost might be suggesting that nature is telling the men something important with its continuous destruction of the walls: that perhaps good fences do not make good neighbors, but instead block our sight from the natural world, or what is truly important.

## CRITICAL OVERVIEW

In the early years of Frost's career, critics positioned Frost as a speaker for America, a connection between nature, art, individual, and nation. His imagery provided every reader with access to the American dream: a life of homespun, real texture and neighborly conversation. In the January 1917 issue of *Poetry*, Harriet Monroe comments on the natural style of Frost in the context of American history by evoking the country's birth: "His New England is the same old New England of the pilgrim fathers—a harsh, austere, velvet-coated-granite earth." Critics shared Monroe's opinion for the next several decades and echoed the patriotic tone, much like G. R. Elliott in the July 1925 issue of *The Virginia Quarterly Review*: "The Frostian humour is peculiarly important for America. No other of our poets has shown a mood at once so individual and so neighborly. . . . His

## MEDIA ADAPTATIONS

In 1956, Robert Frost recorded himself reading "Mending Wall" and other poems at his home. The recording is available online at town.hall.org/radio/HarperAudio/012294_harp_ITH.html.

Robert Frost recorded readings of many of his poems between 1935 and 1962. Many, including "Mending Wall," were released as *Robert Frost: Voice of the Poet* by R. H. Audio Voices in 2003. It is available on compact disc.

poetic humour is on the highway toward the richer American poetry of the future, if that is to be." Others, like Malcolm Cowley in the September 18, 1944, issue of the *New Republic*, focus on Frost's mastery of the everyday power and beauty of nature:

> Let us say that he is a poet neither of the mountains nor of the woods, although he lives among both, but rather of the hill pastures, the intervals [*sic*], the dooryard in autumn with the leaves swirling, the closed house shaking in the winter storms (and who else has described these scenes more accurately, in more lasting colors?). In the same way, he is not the poet of New England in its great days, or in its late-nineteenth-century decline (except in some of his earlier poems); he is rather a poet who celebrates the diminished but prosperous and self-respecting New England of the tourist home and the antique shop in the abandoned gristmill. And the praise heaped on Frost in recent years is somehow connected in one's mind with the search for ancestors and authentic old furniture.

With the advent of modernism, Frost's reviewers focused on the dark realism of Frost's ordinary imagery. Lionel Trilling, in the Summer 1959 *Partisan Review*, calls Frost both a "terrifying poet" and a "tragic poet" while the "universe that he conceives is a terrifying universe." In his 1961 examination of American poetry, Roy Harvey Pearce argues that "Frost's protagonists refuse to live fully in the modern world," while John Ciardi of the *Saturday Review*, March 24,

1962, suggests "the darkness in his poems is as profound as the light in them is long. They are terrible because they are from life at a depth into which we cannot look unshaken." Yet critics were still affected by Frost's style, as shown by a rhetorical question from Denis Donoghue in the Winter 1963 edition of the *Yale Review*: "what are the possibilities for a poetry based upon nothing more than a shared sense of human fact? . . . Frost has spent a lifetime seeing how much he could say on those terms. He is the poet most devoted to bare human gesture."

## CRITICISM

### Zev Trachtenberg

*In the following excerpt, Trachtenberg discusses how Frost thematically reveals the complexities of humanity through the relationship between nature and man, as well as communal and personal space. He asks the reader to contemplate the meaning of the words neighbor and boundary.*

"Mending Wall" has two characters: its narrator and his neighbor, owners of adjacent farms, who meet each Spring to repair the stone wall that stands between their properties. The narrator, at first glance, seems to take a somewhat skeptical attitude toward property. (We shall see that his attitude is in fact more complicated.) The poem opens with his words "Something there is that doesn't love a wall"—a phrase he repeats later, making it a kind of slogan for the position on property he personifies. That position seems to reject human attempts to inscribe the arbitrary divisions of property holdings on the land. The narrator sees in natural processes an attempt to cast off this artificial imposition: that which doesn't love a wall "sends the frozen-ground-swell under it, / And spills the upper boulders in the sun." He recognizes that asserting a separation between the two parcels of property by erecting a wall is futile. For, he recognizes, the two parcels are one, connected underneath the wall by natural forces that work unconsciously but actively against human efforts to divide them.

The neighbor, by contrast, speaks for an individualistic belief in the value of marking property holdings. "Good fences make good neighbors" are his only words in the poem, repeated in the last line like a counter-slogan to

*Wooden crates of apples freshly harvested at an orchard in Middlebury, Vermont* © *James P Blair/Corbis*

the narrator's. The neighbor first offers his slogan in response to the fact that the wall is not needed for the practical purpose of keeping his and the narrator's goods separate. Their goods do not need a wall to be kept apart: they have no cows to wander back and forth across the line, and the narrator's "apple trees will never get across / And eat the cones under [the neighbor's] pines." For the neighbor, that is, the utility of the wall is not economic. Rather it serves to define the sort of relationship he wishes to have with those who surround him: his slogan expresses an ideology of human separation. In the neighbor's eyes, apparently, all that makes a neighbor is the mere fact of owning an adjacent farm, hence what makes a *good* neighbor is his separateness. For what else could characterize the goodness of neighbors who are made good by fences?

The neighbor thus personifies a position on property that disvalues community. Property is marked by walls, whose main function in his view is precisely to divide people—more importantly even than dividing their goods. Thus the neighbor appears to the narrator at the end of the poem as "an old-stone savage," armed with

the rocks to be used for rebuilding the wall, an image that associates walls with weapons. At the same time, this image presents the neighbor as an autarchic figure, an embodiment of human isolation. In both ways the poem shows the neighbor rejecting the human connectedness that constitutes membership in community, in favor of the personal security of his own property. The slogan "good fences make good neighbors" thus encapsulates the notion that property's primary function is to mark off separate domains within which individuals are independent of each other.

What, then, is the value of the wall to the narrator? He understands as well as the neighbor that the wall lacks a utilitarian purpose; it is he who reminds the neighbor of this fact. The neighbor, as we have seen, responds to this fact with the ideological justification that by separating them the wall makes them good neighbors. The narrator responds to it lightheartedly, by conceiving of the shared activity of mending the wall as "just another kind of outdoor game/ One on a side." Because the wall has no practical function, that is, the only justification for the effort of maintaining it must be in the nature of the effort itself. What is important for the narrator is the playful sharing of an activity with his neighbor. Consider his description of their replacing the stones on the wall: "We have to use a spell to make them balance / 'Stay where you are until our backs are turned!'" Here he represents the chore both as a joint enterprise, and as one understood to be justified by the doing of it rather than by the result. Thus, as he says, mending the wall is like a game, in which the opponents are in a broader sense partners in a common undertaking.

In seeing the practice of affirming property divisions as a game, the narrator presents property as a human convention. And, as he witnesses every Spring, this convention sits uneasily on the land. We noted above that the narrator sees in the forces that cast down the wall nature's rejection of the division of land into property. But the narrator also sees in these natural forces the occasion for cooperation with his neighbor. The vulnerability of the wall to natural destruction explains why it constitutes an ongoing opportunity for engagement between his neighbor and himself. Nature tends to obliterate the marks of property; the narrator grasps the effort to reestablish what is their own as an opportunity for human connection. Hence, for him, it is this chance to affirm community in the face of nature that makes mending the wall worthwhile. Recall that he fixes the gaps made by other people himself. By contrast, responding to the forces associated with the land calls for communal activity, carried out and celebrated in the yearly ceremony of mending the wall.

It turns out, then, that the narrator sees a spark of truth in his neighbor's slogan that good fences make good neighbors. But, for him, it is not the simple existence of the fence that does the trick. Rather, to paraphrase Richard Poirier, the narrator sees that while the mere presence of good fences might not make good neighbors, the shared activity of mending fences can. Sharing the chore of mending the wall can transform owners of adjacent properties into neighbors indeed. In the poem that very activity brings the two men together, raising the possibility at least that the narrator can engage the neighbor in the kind of communal interaction the latter seems to disvalue. But we must follow the narrator's position a step further. For, to the extent that he is motivated to "wear fingers rough with handling" stones simply by the chance to enjoy his neighbor's company, we can say that the effort of sustaining their human connection provides the opportunity for the men to reestablish what is their own. The wall stays mended because mending it is the expression of communal attachments. For the narrator, then, the truth of the neighbor's slogan is in its dialectical opposite: in reality, it is good neighbors who make good fences.

How might we classify the narrator's position on property? To underscore the contrast with the neighbor's liberal view, it seems natural to suggest that the narrator frames a "communitarian" conception of property. But we should distinguish between two ways the connection between property and community can be drawn. On the one hand, as Alan Ryan observes, the view of property that stresses its role in the formation and support of personality "is at home with the concerns of so-called 'communitarian' moral and political theories, since personality needs the right communal support if it is to flourish." Note that the focus of this kind of view is on the individual, hence property is conceived as "prior" to community: it contributes to community by helping form the individuals by whom a community is constituted. An example of this sort of connection is the Jeffersonian ideal, in which property enables the individual to participate in the life of the community, which in turn cultivates the civic virtue of its individual members through its property regime.

But on the other hand there is a sense in which community is "prior" to property. For the narrator, as we have seen, the maintenance of a property regime itself relies on communal ties. Few formal theorists of property have developed this sort of connection between property and community. A possible conceptual link can be found in an argument offered by Carol Rose, who has persuasively identified a role for the human connections I associate with community in the creation of a property regime. She treats the institution of a property regime as the collective action problem of providing a public good. To get a property regime going, people must be willing to cooperate reliably with each other, not breaking their mutual agreements even if they are certain they can get away with it. The willingness to enter into cooperative arrangements where it is open to others to cheat can be explained by the existence of some prior human attachments between the erstwhile cooperators. Being part of a community, that is, can inspire the trust needed to initiate and sustain collective action. On this view, community feelings motivate people to respect each other's property holdings, so that good neighbors will make good fences in more than a literal sense.

Although the narrator sees the possibility that property can support community, he also sees that that possibility can go unrecognized. Indeed, by the end of the poem it seems that the neighbor has failed to appreciate the shared activity of mending the wall in the way the narrator would like. The narrator sees the chore as play, and hopes that his banter about his apple trees not eating the neighbor's pine cones will bring his co-worker to acknowledge their connectedness. The neighbor responds with his slogan, endorsing separation. Still, the narrator has hopes that their interaction will make the neighbor question his belief. "Spring is the mischief in me, and I wonder / If I could put a notion in his head / '*Why* do they make good neighbors?'" The narrator wishes, that is, that the neighbor would examine his own understanding of neighborliness. The neighbor should consider that blithely putting up a wall might give offense— building walls requires examination first, of what one is "walling in or walling out." That is, the narrator wants the neighbor to acknowledge that a wall might not make someone a good neighbor, but might sever all connection with him. At this point the narrator repeats his slogan, imagining that the neighbor might see in it a critique of his (the neighbor's) limited conception of human association. The narrator wants the neighbor to grasp that a wall can be like an insult, and that whatever it is that doesn't love a wall might want it down because, like an insult, it disrupts community.

But the neighbor does not entertain these thoughts. He does not even enter into the narrator's play, by, say, joking that the damage the two men repair was caused by elves. Rather, as we noted, the narrator's final image presents the neighbor not as a companion in community, but as "an old-stone savage" who "moves in darkness as it seems to me / Not of woods only and the shade of trees." Far from learning the narrator's lesson, the neighbor, because he "likes having thought of it so well," reaffirms his own slogan. This slogan is the poem's closing line,

indicating that the narrator grasps that their interaction has failed to make the neighbor "go behind his father's saying." The neighbor appears in darkness to the narrator precisely because of this failure: he seems to stand in a shadow cast by his ideology of isolation, blind to the fact that the walls he values are the product of the community he disvalues.

The richness of "Mending Wall" is that it offers a hopeful vision of the role property can play in sustaining community, while fully acknowledging that vision's ambiguous prospect. Though he might convince the reader, the eloquent spokesman for a communitarian conception of property cannot convince his own neighbor. The poem's confrontation between the narrator and the neighbor, and the positions on property they represent, reflect what is perhaps a paradox inherent in the effort to bring the notions of property and community together. A clue is in the poem's title, which yokes a word that evokes reconnection with a word that evokes separation. This paradoxical juxtaposition generates the poem's dialectical power. It is, in effect, reiterated when the narrator tells how he and his neighbor meet to "set the wall between us once again." Together they share an activity that divides them; maintaining the division requires their shared activity. 'Mending Wall' thus displays the dialectic into which we must enter if we are to explore the relation between property and community because it helps us frame a conception of property in which walls are acknowledged as dividers, but are also imagined as seams.

**Source:** Zev Trachtenberg, "Good Neighbors Make Good Fences: Frost's "*Mending Wall*"," in *Philosophy and Literature*, Vol. 21, No. 1, 1997, pp. 114–22.

## SOURCES

John Ciardi, "Robert Frost: An American Bard," in the *Saturday Review*, March 24, 1962. pp. 15–16; excerpted in "Frost, Robert (1875–1963)," in *Modern American Literature*, Vol. 1, 5th ed., St. James Press, 1999, p. 395.

The Charters of Freedom," *U.S. National Archives and Records Administration,* www.archives.gov/national-archives-experience/charters/charters.html (October 29, 2006).

Cowley, Malcolm, "The Case Against Mr. Frost," in the *New Republic,* September 18, 1944, pp. 346–47; excerpted in "Frost, Robert (1875–1963)," in *Modern American Literature*, Vol. 1, 5th ed., St. James Press, 1999, p. 394.

Denis Donoghue, "A Mode of Communicating: Frost and the 'Middle' Style," in the *Yale Review,* Winter 1963. p. 216; excerpted in "Frost, Robert (1875–1963)," in *Modern American Literature*, Vol. 1, 5th ed., St. James Press, 1999, p. 395.

Dragland, S. L., "Frost's Mending Wall," in the *Explicator*, Vol. 25, No. 5, January 1967; reprinted in *Periodicals Index Online.*

Elliott, G. R., "An Undiscovered America In Frost's Poetry," in the *Virginia Quarterly Review,* July 1925, pp. 214–15; excerpted in "Frost, Robert (1875–1963)," in *Modern American Literature*, Vol. 1, 5th ed., St. James Press, 1999, p. 394.

Emerson, Ralph Waldo, "Nature, " *Essays and English Traits,* P. F. Collier & Son, 1909–1914; reprinted on *Bartelby.com,* 2001.

"History of Stone Walls," in *The Stone Wall Initiative,* www.stonewall.uconn.edu/PrimerHist.htm (September 20, 2006).

John Locke, *Two Treatises of Government,* A. Millar et al., 1764; reprinted in the *Online Library of Liberty,* oll.libertyfund.org/Texts/Locke0154/TwoTreatises/0057_Bk.html (April 24, 2004).

Lowell, Amy, "On Imagism," in *Tendencies in Modern American Poetry*, Macmillan, 1917, www.english.uiuc.edu/maps/poets/g_l/amylowell/imagism.htm (October 20, 2006).

Meider, Wolfgang, "'Good Fences Make Good Neighbours': History and Significance of an Ambiguous Proverb, in *Folklore*, August 2003, pp. 155–79.

Monroe, Harriet, "Frost and Masters," in *Poetry,* January 1917. pp. 202–207; excerpted in "Frost, Robert (1875–1963)," in *Modern American Literature*, Vol. 1, 5th ed., St. James Press, 1999, p. 394.

*New Hampshire Division of Parks and Recreation,* "State Parks: Robert Frost Farm," www.nhstateparks.org/ParksPages/FrostFarm/Frost.html (September 30, 2006).

Pearce, Roy Harvey, *The Continuity of American Poetry,* Princeton University Press, 1961, p. 274.

Trilling, Lionel, "A Speech on Robert Frost: A Cultural Episode," in the *Partisan Review,* Summer 1959, pp. 451–52; reprinted in "Robert Frost, an Introduction," Holt, Rinehart, and Winston, 1961, p. 154.

# A Model of Christian Charity

**JOHN WINTHROP**

**1630**

John Winthrop's "A Model of Christian Charity," also known as "A City on a Hill," is often cited to illustrate America's status as the leading nation of the world. It has been quoted by numerous politicians, most notably Ronald Reagan in his 1981 inaugural address, to signify America as a beacon of civilization responsible for guiding the rest of the world into the future. A thorough reading of Winthrop's speech, along with an understanding of the circumstances in which Winthrop wrote it, yields a much deeper understanding of the message he meant to convey.

John Winthrop was selected as governor of the Massachusetts Bay Company in 1629, and he was given the task of leading a fleet of Puritan settlers to establish a community of their own in New England the following year. The speech was given to his fellow travelers on board the *Arbella*, the flagship of this fleet, as they prepared to sail from their native England. Winthrop's words laid out specific guidelines for living together in a Christian community—an important message because many of the settlers came from different regions and did not know each other before the journey. Winthrop also cautioned that the world would be watching them, and that failure to fulfill their duty to God would not only ruin their chances of prosperity, but would also disgrace like-minded Christians across the globe.

Though Puritans are often depicted in popular American culture as cold and unemotional,

"A Model of Christian Charity" provides insight into the warmth and depth with which Winthrop and other Puritans sought to form bonds of community among themselves. Winthrop states to the gathered congregation that "we must love one another with a pure heart fervently," and details the ways in which each member should exhibit charity and mercy to all other members of the community. He emphasizes communal living, with the wealthiest and most prosperous members of society freely giving to the poorest members, as well as charitable lending principles that would require a lender to simply forgive a debt if the borrower had no means of repayment.

It is the final section of "A Model of Christian Charity," however, that has received the most attention. In it, Winthrop compares their new Massachusetts Bay colony to "a city upon a hill": Like a city rising above the surrounding land, it is visible to all, and surely will be subjected to careful scrutiny. Winthrop suggests that if he and his fellow Puritans succeed, they will serve as a shining example for others to follow. However, if they fail, their failure will bring disgrace to all Christians everywhere.

This "city upon a hill" passage is often cited by those who support the notion of American exceptionalism. In the most general sense, exceptionalism is the belief that a certain thing is not bound by established rules or patterns. American exceptionalism is the idea that the United States, with its unique formation and development, is fundamentally different from any other country in the world. The notion of American exceptionalism has been used to hold the United States to higher standards than other countries; it has also been used to justify actions that might otherwise be viewed negatively, such as the appropriation of land from Native American tribes. Supporters of American exceptionalism have used Winthrop's "city upon a hill" passage to suggest that the United States—much like the original Massachusetts Bay colony—serves as a leading example for the rest of the world.

Although the final section of "A Model of Christian Charity" is frequently quoted as a celebration of American uniqueness and idealism, John Winthrop himself remains relatively unknown and unrecognized as one of the earliest architects of the American way of life. In some respects, "A Model of Christian Charity" can be viewed as a precursor to the ideals and notions

# BIOGRAPHY

## JOHN WINTHROP

John Winthrop was born to Adam Winthrop and Anne Brown on January 12, 1588, in Suffolk, England. Educated by a private tutor as a boy, Winthrop attended Cambridge and later studied law at Gray's Inn, where he developed a strong Puritan belief that the Church of England should be cleansed of its Roman Catholic characteristics. Joining with other like-minded men of wealth and influence, Winthrop became a part of the Massachusetts Bay Company, the goal of which was to establish a Puritan community in New England. Before embarking on the trip, Winthrop was selected as governor for this new venture.

Winthrop went on to serve as governor for nearly twenty years, though he was voted out of office and re-elected numerous times during that period. He oversaw the establishment of a democratic governing body that served in conjunction with community church leaders. Though he is most famous for his 1630 speech known as "A Model of Christian Charity," he also wrote extensive journals that chronicled the Massachusetts Bay settlement's first two decades. These journals have proven to be an invaluable record of early American life. He died on March 26, 1649.

later voiced by American icons such as Benjamin Franklin and Thomas Jefferson. As scholar Rick Kennedy writes in his essay "Building a City on a Hill":

> Using the language of later founding fathers, Winthrop wanted to create a "more perfect" society. As he said in the sermon, he wanted to take what was done or what ought to have been done in England and make it better. He wanted to take the politics, religion, and economics of village-life in England and make it better. The end product would be a model to the world.

## PLOT SUMMARY

"A Model of Christian Charity" begins with the following proclamation regarding inequality in human society:

> God Almighty in His most holy and wise providence, hath so disposed of the condition of mankind, as in all times some must be rich, some poor, some high and eminent in power and dignity; others mean and in submission.

He then enumerates the reasons why God would want such inequality to exist. First, Winthrop suggests that this is "to hold conformity" with the differences found in the rest of the natural world. Winthrop also contends that God would prefer to see his work carried out by his followers than by Himself. For that reason, God does not perform miracles to feed the hungry or shelter the homeless; instead, He allows the wealthy to demonstrate charity to those less fortunate, and therefore demonstrate the work of God through themselves. Second, Winthrop argues that by allowing inequality to exist, both the wealthy and the needy are given an opportunity to exhibit some of God's graces. The wealthy may exhibit "love, mercy, gentleness, temperance etc."; the needy can show their grace through "faith, patience, obedience etc." Third, Winthrop asserts that because of this inequality, "every man might have need of others, and from hence they might be all knit more nearly together in the bonds of brotherly affection."

This leads to the general rule of behavior that every man should help any fellow man who appears to need help. The amount of help given should be regulated only by one's own most basic needs: "There is a time when a Christian must sell all and give to the poor, as they did in the Apostles' times." Though giving up all of one's wealth may not always be required, Winthrop encourages Christians to help "beyond our ability rather than tempt God in putting him upon help by miraculous or extraordinary means." Winthrop refers to this as a "duty of mercy" that can be fulfilled through giving, lending, and forgiving debts.

With regard to giving, Winthrop states that under normal circumstances a man should give away whatever he does not reasonably need for himself and his family. He then addresses the argument that a man should save any extra wealth of resources to be prepared for disaster or tragedy. Winthrop argues that a man who gives will be taken care of by God, and that all those he helps will stand as witnesses of his generosity and mercy when his day of judgment arrives. In addition, Winthrop notes that physical objects of wealth "are subject to the moth, the rust, the thief," and that they can cause a person's heart to lose sight of the true treasure of serving God. Finally, Winthrop points out that the interests of God must come before any person's interests, and God's instructions are clear: "If thy brother be in want and thou canst help him, thou needst not make doubt of what thou shouldst do; if thou lovest God thou must help him."

Winthrop delineates specific rules to follow when it comes to lending money or resources to other people. When approached by someone without any possible means of repaying the loan, an upstanding Christian should simply give the person whatever he can afford instead of lending it. If the person has no immediate ability to repay the loan but might be able to repay it in the future, a worthy Christian should lend whatever he can afford—even though he knows the loan may not be repaid. In cases in which a person does have the means to repay, the transaction should be treated purely as a business venture; in other words, the lender should not view his own actions as an exhibition of God's graces, because he has not done anything truly charitable. The rule for forgiving a debt is simple: If the borrower has no means to repay the loan—regardless of the fact that the loan was meant to be repaid—the lender must forgive the debt.

Winthrop also sets forth specific rules for living together as a community. He describes the structure of some older church communities similar to the Puritans where "they sold all, had all things in common, neither did any man say that which he possessed was his own." He compares the Christian community to a single body, with each individual part serving the whole. In such a system, the parts "mutually participate with each other, both in strength and infirmity, in pleasure and pain." The members of the community are united toward a common goal—serving God—and therefore should work to support and protect each other against whatever difficulties they might face. Winthrop provides numerous quotes and examples from the Bible to illustrate the bonds that connect Christians, even those who may not know each other directly.

Winthrop compares the bond between Christians to the love a mother has for her child, noting that "each discerns, by the work of the Spirit, his own Image and resemblance in another, and therefore cannot but love him as he loves himself." Just as a mother gives love without any expectation of receiving something in return, so must a Christian freely dispense love and mercy to other Christians in need. This kindness is sure to be reciprocated, resulting in what Winthrop calls "a most equal and sweet kind of commerce." Similarly, returning to the metaphor of the Christian community as a single body, he observes that the mouth performs most of the work required to nourish the entire body; however, the mouth does not object to this arrangement, because it not only receives pleasure from the work it does, but it also receives a share of the body's nourishment.

Winthrop, speaking to the assembled Christians, notes that even though they have gathered from different places and backgrounds, they are all a part of a single Christian community united by a "bond of love." He then provides some information about what the group should expect in the new community they seek to form. First, the needs of the community must necessarily override the needs of the individual; he notes that "it is a true rule that particular estates cannot subsist in the ruin of the public." In other words, individual households might prosper more than others, but ultimately no one will prosper if the community as a whole fails to thrive.

Winthrop cautions that life in their new American colony will be harder than it was in England, their former home. What serve simply as words of belief for many Christians in England will become the Puritans' daily way of life:

> We must love brotherly without dissimulation, we must love one another with a pure heart fervently. We must bear one another's burdens. We must not look only on our own things, but also on the things of our brethren.

Winthrop also asserts that the Lord will hold their community to higher standards than other Christians due to "the more near bond of marriage between Him and us." For this reason, they must strictly follow their own established laws or risk punishment directly from God. Theirs is a special commission from God, he argues, like the biblical tale of Saul's commission to destroy Amaleck. Saul failed in a small detail of his duties, and therefore did not receive his

> FOR WE MUST CONSIDER THAT WE SHALL BE AS A CITY UPON A HILL. THE EYES OF ALL PEOPLE ARE UPON US. SO THAT IF WE SHALL DEAL FALSELY WITH OUR GOD IN THIS WORK WE HAVE UNDERTAKEN, AND SO CAUSE HIM TO WITHDRAW HIS PRESENT HELP FROM US, WE SHALL BE MADE A STORY AND A BY-WORD THROUGH THE WORLD."

reward. According to Winthrop, in exchange for the fulfillment of their dream to start a new community in a new land, they must serve God according to the doctrines of their religion; if they fail, then "the Lord will surely break out in wrath against us, and be revenged of such a people, and make us know the price of the breach of such a covenant."

In addition, Winthrop points out that God is not the only one who will keep a close watch on the community they seek to establish. He states that they will stand out like "a city upon a hill," adding, "The eyes of all people are upon us." He warns his fellow Puritans that failure on their part will cast shame on not only their colony, but also all those who share their beliefs. Winthrop concludes his speech by again noting their special relationship with God, and by repeating his warning:

> But if our hearts shall turn away, so that we will not obey, but shall be seduced, and worship other Gods, our pleasure and profits, and serve them; it is propounded unto us this day, we shall surely perish out of the good land whither we pass over this vast sea to possess it.

## THEMES

### *American Exceptionalism*

Winthrop's "A Model of Christian Charity" is often quoted as an early example of American exceptionalism. American exceptionalism is the idea that the United States is fundamentally different from other countries, and therefore defies easy comparison of policies or statistics between itself and the rest of the world. In his speech,

*Ronald Reagan gives his farewell address from the Oval Office of the White House* © *Bettmann/Corbis*

Winthrop asserts that he and his fellow colonists have been chosen by God to fulfill a special commission, and that their actions will be watched by the rest of the world. This notion of the elevated importance of Americans and their behaviors is consistent with the idea of American exceptionalism.

A belief in the unique status of the United States was embraced by many supporters of the American Revolution, including author Thomas Paine. In his pamphlet *Common Sense*, Paine asserts that America is blessed with a situation unheard of in the world at the time: "Should an independency be brought about... we have every opportunity and every encouragement before us, to form the noblest, purest constitution on the face of the earth." The popularity of Paine's pamphlet helped to garner public support for the notion that America—at the time, still officially considered a territory of England— should fight for the right to govern itself.

Observers from other nations also attested to the uniqueness of America. In his essay "American Exceptionalism as National History?" Hans

Guggisberg describes how European visitors played an important part in the development of America's unique identity:

> It must also be noted that since the colonial period of American history a very great number of European visitors were deeply impressed with the otherness and uniqueness of mentalities, social structures, and political institutions they had encountered in the New World. In describing what they had seen, many of them became defenders of American exceptionalism.

As Guggisberg points out, French historian Alexis de Tocqueville is credited with inventing the term "American exceptionalism" in his landmark 1835 work *Democracy in America*. In the book, which analyzes American institutions, customs and beliefs from an outsider's point of view, de Tocqueville writes, "The position of the Americans is . . . quite exceptional, and it may be believed that no democratic people will ever be placed in a similar one."

Over the centuries, American exceptionalism has been used to support or defend certain actions that ran contrary to what other nations would consider acceptable. In *American Exceptionalism and Human Rights*, Michael Ignatieff asserts that "Slavery and segregation made America exceptional among liberal democratic states, and southern politicians led the opposition to American adoption of international rights regimes from the late 1940s to the 1960s." Before the Civil War, some southern plantation owners argued that the plantation agriculture system was not feasible without slave labor, and therefore should be seen as an exception to the human rights principles accepted by modern nations around the world.

Manifest destiny is another example of American exceptionalism being used as a justification for actions that might otherwise be viewed negatively. Manifest destiny, popularized throughout the middle of the nineteenth century, is the idea that the United States and its citizens had a duty to claim and populate as much of the North American continent as possible. Those who argued in support of manifest destiny believed that God had chosen the American people to spread and multiply from the Atlantic Ocean to the Pacific Ocean, and that this special mission superceded previous territorial agreements and treaties.

In the twentieth century, the idea of American exceptionalism often appeared in arguments supporting United States involvement in foreign wars. According to Anders Stephanson, author of *Manifest Destiny: American Expansionism and the Empire of Right*, the notion was also used to strengthen public opinion against the Soviet Union during the Cold War: "To refrain from doing one's utmost to extinguish this evil (the Soviet Union) was tantamount to sin and would end in self-destruction. The choice was plain. Only the United States could perform the given task."

In recent decades, a growing number of historians and political scientists have cast criticism on the notion of American exceptionalism. Some, such as Charles Lockhart, point out that America is often exceptional in ways that are not at all praiseworthy; on the first page of his book *The Roots of American Exceptionalism*, Lockhart writes, "The United States is the only advanced industrial society which lacks a public program assuring financial access to a broad range of medical care for the vast majority of its citizens." Historian Howard Zinn, in his essay "The Power and the Glory: Myths of American Exceptionalism," offers these words of caution: "One of the consequences of American exceptionalism is that the U.S. government considers itself exempt from legal and moral standards accepted by other nations in the world."

However, Zinn also notes that the terrorist attacks of September 11, 2001, "gave a new impetus to the idea that the United States was uniquely responsible for the security of the world, defending us all against terrorism as it once did against communism."

## Charity

As the title of the speech suggests, "A Model of Christian Charity" deals primarily with the idea of giving to others in need. According to Winthrop, this is a cornerstone of the new community he and the other Puritans hope to build. For the wealthy colonists, charity is also a measure of their service to God.

At the beginning of the speech, Winthrop asserts that it is God's will that some people are wealthy while others are poor. This imbalance in prosperity is necessary for God to test one's charity; if everyone had the same amount of wealth, then there would be little reason for one person to give to another. In Winthrop's view, God has done this as a two-fold test to ensure "that the rich and mighty should not eat up the poor, nor the poor and despised rise up against and shake off their yoke."

Charity is also shown to be an important part of human interaction. Winthrop argues that although God could simply provide charity Himself, He must be like a king who is "more honored in dispensing his gifts to man by man, than if he did it by his own immediate hands." The act of charity is also depicted as a way of drawing people together into a more tightly knit community, because it requires the formation of meaningful relationships between the giver and the receiver.

Throughout "A Model of Christian Charity," Winthrop indicates the many ways in which a Christian may exhibit charity. First, charity can consist of providing money and material goods to others who need them. As Winthrop points out, such material things "are subject to the moth, the rust, the thief," and therefore should not be held in excess of what one needs for one's own self and family. Second, charity can be exhibited by forgiving a debt that is owed. Winthrop makes a clear distinction between giving freely and lending, and notes that lending should never be viewed as an act of charity in itself. Third, charity can be shown by offering love to others without expecting anything in return. This is a core component of Winthrop's Christian worldview, and he notes that "to love and live beloved is the soul's paradise both here and in heaven."

## Communalism

Communalism is defined as a type of societal organization where the interests of the community as a whole are placed above individual interests. The term also suggests a community in which all resources and duties are shared equally among all members. The principles Winthrop sets forth in "A Model of Christian Charity" reflect these ideas of communalism.

First, although he believes that inequality of wealth exists as a certainty in society because it is God's will, he also believes that it is the responsibility of Christians to correct that inequality as much as they are able to. As he puts it, "If thy brother be in want and thou canst help him, thou needst not make doubt of what thou shouldst do; if thou lovest God thou must help him." Such an exhibition of charity is certainly meant to benefit the individual who serves God as well as the receiver of charity, but it is also meant "for the preservation and good of the whole."

Winthrop states this even more clearly in later portions of the speech. "Hence it was that in the primitive Church they sold all, had all things in common, neither did any man say that which he possessed was his own," he states, comparing their new society to communes of ancient religious tradition. Winthrop suggests that in times of peril, they should strive for "more enlargement towards others and less respect towards ourselves and our own right." This seems to suggest that the interests of the community outweigh the interests of the individual. Similarly, he writes, "We must be willing to abridge ourselves of our superfluities, for the supply of others' necessities." This same message is reflected in the statement, "For it is a true rule that particular estates cannot subsist in the ruin of the public."

The basic principle of communalism, that the success of the whole depends on the success of all involved, is a common thread in the American dream and in American policies. Franklin Delano Roosevelt's New Deal was designed to ensure the success of the country by helping citizens in need. While the Marshall Plan (after World War II) and the Peace Corps (during the Cold War) were global strategies to protect democracy, they rest on the same principle.

Winthrop approaches the notion of communalism not from fairness or equality, but from love. "We must bear one another's burdens," he asserts. "We must not look only on our own things, but also on the things of our brethren." For Winthrop, the principles of communalism reflect the Puritan ideals of love, unity, and charity.

## From Many, One

That the United States is a country of peoples whose common ideals outweigh their individual differences is part and parcel of the American dream. The Latin phrase *E Pluribus Unum*, which means "From many, one," was one of the country's first mottos, appearing on the Great Seal of the United States in 1782. It also appears on all coins produced by the U.S. Mint.

The notion of unity is central to "A Model of Christian Charity." The Puritans who gathered to join Winthrop in the journey to the Massachusetts Bay Colony represented a diverse group united mainly by their opposition to the Church of England. It is through this common link that Winthrop symbolically draws them together in his speech. He points out that although in England they "were absent from each other many miles, and had our employments as far distant," they share a common bond of love through their devotion to God.

Winthrop uses the analogy of a living body and its parts to describe the members of this newly formed Puritan congregation. Although they all represent different parts of the body, they function together as a larger creation, and "the ligaments of this body which knit together are love." If one person is in poverty or pain, the entire group suffers—just as an injury to one part of the body can affect the health of every part:

> All the parts of this body being thus united are made so contiguous in a special relation as they must needs partake of each other's strength and infirmity; joy and sorrow, weal and woe. If one member suffers, all suffer with it, if one be in honor, all rejoice with it.

He continues this analogy with Biblical references to Adam, who refers to Eve as "flesh of my flesh," and to Jonathan and David, whom he describes as being connected by a "ligament of love."

Winthrop views unity not just as a fundamental part of their belief system, but as a necessity for their success and survival. To fulfill their dream of creating a community devoted to serving God, Winthrop's strategy is simple: "For this end, we must be knit together, in this work, as one man."

## HISTORICAL OVERVIEW

### Puritanism

"Puritan" is a term most commonly applied to English Christians who became dissatisfied with the state of the Church of England during the sixteenth and seventeenth centuries. Rather than being a single defined movement, it was composed of many groups of individuals who had differing opinions on what in particular was wrong with the established national church. In general, however, those who were termed Puritans believed that the Church of England had become corrupted by its entanglement with politics, particularly the English monarchy, as well as its adoption of Roman Catholic traditions; they believed it was necessary to "purify" the Church's practices and ceremonies to return to a less elaborate form of worship endorsed in the Bible. The term "Puritan" was originally applied by supporters of the Church of England as an insult, with the label "Dissenter" more commonly being used by members of this religious minority to refer to themselves.

Puritans were largely unsuccessful in effecting religious change within their home country, and they were often openly persecuted and denied jobs in certain professions. This led some Puritans to pursue the notion of forming a new community of like-minded individuals in the New World, where they would be free to worship as they wished. Beginning in the 1620s, Puritan settlers made their way to various settlements along the east coast of North America. The most notable Puritan settlements were established in present-day Massachusetts, where their relative success at maintaining a devout worship-based society lasted well into the eighteenth century.

In England, Puritan dissension was a key factor in the English Civil War, which lasted from 1642 until 1651. During this time, Puritan military leader Oliver Cromwell led the overthrow of the English monarchy that resulted in the execution of King Charles I and the establishment of a permanent parliament. Although Puritanism is often viewed as a reaction to the Church of England as opposed to a specific religious movement, the influence of Puritan ideals was felt throughout Protestant churches across Europe as well as in New England, where it helped shape many modern denominations of Christian worship.

### The Massachusetts Bay Colony

In April 1630, John Winthrop led some seven hundred English settlers on a fleet of eleven ships across the Atlantic Ocean. Winthrop had already been elected governor of the Massachusetts Bay Company, the organization behind the emigration. The settlers were headed to their new home, a colony in present-day Massachusetts. The trip, which took three months, was not the first made by English settlers to the New World, but at the time it was the largest single fleet of settlers ever to depart England. The journey itself was difficult, and more than one-fourth of the settlers died before reaching America. Those who survived the journey still faced the daunting task of forming a new community in an alien environment. A small group of colonists had already set up a post at Salem, but the arrival of this new flood of settlers firmly established Salem, the new settlement of Boston, and the surrounding area as an independent Puritan society in the New World.

Although the motivation for the emigration was primarily religious, many of the settlers came from different backgrounds with slightly different religious traditions and customs, and some made the journey not for religious but for economic reasons. As Francis Bremer points out in *John Winthrop: America's Forgotten Founding Father*, "Even with the most godly men and women other factors influenced the decision to migrate." These different interpretations of Puritanism resulted in conflicts over how to govern the new territory; Winthrop and other community leaders relied on their strict Puritan interpretation of the Bible to guide them in all matters, believing that civic laws should descend directly from Biblical teachings. Those who disagreed, such as Anne Hutchinson and Roger Williams—who believed that this new society should allow freedom to worship in whatever manner one wished, and that civic laws should be independent of religious laws—were often driven out of the community and forced to establish their own settlements elsewhere. Such strict punishment for perceived moral transgressions later fueled the Salem witch trials, a brief period of religious hysteria that led to the deaths of twenty Salem residents.

Still, as the settlement grew in size and success, the governing body adopted more democratic processes that some Puritans, including Winthrop, felt were in conflict with the religious teachings on which the original colony was based. The colony became one of the most successful English settlements in the New World and a cornerstone of New England commerce—a mark of distinction the region continues to enjoy to this day.

## CRITICAL OVERVIEW

Winthrop's "A Model of Christian Charity" was not intended as a timeless piece of literature. Perhaps more than simply a speech he gave to inspire his fellow Puritan settlers to fully commit to their new settlement, and to caution them about the true cost of failing at their commission, its purpose may have been to address a larger audience. As Hugh Dawson suggests in his article "'Christian Charitie' As Colonial Discourse":

> The occasion gave its themes of dependence and reassurance urgency, but beyond seeking to inspire those leaving, Winthrop insisted that all those who had committed themselves to the Colony—those about to sail, the others of the sect now settled ..., and those remaining at home—be faithful to their promises.... Beneath his confident exhortation to those about to sail, it finds another, perhaps more important text directed to the larger community of all those in England and America who had pledged themselves to the project of Massachusetts.

The speech appeared to have little impact at the time it was delivered. In fact, as Francis Bremer notes in *John Winthrop: America's Forgotten Founding Father*, "Despite the relative abundance of source material dealing with the settlement of Massachusetts, not a single individual recorded in letter, diary or other source having heard Winthrop deliver the sermon." The only account survives in Winthrop's own journal.

In the centuries that followed, however, "A Model of Christian Charity" became one of the most well-known Puritan works ever printed. In "Building a City on a Hill," Rick Kennedy

asserts, "In the nineteenth century, the world really was watching America, and Winthrop's speech came to be thought of as prophesy." Ronald Reagan quoted the "city upon a hill" passage as part of his Presidential inaugural speech in 1981, and many other politicians have followed suit. In 1999, Peter Gomes, minister of the Memorial Church at Harvard, selected "A Model of Christian Charity" as the greatest sermon of the previous millennium.

## CRITICISM

### Rick Kennedy

*In the following excerpt, Kennedy explores the broad and lasting resonance of Winthrop's "A Model of Christian Charity" speech.*

In the spring of 1630, John Winthrop composed and delivered one of the most famous speeches in American history, "A Model of Christian Charity." Winthrop was the head of the Massachusetts Bay Company, a corporation that organized a crossing of the Atlantic to establish an English colony. His goal, at its core, was simple. He wanted to create a society out of towns that were economically, politically, and religiously prosperous; thereby, being a model to the world. Adopting an image used by Jesus, his colony was to be a "City upon a Hill" where "the eyes of all people are upon us." Although initially delivered as a speech, "A Model of Christian Charity" was subsequently printed as an essay and widely distributed.

The idea of a watching world may seem a bit egomaniacal; however, a bigger world than Winthrop ever imagined has continued to watch for 370 years. Popular histories of Winthrop's company began to be written within a half century. Within another century, English Whigs and American revolutionaries were regularly referring to the motives and actions of the Puritan migration as they questioned the relationship between England and her colonies. In the nineteenth century, the world really was watching America, and Winthrop's speech came to be thought of as prophecy. In the early twentieth century, Puritan studies became a major cottage industry at American universities, and interest in Puritan society and culture has continued throughout the century. Ronald Reagan, in his first inaugural address as president, quoted Winthrop's famous sentence: "For we must consider that we shall be as a City upon a Hill, the eyes of all people are upon us."

The Puritans of Massachusetts Bay, next to our national Founding Fathers, are probably the most highly studied and talked about group of people in American history. If we consider this, Winthrop and his Puritans are more a city on a hill now than they were then. In this light, it behooves us to look at the "Model of Christian Charity" and see what is in it and in the Massachusetts Bay Company's implementation of it that has such lasting power.

In 1629, Winthrop sold his village and joined with a network of Puritan friends, many of them connected through Cambridge University, in purchasing stock in the Massachusetts Bay Company. Winthrop set sail aboard the *Arbella* and reached Salem in June 1630. As the stockholders of a company to set up a community in America, Winthrop and his friends regained an extensive amount of economic, political, and religious independence.

The stockholders elected the forty-one-year-old Winthrop their governor. Hundreds of farmers and trades people joined the expedition as workers—many of them people who had previously rented from or worked for the stockholders. At this time Winthrop composed his "Model of Christian Charity." Although much would later be said about the motivation for religious freedom that spurred the Puritans to this moment, the essay itself is just as much about politics, economics, and specifically the need to reclaim local autonomy and responsibility against the centralizing tendency of the king.

The greatness of Winthrop's essay, and the Puritan migration in general, is that, though Winthrop and the Puritans sought to regain lost freedom, they succeeded in doing so much more with the freedom they gained than they ever would have been able to do in England even if they had never lost their Elizabethan freedom. The call of Winthrop's words and the actions he led in Massachusetts far exceeded any selfish attempt of a threatened owner of a village to gain control of a new village.

The conclusion of "A Model of Christian Charity" is the most important part of Winthrop's essay. "It rests now to make some application," he declared. First, those who claim to be Christians should be "knit together" in a "bond of Love." Second, church and town governments must work together and the public good must "oversway all private respects." Third, the goal is "to improve our lives, to do more service to the Lord." Fourth, and most significantly, "Whatsoever we did or ought to have done when we lived in England, the same must we do and more also where we go."

Winthrop declared a contract between the Puritans and God. God has "ratified" the contract and further commissioned the Puritans to get to work. God, Winthrop threatened, "will expect strict performance." Given this threat, there is only one way to success: "to do justly, to love mercy, to walk humbly with our God."

It is in this context that Winthrop then closes with the "city upon a hill" line. But note that the line is in the context of failure not success:

> For we must consider that we shall be as a City upon a Hill, the eyes of all people are upon us; so that if we shall deal falsely with our God in this work we have undertaken, and so cause Him to withdraw His present help from us, we shall be a by-word through the world.

With such a speech about such a contract and such a commission, how could anyone expect Winthrop and the Puritans to succeed? In fact, they did not succeed—in the long run. In his own diary, Winthrop reported the frustrations and failures. "As the people increased," he wrote twelve years after arriving in New England, "so sin abounded."

But early on, Winthrop and his company made an heroic effort to succeed. The story of the initial implementation of Winthrop's speech makes it amazing that he did succeed. Winthrop turned his directorship into an annually elected position. Voting was extended more widely among the people than ever before in England. Renters became landowners. Rich people took less than what they could have demanded. Local government was given autonomy. Ministers restrained their political power. Public education was ensured to all children. Virtuous economics was encouraged and price-gouging punished. Surely anyone watching had to admit that the Puritans used their increased freedom to do more political, economic, and religious good in America than was ever possible in England.

We must understand that Winthrop and the Puritans were not egalitarian, but they did believe in community responsibility. Winthrop's "Model of Christian Charity" begins with the simple distinction that there are two ranks of people: the rich and the poor. When giving out land, the Puritans tended to give the people who had been richer in England a little more than the formerly landless. The Puritans did not want to undermine social distinctions. Responsibility was what they were after, not equality. In his speech, Winthrop offered several biblical precedents for "enlargement towards others, and less respect towards our selves and our own right."

Here again, we must see the reality behind the rhetoric of Winthrop's call to do "whatsoever we did or ought to have done when we lived in England, the same must we do and more also where we go." Only this way could the Puritans "improve our lives, to do more service to the Lord." Winthrop wanted everyone in Massachusetts to start "rich" and not "poor." Being "rich" he defined not by estate and servants, rather by the ability "to live comfortably by their own means." The Puritan contract with God needed everyone to have such basic comfort so that they could be "knit together" and spend their days improving Massachusetts instead of worrying about subsistence.

The city on a hill as preached in "A Model of Christian Charity" was not a utopia. Utopias usually depend on the behalf that human nature is good and that a bad environment is what keeps most societies from attaining purity. The Puritan city on a hill was a republic of Christian voters gathered in towns and churches where individual sinfulness could be inhibited by peer pressure. Puritans believed in the inherent sinfulness of individuals and had no illusions about their colony attaining purity.

Using the language of later founding fathers, Winthrop wanted to create a "more perfect" society. As he said in the speech, he wanted to take the politics, religion, and economics of village life in England and make it better. The end product would be a model to the world.

An often-stated irony about the Puritans is that they wanted religious toleration for themselves but refused to extend it to others. While this is superficially true, we should recognize that Winthrop's speech never said anything about religious liberty or toleration. Winthrop's speech was about knitting together people into a web of politics, religion, and economics with underlying assumptions about education. The Puritan creation of a loose republic rooted in independent towns and churches established the web. Those who refused to fully participate in the web were

punished in much the same way English towns punished those unwilling to abide by the social contract.

In 1680, more than a half-century after the founding of the colony, England imposed religious toleration on Massachusetts and demanded that voting no longer be restricted to church members. But the loose town and church structure of the commonwealth was becoming too loose anyway. Success was killing them. As Winthrop noted early: "As people increased, so sin abounded." Too many people wanted to come to the city upon a hill, thus turning it into nothing more than a dynamic English colony. When English imperial policy demanded a break between church membership and the right to vote, the key innovation of the city upon a hill was destroyed. What was left was just the shell of Winthop's model.

But even the shell of the plan has long been influential. By the time of Samuel and John Adams in the 1770s, towns remained the most powerful force in Massachusetts politics. Calling a "town meeting" is still a catch-phrase of participatory democracy. A good case could be made today that it is not Winthrop's speech that is important in American history; rather, it is simply the line about being a city upon a hill. That our town-based, participatory democracy should be exported to the rest of the world.

On the other hand, the deep ideas contained in the "Model of Christian Charity" and their implementation in colonial Massachusetts are inspiring. John Winthrop and his fellow stockholders led one of the greatest events in American history. A small band of rich Protestant men voluntarily diminished their own power in order to launch a social experiment they hoped would inspire the world.

**Source:** Rick Kennedy, "Building a City on a Hill," in *Events that Changed America Through the Seventeenth Century*, edited by John Findling and Frank Thackeray, Greenwood Press, 2000, pp. 59–69.

## SOURCES

Bremer, Francis, *John Winthrop: America's Forgotten Founding Father*, The H. W. Wilson Company, 1952, pp. 164, 174.

Dawson, Hugh J., "'Christian Charitie' as colonial discourse: rereading Winthrop's sermon in its English context," in *Early American Literature*, Vol. 33, No. 2, Spring 1998, p. 117.

de Tocqueville, Alexis, *Democracy in America*, edited by Richard C. Heffner, Signet Classics, 2001, p. 160; originally published in 1840.

Guggisberg, Hans, "American Exceptionalism as National History?", in *Bridging the Atlantic: The Question of American Exceptionalism in Perspective*, edited by Elisabeth Glaser and Hermann Wellenreuther, Cambridge University Press, 2002, p. 265.

Ignatieff, Michael, "Introduction," in *American Exceptionalism and Human Rights*, Princeton University Press, 2005, p. 19.

Kennedy, Rick, "Building a City on a Hill," in *Events that Changed America Through the Seventeenth Century*, edited by John Findling and Frank Thackeray, Greenwood Press, 2000, pp. 59–69.

Lockhart, Charles, *The Roots of American Exceptionalism: Institutions, Culture and Policies*, Palgrave Macmillan, 2003, p. 1.

Paine, Thomas, "Appendix to the Third Edition," *Common Sense*, www.ushistory.org/paine/commonsense/sense6. htm (November 10, 2006).

Stephanson, Anders, *Manifest Destiny: American Expansionism and the Empire of Right*, Hill and Wang, 1996, p. 124.

Winthrop, John, "A Model of Christian Charity," on *The Winthrop Society*, www.winthropsociety.org/doc_charity. php (November 10, 2006); originally delivered in 1630.

Zinn, Howard, "The Power and the Glory: Myths of American Exceptionalism," in the *Boston Review*, bostonreview.net/BR30.3/zinn.html (October 23, 2006).

# Montage of a Dream Deferred

**LANGSTON HUGHES**

**1951**

"What happens to a dream deferred?" That question—one of the most famous lines of poetry to issue from the pen of an American writer—captures the essence of Langston Hughes's 1951 work *Montage of a Dream Deferred*. In this tightly interwoven collection, the "dream deferred" is the collective dream of the African Americans. Although slavery was abolished nearly a century before, black Americans in the 1940s and 1950s were still not seen as equals in the eyes of the general public nor, often, in the eyes of local and state lawmakers. While white Americans were riding a wave of post–World War II prosperity toward the fulfillment of their vision of the American dream, most blacks were left waiting for their opportunity to join in the country's success.

A montage is an artistic work that consists of smaller pieces of art combined into a unified whole that reveals a larger picture or meaning. This is an accurate description of *Montage of a Dream Deferred*, which Hughes preferred to think of as a single, book-length poem. Recurring themes and phrases occur throughout the smaller poetic works that make up the book; in fact, the book begins and ends with the same two lines: "Good morning, daddy! / Ain't you heard?"

*Montage of a Dream Deferred* is, in addition to being a statement about denied opportunities for African Americans, a rich portrayal of the places and personalities that make up the New York neighborhood of Harlem where Hughes lived.

# BIOGRAPHY

## LANGSTON HUGHES

James Langston Hughes was born in Joplin, Missouri, on February 1, 1902. His parents separated while Hughes was still young, and he spent most of his childhood in Kansas and Ohio, sometimes living with his mother and sometimes with his grandmother while his father sought fortune in Mexico. In eighth grade, Hughes was selected as class poet, and during high school he was a frequent contributor to his school's monthly magazine. His first professionally published poem, "The Negro Speaks of Rivers," appeared in the magazine *The Crisis* when Hughes was just nineteen years old. After studying for a short time at Columbia University, Hughes spent the next several years writing poetry and traveling the world as a seaman.

Hughes's first book-length collection of poetry, *The Weary Blues*, was published to critical acclaim in 1926. Over the next four decades, he went on to produce several more volumes of poetry, short stories, novels, plays, and even nonfiction works, including 1959's *Montage of a Dream Deferred*. Hughes died of congestive heart failure on May 22, 1967. He is considered by critics and scholars to be one of the most influential artists of the Harlem Renaissance, and he remains one of America's most popular poets.

According to biographer Arnold Rampersad, from the vantage point of his Harlem home, "Hughes watched the historic evolution of African American culture from its roots in the rural South to its often tangled exfoliation in the cities of the North." More importantly, he documented this evolution for the entertainment and enlightenment of both current and future generations.

One of the most notable stylistic elements of *Montage of a Dream Deferred* is Hughes's use of jazz and bebop musical techniques to infuse his poems with a spirit that is uniquely African American. This includes the use of irregular rhythms and onomatopoetic bursts of sound such as "pop-a-da!" For Hughes, jazz music represented the beating heart of the African American experience. As he wrote in *The Big Sea: An Autobiography* in 1940:

> I tried to write poems like the songs they sang on Seventh Street—gay songs, because you had to be gay or die; sad songs, because you couldn't help being sad sometimes. But gay or sad, you kept on living and you kept on going. Their songs—those of Seventh Street—had the pulse beat of the people who keep on going.

Langston Hughes is beloved for writing poetry, prose, drama, and nonfiction over his four-decade career. His single most famous poem is probably "The Negro Speaks of Rivers," written when he was a teenager, but his most famous concept resonates throughout *Montage of a Dream Deferred*. Though the book is not currently in print as a stand-alone work, it can be found as part of *The Collected Poems of Langston Hughes*, a mammoth anthology of the poet's professional works, edited by Arnold Rampersad and published by Knopf.

## PLOT SUMMARY

*Montage of a Dream Deferred* is a work of free-verse poetry describing different elements of life in Harlem. Although Hughes asserted that the book is intended to be read as a single long poem, it consists of eighty-seven individually titled short works, many of which were previously published as stand-alone poems. The poems are linked stylistically and thematically, with certain phrases appearing as refrains in multiple pieces. Many of the poems consist of less than twenty lines, and some are as short as three lines. In the years after the book's initial publication, Hughes made minor changes to several of the poems that were incorporated into later editions; the versions reprinted in *The Collected Poems of Langston Hughes* reflect these minor changes. The poems discussed here are an overview of the entire work.

### Boogie Woogie Poems

"Dream Boogie" is the first poem in *Montage of a Dream Deferred*, and establishes the musical,

*Langston Hughes* Getty Images

woman in "Lady's Boogie" "ain't got boogie-woo-gie / On her mind—" he believes "she'd hear / . . . / The tingle of a tear," if she would just listen.

"Nightmare Boogie" continues the musical rhythms and imagery found in "Dream Boogie," but it also directly addresses the subject of race. The poem is written in a single stanza of twelve short lines, most of which contain just three or four syllables to create a consistent, driving rhythm. In the first part of the poem, the narra-tor dreams that he sees "a million faces / black as me!" The dream turns into a nightmare, how-ever, when the black faces suddenly turn white. Hughes concludes the poem with imagery of musical instruments, as if the narrator has chan-neled his unease into boogie-woogie music.

The last poem in the book to use the "boogie-woogie" metaphor, "Dream Boogie: Variation" describes a black piano player, his music, and what the poet sees in the musician's face: "Looks like his eyes / Are teasing pain, / A few minutes late / For the Freedom Train." In all these poems, Hughes uses the sound and rhythm of exciting, energetic, complicated music. He hears hardship, grief, sadness, and simmering anger, but also finds a salve for those woes in the music.

### Harlem to Outsiders

Many poems in the collection focus on percep-tions of and interaction between black and white Americans. In "Parade," the poet describes a black marching band that is to take part in a parade and imagines a white observer's reaction: "*I never knew / that many Negroes / were on earth, / did you?*" and concludes that it will be "A chance to let / . . . / the whole world see / . . . / old black me!" He mocks white America's misconception of him in "Movies," which he describes as "crocodile tears / of crocodile art," saying, "(Hollywood / laughs at me, / black— / so I laugh / back.)"

"Ballad of the Landlord" expresses a plight common among those who live in low-income neighborhoods. The first part of the poem is written from the point of view of a black tenant who is upset at his landlord's failure to make repairs to the building where he lives. By way of protest, the tenant refuses to pay rent until the problems are fixed. When the landlord threatens the tenant with eviction, the tenant threatens the landlord physically; this leads to the tenant being arrested and ultimately sentenced to three months in jail.

"be-bop" tone and style found throughout the rest of the collection. In the first two stanzas, Hughes establishes a smooth and rapid rhythm that matches his description of a "boogie-woogie rumble" in the third line. It is just one of several that refer to boogie or boogie-woogie as the sound of a dream deferred. It opens with the line "Good morning, daddy!" addressing not the speaker's father, but using a be-bop era slang term for a fellow hipster man. The mood of the poem at first seems upbeat; however, Hughes uses the phrase "dream deferred" in the last line of the first stanza, which hints at the speaker's frustration. The energetic rhythm of the first two stanzas is broken by an interjectory third stanza that asks, *"You think / it's a happy beat?"* He allows the "daddy" being addressed to go on thinking that boogie-woogie is cheerful music, but he clearly hears discontentment in its rumble.

In "Boogie: 1 a.m." and "Lady's Boogie," Hughes returns to his metaphor for the troubles masked by the music. "Boogie: 1 a.m." repeats the line "The boogie-woogie rumble / Of a dream deferred" from "Dream Boogie," then goes on to describe the "trilling" and "twining" the instruments make to express that mood. Even though the

The first six stanzas of "Ballad of the Landlord" feature a conventional *abcb* rhyme scheme, though the number of syllables in each line varies widely. As with many of the other poems in *Montage of a Dream Deferred*, Hughes uses repetition and parallel structure to create rhythm and mood. For example, the first line of each of the first two stanzas consists of the tenant's plaintive call, "Landlord, landlord"; later, in the first line of the sixth stanza, the landlord's response is, "*Police! Police!*" The tenant also repeats the phrase "Ten Bucks"—the amount of rent that is due—in the third stanza. Hughes chooses to capitalize this phrase, perhaps to indicate its significance to both parties: to the landlord because he is a businessman; and to the tenant because he is poor.

In "Theme for English B," the narrator is a student writing a page about himself for his college English class. The student, a resident of the Harlem YMCA, describes himself as "the only colored student in my class." The narrator lists many of the things he likes, all of which transcend race: "Well, I like to eat, sleep, drink, and be in love." This leads him to wonder: "So will my page be colored that I write?" The narrator realizes that, in America, people of different races become a part of each other simply by interacting and learning from each other—though he does acknowledge that his white instructor is "somewhat more free" than he is himself.

Hughes envisions a racially integrated future in "Projection," and writes that on the day that black and white culture embrace each other, "Manhattan Island will whirl." He concludes, "Father Divine will say in truth, / *Peace!* / *It's truly* / *wonderful!*" A less optimistic view of people of different races coming together is presented in "Mellow," which describes the thrill and danger of interracial dating. One area of life that is already fully integrated for Hughes is New York's public transportation. He describes the mingled crowd in "Subway Rush Hour," as being "so close" there is "no room for fear."

## Harlem to Insiders

With the poem "Children's Rhymes," Hughes trades boogie-woogie rhythms for a cadence more likely to be heard in a schoolyard than a nightclub. In the poem, an older narrator reflects on the chants of neighborhood children as they play. The chants they sing emphasize the gap between the young and old generations; while the narrator remembers innocent childhood chants from days gone by, the rhymes of this new generation carry a message:

> *By what sends*
> *the white kids*
> *I ain't sent:*
> *I know I can't*
> *be President.*

The narrator expresses disapproval at the audacity of the younger generation as they call attention to the inequality they face every day. For the narrator, inequality is simply a fact of life not worthy of comment. Hughes uses this contrast between generations to suggest that the members of the younger generation are less willing to accept inequality without some kind of resistance—even if that resistance is limited to silly rhymes chanted while playing.

The poems "Low to High" and "High to Low" both deal with the dream of achieving a higher social status. In "Low to High," the narrator (the "Low" referred to in the title) speaks to a friend who has achieved success, charging, "Now you've got your Cadillac, / you done forgot that you are black." Then he asks, "How can you forget me / When I'm you?" As the narrator in "High to Low," the achiever ("High") responds to the downtrodden, lower-class friend. The narrator lists all the things that are wrong with the lower-class friend, which include "you talk too loud" and "look too black." The upper-class narrator contends that he is "trying to uphold the race / and you— / . . . / we have our problems, / too, with you."

In "Passing," Hughes offers an ode to his neighborhood. The term "passing"—which appears only in the title and not in the poem itself—is used to describe a light-skinned black person who successfully passes himself or herself off as white in mainstream society, and is therefore freed from the prejudices and inequalities that blacks normally face. In the poem, Hughes describes Harlem on ideal "sunny summer Sunday afternoons," and assures his neighborhood that "the ones who've crossed the line / to live downtown / miss you," even though "their dream has / come true." To those who deny their true selves, Harlem represents comfort and community that they can never again experience. In "Passing," Hughes suggests that those who give up their heritage to achieve their dreams are ultimately left with a sense of loss every bit as potent as a dream deferred.

## Romance

The quartet of poems "Sister," "Preference," "Question," and "Ultimatum" gives four different perspectives on men and women whose romances are complicated by financial worries. In "Sister," a man talks to his mother about why his sister dates a married man. The mother asks, "*Did it ever occur to you, son | the reason Marie runs around with trash | is she wants some cash?*" "Preference" offers a man's point of view about why he would rather date older women: "When she conversations you | it's ain't forever, *Gimme!*" In "Question," a woman asks this question of a man: "*Can you . . . | love me, daddy— | and feed me, too?*" The flip side is presented in "Ultimatum," when a man threatens to stop paying his girlfriend's rent if she does not see him more often.

A much softer side of romance is given in "Juke Box Love Song." Hughes crafts a vision of Harlem through the eyes of a romantic pledging his love to his "sweet brown Harlem girl." Though the poem does not use an established meter, Hughes uses rhyme and parallel structure throughout the poem—for example, the phrase "take the Harlem night" in the first line is mirrored in "Take the neon lights" in the third line—to create a consistent rhythm and flow that is much smoother than the abrupt "boogie woogie" style breaks in many of the book's other poems. The last four lines use an *abba* rhyme scheme, a more formal structure than is found in the rest of the lines. Though the poem differs in rhythm from Hughes's boogie-woogie efforts, the theme still focuses on music: the narrator wants to turn the sounds of Harlem into a song for his girl so that they may dance all day.

## Work

Hughes offers different perspectives on the issue of working in the poems "Necessity" and "Buddy." In the first, the speaker starts with the declaration, "Work? | I don't have to work." He describes his tiny room and how his landlady charges too much for rent, then concludes, "Which is why I reckon I *does* | have to work after all." In "Buddy," a speaker describes his friend who "works downtown for Twelve a week," of which he gives his mother ten, spends the remainder on transportation and clothes, and can spend the rest on "anything he wants."

## Migration

Hughes focuses several poems on the challenges of Southern blacks who move north. The first is "Croon," a three-line poem: "I don't give a damn | For Alabam' | Even if it is my home." In the next poem, "New Yorkers," Hughes presents a dialogue between a man and woman who are from different backgrounds yet have found love in each other. The man states that he is a native New Yorker, born "right here beneath God's sky." The woman—whose words are differentiated by the poet's use of italics—reveals that she has come from a place where "*folks work hard | all their lives*" and yet still never have an opportunity to own anything for themselves. "So I come up here," she says. However, as the woman in the poem tells the man, the opportunities she hoped for in New York have led to only one success: "*Now what've I got? | You!*"

Like "New Yorkers," the poem "Not a Movie" deals with the migration of Southern blacks to more northern parts of the United States, particularly Harlem. In the poem, an unnamed black man is terrorized and assaulted after he tries to vote somewhere in the South. In response, he boards a train bound for New York and takes up residence on 133rd Street, one of the main thoroughfares of Harlem. As the narrator notes, the man will be safe there because "there ain't no Ku Klux | on a 133rd." The poem contains only two rhyming lines, which form a graphic couplet in the middle of the second stanza: "Six knots was on his head | but, thank God, he wasn't dead!" The sing-song meter of the lines presents a stark contrast to the severe violence they describe, and the rather optimistic tone of the narrator suggests that many other Southern blacks suffered a far worse fate.

The meaning of the poem's title, "Not a Movie," is perhaps less clear to modern readers than it was at the time of the book's initial publication. A contemporary reader might take the title to mean that the events of the poem really occurred, or that they are too tragic to be considered entertainment. Within the context of *Montage of a Dream Deferred*, however, the poet seems to suggest a different reason for the title: Such an accurate portrayal of a black man's life would not be considered suitable for a movie, because black characters in movies were often limited to grotesque and insulting stereotypes intended to make white filmgoers laugh.

Two more poems later in the collection portray Southern men working in the North. In "Neighbor," two people discuss a man who goes to a bar after work and debate whether he is a "fool" or a "good man." They agree that he talks too much. It seems to the reader that he is in the bar seeking company more than drinking. In "*Letter*," a man writes to his mother from "up here" and tells her, "*Time I pay rent and get my food / and laundry I don't have much left / but here is five dollars for you / to show I still appreciates you.*"

### War

The poems "Green Memory," "Relief," "World War II," and "Casualty" offer unusual perspectives on the economics of being black in the United States during and after World War II. The narrator recalls World War II with a certain wistfulness—"A wonderful time," as the first line of "Green Memory" states. The narrator explains this fondness for the war by noting in "Green Memory" that it was a time "when money rolled in." This was true for many black workers who were given jobs in industries that supported the war effort. After the war, many of these jobs disappeared or were taken over by white workers returning from the battlefield.

In "Green Memory," the narrator acknowledges that "blood rolled out" as wealth came in—a reference to those soldiers who traveled overseas and died in battle. In "Relief," the narrator envies "them Poles and Greeks / on relief way across the sea / because I was on relief / once in 1933." He admits that it would be fine with him "if these white folks want to go ahead / and fight another war." In "World War II," the narrator repeatedly refers to the war as "a grand time," and is "[s]orry that old war is done!" Only an echoing voice, set off in italics, asks: "*Did / Somebody / Die?*" For the narrators of these three poems, the war and its consequences are distant matters. In "Casualty," the war and its end have a much more personal effect for the narrator. For him, too, times were better during war: He was a black man in uniform and walked tall. Now, he is just a black man again, who "walks like his soldiering / Days are done."

### Gambling

The collection contains a trio of poems about the desperation that drives people to gamble with what little money they have. "Numbers" tells of a man's fantasy of winning some money and that he "ain't gonna / play back a cent." His resolve to stop gambling falters in the next sentence, even before his daydream ends. That dream has come true for the narrator of "Situation," who finds himself with an unexpected problem after a big win: "I was scared to walk out / with the dough."

Gambling is seen as keeping food out of the mouths of the hungry in "Hope." Referring to a method of choosing lucky numbers that gives numerical values to certain dreams and visions, a woman translates her husband's dying wish for fish into a number to gamble with.

### Wisdom

The poems "Motto" and "Advice" are both brief aphorisms that provide suggestions on how to live one's life. Both poems use simple meter and rhyme schemes to allow the reader to quickly commit these short life lessons to memory. In "Motto," Hughes uses terms commonly associated with jazz and boogie-woogie musicians—such as "play it cool" and "dig all jive"—to offer a worldview elegantly simple and universal: "*Dig And Be Dug / In Return.*" The word "dig" is used here to mean both "understand" and "appreciate." The message, then, in less stylized wording, is simply, "Understand and appreciate others, so that others will understand and appreciate you." In "Advice," the narrator points out the hardships encountered at both the beginning and end of a person's life, and concludes "so get yourself / a little loving / in between."

### Dreams Deferred

*Montage of a Dream Deferred* opens, returns to often, and closes with the idea of dreams deferred. It is present in the "Boogie" poems, as well as several others. Early in the collection is the five-line "Tell Me," which asks why the narrator's dream has to be deferred for so long.

In "Deferred," the poet intertwines the voices of people who all wish to achieve some small but significant piece of the American dream. The first would like to graduate from high school, despite the fact that he is already twenty and he received inadequate schooling in the South when he was young. Another would like a white enamel stove that she has dreamed of owning for eighteen years. Yet another voice states, "All I want is to see / my furniture paid for." In this poem, Hughes creates a literal montage of dreams that have been deferred by people who

GOOD MORNING, DADDY!

AIN'T YOU HEARD

THE BOOGIE-WOOGIE RUMBLE

OF A DREAM DEFERRED?"

have not yet been granted the opportunity to achieve the success they desire.

"Harlem" is perhaps the most famous poem in *Montage of a Dream Deferred*. In the first line, the narrator asks, "What happens to a dream deferred?" The narrator suggests that such a dream might "dry up / like a raisin in the sun," or "stink like rotten meat." The similes used by the narrator all suggest that the dream would wither or decay, until the final line offers another possibility: "*Or does it explode?*"

"Good Morning" describes people coming to New York from Caribbean places such as Puerto Rico, Cuba, Haiti, and Jamaica, and from southern states like Georgia, Florida, and Louisiana, all seeking their dreams. The narrator asks again, "What happens / to a dream deferred?" "Same in Blues" answers that question for some. Through different snippets of conversation that reveal people's unfulfilled dreams, the poem explains that "There's a certain amount of" traveling, nothing, impotence, and confusion "in a dream deferred."

The last poem in the book, "Island," describes Manhattan as "Black and white, / Gold and brown— / Chocolate-custard / Pie of a town," where "*Dream within a dream, / Our dream deferred.*" It closes with the lines that open the book's first poem: "Good morning, daddy! / Ain't you heard?"

## THEMES

### Discontent

Discontent with inequality is one of the central themes of *Montage of a Dream Deferred*. The deferred dream to which Hughes refers in the title is the American dream as it applies to African Americans. In Hughes's Harlem, while white Americans are free to pursue their dreams,

black Americans continue to be held back by racism and poverty. Hughes addresses this issue directly in the short poem "Tell Me," when he asks why *his* aspirations have had to wait.

In "Children's Rhymes," the chants of the playing children illustrate a keen understanding of this inequality, even going so far as to proclaim, "*We knows everybody / ain't free!*" In the poem "Harlem," the narrator suggests that such inequality might eventually result in violence or revolt. Although this fundamental unfairness is easily recognized, for many of the characters given voice in *Montage of a Dream Deferred*, it is accepted—for the moment, at least—as an obstacle that must be dealt with on one's own terms.

The "boogie-woogie rumble" present in so many of the poems in the collection, however, reminds readers that the dissatisfaction with the inequalities African Americans face in American life is growing, not shrinking, and makes the explosion predicted in "Harlem" seem near.

### Prosperity

Several poems in *Montage of a Dream Deferred* focus on social status and financial wealth as a measure of success. In "Sister," the narrator laments the fact that his sister Marie is dating a man who is married and has a family. The narrator's mother points out that Marie simply wants to be around someone with money. "Don't decent folks have enough dough?" the narrator asks. The answer is, "*Unfortunately usually no!*" The underlying message in these lines is that working hard does not necessarily lead to wealth and success. In "Preference," the narrator expresses his fondness for dating older women; younger women, he asserts, always ask men to buy them things. Older women are more likely to share their wealth. The narrator fails to realize that he is treating older women the same way younger women treat him. This poem illustrates how both men and women in Hughes's Harlem see money as a path to better lives.

While several poems show people trying to gamble their ways to a better life, wealth is measured on a smaller scale for most of the characters in Hughes's Harlem. In "Dime," a child dares to dream of a spare ten cents that his grandmother simply does not have. In "Relief," the narrator notes that he would not object "if these white folks want to go ahead / and fight another war,"

*Portrait of the Cotton Club Orchestra from the Cotton Club, Harlem, NY, 1924* Getty Images

because it would mean a chance to get a job and earn enough money to survive.

Social status is the main focus of the paired poems "Low to High" and "High to Low." Taken together, the poems represent a dialogue between two old friends, High and Low—one of whom has attained a high-status life, while the other remains on the lower rungs of the social ladder. Both had dreamed of living the high-class life together, and now Low feels cheated and forgotten. However, High reveals that to achieve that success, he has had to adopt a new, "white" way of thinking and abandon the older, "black" perspective—as well as those people it represents.

### Community
The notion of community is a theme that runs through much of *Montage of a Dream Deferred*. The vision Hughes paints of Harlem in "Passing," for example, is a stirring depiction of a tightly knit neighborhood in which residents may face adversity, but they take comfort in knowing that they face it together. The subject of "Neighbor" is a Southern man working in New York who misses the easy community he had back home,

sitting on his porch talking with neighbors. People in New York suspect him of drinking too much because he is in the bar so often, but he is really there seeking company. Throughout the collection of poems, voices frequently overlap and intrude into monologues just as they would if the narrator were talking on the street among friends. This shifting of narrative voice not only suggests an ease and camaraderie among the local residents, but also allows the reader to achieve a sense of community by experiencing Harlem life from many unique viewpoints.

### Future
Although the American dream promises a bright future for those who seek it, there are several poems in *Montage of a Dream Deferred* that look at people for whom the future is more of a chore than a reward. The character in "Wine-O" drinks his days away, "Waiting for tomorrow," when he will drink some more and wait for the next tomorrow. The title character in "Drunkard" drinks not to pass the time, but to forget "the taste of day." The character in "Blues at Dawn" is not drinking to forget, but he is trying to suppress his dread every morning as he faces each new day. He

says, "If I thought thoughts in bed, / Them thoughts would bust my head—" and "If I recall the day before, / I wouldn't get up no more." The future is a concern for the residents in Hughes's Harlem, but it is something to avoid rather than embrace.

## HISTORICAL OVERVIEW

### The Great Migration

Prior to the Civil War, most African Americans living in the United States were slaves in the South, working the plantations that formed the backbone of the Southern economy. During the first half of the twentieth century, however, several factors contributed to a significant geographic shift in the African American population that is often referred to as the Great Migration.

One major factor contributing to the Great Migration was the institution of Jim Crow laws throughout the South. These laws created segregation between the races and were often used as an excuse to exclude blacks from facilities and businesses frequented by whites. In the 1896 Supreme Court case *Plessy v. Ferguson*, the federal government allowed such segregation as long as facilities for whites and blacks were "separate but equal." In reality, African American citizens hardly ever received services comparable to white citizens. They were often threatened or assaulted when simply acting within their rights, particularly when they attempted to exercise their right to vote. In addition, the rising popularity of the white supremacist terror group Ku Klux Klan led many African Americans to leave the South for fear of their own safety. In *Montage of a Dream Deferred*, the unnamed character in "Not A Movie" moves to Harlem after such an assault.

Another important factor in the Great Migration was the rise of factory jobs in the North and Midwest. New York in particular offered a growing urban economy that demanded a constant influx of capable workers. This need only increased during and after World War I, and the New York neighborhood of Harlem became a center of this new urban black population.

### The Harlem Renaissance

Soon after the war, the community that formed in Harlem gave rise to an astounding number of influential African American musicians, poets, authors, and activists; this blossoming of the arts during the 1920s became known as the Harlem Renaissance.

One of the men credited with helping nurture the Harlem Renaissance is civil rights leader, author, and scholar W. E. B. DuBois, who served as the editor of a magazine called *The Crisis*. The magazine, devoted primarily to African American themes and issues, was the first professional publication to print a poem by Langston Hughes. The poem was titled "The Negro Speaks of Rivers," and it turned out to be the first of many poems Hughes wrote for *The Crisis*. Other literary luminaries who called Harlem home during this time included James Weldon Johnson, Countee Cullen, Richard Wright, and Zora Neale Hurston.

The Harlem Renaissance is widely acknowledged as ending in the early 1930s during the Great Depression; though many prestigious members of the Harlem arts community continued to produce work for decades longer, the public no longer viewed Harlem as the vibrant popular destination it once had been. Still, the artists who rose to prominence during the Harlem Renaissance helped to shape the philosophies and viewpoints of an entire generation of African Americans. Historians have asserted that the influential artists of the Harlem Renaissance helped set the stage for the success of the African American civil rights movement in the 1950s.

### The Rise of Jazz and Bebop Music

Jazz is a uniquely American musical style created by drawing from both traditional African and popular American music. The earliest versions of jazz featured elements of ragtime, blues, hymns, and even military marches, and appeared in numerous African American urban and cultural centers across the United States in the first two decades of the twentieth century. New Orleans is generally recognized as the birthplace of jazz music, with the Storyville district—an area notorious for prostitution and other shady cultures—often listed as the center of the burgeoning jazz movement. In 1917, however, the secretary of the navy effectively shut down Storyville in an attempt to keep sailors from engaging in inappropriate behavior while on leave in the port city.

While New Orleans remained an important center for the development of jazz, other cities in the Northeast and Midwest also contributed to the developing sound. Chicago, Washington,

D.C., and New York all produced artists who went on to achieve legendary status within the genre, including Duke Ellington, James P. Johnson, and Jelly Roll Morton. Many of the most famous jazz musicians performed regularly at clubs throughout Harlem during the 1920s, contributing to the notion that the rising popularity of jazz was to some degree a product of the Harlem Renaissance. The white composer George Gershwin, with his jazz-influenced works "Rhapsody in Blue" and *Porgy and Bess*, helped to bring jazz music to a larger, mainstream audience and further cement its standing as a respected and beloved American art form.

Bebop emerged as a variant of jazz in the 1940s and is characterized by fast tempos, improvisation, and an unusual musical interval known as a "flatted fifth" that is derived from traditional African musical scales. The term "bebop" is meant to mimic the sound of the trademark two-note phrase often used to end a song; many of the poems in *Montage of a Dream Deferred* use this same technique, ending with a similar two-syllable line such as "*De-dop!*"

Bebop became one of the most popular forms of jazz throughout the 1940s and 1950s, with performers such as Charlie Parker and Thelonius Monk drawing both black and white audiences to clubs in urban music centers such as Harlem. Two decades after the rise of jazz music, bebop influenced a new generation of writers and artists, including Jack Kerouac and other icons of the Beat Generation in the 1960s.

## CRITICAL OVERVIEW

*Montage of a Dream Deferred* was first published in 1951, at a time when Hughes was already recognized as one of the most important literary figures of the Harlem Renaissance. In addition, many of the poems in *Montage of a Dream Deferred* had already seen publication in various magazines, though some were slightly altered for their appearance in book form. For these reasons, the critical reception of *Montage of a Dream Deferred* was to some extent colored by pre-existing views of Hughes's work and the public's prior exposure to many parts of the book; this might help explain why initial reviews of the book were, according to biographer and anthologist Arnold Rampersad, generally "lukewarm."

## MEDIA ADAPTATIONS

Langston Hughes recorded spoken-word versions of many of his poems, including several in *Montage of a Dream Deferred* in 1958, with accompaniment from jazz legends Charles Mingus and Leonard Feather. The recoding is called *Weary Blues* and was re-released by Polygram records in 1991. It is available on compact disc.

Critics were often quick to note the strong musical influence seen in the book's poems. In an unsigned review for *Booklist*, the critic notes, "The persistent beat and rhythm of jazz, boogie-woogie and other forms of current popular music sound in these kaleidoscopic flashes that make a poem on contemporary Harlem." Babette Deutsch, in a review for the *New York Times*, writes, "Langston Hughes can write pages that throb with the abrupt rhythms of popular music." In his review for the *New York Herald Tribune Book Review*, Saunders Redding notes that the book is filled with "quick, vibrant and probing" imagery, and applauds the author's "spiritually rewarding return" to the subject matter and themes on which he had built his following.

For many critics and academics, however, Hughes's sentimental style and frequent use of everyday vernacular were characteristics of popular writing, as distinguished from works of true literary merit. As Babette Deutsch puts it, "Sometimes his verse invites approval, but again it lapses into a facile sentimentality that stifles real feeling as with cheap scent." Deutsch also argues that the book as a whole reveals "the limitations of folk art," and that although Hughes is "a poet of undeniable gifts," he should make an effort to aim his literary sights higher.

In the decades since *Montage of a Dream Deferred* was first published, academics have come to acknowledge the poet's significant contributions to American literature. He remains one of the most anthologized American poets of the twentieth century, and in an online poll sponsored by the Academy of American Poets in 2002, Langston Hughes was selected above such luminaries as Emily Dickinson, Robert Frost, and Carl Sandburg as America's favorite poet.

## CRITICISM

### Walter C. Farrell and Patricia A. Johnson

*In the following excerpt, Farrell and Johnson examine how Hughes's poetry reflects the mood, tone, and culture of the music of post-WWII Harlem.*

The "bebop era" was also one of unrest, anxiety, and massive discontent in the urban ghetto. Harlem, for example, was the scene of a bloody race riot in 1943. The just indignation of Afro-American people had finally surfaced in the form of massive violence. But the injustice of racism and poverty was only compounded by the injustices of police brutality. Black urban workers found themselves not only trapped in the ghetto but pinned beneath the heel of police repression as well.

Langston Hughes was among the few black intellectuals of this era to sympathize with justly aggrieved poor people in Harlem. In a 1944 edition of *Negro Digest,* he denounced the snobbery of "Sugar Hill" Negroes who viewed the riot as a deterrent to "Negro advancement." Examining the economic determinants of the disturbance, Hughes compared the lifestyles of Harlem's well-to-do Negroes with that of her working poor:

> It is, I should imagine, nice to be smart enough and lucky enough to be among Dr. Dubois' "talented tenth" and be a race leader and go to symphony concerts and live on that attractive rise of bluff and parkway along upper Edgecombe Avenue overlooking the Polo Grounds, where the plumbing really works, and the ceilings are high and airy.
>
> But under the hill on Eighth Avenue, on Lenox and on Fifth there are places like this—dark, unpleasant houses with steep stairs and narrow halls, where the rooms are too small, the ceilings too low and the rents too high . . .
>
> In vast sections below the hill, neighborhood amusement centers after dark are gin mills, candy stores that sell King Kong (and maybe reefers), drug stores that sell geronimoes—dope tablets—to juveniles for pepping up cokes, pool halls where gambling is wide open and barbeque stands that book numbers.
>
> The kids and grown-ups are not criminal or low by nature. Poverty, however, and frustration have made some of them too desperate to be decent. Some of them don't try any more. Slum-shocked, I reckon.

Hughes's poetic commentary on the unrest and anxiety of post-war Black America was presented in a collection published in 1951 entitled *Montage of a Dream Deferred*. In a prefatory note, Hughes explains that his poems were designed to reflect the mood and tempo of bebop. As Hughes puts it:

> In terms of current Afro-American popular music and the sources from which it has progressed—jazz, ragtime, swing, blues, boogie-woogie, and bebop—this poem on contemporary Harlem, like be-bop, is marked by conflicting changes, sudden nuances, sharp and impudent interjections, broken rhythms, and passages sometimes in the manner of the jam session, sometimes the popular song, punctuated by the riffs, runs, breaks, and distortions of the music of a community in transition.

When *Montage* was published, Hughes regarded bebop as a new type of jazz music that drew its strength and substance from a composite vernacular of black musical forms. In conjunction with this notion Hughes incorporated a variety of music-related poems into this collection.

In his prefatory notes, Hughes identifies the entire collection as a "single poem." Similarly, Donald Dickinson, a biographer of Hughes, described *Montage* as "one long interrelated poetic jam session." It is interesting to note that bebop itself evolved out of the jam session of the jazz musicians. Music historians agree that in its nascent stage, bebop was an "after hours" music that Minton playhouse "radicals" performed following their scheduled dates with swing orchestras. The relaxed informal atmosphere of these jam sessions would tend to produce an extemporaneous free-flowing form of musical expression that demanded a creative contribution from each participant. No one can listen to a typical swing number and then a bebop number without realizing that in the latter, the part (individual instrument) makes a singular or distinctive contribution to the ensemble, while in the former the individual component plays a less assertive role.

In *Montage* Hughes took advantage of the structural characteristics of bebop by drastically

*Harlem in the 1950s* AP Images

reordering the traditional limitations imposed on the poem. By breaking down the barrier between the beginning of one poem and the end of another, Hughes created a new technique in poetry. Perhaps one could more accurately describe *Montage* as a series of short poems or phrases that contribute to the making of one long poem. Each poem maintains some individual identity as a separate unit while contributing to the composite poetic message. Movement between passages is achieved by thematic or topical congruency or by interior dialogue.

Hughes developed a form of poetry writing which would allow him to compress a wide and complex range of images into one kaleidoscopic impression of life in Harlem during the 1940s. The fact that these images are historically accurate and the fact that they convey something of what it meant to be black in America during this crucial war-torn era are proofs of Hughes's profound understanding of the events and issues that have shaped the contemporary world.

The idea that America has perennially denied her black working masses the right to life, liberty and the pursuit of happiness is the concentric unifying theme of *Montage of a Dream Deferred*. In practical terms, these rights include access to adequate housing, a decent

standard of living, and fair and profitable employment. Hughes had developed this theme earlier—on a much more general level—in a poem published in 1926 entitled "A Dream Deferred." In *Montage*, Hughes expanded the thematic substance of this poem and injected it with powerful social and political connotations.

*Montage* is divided topically into six main sections: "Boogie Segue to Bop," "Dig and Be Dug," "Early Bright," "Vice Versa to Bach," "Dream Deferred," and "Lenox Avenue Mural." Each section emphasizes a different aspect of life in Harlem—be it social, political, cultural, or economic—but without excluding any of these aspects.

"Boogie Segue to Bach," for instance, glorifies the fullness and richness of black culture, especially black music, through a cogent analysis of its social and political implications. "Dream Boogie," the first poetic passage in this section, identifies a questionable rumbling in the rhythms of bebop and boogie woogie. And since music has always served as the "heartbeat" of the black community, that rumbling becomes symbolic of an underlying state of anxiety and unrest in the urban ghetto:

> Good morning, daddy!
> Ain't you heard
> The boogie-woogie rumble
> Of a dream deferred?
>
> Listen, closely:
> You'll hear their feet
> Beating out and beating out a—
>
>     YOU THINK
>     IT'S A HAPPY BEAT?
>
> Listen to it closely:
> Ain't you heard
> something underneath
> like a - - - -
>
>     WHAT DID I SAY?
>
> Sure,
> I'm happy!
> Take it away!
>
>     HEY, POP!
>     RE-BOP!
>     MOP!
>
>     Y-E-A-H!

Arthur P. Davis's description of the images of Harlem reflected in *Montage of a Dream*

*Deferred* adequately expresses our ideas on this subject. Davis observed that the Harlem depicted in *Montage* had

> ... come through World War II, but [had] discovered that a global victory for democracy [did] not necessarily have too much pertinence at home. Although the Harlem of the 1948–1951 period [had] far more opportunity than the 1926 Harlem ever dreamed of, it [was] still not free; and the modern city having caught the vision of total freedom and total integration would not be satisfied with anything less than the idea. It [was] therefore a critical, a demanding, a sensitive, and utterly cynical city."

That cynicism was part of the overall feeling of disenchantment, of frustration, bewilderment and despair that informed the music—the very life impulse—of postwar urban life in America, as Langston Hughes knew.

**Source:** Walter C. Farrell and Patricia A. Johnson, "Poetic Interpretations of Urban Black Folk Culture: Langston Hughes and the "Bebop" Era," in *MELUS*, Vol. 8, No. 3, Fall 1981, pp. 57–72.

## James Presley

*In the following excerpt, Presley examines the prevasive theme of the American Dream in the poetry of Langston Hughes throughout his career.*

One summer in Chicago when he was a teenager Langston Hughes felt the American Dream explode in his face; a gang of white youths beat him up so badly that he went home with blacked eyes and a swollen jaw.

He had been punished for cutting through a white neighborhood in the South Side on his way home from work. That night as he tended his injuries young Hughes must have mused disturbed thoughts about fulfilment of his American dream of freedom, justice, and opportunity for all.

A few years after that traumatic Chicago afternoon Hughes inaugurated a prolific and versatile writing career. Over the four decades separating then and now, his reaction to the American Dream has been one of his most frequently recurring themes. For many years Hughes, often hailed as "the poet laureate of the Negro people," has been recognized by white critics as an author-poet of the protest genre. Others, more conservative and denunciatory, have assailed Hughes as radical and leftist, to mention the more polite language. In both instances the critics referred to Hughes's treatment of imperfections in the American Dream that we, as a nation, hold so dear.

The American Dream may have come dramatically true for many, Hughes says, but for the Negro (and other assorted poor people) the American Dream is merely that—a dream. If the critics and would-be censors had read further they would have noted that for Hughes the American Dream has even greater meaning: it is the *raison d'être* of this nation. Nevertheless, Hughes was still a regular target for right-wing barbs as recently as the 1960's, having been anathema to the right wing for decades.

As might be expected Hughes has written most frequently, though not exclusively, of Negro characters. Consequently the importance of the color line in America is frequently reflected in his work. The effect of the color line on the American Dream is therefore an integral part of his protest. In one of his biographies for young people, *Famous Negro Music Makers* (1961), Hughes quotes musician Bert Williams as saying: "It is not a disgrace to be a Negro, but it is very inconvenient." In viewing the string of "inconveniences" vitally affecting the dignity of black Americans Hughes voices his reactions to shriveled freedom, dwarfed equality, and shrunken opportunity—blemishes on the essential ingredients of the American Dream. His poetry and prose echo protest and, usually, hope.

Two poems especially reflect his theme of protest and hope. "Let America Be America Again," published in *Esquire* and in the International Worker Order pamphlet *A New Song* (1938), pleads for fulfilment of the Dream that never was. It speaks of the freedom and equality which America boasts, but never had. It looks forward to a day when "Liberty is crowned with no false patriotic wreath" and America is "that great strong land of love." Hughes, though, is not limiting his plea to the downtrodden Negro; he includes, as well, the poor white, the Indian, the immigrant—farmer, worker, "the people" share the Dream that has not been. The Dream still beckons. In "Freedom's Plow" he points out that "America is a dream" and the product of the seed of freedom is not only for all Americans but for all the world. The American Dream of brotherhood, freedom, and democracy must come to all peoples and all races of the world, he insists.

Almost invariably Hughes reflects hope, for that is part of his American Dream. However, some of his poems, apparently written in angry protest, are content to catch the emotion of sorrow in the face of hopelessness and gross injustice. One of his most biting is a verse in *Jim*

*Crow's Last Stand* (1943). Aimed at southern lynch law which had just taken the lives of two fourteen-year-old Negro boys in Mississippi, and dedicated to their memory, the poem cried that "The Bitter River" has

> *... strangled my dream:*
> *The book studied—but useless,*
> *Tools handled—but unused,*
> *Knowledge acquired but thrown away,*
> *Ambition battered and bruised.*

In one of his children's poems, "As I Grow Older," the poet looks at the Dream again. He had almost forgotten his dream; then it reappeared to him. But a wall rose—a high, sky-high wall. A shadow: he was black. The wall and the shadow blotted out the dream, chasing the brightness away. But the poet's dark hands sustain him.

> *My dark bands!*
> *Break through the wall!*
> *Find my dream!*
> *Help me to shatter this darkness,*
> *To smash this night,*
> *To break this shadow*
> *Into a thousand lights of sun,*
> *Into a thousand whirling dreams*
> *Of sun!*

On a similar theme, one of the concluding poems in his child's book, *The Dream Keeper* (1932), treats of the Dream. In "I, Too," the "darker brother" of America eats in the kitchen when company calls. But tomorrow, he says, he'll eat at the table; nobody will dare tell him to eat in the kitchen then.

> *Besides,*
> *They'll see how beautiful I am*
> *And be ashamed—*
> *I, too, am America.*

In *Montage of a Dream Deferred* (1951) Hughes might have been thinking of the wall which blackness had erected in the child's poem. *Montage*'s background is Harlem. There is a wall about Harlem, and the American Dream, as a reality, exists outside Harlem. Harlem (and, one can just as well add, the world of the American Negro) is a walled-in reality where dreams are deferred. The faded Dream pierces black New Yorkers to their hearts. Things which "don't bug ... white kids" bother Harlemites profoundly. White boys cling to the stimulating dream that any American may grow up to be President of the United States. The Negro boy knows better. He also knows that the liberty and justice of the Pledge to the Flag are inherent rights only of white folks. Even in Harlem,

the capital of the North which Hughes once described in a novel as "mighty magnet of the colored race," the American Dream is frayed and ragged.

Throughout Hughes's life—and his literary expression—the American Dream has appeared as a ragged, uneven, splotched, and often unattainable goal which often became a nightmare, but there is always hope of the fulfilled dream even in the darkest moments. During World War II Hughes, commenting on the American Negroes' role in the war, recognized this. " ... we know," he said in a 1943 speech reprinted in *The Langston Hughes Reader* (1958),

> that America is a land of transition. And we know it is within our power to help in its further change toward a finer and better democracy than any citizen has known before. The American Negro believes in democracy. We want to make it real, complete, workable, not only for ourselves—the fifteen million dark ones—but for all Americans all over the land.

The American Dream is bruised and often made a travesty for Negroes and other underdogs, Hughes keeps saying, but the American Dream does exist. And the Dream *must* be fulfilled. In one of his verses he put it more plainly. He might have been speaking to his harshest political critics or to the white youths who beat him up on that long-ago summer day in Chicago.

> *Listen, America—*
> *I live here, too.*
> *I want freedom*
> *Just as you.*

**Source:** James Presley, "The American Dream of Langston Hughes," in *Southwest Review*, Vol. 48, No. 4, Autumn 1963, pp. 380–86.

## SOURCES

Deutsch, Babette, "Waste Land of Harlem (review of *Montage of a Dream Deferred*)," in the *New York Times*, May 6, 1951, p. 23.

Hughes, Langston, *Montage of a Dream Deferred*, Holt, 1951; reprinted in *The Collected Poems of Langston Hughes*, edited by Arnold Rampersad, Alfred A. Knopf, 1994, pp. 387–429.

———, *The Big Sea: An Autobiography*, Knopf, 1940; reprinted, Hill and Wang, 1993, p. 209.

Rampersad, Arnold, "A Chronology of the Life of Langston Hughes," in *The Collected Poems of Langston Hughes*, edited by Arnold Rampersad, Alfred A. Knopf, 1994, p. 15.

—————, Introduction to *The Collected Poems of Langston Hughes*, edited by Arnold Rampersad, Alfred A. Knopf, 1994, p. 4.

Redding, Saunders, Review of *Montage of a Dream Deferred*, in the *New York Herald Tribune Book Review*, March 11, 1951, p. 5; reprinted in *The Book Review Digest: Forty-Seventh Annual Cumulation*, H. W. Wilson Company, 1952, p. 428.

Review of *Montage of a Dream Deferred*, in *Booklist*, Vol. 47, March 1, 1951, p. 233; reprinted in *The Book Review Digest: Forty-Seventh Annual Cumulation*, H. W. Wilson Company, 1952, p. 428.

Younge, Gary, "Renaissance Man of the South," in the *Guardian* (UK), October 26, 2002, books.guardian.co.uk/review/story/0,12084,818715,00.html (September 28, 2006).

# My Kinsman, Major Molineux

**NATHANIEL HAWTHORNE**

**1832**

"My Kinsman, Major Molineux" (1832) is an early short story about American independence—that of an individual as much as of a country—from Nathaniel Hawthorne, a pioneer of the distinctly American voice in literature. Originally published anonymously, as were a number of Hawthorne's early stories and sketches, "My Kinsman, Major Molineux" first appeared in an annual gift book, *The Token*, in 1832 with a few of Hawthorne's other stories. The story was not published again until it was reprinted in Hawthorne's collection of stories *The Snow-Image, and Other Twice-Told Tales* (1851). It also marked the first time "My Kinsman, Major Molineux" was published under his name. Though not considered a major work by Hawthorne during the nineteenth century, it began attracting a great deal of scholarly attention by the mid-twentieth century.

In "My Kinsman, Major Molineux," Hawthorne describes the frustrating journey of young Robin Molineux, a country teen who has come to a Massachusetts city to find the title character. The kinsman is his father's cousin, an officer in the British Army and the gentleman of civil rank in the community. The major, a wealthy man with no heirs, had visited Robin's family a year or two earlier and hinted that he would help establish one of his cousin's two sons in the world. Because Robin's elder brother will inherit their minister-farmer father's farm, Robin has come to the city to take the major up on the offer.

# BIOGRAPHY

## NATHANIEL HAWTHORNE

Born July 4, 1804, in Salem, Massachusetts, Hawthorne (born Hathorne) was the descendent of Puritan settlers. His sea-captain father, also named Nathaniel, died when Hawthorne was four years old. He, his mother, Louisa, and his two sisters then lived with her relatives. An avid reader from an early age, Hawthorne graduated from Bowdoin College in 1825. His first known publication, the novel *Fanshawe* (1828), was self-published anonymously, but it failed; he later suppressed the work. While also writing popular books for children, some with his sister Elizabeth, Hawthorne concentrated on short stories and sketches published in periodicals and annual gift books—including the 1832 edition that featured "My Kinsman, Major Molineux"—for two decades. He spent most of the 1840s working in civil service jobs to support his young family, while still writing when he could.

Hawthorne became more internationally known for first his novel, *The Scarlet Letter* (1850), and then *The House of the Seven Gables* (1851), among others. Beginning in 1853, Hawthorne spent seven years in Europe, first as the U.S. consul in Liverpool, England, then on the continent as a tourist. He returned home to Massachusetts in 1860 and published his last novel, *The Marble Faun*. Hawthorne tried to pen four romances but he found it hard to write fiction again and could not finish them. He died on May 19, 1864, at the age of fifty-nine from cancer.

When Robin arrives in the town, his efforts to find his kinsman are stymied at every turn. For much of the story, the only person who will claim to know the major is a prostitute trying to tempt young Robin. Everyone else hems and haws and laughs after Robin leaves. Growing more and more frustrated by the situation, Robin wanders the streets of the city in the night. He finally meets men who will acknowledge the major's existence at the church. Sitting with a gentleman on the church steps, Robin sees a procession parading a tarred-and-feathered Major Molineux through the streets. Knowing that the major is disgraced and scorned by the townspeople, Robin wants to give up and return home. The gentleman tells him to stay a few days and to see if he can make it in the world without his kinsman's help.

For scholars, a literal reading of "My Kinsman, Major Molineux" focuses on Robin's loss of innocence as he encounters real-world life experiences as well as his transition from adolescence to adulthood. Some critics prefer an allegorical reading of the story. They interpret it as a metaphor for the emergence of the United States, with Robin symbolizes the fledging colonies while the major represents Great Britain and a traditional authority that the colonies must overcome to achieve independence. The townspeople can also be seen as symbols of the colony's rebellion against the mother country, an idea set out in the first page of the story. Also symbolic for some reviewers are Robin's journey of self-discovery and his attempts to find his place in the world. Hawthorne also highlights the differences between rural and urban ideals in "My Kinsman, Major Molineux."

## PLOT SUMMARY

Setting the scene for the story in "My Kinsman, Major Molineux," Hawthorne gives a background of tensions between colonists and appointees of the British king in Massachusetts. Colonists have run off six king-appointed colonial governors in one way or another over the past forty years. The primary story begins one evening as teenaged Robin Molineux rides a ferry into the port of a Massachusetts city. As the ferryman waits for Robin to pay his fare, he notices his lone passenger is young and dressed liked someone from the country who just arrived in town for the first time. After paying the ferryman five shillings, Robin is left with only three pence.

Robin walks to town, full of eager excitement, but soon he realizes that he does not know where exactly he is going. He has come in search of his kinsman, Major Molineux, but because he does not know where he lives, Robin decides to ask the next man he meets. Robin stops an elderly man outside of a barbershop in a nice neighborhood. Holding on to the man's coat, he asks where to find Major Molineux's home. The man rebukes him:

> Let go of my garment, fellow! I tell you, I know not the man you speak of. What! I have authority, I have—hem, hem—authority; and if this be the respect you show your betters, your feet shall be brought acquainted with the stocks, by daylight, tomorrow morning!

As the man leaves, the men in the barbershop laugh at the scene. Confused, Robin concludes that the man was from the country and did not know the major. He believes the men in the barbershop were laughing at him for "choosing such a guide." Robin walks on, coming to the business center of the city. On one corner, he sees an inn with a picture of a British hero outside. The smell of food drifting outside makes Robin hungry but he decides to wait to eat, telling himself, "the Major will make me welcome to the best of his victuals; so I will even step boldly in, and inquire my way to his dwelling."

Once inside, Robin looks over the tavern and groups of men therein, identifying with one group while trying to decide whom to ask about Major Molineux. The innkeeper recognizes Robin as a recent arrival from the country and flatters him. "'The man sees a family likeness! the rogue has guessed that I am related to the Major!' thought Robin, who had hitherto experienced little superfluous civility."

As the whole tavern looks on, Robin tells him he has little money but asks where Major Molineux lives. The innkeeper begins to nervously read a printed "wanted" poster offering a reward for a fugitive who, he claims, is dressed like Robin. "Better trudge, boy, better trudge!", he tells Robin. Reacting to the insult, "Robin had begun to draw his hand towards the lighter end of the oak cudgel, but a strange hostility in every countenance, induced him to relinquish his purpose of breaking the courteous innkeeper's head." After one "bold-featured" patron sneers at him, Robin exits.

Outside, Robin hears everyone inside the tavern laughing. He is still confused by their actions, thinking, "is it not strange, that the confession of an empty pocket, should outweigh the name of my kinsman, Major Molineux?"

Robin walks onto a wide street lined by big houses and shop windows. There are fancy and festive people milling about on the street, and he decides to look in the face of every man his kinsman's age on both sides of the street to try to find him, but he has no success.

As Robin goes down another street to look for the major in another part of town, the young man grows more hungry and tired. He decides to demand the next person he encounters to tell him where the major is. As he turns into a shabby neighborhood, Robin sees a partially open door and a woman dressed in a scarlet petticoat inside. He asks here where to find his kinsman through the door, and the woman comes out. She tells him that the major lives there. Looking at the poor quality of homes, Robin finds it hard to believe her, but he decides she could be the major's housekeeper.

Robin asks her to bring him to the door, but the woman says that he has already been in bed for some time. She also tells Robin that he looks much like the major and that he should come inside. As she takes his hand and tries to pull him inside, she runs inside when another door in the neighborhood opens. A night watchman tries to shoo Robin away, saying, "Home vagabond, home! . . . Home, or we'll set you in the stocks by the peep of day!" As this man walks away, Robin asks after him where the major lives, but gets no answer. When the night watchman is gone, Robin can hear the woman coming down the steps again, "but Robin, being of the household of a New England clergyman, was a good youth, as well as a shrewd one; so he resisted temptation, and fled away."

Robin grows desperate as he looks through streets all over the town. Twice, he comes across groups of men dressed in strange outlandish clothing, but they do not help him. Robin decides to knock on the door of every home that seems like it may be the major's residence. As Robin passes by a church, he stops in front of a man walking with purpose. Robin says, "Halt, honest man, and answer me a question. Tell me, this instant, whereabouts is the dwelling of my kinsman, Major Molineux?" The man threatens him, but Robin insists. He finally tells Robin that if Robin stays here that the major will pass by in an hour. Robin is surprised, especially because he recognizes the man as the "bold-featured" person from the inn, but the stranger's face is now painted red on one side and black on the other.

*Lithograph of the Boston Tea Party by Sarony and Major* National Archives and Records Administration

Robin sits on the steps of the church determined to wait until his kinsman appears. He thinks as he sits and looks around the street on which he waits. Robin notices a mansion, which he thinks might be the major's. He also hears a distant murmur, as well as loud, distant shouts at times. To stay awake, Robin gets up and looks inside the empty church. The sight of the empty church makes him feel very lonely. Noticing the graves around the church, he wonders if the major is buried there, but he dismisses this thought.

To comfort himself, Robin imagines what the family he left behind is doing at that moment. His father, a minister, is probably holding a service with his family and neighbors in his home. Robin also imagines other members of his family, including his mother, elder brother, and his two younger sisters, and how they may be acting.

> Then he saw them go in at the door; and when Robin would have entered also, the latch tinkled into its place, and he was excluded from his home. "Am I here, or there?" cried Robin, starting; for all at once, when his thoughts had become visible and audible in a dream, the long, wide, solitary street shone out before him.

Robin nearly falls asleep on the steps of the church. He is awakened when a man passes by, whom he asks if he must wait all night for the major. The gentleman does not hear the question but "Perceiving a country youth, apparently homeless and without friends, he accosted him in a tone of real kindness, which had become strange to Robin's ears." He asks Robin if he can help him. Robin asks if the major actually lives here. The gentleman inquires how Robin is acquainted with the major.

Robin tells the gentleman about his background. Robin's minister father and the major are first cousins. The major is rich, while Robin's father lives on a small salary as a minister and farmer. The major visited Robin's family a year or two earlier and showed interest in Robin and his brother because the major has no children of his own. The major hinted that he would set up one of them in life. Because his brother is going to inherit the family farm, the family decided

> that Robin should profit from his kinsman's generous intentions, especially as he...was thought to possess other necessary endowments. "For I have the name of being a shrewd youth," observed Robin, in this part of his story.

Robin left home five days earlier to find the major. Robin also tells the gentleman that a man with the painted face said that, if he waited, the major would pass by soon. The gentleman says he does not know the other man well and reveals, "I chanced to meet him a little time previous to your stopping me. I believe you may trust his word." The gentleman decides to wait with Robin for the major to come by and see Robin's reaction himself. As they talk, there is loud shouting coming closer. Robin asks the gentleman if the town is always this loud at night, and he remarks, "There were at least a thousand voices went to make up that one shout." The gentleman asks, "May not one man have several voices, Robin, as well as two complexions?"

As the noisy crowd grows closer, Robin can also hear laughs and the sounds of instruments like trumpets. Robin rises as he believes he is hearing great merrymaking. The gentleman tells him to sit down as the major will be passing by shortly. As the crowd grows closer, windows open on nearby houses wanting to know what is going on. Others leave their homes half-dressed to check out the commotion for themselves.

When the group comes nearer to the church, the gentleman asks Robin if he will be able to pick out the major. Robin is not sure that he can. As the crowd arrives carrying torches, there is a horseman dressed in military gear—the man with a painted face whom Robin encountered earlier—leading the procession. Others are dressed like Indians or in other costumes. The procession stops in front of the church and becomes silent. "'The double-faced fellow has his eye upon me,' muttered Robin, with an indefinite but uncomfortable idea, the he was himself to bear a part in the pageantry."

An uncovered cart stops before him, "and there, in tar-and-feathery dignity, sate his kinsman, Major Molineux!" He is pale and trembling, and trying to keep his composure, "even in those circumstances of overwhelming humiliation." The major and Robin make eye contact. Major Molineux recognizes Robin and feels shame. Robin feels both pity and fear as the events of the night catch up to him:

> Soon, however, a bewildering excitement began to seize upon his mind; the preceding adventures of the night, the unexpected appearance of the crowd, the torches, the confused din, and the hush that followed, the spectre of his kinsman reviled by that great multitude, all this, and more than all, a

> THE PEOPLE LOOKED WITH MOST JEALOUS SCRUTINY TO THE EXERCISE OF POWER, WHICH DID NOT EMANATE FROM THEMSELVES, AND THEY USUALLY REWARDED THE RULERS WITH SLENDER GRATITUDE, FOR THE COMPLIANCES, BY WHICH, IN SOFTENING THEIR INSTRUCTIONS FROM BEYOND THE SEA, THEY HAD INCURRED THE REPREHENSION OF THOSE WHO GAVE THEM."

perception of tremendous ridicule in the whole scene, affected him with a sort of mental inebriety.

He hears some in the crowd start to laugh, including the innkeeper and the woman with the scarlet petticoat. As the laughter spreads through the crowd, Robin "seemed to hear the voices of the barbers; of the guests of the inn; and of all who made sport of him that night." Robin himself joins in the laughter, and he is the loudest of the crowd. After some time, the procession moves on, and the major tries to retain his dignity. "On they went, in counterfeited pomp, in senseless uproar, in frenzied merriment, trampling on an old man's heart."

The gentleman asks, "Well, Robin, are you dreaming?" Robin asks the gentleman to show him the way to the ferry. When the gentleman inquires if Robin is going to look for something else, Robin tells him, "Thanks to you, and to my other friends, I have at last met my kinsman, and he will scarce desire to see my face again." The gentleman will not help Robin leave that night. He says he will help Robin leave in a few days, if he still wants to, "Or, if you prefer to remain with us, perhaps, as you are a shrewd youth, you may rise in the world, without the help of your kinsman, Major Molineux."

## THEMES

### *Forsaking Past Ties*

In "My Kinsman, Major Molineux," a younger generation matures and rejects the authority of the older generation, while the older generation either stands aside and allows or even encourages the new independence. Parents and children must negotiate the delicate shift as they become peer adults. In very much the same way, the young nation acts out against its "parent" and asserts its independence. In the literal action of the story, the colonists are rebelling against British-based authority. Whether the major is personally responsible for the townspeople's grievances, or whether he is merely an unfortunate symbol of their displeasure with the Crown, is a mystery. It is clear that the people Robin meets all over the city that night know of the coming rebellion, feel that the major deserves it, and are prepared to reject Robin by association. The uprising is similar to a teenager's fit of pique, in which he refuses to be told what to do.

Robin's break with his family is less violent but no less final. He has left the countryside and come to the city with his family's help and blessings, but he knows he must now stand on his own. As he imagines those he left back on the farm, "Then he saw them go in at the door; and when Robin would have entered also, the latch tinkled into its place, and he was excluded from his home." In some ways the major represents a surrogate father to Robin, even though they are not closely acquainted. Throughout the evening, Robin imagines himself to be his kinsman's heir apparent, and he prides himself on that connection. When he finally comes face to face with the major's plight, he chooses abruptly to cast his lot with the rebellious "youth" around him. The major, on the other hand, does not struggle and only tries to remain dignified in the face of such pain and humiliation. Like many "parents" who have allowed their "children" to exercise their freedom, the major seems to represent the inevitability of the power shift. As Robin severs his ties with the one he hoped would be his benefactor, he starts to embrace the possibility of making it on his own.

## Coming of Age

Another significant theme in "My Kinsman, Major Molineux" is the concept of making one's way in the world. Robin left the farm (literally) around the age of eighteen and came to the city to find his own place and career, with the support of his family. His older brother will inherit the family farm, which their minister father works to support his family. The rich and then well-placed Major Molineux came to

the visit a year or two earlier and implied that, as a childless man, he would help one of the boys establish themselves. With his family's support, Robin has come to take up the major on his supposed offer. Hawthorne writes of the family's choice, "it was therefore determined that Robin should profit by his kinsman's generous intentions." His father has given him a significant part of his year's salary, while his mother and sister improved his clothes in advance of his voyage.

Robin grows frustrated throughout the story when he cannot find the major nor anyone who would give him direct information concerning his whereabouts. Yet he remains focused on his goal of finding the major and benefiting from his patronage. However, by the end of "My Kinsman, Major Molineux," Robin is ready to give up on his goal as the major is in disgrace because of what he stands for. However, the gentleman who stays with him in the last pages of the story will not let him give up on his dream. When Robin wants to leave and go home, the gentleman insists that he stays for a few days, if not longer. He tells Robin, "if you prefer to remain with us, perhaps, as you are a shrewd youth, you may rise in the world, without the help of your kinsman, Major Molineux." Though Hawthorne does not record Robin's choice, it is clear that Robin's days as a naïve farm boy are over.

In addition to Robin seeking his place in the world, his travels in "My Kinsman, Major Molineux" are a journey of self-discovery, especially as he searches the town for his kinsman. He learns who he is and that the world can be a harsh, unforgiving place.

Robin takes this journey alone. He arrives in town on a ferry with only the ferryman as a companion. Once in town, Robin is on his own as he desperately looks for the major. No one helps him in any discernible way until he reaches the church. Instead, he is laughed at by townspeople when he inquires about the major's whereabouts and nearly taken advantage of by a prostitute, the woman in the scarlet petticoats, who falsely claims the major is in her dwelling. Robin dodges bad situations and grows frustrated by his lack of progress, yet he remains focused on his goal.

While Robin's illusions about the world are shattered when he sees the major paraded about tarred and feathered, he has learned much about himself and the world. Though he repeatedly refers to himself as shrewd in the story, he comes to understand by story's end that he is not as perceptive as he thinks he is. The town has fooled him by repeatedly denying information about the major or lying outright, as the prostitute does. Once he finds the major, Robin sees him humiliated. Robin's journey has not been wasted, as the gentleman encourages Robin to stay and continue on his path.

## *The Unfamiliar*

An underlying tension in "My Kinsman, Major Molineux" is between Robin—with his country ways—and the city life and people that seem so strange to him. The city is sophisticated while the country, of which Robin is the epitome, is basically innocent. To Robin, the city is loud in the night compared to the quiet country where he grew up.

Robin symbolizes country folk with his clothes and cudgel (club) made from an oak sapling. The reader's first impression of Robin through the ferryman's eyes emphasizes his rural background: "He was a youth of barely eighteen years, evidently country-bred, and now, as it should seem, upon his first visit to town." Robin is easily identified as a provincial bumpkin to those he encounters in the more sophisticated town.

Robin's appearance, manners, and ignorance also show through when he deals with townspeople. For example, he is unaware at first that the woman in the scarlet petticoats is a prostitute trying to lure him inside. While Robin tries to be refined when inquiring about the major, he is generally dismissed, not only because he is asking about the major, but also because of his attitude.

When Robin sees the major's fate, he is unsure that he is made for life in the city. He tells the gentleman, "I begin to grow weary of town life, Sir. Will you show me the way to the ferry?" Though the gentleman will not let him give up on his dream right way, life in the city is depicted as a difficult adjustment for the rural-reared Robin.

## HISTORICAL OVERVIEW

### *Colonial America*

British settlement of North America began in 1587 when Sir Walter Raleigh, authorized by Queen Elizabeth I, sent 117 colonists to a territory Raleigh had named Virginia. Though this settlement on Roanoke Island failed and the colonists vanished, the British tried again and established a colony at Jamestown in 1607. Other colonies in what became the American Northeast soon followed when Puritan separatists traveled on the *Mayflower* and landed on Plymouth Rock in 1620. By 1628, the Massachusetts Bay Company had been founded, and two years later, Boston was the largest city in North America.

Because many English colonies, including Massachusetts, were founded as private companies, and because many colonists had been participators in government in England, self-government soon became part of the colonists' identity. During the Puritan Revolution in England, which lasted from 1640 to 1660, the existing American colonies practiced self-government and founded representational government bodies. After the return of the British monarchy in 1660 in the form of King Charles II, the British government began implementing economic and trade policies that favored the mother country.

Colonists' political independence greatly increased early in the eighteenth century when British bureaucrats supervised the colonies' internal affairs much less. Trade growth was more important to Great Britain for several decades. While American political assemblies increased in power and the colonies became more autonomous during the first half of the eighteenth century, this situation was undermined by increasing taxation by the British to pay for its wars with France.

By the 1760s, the American colonies wanted more autonomy and tried to become independent from Great Britain. There were about two million colonists by 1763, and the colonies' economy was growing. The British government, in the form of Parliament, refused to allow their colonies to become free, but instead posed more taxes and tighter controls. Colonists especially resented paying taxes to defray some of the cost of having a standing British army in America. While the British insisted the army was there to protect the colonists, the Americans saw it as an imposition on their rights.

Discontent continued in the American colonies from 1763 until the beginning of the American Revolution in the mid-1770s. Massachusetts was the center of some of the best-known incidents against the British, including the Boston Tea Party. Bostonians protested Parliament's attempt to tax the colonies by dumping a shipment of British tea in Boston Harbor. The British government did not take such acts of rebellion lightly. More controlling laws, known as the Intolerable Acts, were imposed. Massachusetts itself was put under the control of a British officer, Major General Thomas Gage, an act deeply resented by residents of that colony. Within a few years, an all-out rebellion occurred, and the colonists won their independence from Great Britain.

### Boston in 1730

While the episode Hawthorne describes in "My Kinsman, Major Molineux" is fictional, the story incorporates facts and is based on incidents from New England in this time period. Scholars generally assume that the city to which Robin travels is Boston. At the time, Boston was the largest settlement in New England. By 1790, the population of the city was just over 18,000.

In *American Literature*, Robert C. Grayson argues not only that the story is set in Boston but also that Hawthorne set it in a specific time. Grayson believes that it is set in 1730 specifically because the year was the hundredth anniversary of the arrival of John Winthrop with the original colonial charter for Massachusetts as well as Winthrop's co-founding of Boston. Grayson further states that the story takes place on June 23, 1730, mid-summer's eve, which is nearly the exact date that Winthrop arrived one hundred years earlier.

This date is significant because Winthrop's charter allowed people to have a democratic say in their rulers. Boston, especially, resented a second charter that gave the British ruler the right to choose and place a governor in office. The people's treatment of Major Molineux in the story reflects the increasing resistance to the royal governor's authority in Massachusetts, especially Boston, as his power did not originate with them but with the king. It is an act of self-rule that underscores tensions palatable in this time period.

According to Grayson, even the ferry Robin arrived on has historical precedent. The Charlestown Ferry landed on Boston's north end in this time period. Travel was slow in colonial America. Hawthorne writes that it took five days for Robin to travel from his rural community to Boston. Once in Boston, Robin hears the nine o'clock bell. The city had a nine o'clock curfew in this time, and, during his wanderings, Robin encounters a watchman who calls him a "vagabond" and threatens him with the stockades in the morning. This threat and punishment were lawful at the time, as watchmen could hold suspects and put them in stocks in the morning.

Even details of clothing and manners accurately reflect Boston in 1730. The prostitute's hooped petticoats were widely worn, as was the three-cornered hat that adorns Robin's head. Grayson believes that Robin demonstrates his rural roots by not removing his hat when addressing the first old man he encounters. Robin's grabbing the man's coat reveals his lack of knowledge of city manners as well, signifying his country background.

### The United States in the 1830s

By the 1830s, when Hawthorne wrote the story, the United States understood itself as an established country with a growing sense of its history and a sense of patriotic pride. Americans' patriotism was highlighted by a greater awareness and understanding of the rights and responsibilities of the common man. Many people were celebrating America as it came to see itself as more and more of a country. The United States was also growing as more territory was being added, a trend that would occur for several decades.

Thus the United States was a society in transition. Early in the nineteenth century, American farmers fed themselves through their labor, but, by the 1830s, America's industrial economy was growing, and a number of farmers began focusing on producing a particular product for the market economy. More companies were issued charters and became incorporated at such a rate that state laws changed in the 1830s because of the demand. As society became more modern and industrial and the American economy grew larger, urban environments increased in number, especially in the northeast.

Farmers and farm families were not always completely isolated in the 1830s. Many farmers were part of a farm community that often centered on a farm village where farmers and their families could attend church and connect with the outside world. They also organized events like barn raisings and harvesting of crops that helped an individual farmer do work that required more hands but also brought the larger community together in social contact. Women who lived on farms also had bees, collective meetings where they sewed, quilted, or corn-husked together.

There was, however, a growing disparity between city and country as more cities were founded and the American frontier expanded. Established cities, especially those along transportation routes, saw their populations vastly increase. By 1830, Boston's population was over 61,000, making it the largest city in New England; New York City's population was even larger.

As more people moved to cities, overcrowding became an issue, especially in some large cities, as did poverty and an increased crime rate. The disparity between wealth and poverty also became more obvious as slums and mansions often existed in the same vicinity. Those Americans who moved to cities from rural environments often continued rural traditions while living in the city. One problematic habit was throwing trash and relieving themselves in any empty spot. This situation led to horrible smells, disease, and even water pollution in major metropolitan areas. In some cities, people were paid to take away the garbage and human waste, but in others the waste matter would stay where it was deposited.

Urban centers were also being transformed into recognizable American cities. Throughout the 1830s and after, cites began being organized into downtown areas featuring retail shops and businesses, a part of the town dedicated to industry and/or merchant exchanges, and separate home and workplaces for city residents. Entertainment became a commercial enterprise to bring city dwellers together.

Another, more negative way those who lived in the city came together was in urban riots. In the 1830s, riots became common in the cities as people from laborers to skilled craftsmen to merchants to even professionals took out their anger on their adversaries through violent demonstrations. Skilled workers, for example, rioted against new immigrants to the city as symbols of the changing industrial workplace. In 1828 in Philadelphia, American workers raged against Irish weavers. The city also saw dock worker riots between whites and blacks in the mid-1830s.

### American Romantic Literature

"My Kinsman, Major Molineux" is an example of American Romantic literature, a prominent mid-nineteenth–century trend. Although the period, lasting roughly through the middle third of the century, is often referred to as the American Renaissance, "American Naissance" would be a more apt term; the movement marked the birth of truly American literature, not its rebirth. Hawthorne is considered one of the first and the best romantic writers in the United States, promulgating the form in his work with stories in purely American settings and circumstances. Hawthorne was greatly influenced by European writers who emphasized imaginative writing over the more formal writing found in what was then called "the novel." Exploring American themes, ideals, settings, and circumstances, Hawthorne and his contemporaries, including Ralph Waldo Emerson, Edgar Allan Poe, and Herman Melville, laid the foundation for their young country's literary identity and independence from European dominance.

## CRITICAL OVERVIEW

Because "My Kinsman, Major Molineux" was originally published anonymously in an 1832 gift book called *The Token*, little critical attention was initially paid to the short story. Published again under Hawthorne's name in *The Snow-Image, and Other Twice-Told Tales* (1851), this story was not particularly popular among readers or critics of the time. Hawthorne's story did not receive much critical attention until the 1950s. Writing in the *Dictionary of Literary Biography*, William E. Grant explains the story's appeal to scholars of the mid- to late twentieth century. He believes the story "reflects Hawthorne's early fascination with New England history and is his best treatment of the restless period that preceded the American Revolution."

Roger P. Wallins holds in *Studies in Short Fiction* that the criticism of "My Kinsman, Major Molineux" falls into three primary categories:

> the historical critics, who view the story as symbolic of America's struggle for independence; the psychological critics, who view Robin's adventures as a rejection of various father-figures; and the moral critics, who view the story as one of "irresistible gloom."

Many critics focus on the allegorical nature of the story in particular, including its symbolism. Writing in *Explicator* in 2001, Colin D. Pearce interprets "My Kinsman, Major Molineux" as

# MEDIA ADAPTATIONS

"My Kinsman, Major Molineux" was adapted as a stage play by Robert Lowell in 1965. It is one of three such adaptations included in Lowell's *The Old Glory: Endecott and the Red Cross; My Kinsman, Major Molineux; and Benito Cereno,* which was reprinted in 2000 by Farrar, Straus and Giroux.

---

"allegorical of the cultural and civilization shift that had overtaken American life in Hawthorne's lifetime." In *American Literature,* Jerry A. Herndon argues that Hawthorne was emphasizing ethics. He writes,

> The historical situation gave Hawthorne's genius impetus to create a tale dramatizing the complexities of the human heart; once he had launched into the story, he was no longer interested in history *per se* but in moral values.

A number of critics also explored the character of Robin, offering their interpretations of his actions and the actions toward him by those in the town. For example, Robert H. Fossum writes in *Claremont Quarterly* that Robin's character works on two levels. First, "Robin is more than just a young country lad making his first visit to town: he is *any* young man—youth itself at that crucial moment when it wavers between dependence, past and future." Fossum also sees him working on a deeper, more symbolic level as Robin leaves his minister-farmer father and family life behind: "He is the prototypical American rebel, striking out by himself in a world he does not fully understand."

## CRITICISM

### T. Walter Herbert

*In the following excerpt, Herbert asserts that Hawthorne's story goes beyond providing an example of manhood toward which readers can strive, but creates in readers the actual "imaginative experience" that helps them internalize that goal.*

"My Kinsman, Major Molineux" takes part in the cultural process that constructs self-made manhood. The ideal of manly self-reliance and self-sovereignty gained pre-eminent authority in the emerging democratic and competitive society of the early national period, dislodging the hegemony of the colonial seaboard gentry, with its traditions of deferential hierarchy. Hawthorne's tale articulates the symbolic reordering that took place in this cultural transition, which was observed by Alexis de Tocqueville in the 1830s.

Tocqueville found the relations of masters and servants to be a site of conflict between deferential and democratic ideals. "While the transition from one social condition to another is going on," he noted, "there is almost always a time when men's minds fluctuate between the aristocratic notion of subjection and the democratic notion of obedience." Male household servants in America are haunted by "a confused and imperfect phantom of equality...[They] conceive that they ought] themselves to be masters, and they are inclined to consider him who orders them as an unjust usurper of their own rights."

In a frankly hierarchical social system these bafflements do not arise, because a servant's identity is bonded to that of his master. He "detaches his notion of interest from his own person; he deserts himself as it were, or rather he transports himself into the character of his master and thus assumes an imaginary personality." Yet in the transition from the manhood of ascribed status to that of competitive equality, the identities of actual men stand empty, to be haunted by the ghosts that inhabit the two discrepant worlds: on the one side is the vicarious "imaginary personality" generated by habits of deference in an aristocracy; on the other side is the democratic "phantom of equality," whispering to every subordinated man that he is a sovereign.

Tocqueville observes, moreover, that this dilemma is not merely a psychic cost of the transition from one social arrangement to another, but is endemic to democratic society itself, where an ideology of natural equality must contend with the continuing reality of social stratification. "In democracies servants are not only equal among themselves, but...are, in some

*Lithograph by D.C. Johnston showing two American Revolutionaries tarring and feathering an English dandie* © Bettmann/Corbis

sort, the equals of their masters…At any moment a servant may become a master, and he aspires to rise to that condition; the servant is therefore not a different man from the master. Why, then, has the former a right to command, and what compels the latter to obey except the free and temporary consent of both their wills?"

Men who conceive themselves as equal individual sovereigns feel a systemic unrest in the presence of social power, and are strongly disposed to deny its reality, which is a major source of the famous paradox of the middle class, the class that denies the existence of class. It is the formation of just such a manhood—middle-class and self-reliant—that "My Kinsman Major Molinuex" dramatizes, focussing attention upon endemic contradictions that continue to harass exponents of the ideal.

The cultural work of "My Kinsman" may thus be said to continue, and it cannot be finished so long as men continue to understand themselves as democratic individuals. This is true because of an additional dilemma that requires discussion before we turn to Hawthorne's tale.

As Nancy Chodorow has argued, every man—whether a democratic individual or not—

begins life as an infant, in a condition of total dependence upon powerful superiors to whom he looks not only for physical support, but also for his identity. Rather than merely "transporting himself" into the character of his father [or "fathers"], a growing boy receives his personality in large part through imaginative transactions in which he internalizes the possibilities of manhood that are presented to him and arrives at a sense of himself by way of a negotiation among them. A boy comes to know himself as he discovers that he cannot be a mother, gains an impression of the way he is seen by his father and comes to see himself in his father. What Tocqueville dismissed as a conventional feature of aristocratic social relations—the definition of self through the identification with another—is intrinsic to acquiring adult manhood, including the "self-reliant" form of manhood that middle-class society generates.

Democratic men, that is to say, have deferential childhoods: the man who has learned to think of himself as *in essence* an autonomous sovereign—self-made and self-governing—carries with him a primordial memory of total psychic and physical dependency and a more recent memory of his "emergence" as a individual. Hawthorne's treatment of these issues is grounded on the interplay between the historically contingent psychic development of the self-made men and the emergence of political democracy.

"My Kinsman, Major Molineux" portrays the quandary of a young man who carries the social habits of deferential hierarchy into the era of their overthrow. Young Robin comes to town in order to take up the promise of his kinsman, a prominent colonial official who had "thrown out hints respecting the future establishment of…[Robin] in life." What Robin expects is not a competition among democratic equals. He brings with him the deferential responses that are native to hierarchical social arrangements, including the assumption that he himself is due a measure of respect from his kinsman's social inferiors. When an innkeeper addresses him with over-elaborate courtesy, Robin mistakenly concludes that "the rogue has guessed that I am related to the Major" and makes his reply, "with such an assumption of consequence, as befitted the Major's relative."

The social world in Robin's head is sharply at odds with the situation actually surrounding him, where the townspeople are preparing to tar-and-feather Major Molineux because they resent the royal administration he serves. This "temporary inflammation of the popular mind"—fortelling the advent of democracy—triggers off a revolution in Robin's psychic constitution; he is compelled to repudiate, as by an irresistible inborn emotional force, the social habits he brought with him.

The scene in which Robin confronts his ruined kinsman is managed by Hawthorne as an initiation into the emotional realities of self-made manhood. The patricidal ritual—where Robin joins in showering ridicule upon his psychologically shattered and degraded kinsman—is also filicidal. It is aimed at cauterizing the deferential affections of childhood, which must be supplanted if sovereign individualism is to be formed in an adult man. His loyalty to his elderly kinsman once repudiated, Robin enters a new frame of mind, which allows him to join easily in the cheerfully sardonic manner of his new mentor. "Thanks to you, and to my other friends," Robin says, "I have at last met my kinsman, and he will scarce desire to see my face again."

Robin needs help to understand the meaning at stake in the wrenching drama of his initiation, and to this end the mentor acts temporarily *in loco parentis* without the emotional entanglements of kinship. He makes no pretense of arranging Robin's "establishment in life," or of providing him money or land. Instead, he adopts a consultative professional stance, like that Burton Bledstein identifies as a central feature of middle-class culture. He offers Robin insight into his psychological condition, his social environment and his prospects; and this schooling in the new reality is offered in terms that make it clear the mentor assumes no responsibility for the outcome: "perhaps, as you are a shrewd youth, you may rise in the world, without the help of your kinsman, Major Molineux."

David Leverenz has recently discussed the experience of Robin Molineux along similar lines. He describes Robin as a young man "on the edge between his need for patrician protection and his conversion to the new middle-class code of self-reliant competition." To read Leverenz's discussion is particularly instructive because he speaks throughout of his own emotional responses to the narrative. Not only does Robin pass through a psychological transformation as he takes part in

the ritual; the reader is also caught up in the imaginative experience Hawthorne presents. He/she is invited to pass across the threshhold with Robin, as he enacts the transition from deferential dependency and boyishness to self-sufficient manhood.

For readers like the men Tocqueville described, who are enmeshed in the transition—their minds fluctuating between dependence and independence—Robin's performance of the necessary repudiation may have the effect of confirming their grip on the new order of things. Richard Brodhead has written tellingly of this process, by which works of fiction aid in the establishment of emergent cultural patterns by stigmatizing the organization of experience that must be superceded. The psychic bafflement of fluctuating loyalties is thus resolved into a clear-cut battle between the remnants of an oppressive past, and the promise of fulfillment in a bright new day.

The cultural work of fiction thus has a second form, which engages the symbolic creation of selfhood more fully. The story does more than propose an idea for consideration—in this instance that patriarchy should be anathematized and self-made manhood championed—it also generates an imaginative experience that has the effect of "helping readers *think* [such] a social boundary into place" within themselves, as within the body politic. When such work is successfully completed, the picture of reality that before seemed hypothetical and uncertain is now felt to be self-evident, in what Philip Fisher terms a retroactively effective structure of "hard facts." "Where culture installs new habits of moral perception . . . it accomplishes, as a last step, the forgetting of its own strenuous work so that what are newly learned habits are only remembered as facts."

Yet Leverenz's reading vehemently resists this experience; he finds "My Kinsman" to be an attack on the style of manhood depicted in it. Rather than promoting the cultural creation of the self-made man, the story provides an "exceptionally seductive and devious critique."

In reply, I want to propose a third way in which fiction performs cultural work. Here likewise the reader is inwardly divided, not because he/she is unable to commit wholeheartedly to an emerging scheme of things, but because the organization of experience being confirmed is inwardly contradictory. Instead of setting a emergent cultural pattern off against a competitor, the pattern in question is set off against itself. Yet inherent contradiction is now given a paradoxical function. Instead of being invoked to discredit a moribund ideal, so as to consign it to a superceded past, the stresses portrayed are endemic to the emerging model of selfhood, and are made to confirm its truth; the inner conflicts that threaten to undermine the new structure are recruited in its support.

In "My Kinsman" Hawthorne celebrates the social changes heralding the advent of democracy, just as he acknowledges the moral dignity that follows from rising in the world on one's own enterprise. Yet wedded to those assertions is his recognition of the wrong dealt out to Major Molineux. "On they went, like fiends that throng in mockery round some dead potentate, mighty no more, but majestic still in his agony. On they went, in counterfeited pomp, in senseless uproar, in frenzied merriment, trampling all on an old man's heart."

The intensity of this language—as of the entire tale—results from the shift taking place within it; the collision between aristocratic and democratic orders of meaning merges into a structural conflict within democratic standards, which amounts to a dilemma in which patricide is both mandatory and prohibited. Directed against the fraudulent authority of a "potentate," the mockery assailing Major Molineux asserts democratic principle; yet the indelible "majesty" of Molineux's presence redescribes him as an embodiment of the same principle that his humiliation exalts. Hawthorne's concluding phrases protest Molineux's degradation not as an outrage upon the prerogatives of the British throne and its colonial representative, but upon the royalty that democratic doctrine ascribes to all equally-created human hearts, in particular that of an old man in torment. Centrally active here is a contradiction *within* the ethos of democratic self-sovereignty. The filial revolt required of the democratic individual may free him from the entanglements of deferential dependence, but it also strikes a blow against the source of his own identity: to trample on an old man's heart is to defile one's own.

This portrayal of inward contradiction aids in the construction of self-made manhood by offering an occasion on which such system-specific consternations are enshrined as a communion with reality itself. The work encourages the acceptance of what appears to be a somber

yet necessary truth, as it evokes such historically contingent moral distresses as the token of a permanent tragic mystery. The predicaments inseparable from living within a given cultural arrangement are made to appear the blight that man was born for. Evidence that "My Kinsman" effects such a confirmation is available not only in critics who find it an exemplum of Original Sin, but also in Colacurcio's melancholy acknowledgement that Robin's psychic experience, for all its moral defects, simply has to be accepted as portraying a universal law of human maturation, and that "the ugly facts of political life" are indeed ugly.

Leverenz's discovery of a devious protest against self-made manhood in the tale likewise testifies to the imaginative experience at stake here. His discussion amply documents the contention that to read "My Kinsman" is to feel what it's like to become a self-made man. Rather than embracing the story as the talisman of a cherished identity, Leverenz is sharply critical of the competitive self-sufficiency that the tale seeks to confirm, which he terms a "bully-boy" manhood. Yet cultural work still takes place when we become resisting readers, when we seek to consolidate our own identities over-against what the work solicits. If we find that a text tells us who we are and what our world is like better than we can otherwise tell ourselves, we then accord it a consummate value. Yet we may cling to a work because it provides a salutary target, evoking a repellent style of selfhood we don't quite know how to supersede. Our discoveries of supreme imaginative power, like our anxious repudiations, bear witness to the state of our cultural allegiances. Hawthorne's narrative acts upon us as the midnight pageant acted upon Robin, drawing forth more than we knew we had in us.

**Source:** T. Walter Herbert, "Doing Cultural Work: "*My Kinsman Major Molineux*" and the Coustruction of the Self-made Man," in *Studies in the Novel*, Vol. 23, No. 1, Spring 1991, pp. 20–27.

# SOURCES

Fossum, Robert H., "The Shadow of the Past: Hawthorne's Historical Tales," in *Claremont Quarterly*, Vol. 11, No. 1, Autumn 1963, pp. 45–56.

Grant, William E., "Nathaniel Hawthorne," in *Dictionary of Literary Biography*, Vol. 74: *American Short-Story*

*Writers Before 1880*, edited by Bobby Ellen Kimbel, Gale Group, 1988, pp. 143–63.

Grayson, Robert S., "The New England Sources of 'My Kinsman, Major Molineux,'" in *American Literature*, Vol. 54, No. 4, December 1982, pp. 545–59.

Hawthorne, Nathaniel, "My Kinsman, Major Molineux," in *The Portable Hawthorne,*, edited by William C. Spengemann, Penguin Books, 2005, pp. 9–29; originally published in 1832.

Herndon, Jerry A., "Hawthorne's Dream Imagery," in *American Literature*, Vol. 46, No. 4, January 1975, pp. 538–45.

Pearce, Colin D., "Hawthorne's 'My Kinsman, Major Molineux,'" in *Explicator*, Vol. 60, No. 1, Fall 2001, p. 19.

Wallins, Roger P., "Robin and the Narrator in 'My Kinsman, Major Molineux,'" in *Studies in Short Fiction*, Vol. 12, 1975, pp. 173–79.

# On the Road

**JACK KEROUAC**

**1957**

*On the Road* by Jack Kerouac is an autobiographical novel that has come to symbolize the American youth subculture of the 1950s. The book chronicles the cross-country travels of Sal Paradise, the book's narrator, and his wild friend Dean Moriarty over a period of three years. The two hitchhike, party, steal, love, and absorb all the wonders of America and its citizens. Although the novel is in some ways a travelogue of the many places Sal visits—and features breathtaking descriptions of the sights he sees—the story primarily focuses on the rocky relationship Sal and Dean share.

The book is heavily based on Kerouac's actual experiences with his friend Neal Cassady and their mutual friends, including author William Burroughs and poet Allen Ginsberg. All appear in *On the Road* under pseudonyms, since the publisher feared a lawsuit if the names were left unchanged. According to Kerouac expert Ann Charters in her introduction to the Penguin Classics edition of the book, Kerouac had always hoped to publish a collection of his autobiographical works with the original names intact, but he was not able to accomplish this before his sudden, alcohol-related death in 1969.

A legend has arisen around the original manuscript for *On the Road* that is almost as fascinating as the novel itself. According to the legend, to keep his thoughts flowing freely as he wrote, Kerouac taped together twelve-foot-long

# BIOGRAPHY

## JACK KEROUAC

Jack Kerouac was born Jean-Louis Lebris de Kerouac on March 12, 1922, in Lowell, Massachusetts. His parents were originally French Canadian, and Jack did not speak English until he was six years old. His prowess on the football field during high school earned him a college scholarship to Columbia University, where he would later meet many other Beat Generation writers. He left Columbia before graduating, however, to become a merchant seaman.

He wrote a novel about his seafaring adventures titled *The Sea is My Brother* in 1943, but his first published novel was *The Town and the City* (1950). The book was heavily autobiographical, and during its submission and publication Kerouac was busy living out the scenes that would fill his next book, the classic *On the Road* (1957), with his friend Neal Cassady. Kerouac followed this with several more autobiographical novels, including *The Dharma Bums* (1958) and *Lonesome Traveler*. He also published several volumes of poetry.

Kerouac suffered from severe alcoholism throughout his adult life, which led to cirrhosis of the liver and internal bleeding that took his life on October 21, 1969, in St. Petersburg, Florida. He was forty-seven.

sheets of paper to make a continuous roll that would not require stopping to change pages. Kerouac typed feverishly for three weeks, fed by stimulants and coffee, to produce a 120-foot-long single-spaced manuscript of his novel. This is essentially true, and the manuscript still exists; however, Kerouac produced this "spontaneous" manuscript while working from earlier drafts of the novel, and he was well-known for rewriting passages over and over again—a stark contrast to his cultivated image as an artist who operates from the stream of his consciousness.

*On the Road* is the defining novel of the Beat Generation, a subculture symbolized by a group of artists who rejected the rigid societal norms that had developed after World War II. Indeed, the novel caused some controversy upon its release due to its frank depiction of drug use and indecency among young adults. Such controversy only served to heighten the book's appeal to young adults looking for something different from the traditions of their parents. Charters quotes William Burroughs in the introduction to the Penguin edition:

> After 1957 *On the Road* sold a trillion levis and a million espresso coffee machines, and also sent countless kids on the road.... The Beat literary movement came at exactly the right time and said something that millions of people of all nationalities all over the world were waiting to hear.

*On the Road* has remained a favorite for young readers ever since, and has become accepted as an important literary work. As Ann Charters writes in her introduction:

> *On the Road* can be read as an American classic along with Mark Twain's *Huckleberry Finn* and F. Scott Fitzgerald's *The Great Gatsby* as a novel that explores the theme of personal freedom and challenges the promise of the "American Dream."

## PLOT SUMMARY

### Part 1
### Chapters 1–8

The novel begins with a description of Sal's first encounter with Dean Moriarty in 1947. As Sal puts it, "With the coming of Dean Moriarty began the part of my life you could call my life on the road." Dean has traveled from out west to New York with his new wife, Marylou. They move into an apartment in Hoboken, and Dean takes a job parking cars. Soon after, however, they have a fight and Marylou returns home to Denver; Sal agrees to let Dean stay with him in his aunt's New Jersey home for a time. Dean meets one of Sal's friends, Carlo Marx, and they bond immediately. When spring comes, Dean decides to return to Denver, and Sal makes plans to follow him west soon after.

In July, after Sal finishes the first half of a novel he is writing, he leaves New Jersey with fifty dollars and a plan to hitchhike all the way to

*Jack Kerouac* Hulton Archive/Getty Images

San Francisco. He at first plans to follow Route 6 across the entire country but soon realizes this is impractical. He decides to spend most of his money on a bus ticket to Chicago, and just outside Joliet, he hitches his first ride. He hitchhikes across Illinois and Iowa, eating only apple pie and ice cream every time he stops. He meets up with another hitchhiker named Eddie, and the two travel together all the way to Shelton, Nebraska. After Sal buys Eddie a bus ticket for part of the trip and loans him a wool shirt when he is cold, Eddie selfishly takes the only available seat when an old man stops to offer a ride.

Soon after, Sal is picked up by two Minnesotan farm boys driving a truck with a bed filled with hitchhikers. Some of the passengers are young men on their first journey across the country, while others are seasoned hobos with names like Montana Slim and Mississippi Gene. Sal rides to Cheyenne, where he gets off with Montana Slim and the two attempt to woo a pair of local girls. Sal tries to convince one of the girls to make the bus trip with him to Colorado, but she has dreams

of going to New York. Sal tries—unsuccessfully—to convince her that there is nothing worthwhile in New York. He decides to hitchhike the rest of the way to Denver.

Once he arrives in Denver, Sal stays with old friends and anxiously looks forward to reuniting with Dean. Their mutual friend Carlo Marx tells Sal that Dean has been dividing his time between two women: Marylou, his wife, and a new girl named Camille. Carlo also reveals that he and Dean have been taking Benzedrine, a popular amphetamine drug used in inhalers and available in most drug stores at the time. Carlo takes Sal to see Dean, who promises to find Sal a girl and a job.

Eddie, Sal's former hitchhiking partner, meets up with Sal in Denver and the two get jobs working in the market district. Instead of showing up for his first day of work, however, Sal decides to continue living off the charity of his network of friends. He spends his evenings with Carlo and Dean, who has decided to divorce Marylou, marry Camille, and move to San Francisco.

## Chapters 9–14

Sal embarks on a trip to Central City, a former mining town turned tourist destination, with a group of friends that does not include Carlo or Dean. When he returns to Denver, he discovers that Carlo and Dean had also been in Central City, though he did not see them. Carlo tells him that Dean stole a car there and drove it through the mountains back to Denver at ninety miles an hour. Sal is suddenly anxious to continue journeying west to San Francisco, where another friend—Remi Boncoeur—has suggested they both get jobs aboard a merchant ship and sail the world. However, he stays in Denver long enough to spend an evening with a girl Dean has arranged to meet him. As he leaves Denver, he realizes that he "hadn't talked to Dean for more than five minutes in the whole time."

Sal arrives in San Francisco and meets up with Remi, of whom he writes: "When I found him in Mill City that morning he had fallen on the beat and evil days that come to young guys in their middle twenties." Remi works as a security guard watching over sailors' barracks and lives with his girlfriend Lee Ann, whom he describes as "a fetching hunk, a honey-colored creature, but there was hate in her eyes for both of us."

Remi helps Sal get a job as a security guard at the barracks. Sal does not feel comfortable keeping the peace with drunken sailors; he would rather "sneak out into the night and disappear somewhere, and go and find out what everybody was doing all over the country." One night, when a group of sailors gets overly rowdy, Sal ends up joining them and getting drunk; he discovers in the morning that he has put the American flag upside-down on the flagpole. Remi spends much of his guard duty time looking for things to steal from the barracks.

As the weeks wear on, Remi and Lee Ann begin to argue more and more, with Sal often caught in the middle. His friendship with Remi becomes strained, and Sal decides to leave San Francisco. As he makes his way south to Los Angeles, he meets a Hispanic girl named Terry who has just left her young son and abusive husband to stay with her sister in L.A.

After spending a brief time with Terry in what Sal calls "the loneliest and most brutal of American cities," the two decide to travel back to New York and start a new life together. Without money, though, they soon decide instead to hitchhike back to Terry's hometown of Sabinal, near Fresno, and stay with her brother.

Sal eventually finds work as a cotton picker and lives in a tent camp with Terry and her son Johnny near the field where he works. The work is brutally hard, and Sal discovers that he cannot earn enough to feed and house his new family. He tells Terry to move back in with her parents. Terry promises to come to New York soon so they can be together, but Sal knows it will not happen.

Sal receives a money order from his aunt back home, and he uses the money to buy a bus ticket from Los Angeles to Pittsburgh, since he cannot afford the fare all the way to New York. Hitchhiking from Pennsylvania to New York, Sal meets a man he calls "the Ghost of the Susquehanna." The man, an eccentric sixty-year-old hobo, tells Sal that he is on his way to Canada, so Sal follows along. Sal later realizes the man has been leading him the wrong way, and that they are actually going west. The two part ways, and Sal gets a ride into New York.

When he returns to his aunt's house, Sal discovers that Dean has been back in New York, staying with Sal's aunt, awaiting his return. Two days before Sal got back, however, Dean headed west for San Francisco to stay with Camille.

## Part 2

Sal spends the next year finishing his novel and going to school. He begins dating a young married mother named Lucille, and he plans to marry her if she can afford to divorce her first husband. In late 1948, when Sal travels south to Virginia to spend Christmas with his relatives, Dean shows up at Sal's brother's house in Virginia. Marylou and another friend, Ed Dunkel, are traveling with him in a brand-new Hudson he bought before leaving San Francisco.

Dean tells Sal of his life with Camille and his newborn daughter in San Francisco, where he worked on the railroad until he and Ed Dunkel were laid off. He tells of their mad plan to drive across the country to pick up Sal and bring him back to San Francisco. He tells Sal how Ed married a young woman named Galatea just so she would accompany them and pay for gas on the way, and how—when Galatea ran out of money—he and Ed left her in a Tucson hotel and kept driving. After that, Dean made a detour north and met up again with his first love, Marylou, and decided they would try to work things out. From there they drove on to Virginia.

Dean becomes involved in a confusing and ambitious plan to transport some furniture from Virginia to Sal's aunt's house in New Jersey. Sal, Dean, Ed, and Marylou all make the trip in the Hudson, promising to return to Virginia in just thirty hours. When they reach New Jersey to drop off the furniture, Sal discovers that Galatea has called from New Orleans, looking for Ed. Sal tells her to wait in New Orleans, and that they will pick her up on their way back west. Ed and Marylou stay in New Jersey as Dean and Sal race back to Virginia to pick up the rest of the furniture, as well as Sal's aunt.

One night soon after, Dean asks Sal to make love to Marylou while he watches. Marylou agrees, and although Sal tries, he cannot bring himself to do it as long as Dean and Marylou are still in a relationship. He agrees to travel back west with them, hoping to become intimate with Marylou after Dean returns to Camille in San Francisco. Before the group heads west, however, they head to the South—"the washed-out bottom of America"—to pick up Ed's wife Galatea from the home of a mutual friend in New Orleans named Old Bull Lee.

When they arrive, Ed repairs his relationship with Galatea, and the two decide to find an apartment and stay in New Orleans. Sal, Dean, and Marylou continue west, stealing food from gas station markets on the way and picking up hitchhikers to help cover the cost of gas.

When they arrive in San Francisco, Dean returns to Camille, but Marylou is no longer interested in being with Sal. She abandons him in a rundown hotel. Dean finds him days later, starving, and takes him back to Camille's home. After a few days, Sal is ready to return to New York. He and Dean have one last wild night visiting jazz clubs with Marylou, who once again turns up at Dean's call. In the end, though, Sal is happy to be returning home, noting, "We were all thinking we'd never see one another again and we didn't care."

## Part 3

In the spring, Sal travels to Denver with an eye toward moving there permanently. None of his friends are there anymore. He gets a job working at the same fruit market where he had almost worked with Eddie two years before. He longs to see Dean and Marylou again; when a wealthy acquaintance gives him one hundred dollars, he decides to travel to San Francisco and find Dean.

He discovers that Dean is living with Camille and their daughter, and that Camille is expecting a second child. Dean tells Sal how he had gone crazy with jealousy over Marylou and her many lovers, barging into her place with a gun and declaring that either he or she would have to die. After the dust settled, Marylou married a used-car dealer. Before that, however, Dean had tried to hit her across the head one night and ended up breaking his own thumb instead. The wound did not heal properly, and now he cannot work. He takes care of his daughter while Camille supports the family.

The morning after Sal arrives, Camille kicks them both out of the house, knowing the trouble they are likely to cause. Sal convinces Dean to come back to New York with him, and he plans a trip to Italy for both of them after he gets paid for his novel. Dean agrees to go. Before they leave, however, a group of their old friends gather together and criticize Dean for his irresponsible behavior, particularly with regard to Camille and his daughter. Sal tries to defend him, but they insist that Dean is "the worst scoundrel that ever lived." Dean simply ignores them, and he and Sal make their way east.

The two take a travel-bureau car to Denver. There, they take responsibility for delivering a limousine to Chicago. Dean drives the car ragged, getting into two accidents on the way. They deliver the car to the owner's mechanic, who does not even recognize it, and hurry off on a bus to Detroit.

They manage to secure another travel-bureau ride to New York, and soon arrive at Sal's aunt's new home in Long Island. His aunt gives permission for Dean to stay a few nights, but that is all. Sal introduces Dean to a girl named Inez at a party, and within days Dean decides to divorce Camille so he can marry Inez. Soon after, Inez has a baby. Sal states simply, "So we didn't go to Italy."

## Part 4

Sal receives money for his book, and when spring comes, he once again feels the urge to travel. He leaves behind Dean, who now lives with Inez and works as a parking attendant in New York. On the way to Denver, Sal meets an ex-convict named Henry. The two spend time together in Denver, visiting bars and socializing with some of Sal's old friends. As Sal prepares to continue his planned journey, heading south into Mexico, he receives word that Dean is on his way to join him.

Dean arrives in a 1937 Ford automobile he just bought, telling Sal that the official purpose of his trip is to obtain a divorce from Camille in Mexico, which is faster and less expensive than getting one in the United States. The two set off for Mexico with another friend, Stan Shepard, in tow. They spend a wild night at a whorehouse in Gregoria, and then drive on to Mexico City. There Sal contracts dysentery and spends several days falling into and out of consciousness. In the middle of Sal's illness, Dean leaves him and Stan to return to New York. As Sal reflects:

> When I got better I realized what a rat he was, but then I had to understand the impossible complexity of his life, how he had to leave me there, sick, to get on with his wives and woes.

## Part 5

After Dean returns to New York, he marries Inez in Newark and immediately leaves to go see his second wife Camille in San Francisco. Sal gets back to New York and meets Laura, the love of his life. When he writes to Dean to tell him that he and Laura are thinking of moving to San Francisco soon, Dean appears on his

> I WASN'T SCARED; I WAS JUST SOMEBODY ELSE, SOME STRANGER, AND MY WHOLE LIFE WAS A HAUNTED LIFE, THE LIFE OF A GHOST. I WAS HALFWAY ACROSS AMERICA, AT THE DIVIDING LINE BETWEEN THE EAST OF MY YOUTH AND THE WEST OF MY FUTURE, AND MAYBE THAT'S WHY IT HAPPENED RIGHT THERE AND THEN, THAT STRANGE RED AFTERNOON."

doorstep for a visit. He stays for three days. The night Dean leaves, Sal and Laura attend a Duke Ellington concert at the Metropolitan Opera with Remi Boncoeur and his girlfriend. Dean asks to ride in the car with the group, but Remi refuses. Sal cannot enjoy the concert because he is "thinking of Dean and how he got back on the train and rode over three thousand miles over that awful land and never knew why he had come anyway, except to see me." Although this is the last time Sal sees Dean, he reflects that he still thinks of Dean often.

*Neal Cassady in his first suit, New York, circa 1946* © *Allen Ginsberg/Corbis*

## THEMES

### Freedom from Social Conventions

One of the main themes of *On the Road* is freedom. At the beginning of the novel, Sal and Dean both want to live outside the formal social conventions of the time. For example, throughout much of the book, Sal avoids holding a steady job. After he is offered a job in Denver, he fails to show up for his first day of work. In San Francisco, he works as a guard for two and a half months, actively ignoring the rules he is supposed to enforce. To him, such formalized rules are a basic failing of the country's true character: "This is the story of America. Everybody's doing what they think they're supposed to do."

Sal and Dean also defy social conventions in their frequent use of recreational drugs. On several occasions, the two smoke marijuana—which Kerouac refers to as "tea"—and Sal mentions early in the book that both Dean and Carlo have started taking the stimulant Benzedrine.

Although he does not mention Dean taking Benzedrine later in the novel, Dean's hyperactive behavior, free-flowing speech style, and nervous twitches all suggest use of the drug. Sal also suggests that Old Bull Lee is a heroin addict, and his wife Jane is a steady user of Benzedrine.

The characters also show freedom from sexual inhibitions. Dean appears naked to answer his front door on occasion, and even visits an Indian ruin unclothed. He convinces Sal and Marylou to undress in the car as the three ride across Texas together. Dean and Marylou are both open with their sexuality; in one instance, Dean even asks Sal to make love to Marylou while he watches. Dean also spends much of the book romancing more than one woman at the same time. Similarly, Marylou flirts with Sal even as she and Dean plan to solidify their relationship.

### The Spirit of Exploration

One of the themes fundamental to both *On the Road* and the American dream is the spirit of exploration. Throughout the book, Sal and Dean are both drawn by a need to travel across the American landscape with only the most tenuous reasons for doing so. For them, the journey itself is a way to experience the country and its people.

The story of *On the Road* is, as its title implies, primarily a story about traveling back and forth across the country. The narrator, Sal, only briefly summarizes the life-changing events that happen between such trips. Both Sal and Dean are driven not just by a need to move across the landscape, but by a desire to see new things and meet new people, each time expanding their notions of what America means. Throughout the book, Dean often calls attention to specific people they meet and attempts to relate to their life experiences. Passing by a black man in a mule wagon in Virginia, Dean commands his passengers: "Yes! Dig him! Now consider his soul—stop awhile and consider."

The spirit of exploration as shown in the novel is also an expression of absolute freedom and liberty, traits often associated with American ideals. Both Sal and Dean take advantage of their freedom to move back and forth from coast to coast without limits. This free-wheeling spirit is not painted in a purely positive light, however; this is especially clear when Dean is confronted by several friends before he leaves San Francisco to go to New York with Sal. These friends are all upset by Dean's inability to take responsibility for his wife and child. Galatea Dunkel sums up their feelings, saying "Camille has to stay home and mind the baby now you're gone—how can she keep her job?—and she never wants to see you again and I don't blame her."

The desire to explore is depicted as something that can only be done by those outside the mainstream of society. As Sal and Dean's friends—and ultimately Sal as well—become tied to a specific location by commitments and responsibilities, the spirit of exploration no longer drives their actions. Dean, however, remains the embodiment of the traveler to the end—"a sideburned hero of the snowy West."

## HISTORICAL OVERVIEW

### The Beat Generation

The term "Beat Generation" refers not to an entire generation of Americans, but to a group of artists who led a counterculture movement throughout the 1950s. The term is credited to Jack Kerouac, who uses the term "beat" to suggest a number of things about the culture: that they are marginalized and disaffected, as in "beaten down," but also keenly aware of a developing artistic subculture heavily influenced by bebop music and its unusual rhythmic beats.

Other famous members of the Beat Generation include poet Allen Ginsberg, Neal Cassady (who served as the model for the character Dean Moriarty in *On the Road*), and William Burroughs. The core figures in the Beat Generation gathered in and around Columbia University throughout the late 1940s, where they worked to develop a new style of literature that emphasized spontaneous, open form the way jazz had done in music. Much like the characters in *On the Road*, the real-life members of the Beat Generation were greatly influenced by life in both New York and San Francisco, with many living in New York first and later moving west.

The Beat Generation became tightly associated with the subculture in which they lived, so much so that the term suggests a very specific lifestyle. Members of the Beat Generation were considered anti-authority in several respects; for example, the 1956 publication of Allen Ginsberg's poem "Howl" led to an obscenity trial for its publisher. Beat Generation artists were also vocal advocates of illicit drug use and open sexuality. Kerouac wrote openly of Benzedrine and marijuana use—though Benzedrine was legal at the time—and Burroughs later helped Timothy Leary in his campaign to expose mainstream American culture to "mind-expanding" drugs such as LSD. For many Beat artists, drug use was seen as a way to enhance creativity.

The subculture captured by the Beat Generation was later depicted by the stereotype "Beatnik," in which members were stereotyped as wearing berets and black clothing, and to speak in the same unusual slang captured by Kerouac in *On the Road*.

The influence the Beat Generation had on American culture was impressive. Although less a movement than simply a small group of artists with similar ideas, the Beat artists—many of whom would later deny they were members of any sort of "Beat Generation" at all—opened up new avenues of expression for many artists who emerged soon after. In addition to influencing later novelists and poets, the Beat artists had a direct influence on musicians such as Bob Dylan, Jim Morrison, Tom Waits, and even

The Beatles. Many Beat artists later collaborated with these musicians.

In the 1960s, the Beat Generation transformed into the somewhat more mainstream Hippie Generation, with many of its core ideals—such as free expression, open sexuality, and experimental drug use—remaining intact and combining with notions such as pacifism and equal rights. Several key figures from the Beat Generation participated actively in this new subculture. The members of the Beat Generation have continued to influence American culture as subsequent generations have discovered their most important literary works, and many of these works can be found in college literature curricula across the country.

### The Drug Culture of the 1940s and 1950s

A key component of the Beat Generation and the subculture it epitomized was recreational drug use. Although drugs had been used for nonmedical reasons for centuries, the popularity of two drugs in particular led to a substantial population of recreational drug users during the middle of the twentieth century.

Marijuana, referred to as "tea" in *On the Road*, had been legally available as a pain reliever in the United States during the nineteenth century under the name cannabis (taken from the plant it is made from). During the 1930s, marijuana use became the basis for an insanity defense in several high-profile murder cases; defendants claimed that using marijuana had caused them to have psychotic episodes, and argued that they should not be held responsible for their actions. This led to the prohibition of marijuana in 1937 through the Marihuana Tax Act. At the same time, the drug was becoming increasingly popular among jazz musicians and fans. Though the drug had become illegal, the mainstream acceptance of jazz music led to further exposure of the drug throughout American society.

Benzedrine was an amphetamine-based medicine used to treat hay fever and similar ailments throughout the 1920s and 1930s. Benzedrine was usually available in an inhaler, which contained a strip of paper soaked with the medicine inside. Like other amphetamines, Benzedrine was a stimulant that caused feelings of euphoria when ingested. Those who took Benzedrine as a recreational drug usually opened up the inhaler and swallowed the medicine-soaked paper strip for maximum effect. Kerouac describes recreational Benzedrine use in *On the Road*, and he is rumored to have been taking the drug when he wrote the novel. The drug's popularity was helped by its legal and widespread availability at drug stores across the country.

In the 1950s, concerns over the hazards of amphetamine addiction led to the removal of Benzedrine inhalers from the market. Similar amphetamine-based drugs are still available by prescription, though Benzedrine itself is no longer manufactured.

### CRITICAL OVERVIEW

Kerouac finished *On the Road* in 1951, but the novel was not published until six years later. Although he had already published one novel—*The Town and the City* (1950)—few publishers were interested in a book that, aside from its free-wheeling moral attitude, was so autobiographical that it held the real possibility of a libel lawsuit filed by one of the people depicted in its pages. After Kerouac changed the names, locations, and minor details of some of the characters, Viking agreed to publish the book.

The novel received some positive early reviews, including an unsigned review in *Time*. "With his barbaric yawp of a book," the critic writes, "Kerouac commands attention as a kind of literary James Dean." He asserts that the book is important because it creates "a rationale for the fevered young who twitch around the nation's jukeboxes and brawl pointlessly in the midnight streets." The most glowing review came from critic Gilbert Millstein at the *New York Times*, who calls the book's publication "a historic occasion so far as the exposure of an authentic work of art is of any great moment in an age in which the attention is fragmented and the sensibilities are blunted by the superlatives of fashion." Millstein refers to Kerouac's novel as "an authentic work of art" and "most beautifully executed," and claims that the author has become the spokesperson for his generation.

Most reviewers, however, coupled praise with criticism. As David Dempsey writes in his review for the *New York Times*, the author "has written an enormously readable and entertaining book but one reads it in the same mood that he might visit a sideshow—the freaks are fascinating although they are hardly part of our lives." B. R.

# MEDIA ADAPTATIONS

*On the Road* was released as an unabridged audiobook in 2004. It is narrated by Matt Dillon and is available on compact disc from Caedmon.

Redman, writing for the *Chicago Sunday Tribune*, states, "Kerouac possesses a powerful talent, but it is as yet completely uncontrolled." At his worst, the critic notes, the author "merely slobbers words." In a review for the *Atlantic*, Phoebe Adams writes, "Everything Mr. Kerouac has to tell about Dean has been told in the first third of the book, and what comes later is a series of variations on the same theme." Still, Adams notes that the book "contains a great deal of excellent writing."

Carlos Baker, writing for the *Saturday Review*, is less kind in his assessment of the novel, calling Kerouac's vision of America "sad and blank." Baker states, "*On the Road* contains evidence that he can write when he chooses. But this dizzy travelogue gives him little chance but to gobble a few verbal goofballs and thumb a ride to the next town."

While never a breakout success, the book's steady and continuing popularity has earned it a reputation as a life-changing piece of literature for many of its readers. The book was also largely responsible for the widespread adoption of a "Beat Generation" lifestyle among young adults across the country.

## CRITICISM

### Mark Richardson

*In the following excerpt, Richardson argues that* On the Road *presents the idealized America of Kerouac's American Dream.*

*On the Road* involves a familiar American idea about belief: the act of believing in Dean actually brings Dean about—makes him, renews him, creates him. We do not believe in Dean; we believe Dean in, to adapt a phrase Robert Frost once used about God and the future. Dean Moriarty cannot exist apart from our fictions of him, which is why even Neal Cassady, upon whom the character is based, is not essentially real. He had a legendary kind of existence as the "cocksman and Adonis of Denver," as Allen Ginsberg put it. Kerouac, Ginsberg, and Cassady himself were always inventing and reinventing "Neal Cassady," who, as Ginsberg writes in the dedication to *Howl and Other Poems*, had published several books in heaven. Neal is simply too fine a creation for this world; his genius can never be adequately embodied. And the same goes for America, with which Dean Moriarty is mythically identified. (When Carlo Marx addresses America in the person of Dean, he only makes explicit what Kerouac always implies: "Whither goest thou, America, in thy shiny car in the night?")

*On the Road* tells a *Young Goodman Brown* sort of story. We look out on America and see double: promise and piety on the one hand, wickedness and fraud on the other. Dean Moriarty, in all his dubiety, simply is America: "tumbledown holy America," Sal equivocally says, catching the seediness and the grace. On the whole, his fidelity, his affection for Dean, makes *On the Road* an optimistic work in the tradition of Whitman. It says "yes" to America in the way Mark Twain's "road" novel, *Huckleberry Finn*, says "no"—and this despite the fact that *On the Road* invokes dystopian possibilities. Kerouac's is another in a long line of American fiction (and non-fictions) in which utopian and dystopian modes weirdly cooperate. The dubiety of *On the Road* is easy enough to see: it records a long, post-adolescent drunken odyssey that also purports to be a spiritual journey of personal and national dimensions. Those with no faith—for example, the copywriters who marketed early paperback editions of the book as a salacious lurid tale—see only the orgy and the drunkenness, only the kicks. The faithful see something else altogether: Dean Moriarty, new American Saint, as Sal Paradise puts it. Of course, nothing can fulfill the promise of Dean Moriarty. Sal's faith at times seems a deliberately naive refusal to face the truth. His gee-whiz doggedness, taken to an extreme level of

*The City Lights bookstore at the corner of Jack Kerouac Alley in San Francisco's North Beach neighborhood* © Rachel Royse/Corbis

piety, defines a childlike character, a Forrest Gump, whose vast appeal for American audiences is not hard to explain. He flatters our fidelity and optimism. In *On the Road* as in *Forrest Gump* we are invited to admire a faithful, forward-looking hero and discouraged ever from regarding his faith and goodwill as mere gullibility, which we could never respect. *On the Road* is tragically optimistic—a fine figure for the 1950s, a haunted, hopeful, doomed decade.

Kerouac's novel emerged as a new sense of American national identity was consolidating itself: both internally with respect to the possible full Americanness of Black men and women and externally with respect to its conflict with the USSR. Kerouac went west in 1947, and *On the Road* appeared in 1957: the novel imaginatively spans the first decade of the American National Security State and of the Civil Rights struggle. The Internal Security Act became law in 1950, to

be followed in 1954 by the Communist Control Act. 1954 also brought the decision in *Brown v. Board of Education*. In 1949 eleven American Communist leaders were convicted under the Smith Act of 1940. Ethel and Julius Rosenberg were executed in 1953. During the same period, many states considered, and some passed, laws requiring oaths of loyalty for state employees. The U.S. detonated the first hydrogen bomb at Eniwetok Atoll in November 1952. Between 1950 and 1953 defense spending quadrupled as the peacetime economy was partly militarized. By the end of 1950, U.S. soldiers were fighting the Chinese in Korea. In 1955 Emmett Till was murdered in Mississippi, and Rosa Parks was arrested in Montgomery, Alabama.

*On the Road* almost never refers directly to these events, but they are, in a nebulous sort of way, everywhere felt. Dean and Sal pass through Washington on the day of Truman's inauguration in 1949: "Great displays of war might," Sal says, "were lined up along Pennsylvania Avenue as we rolled by in our battered boat. There were B-29s, PT boats, artillery, all kinds of war material that looked murderous in the snowy grass." The next two paragraphs tell how the Virginia police harassed Dean just for the hell of it. Sal points the moral: "The American police are involved in psychological warfare against those Americans who don't frighten them with imposing papers and threats. It's a Victorian police force; it peers out of musty windows and wants to inquire about everything, and can make crimes if the crimes don't exist to its satisfaction." In a more paranoid vein, Old Bull Lee—the character based on William S. Burroughs—rants about predatory "bureaucracies" and what he calls "the big grab" going on "in Washington and Moscow." *On the Road* plainly belongs to the era of containment: containment of the USSR without containment of un-American elements within. All the essential Cold War questions trouble Kerouac's novel: What is America? Who are Americans? Are we the chosen or the damned? Kerouac need hardly address these questions directly, because the structure of feeling of *On the Road* is itself tempered by the Cold War, with its restless anxiety, its troubled optimism, its delirium and depression. Kerouac has Sal say, at a crucial moment late in the novel, when Sal and Dean are in Mexico:

> Strange crossroad towns on top of the world rolled by, with shawled Indians watching us from under hatbrims and rebozos... They

had come down from the black mountains and higher places to hold forth their hands for something they thought civilization could offer, and they never dreamed the sadness and the poor broken delusion of it. They didn't know that a bomb had come that could crack all our bridges and roads and reduce them to jumbles, and we would be as poor as they someday, and stretching out our hands in the same, same way. Our broken Ford, old thirties upgoing America Ford, rattled

through them and vanished in the dust. Sal's peculiar optimism—his "upgoing America"—always has a haggard air of defeat about it.

"Everything was dead," Sal tells us in the first paragraph of the novel. What follows is a story of rebirth—an Emersonian story of the agitation always to redraw the outer boundaries of the soul's horizon. To Sal, Dean appears as "a western kinsman of the sun." Sal speaks of "the coming of Dean" as if it were an advent, saying: "I could hear a new call and see a new horizon, and believe in it at my young age." Dean is a Christ-like, vernal figure, and *On the Road* is a gospel of his life and works.

But after sounding an overture to Dean, *On the Road* presents him to us in equivocal terms. His talk is a kind of hipster-intellectual-comical patois. (Here is how he asks his girlfriend to fix breakfast and clean up their apartment: "In other words we've got to get on the ball, darling, what I'm saying, otherwise it'll be fluctuating and lack true knowledge or crystallization of our plans.") His relations with women are abusive and obtuse enough to occasion wonder. We cannot discredit the judgment of Sal's aunt that Dean is a "madman." And there is no lack of suggestion that Dean is an evangelical fraud. Sal Paradise admits it at the outset: "[Dean] was simply a youth tremendously excited with life, and though he was a con-man, he was only conning because he wanted so much to live and to get involved with people who would otherwise pay no attention to him. He was conning me and I knew it (for room and board and 'how-to-write,' etc.), and he knew I knew (this has been the basis of our relationship), but I didn't care and we got along fine." This perfectly expresses the complexity of the novel: its ambivalence about Dean and its happy, good-humored candor about its own mythology.

It would be hardhearted of us to debunk Sal's faith. Such is the conciliatory position *On the Road* forces us into if we are at all susceptible.

Maybe everyone else but Sal is a Philistine, we say without being able to decide; maybe to lack faith is actually worse than to invest it in a fraud or fiction. All truly valuable things, this novel suggests, come about only through the creative and possibly deceitful agency of belief—through yea-saying, not through skepticism and denial. There are those in *On the Road* who lack faith, but they are always made to seem petty. Sal says early in the novel: "All my other friends [besides Dean] were 'intellectuals'—Chad the Nietzschean anthropologist, Carlo Marx and his nutty surrealist low voiced serious staring talk, Old Bull Lee and his critical anti-everything drawl." He adds by way of summary that these men "were in the negative, nightmare position of putting society down." All of our sympathies lie instead with Dean, whose "criminality," as Sal says, was "a wild yea-saying overburst of American joy." In this book it is un-American not to believe. And belief in Dean becomes belief in the possibility of the mythic "lost America of love" with which he is always identified.

America, Kerouac seems to say, has always been a beautiful fiction believing itself into existence as it unfolds west. Sal gets ready for his first trip west by reading books about "the pioneers." He gives himself over fully to what he calls "hearthside" ideas about America. Once on the road he subsists on apple pie and ice cream: "That's practically all I ate all the way across the country, I knew it was nutritious and it was delicious, of course." Such is the patriotism of *On the Road*, which was a pretty good advertisement for America. Kerouac's novel chooses the West, as the saying used to go, and how different a document it is in this respect from *Howl and Other Poems* (1957), with its tormented, cagey animosities.

In any case, Carlo Marx and Dean, we read in chapter one, "rushed down the street together, digging everything in the early way they had, which later became so much sadder and perceptive and blank." Kerouac is saying that to see "perceptively" is to be "sad" and "blank." He leaves us to infer that to be "digging everything," to live in faith and goodwill, is also to labor under a fortunate illusion—under the dominating power of belief; to be digging everything is somehow willingly to be subject to a con, willingly to turn away from the "whole world of torment" that "naive artists" like Kerouac can't bear to contemplate. The association of disillusion with perception, and of illusion with belief, has great consequence in a novel that in certain respects cannot imperil its belief in its most central and enabling American cultural illusions—illusions that have, it happens, chiefly to do with race. On the other side of the color line lies the world of "horrible importunity" that *On the Road* will not allow itself to register.

**Source:** Mark Richardson, "Pesant Dreams: Reading *On the Road*," in *Texas Studies in Literature and Language*, Vol. 43, No. 2, Summer 2001, pp. 218–44.

## SOURCES

Adams, Phoebe, Review of *On the Road*, in the *Atlantic*, Vol. 200, October 1957, p. 178, reprinted in *The Book Review Digest (Fifty-Third Annual Cumulation)*, edited by Mertice M. James and Dorothy Brown, The H. W. Wilson Company, 1958, p. 492.

Baker, Carlos, Review of *On the Road*, in *Saturday Review*, Vol. 40, September 7, 1957, p. 19, reprinted in *The Book Review Digest (Fifty-Third Annual Cumulation)*, edited by Mertice M. James and Dorothy Brown, The H. W. Wilson Company, 1958, p. 492.

Charters, Ann, "Introduction," in *On the Road*, Penguin Books, 2003, pp. xxvii, xxix.

Dempsey, David, "In Pursuit of 'Kicks' (Review of *On the Road*)," in the *New York Times*, September 8, 1957, p. 4.

Kerouac, Jack, *On the Road*, Viking Press, 1957; reprint, Penguin Books, 2003.

Millstein, Gilbert, "Books of the Times," in the *New York Times*, September 5, 1957, www.nytimes.com (December 26, 2006).

Redman, B. R., Review of *On the Road*, in the *Chicago Sunday Tribune*, October 6, 1957, p. 4; reprinted in *The Book Review Digest (Fifty-Third Annual Cumulation)*, edited by Mertice M. James and Dorothy Brown, The H. W. Wilson Company, 1958, p. 492.

"The Ganser Syndrome (Review of *On the Road*)," in *Time*, Vol. 70, September 16, 1957, p. 120.

# *O Pioneers!*

## WILLA CATHER

## 1913

Willa Cather's 1913 novel, *O Pioneers!*, breathes new life into the American dream narrative using the landscape of the wild Nebraska prairie and a heroic female pioneer to tell a unique American immigrant success story. The title is taken from Walt Whitman's "Pioneers! O Pioneers!", a poem that, like the book, celebrates the spirit of the American frontier. Unlike pioneer tales told from the male perspective—including Whitman's poem—*O Pioneers!* focuses on the powerful connection women have with the land and how that connection affects the settler experience.

Inspired by her own childhood spent on the prairies of Nebraska, Cather began writing her first Nebraska stories after essayist, fiction writer, and acquaintance Sara Orne Jewett advised her in a letter in 1908 to "find your own quiet center of life and write from that." Until she was nine years old, Cather lived near the town of Winchester, Virginia, in the Shenandoah Valley. Her ancestors had cultivated the lush land since the late eighteenth century, so it was a shock when her family left their prosperous farm and moved to wind-swept Red Cloud, Nebraska. According to Amy Ahearn's biography of the writer, Cather "had trouble adjusting to her new life on the prairie: the all-encompassing land surrounded her, making her feel an 'erasure of personality.'" The shock eventually wore off, though, and the immigrant community and geography of the mid-Western plains became for Cather personal touchstones and professional

# BIOGRAPHY

**WILLA CATHER**

Willa Sibert Cather was born in Back Creek Alley, Virginia, on December 7, 1873. In 1883, the Cathers left their lush Shenandoah Valley farm and moved to Catherton, Nebraska. A year later, they moved to Red Cloud, Nebraska, where young Willa tried to acclimate to the near-treeless prairie. Cather's independent spirit led her to take a "man's job" delivering mail on horseback; she also frequently dressed in men's clothing, wore her hair short, and, on occasion, went by the name "William." In 1895, Cather graduated from the University of Nebraska–Lincoln where she was a theater critic and columnist for the *Nebraska State Journal*. From 1906 to 1911, Cather worked as managing editor for *McClure's Magazine*. Encouraged by writer Sarah Orne Jewett, Cather left the magazine to pursue a career in fiction writing. Her first novel, *Alexander's Bridge*, was published in 1912, followed a year later by *O Pioneers!* (1913). The writer went on to become nationally recognized, winning a Pulitzer Prize for fiction in 1923 for her novel, *One of Ours*, and several other literary awards and honorary degrees to colleges, including the University of Nebraska, Yale University, and Columbia University. Cather died of a cerebral hemorrhage in New York City on April 24, 1947.

signatures. Ahearn writes, "It was to this land and these people that her mind returned when she began writing novels."

*O Pioneers!* is Cather's second novel, and the first of her trilogy of Nebraska novels. After *O Pioneers!* came *The Song of the Lark* (1915) and *My Antonia* (1918). Of Cather's many novels, poems, short stories, and essays, the books of the Nebraska trilogy are her most well-loved and critically acclaimed. *O Pioneers!*, published when the author was forty years old, established

Cather as a writer of national significance. According to Kathleen Norris's essay "Willa Cather," the year the book was published one critic wrote, "Here at last is an American novel, redolent of the Western prairies." In 1931, Louise Bogan says of Cather in a *New Yorker* article, the author "used her powers...in practicing fiction as one of the fine arts" and praises her for not being among those "writers of fiction who compromised with their talents and their material in order to amuse or soothe an American business culture."

Cather's allegiance to the people and the land of late nineteenth–century Nebraska make *O Pioneers!* a remarkable book. Her lyrical descriptions of the Nebraska landscape and the detailed characterizations she gives the immigrants that populate her prairie fiction could only be written by someone who had, according to Bogan, "made friends with her neighbors" and "learned all there was to know about the prairie, including how to kill rattlesnakes and how prairie dogs built their towns." This fictionalized dedication and knowledge also provide a view into a world rarely seen in American dream narratives. By teaming a feminist perspective with a disregard for traditional literary ideals— very few writers of the time would dare write fiction about ordinary working people—Cather created a new kind of American literature that continues to resonate with readers and critics to this day.

## PLOT SUMMARY

### Part 1: The Wild Land
### Chapter 1

The first chapter of the novel opens on a cold, windy day in the small town of Hanover, Nebraska, in the late nineteenth century. "Low drab buildings" are "huddled on the gray prairie, under a gray sky." Very few people inhabit the simple main street, except for a few "rough-looking countrymen in coarse overcoats" and a little Swedish boy who sits crying on the sidewalk. His clothes are worn and ill-fitting and he goes unnoticed by passersby. He is distraught because his kitten has been chased up a pole and is now too frightened to come down.

The little boy is relieved to see his sister, "a tall, strong girl," walking "rapidly and resolutely" toward him. The girl chides her brother, Emil, for

*Willa Cather* © *Peter Finger/Corbis*

bringing the kitten into town. Her attempts at trying to lure the kitten down prove unsuccessful, so she goes looking for her friend, Carl Linstrum, believing he might be of help. She finds him in the drug store, and he agrees to climb the pole with the aid of a pair of spikes and rescue the kitten. After retrieving the creature, Carl asks whether Alexandra, Emil's sister, has seen the doctor. She has come into town for the sake of her sick father, whom the doctor has agreed to see the following day. "But he says father can't get better; can't get well," Alexandra explains. Carl is sympathetic and goes to tend to his friend's team of horses in preparation for her and Emil's return home.

Alexandra goes to the general store to fetch her brother and finds him "playing with a little Bohemian girl, Marie Tovesky, who was tying her handkerchief over the kitten's head for a bonnet." The little girl is very pretty and delights everyone in the store with her city clothes and eyes that resemble "that Colorado mineral called tiger-eye."

As Alexandra prepares for the long ride home, she tells her friend, "I don't know what is to become of us, Carl, if father has to die. I

don't dare think about it. I wish we could all go with him and let the grass grow back over everything." Carl, sympathetic though quiet, places a lantern at Alexandra's feet to help light her way home.

## Chapter 2

The second chapter of part 1 begins with a description of the Divide, the plateau situated between the Little Blue and Republican Rivers, where the Bergson family lives. "On one of the ridges of that wintry waste stood the low log house in which John Bergson was dying." After eleven years, the man "had made but little impression upon the wild land he had come to tame," an idea he ponders while looking through his bedside window at his fields, stables, corral, and the grass beyond them. As he lies dying, forty-six-year-old Bergson thinks about his 640 acres and how he acquired and paid for them. Before she was twelve, he learned to trust Alexandra's "resourcefulness and good judgment" and appreciate her "strength of will." Her brothers, Lou and Oscar, were "industrious, but he could never teach them to use their heads about their work." When Alexandra returns from town, he calls her to him and explains that she is to lead the family after his death. She promises to never lose the land and calls Lou and Oscar to their father's room. Bergson tells his sons, "I want you to keep the land together and to be guided by your sister.... I want no quarrels among my children, and so long as there is one house, there must be one head."

## Chapter 3

It is six months after John Bergson's death. Oscar, Lou, Alexandra, and their youngest brother, Emil, stop by Carl Linstrum's home and ask if he would like to join them: "We're going to Crazy Ivar's to buy a hammock." They find Ivar sitting in the doorway of his clay bank dwelling reading the Norwegian Bible. Emil and Alexandra join Ivar in his cave house while Lou, Oscar, and Carl inspect the pond. Once she has selected a hammock, Alexandra asks Ivar's advice about her hogs. He tells her that "the hogs of this country are put upon" and that she needs to "give them only grain and clean feed" and provide them with a sheltered sorghum patch. When Oscar and Lou overhear this, Lou says, "He'll fill her full of notions. She'll be for having the pigs sleep with us, next." That evening,

Alexandra looks "to the sorghum patch, where she was planning to make her new pig corral."

## Chapter 4

The Bergson family had prospered the first three years, but now hard times have "brought every one on the Divide to the brink of despair." Indebted farmers have to give up their land and foreclosures demoralize the county. Carl tells Alexandra that his family is selling their place, auctioning their stock, and moving back to St. Louis:

> You've stood by us through so much and helped father out so many times, and now it seems as if we were running off and leaving you to face the worst of it. But it isn't as if we could really ever be of any help to you. We are only one more drag, one more thing you look out for and feel responsible for.

Alexandra understands that the Linstrums must leave, but she is saddened to lose her only friend. She says, "I can't help feeling scared when I think how I will miss you—more than you will ever know. . . . We've never either of us had any other close friend." Carl promises to write and work for himself as much as for her. "I want to do something you'll like and be proud of. I'm a fool here, but I know I can do something!"

That night, Alexandra tells Oscar and Lou about the Linstrums' plan to leave. At this, Lou replies, "You see, Alexandra, everybody who can crawl out is going away. There's no use of us trying to stick it out, just to be stubborn. There's something in knowing when to quit." This sets off an argument between the siblings. The boys think they should trade their land for a place near the river. Alexandra argues that the people who are running off are bad farmers: "They couldn't get ahead even in good years, and they all got into debt while father was getting out." She reminds her brothers that her father was set on keeping their land, that the family had struggled through harder times than this. Mrs. Bergson, depressed by this talk, cries and says she will never move. After thinking a while, Alexandra decides to investigate the river farms and see if the settlers there are really doing any better than the Divide settlers.

## Chapter 5

The final chapter of part 1 begins with a description of Alexandra and Emil's trip to the river farms. After driving up and down the valley for five days, Alexandra decides the family is better off where they are. She tells Emil on their way back home, "Down here they have a little certainty, but up with us there is a big chance . . . I want to hold on harder than ever, and when you're a man you'll thank me."

The evening of their return, Alexandra holds a family meeting and reports what she found beyond the valley. She explains to the boys her plan to "raise every dollar we can, and buy every acre we can." This includes selling off their cattle and mortgaging the homestead, an idea that upsets Oscar and Lou, who do not share Alexandra's vision of the future. After giving her brothers some time to think, Oscar, as much as he dreads signing "his name to them pieces of paper," declares, "We're in so deep now, we might as well go deeper." He is scared of the uncertainty, but knows that Alexandra is only looking for an easier way for them to get ahead.

## Part 2: Neighboring Fields
## Chapter 1

The first chapter of part 2 finds the Divide "thickly populated" sixteen years after John Bergson's death. Mrs. Bergson now lies buried beside him, the fields above them now a "vast checker-board, marked off in squares of wheat and corn; light and dark, dark and light." Emil Bergson sharpens his scythe "at the gate of the Norwegian graveyard" where his parents lie. Home from college, Emil is now a tall and handsome twenty-one-year-old captain of the track team, interstate record-holder in the high jump, and university band cornet player. Marie Shabata, previously Marie Tovesky, stops by to offer Emil a ride home.

A description of Alexandra's house finishes the chapter. "There were so many sheds and outbuildings grouped about it that the place looked not unlike a tiny village." Her big white house on a hill was marked by a "most unusual trimness and care for detail." The three young Swedish girls Alexandra keeps to cook and clean enjoy a pleasant kitchen, and guests are surrounded by "the old homely furniture that the Bergsons used in their first log house," family portraits, and a "few things her mother brought from Sweden" in the sitting room.

## Chapter 2

Emil finds Alexandra being waited on by her three young Swedish housegirls while lunching with "her men." In attendance is Ivar, a member of Alexandra's household ever since he "lost his land through mismanagement a dozen years ago." Though fuller, Alexandra is much the same. She discusses farm business with her men, especially the silo she had put up months before. One of the men mentions that Alexandra's brother Lou had said "he wouldn't have no silo on his place if you'd give it to him." Alexandra replies, "Lou and I have different notions about feeding stock, and that's a good thing. It's bad if all the members of a family think alike. They never get anywhere." Alexandra, after noticing Ivar's silence over lunch, asks him into the sitting room so that they might talk. He expresses his fear of being sent away to an asylum because he has been "touched by God." He wails, "They say that you cannot prevent it if the folk complain of me, if your brothers complain to the authorities. They say that your brothers are afraid—God forbid!—that I may do you some injury when my spells are on me." Alexandra consoles the old man, saying,

> Ivar, I wonder at you, that you should come bothering me with such nonsense. I am still running my own house, and other people have nothing to do with either you or me. So long as I am suited with you, there is nothing to be said.

## Chapter 3

Alexandra's family comes to dinner. The dining room is set for company, with "colored glass and useless pieces of china" because "her guests liked to see about them these reassuring emblems of prosperity." The party includes Alexandra, Lou, his wife Annie, their three daughters, and Oscar and his four sons. Lou tells Alexandra that he spoke to the superintendent of the asylum about Ivar's symptoms. "He says he's likely to set fire to the bar any night, or to take after you and the girls with an axe." When he tells Alexandra that it is just a matter of time before the neighbors have Ivar "taken up by force" she responds, "I'll have myself appointed Ivar's guardian and take the case to court, that's all. I am perfectly satisfied with him."

Carl Linstrum arrives in a buggy and he and Alexandra share an excited reunion. He asks if he might stay a few days as he is on his way to the coast. He explains that he is a fortune hunter on his way to the goldfields of Alaska and expresses wonder at Alexandra's place. "I would have never believed it could be done. I'm disappointed in my own eye, in my imagination." Oscar and Lou seem apprehensive in Carl's company and

press their old neighbor about his business up north. Out of Carl's earshot, Lou asks Alexandra, "What do you suppose he's come for?" He does not think Carl has made much of himself and sees his traveling as "wandering." Oscar says, "He never was much account."

## Chapter 4

Carl asks Alexandra how she and her neighbors became so successful. Alexandra replies, "We hadn't any of us much to do with it, Carl. The land did it. It had its little joke. It pretended to be poor because nobody knew how to work it right; and then, all at once, it worked itself." The two old friends talk about how they miss the old, wild country and the people who are gone. Alexandra tells Carl about Marie Tovesky, how she married Frank Shabata and moved into the Linstrum's old place. "Your farm took her fancy, and I was glad to have her so near me. I've never been sorry, either."

## Chapter 5

Carl wakes early and walks to where "the Bergson pasture joined the one that had belonged to his father." This was where he and Alexandra used to "do their milking together, he on his side of the fence, she on hers." After a while, he comes upon Emil and Marie duck hunting. Carl does not make his presence known and he watches as Marie is initially thrilled by Emil's successful shot, then tearful when she collects the dead bird. Even though she was the one that invited Emil hunting, she is distressed by the act itself. "I hate to see them when they are first shot. They were having such a good time, and we've spoiled it all for them." Emil tries not to be cross with her, and Carl notices that, "as he looked down into her tearful eyes, there was a curious, sharp young bitterness in his own."

## Chapter 6

Alexandra and Carl visit Marie. The three sit under a white mulberry tree and talk, giving Carl a chance to watch the two women together. As they leave, Carl and Alexandra run into Frank Shabata. He barely acknowledges them and begins yelling at his wife about the hogs he found in his wheat. The guests take their leave, and Marie is left to soothe her furious husband. "She was perfectly aware that the neighbors had a good deal to put up with, and that they bore with Frank for her sake."

## Chapter 7

This chapter describes how Marie and Frank Shabata came to be married. Frank, as a young man, is described as a fancy-dressing, cane-carrying dandy with an eye for Marie Tovesky. When Marie told her father she was to marry Frank, "Albert Tovesky took his daughter, pale and tearful, down the river to the convent." After Marie turned eighteen, she ran away with Frank. Her father forgave her and bought she and Frank the Linstrum farm. "Since then her story had been a part of the history of the Divide."

## Chapter 8

Marie sees Emil mowing on her way to pick cherries. Their conversation turns to Carl Linstrum and Marie says she has always wondered if Alexandra was a little in love with him. Emil is shocked and says, "Alexandra's never been in love, you crazy! She wouldn't know how to go about it. The idea!" He mentions that he would like to talk "to Carl about New York and what a fellow can do there." This sets off an argument between them that ends with Marie saying, "Then all our good times are over." Emil replies, "Yes; over. I never expect to have any more."

## Chapter 9

It is a month after Carl Linstrum's arrival. He and Emil travel to the French country to attend a Catholic fair. Amédée, Emil's best friend, teases Emil for not having a girl. He loves being married and wants his friend to know the same joy. "Are you stuck up, Emil, or is anything the matter with you? I never did know a boy twenty-two years old before that didn't have no girl." Emil thinks it "strange that now he should have to hide the thing that Amédée was so proud of, that the feeling which gave one of them such happiness should bring the other such despair."

## Chapter 10

Lou and Oscar pay Alexandra a visit. They have come to find out when Carl will be leaving. They announce that people in town have begun to talk and accuse her of making their family look ridiculous. When Alexandra suggests she may, in fact, want to marry her old friend, Lou says, "Can't you see he's just a tramp and he's after your money?" This sets off an argument over Alexandra's property—the real source of the boys' concern. They feel her land belongs to the family, but she tells them that if she wants to

marry Carl and leave her property to him, she will. Alexandra tells them, "I think I would rather not have lived to find out what I have to-day."

## Chapter 11

Emil tells Alexandra that he wants to put off law school for another year. He plans "to go down to the City of Mexico to join one of the University fellows who's at the head of an electrical plant" and see about a job instead. Alexandra tells Emil about her fight with Lou and Oscar and how she might want to marry Carl. Emil tells his sister that she should do as she wishes, that he will always support her.

## Chapter 12

Carl, pale and tired-looking, tells Alexandra that, after seeing Lou and Oscar, he has decided to go away. "What a hopeless position you are in, Alexandra! It is your fate to be always surrounded by little men." He counts himself among them because he is "too little to face the criticism of even such men as Lou and Oscar." Alexandra tries to talk Carl into staying, but he feels he needs to have something to show for himself to be worthy. She says, "All at once, in a single day, I lose everything; and I do not know why."

## Part 3: Winter Memories
## Chapter 1

In the first chapter of part 3, winter has settled over the Divide. Emil sends Alexandra weekly letters, but Lou and Oscar have stayed away since Carl took his leave. Old Mrs. Lee comes for her yearly stay with Alexandra. Marie invites the two women to visit when Frank goes into town for the day. Alexandra brings Marie a bunch of Emil's letters to read and Marie gives her a silk necktie to send in his "Christmas box." While looking for crochet patterns for Mrs. Lee, Marie and Alexandra find Frank's old cane. The women laugh over the foolishness of the cane, then Marie turns thoughtful and says, "He ought to have a different kind of wife. . . . I could pick out exactly the right sort of woman for Frank—now." Alexandra believes that speaking so frankly about such things is a bad idea, so she distracts Marie by bringing her attention to the patterns.

## Chapter 2

An omniscient narrator describes Alexandra's one and only fancy. It persisted from girlhood to adulthood, and lately visited her when she was very tired. As a child, it came to her on Sunday mornings, as she lay in bed listening to familiar sounds:

> Sometimes, as she lay luxuriously idle, her eyes closed, she used to have an illusion of being lifted up bodily and carried lightly by some one very strong. It was a man, certainly, who carried her, but he was like no man she knew; he was much larger and stronger and swifter, and he carried her as easily as if she were a sheaf of wheat.

## Part 4: The White Mulberry Tree, Chapter 1

Alexandra escorts Emil, who returned the night before from Mexico, to the French church supper in Sainte-Agnes. As they ride along, Alexandra thinks that all her family's hard work has paid off:

> Both Emil and the country had become what she had hoped. Out of her father's children there was one who was fit to cope with the world, who had not been tied to the plow, and who had a personality apart from the soil.

During dinner, Marie only takes "her eyes from Emil to watch Frank's plate and keep it filled." After playing charades and participating in the auction, Marie retires to her booth and begins telling fortunes. After a while, Emil approaches her booth, gives her a handful of uncut turquoises, and kisses her when the lights go out. "The veil that had hung uncertainly between them for so long was dissolved."

## Chapter 2

This chapter opens at the end of the wedding supper for Signa, one of Alexandra's housekeepers, and Nelse, one of Alexandra's "men." Marie hurries home from Alexandra's, followed by Emil. He asks her why she ran away with Frank Shabata and she answers that she was in love with him. Then he asks her to go away with him. "Emil! How wickedly you talk! I am not that kind of a girl, and you know it. But what am I going to do if you keep tormenting me like this?" Emil promises to leave her alone if she says she loves him. When she admits, in her own way, that she does, he leaves her standing at her gate.

## Chapter 3

A week after the wedding, Emil is packing. Alexandra shares memories of their father, of whom Emil remembers little, and assures him that he would have been proud of their father. "Alexandra felt that he would like to know there was a man of his kin whom he could admire."

## Chapter 4

The fourth chapter of part 4 opens in the kitchen of Angélique and Amédée's house. Emil arrives and Angélique tells that Amédée is out cutting wheat, even though he is very sick. Emil rides out to the wheat field where he finds Amédée sitting atop his new header. The farmer is in obvious pain, but he insists he must keep working. Unable to convince his friend to stop, Emil rides to Sainte-Agnes, where he bids some friends goodbye. On his way home, he sees Amédée staggering out of the wheat field, supported by his two cousins. Emil helps get Amédée into bed.

## Chapter 5

Frank Shabata receives news that Amédée was to be operated on "as soon as the Hanover doctor got there to help." Before heading to Sainte-Agnes, he tells Marie the bad news. After Frank leaves, Marie calls Alexandra who was comforted by her friend's voice. The older woman tells Marie that she already knew about Amédée's appendicitis, and that Emil, who had stayed with Amédé until he was operated on, was sick himself and already in bed. In the morning, Alexandra has to tell Emil that Amédée died hours earlier.

## Chapter 6

Half of the community is dressing in white and preparing for the great confirmation service, while the other is dressing in black in preparation of Amédée's funeral. At the church, Emil notices that Frank arrives without Marie, which makes him begin to worry about her. Before he knows it, he is headed to Marie's house, where he joins her lying beneath the mulberry tree.

## Chapter 7

Frank Shabata arrives home, disagreeable and slightly drunk, to find Emil's mare in his stable. When he steps into the house and hears no sound, he becomes suspicious and fetches his "murderous 405 Winchester from the closet." At the corner of his wheat field, he hears a murmuring. He shoots at two shaded figures lying beneath the mulberry tree, only to discover that he has shot Emil and Marie.

### Chapter 8
Ivar notices that there is something wrong with Emil's mare. Scuttling across the fields to reach the nearest neighbor, Ivar mumbles, "Something is wrong with that boy. Some misfortune has come upon us." Before long, he reaches the Shabata orchard and finds the lifeless bodies of Emil and Marie.

### Part 5: Alexandra
### Chapter 1
Part 5 opens place three months later. A storm has brought rain, dark clouds, and cold winds, and Signa cannot find Alexandra. Ivar takes a wagon to the graveyard thinking he might find her there. She meets him at the graveyard gate and apologizes for worrying him. On their way back home, Alexandra tells Ivar, "I think it has done me good to get cold clear through like this, once. I don't believe I shall suffer so much any more." Once home, Alexandra feels that she is tired of life and longs to be free from her body. Before falling asleep, she experiences, again, the sensation of being lifted and carried by someone very strong.

When she wakes up, she decides to visit Frank Shabata. She blames herself for "throwing Marie and Emil together" and not seeing how they might have had feelings for one another. Her feelings for Carl begin to wane after not hearing anything from him in weeks. She begins to wonder if she might "do better to finish her life alone."

### Chapter 2
Alexandra travels to Lincoln. When she visits Frank in jail, she tells him, "I understand how you did it. I don't feel hard toward you. They were more to blame than you." Frank cries and explains how he never meant to hurt either of them. Alexandra sees that the man's personality has completely changed; he seems to her not altogether human. After they talk for a while, Alexandra promises that she will never stop trying to get him pardoned. "I'll never give the Governor any peace. I know I can get you out of this place." When she arrives back at the hotel, she receives a telegram from Carl. He writes that he arrived in Hanover the night before and will wait for her.

THE HISTORY OF EVERY COUNTRY BEGINS IN THE HEART OF A MAN OR A WOMAN."

### Chapter 3
Carl and Alexandra are spending the afternoon in the sunny fields surrounding her home. Carl never received the letter Alexandra sent that told of Emil's death. As soon as he learned about it from a month-old San Francisco newspaper, he traveled night and day to reach her. He explains that he has to return to Alaska in the spring, but he plans on staying with Alexandra through the winter. She is relieved because, as she tells Carl, he is all she has in the world. She says she would like to travel with him in the spring, but that she cannot go away for good. Carl understands and says, "You belong to the land, as you have always said. Now more than ever." They talk about getting married, and Carl kisses her for the first time.

## THEMES

### Pioneer Spirit
Walt Whitman writes in his poem "Pioneers! O Pioneers!":

> All the past we leave behind;
> We debouch upon a newer, mightier world, varied world,
> Fresh and strong the world we seize, world of labor and the march, Pioneers! O pioneers!
> . . .
> We detachments steady throwing,
> Down the edges, through the passes, up the mountains steep,
> Conquering, holding, daring, venturing, as we go, the unknown ways, Pioneers! O pioneers!

His rugged, celebratory hymn to the pioneer spirit encompasses all that Cather sought to capture in her own ode to the independent, forward-thinking immigrants who tamed the Nebraska plains, especially in the post–Civil War years. America was still trying to define itself, and the influx of immigrants attempting to cultivate the western plains contributed to the country's

*A pioneer family in front of a sod house, circa 1887* © *Corbis*

transformation. After years of labor and thrift, many of these hard-working dreamers reached their goal of wealth and success; they made the American dream come true. Romanticized in Whitman's poem, the challenging land of the prairies is so described by Cather in *O Pioneers!*:

> But the great fact was the land itself, which seemed to overwhelm the little beginnings of human society that struggled in its somber wastes. It was from facing this vast hardness that the boy's mouth had become so bitter; because he felt that men were too weak to make any mark here, that the land wanted to be let alone, to preserve its own fierce strength, its peculiar, savage kind of beauty, its uninterrupted mournfulness.

Anyone who ventured "the unknown ways" and attempted to interrupt the "mournfulness" of the land had to be prepared to fail. Many had no place else to go, and so died as they tried to carve out a life on the unforgiving plains. But while they fought to survive, they exemplified the pioneer spirit by looking forward, digging

in, and making the most of what they had. In *O Pioneers!*, Cather writes,

> Alexandra often said that if her mother were cast upon a desert island, she would thank God for her deliverance, make a garden, and find something to preserve.... She had never quite forgiven John Bergson for bringing her to the end of the earth; but, now that she was there, she wanted to be let alone to reconstruct her old life in so far as that was possible.

The settlers' desire to reconstruct the lives they had known in France, Bohemia, Sweden, and Norway is echoed throughout the novel and is seen in the food they eat, the clothes they wear, the songs they sing, and the rituals they partake in. Over time, the varied cultures become a part of the American soil that is finally, after much struggle and strife, cultivated, fertile, and abundant with life and promise.

### Women's Roles

In *O Pioneers!* Willa Cather creates an iconic American pioneer character that, until 1913, had yet to be imagined. In "Carving an Identity and Forging the Frontier: The Self-Reliant Female Hero in Willa Cather's *O Pioneers!*", Rula Quawas writes,

> Alexandra Bergson is a female hero who shifts the reader's perceptions of heroism, greatness, and nobility. She is a woman who embodies all the attributes admired in the finest of male characters in the American literary canon when faced with trials only a woman could confront. As a hero of the West, Alexandra breaks the concept of the untamed West and the woman's role in it.

Readers learn early on that John Bergson began consulting his daughter about farm issues before she was a teen:

> It was Alexandra who read the papers and followed the markets, and who learned by the mistakes of their neighbors. It was Alexandra who could always tell about what it had cost to fatten each steer, and who could guess the weight of a hog before it went on the scales closer than John Bergson himself. Lou and Oscar were industrious, but he could never teach them to use their heads about their work.

The success of the family, their ability to progress both financially and personally, depended on the success of the farm, and the success of the farm, after her father's death, depended on Alexandra. John Bergson kept the American dream of working hard, saving, and becoming wealthy alive and passed it along to Alexandra because he believed that she, too, understood what it took to hold onto their land, against all odds, and make it grow. Father and daughter may have had different ways of weighing the value of the land—he saw it as the family's future, and she loved it as she loved herself—but both cherished it equally. In a telling passage at the beginning of *O Pioneers!*, Alexandra experiences a connection with the land that gives her faith in its future:

> For the first time, perhaps, since that land emerged from the waters of geologic ages, a human face was set toward it with love and yearning. It seemed beautiful to her, rich and strong and glorious. Her eyes drank in the breadth of it, until her tears blinded her. The the Genius of the Divide, the great, free spirit which breathes across it, must have bent lower than it ever bent to a human will before. The history of every country begins in the heart of a man or a woman.

In "Harvesting Willa Cather's Literary Fields," Beth Rundstrum writes, "Cather portrays harmonious relationships between women and land." She credits social, natural, and economic factors for these harmonious relationships, but lyrical descriptions of the land belie the fact that the author, herself an independent spirit with knowledge of Nebraska's cruel beauty, senses something in the connection that supercedes any single determining factor.

## HISTORICAL OVERVIEW

### *Homesteading*

On May 20, 1862, President Abraham Lincoln signed into law the Homestead Act, a crucial piece of legislation in carving the American landscape and identity. By signing the act, Lincoln encouraged westward migration by offering parcels of 160 acres of public land to any household head over the age of twenty-one. Prospective homesteaders had to be willing to pay a small filing fee and five continuous years of residency on said land before receiving ownership of it. Immigrants, single women, former slaves, and farmers from the East with no land of their own all came forward with the requisite $18—the only money required—and a lot of hope. The parameters of the Homestead Act included a clause that stated that after six months of continuous residency, homesteaders had the option of purchasing land from the government for $1.25 per acre. This made it possible for homesteaders to add acreage to their own parcels over time, which, of course, made the offer that much more attractive. Because of the Homestead Act, eighty million acres of public land was distributed by 1900.

Most pioneers became homesteaders dreaming of a prosperous life on the Western Plains. Some settlers headed to Kansas, Nebraska, Colorado, and Wyoming with their families. Some went alone. They knew farming uncultivated land would be tough, that living in a strange land far from other people would have its drawbacks, but the prospect of owning a piece of the American landscape—their own land—convinced them that the risk was worth it. But many were not prepared for the harsh reality of the homesteader's life. The isolation, with little or no social contact normally provided by schools, churches, or general proximity, was harder to bear than most settlers anticipated.

Homesteaders also experienced the heartbreak of watching helplessly as swarms of grasshoppers devoured entire corn crops. Some lands were located in areas where rainfall was insufficient for successful farming. The soil in other regions was poor and difficult to farm. On the positive side, most settlers thought the country beautiful and worked hard to improve it. They built comfortable homes, sometimes out of sod if timber was unavailable or poor in quality, and accumulated land. Railroad access improved between 1860 and 1880, which made it possible to bring cattle to the homesteaders' farms and ranches. The Homestead Act was repealed in 1976, but provisions for homesteading in Alaska remained in effect until 1986.

## CRITICAL OVERVIEW

In her critical interview with Willa Cather published in the August 8, 1931, *New Yorker*, Louise Bogan writes, "Miss Cather was not a young writer, as such things go, when she wrote *O Pioneers!*. She was thirty-eight. But at that age she found herself so certainly that she never again has needed to fumble about." The writer's sure handling of the story of Alexandra Bergson and her life as a successful homesteader on Nebraska's challenging Divide afforded Cather both an instant and longstanding reputation as a great American novelist. In 1913, one critic writes, "Here at last is an American novel, redolent of the Western prairies." Comparatively, Rula Quawas writes in her 2005 essay, "Carving An Identity and Forging the Frontier: The Self-Reliant Female Hero in Willa Cather's *O Pioneers!*",

> Cather's novel . . . bridges the gap between gender and heroism. In this regional novel, Cather, who shows that women could do something important besides giving themselves to men, captures the essence of the heroic pioneer, the noble American spirit taming the West, in a female character.

Since gender studies came into vogue, *O Pioneers!* has been one of many American novels—and Alexandra Bergson one of many American literary characters— studied for its unique female perspective on a traditionally male-dominated topic. Beyond its reputation as a canonical work of feminist literature, the novel is also widely read as a critique of the effects of

# MEDIA ADAPTATIONS

*O Pioneers!* was adapted as a Hallmark Hall of Farm Productions film in 1992. Jessica Lange and David Strathairn play Alexandra and Carl under Glenn Jordan's direction. The film is available through Hallmark Hall of Farm Productions on DVD and VHS.

*O Pioneers!* was released in an abridged version on audiocassette by Penguin/Highbridge in 1994. It is narrated by Dana Ivey.

nineteenth-century industrialization. Beth Rudstrum wrote in the April 1995 *Geographical Review* article, "Harvesting Willa Cather's Literary Fields,"

> It is . . . useful to analyze Cather's literary imagery. In *O Pioneers* she uses a recurring association of house, home, and homestead in the prairie landscape that symbolizes women. This image reflects the social values and cultural contexts in the United States at the time the novel was written, the early 1900s, and is Cather's prognosis for change in these values and history . . . . It is not unlikely that she used houses and homes to symbolize women on the prairie landscape in order to explicate women's social milieu during the late nineteenth and early twentieth centuries.

Some take issue with Cather's veiled criticism of American industrialization. Kathleen Norris writes, "The doctrinaire socialist and Marxist critics of the 1930s came to see Cather's work (as well as that of Sherwood Anderson, Sinclair Lewis, and other writers depicting small-town America) as reactionary." Michelle Abata quotes Marxist critic Granville Hicks in his scathing 1933 review, "The Case against Willa Cather," in which he disparages Cather's "retreat to the past," derides her work's "supine romanticism," and posits that her fear of technology caused her to "recoil from our industrial civilization." This critique prompted Abate to write in her October 2006 *Hollins Critic* article,

> First uttered more than seventy years ago, Granville Hicks's disparaging remarks about

Willa Cather continue to shape—and even haunt—critical views about her. Indeed, his observation that she "retreated to the past" has become the basis by which she is often critically disparaged and even canonically dismissed to this day.

Despite the criticism, and regardless of the sort of critical lens you use to view *O Pioneers!*, the novel stands as a unique work of American literature that inspires as much attention today as its author did in her time.

## CRITICISM

### Rula Quawas

*In the following excerpt, Quawas argues that* O Pioneers! *presents a new, modern female literary hero: the independent frontier woman.*

In *O Pioneers!*, published in 1913, Cather creates a woman hero who has qualities and actions that make her break the parameters of gender roles. Alexandra, the author both tells and shows us as readers, is brave, strong, independent, and beautiful. At the age of twelve, her father turns to her for advice. She becomes the head of the family at his death because she is the most qualified. Risking the small homestead and planning crops unheard of on the Divide, she creates a successful life upon a land that other people believed fallow. Loving Carl unconditionally, she has a relationship with a man other people believed to be weak. It is my contention that Alexandra is an enduring female hero who shifts the reader's perceptions of heroism, greatness, and nobility. Not the Homeric hero of "extraordinary valor and martial achievements," Alexandra is a woman who embodies all the attributes admired in the finest of male characters in the literary canon when faced with trials only a woman could confront. Her independence, courage, loyalty, and unconventionality are heroic characteristics that make her unequivocally a hero of the American literary canon. As a female hero, she is not only believable and compelling, but she is also vitally important to feminist literature in establishing a pattern of that creature in American fiction—the woman who triumphs alone over intractable surroundings and adversity, shaping a world of order and coherence and achieving for herself identity, nobility, and even fame.

Cather's novel *O Pioneers!* bridges the gap between gender and heroism. In this regional novel, Cather, who shows that women could do something important besides giving themselves to men, captures the essence of the heroic pioneer, the noble American spirit taming the West, in a female character. A love of the land is not a gender-specific quality attributed only to men; the land, Cather states, can be loved by anyone who dares to trust in it and to create it anew. As a hero of the West, Alexandra breaks the concept of the untamed West and the woman's role in it. Traditionally, men were the ones "who forged ahead into the wilderness while the woman came up carrying tablecloths." There are stereotypes about the women who went West; most stereotypes set women in the traditional roles of nurturer or nest-builder (wife, school mistress) or temptress (whores, saloon girls). Even when women prove themselves equal to the challenge of the frontier, in fiction, they are relegated to characters of little worth:

> When female heroism is not condemned, it often is simply ignored ... An obvious example in American history is the women who homesteaded in the West. These women performed the same heroic feats as men, as well as the tasks designated to women; yet western literature generally portrays them as damsels in distress or as unwilling and inadequate companions and victims of the men who conquered the frontier.

Cather's female hero fits neither of the two molds set for women in the novels of the West. Indeed, Alexandra transcends stereotypes traditionally defining and limiting women. She resists the dictates and the limitations of the female frontier. She is proud, resolute, self-sufficient, and most important, successful. Her faith in the potential of the wilderness, which it becomes her task to tame after the death of her father, and her indefatigable patience before the demands of her dottish brothers make her a kind of Earth Mother, a spirited custodian of both the wild frontier lands and the lesser creatures who are independent upon her. Although she faces many challenges and potential scandals as a woman farmer who is both unconventional and successful, she manages to emerge from her brush with the societal and familial pressures a more graceful and dignified person in the reader's eyes. She is an intense, indomitable woman who is determined to expand her horizon and to have her own way.

*A view of the Great Plains prairie near Scotts Bluff, Nebraska, with Dome Rock and the Scotts Bluff National Monument* © *Lowell Georgia/Corbis*

She does what she believes to be right, regardless of the scandal attached to her actions. By doing so, she strips the power away from the very source of scandal. Alexandra is, unquestionably, the novel's life-affirming principle; she has an infinite capacity for living and loving.

Heroism, greatness, and nobility are not gender-defined. Heroism is a condition of character in which the individual is tested by a great physical, social, or moral challenge. For far too long, critics and readers of the American canon have read literary works against a set of value judgments which refuse to accept anything not within a set of specific (male) requirements. However, it is ludicrous to define heroism according to a list of male-specific attributes and actions, when many of the protagonists in western literature are women. So often in the American literary canon, the female character is reduced to a body because there has not been room for her to play any other role. However, when we shift our definition of a literary hero and adjust our vision of it,

we see a new hero emerge in *O Pioneers!*. With a new perception of what a hero is and what heroism entails, we can approach American canonical texts with new eyes because. "there is no ground to till except what we stand on; only by learning to apply feminist principles in particular instances does one make change occur."

With this new "change" in mind, I propose a revisionist reading of *O Pioneers!*—what Rich describes as "the act of looking back, of seeing with fresh eyes, of entering an old text from a new critical direction." I will be "going back into the text" in the sense that *O Pioneers!* (and more specifically its hero Alexandra Bergson) "is no longer an object, a thing-in-itself, but an *event*, something that *happens* to, and with the participation of, the reader.["] That is, the very act of reading can bring about new interpretations of American literary texts thought to be critiqued to the point of exhaustion. I will re-read *O Pioneers!* with a focus upon a new perception of what a hero is and what heroism entails. What we will find in *O Pioneers!* is a female hero, equally as brave and good as Huck Finn. The female heroes are in American literature; however, we have to adjust our vision to find them. We also have to remove the lens through which many readers have read heroism. For many years now, literary critics have not seen female characters as heroes because their journeys apparently lacked the components of the traditional (i.e. male) quest—no dragon, no armies, no wilderness. It should be made clear that nobility and endurance in the face of great adversity make a hero, not gender. Alexandra Bergson is a valiant hero who survives and triumphs. She fights her way against every kind of obstacle, maintains autonomous agency throughout her life, and conquers by sheer power of will and character. We admire her for her heroic self-reliance, an extraordinary independence of spirit manifested with increasing force through the novel. We admire her because she is an American hero whose future holds promise.

Interestingly, Cather gives readers a powerful hero who embodies all the finest attributes of the hero: Alexandra is lofty, beautiful, pure, and wise. This female hero possesses all these fine qualities, and yet she also is a woman of the twentieth century, brimming with vitality and strength. Like Hester Prynne and Lily Bart, Alexandra shows calm self-possession and strength despite a dismal present and an uncertain future. She is endowed with vitality and vigor and is able to endure hardship. There is a sense of pride in the young woman.

Alexandra is independent but not alienated, courageous but not contemptuous of the weak, powerful without dominating others, and rational but not unfeeling. At the end of the hero's path in *O Pioneers!*, Cather yokes Alexandra's life with Carl, who, like her, has been shaped by the timeless tidal rhythms of the land. After her trials, Alexandra finds peace and happiness with Carl. Just as she creates a fulfilling affinity with and a successful life upon a land that other people believed fallow, she unites with Carl in a union that is based on mutual support, affection, and understanding of friendship. Clearly, Alexandra does not accept loneliness as a mode of life, which Ostwalt imputes to her.

> Yet, this all-encompassing orientation to the land is not healthy or proper because Alexandra sacrifices her own identity to the goal of taming and subduing the land. This loss of self to the land is tragic because she also loses her chance at

> meaningful human relationships; she cannot live fully and humanely. . .

Remarkable about Alexandra's way of handling her new life is that she neither forfeits human relationships nor accepts loneliness as her mode of life. She nourishes the land with everything in her personality in the same way that she invests herself in her marriage to Carl. Commenting on her marriage, she says, "When friends marry, they are safe." Love for Alexandra is defined by marriage. Now with her friend, she will find peace on the land she loves. Although Alexandra will remain wedded to the land, as pinpointed by Randall, she will also become a wife whose relationship with her husband is very different from that of the ninettenth-century heroine. Alexandra's marriage is a new type of marriage, not usually seen in literature. According to Mayberry, Alexandra and Carl's is "a partnership of equals." The circle is complete for the woman hero: the land she loves and the friend she so needs are finally both hers. The joy of this moment is evident in the language Cather employs in the conclusion of the novel:

> They [Alexandra and Carl] went into the house together, leaving the Divide behind them, under the evening star. Fortunate country, that is one day to receive hearts like Alexandra's into its bosom, to give them out again in the yellow wheat, in the rustling corn, in the shining eyes of youth.

With her eyes scanning the horizon always looking into the future, Alexandra bequeaths her spirit to the country emblematized in its rustling corn and yellow wheat. She finds inner light, acknowledges her needs of the self, and experiences a spiritual rebirth. She achieves as full and healthy a womanhood as anyone can imagine.

Annette Kolodony, in "Dancing through the minefield," writes that for many years literature offered women readers "a painfully personal distress at discovering whores, bitches, muses, and heroines dead in childbirth where we had hoped to discover ourselves." However, if we shift our definition of the hero and our expectations of the heroic journey (as defined by gender), then within each of these "painfully personal distresses," there may lurk a woman hero. If we free ourselves from an immasculated (Fetterley's 1978 coinage) paradigmatic reading, we see a hero in *O Pioneers!*. As a female hero who is resilient and strong, Alexandra is equally as brave and good as any other male hero in the American literary canon. She depends more and more upon her resourcefulness and good judgment and becomes more noble and heroic. She is one example in literature that nobly confronts, challenges, and acts courageously against all the crushing odds against her. In fact, in the character of Alexandra, one is reminded of Virginia Woolf's *A Room of One's Own* in which she writes about Shakespeare's sister who will one day be the "coming angel" of a literary revelation. Although Woolf's refers to a seventeenth-century woman, she closes her famous essay with a speculation that applies to Cather's hero: "The dead poet who was Shakespeare's sister will put on the body which she has so often laid down. Drawing her life from the lives of the unknown who were her forerunners, as her brother did before her, she will be born." Woolf's prophecy comes true in *O Pioneers!*. In the character of Alexandra, a new Hamlet is born.

**Source:** Rula Quawas, "Carving an Identity and Forging the Frontier: The Self-reliant Female Hero in Willa Cather's *O Pioneers!*," in *Studia Anglica Posnaniensia*, Vol. 41, 2005, pp. 237–50.

## SOURCES

Abate, Michelle, "Willa Cather and Material Culture: Real-World Writing, Writing the Real World," in the *Hollins Critic*, Vol. 43, No. 4, October 2006, p. 16.

Ahearn, Amy, "Willa Cather: A Brief Biographical Sketch," in the *Cather Archive*, www.cather.unl.edu/life/brief_bio.html (November 1, 2006).

Bogan, Louise, "Profiles: American Classic," in the *New Yorker*, August 8, 1931; reprinted at www.cather.unl.edu/writings/bohlke/interviews/1931c.html (November 1, 2006).

Cather, Willa, *O Pioneers!*, Houghton Mifflin, 1913; reprint, Barnes and Noble Classics, 2003.

Norris, Kathleen, "Willa Cather," *PBS American Masters Series*, www.pbs.org/wnet/americanmasters/database/cather_w.html (November 1, 2006).

"Primary Documents in American History: The Homestead Act," *Library of Congress*, www.loc.gov/rr/program/bib/ourdocs/Homestead.html (November 1, 2006).

Quawas, Rula, "Carving an Identity and Forging the Frontier: The Self-Reliant Female Hero in Willa Cather's *O Pioneers!*," in *Studia Anglica Posnaniensia: International Review of English Studies, Vol. 41*, Annual 2005, pp. 237–50.

Rundstrom, Beth, "Harvesting Willa Cather's Literary Fields," in the *Geographical Review*, Vol. 85, No. 2, April 1995, pp. 217–28.

"The Homestead Act: What Was the Homestead Act?" *Homestead National Monument of America*, www.nps.gov/archive/home/homestead_act.html (November 1, 2006).

Whitman, Walt, "Pioneers! O Pioneers!", in *Leaves of Grass*, 1900, bartleby.com/142/153.html (January 11, 2007).

# *Our Town*

## THORNTON WILDER

## 1938

Thornton Wilder won his second Pulitzer Prize for the 1938 drama *Our Town*, with its understated but resonant depiction of the fundamental goal of humanity: to find love and, ultimately, a sense of belonging. In writing *Our Town*, Thornton Wilder joined other writers, such as Robert Frost, who searched for meaning in America after World War I and the Depression years. New England represented traditional American values, as well as the dreams that had built the nation, and by setting the play in New Hampshire, Wilder borrowed from a deeply rooted cultural, social, and political past. Even if readers could not identify with *Our Town*, they could believe that it existed.

Wilder's version of the American dream, as well as a parable about how to attain it, lives in *Our Town*. *Our Town* depicts ordinary lives and ordinary events, yet it leads the reader to contemplate the significance of one's own life. In Wilder's interpretation, the American dream represents that need for acceptance; in achieving the American dream, one is appreciated, valued, and respected, even loved.

By writing *Our Town* in a colloquial style, Wilder makes the story authentic. The everyday speech provides a realistic and believable frame for the everyday tone and activity of the play. *Our Town* eschews pretense for the genuine: In Wilder's world, a reader does not have to read between the lines or translate overblown speech

# BIOGRAPHY

### THORNTON WILDER

Born in Madison, Wisconsin, on April 17, 1897, Thornton Wilder was educated as a young boy in China, where his father was a U.S. consul general to Hong Kong and Shanghai. As a young man, he earned his bachelor's degree at Yale and a master's degree in French literature from Princeton.

Wilder wrote his first play, *The Russian Princess*, during high school in California in 1913, and published his first novel, *The Trumpet Shall Sound*, in 1926. His second novel, *The Bridge of San Luis Rey*, was published in 1927 and earned Wilder his first Pulitzer Prize. In 1938, the play *Our Town* garnered Wilder his second Pulitzer, while another play, *The Skin of Our Teeth* (1942), brought him a third. He served as an officer in the U.S. Army Air Force Intelligence during World War II. Wilder also won the National Book Award in 1968 for *The Eighth Day* and the Presidential Medal of Freedom in 1963. Wilder was a literary celebrity and was friendly with many famous people of his time, from Ernest Hemingway to Ethel Barrymore to Gene Tunney. Although he had many friends, he did not have any enduring romances and never married. He died of a heart attack at home in Hamden, Connecticut, in his sleep on December 7, 1975.

to engage with the text or the experiences. In addition, by focusing on the traditional values and concerns of a community, Wilder creates a story with universal appeal. The town is "our" town, belonging to all.

The play is set before the Depression, between 1899 and 1913, and reflects America's industrial progress. Industrialization marked the decay of small town life as townsfolk whose families had always settled in one place moved to the big city to seek their fortunes. References to the "first automobile," Henry Ford's Model T, as well as to various metropolitan areas such as New York City and Paris, predict a growing desire for mobility and the rural-to-urban exodus. In a way, the play demonstrates the need to appreciate permanent roots and a close-knit community, particularly in the face of certain decline and transience.

Wilder has often been taken to task for ignoring controversial aspects such as racism, suicide, and alcohol abuse in Grover's Corners. The town is a white-washed portrait of America: the fantasy America where everyone aspires to live. But despite the homogeneity of Grover's Corners, the play's characters are far from idealized. Wilder depicts citizens who have real flaws and problems, from Mrs. Gibbs, who waits for life to happen to her instead of actively pursuing what she wants, to Simon Stimson, who commits suicide by hanging himself.

## PLOT SUMMARY

### *Act 1*

Stage directions establish the sparse scene in half-light. The Stage Manager arrives, holding a script. He is an ordinary fellow, with "*hat on and pipe in mouth.*" He arranges tables and chairs on the stage. Finally, the Stage Manager addresses the audience and introduces the play. The dialogue of the play begins here, as the Stage Manager locates the story in Grover's Corners, New Hampshire, "just across the Massachusetts line," and gives the town's exact geographical location.

The Stage Manager explains that "The First Act shows a day" in Grover's Corners, or specifically, "our town." He offers the date, May 7, 1901, and informs the audience that it is "just before dawn." Then he gives the audience a "tour" of the town, beginning with Main Street and "across the [railroad] tracks" to "Polish Town." He points out the community's value of religion in noting the Catholic Church, the Congregational Church, the Presbyterian, the Methodist, the Baptist, and Unitarian. He indicates the Post Office, Town Hall, and jail, then moves on to the "row of stores" along Main Street. He names "our richest citizen," Banker Cartwright, who lives in a large house high above Grover's Corners, and the town doctor, Doc Gibbs.

*Thornton Wilder* Getty Images

Two rose-covered trellises are moved onto the stage. Before the Stage Manager continues his tour, he acknowledges the trellises, suggesting they are onstage "for those who think they have to have scenery." He gestures toward Doc Gibbs's house and describes Mrs. Gibbs's garden. Afterward, he guides the audience to Editor Webb's house and Mrs. Webb's garden, marking the fact that Mrs. Webb has sunflowers and Mrs. Gibbs does not, though their gardens are alike. He comments that the town is a "nice" one, but that "nobody very remarkable ever come out of it." He regards the town's history via the headstones and dates in the cemetery and indicates that the same families still live in the town.

The Stage Manager recounts the early morning routine of Grover's Corners: Joe Junior "getting up so as to deliver the paper," Shorty Hawkins "gettin' ready to flag the 5:45 for Boston," Doc Gibbs "comin' down Main Street" from making a house call. Mrs. Gibbs comes onstage; the stage directions show her coming "downstairs," raising a window shade, and making "a wood fire in the stove." The Stage Manager says, "Doc Gibbs died in 1930," but his

wife "died first"; this observation obviously shows his ability to straddle time and place, particularly because Mrs. Gibbs and Doc Gibbs are alive and well on stage. The Stage Manager continues his omniscient storytelling, revealing that "in our town we like to know the facts about everybody." He comments on each character, Mrs. Webb, Doc Gibbs, and Joe Crowell, as they enter the stage.

Joe and Doc Gibbs exchange morning pleasantries; Joe gives Doc his newspaper and asks politely about the Doc's recent cases. Doc asks Joe how he feels about his teacher Miss Foster's upcoming wedding. Joe shrugs indifference but does say, "if a person starts out to be a teacher, she ought to stay one." Doc also asks Joe about a previous knee injury. The Stage Manager informs the audience that Joe was destined to become a "great engineer" but died in France during World War I. Again, the Stage Manager shows his omniscience. Howie Newsome, a country character wearing overalls, enters the stage with his horse, delivering milk. He engages with Doc in friendly banter about the sick twins in Polish Town and the weather. Mrs. Gibbs wakes the children. Stage directions show Mrs. Webb setting out breakfast and Doc entering his house.

Mrs. Gibbs and Doc talk about Doc's visit to the twins and about a patient, Mrs. Wentworth, "coming at eleven" with a stomach ailment. Mrs. Gibbs chides him for working too hard and asks him to speak to their son George about helping her out around the house. Both Mrs. Gibbs and Mrs. Webb call their children. Doc yells for his boy and girl, George and Rebecca; when they do not appear, he decides to take a nap before his appointment. Mrs. Gibbs tells her children to be quiet while their father sleeps. Rebecca dislikes the dress her mother ironed for her to wear to school, complaining that she looks "like a sick turkey." She and George pick on each other.

According to the stage directions, a "*factory whistle sounds.*" The Stage Manager tells the audience the whistle belongs to a mill in town owned by the Cartwrights. After the whistle blows, the stage directions show the children, Rebecca and George Gibbs, and Emily and Wally Webb, coming downstairs. While Rebecca and George eat their breakfast indifferently, Emily and Wally devour their food. Mrs. Webb chastises them about their animalistic behavior. Emily claims to be "the brightest girl in school" for her age. Mrs. Gibbs talks to George about an allowance of twenty-five cents a week. George grumbles that twenty-five cents is not enough. Rebecca admits she loves money "most in the world." The children hurry out to school as they hear the first school bell." The pairs of children meet each other and go offstage. The mothers follow with last-minute school instructions.

The mothers greet each other, at first discussing innocuous things like the "tickling feeling" in Mrs. Webb's throat. Then, Mrs. Gibbs tells Mrs. Webb that a "secondhand-furniture [man]" came to see her and offered to pay $350 for her grandmother's highboy. She is surprised by the value of the huge piece of furniture and is not sure if she should accept the offer. Mrs. Webb thinks she should, and Mrs. Gibbs reveals her big dream, if she ever has the money: to visit Paris, France. But Doc does not seem the traveling type, she says to Mrs. Webb. He travels to Civil War battlefields, but that is the extent of his need to see the world. Mrs. Webb suggests Mrs. Gibbs drop hints to Doc that she wants to go to France.

The Stage Manager intervenes, thanks the women, and informs the audience that the story will skip forward "a few hours." The women register his comment with surprise, then proceed to follow his instruction. The Stage Manager decides to provide "a little more information about the town" and introduces Professor Willard from the State University. Professor Willard offers "scientific," geological details about Grover's Corners until the Stage Manager interrupts, asking for information on the town "history of man" instead. Professor Willard reports, "Early Amerindian stock, . . . English brachiocephalic blue-eyed stock, . . . some Slav and Mediterranean." He also notes the population, as well as the mortality and birth rates.

The Stage Manager dismisses the Professor and introduces Editor Webb to give the "political and social report." Mrs. Webb says he will be delayed; "he just cut his hand while he was eatin' an apple." Mr. Webb finally appears and talks about how the town is run, by a "Board of Selectmen." While men twenty-one and over can vote, "women vote indirect." He considers the town "lower middle class" and describes the breakdown of political and religious parties. The Stage Manager asks him to comment on society; Mr. Webb calls Grover's Corners a "very

ordinary town" where most people decide to settle down. The Stage Manager then invites the audience to ask questions. An audience member called "Woman in the Balcony" asks, "Is there much drinking in Grover's Corners?" Mr. Webb notes a moderate usage but nothing "*much*." Another audience member, "Belligerent Man at Back of Auditorium," asks something in a muffled tone. The Stage Manager interrupts and tells him to speak louder. The question is, "Is there no one in town aware of social injustice and industrial inequality?" Mr. Webb says everyone constantly gossips about "who's rich and who's poor." The Man wonders why nothing is done about the situation. Mr. Webb admits that everyone tries their best to "help those who can't help themselves" and lets the others alone. "Lady in a Box" asks Mr. Webb about culture in Grover's Corners. "There ain't much," Mr. Webb says. But the citizens do pay attention to nature.

The Stage Manager thanks Mr. Webb and moves back to the town where it is early afternoon. He describes the lazy, post-lunch activity of Main Street, then the scene changes to teasing banter between Emily and Mr. Webb. George enters, tossing a ball. He accidentally runs into Mrs. Forrest, and, in Mrs. Forrest's voice, the Stage Manager chides him for his carelessness. George is sheepish, but he ends up complimenting Emily on a speech she gave in school. He says he can see her through her open bedroom window doing homework at night and suggests they rig a homemade telegraph between their houses so they can compare homework notes. He also praises her for being a "naturally bright" girl, and Emily "figure[s] it's just the way a person's born." George mentions that he will one day inherit his uncle's farm. George leaves and greets Mrs. Webb, who asks Emily to help her string some beans. Emily tells her mother about the successful speech at school, and then asks Mrs. Webb if she is attractive. Mrs. Webb says Emily has a "nice young pretty face." Emily accuses her mother of never telling the truth, obviously worried about George's affections.

The Stage Manager tells the audience about the Cartwrights and their new construction project—a bank built from marble. The Cartwrights are also trying to create a time capsule to put in a cornerstone of the building, and the Stage Manager contemplates what might be included. He says he will include "a copy of this play... [so] the people a thousand years from now'll know a few simple facts about us."

The stage directions note the choir in the orchestra pit, which sings "Blessed Be The Tie That Binds." The Stage Manager guides the audience back to the action in the town. He says the choir music comes from the Congregational Church, and "the day is running down." The scene shifts to the choir and its drunken conductor, Simon Stimson. At the same time, George and Emily catch each other's eye through their bedroom windows and discuss homework. Stimson asks how many people can sing at an upcoming wedding. Doc Gibbs calls George and asks about his future plans. George reveals his desire to run his uncle's farm. Doc Gibbs does not believe he can handle the demands of farm work, especially because he does not even help his mother with responsibilities around the house. He makes George feel guilty, then raises George's allowance because George is growing up. Doc Gibbs begins to get annoyed because his wife is not yet home from choir practice.

Mrs. Webb, Mrs. Gibbs, and Mrs. Soames walk home from choir. Mrs. Soames chatters about Stimson's drunken, scandalous behavior. The women also talk about how the men do not like them staying out late. Doc Gibbs is irritated with Mrs. Gibbs when she arrives home, but Mrs. Gibbs tries to change his mood. She tells him about Mrs. Soames's gossip, and Doc says "some people ain't made for small town life." Mrs. Gibbs worries about her husband because he does not take enough time off. As they go inside, they comment about Mrs. Fairchild, who "locks her front door every night." Doc remarks that the town is becoming "citified."

Rebecca joins George at his window. She thinks the moon is getting closer and soon it is bound to explode. Constable Warren makes sure a few buildings on Main Street are secure for the evening and encounters Editor Webb "after putting his newspaper to bed." They see Stimson wandering down the street, drunk, and say hello to him. Mr. Webb asks Constable to keep an eye on his boy if the Constable ever notices trouble. On the way home, Mr. Webb calls out to Emily, still in her window. Rebecca and George are still talking; Rebecca mentions a letter her friend Jane Crofut received from her minister, telling George,

On the envelope it was addressed like this: It said: Jane Crofut; The Crofut Farm, Grover's Corners; Sutton County; New Hampshire; United States of America; Continent of North America; Western Hemisphere; the Earth; the Solar System; the Universe; the Mind of God.... And the postman brought it just the same.

The Stage Manager announces the end of act 1.

## Act 2

During the short break between acts, the Stage Manager pushes the ladders offstage and rearranges tables and chairs. He leaves the stage but returns to introduce the act. He explains that three years have passed and describes the ordinary changes that have taken place in Grover's Corners. He also informs the audience that act 1 was titled "The Daily Life," while act 2 is about "Love and Marriage." High School graduation has just occurred, the perfect time for most to get married. Mrs. Gibbs and Mrs. Webb enter the scene, and the Stage Manager offers an aside to the women in the audience: "both of those ladies cooked three meals a day,—one of 'em for twenty years, the other for forty—and no summer vacation. They brought up two children apiece, washed, cleaned the house,—and *never had a nervous breakdown*." They greet Howie Newsome delivering the milk and Si Crowell, now delivering the newspapers. Howie and Si are joined by Constable Warren, and all three men talk about how a local baseball player, a grown-up George Gibbs, is giving up his job to get married and settle down. When Doc Gibbs enters the scene, he and Mrs. Gibbs talk about "losing" their son and wonder if he is old enough to be married. Doc recounts memories of their wedding, then they talk about how difficult it is having a family.

George enters the scene, greets his parents, and dashes off to meet his bride, Emily. Mrs. Webb says he cannot see her the day of the wedding. George and Mr. Webb talk about how girls are on the day of their wedding and how a wedding is a tradition created by "women-folk." Mr. Webb passes on the marriage advice that he received: "start out early showing who's boss." He also advises George to "*never* let your wife know about how much money you have, never." George plans to take over his uncle's farm once he is married to Emily; Mr. Webb encourages him to look into raising chickens.

The Stage Manager interrupts the scene, deciding to provide background on George and Emily's relationship. He reverses time to senior year in high school when George was elected senior class president and Emily was elected secretary/treasurer. On the way home, Emily accuses George of being "conceited and stuck-up." She believes a man should be perfect in every way, but George does not believe that is possible because everyone has flaws. But George does think girls are closer to perfect than boys. They go to the drugstore for ice cream. The Stage Manager plays the druggist, Mr. Morgan. Emily has just had a scare on the street when she was nearly hit by a wagon, and Mr. Morgan remarks that Main Street is getting busier every year, and adds, "now they're bringing in these auto-mo-biles, the best thing to do is just stay home."

George asks Emily to write to him when he goes away to college. Emily is worried that he will grow out of touch with the town. Emily's reaction convinces George that he does not need to attend college to learn how to become a farmer and chooses to stay in town after high school. George tells Emily that she is more important to him than college. After awkward hemming and hawing, they establish their relationship. As they leave the drugstore, George says he needs to leave his watch as collateral for money, because he does not have enough to pay for their ice cream sodas. The Stage Manager/Mr. Morgan says he trusts him. As George and Emily head home, the Stage Manager announces that it is time to "get on with the wedding."

The stage is set with extra chairs for the wedding. The Stage Manager takes the role of minister. The stage directions say *The congregation streams into the church and sits in silence. Church bells are heard.* The choir from the Congregational Church enters as well, "*facing the audience under the stained-glass window.*" Mrs. Webb is crying and says that "there's something downright cruel about sending our girls out into marriage this way." She goes on: "It's cruel, I know, but I couldn't bring myself to say anything. I went into it blind as a bat myself." George enters the church, and his baseball player friends call out to him, teasing. The Stage Manager calls them off. George is nervous about the wedding and tells his mother that he does not "want to grow old." Emily confides in

Mr. Webb that she does not want to get married either; she wants to remain exactly who she is. Mr. Webb calms her down and gives her to George. Emily tells George, "all I want is someone to love me. . . . for *ever.*" The Stage Manager performs the ceremony and reveals that he has married two hundred couples. Mrs. Soames comments that in life "the important thing is to be happy." The Stage Manager announces the end of act 2 and a ten-minute intermission.

### Act 3

As act 3 opens, "*ten or twelve chairs have been placed in three openly spaced rows facing the audience. These are graves in the cemetery.* Mrs. Gibbs, Mr. Stimson, Mrs. Soames, and Wally Webb are seated there. The stage direction says that "*the dead do not turn their heads or their eyes* when they speak. The Stage Manager notes that nine years have passed; it is summer 1913. Fords have replaced horses. Not much has changed. In the cemetery, the Stage Manager points out Mrs. Gibbs, Mr. Stimson, Mrs. Soames, and Editor Webb's son, Wallace. He pronounces that "there's something way down deep that's eternal about every human being," and asks "what's left when memory's gone, and your identity?" Joe Stoddard, undertaker, enters the scene to greet Sam Craig, who has returned to town for a funeral after being out west. They chat about some of the dead, most noticeably Stimson, who "hung himself in the attic" after seeing a "peck of trouble." Sam asks how his cousin, Emily, died; Joe says she had complications giving birth to her second child.

The scene shifts to Mrs. Gibbs and Mrs. Soames observing the funeral. They reminisce about life. Emily greets the dead and thanks Mrs. Gibbs for the legacy of money she left George and Emily, which they used for their farm. Obviously Mrs. Gibbs never used the money to go to Paris. Emily wonders how much time will pass before she does not feel like a living person. She notices that living people are so "troubled" and "in the dark." But she wants to return to the living, and though Mrs. Gibbs says it is possible, she advises against it. The Stage Manager agrees. Life as one of the dead is about forgetting. But Emily insists she must understand things for herself and decides to relive her twelfth birthday. She observes conversations on Main Street, sees her mother, and becomes her younger self. Emily has a difficult time watching everyone alive. She is upset that

"THIS IS THE WAY WE WERE: IN OUR GROWING UP AND IN OUR MARRYING, AND IN OUR LIVING, AND IN OUR DYING."

no one has "time to look at one another" and asks if "human beings ever realize life while they live it." She proclaims humans as "blind people." Stimson points out that life is all about a "cloud of ignorance," of "wast[ing] time as though you had a million years." Mrs. Gibbs points to a star, which a Man Among the Dead calls "mighty good company." Emily realizes, after seeing George grieving, that living people "don't understand."

The Stage Manager ends the play by talking about the stars. He says, "one is straining away, straining away all the time to make something of itself. The strain's so bad that every sixteen hours everybody lies down and gets a rest." He advises the audience to go rest as well.

## THEMES

### Life Lessons
Although the play seems to revolve around ordinary and uneventful events in Grover's Corners, Wilder's use of the Stage Manager and stage directions offers commentary that moves the play into parable, or a short moral story. The Stage Manager, as an omniscient narrator, acts as a Greek chorus of sorts, reporting, judging, and participating in the action. The Stage Manager directly addresses the audience, putting the events and characters in a local context with a universal, philosophical slant. Specifically, he details personal relationships and histories and predicts how they will fit into a larger future picture. In addition, he controls time, forcing audience and characters to move backward and forward; with this purposeful movement, he obviously has a goal and message he wants to impart. In this way, the presence of the Stage Manager sets up the play as a cautionary tale: The audience is a character in this play, and as such, must learn and experience the lessons of life exactly as the characters learn and experience

them. In doing so, they might re-examine, adjust, and advance their own American dreams.

### Fleeting Time
The play's three acts combine to illustrate the ordinary cycle of life: the immortality of youth, the uncertainty of adulthood, the regret of age. Act 1, "Daily Life," shows a flurry of daily routine in Grover's Corners. The characters hardly react to ordinary events such as eating breakfast, going to school, delivering milk, and feeding chickens. Everyone in town seems to rush through their day without paying attention to their surroundings. Time, for them, has no end.

Act 2, "Love and Marriage," continues to show the constant, steady progression of life as George and Emily marry, but both Emily and George fear growing old, an indication they are beginning to notice the passing of time and are aware of their choices and experiences. Their elders offer advice, showing that they do not want their children wasting time on the same mistakes.

The dead in act 3 openly disapprove of the living's "ignorance" and believe the living should enjoy the time they still have on Earth. Stimson distills the theme of this act in explaining the meaning of life to Emily: "to move about in a cloud of ignorance; to go up and down trampling on the feelings of those . . . about you. To spend and waste time as though you had a million years." By highlighting the temporariness of everything and the speed with which it passes, Wilder encourages his audience to rethink their own American dreams: to appreciate what they have, and to pursue what they want.

### Success in Human Terms
Although the dead in act 3 do not think the living spend enough time on relationships with loved ones, the bustling daily activity in Grover's Corners shows people constantly connecting with each other. Mrs. Gibbs and Mrs. Webb are active in their children's lives as they chide them about their lazy behaviors; the women bond after choir practice; the children speak about their homework; and Howie and Dr. Gibbs engage in morning small talk. Wilder shows, through these seemingly insignificant relationships, that life is about connections, no matter how small. The Stage Manager is also actively involved, forging an immediate relationship with both the audience and the characters onstage. Additionally, the

*The main street of Peterborough, New Hampshire in November 1950* Getty Images

"our" in the *Our Town* emphasizes the unity and shared experiences within the Grover's Corners community. In the end, the audience must question whether people in Grover's Corners were "blind" to their fellow citizens after all. In act 2, Mrs. Soames says the important thing in life is "to be happy." The play suggests that even the most trivial hello should make our lives fulfilled and "happy." Although the typical idea of the American dream focuses on financial success, this version measures success in terms of love, community, and relationships, and thus outlines a dream that is more fulfilling and more attainable for all American dreamers.

## HISTORICAL OVERVIEW

### *Peterborough, New Hampshire: The Real Our Town?*

Thornton Wilder developed *Our Town* during nine summers spent at the MacDowell Colony in Peterborough, New Hampshire. Peterborough's milkman, Fletcher Dole, and its druggist, Albert E. Campbell, served as models for Howie Newsome and Mr. Morgan. Situated on the Contocook River, the small picturesque community of Peterborough is said to be the inspiration for Grover's Corners with its charming town square and small population.

## Model T Ford

In *Our Town*, the Stage Manager makes several references to the coming of the automobile, namely the Model T Ford created by inventor Henry Ford. The Ford debuted in 1908 and would change the nature of the way people moved and worked, especially since assembly line production made cars more available and affordable. In act 2 of the play, after George fabricates a story about Emily nearly getting run down by a horse and wagon, the Stage Manager comments about the advent of the "auto-mo-bile" and the days when "a dog could go to sleep all day in the middle of Main Street and nothing come along to disturb him." Later in the act, he includes the Ford as an important accessory in the cycle of life: "The cottage, the go-cart, the Sunday-afternoon drives in the Ford, the first rheumatism, the grandchildren, the second rheumatism, the deathbed, the reading of the will,—"

## World War I and Young Men in Their Prime

In act 1, the Stage Manager informs the audience that Joe Crowell dies in France during World War I. "All that education for nothing," he says, and wonders about the purpose of the war. World War I spanned from 1914 to 1918 and was called "The War to End All Wars." The Allied Powers, composed of France, Russia, the United Kingdom, Italy, and the United States, defeated the Central Powers, or Austria-Hungary, Germany, Bulgaria, and the Ottoman Empire. This conflict was sparked by many factors, including the assassination of Archduke Ferdinand in Sarajevo, a naval arms race between Britain and Germany, fervent nationalism in the varying countries involved, and the rise of both Marxism and Communism. America entered the war in 1917 after German submarines attacked American merchant ships. After the summer of 1918, 10,000 troops were arriving in Europe daily. The war began to define what it meant for a young man to be American, because serving the country was an act of patriotic pride and duty. Almost three million men were drafted into the army, and by the end of the war, America had lost nearly 54,000 men in battle.

## Our Town: Touring with the USO

During World War II, the United Service Organization (USO) was employed as the "sole agency to provide civilian entertainment for the Armed Forces," as noted in Lowell Matson's "Theatre for the Armed Forces in World War II." Matson documents that "by the summer of 1945, USO was sending overseas musicals with companies as large as sixty." *Our Town* was one of those plays performed for units stationed across the Pacific as well as Europe. According to Matson, the success of USO shows led to the formation of the Armed Forces Headquarters Theatre Club and its first production was *Our Town*, directed by "Lieutenant Colonel Thornton Wilder."

## CRITICAL OVERVIEW

An "acting edition" of *Our Town* from 1939 reveals positive reviews in major newspapers across the country. Most critics share the opinion offered in the *New York Times*: "One of the finest achievements of the current stage. Mr. Wilder has transmuted the simple events of a human life into universal reverie...A beautifully evocative play." In the same way, the *Chicago Tribune* calls the play "one of the most important theatrical experiences of this generation," while the *Pittsburgh Post-Gazette* finds the work "big, fine and moving—A touching reverie steeped in quiet, humble philosophies." Wilder's straightforward approach to storytelling also impressed the critics; a reporter for the *Philadelphia Inquirer* notes the play's "sincerity and compassionate understanding." The *Cleveland Plain Dealer* goes further in their assessment, praising the "exquisite taste in this writing, a faculty for distilling poetry from tangy and earthy speech, a way of infusing words with the scent of the soil and giving to all a sense of quiet, luminous beauty."

Harold Clurman in the September 3, 1955, edition of the *Nation* hones in on the deceptive simplicity of Wilder's plays:

> What is American in Wilder's plays are their benign humor, their old-fashioned optimism, their use of the charmingly homely detail, the sophisticated employment of the commonplace, their avuncular celebration of the humdrum, their common sense, popular moralism, and the simplicity—one might almost say simplemindedness—behind a shrewdly captivating manipulation of a large selection of classic elements.

Robert W. Corrigan, in his 1961 "Thornton Wilder and the Tragic Sense of Life," follows up with this line of criticism, even stating that "of all

# MEDIA ADAPTATIONS

In 1940, *Our Town* was adapted into a film starring William Holden and directed by Sam Wood. Thornton Wilder was a member of the writing team that adapted the original play. This film was nominated for an Academy Award for Best Picture, Best Actress, and Best Score. It is available on DVD from Focusfilm.

In 1955, *Our Town* became a television musical starring Frank Sinatra, Paul Newman, and Eva Marie Saint. As of 2007, this version is unavailable.

*OT: Our Town* (2002) is a documentary about a high school production of *Our Town* in the Compton neighborhood of Los Angeles. It won several "best documentary" and "audience favorite" awards at independent film festivals in 2002, 2003, and 2004. It is available on DVD from Film Movement.

In 2003, Paul Newman starred as the Stage Manager in another television version of *Our Town*, this one taped from a stage production and distributed by PBS as part of its Masterpiece Theatre collection. It is available on DVD from PBS Paramount.

modern dramatists, none is more difficult to pin down than Thornton Wilder." Corrigan points out that "no one seems to agree about his work. For some he is the great American satirist; for others he is a soft-hearted sentimentalist; and for still others he is our only 'religious' dramatist."

Wilder's play is still being performed across the country, due to its universality and its subtle complexity. PBS, while producing the play as part of its Masterpiece Theatre's American Collection in 2003, called *Our Town* an "American stage treasure" and its executive producer Rebecca Eaton named the work "the quintessential American play." Additionally, though Alvin Klein thought the Bay Street Theater production in Sag Harbor, New York, was less than stellar,

in his review, "In *Our Town*, Wilder Searches for Life's Truth and Balance," he does revere Wilder's original work and claims that "more than any American play of the last century, *Our Town* stands for simple truths and eternal connections."

# CRITICISM

## Malcolm Goldstein

*In the following excerpt, Goldstein discusses how the value in life and existence can be found in the ordinary and universal appeal of* Our Town, *particularly in terms of setting, plot, character development.*

Although the play begins and ends in one precisely described place, Grover's Corners, New Hampshire, it ranges far beyond the village boundaries in each of its three acts. By eliminating scenery and props, except for two small trellises to appease persons who cannot do without scenery, Wilder avoids from the outset any suggestion that the *meaning* of the action relates only to Grover's Corners, and yet, through the dialogue and the expository remarks of the Stage Manager, he retains enough of the New England flavor to remind the audience of the starting point, so to speak, of the nation in which it lives. He begins, then, in the small New England town and from it moves out to embrace all creation.

The plot is the story of two neighboring households, the Gibbs and Webb families. Their lives are in no way sensational or special; nothing has happened to them that might set them off either as heroes or as victims. True, the family heads are professional men—*Dr.* Gibbs an *Editor* Webb—but the distinction implied in the titles serves only to confer upon them a degree of familiarity with human problems, and this they are able to communicate to the audience. As one device out of many to link Grover's Corners to the great world beyond, Wilder also gives the two men distinctive hobbies: Dr. Gibbs devotes all his spare time to studies of the Civil War, and Editor Webb is equally fascinated by the life of Napoleon. The purpose of this quite ordinary information is not to particularize the town; rather, it serves to underline the fact that Grover's Corners, the home of the Gibbses and the Webbs, is just another spot in the cosmos. But at the same time that it is a place of no importance, the town represents the universe, and whatever occurs to its inhabitants is an expression, in very general terms, of the chief events in the lives of all people.

The scenes devised by Wilder are moments of eternity singled out for our attention and played against the panorama of infinity. The first act is titled "The Daily Life," and offers such details as the early-morning milk delivery, the family breakfast, and the children's departure for school. Proceeding from dawn till bedtime, at every turn the action distills poignance from the commonplace, including even so unremarkable an occurrence as the children's struggle with homework.

Of the twenty-two characters who pass across the stage, most are present only to populate the arena whose principal actors are George Gibbs and Emily Webb, the older children of the two families. Through the conduct of their lives, which, as we see them on Wilder's bare stage, they lead in infinite space at a point in the endless continuum of time, emerges in little the general pattern of the human adventure. At the moments when they act out their personal joy and sadness, they present an abstract rendering of these emotions as they come to us all. They are allegorical figures, but, because what they represent is not a special quality or force but the complete sum of the human passions, and because also they speak in an ordinary manner without the aggrandizing self-consciousness of an Everyman, they are completely absorbing as characters in their own right. The two protagonists grow up in houses on adjacent properties, play together as children, fall in love with one another in adolescence, and marry as soon as they graduate from high school. Emily dies in childbirth after nine years of marriage, and as the play ends George grieves hopelessly beside her grave. That is all. But so basic to the life of every civilization are these experiences and the emotions they evoke that their theatrical impact is universally stunning.

To extend the dimensions of the plot, Wilder employs images of vast numbers which with a lightly comic tone the Stage Manager pulls out of his capacious mind. In three years the sun comes up a thousand times, in long marriages husbands and wives may eat as many as fifty thousand meals together, every bride and

*Paul Newman, Maggie Lacey, and Ben Fox in a production of* Our Town *on Broadway* Getty Images

groom have millions of ancestors, all of whom may be spectral guests at the wedding. To take the audience out of the present moment and move the play forward in time, Wilder permits the Stage Manager to use his omniscience in still another way: he mentions not only the past and present of the characters' lives, but their future, including, for many, the dates and circumstances of their deaths. At the end of the first act, after we have listened at length to his observations, we come to understand through the words of another figure, George Gibbs's young sister Rebecca, that over all dates and places and activities such as we have been hearing of, God eternally watches.

In the preface to his *Three Plays*, the collected edition of his major dramatic works, he writes forthrightly of this theme:

> *Our Town* is not offered as a picture of life in a New Hampshire Village; or as speculation about the conditions of life after death (that element I merely took from Dante's *Purgatory*). It is an attempt to find a value above all price

for the smallest events in our daily life . . . Molière said that for the theatre all he needed was a platform and a passion or two. The climax of this play needs only five square feet of boarding and the passion to know what life means to us.

The people of Grover's Corners are the sort whose effect upon the world is slight, slighter even than the effect of such a man as George Brush, since they never move away from their particular piece of the universe. For that reason they are the personages whose lives most clearly reflect the marvelousness of the unheroic.

**Source:** Malcolm Goldstein, "Three Plays of the Human-Adventure," in *The Art of Thornton Wilder*, University of Nebraska Press, 1965, pp. 95–129.

## John Mason Brown

*In the following excerpt, Brown discusses the timelessness, simplicity, and truth in Wilder's idyllic portrayal of small-town America.*

Mr. Wilder's play is concerned with the universal importance of those unimportant details which figure in the lives of men and women everywhere. His Grover's Corners is a New Hampshire *town* inhabited by decent New England people. The very averageness of these quiet, patient people is the point at which our lives and all living become a part of their experience. Yet Mr. Wilder's play involves more than a New England township. It burrows into the essence of the growing-up, the marrying, the living, and the dying of all of us who sit before it and are included by it. The task to which Mr. Wilder has set himself is one which Hardy had in mind in a far less human, more grandiose way, when he had the Chorus in *The Dynasts* say:

> We'll close up Time, as a bird its van,
> We'll traverse Space, as Spirits can,
> Link pulses severed by leagues and years,
> Bring cradles into touch with biers.

Mr. Wilder succeeds admirably in doing this. He shows us the simple pattern behind all simple living. He permits us to share in the inevitable anguishes and joys, the hopes and cruel separations to which men have been heir since the smoke puffed up the chimneys in Greece.

To my surprise I have encountered the complaint that Mr. Wilder's Grover's Corners is not like Middletown, U.S.A. It lacks brothels, race riots, huge factories, front-page scandals, social workers, union problems, lynchings, agitators, and strikes. The ears of its citizens are more familiar with the song of the robin than they are with the sirens of hurrying police cars. Its young people are stimulated to courtship by moonlight rather than by moonshine. They drink soda water instead of gin. Their rendezvous are held in drug stores rather than in night clubs. Their parents are hard-working people. They are quiet, self-respecting, God-fearing Yankees who get up early to do their day's work and meet their responsibilities and their losses without whining. The church organist may tipple, and thereby cause some gossip. But he is a neighbor, and the only good-neighbor policy they care about begins at home.

They do not murder or steal, borrow or beg, blackmail or oppress. Furthermore, they face the rushing years without complaints as comparatively happy mortals. Therefore to certain realists they seem unreal. "No historian," one critic has written "has ever claimed that a town like Mr. Wilder's was ever so idyllic as to be free from intolerance and injustice." Mr. Wilder does not make this claim himself. His small-town editor admits Grover's Corners is "little better behaved than most towns." Neither is Mr. Wilder working as the ordinary historian works. His interests are totally different interests.

He is not concerned with social trends, with economic conditions, with pivotal events, or glittering personalities. He sings not of arms and the man, but of those small events which loom so large in the daily lives of each of us, and which are usually unsung. His interest is the unexceptional, the average, the personal. His preoccupation is what lies beneath the surface and the routine of our lives, and is common to all our hearts and all our experience. It is not so much of the streets of a New England Town he writes as of the clean white spire which rises above them.

There are hundreds of fat books written each year on complicated subjects by authors who are not writers at all. But the ageless achievement of the true writers has always been to bring a new illumination to the simplest facts of life. That illumination has ever been a precious talent given only to a few. It is because Mr. Wilder brings this illumination to his picture of Grover's Corners that I admire *Our Town*. New Hampshire is the state which can claim Mr. Wilder's village, but his vision of it has been large enough to include all of us, no matter where we may come from, among its inhabitants. Personally, I should as soon think of condemning the Twenty-third Psalm because it lacks the factual observation of Sinclair Lewis and the social point of view of Granville Hicks as I would of accusing *Our Town* of being too unrealistically observed.

Anyone who hears only the milk bottles clink when early morning has come once again to Grover's Corners has not heard what Mr. Wilder wants them to hear. These milk bottles are merely the spokesmen of time, symbols for the bigness of little things. In terms of the Gibbses and the Webbs, Mr. Wilder gives the pattern of repetition of each small day's planning, each small life's fruition and decline. He makes us feel the swift passage of the years, our blindness in meeting their race, the sense that our lives go rushing past so quickly that we have scarcely time in which to hold our breaths.

Only once does he fail us seriously. This is in his scene in the bleak graveyard on the hill. Although he seeks there to create the image of the dead who have lost their interest in life, he has not been able to capture the true greatness of vision which finds them at last unfettered from the minutiae of existence. Both his phrasing and his thinking are inadequate here. He chills the living by removing his dead even from compassion.

Nonetheless Mr. Wilder's is a remarkable play, one of the sagest, warmest, and most deeply human scripts to have come out of our theatre. It is the kind of play which suspends us in time, making us weep for our own vanished youth at the same time we are sobbing for the short-lived pleasures and sufferings which we know await our children. Geographically *Our Town* can be found at an imaginary place known as "Grover's Corners, Sultan County, New Hampshire, United States of America, Continent of North America, Western Hemisphere, the Earth, the Solar System, the Universe, the Mind of God." Mr. Wilder's play is laid in no imaginary place. It becomes a reality in the human heart.

**Source:** John Mason Brown, "Wilder's *Our Town*," in *Dramatis Personae: A Retrospective Show*, Viking Press, 1963, pp. 79–84.

## SOURCES

Clurman, Harold, Review of *Our Town*, in the *Nation*, September 3, 1955, reprinted in *Modern American Literature*, edited by Joann Cerrito and Laurie DiMauro, St. James Press, 1999, pp. 388–92.

Corrigan, Robert W., "Thornton Wilder and the Tragic Sense of Life," in the *Educational Theatre Journal*, Vol. 13, No. 3, October 1961, p. 167.

Klein, Alvin, "In *Our Town*, Wilder Searches for Life's Truth and Balance," in the *New York Times*, Long Island Weekly Desk, August 25, 2002, section 14LI, p. 16.

"Masterpiece Theatre: The American Collection: *Our Town*," *PBS*, www.pbs.org/wgbh/masterpiece/american collection/ourtown (October 31, 2006).

Review of *Our Town*, in the *Chicago Tribune*, reprinted in *Our Town*, HarperPerennial, 1998, p. 112.

Review of *Our Town*, in the *Cleveland Plain Dealer*, reprinted in *Our Town*, HarperPerennial, 1998, p. 116.

Review of *Our Town*, in the *New York Times*, reprinted in *Our Town*, HarperPerennial, 1998, p. 111.

Review of *Our Town*, in the *Pittsburgh Post-Gazette*, reprinted in *Our Town*, HarperPerennial, 1998, p. 115.

Review of *Our Town*, in the *Philadelphia Inquirer*, reprinted in *Our Town*, HarperPerennial, 1998, p. 113.

Wilder, Thornton, *Our Town*, Coward-McCann, 1939; reprint, HarperPerennial, 1998.

# Rabbit, Run

**JOHN UPDIKE**

**1960**

*Rabbit, Run* (1960) is the first of John Updike's quartet of novels about Harry "Rabbit" Angstrom, a modern American anti-hero. Later books in the tetralogy are *Rabbit Redux*, *Rabbit is Rich*, and *Rabbit at Rest*. Taken as a whole, the Rabbit novels illustrate the attitudes, joys, and sorrows of the twentieth-century American middle class over the course of four decades. Each written at the end of one decade, published at the beginning of the next, the novels follow Rabbit from early adulthood into old age and death. Because Updike increasingly includes historical and cultural references in each book, they also trace the trajectory of American life and the events that shape and define it over time.

Updike drew from his small-town, middle-class American upbringing as much as his adult sense of domestic claustrophobia when he sat down to write *Rabbit, Run* in 1959. The author was a twenty-seven-year-old husband and father when he wrote the novel, partly as a response to Jack Kerouac's *On the Road*, which was published just two years earlier. As he explains in the introduction to *Rabbit Angstrom*, he believed Kerouac's book was an "instruction to cut loose," and he felt he had to demonstrate what really "happens when a young American family man goes on the road—the people left behind get hurt." In *Rabbit, Run*, twenty-six-year-old Harry "Rabbit" Angstrom, former high school basketball star, becomes so frustrated by his dull existence as husband, father, and kitchen gadget

# BIOGRAPHY

**JOHN UPDIKE**

John Hoyer Updike was born in Shillington, Pennsylvania, on March 18, 1932. His mother was a homemaker with artistic ambitions, his father a high school science teacher. At his mother's urging, Updike applied to Harvard University after graduating co-valedictorian of Shillington High School. He not only got in, he also received a tuition scholarship. After graduating *summa cum laude* from Harvard in 1954, Updike studied drawing and painting at Oxford. He sold his first short story and poem to the *New Yorker* while abroad, but he soon settled in New York City with his wife after E. B. White got him a job as a staff writer for the magazine. He continued writing short stories and poems, then transitioned into writing novels, publishing his first, *The Poorhouse Fair*, in 1959.

Updike wrote *Rabbit, Run* (1960) at the beginning of a very long and successful literary career. Besides the Rabbit books, he has written many novels, including *Couples* (1968) and *The Witches of Eastwick* (1984). Still prolific at the age of seventy-four, Updike has published over fifty books, including poetry, short stories, essays, and criticism. A recipient of numerous literary awards including two Pulitzer Prizes, Updike is considered one of the great writers of his time. As of 2006, he lives with his wife in Massachusetts, where he continues to write.

salesman that he runs out on his pregnant wife and two-year-old son to live for a time with another woman. His rash and irresponsible behavior leads to a series of misfortunes that climax with the accidental drowning of his newborn daughter.

The fight between flesh and spirit is rampant in *Rabbit, Run* as Rabbit desperately searches for some sense of meaning in his life. Youthful minister Jack Eccles befriends Rabbit, believing he can put the broken Angstrom family back together. He and Rabbit discuss religion while they play golf and Rabbit admits "that somewhere behind all this . . . there's something that wants me to find it." He searches for that something by having an extra-marital relationship with Ruth Leonard. In a similar way, he searches for that something in his wife's wounded body and in his flirtation with the minister's wife. Rabbit's tendency to sexualize everything is connected to his fear of death, a fear that propels him toward any hint of grace or spiritual gratification he can find. His quest is selfish at best, but he feels no remorse for hurting those around him. When Ruth asks, "Don't you ever think you're going to have to pay a price?" Rabbit answers, "I'll tell you . . . when I ran from Janice I made an interesting discovery. If you have the guts to be yourself . . . other people'll pay your price." Rabbit's attitude and sense of dislocation are the heart of the novel and the central metaphor for the Updike's take on twentieth-century middle-class America.

## PLOT SUMMARY

### Part 1

Twenty-six-year-old, six-foot-three Harry "Rabbit" Angstrom is walking home from work wearing a business suit. The narrator hints at his nature:

> So tall, he seems an unlikely rabbit, but the breadth of white face, the pallor of his blue irises, and a nervous flutter under his brief nose as he stabs a cigarette into his mouth partially explain the nickname.

He stops and plays basketball with some boys in an alley. He plays well, and he is reminded of his days as a basketball star in high school. Elated because of the March weather and the basketball game, he runs the rest of the way home. He lives in Mt. Olive, "suburb of the city of Brewer, fifth largest city in Pennsylvania." There, he finds his heavily pregnant wife, Janice, drinking Old-fashioneds and watching *The Mickey Mouse Club* on television. She has left their car at her mother's house and their two-year-old son, Nelson, at Harry's mother's house. They bicker a little, both annoyed with the other, but neither seems to take it too seriously. As Rabbit leaves to pick up his son and the car, Janice asks him to bring home a pack of cigarettes.

*John Updike* © *Christopher Felver/Corbis*

Rabbit is reminded of his past as he walks the streets of his hometown. Little landmarks jog his memory and people and events from his youth come to life along the way. As dusk falls, he has trouble deciding which stop to make first. He approaches his parents' home and watches his mother, father, sister, and son eating dinner in the kitchen. He decides their home is a happier for his son than his own and leaves to pick up the car first. Once he gets the car started, Rabbit heads for the highway, letting his instincts guide him. He fantasizes about driving all night, all the way to the Gulf of Mexico, but discovers he is headed east. He stops for gas, and he asks the attendant the distance and direction to several nearby places. The attendant notices Harry's apparent lack of direction and tells him, "The only way to get somewhere, you know, is to figure out where you're going before you go there."

After driving for several hours, listening to news and music on the radio, he stops at a roadside café and feels that he is different from the other customers. Around midnight, back in the car, he realizes he has been angry ever since he left the café. He rips up his map, frustrated with his lack of progress, and heads back to Mt. Judge.

Now morning, Rabbit parks the car in the alley outside the Sunshine Athletic Association, where he knows his former basketball coach lives, and sleeps for a while. When he wakes up, he catches up to his old coach, Marty Tothero, who is walking by. He tells Tothero that he has run out on his wife. Tothero takes Rabbit to his room in the Sunshine and lets him sleep there until he returns at six o'clock that evening. The old man is slightly drunk as he urges Rabbit to get dressed and join him and a couple of girls for dinner in Brewer, the city on the other side of the mountain from Mt. Judge. On the way, Rabbit is nervous about being seen around town, but Tothero assures him that nobody is looking for him. They meet his friend Margaret and her friend Ruth outside a Chinese restaurant. While they eat, Tothero amuses them with his philosophy in basketball terms: "Give the boys the will to achieve. I've always liked that better than the will to win, for there can be achievement even in defeat." After dinner, Rabbit tries to figure out Ruth's situation, and he deduces that she is a prostitute. He goes home with Ruth after she tells him that she will need fifteen dollars.

Upon entering her apartment, Rabbit scares Ruth by lunging at her, kissing and hugging her hard. They scuffle, she tells him to get out, but he convinces her to let him stay. They make love that night, then again the next morning; he convinces her not to use any contraception. Church bells ring and Rabbit looks out the window at the people going to church across the street. He prays silently. He and Ruth discuss their religious beliefs; Rabbit believes in God, while Ruth does not. He finds her attractive and good-natured. Rabbit goes to the delicatessen and buys food for their lunch and suggests they go for a walk that afternoon. Ruth is a better cook than Janice. After lunch, Rabbit leaves to take the car back to Janice and pick up some clothes. Before he goes, he tells Ruth he loves her.

When he arrives back at his empty apartment, he notices the pork chops Janice made for dinner the previous night still in the pan. He hurriedly grabs a few clothes and escapes, leaving his key inside the apartment. On the street, Rabbit is stopped by minister Jack Eccles. The minister urges Rabbit into his car, they drive around, and Eccles tells him how worried

Rabbit's family is. He reports that when he failed to return home after a half hour, Janice called Rabbit's parents. Mr. Angstrom brought Nelson home and then walked around town looking for Rabbit. At two o'clock in the morning, Janice called her own parents. That is when they called Eccles. When Eccles asks what made him leave, Rabbit replies, "She asked me to buy her a pack of cigarettes." Eccles tries to talk Rabbit into returning to his wife. They discuss God, and Eccles suggests that Rabbit needs to grow up. Rabbit replies, "If you're telling me I'm not mature, that's one thing I don't cry over since as far as I can make out it's the same thing as being dead." Rabbit agrees to meet Eccles in a few days for a game of golf.

Rabbit returns to Ruth's apartment, changes his clothes, and wants Ruth to go for a walk with him. She is reading *The Deaths at Oxford*, which annoys Rabbit, who thinks, "What should she care about deaths at Oxford? When she has him here, wonderful Harry Angstrom." She protests, but he convinces her to come outside with him. They walk through town and up the side of the mountain that separates Brewer from Mt. Judge. As they gaze at the city below, Rabbit asks Ruth if she is really a whore. She responds, "Are you really a rat?" They take a bus back to her place. He stays with her, takes her to movies and bowling over the next few days, then goes to Eccles's house on Tuesday. There, he meets the minister's wife, Lucy, and their daughter, Joyce. Rabbit likes the looks of Lucy and gives her a swat on the behind before Eccles comes downstairs. Lucy and Jack Eccles quarrel and Rabbit frightens little Joyce before he and the minister leave the house.

On the way to the golf course, Eccles tells Rabbit that his family knows he is in the county. They talk about religion, about the meaning of Hell, and Rabbit says, "I'll tell you, I *do* feel, I guess, that somewhere behind all this [scenery, 'the un-grandest landscape in the world'] there's something that wants me to find it." Eccles asks Rabbit if he wants a part-time job gardening for an old woman, Mrs. Smith, for $40 a week, then lets Rabbit know he knows about Ruth. On the course, Rabbit feels angry and confused. He cannot explain why he left his family. Eccles tells him he is "monstrously selfish" and "a coward." He goes on to say, "You don't care about right or wrong; you worship nothing except your own worst instincts."

## Part 2

Rabbit has been away from home for two months. He walks Mrs. Smith's acres of flowers with her and listens as she talks about her late husband and the gardens he left behind. The old woman loves Rabbit's company and relishes the fact that they think alike. On Memorial Day, Rabbit and Ruth go to the swimming pool in West Brewer. She tells Rabbit he has it made: Eccles to play golf with, Mrs. Smith in love with him, Ruth to stay and play with. He claims it is because he is lovable. She calls him smug, then becomes upset. Lately she has been crying easily and feeling unbelievably hungry, signs that she is pregnant. Ruth's promiscuous history and disappointments with men are revealed, but she "forgave them all" after making love with Harry. She wants to tell Rabbit she is pregnant with his baby, but she is afraid he will run.

Eccles visits Janice's mother, Mrs. Springer. It has been three weeks since he visited her last and she is upset with him. She accuses him of becoming an expert golfer, a jab at his becoming friendly with her runaway son-in-law. The town gossip about her daughter's inability to keep her husband is getting to her, as is the fact that she called Eccles the night Rabbit disappeared instead of the police. Eccles tries to convince her that Rabbit will return home soon enough, but to call the police if he does not come back after Janice has the baby. He leaves her, feeling thirsty and unsympathetic.

He visits Rabbit's mother next. The big, vigorous woman tells the minister that Harry has not been by, that he is probably too embarrassed. She admits that she never liked Janice and believes the girl got pregnant on purpose, as a way to trap Harry into marrying her. Mr. Angstrom comes home from work and tells Eccles that Harry came back from the army a different boy. He hates what his son is doing and admits to becoming his enemy the night he went looking for him all over town. He does not think Harry will come back, saying, "He's too far gone."

Eccles's third visit is to the Angstroms' Lutheran minister, Fritz Kruppenbach. He wants to talk about what they should do about Harry, but Kruppenbach tells Eccles that meddling in people's lives is not their job. He accuses the young minister of "selling his message for a few scraps of gossip and few games of golf." Eccles, depressed and rebuked, refuses to pray with the Lutheran.

Rabbit and Ruth go to Club Castanet for drinks with Margaret. Ruth's friend shows up with Ronnie Harrison, an old basketball teammate of Rabbit's. Rabbit is not happy to see Harrison, and the two exchange barbs all evening. Harrison, sitting next to Ruth, makes several comments about going to Atlantic City with her years ago. Rabbit sees his sister, Mim, enter the bar and goes to greet her. She tells him that their parents fight about him all the time. Rabbit does not like seeing her in the shabby bar and does not like the looks of her date. He shoves the date, then goes back to his own table and hustles Ruth out of the bar. He picks a fight with her on the way home, asking what she saw in Ronnie Harrison, how many men she had been with, and if she really had been a prostitute. When they get back to her apartment, he coerces her into a demeaning sex act, part out of jealousy and part to punish her. He tells her, "It'd prove you're mine."

Mrs. Springer calls the Eccles' home clearly in a panic, looking for Jack. Lucy, not knowing where he is, spends two hours calling various people trying to reach him. At a quarter past eleven he comes home, light and happy after several hours at the drugstore gossiping with the teenagers from his youth ministry. Though she is furious with him, she simply gives Jack Mrs. Springer's number. Jack calls Rabbit at Ruth's number and tells him that Janice is having her baby.

Rabbit dresses and prepares to leave for the hospital. Ruth, pretending to sleep, does not respond when Rabbit tells her he has to go see Janice through the birth. He suspects she is feigning sleep, and he tells her, "If you don't say anything I'm not coming back, Ruth." When he leaves, Ruth gets up, goes to the toilet, and tries to throw up. Rabbit runs most of the way to the hospital. He waits in the waiting room, and Eccles arrives soon after. They wait together for several hours, Mrs. Springer insults Rabbit, and then the doctor arrives to announce the arrival of his new baby daughter. Janice, still on the painkillers and ether she had been given, is happy to see her husband. He promises her he will return first thing in the morning, and then he tells Eccles he will not be going back to Ruth. Rabbit spends the night at Eccles's house.

Lucy wakes Rabbit so he will not miss visiting hours at the hospital. She feeds him juice and Cheerios and chats confidingly with him as he eats. She tells him how happy Jack is about Rabbit going back to his family, as if the minister had accomplished some great feat by bringing them all back together again. She says that her husband is very fond of Rabbit, as is Mrs. Smith. As they talk, Rabbit thinks that Lucy wants him. She gives him a wink as she says goodbye.

At the hospital, Rabbit runs into Marty Tothero's wife, Harriet. She tells him that Marty has had two strokes and asks if Rabbit would like to visit his room. Tothero cannot speak or move his arms, so Rabbit tells him of his daughter's birth, thanks Tothero for his help while he and Janice were separated, and then leaves to go see his wife. His visit with Janice is disappointing. She complains about her stitches and seems to find his repentant talk boring. Rabbit tells her why he left—she just sat around watching television and drinking all day—and, when he finds out she does not know what has happened to their apartment after not paying rent for two months, he accuses her of not caring about anything. They sit quietly watching television together for a while and then Rabbit goes to see his daughter. He thinks she should be called June, but Janice wants to name her Rebecca, after her mother. They compromise and name her Rebecca June Angstrom.

Janice's father, who had paid the rent while Rabbit was gone, offers Rabbit a job selling cars at one of his four car lots. Rabbit and Nelson move back in while Janice recuperates in the hospital. Rabbit and his son clean the apartment, take walks around town, watch a softball game, and go to the playground together. On a visit to his parents', Rabbit sees how much Nelson loves his grandmother. This makes him like her. On the other hand, his own mother treats Nelson coldly when they visit her. She seems to disapprove of Janice, and Harry thinks, "*What is this anyway? You act like I've gone over to the other side. Don't you know it's the right side and why don't you praise me?*" She makes a comment about the boy having "those little Springer hands," insinuating that he will never be the ballplayer Rabbit was. This makes him love her less.

Rabbit cannot sleep alone and is happy when Janice comes home from the hospital. The first week of her homecoming, Rabbit worships her. He goes to Eccles's church that first Sunday, partly because Eccles invited him, partly because he feels happy and forgiven and wants to give thanks. He accidentally sits behind Lucy and is distracted by her presence. After the service, he walks her and Joyce home, but he declines her invitation to come inside. His desire for her and his confusion about her intentions "has him jazzed up, and he reaches his apartment clever and cold with lust." He arrives home to find the apartment filled with tension brought on by the baby's incessant crying. Janice's milk seems to have dried up, Nelson is fretful and nervous, and Rabbit is full of lust. After the baby calms down and the family eats a late supper, everyone goes to bed. Rabbit tries to convince Janice to make love to him, but she will not. Frustrated, he dresses and leaves.

As soon as Rabbit leaves, Janice falls asleep. At four in the morning, the baby wakes her. She realizes Rabbit is still gone. Afraid that she has lost him again, she begins drinking. When Nelson wakes up hours later, he senses something is wrong and asks if his daddy has gone away. Janice says no, but feels bad for lying and has another drink. Before long, she is drunk. At eleven o'clock, her father calls to ask why Rabbit is not at work. She tries lying to him, but he hears the alcohol in her voice. Soon after, her mother calls to tell her that she is coming right over. Horrified, Janice attempts to pick up the filthy apartment. She finds the crib "smeared with orange mess" and decides to wash the baby. She overfills the tub and loses her grip on the infant. Unable to pull her out of the water in time, the baby drowns: "The worst thing that has ever happened to any woman in the world has happened to her."

## Part 3

Eccles and his wife argue about Rabbit after the minister finds out about the baby's death. Lucy calls Rabbit an animal and Eccles wonders why she speaks so vengefully of him. Rabbit calls from the drugstore, and Eccles gives him the bad news. Rabbit takes the bus back to Mt. Judge from Brewer where he spent the night in a hotel. When he arrives at the Springer's front door, Mrs. Springer slams it in his face but Eccles lets him in. Later, Mr. Springer explains that, while they are hurt and angry, they also forgive him. Rabbit tells his father-in-law, "I promise I'll keep my end of the bargain."

The next day, Janice tells him she cannot stand to look at anyone but him. Visitors come and go all day, including Tothero. When the aggrieved father tells his old coach how guilty

HE HAD THOUGHT, HE HAD READ, THAT FROM SHORE TO SHORE ALL AMERICA WAS THE SAME. HE WONDERS, IS IT JUST THESE PEOPLE I'M OUTSIDE, OR IS IT ALL AMERICA?"

he feels, he replies, "I warned you, Harry, youth is deaf. Youth is careless." The family spends the night at the Springers', then wakes the next day and prepare for the funeral. Janice asks if her dress looks all right, to which Rabbit answers, "What the hell do you think this is going to be? A fashion show?" When she cries and looks to her mother for comfort, Harry thinks,

> The house again fills with the unspoken thought that he is a murderer. He accepts the thought gratefully; it's true, he is, he is, and hate suits him better than forgiveness.

At the burial, Rabbit snaps. "Don't look at *me*," he says aloud, "I didn't kill her." He asks the mourners why they are looking at him, turns to Janice, and says, "I wasn't anywhere near. *She's* the one." Embarrassed and full of hate for his wife, he runs from the cemetery.

He makes his way to Ruth's apartment. She tells him she is pregnant, and he says he wants to marry her and have the baby. She asks,

> How many wives can you support? Your jobs are a joke. You aren't worth hiring. Maybe once you could play basketball, but you can't do *any*thing now. What the hell do you think the world is? . . . You divorce that wife you feel so sorry for about once a month, you divorce her or forget me.

He agrees, and thinks, "If he can just bury himself in her he knows he'll come up with his nerves all combed." He leaves the apartment to get them lunch and becomes afraid. Once he starts walking, trying to decide what to do, he starts to feel light. Without deciding which way to go, Rabbit begins to run.

## THEMES

### *Spirituality and Religious Belief*

Marshall Boswell writes of John Updike, "At the same time that he was discovering his own literary

*A parking lot full of cars circa 1950* Al Fenn/Time Life Pictures/Getty Images

voice, he was also undergoing a debilitating spiritual crisis." Updike told *Time* magazine in 1968 that during the writing of *Rabbit, Run* he felt a "sense of horror that beneath the skin of bright and exquisitely sculpted phenomena, death waits." Seeking solace, he found comfort in the writings of Danish philosopher Soren Kierkegaard and theologian Karl Barth. Kierkegaard, widely recognized as the first existential philosopher, taught that doubt was an integral part of faith. Without doubt, a rational component of human thought, there could be no real faith. Barth, a leading thinker of twentieth-century Protestantism, called for a theological return to neo-orthodoxy, or a rejection of what he believed was indifference to God's word. The writings of Kierkegaard and Barth shaped the author's artistic vision as well as his spiritual belief system. *Rabbit, Run*, writes Boswell, "gives direct voice to all these influences, from its Joycean use of internal monologue to the protagonist's status as a Kierkegaardian 'Knight of Faith.'"

Harry Angstrom's spiritual angst—which his very name suggests—is the heart of the novel. He describes his quest for meaning while playing golf with Episcopalian minister Eccles: "Well I don't know all this about theology, but I'll tell you, I do feel, I guess, that somewhere behind all this ... there's something that wants me to find it." He wants it so badly, "it" appears almost everywhere—even in a well-hit ball.

> Very simply he brings the clubhead around his shoulder into it. The sound has a hollowness, a singleness he hasn't heard before. His arms force his head up and his ball is hung way out.... It hesitates, and Rabbit thinks it will die, but he's fooled, for the ball makes its hesitation the ground of a final leap: with a kind of visible sob takes a last bite of space before vanishing in falling. "That's it!" he cries.

His spiritual quest leads him away from his Christian family into the arms of a non-believing adulteress. Confusing worship of the flesh and belief in his own instincts for religious faith, Rabbit feels, for a time, that he is on the right track. He says, "Funny, the world just can't touch you once you follow your instincts."

Similarly, when Ruth asks, "Don't you ever think you're going to have to pay the price?"—referring to his list of misdeeds—he answers, "When I ran from Janice I made an interesting discovery. If you have the guts to be yourself, other people'll pay your price." His arrogance is repaid in the end, but his spiritual quest seems not to end. He runs from his family, and from a pregnant Ruth, shortly after he returns to them.

If Rabbit's spiritual crisis is the heart of the novel, spirituality in the twentieth-century is a subtheme. A range of beliefs is exposed, from Eccles's liberal Episcopalianism, to Kruppenbach's thundering Lutheranism, to Ruth's studied atheism. These beliefs coupled with the quest for meaning paint a revealing portrait of religious freedom in America at the end of the 1950s.

## Responsibility

The prosperity following World War II and the Korean War caused a shift in America's sense of responsibility. Previously devoted to their country, young servicemen were now coming home to start families and work in corporate jobs. No longer heroes, the men traded their military uniforms for business suits and concentrated their efforts on supporting wives and children. Women could choose to work as homemakers, but increasing numbers of them began working outside the home. Conformity was expected at the beginning of the decade, but societal and political changes informed a growing counterculture that attempted to smash the uniformity. The responsibility of individuals to society was beginning to be seriously questioned.

Rabbit Angstrom's desertion illustrates this spreading doubt. Smothered by the claustrophobic domesticity and utter ordinariness of his life, Rabbit abandons job, family, home, and all adult responsibility. Frustrated with what he sees as a colorless existence, he longs for his days as a high school basketball star. He tells Eccles, "I once did something right. I played first-rate basketball. ... And after you're first-rate at something, no matter what, it kind of takes the kick out of being second-rate." By shirking responsibility, Rabbit distances himself from his "second-rate" job as a kitchen gadget demonstrator and husband to an alcoholic wife. He resents having to work at all, "to earn a living to buy sugar for her to put into her rotten old Old-fashioneds."

Rabbit's disregard for his responsibilities as salesman, husband, father, and son bring into sharp focus the responsibilities those around him continue to carry out. His dropping out actually increases the burden carried by some. Jack Eccles, troubled by the weight of responsibility he feels for bringing Rabbit's family back together again, wanders from home to home, disrupting his own family life for the service of others. Mr. Springer pays the rent when Rabbit does not so his daughter and son-in-law do not lose their home. Mrs. Springer takes on the burden of caring for her daughter and grandson, at the expense of her own health. Rabbit's leaving makes him his father's enemy, so strong is the old man's sense of responsibility. Even Ruth takes a job. But Rabbit sees no worth in all this work. At the hospital, during the delivery of Rabbit's daughter, Mr. Springer gives Rabbit "a painfully complex smile." Rabbit responds by thinking, "*You crumb*; hurls the thought at the slammed door. *You slave.* Where is everybody going? Where are they coming from? Why can't anybody rest?"

## HISTORICAL OVERVIEW

### The Eisenhower Era

*Rabbit, Run* is set in 1959, as evidenced by the radio news Rabbit listens to as he leaves Mt. Judge:

> President Eisenhower and Prime Minister Harold Macmillan begin a series of talks in Gettysburg, Tibetans battle Chinese Communists in Lhasa, the whereabouts of the Dalai Lama, spiritual ruler of this remote and backward land, are unknown.

Dwight D. Eisenhower was president during this time, his administration stretching from 1953 to 1961. Eisenhower was inaugurated the same year the Korean War ended, which happened just eight years after the end of World War II. It was peacetime, which meant a sharp rise in industry. Corporations flourished, jobs were plentiful, and goods that were previously unavailable were now easily accessible. America was experiencing a time of great energy, expansion, and prosperity, but that is where the happy nostalgia most people equate with the 1950s stops. The Eisenhower administration was actually a time of great tumult and swift change.

At the beginning of the decade, Senator Joseph R. McCarthy instigated a "Red Scare" by conducting hearings on communist subversion in the government and the private sector. The climate of deep suspicion he aroused would linger for years to come. After Stalin's death and Nikita Khrushchev's rise to power in the Soviet Union, the cold war was under way. Events leading up to the Vietnam War began soon after. Racial tensions were also on the rise. In 1954, the Supreme Court overturned the "separate but equal" ruling of *Plessy v. Ferguson* and made racial segregation illegal. A year later, Rosa Parks's act of nonviolent protest on a bus in Montgomery, Alabama, sparked the U.S. Civil Rights movement. Culturally, the face of music was forever changed when Sun Records released Elvis Presley's first rock 'n' roll record in 1954. Around the same time, Jack Kerouac's novel *On the Road* jumpstarted the postwar counterculture, which influenced the rise of rebellious new movie stars like Marlon Brando and James Dean.

The events and rapid societal changes experienced during the Eisenhower administration shape *Rabbit, Run* in a number of ways. For example, the explosion in mass marketing and advertising brought about by the sudden and widespread ownership of the television has much to do with Rabbit's occupation as well as his opinion about the effects of advertising on American society. At the beginning of *Rabbit, Run* he watches *The Mickey Mouse Club* over Janice's shoulder, expecting "to learn something . . . helpful in his own line of work, which is demonstrating a kitchen gadget in several five-and-dime stores around Brewer." After the Mouseketeer on television explains a proverb, "he pinches his mouth together and winks."

> That was good. Rabbit tries it, pinching the mouth together and then the wink, getting the audience out front with you against some enemy behind, Walt Disney or the MagiPeel Peeler Company, admitting it's all a fraud but, what the hell, making it likable. We're all in it together. Fraud makes the world go round. The base of our economy.

The "enemy" was omnipresent during the Eisenhower era. The cold war was in full swing since relations with the Soviet Union and Nikita Khrushchev were tense. The very real threat of a nuclear war between the superpowers led many Americans to build bomb shelters. At school, children were told what to do in case of a nuclear attack. The pervasive fear of war led to the execution of the largest American public works program on record. Thanks to Eisenhower's

ambitious Interstate Highway System program, highways soon connected the nation's towns and cities. Intended as a means to enhance defense capabilities, America's new roadways made it even easier for the automobile-loving, mobile society to hit the road. The accessibility and ease of movement provided by these newly built roads allow Rabbit to fantasize:

> He wants to go south, down, down the map into orange groves and smoking rivers and barefoot women. It seems simple enough, drive all night through the dawn through the morning through the noon, park on a beach take off your shoes and fall asleep by the Gulf of Mexico. Wake up with the stars above perfectly spaced in perfect health.

Updike admits to not reading Jack Kerouac's *On the Road* before deciding to write a novel about the repercussions of going "on the road." This fact says much about the impact the 1957 novel had on the American psyche at the time. *On the Road* was as much a cultural phenomena as it was a critical work of American literature. But Kerouac was not Updike's only inspirational contemporary. He was also influenced by the short stories published in the *New Yorker* by J. D. Salinger and John Cheever. The middle-class frustration and marital tension found in *Rabbit, Run* closely mimic similar themes found in such stories.

## CRITICAL OVERVIEW

Decades after its publication, *Rabbit, Run* remains one of John Updike's most critically acclaimed and popular novels. For all its accolades, though, Updike's masterpiece was initially received with mixed reviews. Alfred A. Knopf personally agreed to publish the book, but he had reservations. Books were still being banned in 1959, and Knopf was afraid the book's sexual explicitness would land author and publisher in jail. Working with a lawyer, Updike cut the more lascivious parts from the *Rabbit, Run* manuscript, and Knopf published the revision in late 1960. No one went to jail. In fact, several years later Penguin Books agreed to publish a restored edition. Updike made further corrections in following editions and says in his introduction to *Rabbit Angstrom: A Tetralogy* (1995), "*Rabbit, Run*, in keeping with its jittery, indecisive protagonist, exists in more forms than any other novel of mine."

# MEDIA ADAPTATIONS

*Rabbit, Run* was adapted as a film in 1970 by Warner Brothers, starring James Caan in the role of Rabbit Angstrom. As of 2007, it is not available.

In his essay, "Rabbit Loses the Race," Rand Richards Cooper captures the most widely and insistently held criticism against Updike—that the author "is all medium and no message, a man who writes beautifully about nothing." Others, though, feel just as strongly that Updike's lyrical prose is what elevates him above other writers of his generation. According to Paul Gray in a *Time* magazine article about the author, "No one else using the English language over the past 2 1/2 decades has written so well in so many ways as he."

Updike's prose style was not the only thing *Rabbit, Run* critics objected to. The subject matter offended more than one reviewer. David Heddendorf, in notes in his *Southern Review* article "Rabbit Reread,"

> When *Rabbit, Run* first appeared, the explicit sex obliged Updike to consult a lawyer. The threat of legal repercussions had abated by the time of *Rabbit Redux*, but Updike still wonders if that novel didn't contain a "possibly inordinate emphasis on sexual congress."

As forcefully lauded as it was panned, *Rabbit, Run* was significant enough, and Harry "Rabbit" Angstrom interesting enough, to warrant both public and critical interest in three more Rabbit books. *Rabbit Redux*, *Rabbit is Rich*, and *Rabbit at Rest* remain Updike's best known and critically praised books. *Rabbit is Rich* earned a Pulitzer Prize and the National Book Award and *Rabbit at Rest* brought another Pulitzer and a National Book Critics Award. In her review of the entire Rabbit saga, Margaret Sullivan praises the scope of the works and the author's great accomplishment:

> John Updike's four books about Harry Angstrom . . . are not only one of the signal

literary accomplishments of the past half-century. They are not only the most identifiable work of America's best postwar novelist. They're also prime time-capsule material. Written at the end of four decades, starting with the late '50s, the four novels tell us all we need to know—sometimes more than we want or can stand to know—about life in these United States.

## CRITICISM

### David Heddendorf

*In the following excerpt, Heddendorf reflects on the four novels of Updike's "Rabbit" tetrology and the protagonist who has remained a "repugnant but beloved" American character, striving for individuality in an increasingly generic world.*

For the first time since 1950, Americans are leaving a decade behind without the company of Harry "Rabbit" Angstrom, John Updike's fictional Toyota dealer and former high-school basketball star. Not only is Rabbit dead, he's been ceremonially interred in *Rabbit Angstrom* (1995), the one-volume Everyman's Library edition of the four novels that bear his name. In the forty years since, the publication of *Rabbit, Run*, a literary phenomenon that began life as a scandal has achieved a kind of revered, grand-old-man status—still delighting and surprising, certainly selling, but no longer capable of shocking. By 1990 there was something inevitable and almost taken for granted about the Rabbit books, as though Updike owed the world another installment as surely as the world owed Updike another round of awards. The arrival of the next in the series was one of those comforting recurrences like spring or a visit from a favorite uncle. Now, with no further novels to anticipate, we can finally look back and see Harry whole, from the young man crashing a back-alley pickup game to the sad retiree literally playing his heart out on a dusty Florida playground.

To which Rabbit, though, do we look back? Do we reread the originals or the collected, corrected *Rabbit Angstrom?* It's like trying to decide between the 1881 version and the New York Edition of *The Portrait of a Lady*. But where Henry James's late manner superseded his earlier style, charting a new course of indirectness and qualification. Updike's career, while remarkably varied, follows a more continuous line. His aim with the new edition seems restorative rather

*Lew Alcindor (Kareem Abdul-Jabbar) blocks a shot during a high school basketball game* © *Bettmann/Corbis*

than revisionary, the alterations limited mostly to repairing "automotive glitches" (as he calls his mistakes with cars) and correcting other minor errors.

What astonishes, on rereading the novels in their original versions, is how much Updike got right the first time. To return again and again over decades to a detailed chronicle, picking up where one left off and bringing a unified work to completion, must feel like doing a lifelong crossword puzzle in indelible ink. Yet not only do Harry, his wife Janice, and son Nelson endure, looking and sounding like the same complex characters; Updike's language as well—the ever-youthful hero of the tetralogy—reverberates through the novels with widely scattered refrains and sly internal references.

Sometimes a word or phrase from a major scene is repeated from book to book, as with Rabbit's surprised "Hey" from his first night with Ruth in *Rabbit, Run*. Elsewhere a line

rings such a faint bell that only a hunch and some backward paging can locate the source. In *Rabbit at Rest*, for example, Harry contemplates the perfect golf swing, the way the ball makes "a tiny tunnel into the absolute." "That would be *it*," the rapturous paragraph concludes—oddly, yet with something familiar the phrase. Sure enough, in *Rabbit, Run* Harry hits a gorgeous tee shot, admires the ball's protracted flight, and exclaims, "That's *it*!" to the minister Jack Eccles, who has been asking Rabbit what mysterious presence he seeks.

Later in *Rabbit, Run*, after the birth of the doomed baby, one of the novel's showier sentences occurs: "Sunshine, the old clown, rims the room." It reappears verbatim in *Rabbit, Redux*, again placed prominently at the beginning of a section. (In the new *Rabbit Angstrom* the echo is clipped to "Sunshine, the old clown"—as in the golf epiphany only grazing the ear, stirring memory like a symphony theme.)

Since the novels are narrated, with occasional exceptions, from Rabbit's expansive point of view, these verbal echoes occur as Harry remembers words of warning, command, joy, and love. He hears his mother whispering "Hassy," Ruth in bed saying "Work," and a gruff gas-station attendant telling him, his first time on the road, "The only way to get somewhere, you know, is to figure out where you're going before you go there." These catchwords and aphorisms lodge in Harry's teeming mind, to surface unpredictably as the decades pass. The wholeness Rabbit feels in his life derives, like the novelistic wholeness wrought by Updike's brimming language, from a lengthy accretion of verbal textures.

In *Rabbit, Run* more than in the later novels, Harry is the central problem, the baffling source of all the action. He leaves Janice before we quite know who he is, tells Ruth he loves her when she's little more to him than a prostitute, returns to Janice for the baby's birth, and runs again. Where the later novels bulge with events and people to whom Rabbit must respond, *Rabbit, Run* dwells probingly on Harry himself, introducing others mainly so they can try to figure him out. "Oh, my Rabbit," Ruth laughs, charmed yet mystified. "You just wander, don't you?" Jack Eccles, sent by Janice's parents to bring Harry home, winds up on the golf course soliciting his views about God.

Updike has said he intended his hero to show the cruelty of unrestrained, Kerouac-inspired romanticism, a temperament that characterizes one side of Rabbit. "All I know is what feels right," says this selfish, impulsive Harry to Ruth. But because his feelings are torn between the flesh and the spirit, he can also embody what his earthly creator calls "our heart's stubborn amoral quest for something once called grace." The novels issue periodic bulletins on this quest of Rabbit's, monitoring his spiritual state as, in his fashion, he nurses a wavering, unfocused faith. On the night his child is born he stands in the hospital parking lot, praying to the moon. Flying to the tropics with adultery on his mind, he is filled with religious awe: "God, having shrunk in Harry's middle years to the size of a raisin lost under the car seat, is suddenly great again, everywhere like a radiant wind." There is nothing phony or hypocritical about these transports of Harry's. They simply come over him, out of the blue as it were, moving him with the same irresistible force as lust. All he knows is what feels right.

The relatively empty, God-haunted universe of *Rabbit, Run* gives way to the worldly incursions of the later novels: the Apollo 11 landing of *Rabbit Redux*, the gas shortage of *Rabbit Is Rich*, the Pan Am bombing of *Rabbit at Rest*. AIDS and cocaine add their destructive plot engines, while hurricanes and Super Bowl crowds roar offstage. Harry, who began as a cryptic central presence, diminishes to a ten-year time capsule. We learn what's on TV, what songs are on the radio, how Mike Schmidt and the Phillies are doing. Harry starts to react with his familiar surly grow—rereading *Rabbit, Run*, one is startled by the boyish voice—as celebrities, headlines, and commercial jingles compete for his sensitive notice. A marked change comes over the novels. Details that once appeared as background, fixing us in time and space, become prominent in their own right. We still get the news and hype through Harry's point of view, with his opinions as our escort through the cultural landscape, but both the landmarks and the minutiae claim considerable space on their own.

Rabbit participates in his inundation—rushing to catch the nightly news, annoyed when family duties delay him. The Toyotas he selects for his personal use must have high-quality radios among their features. Yet even as Harry invites the media tide, he resents and fears a dark undercurrent he can't help hearing. Vacationing in the Poconos in *Rabbit Is Rich*, he remembers boyhood summer drives to the Jersey Shore: "Town after town numbingly demonstrated to him that his life was a paltry thing, roughly duplicated by the millions in settings where houses and porches and trees mocking those in Mt. Judge fed the illusions of other little boys that their souls were central and dramatic and invisibly cherished." The older Rabbit gets, the more his soul feels squeezed by multitudinous America. Duplication, it turns out, was just getting warmed up. With his copy of *Consumer Reports* promising a world of choices, he watches his surroundings collapse into wearying sameness, a boulevard of malls and fast-food chains. His daily joys, robbed of singularity, seem transient as the songs that clog the memories of millions like himself.

Harry can't endure immersion in the crowd—he used to be the crowd's high-scoring favorite. As an older man he relinquishes local fame, reduced to a benevolent Uncle Sam in a Fourth of July parade, but he still demands some minimal notice, as if proving to himself he exists. He needs the reassurance of "earning his pay-check, filling his slot in the big picture, doing his bit, getting a little recognition. That's all we want from each other, recognition."

After four lengthy volumes we readers, at least, do recognize Harry. We're acquainted with his uncircumcised penis, his tendency to sneeze, his queasiness about eating animals. We've been told the address of every place he's lived. We know the eyebrow cowlick he's handed down to his son, Nelson, and granddaughter Judy. These enumerated particulars begin to seem insistent, as if claiming more than the conventional roundedness of fictional characterization. "Here stands (walks, talks, copulates) an individual," say these traits, "despite the best efforts of mass society." But Harry requires the ultimate recognition, the one he believes in as the ground of all others. To his friend and fellow heart patient Charlie Stavros, who asks what *else* Harry is but a machine for pumping blood, Harry replies silently, defiantly, "A God-made one-of-a-kind with an immortal soul breathed in." In a uniform, flattening America of disposable identities, Rabbit calls on a resource that exceeds his traits: his dogged faithfulness in being himself.

As Updike observes in the *Rabbit Angstrom* introduction, the first of the novels contains the fewest topical references. After the strange and faraway *Rabbit, Run*, *Rabbit at Rest* can feel almost pushily familiar, accosting us with our own obsessive murmurings and daydreams. But the sense of being overrun by brand names and current events might be partly a trick of historical perspective. Compared to Deion Sanders and Toyota slogans, the pop culture of thirty and forty years ago will sound faintly, if at all. The voices buzzing around us might amount to little more than static, but *Cheers* and *Night Court* remain, after a little over a decade, *our* static. Reading the novels in succession, gradually nearing our own time, we see Harry's world grow larger and more distinct book by book, like an object approaching from beyond the horizon.

But what of Harry himself? To recognize him by his quirks isn't necessarily to know him,

and his noisy, garish world, much of it with us still, threatens to obstruct our view of the man. In forty more years, the gleam of the contemporary having rubbed off at last, Harry might emerge in a clearer light, if at a greater distance. Perhaps he'll join on the remote heights of literature such flawed idealists as Ahab, Hester Prynne, and Huckleberry Finn—ambiguous yet unmistakable, repugnant yet beloved. Already Harry seems destined for such an afterlife, with his contradictions, his moral failures redeemed by moral outrage, his American distrust of collective identity. To know and understand these tendencies in Harry—loving him one moment, fearing him the next—is to recognize ourselves in his disappointed faith, his alert and articulate pain.

**Source:** David Heddendorf, "Rabbit Reread," in *Southern Review*, Vol. 36, No. 3, Summer 2000, pp. 641–47.

## SOURCES

Boswell, Marshall, "John Updike," in *The Literary Encyclopedia*, March 18, 2004, www.litencyc.com (August 19, 2006).

Bradley, Becky, "American Cultural History," in *Kingwood College Library*, updated June 2005, kclibrary.nhmccd.edu/decade50.html (August 19, 2006).

Cooper, Rand Richards, "Rabbit Loses the Race," in *Commonweal*, May 17, 1991, pp. 315–21.

Heddendorf, David, "Rabbit Reread," in the *Southern Review*, Vol. 36, No. 3, Summer 2000, p. 641.

Gray, Peter, "Perennial Promises Kept," in *Time*, October 18, 1982, www.time.com/time/magazine/article/0,9171,949600,00.html (November 25, 2006).

Sullivan, Margaret, "Rabbit's Window on America," in the *Buffalo News* (Buffalo, New York), January 7, 1996, p. G5.

Updike, John, "Introduction," in *Rabbit Angstrom—The Four Novels*, Everyman's Library, 1995, pp. x, xi.

———, *Rabbit, Run*, Knopf, 1960; reprint, Ballantine Books, 1996.

"View From the Catacombs" in *Time* April 26, 1968, Vol. 91, No. 17, p. 10, www.time.com/time/magazine/print out/0,8816,838313,00.html, (November 25, 2006).

# Self-Reliance

## RALPH WALDO EMERSON

## 1841

In "Self-Reliance" (1841), Ralph Waldo Emerson, the premier American poet, philosopher, and lecturer of the nineteenth century, sums up the most basic and pervasive idea of the American dream and gives expression to many prominent and long-lasting American ideals. From individualism to entrepreneurialism, Emerson's writings emphasize the responsibility of each citizen to the self rather than to an outside authority. Living at a time when America is undergoing vast social and economic changes, Emerson provides an image of the young nation as enterprising, imaginative, and full of opportunity. A person's destiny lies in his or her own hands, according to this giant of American literature, and therefore Emerson helps establish much of the rhetoric surrounding the American dream.

"Self-Reliance" remains one of Emerson's most popular essays. In it, he describes the many distractions of society and culture that attempt to draw attention away from personal introspection. Looking within the self is the only path to true enlightenment, Emerson writes, and therefore anything that calls one away from the self should be shunned. Similarly, each person must define life individually, boldly casting off any external pressures to conform. "Self-Reliance" helps articulate the rallying cry for the nineteenth-century philosophical movement called Transcendentalism, in which many other prominent writers and artists participated and

which focused energy away from cultural institutions such as the church and toward the inner workings of each individual soul. Emerson's essay claims that success lies in remaining true to the divine directing voice within each person's soul and not to any outside influence.

Emerson was raised and educated in Massachusetts, living in Boston while young and making his adult home in Concord. Having grown up around the elite intellectual circles of Boston, Emerson enjoyed social prominence because his family included several generations of respected Unitarian ministers. Financial stability was elusive, however, due to Emerson's father's untimely death. Until his early adulthood, Emerson worked to help support his mother and siblings. It was not until his inheritance from the unfortunate death of his first wife that the aspiring writer was able to retire from the ministry and pursue intellectual efforts. Despite his family legacy and his Harvard degree in ministry, Emerson's heart was not in his pulpit but instead in a philosophical life.

Despite his early connection to elite society, Emerson became highly critical of such traditional communities later in life. *Nature*, published in 1836, was one of Emerson's first major literary efforts and began his rise to national prominence. His later works include collections of essays, books of poems, and many recorded speeches. Calling on life as a man's best educator (and Emerson speaks almost exclusively about *men*), this philosopher praises the highly adaptable, resilient, and ultimately self-reliant man as the best model. Emerson's influence is so widely felt that his articulation of the self-reliant individual has become mythic in American culture. Emerson's self-reliant man has access to the American dream because he asks for little help and instead finds resources for success within himself.

Becoming one of America's most beloved writers during his lifetime, Emerson personally influenced an entire generation of artists. Helping establish the emerging literary scene in America, Emerson followed his own philosophy of the individual and pursued friendships with many young writers. Most famously, he maintained lifelong relationships with fellow essayists and Transcendentalists Henry David Thoreau and Margaret Fuller. Emerson mentored his Concord neighbor, Thoreau, encouraging his work and even financially supporting him on

# BIOGRAPHY

## RALPH WALDO EMERSON

Born May 25, 1803, Massachusetts native Emerson became America's preeminent literary figure in the nineteenth century. "Self-Reliance" (1841) was written during Emerson's most productive years, and it remains one of his most read pieces. His poems and essays catapulted Emerson to international fame and established him as the authority on American letters. With generations of ministers in his family, Emerson followed in his father's footsteps and trained at Harvard Divinity School. He became an ordained minister in the Unitarian church, serving as a preacher for a short time.

After a crisis of faith, however, he left the pulpit and went on to become a poet, essayist, and lecturer. Helping launch the American Transcendentalist movement, a philosophy that espoused spirituality based within the individual, he strongly influenced the younger writers of his time. Emerson championed many of the concepts that have become mainstays of the American consciousness: individualism, personal responsibility, and nonconformity. He survived many tragedies in his life, including the deaths of his father, brothers, wife, and first son. Emerson wrote copiously throughout his long life, including innumerable journals, and he died peacefully on April 27, 1882, among friends.

occasion. Similarly, Fuller and Emerson regularly corresponded and discussed their current writing projects as well as the political and social issues of the day. Beyond such intimate personal interactions, Emerson's endorsement was constantly and eagerly sought after among nineteenth-century writers. Walt Whitman and Louisa May Alcott, among numerous others, mentioned the profound shadow Emerson cast on their own writing as well as on the American literary tradition more generally.

Emerson has become canonized as a primary figure in Western literary history, often referred to as the father of American literature. And while his specific contributions are still debated among academics, his literary legacy remains solid. Emerson's reputation was not strictly positive during his lifetime, however. While some negative reviews arose in the North among those who disliked Emerson's attacks on institutions such as church and government, the New England writer's most virulent critics grew out of the South. Emerson seemed to attack the entirety of southern culture in his rejection of community, his suspicion of religion, and his denouncement of slavery, and southern readers took notice. Emerson and his southern critics traded jabs throughout his career, illustrating how controversial Emerson's ideas of America and self-reliance truly were. But his fame remained constant throughout his lifetime and since, despite these critical detractors.

Studied alongside Emerson's other famous text, the Harvard Phi Beta Kappa speech, "The American Scholar," "Self-Reliance" is now widely available online and in print. Consistently anthologized, Emerson's essay may be found in such popular college texts as *The Norton Anthology of American Literature* and *The Heath Anthology of American Literature*. And although Emerson's larger influence on American literature and culture cannot be understated, "Self-Reliance" often stands as one of the few texts by this literary icon students ever read.

*Ralph Waldo Emerson* © *Corbis*

## PLOT SUMMARY

Emerson focuses his essay on all the external ways men distract themselves from their true, internal genius (Emerson exclusively uses the masculine pronoun). Only the self-reliant man will find success; all outside influences only take away from personal fulfillment. He begins by emphasizing the value of individual expression. The more personal and honest a man's sentiment, the more universally applicable that sentiment will be. Anyone who has ever recognized his own idea in another's words understands the truth of this phenomenon. Therefore, man must begin to trust himself and discover his own journey in life, because no one else can live his particular life for him. And when he follows

someone else's path, he feels downtrodden and deflated; therefore, he must trust himself and trust the goodness of his specific experience.

Man cannot bow to the pressures of society if he wants to follow his own genius. No government or church can explain a man's heart to him, and so each individual must resist institutional authority. Even when following one's own path may be offensive to others, Emerson charges readers to do so. Seemingly good relationships may undermine individual genius as well, and so Emerson charges individuals to disregard how they will appear to others. "My life is for itself," he writes, "and not for a spectacle." The danger of trying to please others is that it buries the true self, making it more difficult to discern later. The self ends up becoming part of the group, leaving little individuality and creating a herd mentality. But remaining separate from social pressures will not win friends; in fact, the man who follows his own path will likely bother those around him.

A man should be bold in his words and actions, even if they are either offensive or contradictory. There will always be the potential that what one says or does today will clash with what one says or does tomorrow, but Emerson states that a concern for contradiction is futile. "A foolish consistency is the hobgoblin of little minds. . . . With consistency a great soul has simply nothing to do," Emerson says, "He may as well concern himself with his shadow on the wall." In the same way, one cannot be worried about being misunderstood: "To be great is to be misunderstood." All important men have faced public scrutiny; such criticism is often evidence of the genius of a man's actions. Even when distinct choices may not seem to make sense, if a man follows his own inspiration, a larger pattern will eventually emerge.

Great men all exhibit similar characteristics of self-reliance, but still one should not be overly impressed by any historical figure. Men of the past are no more important than men of the present; they only provide an example of how one may be true to oneself. Nothing can be true in the past alone, but if something is true, it will be true for all time: "it lives now, and absorbs past and future in the present hour." Therefore, history should not become an authority in an individual life. Instead of quoting famous men of the past, Emerson encourages individuals to project their own ideas in their own words. Further, the study of history cannot help a man understand his own inspiration. When a flash of genius occurs, it is completely new and cannot be compared to anything that came before. History serves no purpose in the face of present enlightenment. No matter how much one wants the past to influence the future, it cannot: "This one fact the world hates, that the soul *becomes*; for that for ever degrades the past, turns all riches to poverty, all reputation to shame."

Self-reliance is the only law of nature; men that find all truth within themselves have consistent access to survival. Distractions such as society, work, and family only take away from a man's ability to survive and thrive. To nurture self-reliance, men should attempt to make their outside relationships more truthful. It takes courage to be so honest, and most men do not succeed. For most people, "we have not chosen, but society has chosen for us. We are parlour soldiers." Because of social pressure, men succumb to failure too quickly. Emerson praises the resilient man, the man who can turn adversity into opportunity. Describing a multi-talented and quick-thinking representative man, Emerson encourages readers to continually reinvent themselves according to their own inspiration. A self-reliant man exhibits

> WHAT I MUST DO IS ALL THAT CONCERNS ME, NOT WHAT THE PEOPLE THINK. THIS RULE, EQUALLY ARDUOUS IN ACTUAL AND IN INTELLECTUAL LIFE, MAY SERVE FOR THE WHOLE DISTINCTION BETWEEN GREATNESS AND MEANNESS."

eternal optimism in the face of difficulty, and he tries many different avenues to achieve success.

While pursuing success, society encourages men to use religion as a crutch. Prayer, for example, misdirects a man's focus away from his internal inspiration. If prayer helps an individual understand the vastness of creation, then it is an appropriate spiritual expression. But if it seeks only short-term gain, prayer remains petty. Similarly, men fall victim to regret as they pursue success. Instead of regretting past mistakes, Emerson encourages men to use that energy toward correcting the actual problem. "Welcome evermore to gods and men is the self-helping man," Emerson writes, "For him all doors are flung wide."

The self-reliant man also shuns travel. Despite the popularity in Emerson's time of visiting Europe, Emerson asserts that all truths can be found locally, within the individual. The thinking man, therefore, remains true to himself in all situations and does not require the distraction of travel to occupy him: "The soul is no traveller; the wise man stays at home." A man's internal state remains the same no matter where he is, and, unfortunately, his problems will follow him throughout his travels. Travel only distracts a man from himself and discourages his originality. "Insist on yourself," Emerson writes, "never imitate."

Finally, despite the many advances of civilization, Emerson states that society always loses when it gains. Whereas modern society has more advanced modes of living, it has lost much of its physical strength. "Society is a wave," he explains, "The wave moves onward, but the water of which it is composed does not." Too much concern for the progress of civilization as well as the accumulation of property only distracts the individual from his own genius. One must cast aside consumerism and embrace the unique work set in front of him; such is the only path to both enlightenment and happiness. The self-reliant man does not need good luck to succeed because his devotion to his own genius makes luck superfluous. Emerson concludes, "Nothing can bring you peace but yourself."

# THEMES

## *Authority of the Individual*

Emerson explores and expounds on some of the oldest and most basic of American ideals in his essay. That church and state should be separate, and that the wisdom to govern rests within each member of the democracy are tenets that form the basis for American life. Emerson wants every person to embrace and acknowledge that individual authority. Because Emerson believes that all the truths of the universe reside in the individual soul, he debunks tradition as an authority in a person's life. Religion and history, therefore, should hold little sway over an individual's decisions. Instead, Emerson calls religious tradition and historical study distractions, keeping the true self from expressing its own spirit.

Religion provides life answers that Emerson believes individuals should seek out for themselves. Certainly not against spirituality, Emerson instead believes that enlightenment lies within personal experience rather than among centuries-old religious traditions. Above all, however, Emerson rails against religious authorities that require community obedience. Nothing has authority over the self, he writes, but the honest internal revelations of a true seeker. Any ideas or inspirations that an individual has should be pursued and should not be tested against an external authority such as a minister or a sacred text. Such actions only serve to undermine the individual quest for truth and make a person doubt himself. Emerson believes that the individual is sufficient to encounter truth and should not rely on a church for mediation.

Similarly, history often becomes an idol and a distraction in directing people's lives. Emerson strongly believes in studying history for knowledge but not for authoritative answers in the individual life. History shows that great individuals always follow their own path and create their own followers. Anyone who attempts to mimic those great individuals goes against that very teaching, Emerson explains; great individuals are always originals. History cannot bring enlightenment; only individual searching can. Thus the only authority in people's lives resides in the truth that exists within their souls and not in revered institutions such as religion or history.

## *Nonconformity*

Emerson writes, "Whoso would be a man must be a nonconformist." Therefore, he encourages every person to follow his or her own path at the expense of any other commitments. While not all versions of the American dream envision or encourage individualism, the counter-culture ethos has been the driving force behind generations of Americans' quests for themselves. "Self-Reliance" harshly condemns the herd-like functioning of many communities and instead insists that individuals withdraw from such conformity and enter into their own sphere of influence. From institutional pressures such as government or religion to personal obligations such as family and friends, Emerson espouses radical solitude. He writes, "the great man is he who in the midst of the crowd keeps with perfect sweetness the independence of solitude." Often intending that solitude to be understood more metaphorically than literally, Emerson desires for each individual to cultivate an internal peace that repels outside influence.

Emerson claims that everyone has a spirit of genius within them waiting to be explored. The path of exploration may lead in various and ever-changing directions, he explains, but such inconsistency should not be feared. In fact, Emerson encourages the individual to embrace whatever inspiration may arise at that moment, and then change direction willingly if inspiration so determines. "Speak what you think now in hard words," he insists, "and to-morrow speak what to-morrow thinks in hard words again." A fierce commitment to truth is required to achieve enlightenment, Emerson believes, because one cannot fear looking foolish to others. Despite other people's impressions, one must seek one's own truth. Neither social custom nor even one's own past actions should determine an individual's genius, according to Emerson, but instead ever-present internal inspiration should direct one's choices.

## Community and Solitude

Emerson repeatedly discusses the merits of being alone, both literally and metaphorically, throughout his essay. He believes enlightenment can only develop within the individual when there is adequate time for contemplation and meditation, and community often threatens that opportunity. Solitude provides Emerson with the peace to consider his own thoughts, following them from initial inspiration to mature development. Community, on the other hand, often distracts the individual from the project of self-discovery. Distractions take many forms, including friendly social visits, spouse and child needs, as well as community pressures to become involved with local governments; all of these forms of personal invasion interrupt individual thought. Because Emerson recognizes that pressures such as work and family often impede on individual solitude, he encourages people to fend off such intrusions. Be less involved with the community, he instructs, and take abundant time for internal reflection.

But solitude does not only reside with the individual who remains alone, according to Emerson. The individual can indeed cultivate an internal solitude even among a crowd by developing a strong sense of self. This solitude is the very core of self-reliance, which is the core of the American dream for Emerson. By fostering one's own thoughts deeply and thoroughly, Emerson believes that a person may gain adequate self-confidence to avoid being swayed by a group of people. Considering Emerson's own very active social circles, it is not surprising that his views on community seem somewhat contradictory. On one hand, he praises solitude and, on the other hand, he cultivates numerous personal relationships. Emerson concludes that the individual who knows one's own mind can remain strong among life's distractions and can keep that mind free from whatever external clutter surrounds it. Developing an internal solitude, for Emerson, helps the individual reach enlightenment by not allowing trivial details to crowd out important personal revelation.

## Spirituality

Emerson was raised with the legacy of New England tradition and Puritan Christianity. Among the principles of this inheritance of faith are a strict adherence to moral piety and a reverence for the Bible as an authority. Further, religious revivals grew popular throughout America in the late eighteenth century, causing his contemporary culture to be saturated with various forms of Protestant Christianity. Because Emerson himself came from a family of Unitarians, both the specific denomination and the larger tradition of Christian faith weighed heavily on his community and on his early life.

As Emerson reviews an increasingly wide range of texts in his writing, he develops an argument against such strict Christian religions. He finds truth in the religions from other lands, such as Buddhism and Hinduism, and also finds inspiration in literary texts from other cultures. Emerson presents illustrations from such varying sources to explain how truth can be found in many different locations, not just in the Judeo-Christian heritage of New England culture. In fact, in the end, truth really resides within the individual soul. His belief is that soul that recognizes truth within literature, art, and nature, and thus becomes enlightened by those inspirational encounters.

Emerson views religion as often standing in the way of personal enlightenment. But he does not merge the restrictive idea of organized religion with what he views as the positive idea of personal faith. Whereas religion seeks to bind and control a person, faith instead serves to inspire and free an individual. For Emerson, faith indicates a belief in a universal God who permeates all of creation and inspires the individual to enlightenment. Any idea, whether from one's own mind, another person, a piece of literature, or a simple walk in the woods, that rings true to the individual reflects a connection with this all-encompassing God. Emerson's goal, then, is to encounter truth wherever it may appear. Religion, Emerson believes, by contrast exists on a small scale and only discourages people from finding truth for themselves. Faith and religion are very different entities for Emerson, faith being crucial to his philosophy and religion often impeding it. Emerson, like countless Americans before him and since, enjoys the freedom to develop and exercise his own view of what his spiritual life should be.

## HISTORICAL OVERVIEW

### Emerson and the American Literary Renaissance

Emerson's life spanned the nineteenth century, a century full of major changes for the then young nation. Emerson's early education brought him into contact with the elite Boston Brahmin society of his father's circles. His college and seminary education at Harvard continued his access to the traditional and privileged world of high academia. But by his young adulthood, Emerson became disenchanted with this social and cultural atmosphere; as a result, he began conceiving and writing about his perspective on individual enlightenment and its free access to all mankind, regardless of life position. This democratic approach to education, claiming that the only true knowledge comes from internal investigation and loyalty to the self alone, helps develop the larger American persona of rugged individualism that lasts throughout the next century.

"Self-Reliance" extends the philosophy of the individual Emerson made famous in his 1837 Harvard Phi Beta Kappa address, "The American Scholar." In this speech, Emerson encourages Americans to throw off the fetters of tradition and live an original life. Despite his own education at Harvard and his very presence at the institution while delivering the speech, Emerson decries conventional education, instead favoring the education only true living can bring. Emerson praises the individual spirit and thus builds his career, and reputation, on the shaping of the American character.

Only an independent nation for several decades, nineteenth-century America sought to define itself in relation to England and the rest of Europe. Competing with centuries-old cultures often left the United States looking not only inexperienced but also naive and unsophisticated. In literature especially, America lacked a respected tradition, causing British and French literature to remain preferable to domestic writers. Emerson emerged within this ongoing battle for an American place on the literary stage, and expressed a new approach, eventually becoming one of the first American writers recognized on an international level. Emerson's philosophy enabled American literature to compete with European literature, by claiming that inspiration and genius develop from individuals rather than from any longstanding national pedigree. Emerson asserts that every individual has access to the divine spirit, a tenant of Transcendental thought, and that true fulfillment comes only with the liberation of custom and culture. By encouraging the individual to resist society's rules, he underscores the idea that Americans can succeed on their own terms. Emerson, then, helps build the concept of American opportunity, free and open to anyone willing to follow personal inspiration.

Amid this new spirit of American individualism, many young literary voices arose and helped establish the American Renaissance. During this time, an unprecedented number of writers published essays, novels, shorts stories, and poems, all of which began establishing the United States as a distinct literary tradition. Among the Renaissance writers are Henry David Thoreau, Margaret Fuller, Nathaniel Hawthorne, Herman Melville, Edgar Allan Poe, Harriet Beecher Stowe, and Walt Whitman. Famous slave narratives by Frederick Douglass and Harriet Jacobs were also written and published during the mid-nineteenth century, adding the slave voice to the emerging character of American literature.

Early to mid-nineteenth-century American literature is also often referred to as America's Romantic period. Romanticism is a broad category in literary studies, used to denote a time span in which writers focus, broadly speaking, on the feelings or emotions associated with a text. Focal points often include nature, individualism, mysticism, and history. Generally, Romanticism deals in imagination while realism deals in the unadorned details of everyday life. French and English cultures both had periods of romantic literature in the eighteenth century, and America's Romanticism emerged in the mid-nineteenth century. American Romanticism is often understood to be a reaction to the Enlightenment period of the eighteenth century, in which rationality prevailed.

### Transcendentalism

Emerson also helped found the popular Transcendentalist movement in the northeastern United States. Steering its followers away from reliance on cultural institutions such as the church or the government, Transcendentalism sought to uplift the individual soul. In part a reaction against Unitarianism, the Transcendentalists attempted to connect to nature's and the soul's overarching and spiritual energy. Whereas Unitarianism promoted controlled and rational expression of religious experience, the Transcendentalists sought a more animated spiritual response. Instead of locating the subject of their worship in a deity, however, the

Transcendentalists experienced inspiration from both the individual soul and from nature. Often including a near-worship of the natural world, Transcendentalists regularly located their meditations and even their conversations outside. And physical labor was prized among the group as a vehicle for enlightenment, with the Transcendentalists praising simple work to clear the mind.

Emerson stood as a leading figure in the Transcendentalist movement, as did many other public intellectuals of the time including writers Henry David Thoreau, Margaret Fuller, Bronson Alcott, William Ellery Channing, and Lydia Marie Child. The Transcendentalists met regularly to discuss ideas, politics, and writing, and they even established their own literary journal, *The Dial*. Although lasting only four years and not particularly popular in its time, *The Dial*, and the Transcendentalists more generally, became significant and often-studied contributors to the American literary tradition.

Devotees of Transcendentalism were so passionate about their new American philosophy that they even established a short-lived commune called Brook Farm, located outside of Boston. A utopian community, Brook Farm incorporated both manual labor and intellectual stimulation into the daily lives of its residents; the hope was that individuals could pursue a freedom of mind and body on the farm, unrestrained by traditional constraints of society and yet with the support of an ever-present community. While Emerson did not participate in the Brook Farm experiment, Nathaniel Hawthorne was involved early on. Hawthorne, however, developed into a most notable opponent to Transcendentalism after his initial support of Brook Farm, later finding such profound optimism troubling and preferring to investigate the darker side of individuals in community.

## Social Change and Upheaval in a Young Nation

During Emerson's career, the biggest crisis of the young United States, the American Civil War (1860–1865), occurred. With the abolitionist movement swelling in the northern states throughout the decades preceding the war, Emerson faced frequent criticism for his lack of involvement to free the slaves. His early philosophy, however, warned citizens of joining political movements because of the potential for lost individualism. With many political causes growing during the early to mid-nineteenth century, also including the fight for women's suffrage, Emerson watched as activist groups seemed to overtake the individual person. To stay loyal to himself, Emerson initially rebuffed political involvement. However, several national incidents such as the passage of the 1850 Fugitive Slave Law, requiring northern states to return escaped slaves to their owners in the South, stirred Emerson to action. Still conflicted about activism more generally, he believed the slave law to be unfair and publicly denounced it. All of Emerson's writings exhibit the tension between personal inspiration and communal responsibility, as did his own life during the century that witnessed so many changes.

Emerson's lifetime also saw the expansion of America westward, the growth of immigration, and the building of railroads. Such changes brought vast upheaval to the idea of America because its very borders, the modes of economic support, and the ways to travel between those borders, were rapidly transforming. As the United States acquired new territory, tripling its size by mid-century, the main question remained whether each new territory would be deemed a slave or a free state. For the average citizen, greater expansion meant more opportunity. Pioneers regularly set out to make a better life in the territories as yet unpopulated by Americans; life proved harsh for those early explorers, but the promise of land and a new life continued to attract frontier families.

Furthermore, mass immigration completely changed the face of America and vastly increased its workforce. Largely from Ireland and western Europe, great numbers of foreigners moved to the United States in search of a better life. Industrialization, marked by textile manufacture and increased mining, harnessed this growing workforce in mills and factories of various sorts. Working conditions for everyone, immigrants and non-immigrants alike, began to decline rapidly because of unregulated markets and competition for jobs. The newly established railroad system provided even more jobs for the changing American workforce and even more profit for the giants of American business. With railroads came enormous new opportunities for fast travel, while at the same time increasing the wealth, and ultimately corruption, of the few owners of industry.

All of these additions to the young nation caused a feeling of constant tumult in society. Emerson generally sided with progress in many cases, as did poet Walt Whitman, both exhibiting their characteristic optimism. Other writers, such as Thoreau, remained skeptical of such changes. Emerson grew into an outspoken critic of slavery, thus promoting national expansion without human bondage. He touted the new railroad as a transportation wonder, singing its praises and becoming a champion of technological progress. The main focus for Emerson, throughout the many changes appearing in his lifetime, was to retain the supremacy of the individual, though. He believed that no positive change would come without an enlightened individual soul. Numerous enlightened souls might be able to affect change, but the individual enlightenment comes first. Technology and progress transform with the times, he believed, so there would be little morality in the changes themselves; instead, meaning could be found in the ways an individual harnesses progress for one's own edification and how one finds inspiration amid the progress.

## CRITICAL OVERVIEW

The critical work surrounding Emerson is rich and varied, first and foremost establishing him as one of the most influential writers in American history. Critics focus on Emerson's vast contributions to American culture, citing his elevation of democratic ideals and his focus on individualism. As these elements become synonymous with the American character, Emerson's place in literary tradition, and American history more generally, can hardly be understated.

Specific analyses of Emerson's writings vary widely. Politics, for example, offer a fertile ground for Emersonian critical inquiry. Whereas some writers claim that Emerson rejects all politics on a philosophical level, others link him to a variety of specific political causes. "Self-Reliance" illustrates well the difficulty of establishing Emerson within the political realm; on one hand, he encourages the individual to remain aloof from society and answer only to the self; on the other hand, he preaches a gospel of individual freedom two decades before the American Civil War. With various methods, critics generally agree that Emerson did not endorse politics without serious personal examination. Political positions might be established through individual enlightenment but, for Emerson, could not be entered into without such deep contemplation and personal integrity.

From classifying him as an apolitical inspiration of the nineteenth century's American literary Renaissance to drawing connections between his writings and social issues such as abolition and, later, the U.S. Civil Rights movement, academics continue to analyze Emerson's writings on various levels. Emerson also provides a lightening rod for women's issues both in his time and beyond, as writers and critics question how his view of self-reliance may or may not be accessible to minority members of society, especially African Americans and women.

Emerson is most typically placed within the larger scope of the development of American literature, initially by Perry Miller and William Hedges, who read Emerson as following and extending the ideas of earlier writers such as Puritan preacher Jonathan Edwards and philosopher and statesman Benjamin Franklin. Emerson becomes understood as helping create a distinctly American literature, as differentiated from the then more-prestigious British and European writing. Buell, Emerson critic and biographer, contextualizes this understanding of the New England writer and of American literature more specifically, by illustrating how Emerson remains indebted to global influences throughout his body of work. "Self-Reliance," like much of Emerson's writing, uses numerous examples from international literature and philosophy to make his arguments about individuality. Buell writes in "Emerson and His Cultural Critics," "not New England alone but the whole world was to be his workshop." Emerson, then, not only helps establish the tradition of American literature as centered on the individual, with a strong emphasis on originality, but also relies on and respects vast world cultures to solidify his philosophy.

Emerson critics also focus on the writer's literary voice. Despite Emerson's enormous popularity with readers during his lifetime, many critics cite the difficulty modern readers have in understanding and enjoying some of Emerson's more extensive ideas. Finding his writing, at times, dense, full of allusions, and

# MEDIA ADAPTATIONS

"Self Reliance and Other Essays" was released as an audio CD in 2005. It is available from bnpublishing.com.

"Thoreau and Emerson: Nature and Spirit" is a two-cassette set featuring both authors' best-known essays. It is read by Russ Barnett and is available from Audio Partners Publishing.

"Self-Reliance" is available as an audio cassette or MP3 download from Recorded Books. It is read by Richard Wulf and was published in 1988.

difficult to follow, twenty-first century readers often study only his short essays and inspirational quotes. George Kateb, according to Gregory T. Garvey, "emphasizes distinctions between 'mental' and 'active' self-reliance to assert Emerson's importance to theories of democratic citizenship." Garvey goes on:

> Kateb politicizes Emersonian Transcendentalism by making a direct connection between mental self-reliance and the preservation of democracy. Because mental self-reliance denotes an independent and imaginative construction of identity, Kateb gives it a unique importance to the theory of democratic citizenship.

In the twenty-first century, critics see a parallel between Emerson's ideal and modern Americans, who may be less than ideal. In a *New York Times* editorial, Adam Cohen writes:

> Emerson's vast body of work is credited with playing a large part in shaping the American character. It provides, in particular, an intellectual basis for one of America's great traditions, rugged individualism. But also embedded in his writings are the stirrings of a more pernicious, and currently thriving, philosophy, of American individualism run amok—call it American self-absorption. . . . [H]is writings on individualism speak not only to our highest natures, but to our lowest. Two hundred years after his birth, Emerson the secular preacher still matters not because he has all the answers for how we should live, but because he so intriguingly reflects who we actually are.

## CRITICISM

### Hildegard Hoeller

*In the following excerpt, Hoeller illustrates how gender and class influence Emerson's concepte of sel-reliance, despite the transcendentalist's claims to universalism. Hoeller uses Frances Harper's writings to flesh out self-reliance for those not included in Emerson's elite world, that is, for women, African Americans, and the working class.*

In "Self-Reliance" Emerson undoubtedly envisions a self-reliant man, not a self-reliant woman. "Man is his own star," the essay opens, and it never wavers in its assumption that the self-reliant person Emerson invokes is male. While at one moment Emerson writes that "we want men and women who shall renovate life and our social state," his essay does little to imagine or name such women. His models for self-reliance—such as Moses, Plato, Milton, Pythagoras, Socrates, Jesus, Copernicus, Newton, Hermit Anthony, Luther, Wesley, Clarkson, Scipio and others— are all men. Throughout the essay, Emerson uses the terms "every man" and "a man," and the "I" of the essay announces that he "will shun father and mother and wife and brother when my genius calls me." Indeed, Emerson underscores the maleness of his self-reliant man when he labels the "decorous and prudent rage" of the "cultivated classes" who might oppose the self-reliant man with "their feminine rage." As Carolyn Sorisio argues, "the radical implications of [Emerson's] philosophy are undercut when considered in relation to women by his consistent use of gendered language that highlights difference." To Sorisio, "'Self-Reliance'...exhibits Emerson's suspicion of the feminine/domestic realm's potential tyranny" and its ability to "[entrap] the young male in stifling societal roles." Emerson imagines that the self-reliant man, while staying "the chaste husband to one wife", may need to assert himself against his family in order to be on the side of truth rather than appearances. "Self-Reliance" is without a doubt written from man to man, underscoring that self-reliance is an ideal of manhood.

This manly ideal is, to a large degree, seen in opposition to family as well as sympathy and charity. Emerson emphasizes the individualism of the self-reliant man and questions his social ties and obligations. When the speaker of the essay declares that he will "shun father and mother and wife and brother when my genius

*The historic home of Ralph Waldo Emerson, now a museum, in Concord, Massachusetts* © *Mark E. Gibson/ Corbis*

calls me," he begins a longer, somewhat vexed and ironic inquiry into his relation to others:

> Expect me not to show cause why I seek or why I exclude company. Then, again, do not tell me, as a good man did today, of my obligation to put all poor men in good situations. Are they my poor? I tell thee, thou foolish philanthropist, that I grudge the dollar, the dime, the cent, I give to such men as do not belong to me and to whom I do not belong. There is a class of persons to whom by all spiritual affinity I am bought and sold; for them I will go to prison, if need be; but your miscellaneous popular charities; the education at college of fools; the building of meeting-houses to the vain end to which many now stand; alms to sots; and the thousandfold Relief Societies;—though I confess with shame I sometimes succumb and give the dollar, it is a wicked dollar which by and by I shall have the manhood to withhold.

Emerson does not imagine his self-reliant man to be entirely on his own—indeed even when the "I" of the essay declares to his family that he will live according to his truth and not their rules, he always envisions taking care of them.

But, responding to the foolish philanthropist, he does define self-reliance and manhood in opposition to charity and sympathy. The essay wonders: to whom does the self-reliant man belong and whom should he support? There is no easy answer since spiritual affinity is hard to define and to find—as Emerson also makes abundantly clear in his beautiful and meandering essay on "Friendship." While he will go to prison for those with whom he shares such spiritual affinity, Emerson's self-reliant man confesses that he needs to resist the temptation of the central nineteenth-century (feminine) concepts of sympathy and charity; indeed, it is part of his manhood to be able to do so. In that sense, too, Emerson constructs self-reliance as a male ideal, even a sign of manhood.

But Emerson is not writing to or for all men; his essay does not seem to envision self-reliant African-American men or working-class men, and, surprisingly, Emerson offers few American models of self-reliance. When he invokes "our Saxon breasts," Emerson's call for a new manhood "was a racialized call for a Saxon brotherhood."

Indeed, Sorisio argues, "his desire to reclaim the American males' manhood, to emancipate them from the captivity of the feminized parlor, coincides with some of the most pronounced language of racial difference." In the same vein, while consciously encouraging every man to value his own thoughts, Emerson unconsciously situates his self-reliant man above the lower class when he imagines him in opposition not just to the "feminine rage" of the "cultivated classes" but more forcibly to "the ignorant and the poor," "the unintelligent brute force that lies at the bottom of society." Finally, while Emerson mentions with admiration "Washington's dignity" and "Adam's eye," his essay looks for most of its examples of self-reliant men into the past and outside of America. Thus, Emerson's essay, while outlining self-reliance as a crucial American principle, does not flesh out visions of self-reliant Americans that would include the poor, African Americans, and women.

To flesh out these visions is a central project of Frances Ellen Watkins Harper's work. Self-reliance is a consistent key term in Harper's writings, from her early short story "The Two Offers" (1859) to her late novel *Iola Leroy* (1892). As if directly answering Emerson's essay, Harper's work addresses precisely those questions that Emerson's essay rhetorically excludes: What does self-reliance mean for women and others who are dependent and oppressed? How exactly can we envision the lives of self-reliant African Americans, working-class people, and, most importantly, women? Harper's work offers a critical extension and revision of Emerson's original concept of self-reliance in terms of race, class, and gender. Consequently, tracing Harper's use and re-definition of the term self-reliance in her fiction and nonfiction allows us to explore her contribution to American Renaissance writing and to open up connections between these two eminent nineteenth-century writers.

Despite the fact that Emerson and Harper both were foremost public intellectuals and writers in nineteenth-century America and both were involved in the abolitionist and the women's movements, they are seldom mentioned in the same breath. The MLA bibliography yields not a single entry in a recent combined search of the two writers, and Harper receives virtually no mention in criticism about Emerson and vice versa. Her work is mostly discussed within the realm of late nineteenth-century realism and in the context of other African-American women

writers. She is rarely discussed in connection to any American Renaissance writing, even though she if finally included in Denise Knight's reference work *Writers of the American Renaissance: An A-to-Z Guide* (2003). Thus, while their spheres did overlap in reality, in literary history the two writers have inhabited mostly separate spheres. Yet, Harper's work is clearly in dialogue with Emerson's. If we can read Whitman as producing the kind of radically new American poetry that Emerson envisions in his essay "The Poet" and Thoreau as exemplifying Emerson's concept of self-reliance in his life experiment at Walden, then we can read Harper as transforming Emerson's initial conception of self-reliance into a politically viable concept for minorities. Harper's self-reliance allows women (and African Americans) to rely on themselves in full recognition of their systematic oppression and their specific historical and economic situation. For Harper self-reliance implies both a sense of self and of solidarity with others. In her writings, Harper exemplifies how the "self" Emerson posits in "Self-Reliance" can be compatible with a politically responsible "identity," and how it can be re-conceived in such a way that it may include and speak to all Americans; she not only imagines in her work what self-reliance means for women, but, in the process, she also democratizes Emerson's idea of self-reliance, transforming it into a truly American concept: a workable vision for all Americans.

Harper's 1859 short story "The Two Offers" offers a model of a self-reliant woman in her "old maid" character, Janette Alston. The opening dialogue between two cousins, Laura Lagrange and Janette, picks up the central theme of Emerson's essay on self-reliance—appearances versus truth, conformity versus self-reliance—within a feminized frame. The two women discuss the two offers of marriage Laura has received. Echoing Emerson's sense of "spiritual affinity," Janette insists that marriage should be based on an "affinity of souls and a union of hearts, and that it should not be a mere matter of bargain and sale, or an affair of convenience and selfish interest." Laura counters that, even though neither man truly appeals to her, refusing both bears the "risk of being an old maid, and that is not to be thought of." While Laura is afraid of public opinion and thus marries one of the suitors, Janette walks her path "with unfaltering steps" according to her own sense of truth and right. Like Emerson's self-reliant man, she knows that "what I must do is all that concerns me, not what the people think." Laura withers and dies in an unfulfilled marriage because her husband cannot respond to "the deep yearnings of her soul," which is "overflowing with a sense of the good, the beautiful, and the true." In contrast, Janette, "the true woman," blooms and lives to the fullest as "an old maid." Harper's story aims at having women overcome one of their greatest and most conventional fears of becoming "old maids." The story encourages women to stay on their own and enter marriage only when it offers the kind of spiritual affinity Emerson's self-reliant man seeks as well; female self-reliance, to Harper, is finding an ideal marriage or being an "old maid" by conviction and against all public opinion and pressures. Through the juxtaposition of the two cousins, Harper provokes women into becoming radically independent of public opinion and of the institution (but not the ideal) of marriage that may hold them in shackles and destroy them; she celebrates the role of the "old maid" as one viable option of female self-reliance.

Harper shows how Janette manages to be self-reliant. After having had a romantic disappointment in her life, Janette stays on her own. She is not only without husband but also without other family or inheritance. Both her parents, while good and affectionate, failed in their lives: "her father had been unfortunate in business," and his widow was unable to defend herself against creditors and lawyers and ended up "homeless and almost penniless." But, Harper stresses, Janette, "too self-reliant to depend on the charity of relations, endeavored to support herself by her own exertions, and she succeeded." She supports herself as a writer, and, Harper promises her readers in contradistinction to prevailing views, she is neither lonely nor ugly. Emerson posits that "the great man is he who in the midst of the crowd keeps with perfect sweetness the independence of solitude." Harper explores this concept for her "old maid":

True, she was an old maid, no husband brightened her life with his love, or shaded it with his neglect. No children nestling lovingly in her arms, called her mother. No one appended Mrs. to her name; she was indeed an old maid, not vainly striving to keep up an appearance of girlishness, when departed was written on her youth. Not vainly pining at her loneliness and isolation, the world was full of warm, loving hearts and her own beat in unison with them.

Janette has found her place in the world, not within the domestic realm but in the public sphere. Her decision to live according to her own truth has given warmth and love as well as both inner and outer beauty. "The bloom of her girlhood had given way to a higher type of spiritual beauty, as if some unseen hand had been polishing and refining the temple in which her lovely spirit found its habitation; and this had been the fact. Her inner life had grown beautiful, and it was this that was constantly developing the outer." Thus, in this old maid, Harper offers a model for female "self-reliance" that promises great and unexpected rewards to her female readers and that encourages women to live according to their own truth.

**Source:** Hildegard Hoeller, "Self-Reliant Women in Frances Harper's Writings," in *American Transcendental Quarterly*, Vol. 19, No. 3, September 2005, 205–220.

## SOURCES

Buell, Lawrence, "Emerson in His Cultural Context," in *Emerson: A Collection of Critical Essays*, edited by Lawrence Buell, Prentice Hall, 1993, pp. 48–60.

Cohen, Adam, "It's Emerson's Anniversary and He's Got 21st-Century America Nailed," in the *New York Times*, May 4, 2003, p.WK12.

Emerson, Ralph Waldo, "Self-Reliance," in *Ralph Waldo Emerson: Essays and Lectures*, The Library of America, 1983, pp. 257–82; originally published in 1841.

Garvey, T. Gregory, "Emerson and Self-Reliance," in *College Literature*, Vol. 25, No.1, Winter 1998, pp. 261–75.

# Sister Carrie

**THEODORE DREISER**

**1900**

Considered by many to be the first great novel of the twentieth century, *Sister Carrie* (1900) has nevertheless been a troubled—and troubling—work from its very beginning. The inspiration for Dreiser's debut novel is a scandal within his own family, as his sister Emma once ran away with a man who had stolen from his employer's safe, a situation recreated in the most dramatic moment of the novel. The novel's original publisher, Frank Doubleday, was scandalized by a work that seemed to reward immorality, and tried to bury the book with a small print run. Discouraged by a seeming lack of critical or popular response, Dreiser did not complete another novel for ten years.

It is often noted that Carrie's story is quite similar to other literature quite popular at the time, the "rags to riches" tales of Horatio Alger. Carrie begins in poverty, gets a glimpse of a better world than what she is used to, works hard to succeed, faces major setbacks, but is finally rewarded with a meteoric rise to unimagined heights. In Carrie's case, however, "work" is a very broad term, as it is her feminine charms, her ability to charm and win over men—and in turn, be won over by them—that is her main occupation. This is true in her relationships with Charles Drouet and G. W. Hurstwood, as well as in the attention she earns as an actress on Broadway.

However, where material success and spiritual fulfillment are conflated easily in Alger's

stories, the two often seem opposed in *Sister Carrie* and in other works by Dreiser. If anything, this opposition signifies an innate dissatisfaction within human nature that has several roots: a personal sense of entitlement or the belief that the world owes one something; the related belief that there are always others who are doing better than oneself, summed up best in the saying about the grass always being greener on the other side of the fence; and outside influences such as the mass media and modern commerce, which were only starting to blossom when Dreiser wrote his novel but have become ubiquitous in our own times as arbiters of "the good life."

As a result, the dreams described in the novel are indeed indicative of the American dream in the twentieth century—and the discontent feels just as modern, a century later. Right after Carrie leaves her sister's home to be Charles Drouet's kept woman, her sister Minnie has a dream of Carrie drowning. During his downward slide into poverty and obscurity, Hurstwood dreams of his previous life as a prominent member of the Chicago upper middle class. He had the American dream in his grasp, in true Dreiserian fashion was unsatisfied, and in seeking a new bliss brought about his own eventual demise.

In Dreiser's fictional world, there is a sense of inevitability in these progressions, whether characters are moving up or sliding down. This is a reflection of the scientific beliefs that infuse the literary naturalism he both defined and personified as an author: Heavily influenced by philosopher Herbert Spencer, Dreiser considers the human animal caught between a truly rational perspective of the world and the base instincts of other creatures. As a result, social forces and the base needs of all creatures define the individual, who is unable to control her destiny as much as she would choose to believe. So even though Carrie's rise from chorus girl to featured player to Broadway star is often described in a happenstance manner—she is coincidentally noticed and given a better assignment—it is because of innate characteristics she displays, characteristics developed meticulously by Dreiser over the course of the novel.

With its conflicted attitude of morality and the impassioned search for the higher purpose hidden behind the bland exterior of conventional aspirations, *Sister Carrie* can be likened to other

# BIOGRAPHY

### THEODORE DREISER

Herman Theodore Dreiser has born on August 27, 1871, in Terre Haute, Indiana. His early years were defined by poverty and instability: His father had fallen from prosperity as a factory manager and became intensely religious, frequently moving his family to pursue work and to preach. As a young man, Dreiser attended college briefly before becoming a journalist, working for various publications before settling in New York. It was at the encouragement of wife Sara "Jug" White and friend Arthur Henry that Dreiser wrote his first novel, *Sister Carrie*, based on a real-life incident in which Dreiser's sister Emma ran away with a man who had stolen from his employer. The poor reception of the novel greatly upset Dreiser, causing a breakdown and delaying his next novel, *Jennie Gerhardt*, almost a decade.

Slowly, *Sister Carrie* and Dreiser would earn increasing acclaim, thanks to his friend H. L. Mencken and others who saw Dreiser as the head of a new literary movement dubbed "naturalism." A highly productive novelist in the years following his return, Dreiser in 1925 wrote his masterwork *An American Tragedy*, which defined him as one of the great literary figures of his time. In later years, Dreiser focused less on fiction and more on political and philosophical writings; he died of a heart attack in Los Angeles on December 28, 1945.

novels that deal in the American dream in radically different ways throughout the twentieth century, including Vladimir Nabokov's *Lolita*, Philip Roth's *Portnoy's Complaint*, and William Vollmann's *The Royal Family*. As with Dreiser's novel, all these works revolve around the very personal and idiosyncratic nature of sexual desire, exploring aspects that even now are considered unsuitable for discussion in polite company. However, these are also quintessentially American works in that such sexual desire defines the ambitions some people set for themselves, the way they identify themselves in relation to their community, and how the pursuit of happiness—the very cornerstone of the American dream—can become tragedy, farce, and cautionary lesson all at once.

Certainly, this is reflected in the complex reactions evoked by Carrie at the end of the novel: Successful beyond her wildest dreams, adored by strangers for her work onstage, she rocks in her chair in a symbolic expression of moral and spiritual paralysis. Readers are invited to feel pity for her, but it is just as easy to feel anger, revulsion, or indifference to her plight. There is no noble attempt on her part to give up wealth and fame in favor of some more profound enrichment, as that would be unrealistic (albeit morally sound for readers of a previous era); indeed, much earlier in the novel, Carrie idly comments on the notion that no one is happy, only to have a friend retort, "I notice . . . that they all try mighty hard, though, to take their misery in a mansion." Dreiser thus exposes the realpolitik of the American dream: that for many, the accoutrements of successful living and achievement, the status symbols and luxurious surroundings, are often meant to stand in for the deeper feeling of satisfaction that achieving the American dream is supposed to instill in people, a satisfaction that often remains out of reach. More than a century later, this observation and its particular example in Carrie Meeber Wheeler Madenda remains as insightful an observation as can be found anywhere in literature.

*Theodore Dreiser* Public Domain

## PLOT SUMMARY

### Chapters 1–4
In 1889, eighteen-year-old Carrie Meeber takes a train from her home in Columbia City, Wisconsin, to Chicago to stay with her sister. During the ride, she is approached by a charming, well-dressed traveling salesman named Charles Drouet. As they approach Chicago, Drouet asks to see Carrie again, and they agree to meet at her sister's place the following Monday night.

Carrie's sister, Minnie Hanson, meets the train. She lives in a small flat with her husband and baby, where Carrie, "felt the drag of a lean and narrow life." She decides not to see Drouet

until she has started contributing to her new household, and she writes him to put off their date. The next day, Carrie goes to several places seeking a job. Among the potential employers she visits is a department store, a new phenomenon at the time, and the wide offering of apparel enchants her even as she is turned away yet again in her job hunt. Finally, a Mr. Brown at a shoe factory offers her work for $4.50 a week and tells her to report there Monday morning.

Carrie imagines the spending power of her new job far beyond the reality of her situation. She wants to go out, but Minnie worries and Hanson disapproves of her urge to be frivolous. "She oughtn't to be thinking about spending her money on theaters already," he remarks. Carrie decides to simply go downstairs and look out the front door. Monday morning, Carrie learns how to work one of the leather fastening machines at the factory: The job is physically demanding and Carrie finds her co-workers vulgar and crude.

### Chapters 5–8
Drouet goes out for dinner by himself on Monday evening and then visits the popular bar Fitzgerald and Moy's. Drouet and the bar manager, George

Hurstwood, chat amiably. That same evening, Carrie returns from her first day of work, tired and dispirited. The lack of sympathy from Minnie and Hanson makes her feel worse, while her discontent annoys them:

> She began to see that they looked on her complaint as unwarranted, and that she was supposed to work on and say nothing. She knew that she was supposed to pay four dollars for her room and board, and now she felt that it would be an exceedingly gloomy round, living with these people.

She spends the evening looking out the front door again, which Hanson considers unseemly. As the weather gets colder, Carrie's clothes are not warm enough, and she falls sick. She loses her job after missing work for a few days. Finding work is harder this time. On the fourth day of her new job hunt, she runs into Drouet, who cheers her with a sumptuous lunch and solicitous attention. He notices her shabby clothes and unhappiness with her sister, and he insists on lending her $20.

At home, Minnie hints that if a new job does not materialize, Carrie should return to Columbia City. Carrie wants to buy new clothes, but she worries about how she can explain new purchases to Minnie and Hanson. Carrie meets Drouet to return his money but he talks her out of that and helps her shop instead. He then rents her a room of her own where she can keep her new things, and he convinces her to move in that night. After dinner at home, Carrie writes Minnie a note explaining that she is going off on her own, and she leaves it for her sister to find later. She tells Minnie she is going to stand at the front door, then leaves with Drouet.

Drouet keeps Carrie busy with shopping, sightseeing, dining, and theater. Carries tries to believe she has not put herself in a compromising situation with Druet, who the story's narrator reveals, "would need to delight himself with Carrie as surely as he would need to eat his breakfast." Minnie has a dream of Carrie slowly drowning. A week later, Drouet invites Hurstwood to visit his home, ostensibly to meet Carrie.

## Chapters 9–12
George Hurstwood lives in a ten-room house with his wife Julia, son George Jr., and daughter Jessica, all comfortable and feeling entitled to their affluent lifestyle. Hurstwood is aware of the importance of avoiding scandals to keep his job as manager of Fitzgerald and Moy's, and his social life with his wife is primarily meant to maintain that spotless image. However, Hurstwood is unsatisfied with his family and once took to a trip to Philadelphia just to enjoy himself without the pressure of keeping up appearances.

Carrie and Drouet have become lovers and moved into a three-room flat together. Despite the comforts of her new situation, Carrie remains morally conflicted about what she has done. She asks Drouet if they will marry, but he keeps putting her off. Carrie is not deeply enamored of Drouet, and his shortcomings as a man becomes clear when George Hurstwood comes to call on the couple. Drouet claims he and Carrie are married, and Hurstwood plays along with the lie. Hurstwood charms Carrie, and both Carrie and Drouet are flattered by the attention.

Carrie has a highly refined sensibility, and although Drouet thought he possessed such refinement, he is not as sensitive or as clever as Carrie. Hurstwood is drawn to Carrie and wonders how Drouet won her. Drouet flirts with other girls, and Hurstwood flirts with Carrie. Hurstwood's son sees the three of them together at the theater one night, and he mentions it to the family at breakfast the next morning. Hurstwood explains his outing as a business obligation, but his wife uses the incident to subtly coerce Hurstwood into social appearances with her in the coming days, events that he would have otherwise avoided.

Hurstwood is growing increasingly interested in Carrie, who in turn is learning to appreciate the finer points of a wealthy lifestyle from her neighbor Mrs. Hale. Hurstwood visits Carrie while Drouet is out of town on business. Hurstwood expresses his affection for Carrie and asks if she is unhappy, which she affirms without meaning to. Hurstwood pushes no further for the moment, satisfied in knowing she is interested in him. Carrie is troubled by the encounter.

## Chapters 13–16
Won over by Carrie's youthful innocence, Hurstwood drops by Carrie's home again two days later, leaving work in the afternoon to do so. The two go for a walk and, reaching a stable, take a horse and buggy for a drive. Hurstwood tells Carrie he loves her. Carrie resists, but she finally admits her own love by kissing him.

At Ogden Place, where Carrie lives, people note Carrie's outings while Drouet is away. Hurstwood and Carrie dine together and agree to meet again. When Drouet returns to Chicago from his business trip, he stops by Fitzgerald and Moy's first, where Hurstwood tells him he had checked in on Carrie once. Returning to Ogden Place, Drouet bores Carrie with details of his trip and again makes empty promises of soon marrying her, which she openly scoffs. Carrie also accidentally reveals a second visit by Hurstwood, which Drouet notes but quickly dismisses. Hurstwood writes to Carrie about getting their stories straight; they meet and Hurstwood assures Carrie that she need not worry. The three go out to the theater and Drouet unwittingly insults himself when he says that the cuckold in the show they watch deserved his fate. Later, Drouet gives a dime to a beggar that Hurstwood and Carrie barely notice.

At his own home, Hurstwood feels the respect he gets from his family is diminishing, especially as his children grow older and more independent. One afternoon during a meeting in the park, Hurstwood asks Carrie to leave Drouet for him. Carrie says they would have to leave Chicago as she could not bear to see Drouet after such a thing; Hurstwood assures her that a move to the South Side would more than suffice. He asks Carrie a hypothetical question: If he goes to her and says they must leave immediately, would she join him, even if there was no time to marry her? Carrie says yes, as long as they marry at their eventual destination. Hurstwood is determined to win her from Drouet, but he does not intend to marry her or leave Chicago.

Drouet is enlisted to find a woman to perform in the play *Under the Gaslight* for a fundraiser at his Elks lodge. Carrie agrees reluctantly but in practicing for the role is excited by the prospect.

### Chapters 17–21

Carrie writes Hurstwood of her upcoming dramatic role, and her enthusiasm delights him. He feigns ignorance about Carrie's role when Drouet tells him, then offers to send flowers and take them out to dinner afterward. At the first rehearsal, Carrie stands out among all the other performers in this amateur production. Hurstwood meets Carrie and encourages her to succeed. Working unnoticed in the background, Hurstwood boosts sales for the show, even

getting it a notice in the papers. The night of the fundraiser, Carrie prepares nervously in the dressing room while Hurstwood talks with the various affluent attendees, feeling important that his influence prompted their attendance.

When the drama *Under the Gaslight* begins, the actors are weak but improve slightly. Carrie is nervous when she appears and is the least engaging of the group. Drouet goes backstage to encourage her, reminding Carrie how well she had done in rehearsals at home. Slowly, Carrie becomes the audience's center of attention, providing a competent performance that the crowd considers even better than it is. Both Hurstwood and Drouet feel their passions further aroused by Carrie's performance, and Hurstwood grows to resent his rival. He keeps his composure, however, when the three go out for dinner afterward as planned, though he is now more determined to have Carrie all to himself.

The next morning, Hurstwood gets in an argument with his wife over when they will take their vacation. Jessica wants to go to Waukesha to meet boys in her social circles, and Julie agrees, stressing that they will go without Hurstwood if necessary. The same morning, Drouet again promises to marry Carrie, who has now long stopped believing him. After Drouet leaves for work, Carrie goes to meet Hurstwood. However, when Drouet returns to collect something he had forgotten, the maid slyly tells Drouet that Hurstwood has visited Carrie repeatedly when Drouet was out of town. Drouet becomes jealous.

Carrie meets with Hurstwood in the park. He asks her to go away with him on Saturday. She agrees on the condition that they marry, to which he outwardly agrees.

### Chapters 22–25

Julia Hurstwood learns from a friend that her husband was seen taking a drive with a woman. Later, Julia encounters several friends who attended the previous night's fundraiser at Drouet's secret lodge; they mention that Hurstwood said Julia could not attend because she was sick. Piecing these deceptions together, she suspects an affair and confronts Hurstwood. She demands the money for the Waukesha trip by the next morning. "Somehow he felt evidence, saw the remembrance of all his property which she held in her name, to be shining in her glance."

Meanwhile, Drouet confronts Carrie about Hurstwood's visits. Carrie says Drouet is the one at fault, as he introduced her to Hurstwood in the first place and under false pretenses. Drouet accuses Carrie of being ungrateful, and Carrie counters by saying she never asked for anything. Drouet reveals that Hurstwood is married, something Carrie did not know and which shocks her. Carrie threatens to leave, softening Drouet's stance as he asks her to at least stay until the end of the month, since she has no other real options. Drouet tries to be conciliatory, but, when he discovers that Carrie does have feelings for Hurstwood, he leaves in anger.

Hurstwood is aware of the threat a scandal poses to his property and position but comforts himself with thoughts of Carrie. The next morning, a Friday, Hurstwood neither receives a letter from Carrie nor is she there to meet him in the park as they planned. That afternoon, he receives a message from Julia demanding the money for the Waukesha vacation. He tells the messenger boy there is no reply, and later that afternoon the boy returns with another message from Julia Hurstwood: If she does not receive the money, she will take the matter to Hurstwood's employers. He decides to go home and confront his wife, but he arrives by cab only to find out the locks have been changed.

At his office, Hurstwood wonders what has happened to Carrie and sends an employee to Julia with the money. Saturday and Sunday pass with no word from Carrie; on Monday, Hurstwood receives a letter from a law firm Julia hired, seeking to adjust certain matters. On Wednesday, Hurstwood receives another letter from the same law firm, threatening to file for divorce and alimony if no reply is made by the next day.

### Chapters 26–30

After being abandoned by Drouet, Carrie considers her options. She looks for work as an actress, and she learns that New York would be a better place to break into the business than Chicago. She receives a letter from Hurstwood from Saturday and finds her emotions stirred despite what she now knows about him. She writes to him, saying, "How could you deceive me so? You cannot expect me to have any more to do with you."

Hurstwood is encouraged by the fact that Carrie bothered to write him at all. He is even more encouraged when he happens to learn that

she and Drouet have separated. Hurstwood goes to Fitzgerald and Moy's, where he begins drinking with friends. After the bar closes at midnight, an inebriated Hurstwood finds that the cashier had not locked the safe and that $10,000 is unprotected. He resists the urge to steal the money, but as he decides to return the money to the safe, its door accidentally shuts and locks. He leaves with the money, learns that a mail train to Detroit leaves at three o'clock in the morning, and hurries to Carrie. He tells her that Drouet is in the hospital, and he whisks her away to the train station.

On board the train, which Hurstwood told her they were taking to the South Side, he admits that Drouet is not sick and that they are actually bound for Detroit. Hurstwood convinces her to stay by promising to divorce his wife and marry her. They travel on to Montreal, where Hurstwood believes he will be out of reach from those pursuing him.

Hurstwood writes to Fitzgerald and Moy explaining what happened, offering to return the money if no charges are pressed, and even asking to be reinstated as manager. He convinces Carrie to start a new life with a new name, and they marry under the name Wheeler. Mr. Moy writes back to Hurstwood, agreeing to the return of the money but declining to rehire him. He keeps $1,300 and returns the rest, then leaves for New York with Carrie. There, he then secures a partnership in a saloon with less prestige than Fitzgerald and Moy's, and he must worry about generating enough income from this new business venture. Carrie notices that he is no longer as free with money.

### Chapters 31–35

Though initially quite affectionate to Carrie, as the years pass in New York, Hurstwood again gathers a circle of friends with whom he stays out at night. Meanwhile, Carrie befriends Mrs. Vance, her neighbor. When Hurstwood meets Mrs. Vance and her husband, he displays his old charm again, something he had not done for some time. Carrie and Mrs. Vance attend a Broadway matinee together, which makes Carrie sharply aware of her deficiencies in attire and other luxuries. Later, Mrs. Vance introduces Carrie to her cousin Mr. Ames. His refined opinions on life and the arts make a lasting impression on Carrie, including his belief that theater is a great thing.

Hurstwood's fortune slowly declines. The narrator explains that a man must be either increasing or decreasing in vitality, that there are no other states. In their third year in New York, Hurstwood convinces Carrie that they should leave their apartment and move to a cheaper flat. Later, Hurstwood's partner Shaughnessy breaks the news that the building where they maintain their business will be torn down, meaning Hurstwood will lose the money he invested once the lease expires and they are forced out. By the time the bar finally closes, he has not made any new arrangements. He has $700 left.

Hurstwood follows several newspaper leads for jobs, to no avail. He exaggerates his prospects to Carrie, who pretends to remain hopeful, though she begins to worry when he starts volunteering to run household errands for her. As winter sets in, Hurstwood stays in more and more instead of seeking work, and he becomes more frugal about the household expenses. He stops caring about his appearance and Carrie starts sleeping separately from him.

## Chapters 36–42

Hurstwood tries his hand at poker and loses some more of his money. Carrie is distressed when she finds out that a friend had dropped by when Carrie was not home, and Hurstwood was unshaven and shabby looking. During an argument with Hurstwood Carrie discovers that their marriage ceremony was a fraud. Hurstwood leaves the flat angry and loses still more money playing poker. Later, down to $50 from his reserves, Hurstwood lies to Carrie, telling her he will have a good job opportunity in a few months at a new hotel. In the meanwhile, he asks that Carrie find work and helps her in looking for a position in the theater. She gets a job as a chorus girl for $12 a week, which only makes her more critical of Hurstwood and his fruitless search for employment. On the first day of her job, Carrie uses the stage name Carrie Madenda, the same name Drouet used when she was in the play at the Elks lodge in Chicago. The chorus girls are worked mercilessly and Carrie is exhausted; on the first night of performance, she must again get over her stage fright but does so, realizing she is better than some of the other girls. One evening, Hurstwood tells Carrie his reserve of money is almost depleted, and so Carrie starts paying for their expenses. He assures a disbelieving Carrie that it is only temporary until the hotel job is available for him in September.

At the theater, Carrie is befriended by a fellow performer, Lola Osborne. Carrie's good looks gain the attention of the manager, and she is moved to the head of the chorus line and gets a commensurate raise for the promotion. Assuming Carrie is a single girl like herself, Lola persuades Carrie to go on a drive with two young men. Carrie is unimpressed by these boys, given her past experience with men.

Carrie's indifference to Hurstwood and her home with him grows. As her show prepares to go on the road, Lola advises that she stay in the city and apply for another local show. She does so successfully, feeling validated in her new profession. She soon becomes aware of the debts Hurstwood was incurring with local merchants, and her disapproval spurs Hurstwood to look for work. He reads about striking trolley railcar workers in Brooklyn and decides to become a scab motorman, working for the railcar companies and being paid by the run. Carrie is concerned that it is dangerous but Hurstwood assures her that the companies promise protection. He walks to Brooklyn and applies for a job, where he is readily accepted.

At the rail yard barn, Hurstwood overhears talk of other scabs who have been injured by angry strikers. He learns how to drive a railcar, sleeps overnight at the yard, and the next day is sent off on a run with two policemen to protect him. There are attempts to stop the car by strikers who wish to do harm, and a pile of rocks had been set up to block the rail. He returns safe on this first run, but on the second run he is accosted by a mob that stops the car and attacks him. Hurstwood runs away from the car and decides to head home, where he reads the newspaper articles about the riots breaking out in the city over the strike.

During a performance, Carrie adlibs a line when she is addressed onstage by a comedian in her show. Instead of being fired, she is told to keep the line in future performances and rewarded with a raise. When she presses Hurstwood about working as a scab, he says little, making her think he is simply lazy. Lola Osborne invites Carrie to share an apartment with her, and Carrie agrees. Carrie leaves a note and money for Hurstwood, breaking off her relations with him. Hurstwood is shocked, believing he tried his best.

## Chapters 43–47

Carrie becomes absorbed in her work. Lola advises Carrie to stay in New York when the show goes on the road, and by doing so, she gets a minor role as a Quakeress at a new production at her theater. She receives minor attention from the theatrical press but her role is in jeopardy of being cut by the author when he notices her intensely frowning during a scene because she was worried over her fate. Finding this humorous, he and the stage manager encourage her to do this on purpose: On opening night Carrie's frowning delights the audience and angers the show's star. Carrie becomes the center of the show, and she is praised as the best thing about the show by the theater critics in attendance. She is given a song of her own to sing and is asked to sign a contract for $150 a week for one year. Hurstwood sees Carrie has struck it big but decides not to bother her.

Now the star of the show, Carrie is given a large dressing room, and she is offered a lavish suite at the prestigious Wellington Hotel for a token fee. Carrie and Lola move in to their new home. Several nights later, she is met in her dressing room by Mrs. Vance, who renews her friendship with Carrie. Carrie receives many romantic offers from men she does not know, which intrigues Lola but simply bores Carrie after her own experiences with Drouet and Hurstwood. Despite the attentions from fans and the press, she tells Lola she still gets lonely, which puzzles her friend.

Hurstwood continues to deteriorate, having waking dreams of his more prosperous life in Chicago. He gets a job running errands for a hotel but falls sick and loses the position. He takes advantage of the charity of "the captain," who lines up homeless men and asks passersby for enough money to give each one a bed for the night.

Drouet unexpectedly visits Carrie in her dressing room one night. He tries to re-ignite a romance with her but fails. Hurstwood manages to contact Carrie on the street, who gives him what money she has with her. Mrs. Vance's cousin Mr. Ames advises Carrie to work in comedy-drama (the term for dramas at the time) instead of comedies, believing it better suits her. Carrie mentions this to Lola but does nothing about it.

Hurstwood takes advantage of the charities available to him, but the hardships of his life make him want to give up. He tries one last time to contact Carrie but fails. While he is out

THERE IS NOTHING IN THIS WORLD MORE DELIGHTFUL THAN THAT MIDDLE STATE IN WHICH WE MENTALLY BALANCE AT TIMES, POSSESSED OF THE MEANS, LURED BY DESIRE, AND YET DETERRED BY CONSCIENCE OR WANT OF DECISION."

in the cold and slips in the snow, Carrie and Lola are warm and comfortable in their quarters, where Lola sees Hurstwood fall but does not know the man. Drouet decides to forget about Carrie; Hurstwood commits suicide, allowing gas fumes to fill his rented room. The book ends with Carrie sitting in her rocking chair, alone and unhappy despite gaining all that she desired.

## THEMES

### Success

Hard work is rewarded in Dreiser's novel, but not equally—different kinds of work are rewarded to different degrees, depending as much on prestige as on the ambition of the worker. Defining what work is, exactly, is one of the more subversive elements of *Sister Carrie* and Carrie's journey throughout. Her time as Drouet's mistress has the classic dimension of any such arrangement: She provides pleasure for Drouet, sexual and social, in return for the basic necessities as well as whatever luxuries she desires that he can provide. This may not be seen as "legitimate" work but it is clearly portrayed as a materialistic step up from her previous situation with her sister Minnie. Furthermore, it allows her to cultivate the sensitivity and feelings that would help make her a distinctive stage presence on Broadway, where her hard work pays off well beyond her wildest dreams.

While it is a sexist cliché that women—especially young women—are fond of clothing and the latest fashions, this is actually in keeping with the complex personality Dreiser creates for Carrie. Carrie is attracted to what is aesthetically beautiful—and one of the most obvious manifestations is her fondness for looking stylish

*Marion Davies being squeezed into her dress in the film* The Gay Nineties *(aka,* The Florodora Girl*)*

*Hulton Archive/Getty Images*

and enjoying the luxuries of fine clothing. This is only the most obvious manifestation of material success in the novel: There are also sumptuous meals and spacious living areas. Dreiser strongly argues the possible emptiness of such achievement—that is, the notion that money or material goods cannot buy happiness—but also the corollary that wealth and luxury are nevertheless more desirable than poverty even if one is miserable. In keeping with the naturalist ethos, material goods are at least an assurance of creature comforts, and a basic need before more abstract needs can be met.

Dreiser offers a wide range of ambitions to reflect different characters' American dream: Minnie's husband Hansen wishes to build a house on a lot for his family, Drouet wishes to simply be admired by those around him and have a good time, Hurstwood has already achieved material prosperity but still desires romantic conquest, while Carrie's desires seem deceptively simple—pretty clothes and a comfortable life—but grow increasingly complex as she gains experience.

### Happiness

*Sister Carrie* ends with the titular character in a rocking chair, having achieved fame and fortune but nonetheless still intensely unsatisfied with her life. The rocking is symbolic of a lack of movement in her life—despite all she has achieved as an independent woman and a star of the Broadway stage, she feels a dissatisfaction about her life, believing something is eluding her. Options are weighed toward making her life more fulfilling—a romantic involvement, or a change in her career direction—but Carrie casually dismisses the former (for good reason, given her experiences over the course of the novel) and is unsure of the validity of the latter, as expressed in the common sense advice of Lola.

While it is tempting to refer to Carrie as a victim of anhedonia—the malaise of never being happy despite whatever good one achieves or is given—this would be simplifying and ignoring all that Dreiser set out in the novel. Carrie is often described as possessing a sensitive soul—and the lack in herself is something she becomes attuned to early in the novel but can never quite fulfill.

One of the fondly held tenets of the American dream is the possibility to start over in life, to set aside past mistakes and have a second (or third or fourth) chance at living and succeeding as a new person. The novel begins with an act of re-invention: Carrie moves from her hometown of Columbia City, Wisconsin, to Chicago. Carrie Meeber takes on other names in the course of the book. Her stage name is Carrie Madenda, first in Chicago as an amateur thespian and later in New York as a professional. At the end this is the name and the identity she has assumed, but it ultimately proves as empty and unsatisfying as all the identities she had before: In effect, the re-invention of self has simply become a shell game for a lonely soul.

## HISTORICAL OVERVIEW

### The Gilded Age

Recovering from the Civil War, the United States emerged in the remaining decades of the nineteenth century as the world's leading industrial nation, its gross domestic product going from $10 billion at the beginning of the century to $350 billion at its close. With major innovations in transportation, manufacture, communications, and the sciences, the so-called Second Industrial Revolution allowed for greater organization and coordination in many industries, creating a new scalability of production that had never been seen before.

The Gilded Age was a term coined by Mark Twain and Charles Dudley Warner in their 1873 novel of the same name, indicating a layer of ostentatious wealth that creates a false sense of prosperity. With immigrants continuing to arrive in America in large numbers throughout this era, there was never a shortage of cheap labor to exploit, such as Chinese railroad workers in the West. As a result, the prosperity of the Gilded Age was not widely shared by the populace: Only a small percentage became wealthy and a growing economic inequality became evident as a de facto plutocracy—a social and political hierarchy built on wealth and affluence—emerged to cement this new order.

The so-called "Robber Barons" were prominent industrialists who amassed great power and personal fortunes by engaging in unethical business practices. Corporations were financed by stocks, with the most successful combining into trusts and forming monopolies to gain leverage in their respective industries. Attempts to keep the excesses in check, such as the Interstate Commerce Act of 1887 and the Sherman Antitrust Act of 1890, were only mildly successful at best.

Carrie climbs from the bottom of the social ladder to the only respectable peak available for a single woman: as a star on Broadway. Though her personal wealth was only a fraction of a wealthy industrialist's, her status was commensurate to the privileged few; she even spurns the advances of millionaires who wish to marry her. That said, her ascendancy to fame and fortune is indeed a Gilded Age—despite the fine trappings, Carrie still feels hollow and unfulfilled, trapped in a life that others envy but that offers her little solace.

## Consumer Culture
The latter half of the nineteenth century marked a change in the economy from production to consumption. Innovations in production meant that it was easier and cheaper for families to purchase mass-produced goods, such as clothing and food, that they previously made for themselves. The usefulness of such goods was often augmented by the status they could bestow on its buyers, as

manufacturers sought to differentiate themselves. The marketing of goods—especially luxury items now accessible to a wider audience—became a key part of the consumer culture that emerged.

The first department stores in the United States were established in Chicago and described in great detail by Dreiser, becoming a metonym for the way material goods define the way people understand themselves and their needs. Carrie's sensitivity for what is aesthetically pleasing first manifests itself in a desire to own fashionable clothing, and it is a passion that continues unabated throughout the novel. This attitude is what attracts Carrie to Drouet, a "drummer" who travels extensively to sell the wares of his company, as well as to Hurstwood, who caters to the influential and prosperous citizens of Chicago as manager of a popular resort. For Carrie, wealth and affluence reflect not only the acquisition of material goods but also an unarticulated but powerfully felt philosophy of what a happy life entails.

Carrie is by no means alone in her susceptibility to consumerism. Most everyone in the novel is interested in whatever material gain can be found, from the factory girls whose romances reap them gifts to Mrs. Vance, who introduces Carrie to the fineries paraded on the streets of Broadway. The only major exceptions to this ostentatious materialism are Minnie and her husband: Theirs is an old-fashioned work ethic based on careful economizing and hard work, not of living or aspiring beyond their means. When readers last see Minnie, she is dreaming of Carrie drowning: symbolic of how Carrie is not only lost to Minnie from the choices she made but also awash in a need for material acquisitions that will only consume her in turn.

## Depression of 1893–1894
The Panic of 1893 was the worst economic crisis to face the United States up to that point: The unemployment rate peaked at 18 percent by some estimates and exceeded 10 percent for five or six straight years, leading to nationwide unrest such as the May Day Riots of 1894.

During the close of Benjamin Harrison's presidency, the national treasury's gold reserve was under siege by outstanding notes being redeemed by fearful investors. Finally, on April 15, 1893,—with Grover Cleveland returning for a second term as president, after being voted out in 1888—the redemption of Treasury gold certificates was suspended. At the same time, investments in bonds issued by corporations were buoyed by rampant speculation, and two major companies favored by speculators were among the first to fall: Philadelphia and Reading Railway Company went into bankruptcy in February 1893, with National Cordage Company (the most traded stock at the time) following in May. Smaller businesses dependent on larger companies were in turn affected by these events, with 15,000 companies and 500 banks failing during this depression.

Financial downturns have long been part of the American economy, occurring every two decades or so since the Panic of 1819. For this reason, the government did not first react as vigorously as it could have, at first believing the panic to be cyclical. As the seriousness of the situation became clear, Cleveland repealed the Sherman Silver Purchase Act passed under Harrison, which was a key factor in the depletion of the Treasury gold reserve, and tried to reform highly protective tariff policies but failed to do so. The economy started to recover fully under President William McKinley, elected in 1896; ironically, the McKinley Tariff of 1890 was considered another contributing factor to the Panic.

The fragile nature of the economy is reflected in Hurstwood's fall from grace after fleeing to New York with Carrie. As a scab during a trolley workers strike, he finds others also forced to seek whatever work they can, evoking Herbert Spencer's notion of Social Darwinism, which was hugely influential on Dreiser. The ever-increasing gap between Hurstwood's life and Carrie's after they part ways is not only an important narrative irony in the novel, but it also symbolizes the social inequality created by pressing economic circumstances.

## CRITICAL OVERVIEW

The most memorable critical response to *Sister Carrie* came from its first publisher, Doubleday, Page: Though the novel was championed by Walter Page and author Frank Norris, Frank Doubleday was offended by the book's subject matter and allowed a print run of only 1,000 copies—nearly half of those copies unbound, pending further orders—and kept the book from being listed in the publisher's catalog. Norris sent out numerous copies for review and the general reaction of those who read and wrote about *Sister Carrie* was not as extreme as

Doubleday's. Describing the initial reaction to *Sister Carrie*, Donald Pizer explains:

> The implication that sex for a young woman of Carrie's class and background was intimately linked to survival and success, and that a woman using her sex was not necessarily a fallen woman, ran counter to almost every conventional nineteenth-century belief about the nature of women and the inevitability of moral retribution.

Reviewing a biography of the author, Martin Northway offers another summary of the initial reaction:

> Setting the stage for the naturalism of the 20th century, *Sister Carrie* was derided for what some considered too-frank sexuality. Other critics praised its portrayal of the precipitous decline of male protagonist George Hurstwood, but at least one objected to its picture of "the godless side of American life."

In an introduction to a critical survey of Drieser, Alfred Kazin claims, though, that the challenge to the novel was more one of the reviewers' timidity than their disgust: "*Sister Carrie* did not have a bad press; it had a frightened press, with many of the reviewers plainly impressed, but startled by the concentrated truthfulness of the book."

If anything, then, the debut of *Sister Carrie* was met with more indifference than revulsion by the critical and popular readership. In its first decade, the novel garnered further critical recognition in England even as it was championed in America by a small coterie of literary figures—most notably H. L. Mencken—who saw the work and its author as ushering a fresh new perspective on literature as a social force.

In an article in *American Heritage*, Richard Lingeman describes the book's revolutionary impact on modern literature:

> Other novelists of Dreiser's generation, such as Frank Norris and Stephen Crane, chipped at the Victorian code, but *Sister Carrie* threatened to blow it away. William Dean Howells, a pioneer realist and an editor at *Harper's Magazine*, said to Dreiser, "You know I didn't like *Sister Carrie*." His comment typified the reception from the old guard. To a new generation *Sister Carrie* struck a blow for freedom.

Not only did the novel herald changing social and artistic mores, it presented the coming modern age. Examining U.S. history through literature, Leonard Cassuto explains the novel's lens on its time:

# MEDIA ADAPTATIONS

*Sister Carrie* was adapted for the screen in the 1952 film *Carrie* was directed by William Wyler, starring Jennifer Jones as Carrie Meeber and Laurence Olivier as George Hurstwood. It is available on DVD from Paramount.

In 2002, *Sister Carrie* was adapted to the stage by playwright Charles Smith. It was commissioned and performed by the Indiana Repertory Theatre.

---

> Appearing at a time of profound social and economic transformation in the United States, *Sister Carrie* looks forward to an urban, industrial future and backward to a rural, sentimental past. It stands as an American classic, a work utterly representative of its fraught and dynamic time.

In more recent decades, critical opinions on Dreiser and *Sister Carrie* have solidified. The political and social controversy surrounding *Sister Carrie*, naturalism, and even Dreiser himself in the first half of the twentieth century have subsided with the passing of time. The mechanistic view propounded by naturalism is considered less conceptually threatening in this day and age compared to the more chaotic spirit of various strains of postmodernism. In *Studies in the Novel*, Karl Zender explains why *Sister Carrie* is as relevant today as is was when it was published more than a century ago:

> Dreiser's fiction speaks to our own age. In an America still torn between the twin gods of "family values" and of rampant consumerism—of nostalgia and desire—Hurstwood's and Carrie's evasions and denials, and the instabilities of identity they conceal, should seem uncannily familiar.

## CRITICISM

### David E. E. Sloane

*In the following excerpt, Sloane considers Dreiser's intentions in his characterization of Carrie, and how she epitomizes a kind of ambition and success that reflects the darker aspects of the American dream.*

Carrie is a special fusion of female traits that represents what Dreiser conceives of as the creative spirit. To some extent, she even represents the author himself, including a number of sympathetic traits that the author used in portraying his later heroes. Carrie's femininity is part sexuality—the allure of innocence and freshness—and part her special spiritual quality, which sets her above Drouet and Hurstwood. Although Carrie is portrayed as the opposite of the "pythoness" Julia Hurstwood in most respects, but especially because Carrie lacks Julia's moral strength and outrage, some argument could be made for seeing the two figures in similar terms. Mrs. Hurstwood reveals the unbridled mendacity of her economic position but wishes to rise socially and materially as does Carrie; Carrie's impoverished origins and vulnerability to small economic reverses make her tentative and sympathetic, but she too abandons Hurstwood once he no longer fits into her need to rise materially. Rudyard Kipling, among other writers, would have no trouble envisioning such a pair, like the Colonel's lady and Rosie O'Grady, as "sisters under the skin."

Stephen Crane had described the title character of *Maggie, a Girl of the Streets* (1893) as having "blossomed in a mud-puddle" with options that anticipate Carrie's: go to hell or go to work. In a line or two, Crane assigns Maggie to a stool and machine and the dull and dark life of a factory girl, making her eventual seduction all but inevitable. Dreiser ponderously embroiders a similar reference for Carrie when he describes Hurstwood's fascination with "this lily, which had sucked its waxen beauty and perfume below a depth of waters which he had never penetrated and out of ooze and mould [*sic*] which he could not understand." Hurstwood's inability to conceptualize Carrie's background establishes the grounds for her emotional superiority. Carrie's sympathy with the "under-world of toil" from which she derives her memories is like her yearning for clothes, "the essence of poetic feeling." Her poetry derives not from high idealism and moral purpose, as in the Horatio Alger novels, but from the cellars and narrow factory windows and blast-furnaces— "Her old father, in his flour-dusted miller's suit"—haunting her at odd moments. Carrie's poetry is the poetry of a materialistic girl who understands what it means to have to work so hard and have so little. Thus, the sociological

*State Street looking north from Madison Street, Chicago, IL, circa 1890* © *Bettmann/Corbis*

elements in the novel are folded into the consciousness of the title figure.

With all these elements at work, Dreiser "types" Carrie and rounds out her character. Through Carrie Dreiser raises questions about the well-being and progress of the limited American working class, although in the first few words of the novel we are led to believe that she represents a "middle" class. Out of the potential for her "fall," a concept Dreiser confuses apparently on purpose, comes the drama of her story. Carrie is an unsophisticated and natural mind in a general predicament, for she is confronted by an equivocal and undoing superhuman force, like music, the "roar of life." The city suits Dreiser's purpose, for it offers forces of guile and power that can be embodied in wealth and material objects so that he does not have to personalize them in a villain. Not only Drouet and Hurstwood but also the department store and the gaslit restaurant seduce the poor and the weak.

Dreiser's description of Carrie in animal terms tends to move her problem from the moral to the physical realm. As early as chapter 1, Carrie looks at Drouet with "the instincts of

self-protection and coquetry mingling confusedly in her brain." Thus, Dreiser's later depreciations of Carrie's intellect have been fully foreshadowed, and Dreiser fulfills this contract when he proposes that "The unintellectual are not so helpless. Nature has taught the beasts of the field to fly when some unheralded danger threatens. She has put into the small, unwise head of the chipmunk the untutored fear of poisons. . . The instinct of self-protection, strong in all such natures, was roused but feebly, if at all, by the overtures of Drouet." At the same time he characterizes her as partially protected "like the sheep in its unwisdom, strong in feeling" and then adds a paradoxical biblical reference: "He keepeth his creatures whole." This suggests that the animal images are not intended as totally degrading naturalistic allusions, but neither is Carrie guided by religious principles or religious authority despite the misleading implication.

The worsening moral ramifications of Carrie's affairs are blamed on her circumstances, but the ultimately amoral position of the book derives from the choices she makes of her own volition. Having become Drouet's mistress, the heroine, "looked into her glass and saw a prettier Carrie than she had seen before; she looked into her mind, a mirror prepared of her own and the world's opinions, and saw a worse. Between these two images she wavered, hesitating which to believe." Her psychology exists within her social context. Consistent with Dreiser's use of the sociological metaphor we have a corresponding social psychology in the heroine. Carrie judges herself by the world's opinions, but external documentation of them tells her they are counter to her welfare. To further elaborate this point about Carrie's psychology, we need only move down the same page to the point where Carrie argues, pleads, and excuses herself with her own conscience, which is "not a Drouet": "It was only an average little conscience, a thing which represented the world, her past environment, habit, convention, in a confused way. With it, the voice of the people was truly the voice of God." The interplay of the great and the little that has distinguished Carrie from the wealth of the city is continued in this passage. Once again, blame is shifted from Carrie the person to the conventional popular ideal, with some suggestion that "God" is implicated, although the text carefully makes no such claim. This is yet another of the many marvelous passages in which Dreiser deftly undercuts the character's mind but still allows us to retain our sympathy for her as a victim of forces far beyond her control. The reader becomes attached to her even though she lacks the ability to transcend the forces of her world, for she is its victim, not its manipulator.

Elsewhere, images such as the "deep pit," the "vague shadows," and "the mystic scenery" provided in Minnie's dream establish melodramatic alternatives for the mundane Carrie. Such mental images help the blank-minded Carrie become an exciting heroine; her life holds the potential for her dramatic rise to stardom, neither through self-protection nor strength of will, but rather through her "drift" and the effect of her emotional "greatness" on the minds of others. The real complexity of Carrie lies in this opposition: the limited spirit and understanding that follows safe moral conventions and understands the danger of the fall versus the questing soul of the vaguely immoral and unconventional drifter—Carrie. The "essence of poetic feeling" in Carrie is compounded by her wistfulness and her desire for pleasure and social position—all terms applied to her in chapter 15. In these traits, Carrie's spirit is indeed parallel to Theodore Dreiser's, and in this she becomes a heroine the reader can become attached to and empathize with. Even a physical characterization is included: "Experience had not yet taken away that freshness of the spirit which is the charm of the body" in such a way as to clearly imply her physicality. Carrie includes all possibilities for interpretation.

Carrie's rise in the theater projects the anomalies of her place in American society even as it appears to be a fulfillment of the American dream. Her success is owing to chance, the American pluck born of necessity, and her experience, blended with her special spiritual power to reflect her world. Despite the cloying falsity of the plot of *Under the Gaslight*, Carrie earns sympathy because she identifies with the emotional loss of the character she plays, being herself an outcast. True, Carrie is a sinner, not a wronged innocent, but Dreiser has taken pains to lighten the reader's perception of evil in Carrie and has, in fact, tended to justify her against the conventional social interpretation of a woman in her situation. When Mrs. Vance actually calls her a "little sinner," as mentioned previously, it is merely a casual reference to Carrie having dropped out of contact; the religious idea has been secularized by the worldly woman of New York society. Since Carrie will strongly emphasize the desire for marriage in her liaison with Drouet and her affair with Hurstwood, Dreiser even builds into his plot her recognition that such a marriage should take place. Meanwhile Dreiser, who is notable for his philosophical intrusions, never once intrudes to discuss whether Carrie's desire for marriage is wrong or right, although he does at times point out her naïveté. Wanting to get married is her reflection of appropriate social behavior.

Carrie's personality is somewhat stronger later in the novel as compared to earlier in the novel, but she is still not wholly without self-delusion. Having been given in Ames "an ideal to contrast men by," "not without great gloom," she begins to look at Hurstwood, who is no longer young, strong, and buoyant, "wholly as a man, and not as a lover or husband." Recognizing her "mistake" in being involved with Hurstwood, she also recalls the force with which she was removed from her former life, although she had been in a precarious position. When Hurstwood gives up looking for a job and settles for staying around the house and looking disheveled, Carrie loses her respect for him, yet she wavers between drifting along with him and being assertive. Ultimately their relationship is severed when he falls ill and Carrie is unable to be "good-natured and sympathetic" as she wishes, owing in part to his nature. Carrie's weariness and discontent with Hurstwood derive from a combination of her yearning for wealth and his knavishness. The heroine is never completely independent of her needs, and when Hurstwood storms out the door after revealing that their marriage is a fraud, "she thought, at first, with the faintest alarm, of being left without money—not of losing him." Truly, Carrie is driven by the need for survival more than by love, but Carrie has lived without real love from the beginning, when her sister emerges from the throng at the railway station bringing "the change of affectional atmosphere" that represents the "cold reality" of the family life of the poor. Carrie's abandonment of Hurstwood is ultimately a coldly economic decision, and it shows her as an unpleasantly self-centered human being, but one whose actions derive from needs unrecognized and unmet by the people surrounding her.

Perhaps it is the absence of familial warmth that makes the larger myth of the star so compelling, for a long-standing maxim is that everybody wants to be the darling of everybody's darling. Carrie's humble beginnings and fictional rise fit the historical myths of Broadway perfectly. She is advanced by her natural beauty, luck, and determination, but she is not free from the sadness of the past even once she has achieved great success. Similar patterns show up frequently as the lot of the "star," not only in our contemporary myths, but also as early as the 1880s. One need only turn to the pages of the July 1886 *Demorest's Monthly Magazine* to find in "The American Drama and Its Typical Stars" such an American icon in "Clara Morris, the Emotional Actress." Clara was an orphan, fled advances from an older man at the age of 12, was identified in the chorus line of a Midwest theater as having talent, and made her way to New York and stardom, carrying with her the pain of physical illness. Parallels to Carrie do not extend so far as to suggest that Clara is an outright source, but Clara's story suggests a generalized ethos into which Carrie fits perfectly as an ideal of popular American culture. At the same time the other problems of a dubious sexual history and the haunting sadness of the great, which run through American star worship from Clara Morris to Marilyn Monroe, do not stand in the way of fame but enhance its mystery. Dreiser had already explained Carrie's situation at the time that she had her first success as Laura: the thought of success "hummed in her ears as the melody of an old song," longing for the better life, but she rather modestly states it as a dream of "sometime" getting a place as a "real" actress. This haunting sense of unworthiness and the involvement of hidden personal pain and a troubled personal history enlist our sympathies on the side of the successful star.

**Source:** David E. E. Sloane, "Carrie," in *Sister Carrie: Theodore Dreiser's Sociological Tragedy*, Twayne Publishers, 1992, pp. 95–114.

## SOURCES

Cassuto, Leonard, "Sister Carrie," in *American History Through Literature 1870–1920*, Vol. 3, edited by Tom Quirk and Gary Scharnhorst, Charles Scribner's Sons, 2006, pp. 1046–51.

Dreiser, Theodore, *Sister Carrie*, Doubleday, Page, 1900; reprint, Signet Classic, 2000.

Kazin, Alfred, "Introduction," in *Stature of Theodore Dreiser: A Critical Survey of the Man and His Work*, edited by Alfred Kazin and Charles Shapiro, Indiana University Press, 1955, pp. 3–12.

Lingeman, Richard, "The Titan (Author Theodore Dreiser)," in *American Heritage*, Vol. 44, No. 1, February–March 1993, pp. 72–80.

Northway, Martin, "Dreiser Biography Spells Out Why His 'Realistic Fiction' Caught On," in *St. Louis Post-Dispatch*, April 3, 2005, p.G8.

Pizer, Donald, "Theodore Dreiser," in *Dictionary of Literary Biography, Volume 12: American Realists and Naturalists*, edited by Donald Pizer and Earl N. Harbert, Gale Research, 1982, pp. 145–65.

Zender, Karl F., "Walking Away from the Impossible Thing: Identity and Denial in 'Sister Carrie,'" in *Studies in the Novel*, Vol. 30, No. 1, Spring 1998, pp. 63–76.

# *Song of Myself*

## WALT WHITMAN

## 1892

Walt Whitman's "Song of Myself" is the most famous of the twelve poems originally published in *Leaves of Grass*, the collection for which the poet is most widely known. First published in 1855, Whitman made extensive revisions to the book, changing titles, motifs, and adding whole poems until 1881, and tinkering further until his death in 1892. The title "Song of Myself" did not come about until 1881, going through various permutations that include "Poem of Walt Whitman, an American," "Walt Whitman," and "Myself." Its changing title hints at the shifts found within the sprawling epic. From the obvious "Walt Whitman" to the abstract "Myself," Whitman reveals his desire to examine the individual, the communion between individuals, and the individual's place in the universe. The poem is at once a meditation on what it is to be human, a song to the America that Whitman felt so passionately about, and a sermon about the equality of man. Its free-verse construction, devoid of conventional meter and rhyme, mirrors the expansive, sensual, often sexual, language that marked the poem as something totally new. An early criticism of *Leaves of Grass* in the September 15, 1855, edition of the *Brooklyn Daily Eagle* explains,

> Here we have a book which fairly staggers us. It sets all the ordinary rules of criticism at defiance. It is one of the strangest compounds of transcendentalism, bombast, philosophy, folly, wisdom, wit and dullness which it ever catered into the heart of man to conceive. . . . It is a

# BIOGRAPHY

**WALT WHITMAN**

Walt Whitman was born in West Hills, New York, on May 31, 1819, and settled with his family in Brooklyn soon after. Frequent visits to the city's museums, libraries, and lecture halls supplemented the future poet's lackluster public school education. He worked as a newspaper apprentice, schoolteacher, journalist, fiction writer, and editor of a New Orleans paper. It was in New Orleans that Whitman witnessed a slave auction firsthand. He vowed to never forget the dehumanization that was a regular occurrence in the United States.

He began writing uninspired, conventional poetry in the 1840s, then, toward the early 1850s, mysteriously abandoned convention and started creating utterly original poems. These were published anonymously in 1855 in a collection titled *Leaves of Grass*. The poems, especially "Song of Myself," changed the face of American poetry forever. Whitman revised, rearranged, and added poems to the book throughout the rest of his life, issuing a total of nine distinct editions between 1855 and 1892.

The Civil War and its attendant brutality shocked the poet, whose deeply held beliefs about humanity were now being challenged on the battlefields of America. He spent time comforting sick and injured soldiers on frequent hospital visits and writing poems about the war. He suffered a paralyzing stroke in 1873, but published four additional editions of *Leaves of Grass* before he died on March 26, 1892, in Camden, New Jersey.

poem; but it conforms to none of the rules by which poetry has ever been judged.

Born in West Hills, New York, just thirty years after George Washington was inaugurated, Whitman was raised by working-class, liberal parents during the most nationalistic period in American history. Pride in the newly formed country's success was widespread, yet no indigenous work of literature existed to reflect the native culture, the landscape, or the political idealism of America. In his 1837 "American Scholar" address, Ralph Waldo Emerson challenged his listeners: "Our day of dependence, our long apprenticeship to the learning of other lands, draws to a close. . . . We have listened too long to the courtly muses of Europe." In the 1955 introduction to Whitman's *Leaves of Grass*, Gay Wilson Allen tells that the challenge sparked the poet's imagination. In 1849, one of the characters from Henry Wadsworth Longfellow's *Kavanagh* shouted, "We want a national literature altogether shaggy and unshorn, that shall shake the earth, like a herd of buffaloes thundering over the prairies!" Whitman responded to the call with the earth-shaking *Leaves of Grass*, the first truly American collection of poetry written by a great American poet.

Before publishing *Leaves of Grass*, Whitman worked as a newspaper apprentice, a teacher, a journalist, and a writer of short fiction. His working-class background gave him compassion for the disenfranchised. His passion for democracy and equality made him detest slavery. His frustration with the political climate leading up to the Civil War inspired him with poetic fervor. It is interesting, then, that these elements come together in an utterly indefinable work of poetic genius. Poets, critics, lecturers, and educators have failed to come up with a definitive interpretation of "Song of Myself," though not for lack of trying. Countless books and papers have been written in an attempt to unlock the mysteries of Whitman's mystical, lyrical, poetic journey of the soul. In the end, most agree that the independent reader is responsible for making his or her way through this innovative, challenging, and thoroughly American poem. The version explored here is the final, 1892, or "Deathbed" edition.

## PLOT SUMMARY

### Section 1

The opening lines of the poem prepare the reader for what lies ahead: "I celebrate myself, and sing myself, / And what I assume you shall assume, / For every atom belonging to me as good belongs to you." This introduces the universal "I," sets the celebratory tone, and foreshadows the themes of equality, nature, and goodness. He goes on, "I

*Walt Whitman in the late 1880s* © *Corbis*

loafe and invite my soul, / I lean and loafe at my ease observing a spear of summer grass," equating the natural ease and comfort with which the "I" observes a blade of grass to communing with the soul. Though the universal "I" is invoked, Whitman appears as himself in the third stanza, "form'd from this soil, this air, / Born here of parents born here from parents the same... / I, now thirty-seven years old in perfect health begin." As Whitman the man is born of the earth and the air, Whitman the poet is emerging as himself, as the poem itself, in these very lines.

## Section 2

In this section, the poet exalts the beauty of nature, writing, "The atmosphere is not a perfume, it has no taste of the distillation, it is odorless, / It is for my mouth forever, I am in love with it." Whitman equates fresh air with all that is good. "I will go to the bank by the wood and become undisguised and naked, / I am mad for it to be in contact with me." Nakedness is honesty. Whitman rejoices in simplicity and vitality as much as in honesty. The introduction of the senses begins with air on skin and progresses to "My respiration and inspiration, the beating of my heart, the passing of blood and air through my lungs, / The sniff of green leaves and dry leaves, and of the shore." The celebration of the self and of the soul continues. Whitman expresses the miracle of the body and its functions while the soul rejoices in its existence on earth. "The sound of the belch'd words of my voice loos'd to the eddies of the wind / . . . / The feeling of health, the full-noon trill, the song of me rising from bed and meeting the sun." He then claims that the reader can "possess the origin of all poems," and will learn to "listen to all sides and filter them from your self."

## Section 3

Whitman invokes the urgency of the present early in this section:

> There was never any more inception than there
>   is now,
> Nor any more youth or age than there is now,
> And will never be any more perfection than
>   there is now,
> Nor any more heaven or hell than there is now.

The mystery of the self as a present being in both body and soul is expressed in the lines, "I and this mystery here we stand / Clear and sweet is my soul, and clear and sweet is all that is not my soul." Whether in body or soul, the present is all that matters. With, "I am satisfied—I see, dance, laugh, sing; / As the hugging and loving bed-fellow sleeps at my side through the night, and withdraws at the peep of the day with stealthy tread," he repeats the love of the present in sexual language. The emphasis falls on the fact that Whitman is satisfied in his body, seeing, dancing, laughing, singing, hugging, and loving. This joyful expression carries into the next section.

## Section 4

The poet recalls good times and bad, including "Battles, the horrors of fratricidal war, the fever of doubtful news, the fitful events; / These come to me days and nights and go from me again, / But they are not the Me myself." Whitman will not let the evils of the earth strip him of his joy. The "myself" of which he speaks is his essence, his soul, as well as the soul of mankind. The soul is naturally good. It naturally seeks joy and equanimity and does not dwell on "fitful events." "Looking with side-curved head curious what will come next, / Both in and out of the game and watching and wondering at it." Whitman seems to believe it best to let life unfold on its natural progression.

## Section 5

In this section, Whitman the individual becomes the abstract "myself" of the poem's title. The identities of "I," "you," and "myself" evolve into a universal self brought about by the birth of Whitman the poet. As introduction to his poetic birth, Whitman writes,

> Loafe with me on the grass, loose the stop from
> your throat,
> Not words, not music or rhyme I want, not
> custom or lecture, not even the best,
> Only the lull I like, the hum of your valvèd
> voice.

The reader may ask, "Whose voice? And why not words, or music, or rhyme?" The following stanza, one of the most surreal verses in the whole poem, describes Whitman's poetic birth in highly sensual language:

> How you settled your head athwart my hips
> and gently turn'd over upon me,
> And parted the shirt from my bosom-bone, and
> plunged your tongue to my bare-stript
> heart,
> And reach'd till you felt my beard, and reach'd
> till you held my feet.

In an essay in *Walt Whitman: An Encyclopedia*, James E. Miller Jr. writes, "This event may best be described as the organic union of the poet's body and soul, the latter appearing first in the disembodied 'hum' of a 'valvèd voice.'" The newly born poet finds himself with "the peace and knowledge that pass all the argument of the earth." He continues:

> And I know that the hand of God is the
> promise of my own,
> And I know that the spirit of God is the brother
> of my own,
> And that all the men ever born are also my
> brothers, and the women and my sisters
> and lovers,
> And that a kelson of the creation is love.

## Sections 6–7

In section 6, Whitman introduces the first key image after his poetic awakening. The spear of grass image from the beginning of "Song of Myself" reappears here. "A child said *What is the grass?* fetching it to me with full hands, / How could I answer the child? I do not know what it is anymore than he." With these words, the journey into understanding begins. From here through the mid-section of the poem, the democratic symbolism of grass ("Sprouting alike in broad zones and narrow zones, / Growing among black folks as among white") expands to celebrate daily scenes of American life with Whitman as guide.

The last lines of the section, "All goes onward and outward, nothing collapses, / And to die is different from what any one supposed, and luckier," act as a bridge between sections 6 and 7. In section 7, the song continues, "Has any one supposed it lucky to be born? / I hasten to inform him or her it is just as lucky to die, and I know it." Here, Whitman refers to his poetic rebirth, the birth of the new self that depended on the death of his previous self.

## Sections 8–10

"The little one sleeps in its cradle" marks the official beginning of Whitman's poetic journey through America as he catalogs the American experience. He explores the commonalities shared by the human race, the celebration of everyday life, and the indignities and difficulties suffered by humanity:

> The runaway slave came to my house and stopt
> outside,
> I heard his motions crackling the twigs of the
> woodpile,
> Through the swung half-door of the kitchen I
> saw him limpsy and weak,
> And went where he sat on a log and led him in
> and assured him,
> . . .
> He staid with me a week before he was
> recuperated and pass'd north,
> I had him sit next to me at table, my fire-lock
> lean'd in the corner.

This image follows one describing the marriage of a trapper to a "red girl . . . her head was bare, her coarse straight locks descended upon her voluptuous limbs and reach'd to her feet." Boatmen, clam-diggers, Native Americans, runaway slaves: Whitman makes plain the fact that one man or woman works, lives, seeks love, and seeks freedom as well as the next.

## Section 11

Section 11 opens with the image of the twenty-ninth bather, a female spectator longing to leave her proper place and join twenty-eight young male bathers by the shore. He implies that to fully experience the world, one must be of it, yet apart from it enough to maintain some perspective and without interfering. The voice, at first, belongs to the twenty-eight-year-old woman, hiding behind the blinds inside her fine house. Then, Whitman takes over, describing what it would be like if she were to join them as she has in her imagination. His reverence for the communion of bodies and souls is richly detailed here, and, due to the highly sensual language being employed, one might be led to consider the melding of bodies and souls in the act of lovemaking. The description of the men bathing invites the comparison of two people becoming one in a purely physical though transcendent moment, the hidden twenty-ninth bather the metaphor for the self that exists when the moment has passed.

## Sections 12–19

In these sections, Whitman describes the people he meets as he travels, as well as his philosophy of accepting them all. Section 12 describes workers in a marketplace. In section 13, Whitman describes himself as the "caresser of life wherever moving, backward as well as forward sluing. . . . Absorbing all to myself and for this song." From this point on through section 17, Whitman "absorbs" a litany of snapshots of American lives and people and spreads them before the reader as proof that all these actions, and places, and people, and moments truly exist:

> The half-breed straps on his light boots to
>    compete in the race,
>
> . . .
>
> The groups of newly-come immigrants cover
>    the wharf or levee,
>
> . . .
>
> The child is baptized, the convert is making his
>    first professions,
>
> . . .
>
> The bride unrumples her white dress, the
>    minute-hand of the clock moves slowly,
>
> . . .
>
> The stumps stand thick round the clearing, the
>    squatter strikes deep with his axe.

Whitman's list ends in section 17 with these words: "This is the grass that grows wherever the land is and the water is, This the common air that bathes the globe." In sections 18 and 19, Whitman illustrates his egalitarian approach, writing "I play not marches for accepted victors only, I play marches for conquer'd and slain persons," and "I will not have a single person slighted or left away."

## Sections 20–24

Whitman's song becomes metaphysical in section 20: "Who goes there? Hankering, gross, mystical, nude; How is it I extract strength from the beef I eat? What is a man anyhow? what am I? what are you?" He goes on to attempt

answers and comes up with, "In all people I see myself, none more and not one a barley-corn less, And the good or bad I say of myself I say of them." This continues through to section 21, "I am the poet of the Body and I am the poet of the Soul, the pleasures of heaven are with me and pains of hell are with me." The next sections seem egotistical as he asserts his importance in the world, but he soon reveals that he believes the same is true for all: "I speak the pass-word primeval, I give the sign of democracy / By God! I will accept nothing which all cannot have their counterpart of on the same terms."

## Sections 25–29

Whitman introduces the ideas of seeing and speaking in section 25. These acts may reveal an attempt at expression, even as they conceal "what I really am":

> My voice goes after what my eyes cannot reach,
> With the twirl of my tongue I encompass world
>    and volumes of worlds.
>
> Speech is the twin of my vision, it is unequal to
>    measure itself,
> It provokes me forever, it says sarcastically,
> *Walt you contain enough, why don't you let it out
>    then?*

Deciding he has spoken too much, Whitman decides to listen. Section 26 begins, "Now I will do nothing but listen, To accrue what I hear into this song, to let sounds contribute toward it." This leads to a lengthy pattern of sounds, from "The ring of alarm-bells" to "The steam-whistle" to "The orbic flex of [the tenor's] mouth is pouring and filling me full."

Touch, though hinted at throughout, is given its own section in section 28. These surreal lines suggest sexual arousal in the context of the search for self-identity:

> Is this then a touch? quivering me to a new
>    identity,
>
> . . .
>
> You villain touch! what are you doing? my
>    breath is tight in its throat,
> Unclench your floodgates, you are too much
>    for me.

## Sections 30–32

Section 30 returns to the idea that truth can be found in natural things. This exploration leads the reader to section 31 ("I believe a leaf of grass is no less than the journey work of the stars") where the frenetic journey reaches a resting point. Here, Whitman breaks out the lofty language of the sage: "In vain the plutonic rocks send their old heat against my approach, / In vain the mastodon retreats beneath its own pow-der'd bones." The section ends, "I follow quickly, I ascend to the nest in the fissure of the cliff."

He turns to animals next, praising their peacefulness, and denounces the earthly frustra-tions of man in this section. "I think I could turn and live with animals, they are so placid and self-contain'd, I stand and look at them long and long." He goes on:

> They do not sweat and whine about their
>     condition,
> They do not lie awake in the dark and weep for
>     their sins,
> They do not make me sick discussing their duty
>     to God,
> Not one is dissatisfied, not one is demented
>     with the mania of owning things,
> Not one kneels to another, nor to his kind that
>     lived thousands of years ago,
> Not one is respectable or unhappy over the
>     whole earth.

As much as Whitman loves men and women, he also fully embraces their faults. This section reveals the failings of man the poet finds particularly unsavory. The self in its rising must then rise above the faults he addresses here.

## Sections 33–39

In section 33, the poet presents the vastness of his poetic world, writing, "My ties and ballasts leave me, my elbows rest in sea-gaps, / I skirt sierras, my palms over continents, / I am afoot with my vision." He puts himself in the place of many different people who have suffered, from doomed sailor to burned martyr to "hounded slave." He describes events from the Texas War of Independence and the American Civil War, and finally declares, "I am possess'd! / Embody all presences outlaw'd or suffering." He seems to wake from a dream in section 38, and in section 39 refers to himself in the third person: "Wherever he goes men and women accept and desire him, / They desire he should like them, touch them, speak to them, stay with them."

## Sections 40–43

Whitman examines his own role as poet and truth-seeker in these sections: "Flaunt of sun-shine I need not your bask—lie over! / You light surfaces only, I force surfaces and depths also." He asks, "And what is reason? and what is love? And what is life?" He goes on to assure the

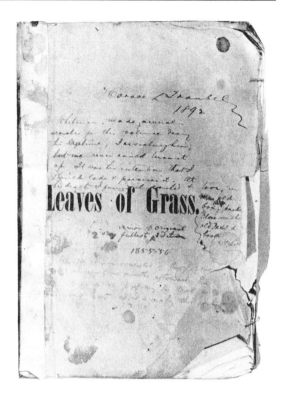

*The cover of Whitman's own copy of the first edition of his 1855 collection* Leaves of Grass
*Getty Images*

world's priests that he does not despise them, and says, "My faith is the greatest of faiths and the least of faiths."

## Section 44

In section 44, Whitman writes,

> It is time to explain myself—let us stand up.
> What is known I strip away,
> I launch all men and women forward with me
>     into the Unknown.
> The clock indicates the moment—but what
>     does eternity indicate?

The sprawling epic that preceded this moment made this moment possible. Without the journey, the destination would just be another place. Instead, Whitman has brought his readers to this place after carrying them to richerplaces. Now is the time to decipher the images, sift through the sand to reveal the treas-ures. He explains:

> Immense have been the preparations for me,
> Faithful and friendly the arms that have help'd
>     me.
>     . . .

"I CELEBRATE MYSELF, AND SING MYSELF,

AND WHAT I ASSUME YOU SHALL ASSUME,

FOR EVERY ATOM BELONGING TO ME AS GOOD

BELONGS TO YOU."

All forces have been steadily employ'd to
  complete and delight me,
Now on this spot I stand with my robust soul.

## Sections 45—47

The poet counsels the reader, "See ever so far,
there is limitless space outside of that, / Count
ever so much, there is limitless time around
that," and, "Not I, not any one else can travel
that road for you, / You must travel it for yourself." "Song of Myself" has thus become a road-
map as much as a journey. Having brought the
reader this far, Whitman has become more than
a guide. He has become a father and a mother, a
nurturing self wanting nothing more than for his
child to find his or her way in the world alone:

Sit a while dear son,
Here are biscuits to eat and here is milk to drink,
But as soon as you sleep and renew yourself in
  sweet clothes, I kiss you with a good-by
  kiss and open the gate for your egress
  hence.

## Sections 48–52

Whitman ponders God, which he sees in everyone and everything around him, and Death,
which he does not fear, and finally falls into a
deep sleep, exhausted from his vision. "To it the
creation is the friend whose embracing awakes
me. . . .—it is Happiness." He is eager to continue
with new people and new experiences.

The journey concluded, the reader is taken
back to the beginning, to where Whitman loafes
and leans, wondering over a spear of grass. "The
spotted hawk swoops by and accuses me, he
complains of my gab and my loitering. / I too
am not a bit tamed, I too am untranslatable, / I
sound my barbaric yawp over the roofs of the
world." He leaves the reader with these lines:

Failing to fetch me at first keep encouraged,
Missing me one place search another,
I stop somewhere waiting for you.

## THEMES

### Equality

In "Song of Myself," Whitman uses "I" to refer not
only to himself, but to a larger "I" that includes the
reader and humanity in general. Invoking the universal "I" brings a sense of equality to the poem
without directly addressing that theme. In its own
mysterious way, though, the poem does deal
directly with equality and democracy, primarily
through Whitman's imagery and language.

Whitman's belief in equality is so strong, he
dedicates the first lines of "Song of Myself" to it:

I celebrate myself, and sing myself,
And what I assume you shall assume,
For every atom belonging to me as good
  belongs to you.

Here, "I" and "you" are used symbolically,
not unlike the "myself" from the title that repeats
itself in the first line.

The grass is used symbolically to indicate
equality later in the poem:

A child said *What is the grass?* fetching it to me
  with full hands;
How could I answer the child? I do not know
  what it is any more than he.

Whitman seeks an answer. He speculates
upon a number of possibilities before suggesting
the following:

Or I guess it is a uniform hieroglyphic,
And it means, Sprouting alike in broad zones
  and narrow zones,
Growing among black folks as among white,
Kanuck, Tuckahoe, Congressman, Cuff, I give
  them the same, I receive them the same.

Here, the grass represents that which is
equal among all people. By sprouting everywhere, in both broad and narrow zones, among
black and white people, given and received
equally, the grass is a symbol of democracy.

One of the most powerful and elusive segments of the poem addresses the theme of equality by virtue of its imagery alone. Whitman
paints a vibrant picture of democracy by compiling a descriptive list of Americans in action:

The duck-shooter walks by silent and cautious
  stretches,
The deacons are ordain'd with cross'd hands at
  the altar,
The spinning-girl retreats and advances to the
  hum of the big wheel.

Without commentary or elaboration, Whitman illustrates the essence of equality in this

catalog of humanity, which includes the farmer, the lunatic, the malform'd, the quadroon, the connoisseur, the bride, and the prostitute, among many others. The segment ends with the following:

> And these tend inward to me, and I tend
> outward to them,
> And such as it is to be of these more or less I
> am,
> And of these one and all I weave the song of
> myself.

The song of the poet and his subjects, then, becomes the song of America and its lofty ambitions of egalitarianism.

Finally, the poet declares himself "a kosmos" as a way of representing his and our universality:

> Walt Whitman, a kosmos, of Manhattan the
> son,
> . . .
> Whoever degrades another degrades me,
> And whatever is done or said returns at last to
> me.
> . . .
> I speak the pass-word primeval, I give the sign
> of democracy,
> By God! I will accept nothing which all cannot
> have their counterpart of on the same terms.

## Sex and Sexuality

Sex and sexuality are prominent themes in "Song of Myself." Whitman's passionate belief in the goodness of nature fuels his eroticism as much as his belief in the intrinsic connection of body and soul. Whitman's belief in egalitarianism and the communion of individuals is further reflected in his sensuous language and imagery:

> I have said that the soul is not more than the
> body,
> And I have said that the body is not more than
> the soul,
> . . .
> And there is no object so soft but it makes a
> hub for the wheel'd universe,
> And I say to any man or woman, Let your soul
> stand cool and composed before a million
> universes.

Sex and sexuality are bound to nature as well as to spirituality. Whitman proves this by pointing out that the senses, though natural, are also supernatural in the miraculous abilities they impart. Though not overtly sexual, the following example of his earthy rhetoric illustrates how Whitman connects flesh, desire, bodily function, and spirituality:

> I believe in the flesh and the appetites,
> Seeing, hearing, feeling, are miracles, and each
> part and tag of me is a miracle.
> Divine am I inside and out, and I make holy
> whatever I touch or am touch'd from,
> The scent of these arm-pits aroma finer than
> prayer,
> This head more than churches, bibles, and all
> the creeds.

Whitman also uses the body as a metaphor for the dramatic and varied American landscape. In the following passage, the use of "I" and "you" reflect the universal "myself" of the poem's title:

> Mix'd tussled hay of head, beard, brawn, it
> shall be you!
> Trickling sap of maple, fibre of manly wheat, it
> shall be you!
> . . .
> Winds whose soft-tickling genitals rub against
> me it shall be you!
> Broad muscular fields, branches of live oak,
> loving lounger in my winding paths, it
> shall be you!
> Hands I have taken, face I have kiss'd, mortal I
> have ever touch'd, it shall be you.

Whitman's ambiguous sexuality—critics have referred to his language as being everything from autoerotic to omnisexual—point to the possibility of his homosexuality as well as his desire to convey "the largeness and generosity of the spirit of the citizen" (as he described his countrymen in his preface to the 1855 edition). In the same way that "Song of Myself" defies absolute interpretation, Whitman's sexuality, and the manner in which he uses it in the poem, is too sprawling, too unwieldy to categorize. Or as Whitman says, "Do I contradict myself? Very well then I contradict myself, (I am large, I contain multitudes.)"

## HISTORICAL OVERVIEW

### Nationalism

Walt Whitman was born during a time of unrivaled American nationalism. His generation was the first to witness growing stability and expansion of the territories. Patriotism was rampant. Walt's father, Walter Whitman Sr. an admirer and acquaintance of Thomas Paine, had such reverence for the heroes of the American Revolution that he named three of his nine children Andrew Jackson, George Washington, and Thomas Jefferson. The new nation was being

*A drawing of New York and Brooklyn, circa 1855, by Simpson* © *Museum of the City of New York/Corbis*

invented with every passing day, and American citizens were filled with political idealism.

According to Gay Wilson Allen in the introduction of Signet Classic's 1955 edition of *Leaves of Grass*, Whitman's success was aided

> by the sanguine nationalism of the American people in the mid-nineteenth century. From the Puritans the young nation had inherited the belief that God had ordained a special, fortunate destiny for it. The Puritans had intended the Theocratic State of Massachusetts to be God's Own Government on earth. And the successes of the American people in their two wars with England had increased their confidence in a Providential destiny.

By the time Whitman had reached middle age, Ralph Waldo Emerson and Henry Wadsworth Longfellow had clarified the need for an original American literature. Emerson wrote in his essay "The Poet" (1844), "Our log-rolling, our stumps and their politics, . . . the southern planting, the western clearing, Oregon and Texas, are yet unsung." The call for a wholly new American literature—one that would define and describe the as-yet undefined American

culture, landscape, and psychology—had been sounded. It was the vibrant, heady climate of these times that inspired Whitman to write *Leaves of Grass.*

### Slavery

The optimism and enthusiasm for American expansion was tempered by the institution of slavery. Africans and their descendants had been enslaved on American soil since the early seventeenth century. By the time the U.S. Constitution was adopted, slavery had become a dying institution. The northern states began to abolish the practice and the founding fathers declared that the importation of slaves into the United States would end by the year 1808, but slavery was reinvigorated in the southern states after the invention of the cotton gin in the early 1800s. Cotton, a crop that requires a massive labor force to raise, suddenly became profitable. Slavery was once again on the rise.

During Whitman's lifetime, the problem of slavery begged a solution. The contradiction of enslaved peoples living in a supposedly free country was just too great. As a journalist, Whitman wrote primarily about class issues and the interests of white workingmen. He made his anti-slavery stance known, but he never focused his attention on the issue. Critics speculate about what may have caused him to address the issue as a poet. Some say witnessing a slave auction in New Orleans while working as an editor for the *Crescent* was a turning point. Others point to the fact that Whitman was beginning to attract a circle of radical thinkers and writers as friends. Ed Folsom and Kenneth M. Price, in their biography of Whitman for the *Whitman Archive*, write, "Whatever the cause, in Whitman's future-oriented poetry blacks become central to his new literary project and central to his understanding of democracy."

The first edition of *Leaves of Grass* was published in 1855, just six years prior to the attack on Fort Sumter—the start of the American Civil War—and the inauguration of Abraham Lincoln as the sixteenth U.S. president. Slavery was the most divisive issue facing American citizens at the time. Whitman was prompted to write a political tract called "The Eighteenth Presidency!" in 1856 denouncing the fact that slave owners persisted in dominating both the national judiciary and the legislature. He wrote, "At present, the personnel of the government of these thirty millions, in executives and elsewhere, is drawn from limber-tongued lawyers, very fluent but empty feeble old men, professional politicians," not "the solid body of the people." He was not the only American to prophesy the coming civil war and condemn hypocritical leaders. The powder keg that was slavery was ready to blow, and every American citizen, whether free or enslaved, was affected.

## CRITICAL OVERVIEW

The first edition of Walt Whitman's 1855 *Leaves of Grass* was an anonymous, slim volume boasting a curious frontispiece. It featured an engraving of Whitman in full beard and working clothes, one hand in his pocket, the other on his hip. The jaunty, earthy image he presented was meant to emphasize the informal, personal nature of the poems.

The strange book was sold in a handful of bookstores around New York. Of the eight hundred copies printed, only two hundred were bound. In the introduction of Signet Classic's 1955 edition of *Leaves of Grass*, Gay Wilson Allen wrote, "Today Walt Whitman's *Leaves of Grass* is almost universally recognized as one of the masterpieces of world literature, but it did not have an impressive beginning." Its free verse was lost on many of Whitman's critics. In 1856, the reviewer in *Crayon 3* writes,

> With a wonderful vigor of thought and intensity of perception, a power, indeed, not often found, *Leaves of Grass* has no ideality, no concentration, no purpose—it is barbarous, undisciplined, like the poetry of a half-civilized people, and, as a whole, useless, save to those miners of thought who prefer the metal in its unworked state.

Others, such as Charles Dana of the *New York Daily Tribune*, found Whitman's sensual language offensive:

> His words might have passed between Adam and Eve in Paradise, before the want of fig-leaves brought no shame; but they are quite out of place amid the decorum of modern society, and will justly prevent his volume from free circulation in scrupulous circles.

Anonymous reviews trumpeting the glowing collection appeared in various New York papers ("An American bard at last!" read one; another hailed it as "transcendent and new"), but they were obviously penned by Whitman himself. He sent copies to several well-known writers, but only Ralph Waldo Emerson responded. In a personal letter addressed to Whitman, Emerson expresses his enthusiasm for *Leaves of Grass* (quoted in "Whitman as Transcendentalist"):

> I greet you at the beginning of a great career, which yet must have had a long foreground somewhere, for such a start. I rubbed my eyes a little to see if this sunbeam were no illusion; but the solid sense of the book is a sober certainty.

Emerson's praise gave Whitman the confidence to forge ahead with a second edition of *Leaves of Grass*. He continued to rework and revise "his experiment" throughout the rest of his life. *Leaves of Grass* swelled from twelve poems in 1855 to 389 in 1881. According to Ivan Marki in his paper, "*Leaves of Grass*, 1855 Edition,"

> When Malcolm Cowley reprinted [the 1855 edition] in paperback in 1959, he had to introduce it as "the buried masterpiece of American writing." Until then, the text was not easily available and, except in Jean Catel's French study in 1930, received little scholarly or critical

# MEDIA ADAPTATIONS

The 1855 edition of *Leaves of Grass* was made available on audiocassette from Blackstone Audiobooks in January 1996. It is read by Noah Waterman.

attention. That the situation has radically changed is due, to a large extent, to Gay Wilson Allen, who, even before Cowley, gave the first edition its due both in his handbook in 1946 and in his exemplary biography of Whitman, *The Solitary Singer* in 1955. No serious study of Whitman has appeared since in which the 1855 text is not extensively discussed and its significance in Whitman's achievement not recognized. . . . [T]he fascination with the 1855 edition continues, and the book is unlikely to become a buried masterpiece again.

"Song of Myself," untitled at the time, is the heart of every edition of *Leaves of Grass* from 1855 onward. The poem is not only Whitman's best, it is Whitman. Marki writes, "the poetic self named Walt Whitman is born. . . . *Leaves of Grass* is dominated by this presence emerging from 'Song of Myself.'"

## CRITICISM

### William Birmingham

*In the following excerpt, Birmingham presents "Song of Myself" as the idealization of the potential American being: egalitarian, relational, and loving.*

My suggestion is this: religious Americans might profit spiritually from a committed reading of Walt Whitman's "Song of Myself." By a committed reading I mean one in which, having suspended disbelief, readers allow themselves to experience the text as meaningful aesthetic event, bringing to bear only later their critical faith practice.

Whitman, I should warn, was a great poet of experience and the possibilities it contains, but a terrible philosopher. A stanza from the last poem in the first edition (1855) of *Leaves of Grass* only slightly exaggerates how badly he often wrote when a philosophical mood came upon him:

> Great is justice;
> Justice is not settled by legislators and laws . . .
>     it is in the soul,
> It cannot be varied by statutes any more than
>     love or pride or the attraction of gravity
>     can,
> It is immutable . . . it does not depend on
>     majorities . . . majorities or what
> not come at last before the same passionless
>     and exact tribunal.

The ungainly and demotic "what not" instances, however, one of Whitman's great gifts to later poets—license to replace conventionally poetic English with the language and rhythms of common American speech. Examples from two minor African-American poets may clarify the effect of this democratization of language. (Other groups and other poets could as easily be used.) Three or four decades before Whitman's birth in 1819, Phyllis Wheatley, doing her best to work in a language foreign both to her African and to her American heritage, writes that her love of freedom springs from having been "snatch'd from *Afric's* happy seat" and concludes, "Such, such my case. And can I then but pray / Others may never feel tyrannic sway?" However valid Wheatley's generous sentiment, the language rings untrue. (Its falseness brings to the poem an aura of cultural imperialism that may, paradoxically, enhance its effectiveness.) Three decades after Whitman's death in 1892, the congregation in James Weldon Johnson's "Listen, Lord—A Prayer" prays that the minister "Who breaks the bread of life this morning" be kept "out of the gunshot of the devil":

> Wash him with hyssop inside and out,
> Hang him up and drain him dry of sin.
> Pin his ear to the wisdom post,
> And make his words sledge hammers of
>     truth—
> Beating on the iron heart of sin.

Johnson is not writing dialect poetry, yet his language rises from within the congregation's experience, capturing the black Baptist sacramentalization of the sermon. He can do so because the tradition Whitman began opened up poetry to the varieties of American language.

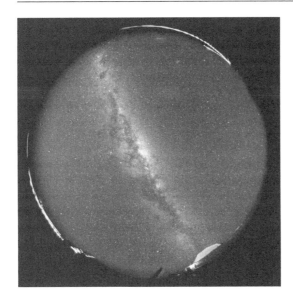

*The center of the Milky Way Galaxy as seen over Las Campanas Observatory* Getty Images

Literary language no longer reigns. Or, better, every language feeds the poetic imagination.

I cite the African-American tradition because it has been marginalized by our culture as a whole, and Whitman's aesthetic vision—not only of language but of the possible American self—comprehends those relegated to society's edge. In her preface to *Passion* June Jordan, alluding obliquely to Whitman's homosexuality, speaks of him as "the one white father who shares the systematic disadvantages of his heterogeneous offspring trapped inside a closet that is, in reality, as huge as the continental spread of North and South America" and ultimately asserts that "[a]gainst self-hatred," which is what those at the margins are so often taught, "there is Whitman." At its best, Whitman's poetic vision affirms, against self-hatred, a possible American self that is inclusive rather than exclusive, trusting rather than suspicious, egalitarian rather than hierarchical, relational rather than individualistic.

Whitman's inclusive vision of the possible self will surely appeal to those at home with contextual theology, though it is in other ways disquieting to the religious mind. It discovers the transcendent, if at all, in the immanent—in the spirit (but not the Spirit) with whose grandeur the world is charged. In "Song of Myself," the self experiences the divine not as Other but as merged with the cosmos, with which the self merges as well. Further—and this limitation is secular as well as religious—that cosmos seems closed to evil and to tragedy. There is more here than facile optimism, however; "Song of Myself" offers not an ideal self, realized or to come, but a delineation of what the empirical American self and its world may become if it follows the trajectory of the best in its democratic experience. If taken as optimism from below, this bears a close resemblance to hope.

Whitman's was, to borrow the aesthetic theologian John Dixon's term, a horizontal imagination, polar to the vertical, hierarchical imagination dominant in Western culture. (Dixon notes that the Reformation belief in the priesthood of all believers was the product of the horizontal imagination, but as decades passed, the pulpit rose higher and higher, creating in Protestant church architecture a visual hierarchy that implicitly denied the belief.) The horizontal imagination is democratic; it prizes each reality for what it is, not for the height of the step it occupies on the stairway to the heavens. When Walt proclaims "Every kind for itself and its own [...]" he is not insisting on the superiority of human to beast but stating his primary affinity with the human.

*Leaves of Grass*, more than any of the other seminal works published during the half-decade of 1850–1855, addresses America as a geographical and cultural totality in the process of self-creation. The Union was threatened; Whitman envisions unity present. Greed was manifest; he supposes heroes "pocketless of a dime" and originates delight in the common grass and air. American individualism was raw; he raises egocentricity to impossible heights on the one hand and affirms the inherently relational nature of the self on the other. Democracy was, given the depredations of slavery and the deprivations of women, unrealized; he imagines equality of dignity and respect. He loves and finds hope in both city and countryside.

The angel, however, is in the details, what Zweig calls "the unvarnished, shaggy particulars of the everyday world." Whitman perceives, Zweig says, "a sexual prodding from within life to produce more and better life." In "Song of Myself," Walt witnesses the particulars and waits, observing with ear and touch as well as eye—trusting in the inner capacity of each thing to make itself new. One essential element is patience. Those who loiter instead of rushing by see the "butcher-boy [put] off his killing clothes" and dance "his shuffle and breakdown." Another is compassion, which Walt exercises without the pity that reduces sufferers to their pain, whether it is the "child that peeped in at the door and then drew back and was never seen again" or a man "in the poorhouse tubercled by rum." But the most important is trust. To readers, Walt says:

> [. . .] each man and woman of you I lead upon a
> knoll,
> My left hand hooks you round the waist,
> My right hand points to landscapes of
> continents, and a plain public road.
>
> Not I, not any one else can travel that road for
> you,
> You must travel it for yourself.

**Source:** William Birmingham, "Whitman's Song of the Possible American Self," in *Cross Currents*, Association for Religious and Intellectual Life, Vol. 43, No. 3, Fall 1993, pp. 324–57.

# SOURCES

Allen, Gay Wilson, "Introduction," in *Leaves of Grass*, Signet Classics, 1980, pp. v–xx; originally published in 1955.

Dana, Charles A., "New Publications: Leaves of Grass," in the *New York Daily Tribune*, July 23, 1855, reprinted in *Whitman Archive*, www.whitmanarchive.org/criticism/reviews/leaves/leaves55/nytrib.html (August 7, 2006).

Emerson, Ralph Waldo, "American Scholar," on *American Transcendentalism Web*, www.vcu.edu/engweb/transcendentalism/authors/emerson/essays/amscholar.html (October 18, 2006); originally published in 1837.

———, "The Poet," www.vcu.edu/engweb/transcendentalism/authors/emerson/essays/poettext.html (October 19, 2006); originally published in 1844.

Folsom, Ed, and Kenneth M. Price, "Walt Whitman," in *Whitman Archive*, www.whitmanarchive.org/biography/biographymain.html (August 7, 2006).

"Leaves of Grass—An Extraordinary Book," in the *Brooklyn Daily Eagle*, September 15, 1855, reprinted in *Whitman Archive*, www.whitmanarchive.org/criticism/reviews/leaves/leaves55/eagle.html (August 7, 2006).

"Leaves of Grass," in *Revising Himself: Walt Whitman and Leaves of Grass*, www.loc.gov/exhibits/treasures/whitman-leavesofgrass.html (December 21, 2005).

Longfellow, Henry Wadsworth, *Kavanagh, A Tale*, Ticknor, Reed and Fields, 1849, p. 114; reprinted on etext.lib.virginia.edu/railton/enam315/kavanagh.html (October 18, 2006).

Marki, Ivan, "Leaves of Grass, 1855 Edition," in *Walt Whitman: An Encyclopedia*, Garland, 1998, pp. 354–58.

Miller, James E., "Song of Myself [1855]," in *Walt Whitman: An Encyclopedia*, Garland, 1998, pp. 654–57.

"Studies Among the Leaves: The Assembly of Extremes (Review of *Leaves of Grass* and Tennyson's *Maud*)," in *Crayon 3*, January 1856.

Whitman, Walt, *Leaves of Grass*, Signet Classics, 1980; originally published in 1892.

———, "Preface" to *Leaves of Grass*, 1855; reprinted in *The Oxford Book of American Essays, 1914*, www.bartleby.com/109/15.html (October 19, 2006).

———, "The Eighteenth Presidency!" in *Whitman: Poetry and Prose*, edited by Justin Kaplan, Library of American, 1996, p. 1331.

"Whitman as Transcendentalist," in *American Transcendentalism Web*, www.vcu.edu/engweb/transcendentalism/roots/legacy/whitman/index.html (October 19, 2006).

# White House Correspondents' Association Dinner 2006 Speech

**STEPHEN COLBERT**

**2006**

In April 2006, Stephen Colbert was a late-night cable-television comedian; by May, he was revered as the truth-telling jester in the farce of modern American media and politics. He delivered his speech at the White House Correspondents' Association Dinner on April 29, 2006. Although comedians and other entertainers have been invited to the annual dinner before, and while both the press and the presidency have always been open for some gentle ribbing, Colbert was the first speaker to so harshly and hilariously attack those honored institutions. As a result, Colbert found himself condemned in some circles as a tasteless bully while being venerated as a great American satirist in others. As Adam Sternbergh of *New York Magazine* put it:

> [Colbert] wound up delivering a controversial, possibly very funny, possibly horribly unfunny, possibly bravely patriotic, and possibly near-seditious monologue that earned him a crazed mob of lunatic followers who await his every command.

Since 1914, the White House Correspondents' Association has promoted the interests of reporters whose regular assignment is the presidency. The WHCA held its first dinner in 1920, and Calvin Coolidge established a tradition when he became the first sitting president to attend the dinner a few years later. Colbert, an actor and comedian best known for his satirical television show *The Colbert Report*, which pokes fun at popular but often

uninformed political commentators on television, was evidently invited to address the White House Correspondents' Dinner because of his popularity among younger, hipper fans.

Colbert's show regularly displays the host's earnest stance on ridiculous topics, such as his list of individuals, organizations, and even concepts that are "On Notice," which is a form of chastisement. The list of those "on notice" has included singer Barbra Streisand, the British Empire, and grizzly bears (a running joke on the show is Colbert's fear and distrust of bears). Even more daunting is the list of those people and concepts that are "Dead to Me," in Colbert's parlance. This list includes New York intellectuals, bowtie pasta, and owls. Colbert coined the term "truthiness" to describe his brand of comic hot air. "Truthiness is 'What I say is right, and [nothing] anyone else says could possibly be true.' It's not only that I *feel* it to be true, but that *I* feel it to be true. There's not only an emotional quality, but there's a selfish quality," Colbert explained in a 2006 interview with the *Onion's A.V. Club*. "Truthiness" was declared the Word of the Year 2005 by the American Dialect Society.

Stephen Colbert (the actor) explained the core of his show's humor to New York Magazine:

> Language has always been important in politics, but language is incredibly important to the present political struggle. Because if you can establish an atmosphere in which information doesn't mean anything, then there is no objective reality. The first show we did, a year ago, was our thesis statement: What you wish to be true is all that matters, regardless of the facts. Of course, at the time, we thought we were being farcical.

In interviews, Colbert has repeatedly stressed that his TV persona is not himself but rather a character named "Stephen Colbert" who is an idiotic blowhard convinced of his own brilliance. "Stephen Colbert" is an overbearing, know-it-all jingo who takes the cotemporary culture of American politics and journalism to a ridiculous extreme. "We share the same name," Colbert says of "Colbert." "But he says things I don't mean with a straight face. On the street, I think people know the difference. But I'm not sure, when people ask me to go someplace, which one they've asked."

It is easy for some people to confuse the actor and his act. While many argued that Colbert's comments at the dinner were not his

# BIOGRAPHY

**STEPHEN COLBERT**

Stephen Colbert was born May 13, 1964, in Charleston, South Carolina. He was the youngest of eleven children born to James and Lorna Colbert. When he was ten, his father and two of his brothers died in a plane crash on September 11, 1974. After a somewhat lonely childhood during which he developed a passion for science fiction, fantasy, and role-playing games, Colbert studied philosophy at Virginia's Hampden-Sydney College before transferring to Northwestern University to study acting. Eventually he joined Chicago's famous Second City Comedy group, where he met fellow performers Amy Sedaris and Paul Dinello. With Sedaris and Dinello Colbert developed *Strangers With Candy*, which debuted in 1998, for the basic cable Comedy Central television network. By this time, Colbert was a regular correspondent on Comedy Central's *The Daily Show*, a parody of TV news programs.

After Jon Stewart started hosting *The Daily Show*, Colbert perfected his screen persona of the know-it-all-idiot. In the fall of 2005, Colbert got his own show on Comedy Central, *The Colbert Report*, which is pronounced "col-bare repore" for additional comic effect. Primarily inspired by politically conservative TV personality Bill O'Reilly, Colbert's persona is obnoxious, bullying, and blatantly ignorant. He burst into the mainstream American awareness with his speech at the White House Correspondents' Dinner on April 29, 2006. As of 2007, Colbert lives with his wife Evelyn McGee-Colbert and their three children in New Jersey, where he also teaches Sunday school.

actual opinions but the absurd ramblings of a blustery but fictional construct, others took his pointed jokes at the expense of President Bush and the journalists assigned to cover the White House to be Colbert's true opinions about the relationship between the press and the president.

Because the press is considered the watchdog of democracy, the public's primary defense against excessive government power and corruption, its independence and reliability are considered among the most precious hallmarks of the American way of life. If it is the press's job to keep an eye on the government, Colbert's gutsy speech reminded the press that his job as a comedian is to keep an eye on them.

## PLOT SUMMARY

Stephen Colbert begins his speech by jokingly announcing that a throng of conspicuous high-security vehicles need to be moved to make way for another identical throng of vehicles. Colbert goes on to describe President Bush as "my hero" and asks somebody to pinch him because he must be dreaming. Appearing to second-guess himself, Colbert recommends that somebody shoot him in the face, alluding to Vice President Cheney's recent hunting accident. He also recommends that anyone who needs anything lean over and speak slowly and clearly into their table numbers so that operatives of the National Security Administration can take their orders—an allusion to the rumors that the Bush administration engaged in unlawful spying on American citizens.

Colbert claims that he and the president approach the truth in the same way: "We're not brainiacs on the nerd patrol. . . . We go straight from the gut, right sir? That's where the truth lies, right down here in the gut."He goes on to explain that there are more nerve endings in the gut than in the head and that on his show he gives people "the truth, unfiltered by rational argument." He has created what he calls the "No Fact Zone," then warns Fox News that the term is copyrighted, hinting that the network might want to use it as well. This is an allusion to the right-leaning network's use of the term "No Spin Zone" on *The O'Reilly Factor*, Bill O'Reilly's popular but controversial Fox program.

Colbert then claims that he is a simple man, like the president, and rattles off a list of fundamental beliefs. This list is absurd because it consists of easily verifiable facts rather than actual philosophical positions. Next he claims that democracy is America's number one export, "at least until China figures out a way to stamp it out

of plastic for three cents a unit." Colbert then greets the Chinese ambassador, Ambassador Zhou Wenzhong, who is in attendance. Next on his list of beliefs is Thomas Jefferson's famous line, "The government that governs best is the government that governs least," then uses that line of reasoning to assert that the United States has "set up a fabulous government in Iraq."

Before rounding out his list, Colbert, with great apparent magnanimity and sincerity, tells the crowd he respects all religions, noting, "I believe there are infinite paths to accepting Jesus Christ as your personal savior."

Colbert returns his attention to President Bush, specifically addressing Bush's low approval rating in many polls. "Sir, pay no attention to the people who say the glass is half empty, because 32 percent means it's two-thirds empty." Colbert then goes on to compare Bush to the protagonist of the movie *Rocky* before appearing to suddenly recall that Rocky loses his fight at the end of the film.

Colbert next claims he stands by the president: "I stand by this man because he stands for things. Not only for things, he stands on things." Colbert alludes to several of President Bush's widely covered public appearances: aboard the aircraft carrier *Abraham Lincoln* during which the flight-suited president proclaimed "mission accomplished" in Iraq, among the ruins of the World Trade Centers following the 9/11 attacks, and in the aftermath of Hurricane Katrina in New Orleans's Jackson Square. He says these events send "a strong message: that no matter what happens to America, she will always rebound—with the most powerfully staged photo ops in the world."

Colbert discusses the Chief Executive's awareness of the energy crisis. Colbert notes that Bush spends a lot of time cutting brush on his ranch in Texas. Because of this, Colbert claims, by 2008 the country will have "a mesquite-powered car." Colbert mentions that the president is a regular guy who loves his wife, Laura. Unfortunately, the First Lady's "reading initiative" does not sit well with Colbert, who does not like, trust, or believe in books because they "[tell] us what is or isn't true, or what did or didn't happen." He claims that it is the right of all Americans, like the president, to make up "facts" to suit them.

Returning to the president, Colbert praises his firmness of mind: "He believes the same thing Wednesday that he believed on Monday, no matter what happened Tuesday. Events can change; this man's beliefs never will."

Having thoroughly mocked President Bush while pretending to praise him, Colbert turns his attention to the press. He claims he is appalled to find representatives of the press at a White House dinner, explaining:

> I am appalled to be surrounded by the liberal media that is destroying America, with the exception of Fox News.

Colbert continues in his ironic vein, celebrating the news industry for not depressing the American people by spending time covering tax cuts, weapons of mass destruction, and the environment. Colbert says, "Americans didn't want to know, and you had the courtesy not to try to find out. Those were good times, as far as we knew." He sums up the apparent relationship between the White House and the press corps, saying their job is to print what the White House tells them, and that they can daydream about bold reporters who challenge the administration if they take up a career writing fiction.

He chides the reporters for saying the administration is "just rearranging deck chairs on the *Titanic*" when the White House does something that the public has clamored for. "This administration is not sinking. This administration is soaring." He quips that the administration has more in common with a doomed 1937 airship that burst into flames and fell from the sky than a doomed 1912 ocean liner.

After noting certain journalists are "heroes" (Colbert's term for fans of his show), such as Christopher Buckley, Ken Burns, and Bob Schieffer, Colbert points out that these men have appeared on *The Colbert Report*. He then alludes to a controversy in which it appeared that President Bush would appear on the show but did not do so. Colbert remarks that he will bump liberal commentator Frank Rich to make room for Bush.

Colbert focuses on various notables in attendance at the dinner. Specifically he notes the presence of Generals Moseley and Pace: "They still support Rumsfeld. Right, you guys aren't retired yet, right?" Both men remained supportive of the Bush White House and then-Secretary of Defense Donald Rumsfeld, even while many retired generals have criticized the handling of the war in Iraq. He also mentions the presence of civil rights activist Jesse Jackson, whose determination to speak his mind Colbert compares to boxing a glacier. "Enjoy the metaphor," Colbert adds, "because your grandchildren will have no idea what a glacier is," a swipe at Bush's environmental policies.

Supreme Court justice Anthony Scalia is in attendance and Colbert greets him while making hand gestures. Scalia had recently drawn criticism for apparently making obscene gestures to a reporter while discussing political enemies. The justice laughs heartily in response to Colbert. Colbert greets maverick Republican Senator John McCain by mentioning the Senator's plans to speak at Bob Jones University, a very conservative Christian school in South Carolina, where Colbert claims to still have a summer home. This quip is a subtle jab at McCain, often a vocal critic and opponent of President Bush, who seems to be returning to more conventional Republican behavior.

Colbert greets former ambassador Joe Wilson and jokes about Wilson's wife, Valerie Plame, whose status as an undercover CIA agent was famously (and possibly illegally) revealed through a government leak. Many observers believe the leak was a deliberate attempt to punish Wilson for criticisms he had earlier made about the Bush administration. Colbert pretends to inadvertently reveal Plame's identity, then breathes a false sigh of relief that special prosecutor Patrick Kennedy, who was appointed to investigate "Plamegate," is not present. Colbert also kids newly appointed press secretary Tony Snow, cautioning Snow that he has "big shoes to fill. Scott McClellan could say nothing like nobody else." McClellan was the previous press secretary.

Colbert then complains that he wishes President Bush had not rushed to choose Snow; Colbert claims he wanted the job of press secretary for himself. At this point, Colbert screens an "audition tape" he allegedly prepared. The tape features clips of White House journalists asking tough questions spliced in with footage of Colbert dodging or ignoring them. However, the tables turn on Colbert when veteran correspondent Helen Thomas begins to stalk him. The tape then becomes a parody of horror movies, with Colbert fleeing the slow-moving yet relentless Thomas while scary music plays on the soundtrack. Eventually Colbert seems to

❝

**BUT, LISTEN, LET'S REVIEW THE RULES. HERE'S HOW IT WORKS: THE PRESIDENT MAKES DECISIONS. HE'S THE DECIDER. THE PRESS SECRETARY ANNOUNCES THOSE DECISIONS, AND YOU PEOPLE OF THE PRESS TYPE THOSE DECISIONS DOWN. MAKE, ANNOUNCE, TYPE. JUST PUT 'EM THROUGH A SPELL CHECK AND GO HOME.❞**

escape by taking a shuttle from Washington to New York. However, when he gets into his car and asks the uniformed driver to take him home, the driver turns around and says, "Sure thing, hon." The chauffeur is in fact Helen Thomas, and the skit ends with Colbert pressing his terrified face against the car window and screaming. After the mock audition tape ends, Colbert thanks the president and the audience, apparently with total sincerity.

## THEMES

### The First Amendment

The U.S. Constitution, as it was accepted in 1787, focuses on the organization, power, and responsibilities of the federal government. The Bill of Rights, as the first ten amendments to the Constitution are collectively known, explicitly grants important personal freedoms to individuals. The Bill of Rights became the law of the land in 1792. The first of these amendments protects people's right to believe and say what they wish with this single sentence:

> Congress shall make no law respecting an establishment of religion, or prohibiting the free exercise thereof; or abridging the freedom of speech, or of the press; or the right of the people peaceably to assemble, and to petition the government for a redress of grievances.

Not all speech is protected: that which may pose a "clear and present danger" to the government, obscene or pornographic art, and libel and slander against public or private persons are some types of restricted expression. Furthermore, not every citizen supports every First Amendment

safeguard in American society. The issues of prayer in school, the Ten Commandments in courthouses, flag burning, offensive art, conscientious objection, and tabloid journalism are all quandaries posed by the First Amendment. However, Americans' freedoms to worship as they please, exchange ideas, and question the government are cornerstones of the American dream By exercising his rights to express himself and question the government, and by rebuking the press for slacking in their responsibilities, Stephen Colbert championed the First Amendment and dared others to do so as well.

### Satire and Political Humor

Satire is a form of social commentary that attacks human failures and shortcomings, often through the use of verbal irony. In essence, verbal irony means that what is said is the opposite of what is meant; thus when a person says "boy, what a nice day" during a violent thunderstorm, he really means the day is ugly and miserable. Satirists often employ vicious irony in their attacks on human nature and institutions, sometimes using greatly exaggerated examples and characters for comic effect. Satire is one of the most important elements in political humor, which makes fun of government personnel, agencies, or activities.

The satiric tradition is as old as human literacy itself. The leading satirists of the Classical period were the Romans Horace and Juvenal. To this day, works of satire are classified as either Horatian (gentle and urbane) or Juvenalian (biting and more vulgar). During the Age of Enlightenment (the seventeenth and eighteenth centuries), the English poet and satirist John Dryden published a translation of Juvenal in 1693. This translation included Dryden's "A Discourse on the Original and Progress of Satire," which became the standard definition of satire in English. Best known as the author of *Gulliver's Travels*, which in spite of its reputation as a children's book is actually a sophisticated piece of adult satire, Jonathan Swift (1667–1745) is often cited as the greatest satirist in English literature. Perhaps Swift's most influential work is his "A Modest Proposal" (1729), in which the author appears to advocate cannibalism of poor children as a means of alleviating overpopulation and reducing poverty. "A Modest Proposal" is a masterpiece of irony because Swift's outrageous plan is presented with a straight face. In fact, Swift's

*Stephen Colbert delivering his speech with President George W. Bush looking on during the 2006 White House Correspondents' Association Dinner* © *Hyungwon Kang/Reuters/Corbis*

apparent sincerity inspired controversy, because many readers thought he was serious; even today many students are convinced Swift actually believes that eating children is a good idea, although a careful reading of the essay reveals Swift's true motivation, which is to support reasonable reforms in society to alleviate human suffering.

The American satirical tradition can be traced back at least to 1707, when Ebenezer Cooke published "The Sot-Weed Factor," a Juvenalian attack on the attitudes and activities of both early settlers and American Indians. In the nineteenth century, Samuel Langhorne Clemens, aka Mark Twain, wrote many satirical pieces, though many did not appear in print until after his death. Among his most famous is *A Connecticut Yankee in King Arthur's Court*

(1889), which mocks both political and social folly. Former Civil War officer Ambrose Bierce is best remembered for his war and horror stories, which are often laced with grim irony. However, Bierce's *The Devil's Dictionary*, first published in book form as *The Cynic's Work-Book* in 1906, is his sharpest satirical work. *The Devil's Dictionary* contains such definitions as "Idiot" ("a member of a large and powerful tribe whose influence in human affairs has always been dominant and controlling") and "Love" ("a temporary insanity curable by marriage").

In more recent times, satire has been associated with the mass media, including movies and television. Based on a short story by Budd Schulberg, Elia Kazan's *A Face in the Crowd* (1957) features legendary television star Andy

Griffith as a vile thug who manages to become a powerful television star by presenting a charming, folksy persona to millions of viewers. The film's depiction of television's often pernicious influence on the general public is still powerful today. Robert Altman's *M.A.S.H.* (1970), based on Richard Hooker's novel, lampooned the Vietnam War by presenting a story set during the Korean War of the 1950s. Alex Cox's *Walker* (1987) uses a similar technique of mocking current events with a story set in the past. Based on the life of William Walker, a nineteenth-century military adventurer who became president of Nicaragua in 1857, the film satirizes the Reagan Administration's involvement in the Iran-Contra affair, a scandal in which elements of the U.S. government sold arms to the rogue nation of Iran to fund anti-Communist guerillas (the Contras) in Nicaragua.

Television comedies have always incorporated a degree of satiric humor, but sketch comedy shows such as *Saturday Night Live* and *MadTV* have regularly mocked politicians, celebrities, and life in general. The often absurd and exaggerated humor of these programs can be directly traced to the British TV show *Monty Python's Flying Circus*, although other influences from popular culture have also had an impact. With the rise of original cable television programming, such programs as *South Park* and *Robot Chicken* have reached comparatively small but extremely devoted audiences; like *The Daily Show* and *The Colbert Report*, these shows frequently make fun of politicians and the government.

Political humor has been a mainstay of American culture since before the American Revolution. Highly satiric political humor was a primary trait in the English tradition of journalism, which itself was influenced by the writings of ancient Roman satirists. All American chief executives have been attacked by political humorists, usually by artists and writers in the employ of opposition parties. America is a country founded on protest, and it remains a traditional part of the society that even the most powerful and respected people and institutions are never above being targeted for criticism. Like it or loathe it, Colbert's speech is a demonstration of Americans' national right to satirize their leaders and the mechanisms of their culture.

## Freedom of the Press

Stephen Colbert's speech at the White House Correspondents' Dinner gained notoriety because it seemed like a comic attack on President Bush. However, Colbert's speech is just as critical of the mainstream press—perhaps more so. It is one of the basic principles of American democracy that the press is responsible for keeping the voting populace informed by keeping tabs on the government, watching carefully for abuse, corruption, misinformation, and incompetence on the part of elected or appointed officials. Colbert's remarks to the press corps are particularly caustic, implying that the assembled journalists had not been sufficiently skeptical of the Bush administration's policies in particular, and of government in general.

Since the earliest days of the republic, journalists have been charged with keeping an eye on the government and encouraging dissent when authorities have shirked or failed in their duties. Writers such as Thomas Paine published pamphlets that encouraged the weary colonists to continue their support for the Revolutionary movement that resulted in American independence from Great Britain, and ever since then journalists have crusaded for social justice and the punishment of wrongdoing on the part of elected officials. The best-known example of American journalists performing their watchdog role is the Watergate scandal of the 1970s, which resulted in the downfall of President Richard M. Nixon. Two reporters for the *Washington Post*, Carl Bernstein and Robert Woodward, investigated the break-in of the Democratic National Committee headquarters at the Watergate Hotel in 1972, a burglary committed by associates of prominent officials of the Nixon White House. At attempt to cover up the connection between the burglars and the Nixon administration failed, and ultimately President Nixon resigned in 1974 rather than face impeachment.

Woodward and Bernstein became heroes of a sort among young journalism students, but in the years since there have been indications that the press has failed to watch the government as carefully as it should. For one thing, the rise of television news eroded newspaper readership; the decline in circulation has encouraged major news dailies to focus less on "hard" news and more on "feature" news, such as entertainment. At the same time, more and more newspapers closed down or combined with other papers, and increasing numbers of papers were bought by major media conglomerates whose focus is more on the bottom line than reporting the news.

Some liberal critics have charged that the contemporary press corps seems unwilling or unable to push the Bush administration to fully disclose information relevant to the public good. On the other hand, many conservatives believe the mainstream media are biased against President Bush in particular and conservative politicians in general. Indeed, many polls suggest that the American public believe major print and television journalists are biased in favor of liberal causes and politicians. Mainstream journalists are supposed to be objective in their reporting; charges of bias on either or both sides of an issue often clouds both the media's and the public's perception of the goings-on in the modern world.

## HISTORICAL OVERVIEW

### The White House Correspondents' Association Dinner

Formed by eleven charter members on February 25, 1914, the White House Correspondents' Association exists for "the promotion of those reporters and correspondents assigned to cover the White House." The organization was formed in response to a rumor that President Woodrow Wilson was planning a series of press conferences to which only certain reporters would be invited. The WHCA hosted its first Correspondents' Dinner in 1920; in 1924, Calvin Coolidge became the first president to attend the dinner, thereby establishing a tradition followed by almost every chief executive since.

For many years the annual dinner emphasized entertainment, which was often provided by popular singers and other performers of the Great Depression. The dinner became more subdued during World War II, but by the 1990s entertainers were once again being invited to address the WHCA and its guests. Such performers as Jon Stewart, Aretha Franklin, Ray Charles, Jay Leno, and Cedric the Entertainer have provided the entertainment in the years since. Comedians often "roast" the president and his administration, and White House residents have even gotten in on the fun: In 2000 President Clinton appeared in a short film

spoofing his last days in office, and in 2005 First Lady Laura Bush delivered a well-received comedy routine that gently mocked her husband and his cabinet.

The WHCA has always operated outside of the normal White House credentialing process, a decision the organization feels is necessary to safeguard journalists' responsibility to cover presidents objectively. According to the WHCA website, the organization "stands for inclusiveness in the credentialing process so that the White House remains accessible to all journalists," a mission that is "consistent with the First Amendment." It is a bedrock principle of American culture that newspapers and other news outlets serve as watchdogs of the government; by protecting and promoting the First Amendment to the Constitution, journalists fulfill their role as promoters of the American dream of open and accessible government.

### Political Punditry

In 1987, the Federal Communications Commission repealed its "fairness doctrine," which required broadcasters to present balanced coverage of controversial matters of public importance. The decision allowed television and radio stations to begin airing political commentary without having to necessarily feature opposing points of view.

Although the United States, like any other free country, has always been home to various factions that argue among themselves, it seems that the nature of public debate has abandoned the high road in the late twentieth and early twenty-first centuries. There is no single explanation or cause for these tendencies, but cultural critics place a lot of blame on the rise of television talk shows that present contentious, even combative, guests and hosts. So-called "trash TV" programs such as *The Jerry Springer Show* rarely pertain directly to serious political issues, but the circus-like atmosphere of these shows has spilled over into the new generation of news and current-events programming.

Foremost among the broadcasters who benefited from the repeal of the "fairness doctrine" was veteran radio personality Rush Limbaugh, who rose to unprecedented levels of national success following the syndication of his talk show in 1988. Unapologetically conservative and given to making sarcastic, often highly controversial on-air pronouncements,

Limbaugh emerged as the symbol of the "neo-conservative" movement of the 1990s. Inspired by Limbaugh, a number of other conservative commentators emerged, finding success on radio, television, and the Internet. Like Limbaugh, these commentators incorporated irony, satire, and often inflammatory statements to get the attention of supporters and opponents alike. Bill O'Reilly and Anne Coulter have been among the most popular—and at times polarizing—of these neoconservative personalities during the George W. Bush era.

## CRITICAL OVERVIEW

Time enough has not yet passed for cultural and political critics to examine Colbert's 2006 speech at the White House Correspondents' Dinner with the benefit of hindsight. Initially, most of the mainstream newspapers neglected to discuss the Colbert speech in any great detail. However, the speech did inspire passionate responses from both liberal and conservative bloggers on the Internet, leading one group of fans to start the website thankyoustephencolbert.org to express their admiration. "Stephen Colbert delivered a biting rebuke of George W. Bush and the lily-livered press corps," announces blogger Peter Daou the day after the speech. The editors of the *American Federalist Journal* comment on their blog, "The Unalienable Right," that Colbert's speech was "mostly unfunny" and "tedious." By contrast, Joan Walsh on salon.com remarks of her reaction to Colbert's speech:

> I'm enjoying watching apologists for the status quo wear themselves out explaining why Colbert wasn't funny.... For those who think the media shamed itself by rolling over for this administration, especially in the run-up to the Iraq war, Colbert's skit is the gift that keeps on giving.

The major papers eventually picked up the story, but as television critic Doug Elfman writes in the *Chicago Sun-Times*, "The media's implosion of silence could be one of the final reasons many liberals use to not turn on TV news," getting their information from blogs and websites instead. In the pages of the *Christian Science Monitor*, Dante Chinni claims that the debate over Colbert's remarks suggested that the traditional Correspondents' dinner should be ended, since it merely celebrates the "coziness" of

## MEDIA ADAPTATIONS

Clips of Stephen Colbert delivering his speech at the 2006 White House Correspondents' Association Dinner are widely available on the Internet, and the C-SPAN network sells a DVD of the Dinner at www.c-spanarchives.org/shop and through other websites.

Washington media with political figures. Chinni observes that "Journalists have slid in the public's estimation over the past 20 years, and if they want to try to recapture their standing, they need to reassert their independence" from the political establishment. The attacks on Colbert seemed to confirm that most journalists would rather not deal with the thorny issues raised by his critiques of the Bush administration—and modern journalism.

## CRITICISM

### Julie Hilden
*In the following article, Hilden explores the importance of parody and free speech in public discourse.*

Stephen Colbert's April 30th keynote address to the White House Correspondents' Association Dinner continues to spark commentary even now, more than a week later—with the video and the transcript still widely circulated on the Internet. Why?

One reason the story has had "legs," it seems, is the contention that Colbert crossed an invisible line, and the retort that either such a line shouldn't exist, or that Colbert was entitled to cross it. (For those unfamiliar with Colbert, he's the satirical host of *"The Colbert Report"*—a parody of a pundit show, lampooning the likes of Fox's "The O'Reilly Factor" and MSNBC's

"*Scarborough Country*"—appearing four nights a week on the cable network Comedy Central.)

Interestingly, Bush supporters aren't alone in claiming that Colbert went too far in his routine. Indeed, even Democratic House Minority Whip Steny Hoyer said, "I thought some of it was funny, but I think it got a little rough. He is the President of the United States, and he deserves some respect." Hoyer felt Colbert "crossed the line" with many jokes that were "in bad taste."

In this column, I'll draw on ideas from First Amendment doctrine to try to explain many people's intuition that Colbert crossed a line, but also, using the same doctrine, I will argue that Colbert's performance reaffirms the importance and power of parody to free speech and public debate.

### Was the President Effectively a Captive Audience?

I think part of the intuition arises from the fact that the unhappy—and seemingly insulted—president couldn't practically leave while the speech was going on.

Recently, Michael Dorf wrote a perceptive column for this site on the role of the "captive audience" in First Amendment doctrine. As Dorf suggests, an audience may be deemed "captive," in free speech doctrine, when its attendance is either legally required (Dorf's example is teens' attendance at public school), or socially required (Dorf's example is family members' attendance at a funeral). Speakers' First Amendment rights to reach the ears of such audiences may be less than their rights to reach the ears of, say, passersby in the public square.

The Correspondents' Dinner was the rare instance where the president was himself a captive audience of one. By comparison, the president has the ability to stop taking questions at a press conference at any time, or simply to send new White House Press Secretary Tony Snow to field questions on his behalf. (Even presidential candidates can now be insulated from criticism—thanks to "free speech zones" at conventions, which I wrote about in a prior column.)

But the president could not have fled Colbert's speech, except at great cost. The Correspondents' Dinner was being broadcast on C-SPAN, with the media attending in full

force. And there has long been a presumption that, at the dinner, the president will take the mockery handed out graciously. In sum, the president doesn't really have the option to leave the Correspondents' Dinner: Whatever happens, the tradition is that he must grin and bear it.

At some point, though, Bush stopped grinning and, by most accounts, looked annoyed; *Salon's* Michael Scherer described him as "tight-lipped," and warned that Colbert, who'd violated the protocol of a typically "fawning" event, was unlikely to be invited back.

I think the "captive audience" aspect of the event was one reason why Colbert's speech had the breath-holding, sickening/thrilling quality of wedding speeches that tread much too close to the bone. The audience could almost be overheard wondering to themselves, "What will he say next, and what will his target do?" And the president was just as unlikely to walk off the podium, as a bride and groom would be to walk out of their own reception.

### Was Colbert's Speech a Comedy Routine, or a Political Attack?

Many observers intuitively feel that the president suffered a political attack, rather than merely enduring a comedy routine.

As Americans, we're used to comedy that is observational—aren't people funny?—not comedy that is pointed: Isn't the president ignorant and out of touch with reality? We're also not used to satire—as Scherer points out in his Salon.com piece. Indeed, Scherer himself goes back to "the Situationists in France" to find a fit parallel for Colbert's "ironic mockery."

Moreover, we are used to comedy routines that string together bite-sized, stand-alone jokes—routines that can be reduced to individual "bits"—not themed attacks like Colbert's, where one joke refers back to the next, and jokes are repeated, with variations.

Colbert was relentless. He repeatedly targeted, for instance, Bush's 32% approval rating. Indeed, Colbert even suggested that the president's scant remaining support is worthless, advising him, "Sir, pay no attention to the people who say the glass is half empty, because 32% means it's 2/3 empty. There's still some liquid in that glass is my point, but I wouldn't drink it. The last third is usually backwash."

A little later, Colbert flipped the statistic—referring to the disapproving 68%: "Don't pay attention to the approval ratings that say 68% of Americans disapprove of the job this man is doing. I ask you this, does that not also logically mean that 68% approve of the job he's not doing?"

Colbert also repeatedly suggested that the president ignores facts ("Events can change; this man's beliefs never will."), that he doesn't read books, and that his embattled Administration is only headed for further, worse trouble.

In sum, with the president effectively trapped, and at his mercy, Colbert chose to inflict blows upon bruises—smashing Bush at length on topics that must already smart, from Iraq war debacles, to warrantless wiretapping, to the Valerie Plame scandal, where allegations have now reached up to the level of the president and Vice president themselves.

### If the Speech Was an Attack, Was it Fair to Launch It In A Setting Where The president Couldn't Leave?

Colbert launched his vituperative parody when there was no forum for the president—or anyone speaking on his behalf—to reply. Again, First Amendment doctrine seems relevant: While concepts like "equal time" now seem relics of the Sixties and Seventies, and the FCC long ago junked the "fairness doctrine," we still remain more comfortable with harsh speech when the target has a chance to quickly respond.

All else being equal, the situation would seem especially unfair in First Amendment terms because the brand of irony of which Colbert is a master serves—as Scherer points out, quoting David Foster Wallace—"an almost exclusively negative function" for which there is no easy response.

However, all else is not equal. The president, with his "bully pulpit," has a platform from which to command attention, and a national audience, as no other individual can. If he decides to address the nation, his remarks will be televised on all networks, and will pre-empt other programs.

Not only does the Bush Administration command an audience virtually at will, but this particular administration has controlled criticism and discussion to a remarkable degree. To cite but a few examples: during his campaigns and in promoting his major initiatives, the president has held scripted "town meetings" in which the audiences are carefully screened so there's little chance of critical questions; he has censored scientific reports of the Environmental Protection Agency and NASA that don't toe the Administration line about global warming; and he has held the fewest number of press conferences of any modern president.

Considering the extensive limitations imposed on the ability to question or criticize this president, it is understandable that given the once-in-a-lifetime opportunity to publicly roast him, Colbert seized it. Colbert's in-the-President's-face parody followed the tradition of Nineteenth and early Twentieth Century political cartoonists whose caustic renderings of public figures and officials were devastating, as the newspapers they were printed in were the near-exclusive sources for the public's news.

As the late Chief Justice Rehnquist recognized, in discussing Nineteenth Century political cartoonist Thomas Nast, "The success of the Nast cartoon was achieved 'because of the emotional impact of its presentation. It continuously goes beyond the bounds of good taste and conventional manners.'" According to Rehnquist, despite the caustic nature of such satires—ridiculing the presidents of the time—they "played a prominent role in public and political debate" and "[f]rom the viewpoint of history it is clear that our political discourse would have been considerably poorer without them."

Despite the caustic nature of Colbert's satire, it is clear that given the extent to which the Bush Administration, elected officials, the news media, pundits, and the public have continued to talk about and debate his keynote—more than a week after Colbert delivered it—Colbert, like Nast before him, has enriched our political discourse.

That he did so with the president as a captive audience may have defied protocol, but in light of the protocols regarding public debate that this president has defied, it should be viewed as fair play.

In the end, we shouldn't so automatically accept contentions like Hoyer's claim that "He is the president of the United States, and he deserves some respect." Respect ought to be based on what one does and says, not on the office one occupies. And even when the president deserves respect, he must also be accountable. Seeking to hold a president accountable through use of a caustic parody that exploits politically embarrassing events is in the best tradition of the First Amendment and encourages the robust public debate democracy requires.

**Source:** Julie Hilden, "Did Stephen Colbert Cross a Free Speech Line at the White House Correspondents' Dinner? And If So, What Defined the Line?", in *FindLaw's Writ*, May 9, 2006, p. 1.

# SOURCES

"About the WHCA," on *White House Correspondents' Association*, www.medill.northwestern.edu/whca (May 2, 2006).

The Charters of Freedom," *U.S. National Archives and Records Administration*, www.archives.gov/national-archives-experience/charters/charters.html (October 29, 2006).

Chinni, Dante, "Pulling the Plug on the White House Correspondents Dinner," in the *Christian Science Monitor*, www.csmonitor.com/2006/0509/p09s02-codc.html (May 9, 2006).

Daou, Peter, "Ignoring Colbert: A Small Taste of the Media's Power to Choose the News," in the *Daou report*, April 30, 2006, daoureport.salon.com/default.aspx?archive Date = 4/30/2006 (November 6, 2006).

Donovan, Bryce, "Great Charlestonian? . . . Or the Greatest Charlestonian?", in the *Charleston Post and Courier*, April 29, 2006, p F 1.

Elfman, Doug, "Did Media Miss Real Colbert Story?", in the *Chicago Sun-Times*, www.suntimes.com (May 7, 2006).

Frederick, "Re-improved Colbert Transcript (Now With Complete Text of Colbert-Thomas Video!)," *Daily Kos*, dailykos.com/storyonly/2006/4/30/1441/59811 (April 30, 2006).

"On Notice/Dead to Me," on the *Colbert Nation*, www.colbertnation.com/cn/notice-dead.php (October 3, 2006).

Rabin, Nathan, "Interview: Stephen Colbert," in *A. V. Club*, www.avclub.com/content/node/44705 (January 25, 2006).

Solomon, Deborah, "Funny About the News," in the *New York Times*, www.nytimes.com (September 25, 2005).

Sternbergh, Adam, "Stephen Colbert Has America by the Ballots," in *New York Magazine*, newyorkmetro.com/news/politics/22322 (October 12, 2006).

"The White House Correspondents Dinner," on *The Unalienable Right*, www.federalistjournal.com/fedblog/?m = 200604 (April 30, 2006).

Walsh, Joan, "Making Colbert Go Away," on *Salon.com*, www.salon.com/opinion/feature/2006/05/03/correspondents (May 3, 2006).

# Subthemes

THE AMERICAN DREAM IN THE NINETEENTH
CENTURY

THE AMERICAN DREAM IN THE TWENTIETH
CENTURY

THE AMERICAN DREAM TODAY

THE AFRICAN AMERICAN DREAM

THE AMERICAN DREAM ABROAD

THE AMERICAN FEMINIST DREAM

THE AMERICAN POLITICAL DREAM

THE ASIAN AMERICAN DREAM

THE COLONIAL AMERICAN DREAM

THE FRONTIER AMERICAN DREAM

THE HISPANIC AMERICAN DREAM

THE IMMIGRANT AMERICAN DREAM

THE NATIVE AMERICAN DREAM

THE SOUTHERN AMERICAN DREAM

# The American Dream in the Nineteenth Century

## Introduction

The American dream of the nineteenth century was marked by a heightened sense of individualism and self-interest—a natural response to America's relatively new freedom from British rule. With a mere twenty-five years of independence behind them, Americans entered the 1800s intent on exploring the vast wilderness that lay west of their former colonies. This frontier mindset called for a rugged individualism that quickly replaced the community-oriented thinking that once motivated the American colonists. With the push west came the forced expulsion of Native Americans and, later, a frenzied scramble for California gold. Nineteenth-century Americans also witnessed wave upon wave of immigration, the nightmare of the Civil War, and a period of industrialization that seemed to alter the American economy and culture overnight. Competitiveness took the place of cooperation as Americans fought to control the development and seize the wealth of their hard-won country. In this century of rapid expansion, the notion of the "self-made man" took on a new meaning.

## The American Frontier

One of the first to explore the American West was Meriwether Lewis. Raised between Virginia's frontier and its settlements, young Lewis learned wilderness skills, including how to hunt and fish, and was also exposed to refined plantation society, from which he acquired knowledge about

surveying, geography, and natural history. After serving in the Virginia militia, Lewis rose through the ranks to become President Thomas Jefferson's private secretary. In 1803, Jefferson sent Lewis to Pennsylvania to be trained in the areas of astronomy, mathematics, botany, paleontology, and biology. Lewis, his expeditionary partner, William Clark, and their men set off for the western wilderness in the spring of 1804 to explore the Louisiana Purchase—land west of the Mississippi river recently acquired from France. On November 8, 1805, Lewis and Clark reached the Pacific Ocean; when they returned home on September 23, 1806, they brought with them a wealth of information.

Lewis and Clark recorded their findings in minute detail in a series of journals that have come to be known as *The Journals of Lewis and Clark*. Excerpts such as the following reveal how respectful and friendly relations were between the white explorers and their Native American counterparts:

> While Sacajawea was renewing among the women the friendships of former days, Captain Clark went on, and was received by Captain Lewis and the chief, who after the first embraces and salutations were over, conducted him to a sort of circular tent or shade of willows. Here he was seated on a white robe; and the chief immediately tied in his hair six small shells resembling pearls, an ornament highly valued by these people, who procure them in the course of trade from the sea-coast. The moccasins of the whole party were then taken off, and after much ceremony the smoking began.

Meriwether Lewis and his expeditionary journals provided fodder for proper writers to explore the nineteenth-century American dream of taming the West—if only on paper. James Fenimore Cooper, credited as being one of America's first professional writers, did just that in his historically influenced novels. His most widely recognized work, *The Last of the Mohicans* (1826), draws from wilderness themes borrowed from Lewis and actual events that occurred before, during, and after the War of 1812. Cooper's epic was one of the most popular English-language novels of the era. The novel's main character, Nathaniel "Natty" Bumppo, or "Hawkeye," personifies the rugged individualism that was quickly defining the new American identity. In her biographical essay on Cooper, Jill Anderson describes the Bumppo character as "a white man who resisted the onslaught of American civilization and law and who wanted only to live in harmony with nature like his Indian friends."

*Davy Crockett* © *Bettmann/Corbis*

A survey of American frontier literature would not be complete without mentioning *A Narrative of the Life of David Crockett*. According to Paul Andrew Hutton's introduction from the 1987 University of Nebraska Press edition of the autobiography,

> [*The Narrative*] falls within the tradition of American autobiography pioneered by Benjamin Franklin. Like Franklin's work, it is peculiarly American in form and tone, recounting one of the most beloved of our national obsessions: the success story of the self-made man. It is also a literary and folk document, capturing the humor and backcountry dialect eventually enshrined in our highest literary traditions by Mark Twain.

The autobiography, co-authored by Crockett's congressional colleague, Thomas Chilton, documents the American frontier experience of the first half of the 1800s. It describes Crockett's early life growing up in eastern Tennessee through his moves westward, his experiences in the Creek War, his infamous hunting trips—he allegedly killed 105 "b'ars" in one season—and his political appointments as Tennessee House Representative and U.S. congressman. The book ends before his fateful journey to the Alamo, where he died in 1836.

## *Transcendentalism*

Once the American geographical landscape had been conquered, time was ripe for an exploration of the American psyche. If the literature of Lewis and Cooper is regarded as a study of the difference between the old and the new America, then Ralph Waldo Emerson was one of the first new American writers. Once the frontier was tamed, rugged individualism became somewhat more refined and the wilderness was given a far less fearsome name: nature. This happened in 1836 when Emerson, a self-described "naturalist," anonymously published "Nature," a powerfully lyrical essay that renounced both conventional religion and materialism and declared nature the source of endless human possibility and fulfillment. An excerpt from the first chapter hints at Emerson's vision:

> I become a transparent eye-ball; I am nothing; I see all; the currents of the Universal Being circulate through me; I am part or particle of God. The name of the nearest friend sounds then foreign and accidental: to be brothers, to be acquaintances,—master or servant, is then a trifle and a disturbance. I am the lover of uncontained and immortal beauty. In the wilderness, I find something more dear and connate than in streets or villages. In the tranquil landscape, and especially in the distant line of the horizon, man beholds somewhat as beautiful as his own nature.

Soon after the essay was published, Emerson became the voice for the Transcendental movement, a generation of American men and women who sought to create a wholly new literature divorced from European influence. Their poetry, essays, and philosophical writings were defined by their reliance on intuition rather than rationality, individuality rather than conformity. Many Transcendentalists went on to become social reformers, especially anti-slavery and women's rights advocates.

Henry David Thoreau, a friend of Emerson's and a fellow Transcendentalist, was profoundly affected after reading "Nature." As important as "Nature" was is in the canon of nineteenth century American literature (and American literature in general), Thoreau's *Walden* (1854) is widely considered the best representation of American Transcendentalist thought.

*Walden* is Thoreau's account of the two years he spent living in solitude on the shore of Walden Pond in Concord, Massachusetts. According to the first lines of the first chapter, "I lived alone, in the woods, a mile from any neighbor, in a house which I had built myself ... and earned my living by the labor of my hands only." The book's chapter headings hint at Thoreau's general topics of interest—economy, reading, sounds, solitude—but at its heart, *Walden* is a call for higher living. In the appropriately titled chapter, "Higher Laws," Thoreau writes,

> All nature is your congratulation, and you have cause momentarily to bless yourself. The greatest gains and values are farthest from being appreciated. We easily come to doubt if they exist. We soon forget them. They are the highest reality. Perhaps the facts most astounding and most real are never communicated by man to man. The true harvest of my daily life is somewhat as intangible and indescribable as the tints of morning or evening. It is a little star-dust caught, a segment of the rainbow which I have clutched.

Like Thoreau, Herman Melville was supremely affected by the writings of Ralph Waldo Emerson. Unlike Thoreau, Melville did not become a devoted Transcendentalist, even though his short story "Bartleby the Scrivener" (1853) exhibits similarities to Emerson's essay "The Transcendentalist." "Bartleby" is Melville's commentary on reason and common sense. Experimental in style, the short story rates as one of Melville's most important works and has been cited as a precursor to both Absurdist and Existential literature.

## *Slave Narratives*

The proliferation of slave narratives published throughout the mid- to late 1800s shed new light on the human tragedy of slavery. The best-known authors of nineteenth century slave narratives are Frederick Douglass, William Wells Brown, and Harriet Jacobs. Jacobs's *Incidents in the Life of a Slave Girl* (1861), according to Linda M. Carter, "is an important work in that it is the most comprehensive slave narrative by a woman." Read in the context of the nineteenth-century American dream, these narratives parallel the emphasis on individualism and freedom found in the literary works of free white American writers. Carter writes,

> The nineteenth-century slave narratives continued the tradition of black self-definition and self-assertion that was established by the

eighteenth-century slave narratives. The slave narratives of both centuries served as a preface and a foundation for subsequent expression through fiction, poetry, autobiography, essays, and other genres.

Jacobs's story is told in rich, vivid detail, giving the reader a firsthand account of the daily humiliations and punishments meted out by her cruel masters. In the preface to *Incidents in the Life of a Slave Girl*, written after her escape to the North, Jacobs writes,

> I have not written my experiences in order to attract attention to myself; on the contrary, it would have been more pleasant to me to have been silent about my own history. Neither do I care to excite sympathy for my own sufferings. But I do earnestly desire to arouse the women of the North to a realizing sense of the condition of two millions of women at the South, still in bondage, suffering what I suffered, and most of them far worse. I want to add my testimony to that of abler pens to convince the people of the Free States what Slavery really is. Only by experience can any one realize how deep, and dark, and foul is that pit of abominations. May the blessing of God rest on this imperfect effort in behalf of my persecuted people!

### The Civil War

Another woman who took great pains to document the events that shaped her life and reflected the nation at large was Mary Boykin Chesnut. Her *Diary from Dixie* (1905), published nearly twenty years after her death, is a record of the events, issues, and people involved in the tragic occurrences related to the Civil War. Chesnut, wife of Senator James Chesnut, began a diary in February 1861 in which she recorded her thoughts about the war as it unfolded. What makes the *Diary* especially fascinating is Chesnut's spirited personality, her wide literary knowledge, her proximity to the events of the war and the politicians who guided its course, and her anti-slavery stance supported by her belief that southern women, such as herself, suffered enslavement by the male-dominated culture of the region. Her outspokenness regarding female equality echoed a growing trend among women across the country; an all-out fight for women's rights loomed on the horizon.

### Unlikely American Heroes and Heroines

As the nineteenth century waned, popular literary characters of the day revealed a shift in cultural heroes and heroines. At the beginning of the century, frontiersmen and larger-than-life folk heroes dominated the pages of popular books. Toward the end, beloved literary characters started to look more like everyday people who possessed independence, individuality, and a willingness to make their own way in the world, despite traditional cultural mores.

One of the most beloved of these characters is Jo, Louisa May Alcott's timeless creation who plays the leading role in her 1868 novel, *Little Women*. According to Elizabeth Janeway in her 1968 *New York Times* book review,

> Jo is a unique creation: the one young woman in nineteenth-century fiction who maintains her individual independence, who gives up no part of her autonomy as payment for being born a woman—and who gets away with it. Jo is the tomboy dream come true, the dream of growing up into full humanity with all its potentialities instead of into limited femininity: of looking after oneself and paying one's way and doing effective work in the real world instead of learning how to please a man who will look after you, as Meg and Amy both do with pious pleasure.

Another nineteenth-century literary favorite is Tom Sawyer, Mark Twain's eternally beloved ruffian from *The Adventures of Tom Sawyer* (1876). It is Tom's vivid imagination and quick wit that define him as a loveable prankster, a conformist who behaves like a rebel, an adventurer who seeks the approval of the adults in his life. Nineteenth-century readers of fiction, especially young readers, had never met a character like Tom. Tom's complexities coupled with Twain's exposure of the inherent hypocrisy of institutions such as church and school signaled a break in American literary traditions. The American dream of individuality and self-interest was beginning to include a rejection of institutions and moral laws.

### The Implications of Rapid Change

*The Education of Henry Adams* (1871) is more than the autobiography of the great-grandson of American founding father John Adams, the grandson of U.S. President John Quincy Adams, and the son of U.S. Senator and Ambassador to the United Kingdom Charles Francis Adams. It is a critical review of the political, social, intellectual, and technological changes this aristocratic American witnessed over the course of his life. A fervent individualist and product of a life of observation, education,

*Walden Pond as seen from Henry David Thoreau's hut* © *Bettmann/Corbis*

and writing, Adams was imminently qualified to write what is essentially a critique of intellectual and political life in the nineteenth century. Written in the third person, *The Education*, though somewhat dark, is full of wit and humor, as witnessed from this excerpt from the chapter titled "Failure":

> Not that his ignorance troubled him! He knew enough to be ignorant. His course had led him through oceans of ignorance; he had tumbled from one ocean into another till he had learned to swim; but even to him education was a serious thing. A parent gives life, but as parent, gives no more. A murderer takes life, but his deed stops there. A teacher affects eternity; he can never tell where his influence stops.

Adams levels the bulk of his criticism at the American educational model—thus the title of his autobiography. He fully intends his life experiences to be used as an educational tool to be used by those who have been failed by a cynical nation overrun with materialism, civility, and vulgar exploitation.

## Conclusion

The American dream at the beginning of the 1800s was defined by rugged individualism of those standing on the brink of a vast and wild frontier. As the land was tamed, so was the independent spirit that had come to characterize the American character; it was not lost, it simply turned inward. Independent thinking replaced land-grabbing and the Transcendental movement was born. This independent spirit was shared by slaves and expressed in slave narratives that exposed the violence and fear experienced by millions held in bondage so that the horror of the institution might be seen for what it truly was. The Civil War shattered the American dream for many, though those left standing were inspired to speak out against rampant inequalities between the races and the sexes. Finally, individualism and the American dream reached a crossroads; once society excoriated the individual for not conforming to a standard of behavior. At the end of the nineteenth century, it was

TOM WAS A GLITTERING HERO ONCE MORE—THE PET OF THE OLD, THE ENVY OF THE YOUNG. HIS NAME EVEN WENT INTO IMMORTAL PRINT, FOR THE VILLAGE PAPER MAGNIFIED HIM. THERE WERE SOME THAT BELIEVED HE WOULD BE PRESIDENT, YET, IF HE ESCAPED HANGING."

**Source:** Mark Twain, *The Adventures of Tom Sawyer*

society that was faulted for failing to live up to the standards of its citizens.

## SOURCES

Adams, Henry, "Chapter 20: Failure (1871)," *The Education of Henry Adams*, Houghton Mifflin, 1918; reprint, Bartleby.com, 1999, www.bartleby.com/159/20.html (December 10, 2006).

Anderson, Jill E., "Cooper, James Fenimore (1789–1851)," in *American Eras, Volume 5: The Reform Era and Eastern U.S. Development, 1815–1850*, edited by Gerald J. Prokopwicz, Vol. 5. Gale, 1998.

Carter, Linda M., "The Slave Narratives," in *African American Almanac*, edited by Jeffrey Lehman, 9th ed., Gale, 2003, Gale Trial Site (December 9, 2006).

Emerson, Ralph Waldo, "Nature," in *Essays and English Traits*, P. F. Collier & Son, 1909–1914; reprint, Bartleby.com, 2001, www.bartleby.com/5/114.html (December 26, 2006).

Hutton, Paul Andrew, "Introduction," in *A Narrative of the Life of David Crockett of the State of Tennessee*, University of Nebraska Press, 1987, p. i.

Jacobs, Harriet, *Incidents in the Life of a Slave Girl*, xroads.virginia.edu/~Hyper/JACOBS/hj-preface.htm (December 26, 2006), originally published in 1861.

Janeway, Elizabeth, "Meg, Jo, Beth, Amy and Louisa," in the *New York Times Book Review*, September 29, 1968, pp. 42, 44, 46.

Lewis, Meriwether, *The Journals of Lewis and Clark*, edited by Bernard DeVoto, Mariner Books, 1997, p. 203.

Thoreau, Henry David, *Walden*, xroads.virginia.edu/~HYPER/WALDEN/walden.html (December 26, 2006), originally published in 1854.

Twain, Mark, *The Adventures of Tom Sawyer*, American Publishing, 1876; reprint, Penguin Classics, 1986, p. 151.

# The American Dream in the Twentieth Century

## Introduction

The American dream has long been an ideal of prosperity not just for Americans, but for people across the globe. The promise of freedom and a better life drew hopeful immigrants before there was even a country to call home, and has continued to draw countless millions ever since. In the 1900s, the backgrounds of people dreaming the dream had never been broader. The economic ups and downs of a century had never been sharper. The scope of international interest and impact had never been wider. As the modern age arrived and cynicism began to rival idealism in the national mindset, the dark lining of the American dream loomed large in twentieth-century literature.

## Small-Town Life

Just after the beginning of the twentieth century, one widely accepted literary vision of the American dream involved life in a small, tightly knit community where residents were free from secrets and ill will. This idealized vision of a perfect American town, far removed from the tumult of the rest of the world, became a symbol for how the United States viewed itself in the larger community of the world. The reality of American small-town life may not have matched this vision very closely, but it was not until just prior to World War I that American writers began to explore this discrepancy in a meaningful way.

*A sharecropper's family circa 1930* © *Corbis*

Edgar Lee Masters, in his poetry collection *Spoon River Anthology* (1915), employs an ingenious technique for stripping away the rigid customs and traditions of American small-town life: Each poem is narrated from beyond the grave by a resident of the local Spoon River cemetery. These narrators are free to speak the truth about their own dreams and habits, and to expose the ways in which their seemingly idyllic town falls short of the idealized American dream. In "Doc Hill," the town caregiver admits he worked long hours because "My wife hated me, my son went to the dogs." In "Margaret Fuller Slack," the mother of eight recalls that, though she wanted to be a writer, her choices were "celibacy, matrimony or unchastity," and concludes, "Sex is the curse of life!" In "Abel Melveny," an apparently wealthy man laments the things he bought but never needed or used and sees himself "as a good machine / That Life had never used."

Even as he exposes the dark side of Spoon River, however, Masters affirms the intimate nature of the community by showing connections between many of the deceased characters. With the advent of World War I, the notion of America as a tightly knit community isolated from the rest of the world came to an abrupt end.

## Questioning Conventions

F. Scott Fitzgerald's first novel, the semi-autobiographical *This Side of Paradise* (1920), was published after World War I. At the time, the horrors of modern warfare had led many people to question their traditional beliefs in a number of ways; in *This Side of Paradise* Fitzgerald introduces themes that would capture the public's growing disillusionment with the conventional American dream. In the novel, Amory Blaine, an intelligent but restless young man from a wealthy family, embarks on a quest to discover his own definition of what makes a meaningful existence. Blaine's family falls upon hard times financially, and he leaves Princeton without finishing his degree so that he can fight in the war. When he returns, he falls in love with a socialite named Rosalind. Like Blaine, Rosalind at first appears to reject the conventions of the wealthy social circles in which she lives; she tells Blaine of the many men she has kissed, and she even kisses him after knowing him only briefly. Rosalind—who has so strongly rebelled against her mother's views on marrying into wealth— eventually breaks up with Blaine because he is too poor. Having lost both love and wealth by the end of the novel, Blaine is finally free to discover his true self. In this way, Fitzgerald depicts the new American dream as a search for one's identity. "It was always the becoming he dreamed of, never the being," Fitzgerald writes of Blaine.

## The Depression

At his poorest, Fitzgerald's Amory Blaine embraces the ideals of socialism: the belief that citizens should collectively share ownership of resources in a society, rather than allowing a small number of wealthy individuals to own most of the resources. This notion, an important facet of the American dream since Winthrop's Massachusetts Bay Colony in the early seventeenth century, gained popularity throughout the Great Depression of the 1920s and 1930s. Folk singer Woody Guthrie, who spent years living among the impoverished Okies and other migrant workers in California, wrote "This Land is Your Land" in 1940; the song has endured as one of the most popular American folk songs of all time. Guthrie's patriotic tribute emphasizes themes of community and cooperation among all Americans, and celebrates the freedom to explore the vast and varied geography that makes up the United States, with its familiar refrain, "This land was made for you and me." The song has appeared in many slightly altered versions over the years; verses that criticize private land ownership and the government's failure to look after the poor are often left out.

*Let Us Now Praise Famous Men* (1941) by James Agee and Walker Evans explores some of the same issues Guthrie memorialized in song. The book documents in words and pictures the lives of three families of white tenant farmers in the South during the Great Depression. Agee's rich descriptions and Evans's stark photographs highlight the harsh life faced by millions during the 1930s, when dreams of prosperity were replaced with nothing more than simple hope for survival. Agee also reflects on the split American identity represented by the "haves"— which included in some ways the Harvard-educated Agee himself—and the many desperate "have nots."

## Emerging Superpower

"The Gift Outright" (1942) by Robert Frost directly addresses the idea of establishing an American identity. "The Gift Outright" can be read as a brief synopsis of early American history. The first line sums up America's colonial roots: "The land was ours before we were the land's." In the poem, Frost contends that only after Americans fully gave themselves to this new land—by breaking free of ties to England and other European empires—could an American identity truly be formed. Frost describes this as "salvation in surrender" and suggests that the legacy of what it means to be an American has proven more valuable than the land on which the country was founded. Frost recited the poem from memory at President John F. Kennedy's inauguration in 1961, after the aged poet was unable to read another poem he had written specifically for the occasion. Composed as the country entered World War II, and invoked amid Cold War anxiety twenty years later, the poem captures the feeling that the United States has a great destiny yet to fulfill.

## Disillusionment

J. D. Salinger's *The Catcher in the Rye* (1951) presents Holden Caulfield, an anti-hero who has been the model for disaffected American youth for half a century. He is a bright young man who nonetheless finds himself failing academically. After he is expelled from prep school, he spends a few unchaperoned days in New York, killing time until his family expects him home for the Christmas holiday. He drifts into and out of the lives of several friends and acquaintances, making no meaningful connections with anyone except his younger sister Phoebe. He toys with grown-up ideas and situations and uses cynicism to mask his juvenile befuddlement about such adult things. He dismisses adulthood—and all the conventional notions of the American dream that accompany it—as phony.

The novel's frank language and discussion of sexuality and its anti-establishment tone created controversy in the idyllic prosperity of

*A family watching television at home circa 1950* © Bettmann/Corbis

post–World War II America. *The Catcher in the Rye* became and remains one of the premier works defining the mid-century counterculture and its disillusionment with the American dream. Counterculture and disillusionment are also important themes in Allen Ginsberg's poem "Howl" (1955). Beginning with the line "I saw the best minds of my generation destroyed by madness," the poem is a rambling, hallucinatory epic that covers topics such as the evils of industrialization and the role of the artist in modern society. Ultimately, it challenges the accepted notions of American traditions and ideals, using profane language, challenging religion, and depicting graphic sex. Shortly after the poem was published, the publisher was charged with indecency. Although "Howl" is often regarded primarily as a statement against conformity and the status quo, it also embodies the themes of searching for identity and meaning,

much like Fitzgerald's more straightforward *This Side of Paradise.*

## Modern War

In the mid-1960s, a generation raised in unprecedented prosperity and still searching for its own identity found itself embroiled in the Vietnam War. Kurt Vonnegut's *Slaughterhouse-Five* (1969) is often cited as a literary response to events in Vietnam, though Vonnegut was writing of his personal experiences surrounding the Allied bombing of Dresden during World War II. The central gimmick of the novel is that main character Billy Pilgrim has become "unstuck" in time and experiences scattered moments from throughout his life in no particular chronological order. This allows Vonnegut to tell his semi-autobiographical story obliquely, to convey the full experience of war without using a traditional story structure; as Pilgrim notes, "there is nothing intelligent to say about a massacre." Similarly, Tim O'Brien based the stories contained in his collection *The Things They Carried* (1990) on his own experiences in Vietnam, but he was careful to select story "truth" over fact to make his points. As O'Brien himself puts it, "You start sometimes with an incident that truly happened . . . and you carry it forward by inventing incidents that did not in fact occur but that nonetheless help to clarify and explain." Both authors drive home the message that war has no winners; even those who survive carry the burden of their experiences with them until they die. Though the two works were published more than twenty years apart, *Slaughterhouse-Five* and *The Things They Carried* both illustrate an important shift in how Americans viewed war in the decades following World War II.

## Counterculture

War was just one of many topics considered from a fresh perspective during this time. Appearing at the end of the 1960s, *Portnoy's Complaint* (1969) by Phillip Roth reflects the American public's growing openness about sexuality as an important element in a happy life. In the novel, which is an extended monologue issued by Portnoy to his psychoanalyst, the main character reveals that his more virtuous impulses are constantly at war with his increasingly perverse sexual urges. An uneasy mix of guilt, openness, titillation, and shame, Portnoy is the embodiment of the sexual revolution that shaped the American dream of the latter part of the twentieth century.

Like *Portnoy's Complaint*, journalist Hunter S. Thompson's *Fear and Loathing in Las Vegas: A Savage Journey to the Heart of the American Dream* (1971) reflects a fundamental shift in the values and dreams of America as a whole. The book, which is loosely based on Thompson's own experiences, shattered taboos with its open and detailed discussion of drug use. The two main characters, Raoul Duke and Dr. Gonzo, engage in a comic, frightening, drug-fueled search for the true nature of the American dream (literally, as it is Duke's journalism assignment and the impetus for the trip and the story). At the same time, they repeatedly attack elements and symbols of what they consider mainstream American culture. For these characters, the essence of the American identity is not what exists in the most popular public arenas, but what exists at the fringes of American society.

*Anti-Vietnam protestors marching with signs down Pennsylvania Avenue* © *Wally McNamee/Corbis*

## Age of Excess

During the 1980s, the popular notion of the American dream shifted once again: While the traditional notion of success included little more than a family, a home, and a secure means of supporting both, toward the end of the twentieth century the American dream of prosperity became increasingly associated with wealth, fame, and power. Thomas Wolfe captures the timbre of the time in his novel *The Bonfire of the Vanities* (1987), which tells the tale of a wealthy New York bond trader named Sherman McCoy whose mistress runs over a black man while driving McCoy's car. The incident brings out the worst in many of the characters, who each see it as a way to achieve their own personal ends at the expense of others. Wolfe's novel is a clear condemnation of the shallowness and materialism of the 1980s.

## The Dream versus Reality

The final decade of the twentieth century saw the publication of two works that emphasize the distance between the accepted notions of the American dream and the reality of American society. In *Generation X: Tales for an Accelerated Culture* (1991) by Douglas Coupland, the three main characters, dismayed at their bleak futures in mainstream society, "opt out" and live a simple existence outside the normal bounds of American culture. The narrator says of Tobias, an age-peer who opts to pursue the American dream of prosperity,

> I realize that I see in him something that *I* might have become, something that all of us can become in the absence of vigilance. Something bland and smug that trades on its mask, filled with such rage and such contempt for humanity, such need that the only food left for such a creature is their own flesh.

Coupland's characters are apathetic about the traditional American dream, which they feel is simply no longer attainable. Others of the same generation reacted to the same sense of disenfranchisement with rage. In *Twilight: Los Angeles 1992* (1994), playwright Anna Deveare Smith offers a piece constructed from the actual words of Los Angeles residents who experienced the effects of the 1991 Rodney King assault, the 1992 trial, and subsequent citywide riots firsthand. Smith suggests that the riots are more than a failure of the American dream, however. They represent an opportunity to open a dialogue about issues of race, justice, and social class that have been ignored because they do not fit comfortably into the mainstream American identity.

## Conclusion

From 1900 to 2000, the notion of the American dream assumed more forms, affected more dreamers, and encountered more backlash than ever before. In the twentieth century, Americans dreamed of the same things as their forebears— things such as freedom, wealth, and meaning. It is hard to say whether twentieth-century Americans were any more or less successful achieving their wishes than the generations that came before them. The undercurrent of disappointment explored in these few titles should not be taken to mean that the American dream has been rejected. Whether their dreams led to joy or heartbreak, the fact that writers return to the theme

THIS FALL I THINK YOU'RE RIDING FOR—IT'S A SPECIAL KIND OF FALL, A HORRIBLE KIND. THE MAN FALLING ISN'T PERMITTED TO FEEL OR HEAR HIMSELF HIT BOTTOM. HE JUST KEEPS FALLING AND FALLING. THE WHOLE ARRANGEMENT'S DESIGNED FOR MEN WHO, AT SOME TIME OR OTHER IN THEIR LIVES, WERE LOOKING FOR SOMETHING THEIR OWN ENVIRONMENT COULDN'T SUPPLY THEM WITH. OR THEY THOUGHT THEIR OWN ENVIRONMENT COULDN'T SUPPLY THEM WITH. SO THEY GAVE UP LOOKING. THEY GAVE IT UP BEFORE THEY EVER REALLY EVEN GOT STARTED."

**Source:** J. D. Salinger, *The Catcher in the Rye*

again and again with new aspects to explore and new perspectives to present tells readers that Americans continue dreaming the dream.

## SOURCES

Coupland, Douglas, *Generation X: Tales for an Accelerated Culture*, St. Martin's Press, 1991, p. 81.

Fitzgerald, F. Scott, *This Side of Paradise*, Scribner's Sons, 1920; reprint, Signet Classics, 1996, p. 33.

Frost, Robert, "The Gift Outright," in *The Poetry of Robert Frost: The Collected Poems, Complete and Unabridged*, edited by Edward Connery Lathem, Henry Holt, 1969, p. 348.

Ginsberg, Allen, "Howl," in *Howl and Other Poems*, City Lights Publishers, 1956; reprint, in *Collected Poems 1947–1980*, Harper & Row, 1984, p. 126.

Masters, Edgar Lee, *Spoon River Anthology*, Macmillan, 1915; reprint, Signet Classics, 1992, pp. 32, 48, 159.

O'Brien, Tim, *The Things They Carried*, Broadway, 1998, p. 158.

Salinger, J. D., *The Catcher in the Rye*, Little, Brown, 1951; reprint, Bantam, 1981, p. 187.

Vonnegut, Kurt, *Slaughterhouse-Five*, Delacorte Press, 1969; reprint, Laurel, 1991, p. 19.

# *The American Dream Today*

## *Introduction*

The American dream has always been a significant theme in literature throughout the nation's history, so it is no surprise that writers at the dawn of the twenty-first century are exploring issues and questions associated with our most basic principles as a country. By analyzing the meaning of the phrase "American dream," modern writers help define (or redefine) the promises the United States makes to its citizens. Writers in the new century find themselves in the difficult position of incorporating modern phenomena, such as family, history, faith, industry, and politics, into a new understanding of what, exactly the American dream constitutes today.

## *Family Life*

Jonathan Franzen's *The Corrections* (2001) became a bestseller and won the 2001 National Book Award. Franzen tells the story of the dysfunctional Lambert clan and their attempts to "correct" the various problems in their lives. Elderly father Alfred suffers from Parkinson's disease and is succumbing to dementia; his long-suffering wife, Enid, deals with his slow decline while planning a final Christmas gathering with her husband and their three adult children. The three Lambert progeny—Gary, Chip, and Denise—are all undergoing various traumas, including divorce, unemployment, and depression. The result is a funny look at the modern American family, in all its dysfunctional glory.

Much of the praise for *The Corrections* is due to its reputation as a "Great American Novel." Earlier authors such as Sinclair Lewis and Booth Tarkington crafted sprawling tales of American families working through their conflicts with themselves and their culture; Franzen's story explores similar literary and social terrain. Of particular interest is Franzen's method of commenting on the ways contemporary society has undermined the American dream, replacing traditional values with materialism, technology, and "quick fixes" to various problems, especially emotional issues. As one character notes:

> A lack of desire to spend money becomes a symptom of a disease that requires expensive medication. Which the medication then destroys the libido, in other words destroys the appetite for the one pleasure in life that's free, which means the person has to spend even *more* money on compensatory pleasures. The very definition of mental "health" is the ability to participate in the consumer economy.

While the white, Midwestern Lamberts constitute the "traditional" nuclear family of Normal Rockwell's Americana, they do not represent the typical twenty-first-century Americans trying to live their dreams. Suzan-Lori Parks presents a different view with her two-man show *Topdog/Underdog*, a play for which she won the 2002 Pulitzer Prize. The two characters, brothers Lincoln and Booth, are named after the president and his assassin, but the play is much more a study of sibling rivalry than American history. Lincoln was a legendary hustler who has given up three-card monte to portray Abraham Lincoln—and get "assassinated" by patrons every day—in a carnival. Booth is a shoplifter who lacks his brother's cool head or talent with cards, and wishes Lincoln would teach him the art of the hustle. The play depicts their attempts to cope with their difficult upbringing and frustration with each other despite their closeness, all in the context of growing up poor and black in contemporary America. The play's predictably tragic ending stems from societal and family dynamics, as one underdog reaches for higher status in his world.

## Echoes of the Past

In *Everything is Illuminated* (2002), Jonathan Safran Foer exemplifies the highly modern—some would say postmodern—technique of writing a fictional account of actual events involving fictionalized versions of real people. The protagonist, also named Jonathan Safran Foer, journeys to the Ukraine to find the woman who saved his grandfather's life during the Holocaust. His guide on the journey is a young man named Alex whose broken English and awareness of America is attributed to his familiarity with American popular culture. The story is told through a combination of letters from Alex and excerpts from the novel Foer (the character) has tried to write about life in his grandfather's community before the Holocaust.

Foer's technique makes for an interesting reading experience, as readers must get used to reading Alex's letters—one starts off "I luxuriated the receipt of your letter"—then switching to the more formal style of the novel-within-a-novel. Yet the story is always intriguing, and the emphasis on making a journey to discover one's roots and to understand the past forges a strong connection to the American literary tradition. Foer's novel, then, symbolizes the journey of Eastern European Jews to America and their dream of finding a hospitable new country while maintaining memories and respect for the "old country"—even when those memories involve painful recollections of Nazi atrocities.

Colson Whitehead's 2001 novel *John Henry Days* is also concerned with the conflict between the past and the present, albeit from a different perspective. It is the story of J. Sutter, a freelance journalist who describes himself as a "junketeer," a freeloader who travels around the country sponging off the free items available at publicity events or living off his expense account. Writing in second person, Whitehead observes of his protagonist,

> Everything on him is free. His black Calvin Klein jeans hard won years prior at a party celebrating the famous designer's spring line. . . . His T-shirt arrived in the mail one day with an advance copy of Public Enemy's latest release. Mickey Mouse heads festooned his socks, Goofy his boxer shorts. His shoes bounty from a Michael Jordan–Nike charity event, intended for disadvantaged kids but everybody helped themselves so J. figured why not.

When Sutter is assigned to write an article about the "John Henry Days" celebration in West Virginia, Sutter is reintroduced to folk hero John Henry, the legendary "steel drivin' man" who died immediately after winning a drilling contest with a steam drill. In the John Henry legend, Sutter sees a symbol of man's losing battle with mechanization in the Industrial Age; in his rootless modern life, Sutter is fighting a similarly losing battle against the depersonalization of the Digital Age. Like John Henry, Sutter is black; his place within the context of the nation's conflicted racial history and as a professional black man participating in an empty materialist culture is one of the novel's most significant themes.

### Tomorrow's Dreamers

Young writers offered unsettling views of young Americans in the early 2000s. Nick McDonell was just seventeen years old when he wrote his debut novel, *Twelve* (2002). Writing in first person, McDonell chronicles a week in the life of White Mike, a rich kid who does not smoke, drink, or do drugs but does sell drugs to other New York prep schoolers. McDonell includes numerous references to actual companies and products, acknowledging the pervasiveness of modern consumer culture and its impact on young adults. The title refers to a trendy new drug that White Mike sells. At various points hilarious, thoughtful, and violent, the novel captures the frustration and ennui frequently prevalent among American youth, apparent when the wealthy Jessica makes her first drug buy:

> She keeps looking around but doesn't notice the two drug dealers until they are almost right on top of her. She is trying to play it cool, but she has never done this before. . . . Jessica, eager to get away from them now, says good-bye and turns the corner hurrying toward Fifth Avenue. *That was easy. I am so cool.*

While McDonell's shocking, violent novel is a fictional account of tragic youth, Koren Zailckas's *Smashed: Story of a Drunken Girlhood* (2005) is the common real-life story of a teenaged binge drinker. "To this day I can't remember when I had my first kiss. . . . But like most women, I remember my first drink in tender minutiae," Zailckas recalls. This frequently disturbing book not only traces Zailckas's relationship with alcohol, which began at age twelve, but also the surprising extent of underage female drinking in America today. Years of hangovers, blackouts, and drunken, risky behavior followed Zailckas, who ultimately figures out that she does not possess the usual genetic indicators of alcoholism. Ultimately she concludes that it is society's emphasis on alcohol consumption, the expectation that young people drink (and drink a lot), that led to her problem. This is a sobering realization, for the nation as well as the author,

for the American dream has always been that our children are healthy and prepared to take their place in society free from the horrors of alcohol abuse.

### Questions of Faith

Marilynne Robinson's *Gilead* (2004) is the story of John Ames, an elderly, dying minister in the town of Gilead, Iowa, in 1956. Ames has a much younger wife and six-year-old son; knowing he will not be around when the boy grows up, Ames decides to write for him an account of Ames's life and times. This account spans more than a century, for it covers the conflicts between Ames's father and grandfather, who quarreled over the issue of slavery prior to the Civil War. While Ames is writing, he must also deal with the reappearance of his best friend's son, a troubled fellow named after Ames.

Like other great American novels, *Gilead* spans a long period of time and represents the long and sometimes troublesome history of the United States. Robinson is concerned with family conflicts, especially the gulf that sometimes emerges between fathers and sons. She is also very interested in the true nature of the Christian faith, as demonstrated by the many theological digressions her dying clergyman protagonist includes in his letter. At one point, he writes,

> Calvin says somewhere that each of us is an actor on a stage and God is the audience. That metaphor has always interested me, because it makes us artists of our behavior, and the reaction of God to us might be thought of as aesthetic rather than morally judgmental in the ordinary sense. How well do we understand our role? With how much assurance do we perform it?

Questions about religion permeate Pete Hautman's *Godless* (2004), a National Book Award winner. Hautman's novel concerns Jason Block, an atheist teen who starts his own religion after troubles with a bully. Jason's plan seems light-hearted at first, but as his new faith gains acolytes, including the bully, different interpretations of the "faith" leads to trouble. *Godless* is a thoughtful investigation of religious thought among young people and suggests the importance of faith—any faith—in a society that claims to be religious but often seems highly secular.

*An Enron employee walks out of the Enron building carrying a box* © *Reuters/Corbis*

## Media and Politics

Chris Bachelder's 2006 novel *U.S.!* is a thoughtful and often hilarious satire about the ideological struggle between political extremists in the United States. The novel centers on Upton Sinclair, the real-life writer whose novel *The Jungle* (1906) spurred reform in the American meat-packing industry. Bachelder has the crusading journalist being endlessly killed by Americans who fear his socialist ideas, only to be resurrected by others who want him to bring attention to their causes. Sinclair's liberal idealism becomes a symbol of the failure of liberalism among contemporary Americans, who are too conservative to embrace Sinclair's proposals. The character Sinclair mocks capitalism during a rant:

> Everyone can be rich! Everyone can go to Harvard! Everyone can have a corner office! Nobody need be poor or jobless. As if any of this were possible under this system that we are not allowed to speak of!

Sinclair is the archetypal crusading journalist, a type that many Americans feel is lamentably absent from public discourse at the beginning of the new millennium. Comedians have found it just as easy to make fun of the press as the politicians they are supposed to report on. In fact, surveys indicate that Comedy Central's "fake news" program *The Daily Show with Jon Stewart* is actually a leading source of information about politics and current events for many college-age viewers. Stewart and the other *Daily Show* writers published *America (The Book): A Citizen's Guide to Democracy Inaction* (2004), a textbook-style satire about American government, which met with immediate critical and popular success.

*America (The Book)* is filled with satirical observations on American history, culture, and politics. Photographs, maps, and other illustrations are used to poke fun at politicians and celebrities, living and dead alike. Although written in the comparatively simple and straightforward style of a real textbook—complete with key words and concepts in bold-face type for emphasis—Stewart's fake textbook is laced with ironic comments, observations, and puns. Among the outrageous highlights of the book are a section on presidential nicknames (in which Stewart alleges that thirteenth president Millard Fillmore "lived for eighteen years with a pair of magical talking cats, who for reasons known only to them insisted on calling their human master 'Mr. Norris'") and paper dolls representing the nine Supreme Court justices—in the nude.

What *America (The Book)* suggests about the American dream is that many of our principles have been compromised by corrupt politicians and media moguls and abandoned by apathetic citizens. Chapter 7, "The Media: Democracy's Guardian Angel," begins,

> A free and independent press is essential to the health of a functioning democracy. It serves to inform the voting public on matters relevant to its well-being. Why they've stopped doing that is a mystery.

It is no wonder that a group of comedians with a "fake news" show that many fans believe is more honest and relevant than the "real news" are bewildered by the culture of media and politics that made them stars. Like earlier satirists, Jon Stewart and his collaborators hope that making fun of society will inspire people to improve it.

## Corporate America

Jon Stewart makes serious points with his humor, but another writer, Barbara Ehrenreich, often uses humor to relieve the very grim discoveries she makes about working in this country. Having previously explored how hard it is to make a living on minimum wage in *Nickel and Dimed* (2001), Ehrenreich investigates the difficulties of landing a professional "white collar" job in her 2005 book *Bait and Switch: The (Futile) Pursuit of the American Dream*. Ehrenreich spent months trying to land a so-called "good job" in a corporate setting; to her shock, she found that even a college degree and professional credentials were not enough to get the kind of career position she once believed was practically the birthright of hardworking, educated Americans. Ehrenreich is never offered the kind of job she expects to find; her only tentative opportunities are in commissioned sales, jobs that are highly stressful, offer no security, and provide no fringe benefits such as health insurance.

Ehrenreich tries everything, from services that promise to help her improve her résumé to image consultants to "career coaches," all people who make their living by helping other people to find jobs. The amount of time and money the author spends experimenting with these individuals, plus

> DEMOCRACY SOUNDS GOOD "ON PAPER," BUT HOW DO WE KNOW IT WON'T EXPLODE WHEN WE START IT? CAMPAIGNS AND ELECTIONS ARE WHERE THE IDEALISM AND ELEGANT DESIGN OF THE AMERICAN EXPERIMENT ARE SET FREE, TO SEE IF THEY CAN SURVIVE IN THE WILD."

**Source:** Jon Stewart, *America (The Book): A Citizen's Guide to Democracy Inaction*

the vain efforts she puts into networking, is very disheartening. Ultimately the conclusion that must be drawn from *Bait and Switch* is that the American dream of secure employment is dying out, and fewer and fewer people will enjoy the security that Americans enjoyed for generations.

On the other side of the coin, while workers like Ehrenreich struggled at the turn of the twenty-first century, those in the country's corner-offices thrived. Bethany McLean and Peter Elkind investigated the infamous collapse of Enron in *The Smartest Guys in the Room: The Amazing Rise and Scandalous Fall of Enron*. This book explores how the managers of the company lied about the firm's financial stability; eventually Enron declared bankruptcy, the costliest such filing in American business history. Thousands of employees lost their jobs and life savings in the wake of the scandal. Although a nonfiction book, *The Smartest Guys in the Room* offers an important insight into the nature of contemporary business and the corporate culture that affects all the members of the nation's economy.

## Conclusion

There are of course many other works, fiction and otherwise, that are concerned with the American dream. Some works demonstrate that it still exists, although perhaps in new and different forms. Many suggest that the dream is dead, or at least out of reach for most Americans today. That the first few years of the new century produced books that examine the modern dream from all the traditional angles should at least indicate that the dream is as relevant as it has ever been. It evolves as the country and its people evolve, and it shows no signs of losing its power to inspire Americans, writers and dreamers alike.

## SOURCES

Bachelder, Chris, *U.S.!*, Bloomsbury USA, 2006, p. 182.

Foer, Jonathan Safran, *Everything is Illuminated*, Gardners Books, 2002, p. 100.

Franzen, Jonathan, *The Corrections*, Picador, 2001, p. 31.

McDonell, Nick, *Twelve*, Grove/Atlantic, 2003, pp. 64–65.

Robinson, Marilynne, *Gilead*, Farrar, Strauss, and Giroux, 2004, p. 124.

Stewart, Jon, and the Writers of *The Daily Show*, *America (The Book): A Citizen's Guide to Democracy Inaction*, Warner Books, 2004, pp. 103, 131.

Whitehead, Colson, *John Henry Days*, Anchor Books, 2001, p. 28.

Zailckas, Koren, *Smashed: Story of a Drunken Girlhood*, Viking Adult, 2005, pp. 3–4.

# *The African American Dream*

### *Introduction*

As any broad survey of American literature can attest, the notion of the American dream has often meant something different to African Americans than it has to any other segment of the population. This is due to the changing status of African Americans in society and to fundamental changes in the collective viewpoint of white Americans over the past three centuries. Even in this ever-shifting human landscape, however, the core concepts of equality and identity have been enduring components of the African American view of the American dream.

### *Freedom*

Since many of the first Americans of African descent were brought to the United States as slaves, the African American dream in its earliest form is perhaps best expressed by a single word: freedom. *The Interesting Narrative of the Life of Olaudah Equiano* (1789) was the first widely read autobiography written by a former African slave. In his narrative, Equiano tells of his early life in what is now Nigeria and of his horrific journey to the New World aboard a slave ship. His was one of the first well-known descriptions of a slave ship as experienced by one of its slave passengers:

> The closeness of the place, and the heat of the climate, added to the number in the ship, which was so crowded that each had scarcely room to turn himself, almost suffocated us.... The

*The Sale of Uncle Tom at the Slave Market by Henri-Desire Charpentier, lithograph from the book* Uncle Tom's Cabin © *Historical Picture Archive/Corbis*

shrieks of the women, and the groans of the dying, rendered the whole a scene of horror almost inconceivable.

After spending some time as the property of an officer of the Royal Navy, Equiano was sold to a Philadelphia Quaker who introduced him to Christianity and taught him to read and write in English. Equiano was eventually able to buy his own freedom and become a successful seaman; he ultimately settled in England, where he married and became an important voice in the abolition movement.

Although Vincent Carretta's 2005 biography questions Equiano's assertion that he lived part of his early life in Africa—claiming at least one official record lists his birthplace as South Carolina—there is no doubt that his journey from slave to free man served as a compelling proof of concept for those African Americans who read it. Equiano's story showed that it was possible, through years of hard work and determination, for a black American to achieve not

only his own freedom but financial success comparable to that of white Americans.

Equiano's work also served to influence subsequent generations of white Americans who supported the abolition of slavery. One such white abolitionist was Harriet Beecher Stowe, whose experiences with the Underground Railroad led her to write one of the most famous anti-slavery works ever put on paper. *Uncle Tom's Cabin*, serialized in an abolitionist magazine starting in 1851 and published separately as a novel in 1852, focuses primarily on Tom, a pious, faithful, middle-aged slave who endures tremendous suffering with grace after being sold by his decent but debt-plagued owner to the cruel Simon Legree.

Stowe's idea of the African American dream—a white-abolitionist's fiction—is a different point of view from Equiano's; while many of the African American characters in *Uncle Tom's Cabin* seek freedom from slavery, they only do so when faced with the prospect of serving violent and ruthless owners or slave traders instead of more benevolent owners like George Shelby and Augustine St. Clare. Those that do escape have little hope of achieving true freedom and equality in the United States and eventually flee to the newly formed African nation of Liberia, created as a safe haven for former slaves. Uncle Tom—the heroic slave who chooses not to run away, instead finding strength in his Christian faith—is killed outright by his cruel owner. Taken as a whole, Stowe's novel offers a rather cynical view of black-white relations in the United States before the Civil War, and suggests that, without sweeping and fundamental societal changes, the African American dream of a better life might only be possible somewhere other than America.

## Equality

After the Civil War, American society underwent sweeping changes that resulted in the emancipation of slaves in the United States. However, it soon became clear to many African Americans that freedom in the legal sense did not necessarily equal fair treatment and opportunity, especially in the South. When Reconstruction came to an end and federal troops withdrew from the region in the 1870s, the backlash against Southern blacks was swift and often devastating. One particular brand of injustice was documented by a black journalist named Ida Wells-Barnett, whose pamphlets in the 1890s exposed the horrors of lynching—a form of mob justice where individuals, usually African Americans, were publicly punished and often executed by hanging for crimes, petty or grievous, they may or may not have committed. The most important works related to her anti-lynching crusade were later brought together in the collection *On Lynching* (1969). Often, lynching tactics were used against Southern blacks who opposed segregation or were perceived as an economic threat to whites, those African Americans who dreamed not just of freedom, but of being treated as equals by other Americans.

This same dream was shared by Booker T. Washington, though his strategy for achieving that dream differed markedly from the views of many other African American activists, including Wells-Barnett. Washington, a former slave who was freed by the Emancipation Proclamation at the age of nine and ultimately built and ran the Tuskegee Institute, documents his journey in the autobiography *Up From Slavery* (1901). Though Washington believes that equality will come for African Americans, he does not believe that blacks should demand it, but rather that they should earn respect and equality through their own actions. Washington knew that black Americans would continue to face hardships in what he calls "the severe American crucible" for many years to come, and forewarns:

> We are to be tested in our patience, our forbearance, our perseverance, our power to endure wrong, to withstand temptations, to economize, to acquire and use skill; in our ability to compete, to succeed in commerce, to disregard the superficial for the real, the appearance for the substance, to be great and yet small, learned and yet simple, high and yet the servant of all.

In contrast, *Philosophy and Opinions of Marcus Garvey* (1923) offers an entirely different solution to the problem of inequality. Garvey, a Jamaican-born activist who founded the Universal Negro Improvement Association, believed that true equality for blacks was not likely to be achieved in the United States or any other country that maintained a white majority in its population. For that reason, he calls for African Americans to return to Africa and assert their independence in their respective ancestral lands. His views were controversial; however, his attempt to unite all people of African descent toward a common cause—the redemption of Africa from European colonialism—helped shape the way in which later generations of African Americans viewed themselves as an extension of their African ancestors.

## Identity

Ralph Ellison's *Invisible Man* (1952) also expresses doubt about the likelihood of African Americans ever achieving equality in the United States. One of the main themes of the novel is the inability for whites to truly see the black narrator as a person at all—hence the title. For Ellison, however, the situation is hardly "black versus white." Although whites are often depicted as the controlling force, the narrator's greatest immediate conflicts are with other blacks. This is especially well depicted in the "battle royal" sequence, where the narrator must fight other black men while blindfolded—solely for the amusement of white men—before he is given a college scholarship. Later, a black rival calls for the narrator's lynching during a Harlem riot that was secretly instigated by white leaders.

Throughout the novel, the unnamed narrator is on a search for his own identity through various groups, communities, and institutions. It is only when he becomes completely invisible to others—and therefore beyond their reach—that he is able to begin to understand himself. Ellison seems to suggest that such an establishment of personal identity should be the true aspiration of African Americans; that it is only through the establishment of identity that other progress can be made; and that as long as African Americans allow others to determine their identities, true freedom and equality will be hard to achieve.

## *Opportunity*

The characters depicted in the Gwendolyn Brooks poem "We Real Cool" (1966) embrace their collective identity with bravado. The poem summarizes the attitudes, beliefs, and fears of young inner-city pool players—all a part of the repeated collective "we"—with just two dozen words arranged in alliterative three-word sentences. According to their own declarations, the young men spend their time engaging in frivolous activities instead of trying to better themselves. The reason becomes clear in the devastating final sentence of the poem: "We / Die soon." The young men see no future for themselves, and therefore see no reason to prepare for such a future:

Lorraine Hansberry's play *A Raisin in the Sun* (1959) portrays an African American family in which each member has his or her own idea about the American dream. The title of the play refers to the Langston Hughes poem "Harlem," which posits that the delayed dream may burst rather than shrivel. After the death of her husband, Mama Younger wants to use the life insurance money to move her family from their cramped Chicago apartment and into a house in a respectable neighborhood. Her son, Walter, would rather use the money to start a business he hopes will secure the family's financial future. Daughter Beneatha feels that both Walter and Mama try too hard to live like white Americans; for her, ultimate achievement lies in embracing the family's African roots. All have their dreams challenged: Walter loses much of the insurance money to a con artist; Beneatha is courted by a wealthy black man who she feels has lost himself in the white culture; and after Mama places a down payment on a house in a white neighborhood, a neighbor representing the community offers the Youngers additional money to *not*

move into the area. By taking a stand and moving to their new house, the Youngers know they will face opposition and adversity. However, Hansberry suggests that it is through small struggles such as these that all African Americans move forward toward the dream of equality.

LaVaughn, the fifteen-year-old narrator of Virginia Euwer Wolff's verse novel *True Believer* (2001), is on a quest to fulfill her potential as well. She is a rarity in her inner-city neighborhood: a student who not only intends to finish high school but also plans on attending college. Though her environment certainly seems to offer more promise than those of Uncle Tom and Ellison's invisible man, her challenges are hardly less daunting. For the African Americans in LaVaughn's community, opportunity remains as rare is it was for the Youngers in 1950s Chicago.

## *History*

Alice Walker's short story "Everyday Use" (1973) explores similar territory, though the work—coming more than a decade after Hansberry's play—turns some earlier notions of heritage and identity upside down. In "Everyday Use," Mama, a simple and hard-working mother, lives on a small farm with her modest and physically scarred daughter Maggie. Both prepare for a visit from Mama's older daughter, the successful, beautiful, and urbane Dee. When Dee arrives, she is wearing a bright African-print dress and informs her mother and sister that she has adopted the name Wangero in place of Dee. She seeks her African heritage, but only in the most superficial and fashionable way; she renounces her given name, which reflects several generations of her family's own personal history, in exchange for an African name that carries no significance to her known ancestors. Similarly, she embraces her American roots only so she can acquire family heirlooms to be displayed as trendy artifacts in her stylish home. Unlike Mama and Maggie, Dee does not consider her heritage a fundamental part of her everyday life.

After undertaking a search for his own heritage, author Alex Haley created a fictionalized version of his family's history based on oral and historical accounts. The resulting book, *Roots: The Saga of an American Family* (1976), is a two-century chronicle of the African American

*Oprah Winfrey* © *Keith Bedford/Reuters/Corbis*

experience from the perspective of Haley's ancestors. *Roots* represents the realization of a dream held by many African Americans: the desire to discover one's place in both American society and human society as a whole. The book's enormous success also helped create an appreciation among white readers of the long struggle endured by African Americans in search of equality. Although the historical accuracy of some elements of Haley's novel have been called into question—most notably the facts surrounding the Gambian patriarch Kunta Kinte—its power as an agent for social awareness are undisputed.

### Dignity

In Ernest Gaines's *A Lesson Before Dying* (1993), elderly matrons Miss Emma and Tante Lou have a simpler dream: They want Emma's godson Jefferson, who awaits execution for a murder he did not commit, to discover that he is worthy of dignity and self-respect before he dies. The novel takes place in Louisiana in the 1940s, where the idea of equal justice is almost unfathomable to the black residents. Rather than defend Jefferson with facts and truth, his lawyer simply tries to keep the young man alive by convincing the white jurors that Jefferson is like a hog—not aware, and not even worth the trouble of killing. In jail, Jefferson begins to see himself as no better than an animal. Grant, the plantation schoolteacher, works to convince Jefferson that he is indeed a man, and tells Jefferson:

> I want you to show them the difference between what they think you are and what you can be. To them, you're nothing but another nigger—no dignity, no heart, no love for your people. You can prove them wrong.

By asserting his humanity before he is executed, Jefferson fulfills his potential and becomes an example for other African Americans who have become convinced that they are somehow less than human. In the end, Jefferson teaches as much as he learns.

Aaron McGruder's comic strip *The Boondocks*—the first several years of which are collected in the book *A Right to Be Hostile* (2003)—is in many ways a spiritual successor to Hansberry's *A Raisin in the Sun*. In *The Boondocks*, the Freeman family—a retired middle-class black man and his two grandsons—move from the inner city to a large house in the suburbs. For the grandfather, much like Mama Younger, this is the achievement of the American dream: a beautiful house in a peaceful neighborhood, and the perfect place to raise children. For his grandsons, the black radical Huey and the wannabe thug Riley, however, it is the worst situation imaginable: They feel completely cut off from the excitement and cultural stimulation of their former urban neighborhood and their culture. Their idea of the American dream is the opposite of their grandfather's. The fact that the strip is a funny cartoon centered on children has not dampened controversy about the characters' opinions and observations: The strip is often moved to newspapers' editorial pages or dropped altogether when topics become particularly charged.

### Conclusion

The American dream means different things to different people. Literature representing the African American perspective is as diverse as the people it attempts to speak to and speak for. The enduring themes of justice and identity are a fundamental part of nearly every American

**" "**

BIG WALTER USED TO SAY, HE'D GET RIGHT WET

IN THE EYES SOMETIMES, LEAN HIS HEAD BACK WITH

THE WATER STANDING IN HIS EYES AND SAY, "SEEM LIKE

GOD DIDN'T SEE FIT TO GIVE THE BLACK MAN NOTHING

BUT DREAMS—BUT HE DID GIVE US CHILDREN TO MAKE

THEM DREAMS SEEM WORTHWHILE." "

**Source:** Lorraine Hansberry, *A Raisin in the Sun*

group's attempt to construct its own archetypal version of an ideal existence. The unique experience of having literally been denied personhood for centuries weights the literature of the African American dream with tragedy, while having demanded and won the recognition, assertion, and celebration of individual human dignity buoys the canon with triumph. The voices that make up the chorus of the literature of the African American dream echo with one refrain:

The dream is overdue and can no longer be deferred.

## SOURCES

Brooks, Gwendloyn, "We Real Cool," *Blacks*, Third World Press, 1987, p. 331; originally published in *The Bean Eaters*, Harper, 1960.

Equiano, Olaudah, *The Interesting Narrative of the Life of Olaudah Equiano*, printed by the author, 1789, www.gutenberg.org/files/15399/15399-h/15399-h.htm (August 22, 2006).

Gaines, Ernest J., *A Lesson Before Dying*, Knopf, 1993; reprint, Vintage, 1997, p. 191.

Hansberry, Lorraine, *A Raisin in the Sun*, Random House, 1959; reprint, Vintage Books, 1988, pp. 45–46.

Hughes, Langston, "Harlem," *Montage of a Dream Deferred* originally published in 1951, reprinted in *The Collected Poems of Langston Hughes*, edited by Arnold Rampersad, Alfred A. Knopf, 1994, p. 426.

Washington, Booker T., *Up From Slavery: An Autobiography*, Doubleday and Company, 1901, p. 300, reprinted on *Documenting the American South*, docsouth. unc.edu/washington/washing.html, (August 22, 2006).

# *The American Dream Abroad*

## *Introduction*

Since the Pilgrims emigrated from England in 1620, America has represented a place of freedom and financial gain. While the Separatists fled to the New World for religious acceptance, cultural identity, and civil autonomy, merchant investors in the Virginia Company of London looked to make a profit on exploration and newly found territory. Both groups saw the potential for expansion and wealth; the untouched land offered fulfillment financially and spiritually. As the pilgrims sought to spread their church doctrine and populate their faith, the merchants sought new ways to fill their monetary coffers. The New World symbolized a new life, nearly free from tyranny.

But the dream built on American democracy has inspired mixed emotions, from admiration to distrust. In 1833, Frenchman Alexis de Tocqueville wrote *Democracy in America*, a study of why the republican representative democracy in America is successful. In the book, he discusses why this particular form of government fails elsewhere, including in his home country, and hypothesizes about the future of American democracy. Though Tocqueville mused on what worked about the system, he also pointed out possible dangers, including the tyranny of majority. But ultimately, Tocqueville recognized the potential for America to one day become a global force of power.

As a nation so powerful, America continued to prompt curiosity and interest abroad, especially

*Still from the movie* Not Without My Daughter *with Sally Field* Pathe/The Kobal Collection

with men of letters. In 1842, Englishman Charles Dickens, though primarily known for his fiction, wrote *American Notes for General Circulation*, a travelogue that not only described geography and landscape for his British readership, but also provided an outsider's look at American society. He chronicled his experiences visiting mental institutions, prisons, and even tobacco spitting contests. He criticized copyright laws as well as slavery, and tried to be fair in his assessment of the country, or even favorable, as noted in his preface: "Prejudiced, I am not, and never have been, otherwise than in favour of the United States.... To represent me as viewing AMERICA with ill-nature, coldness, or animosity, is merely to do a very foolish thing."

At the turn of the twentieth century, the American dream called to people worldwide. Between 1900 and 1910, over nine million immigrants entered the United States. Though centuries had passed since the arrival of the pilgrims, people still came to America because of religious persecution, as well as social and economic

opportunities. In 1917, President Woodrow Wilson reminded people about their patriotic duty and global responsibility as Americans. During his second inaugural address, he prepared the country for its participation in World War I, clearly stating what the United States would "stand for, whether in war or in peace":

> That all nations are equally interested in the peace of the world and in the political stability of free peoples, and equally responsible for their maintenance; that the essential principle of peace is the actual equality of nations in all matters of right or privilege; ... that governments derive all their just powers from the consent of the governed and that no other powers should be supported by the common thought, purpose or power of the family of nations; ... that national armaments shall be limited to the necessities of national order and domestic safety; that the community of interest and of power upon which peace must henceforth depend imposes upon each nation the duty of seeing to it that all influences proceeding from its own citizens meant to encourage or assist revolution in other states should be sternly and effectually suppressed and prevented.

Wilson's rhetoric of international unity is exemplified by the American Field Service's involvement with the French Army between 1915 and 1917. The AFS, a group of approximately twenty-five American men, served in the ambulance and automobile services, helping transport troops both on and off the battlefields. In his history of the AFS, A. Piatt Andrew quotes a French officer who praised the American volunteers in 1916:

> The American Field Service is the finest flower of the magnificent wreath offered by the great America to her little Latin sister. Those, who like you and your friends have consecrated themselves entirely to our cause, up to and including the supreme sacrifice, deserve more than our gratitude. We cannot think of them in the future as other than our own.

Andrew notes that the admiration was mutual, quoting President Sills of Bowdoin College the same year: "The drivers in the American Ambulance Field Service showed France that chivalry was not dead in America, and carried to the gallant and hard-pressed French people the sympathy of the United States that was never neutral."

The strength, sympathy, and support of America were summoned once again during World War II when Hitler and his Nazi Party systematically invaded and conquered Europe. Though America did not officially enter the war until 1941 after the Japanese bombing of Pearl Harbor, the nation was already supplying Europe and Asia with war resources to sustain the efforts. America's victory in World War II cemented its reputation as a superpower. A leader in spearheading the United Nations, the United States was instrumental in implementing peace treaties, re-parceling territories, and drawing new boundaries. From 1948 to 1952, U.S. Secretary of State George Marshall's "European Recovery Program," commonlny known as the Marshall Plan, spent $13 billion in aid to rebuild Western Europe. With this plan's American values, ideals, and trade relations, war-torn Europe prospered.

In the coming decades, the diplomatic and economic authority of the United States made the nation even more of a haven for immigrants than it had been for the pilgrims. The country's participation in the Korean War and the Vietnam Conflict demonstrated American strong-arm, and although many people protested America's involvement, the undeniable might showed people around the world that the nation would not easily back down. Seeking refuge in a country that faced its battles and fought for citizens beyond its borders seemed a logical choice. Despite the controversy of the Iraq War and Middle Eastern politics, the twenty-first century still finds the American dream alive overseas. But in some ways, American prosperity and success has tempered the golden image; what represents a hopeful dream for many is seen as excessive and materialistic by others.

### America the Beautiful

Though the chance for personal freedom and democracy beckoned most immigrants to the New World, the idea of wide open spaces and unique landscape was another incentive. Just as Charles Dickens visited in the nineteenth century, Simone de Beauvoir, French intellectual, theorist, and writer, headed for the United States in 1947 on a four-month tour of American culture. After traveling from college to college on a lecture circuit, she wrote *America Day by Day*, a journal comprised of souvenirs, memories, letters, and notes from her trip on buses, cars, and trains. Though she was intrigued and impressed by America's landscape, she explored the nation's true colors and textures through a variety of cultural experiences, socializing with people everywhere from drugstores and Ivy League schools to slaughterhouses and burlesques. In the book, she provides a keen look at America not only from a foreign woman's perspective, but also from the perspective of those interesting characters she meets. De Beauvoir is both fascinated and repelled by the American scene. "America is so vast," de Beauvoir writes, "that nothing anyone can say about it is true." When dining with some friends who emigrated from Spain, she also recognizes that beauty may be in the eye of the beholder: "I know that for many refugees, America has been a land of exile, not a place they've come to love. . . . They say life is cruel in New York for immigrants and for the poor."

Nearly fifty years later, America possesses that same contradicting allure for Beppe Severgnini, an Italian writer who moved to the United States with his wife. Severgnini, unlike de Beauvoir, appreciates the United States with a humorous outlook in his book, *Ciao, America!*. Renting a house in Washington, D.C., Severgnini and his wife develop a fascination with ice cubes, recliner chairs, and yard sales, and along the way, observe

American mannerisms, morals, and social customs. The Severgninis, like Dickens and de Beauvoir, sought the "real" America and left no stone unturned in their quest, making even a simple shopping trip a lesson in what it means to be American. But the best thing about America, Severgnini muses, is the facility of American bureaucracy:

> For Italians coming to live in the United States, the greatest satisfaction derives not from seeing films six months before they are released in Italy, or choosing from fifty different kinds of breakfast cereal, or reading two kilos of newspaper on a Sunday morning. What really tickles our epiglottis is grappling with American bureaucracy. Why is that? It's because, having trained on the Italian version, we feel like a matador faced with a milk cow. It's a pushover.

## America Goes Abroad

In Henry James's *The American*, written in 1877, France plays host to retired young American Christopher Newman as he takes his first tour of Europe. He falls in love with Claire, but her family cannot tolerate his materialistic and gauche ways. Essentially, this novel deals with the clash between old world European traditions and the corruption of new world American manners. Newman's experiences are loosely based on those of the author, who had spent his youth traveling between the United States and Europe and was educated in cities such as Paris, Bonn, and Geneva.

Paul Bowles's *The Sheltering Sky* (1949), though published more than seventy years after *The American*, also tells the story of three wealthy Americans and their experiences in a foreign land, this time North Africa. In contrast to James's witty, social tale, Bowles tells the edgy, sensual, existentialist story of married couple Port and Kit Moresby and their friend George Tunner. The theme familiar in James's novel—corruption of American values—also takes hold in this novel as Port, Kit, and Tunner desire intimacy with one another but can never connect emotionally. By the end of the book, the characters' lack of appreciation for time, life, love, or even death leads them to tragedy. Their lives are boundless, a very American notion, as shown in this musing from Port:

> Because we don't know [when we will die], we get to think of life as an inexhaustible well. Yet everything happens only a certain number of times, and a very small number really. How

many more times will you remember a certain afternoon of your childhood, some afternoon that is so deeply part of your being that you can't even conceive of your life without it? Perhaps four or five times more, perhaps not even that. How many more times will you watch the full moon rise? Perhaps twenty. And yet it all seems limitless.

Several years later, in 1955, Graham Greene uses his personal experiences in Vietnam to write *The Quiet American*, a novel set in 1950s Saigon. In this story about the conflict mounting in Vietnam, British journalist Thomas Fowler, young American Alden Pyle, and Fowler's Vietnamese mistress Phuong make up the triangle of main characters. Their complex relationship provides a framework for the novel as Fowler and Pyle's battle for Phuong's attentions mirrors the idea of the United States' potential colonization of Vietnam. Idealistic and driven, Pyle wants to "save the east for democracy" and does not mind killing innocent people for the greater good of social and national development. American patriotism motivates his sense of social justice: "He was absorbed already in the dilemmas of democracy and the responsibilities of the West; he was determined ... to do good, not to any individual person but to a country, a continent, a world. Well, he was in his element now with the whole universe to improve." Greene criticized American involvement in Vietnam and offers Pyle as a critique of foreign policy.

In contrast to *The American*, *The Sheltering Sky*, and *The Quiet American*, Betty Mahmoody's book *Not Without My Daughter* is not about an American touring a foreign country for pure pleasure and cultural awakening. However, like the novels by Bowles and Greene, Mahmoody's novel is based on personal experiences and deals with the challenges and harsh realities of crossing cultures. Written in 1987, the true story recounts Mahmoody's difficult journey, from the moment her Iranian husband convinces her to bring their daughter Mahtob to visit his family in Iran to the moment she must flee the country with Mahtob, eighteen months later. Mahmoody's emotional struggle begins when her husband says she can return home, but Mahtob must remain. Mahmoody and her daughter stay in Iran for eighteen months, imprisoned by Islamic fundamentalism and misogyny. In Iran, Mahmoody becomes the property of her husband; she cannot do anything without his permission.

*Fidel Castro speaking to the U.N. General Assembly in 1979* © *Bettmann/Corbis*

Again, the idea of America and being American disintegrates on foreign soil; its power and patriotism dissolve into the old world strength of another homeland, another culture, and other traditions.

## U.S. Foreign Policies, a Foreign Perspective

Like Graham Greene, Canadian writer and feminist Margaret Atwood uses her poetic and fictional work to criticize and comment on political issues. But just after the turn of the twenty-first century, on March 27, 2003, she wrote "A Letter to America," a personal letter to the newspaper the *Nation*, wagging her finger at the deterioration of American strength, morality, and leadership and attacking American action in Iraq. In directly addressing America, she points out how the nation used to set the intellectual and entertainment trends with Mickey Mouse, Marlon Brando, Walt Whitman, and Ernest Hemingway. She notes how she used to admire, even revere America. But America, by "gutting its Constitution," "torching the American economy," and "running up a record level of debt,"

is slowing losing its power and prestige. Adressing America directly, Atwood writes,

> If you proceed much further down the slippery slope, people around the world will stop admiring the good things about you. They'll decide that your city upon the hill is a slum and your democracy is a sham, and therefore you have no business trying to impose your sullied vision on them. They'll think you've abandoned the rule of law. They'll think you've fouled your own nest.

Margaret Atwood uses humor, satire, nostalgia, and personal sentiment to present her case and express her feelings about the direction of American policies, foreign and domestic. In 2006, Gary Shteyngart combined similar rhetorical styles in *Absurdistan*, a clever satire about what America means to Russian Misha Vainberg, who attended college in America and fondly remembers those optimistic days of excess and pleasure. He now leads a luxurious life in Russia on an inheritance from his murdered mobster father, but he longs to return to the States where his girlfriend lives in the Bronx. Because of his father's shady actions, Vainberg cannot obtain a visa. He heads for the minor republic Absurdistan in hopes of rectifying the

> MAHTOUB AND I EXCHANGED GLANCES,
> READING EACH OTHER'S MIND. THIS VACATION WAS A
> BRIEF INTERRUPTION OF OUR OTHERWISE NORMAL
> AMERICAN LIVES. WE COULD ENDURE IT, BUT WE DID
> NOT HAVE TO LIKE IT. FROM THAT VERY MOMENT, WE
> BEGAN COUNTING THE DAYS UNTIL WE COULD GO
> HOME."

**Source:** Betty Mahmoody, *Not Without My Daughter*

situation, but political conflict in the territory, ironically backed by American dollars and democracy, stops his dream cold. Rather than providing a direct hit like Atwood, Shteyngart employs farce to show, from a global perspective, how absurd people are in their biases, prejudices, and opinions of each other. Echoing the same themes as James's *The American*, yet told in a more contemporary, more preposterous fashion, *Absurdistan* reveals the ways in which foreign and American attitudes clash and affect each other socially and politically.

The inverse of outside opinions about the pursuit of the American dream at home is inside opinions about the fostering of the American dream abroad—American influence in foreign affairs, that is. Never has one opinion been so contrary to the American notion of its righteousness in the world than when Fidel Castro denounced imperialism and colonialism at the United Nations in a speech delivered before the U.N. General Assembly in September 1960, blaming the United States for the plight of impoverished Cubans:

> Of course, as far as the President of the United States is concerned, we have betrayed our people, but it would certainly not have been considered so, if, instead of the Revolutionary Government being true to its people, it had been loyal to the big American monopolies that exploited the economy of our country. At least, let note be taken here of the wonders the Revolution found when it came to power. They were no more and no less than the usual wonder of imperialism, which are in themselves the wonders of the free world as far as we, the colonies, are concerned!

Carlos Fuentes's novel *The Eagle's Throne* (2006) uses a satirical strategy to comment on

America's fictional political positioning in 2020. Though the world has not changed much, Condoleeza Rice is the U.S. president, the United States has conquered Colombia, and Mexico is demanding its withdrawal. In reply to Mexico's demands, the United States shuts down Mexico's communication systems. Written in epistolary style, as the characters communicate by letters, this futuristic tale veils Fuentes's commentary on the authoritarian morphing of "American" democracy in Mexico. As Fuentes said wryly at a February 2006 talk in London, "We always know who will be president [of Mexico], because we know it a year ahead of elections."

## Conclusion: The American Dream, A Global Tangle

The American dream is still famous around the world. The land of opportunity and instant success continues to gleam with certain promise, encouraging immigration and subsequently stirring that nation nicknamed "the melting pot." America, as in the lyrics to the national anthem, remains "the land of the free and the home of the brave," and in the Statue of Liberty's signature poem, those "yearning to breathe free" continue to land on American shores. But globally, the idea of America, or Americans, will forever evoke a complicated tangle of social, political, and geographical assumptions and expectations.

## SOURCES

Andrew, A. Piatt, "History of the American Field Service, Part 1," net.lib.byu.edu/~rdh7/wwi/memoir/AFShist/AFS1a.htm (December 15, 2006).

Atwood, Margaret, "A Letter to America," in the *Nation*, March 27, 2003, www.thenation.com/doc/20030414/atwood (January 9, 2007).

Bowles, Paul, *The Sheltering Sky*, Harper Perennial, 1998, p.238; originally published in 1949.

Castro, Fidel, "Address to the United Nations General Assembly, 1969," Castro Speech Data Base: Speeches, Interviews, Articles: 1959–1996, lanic.utexas.edu/la/cb/cuba/castro/1960/19600926 (December 15, 2006).

de Beauvoir, Simone, *America Day by Day*, University of California Press, 1999; originally published as *L'Amerique on Jour le Jour*, Editions Gallimard, 1954.

Dickens, Charles, "Preface to the Charles Dickens Edition," in *American Notes for General Circulation*, Kessinger Publishing, 2004, p. 3; originally published in 1850.

Greene, Graham, *The Quiet American*, Penguin, 1991, p. 13, originally published in 1955.

Mahmoody, Betty, *Not Without My Daughter*, St. Martin's Press, 1991, p. 16.

Severgnini, Beppe, *Ciao, America!*, Broadway Press, 2003, p. 13.

Wilson, Woodrow, "Second Inaugural Address," March 5, 1917, *The Avalon Project at Yale Law School*, www.yale.edu/lawweb/avalon/presiden/inaug/wilson2.htm (December 15, 2006).

# The American Feminist Dream

### Introduction

In the early years of the country, the traditional American dream of forging a new frontier, achieving instant success, and assuming a new and prosperous identity was not readily available to women. Men would take the lead in building the United States, claiming property, forming a legal system, and declaring their independence. Women certainly supported these ideals, working alongside their husbands, brothers, and sons to hoe the progress of a new nation. However, their unyielding efforts did not automatically grant them a voice in determining the direction America would grow. Because the opinions of women were not taken into consideration professionally, socially, or politically, women had to fight to be heard and seen.

The American Revolution gave many women the opportunity to contribute to the birth of the nation as men left their homes for war. Women raised funds to support the republic, kept family businesses running successfully, and took care of domestic activity. Abigail Adams tried to encourage her husband, John, then a member of the Continental Congress, to recognize this emerging independence. In 1776, in a letter to John, Abigail tells him to "Remember the Ladies" as he and the other congressmen create a new code of laws following the colonists' break from Britain.

In the 1830s, the abolitionist movement inspired women to examine the similarities

*Sojourner Truth* Getty Images

women into civilian and military efforts; however, when men returned home from the fronts, women lost their status in the workforce. For the next few decades, women not only battled to maintain a presence in industry, but also rallied for equal pay. During the 1960s and 1970s, the second wave of feminism swept across America, demanding equal treatment for women. Literature of this time promoted activism and solidarity, introducing public conversations about taboo subjects such as abortion, contraception, homosexuality, and domestic violence. In 1963, Eleanor Roosevelt was the chairperson on the Commission on the Status of Women, which chronicled discriminatory practices against women, while Betty Friedan wrote *The Feminine Mystique*, a manifesto commenting on the undeniable restriction in traditional female roles.

Feminism soon became a hotbed of antagonism as some thought the term reflected an anti-male philosophy, rather than one based on women's empowerment. Many women also believed that the feminist movement focused too much on the experiences of white women and assumed a universal female identity. In the 1980s, the third wave of feminism emerged and embraced advocacy for all genders, races, and sexualities.

## The Woman Question

Margaret Fuller, a famous woman of letters in the nineteenth century, started public "conversations" for women, which borrowed from the model of study groups and reading parties. During these gatherings, Fuller encouraged women to express themselves freely and to act on their ideas. In discussing the "woman question" in her piece "Woman in the Nineteenth Century" (1845), Fuller argues the importance of women's roles in the future if "every path [were] laid open to woman as freely as man":

> We believe the divine energy would pervade nature to a degree unknown in the history of former ages, and that no discordant collisions, but a ravishing harmony of the spheres would ensue.

Between 1851 and 1872, Fanny Fern (the pen name of Sara Willis) published a weekly syndicated newspaper column that also addressed problems relative to women. Fern covered the topics of women's suffrage, women's rights within the family unit, and female perseverance, in addition to depression, matrimony, and feminine attire. In her semi-autobiographical *Ruth*

between how society regarded slaves and women. For many women, the struggle for slaves' rights was a struggle for human rights. Following the Civil War, Elizabeth Cady Stanton and Susan B. Anthony formed the National Loyal Women's League, which argued for the right to vote, not only for women but also for people of any race or color. However, despite the progressive leadership of Stanton and others, the women's vote was not secured until 1920 with the Nineteenth Amendment to the Constitution.

Like the American Revolution, both World Wars opened doors for women to actively participate, both vocally and physically. Edna St. Vincent Millay, the first woman to receive a Pulitzer Prize for poetry, dared to offer her bitter take on the state of the world, anticipating World War II with her poem, "Apostrophe to Man." Millay unequivocally points a finger at "Homo called sapiens," the entity she believes responsible for humanity's downfall. Millay is brutally honest, even harsh, about a topic of universal concern, reflecting women's growing boldness in society.

Socially and economically, the demands of World War II pulled hundreds of thousands of

*Margaret Fuller* © *Corbis*

*Hall: A Domestic Tale of the Present Time*, Fern portrays a young widow and single mother who uses her wits, not her wiles, to support her family.

### Freedom and Equality

Like Fuller and Fern, Sojourner Truth spoke to her audience about equality and rights for women, as well as for all genders and races. However, as a former slave, Truth presented a personal and powerful perspective on the privileges and rights denied women. In 1851, while Fern united women through print, Truth urged those who stood before her at a women's rights convention in Akron, Ohio, to listen and act, dismissing the argument that women and blacks were less capable: "What's [intellect] got to do with women's rights or negroes' rights? If my cup won't hold but a pint, and yours holds a quart, wouldn't you be mean not to let me have my little half measure full?" She went on to rally the audience by telling them, "If the first woman God ever made was strong enough to turn the world upside down all alone, these women together ought to be able to turn it back, and

get it right side up again! And now they is asking to do it, the men better let them."

In Zora Neale Hurston's *Their Eyes Were Watching God*, Old Nanny seems to channel Sojourner Truth's "Ain't I a Woman?" speech as she comforts her granddaughter Janie Crawford and talks about the past: "Ah was born back due in slavery so it wasn't for me to fulfill my dreams of what a woman oughta be and do. Dat's one of de hold-backs of slavery. But nothing can't stop you from wishin." Hurston wrote her novels at the height of the Harlem Renaissance in the 1930s, but she echoes Truth's affirming view of the future. But in contrast to Truth, Hurston's Old Nanny seeks a different type of action from her young listener. She ultimately sees the wealth and security that a man can offer as the keys to Janie's happiness. Janie, on the other hand, grows into an independent woman who speaks her mind, relies on her instincts, and even plays checkers, much to men's chagrin. Janie challenges the male chauvinism in her town, and during a public

*George McGovern addressing a woman's caucus, with Gloria Steinam and Bella Abzug* © *Bettmann/Corbis*

conversation when Joe Lindsay reports that a friend "says beatin' women is just like steppin' on baby chickens," Janie calls the men on their righteousness: "It's so easy to make yo' self out God Almighty when you ain't got nothin' tuh strain against but women and chickens."

### Social, Sexual, and Spiritual Awakening

Like Janie Crawford, Edna Pontellier in Kate Chopin's *The Awakening* is desperate to find herself and surges against the restrictions placed against her. A young white wife and mother in New Orleans at the turn of the twentieth century, she travels a hard road to self-discovery and begins to recognize her own desires. Both Edna's and Janie's awakenings grow from their relationships with men; just as they become more aware of their sexuality, they become more aware of themselves as viable human beings. A "true woman," they realize, does not have to be pure and pious. She can acknowledge her body and the sensations incited within it. Edna sees something beyond her "colorless existence" and "blind contentment," and at the end of the story, she stands nude on the beach like a "new-born creature opening its eyes in a familiar world that it had never known." As she swims out to sea and drowns from exhaustion, Edna represents a cohort of women who felt impossibly trapped in their bodies and unfulfilled by their expected roles. Although they saw the possibility of empowerment, they did not see the reality of it.

More than sixty years later, Betty Friedan addresses a similar sense of hopelessness in *The Feminine Mystique*:

> If a woman had a problem in the 1950's and 1960's, she knew that something must be wrong with her marriage, or with herself. Other women were satisfied with their lives, she thought. What kind of a woman was she if she did not feel this mysterious fulfillment waxing the kitchen floor? She was so ashamed to admit her dissatisfaction that she never knew how many other women shared it.

By exposing the inner conflicts of women in traditional roles, Friedan gave hope to those who felt limited by their responsibilities as "dutiful" females. *The Feminine Mystique* was the catalyst for the second wave of feminism and helped amplify the discussion about civil rights for women.

## Dreams in Reality

Friedan's study of conventional roles paved the way for activists like Angela Davis, whose progressive *Women, Race, and Class* (1981), went one step further in expanding conversations about women's rights. In chronicling the women's movement, Davis discusses how race and class affect the movement as a whole and shows how the first and second waves of feminism neglected to embrace all women in its goals and achievements. She explores the oppression of African American women, as well as working-class women and immigrants, and suggests that the differences in race, class, and sex need to be acknowledged to achieve equality.

Joyce Carol Oates speaks to the reality of the working class in her novel *Them*, with a fictional portrait of a family from Detroit whose failed plans and broken dreams from the 1930s to the 1960s are rooted in the slums. Oates tells the story of the Wendall family, whose women experience the American dream through the nightmares of rape, prostitution, and domestic violence. Maureen and Loretta have few chances and even fewer opportunities to free themselves. They symbolize the women Davis identifies in her book: those women who have been forgotten in the quest for women's liberation.

Throughout her career as a poet, Adrienne Rich has spoken for those people who have been forgotten, or denied a voice. In 1997, she refused an invitation to accept the National Medal of the Arts award at the White House, prompted by the elimination of federal arts funding. In her commentary about her refusal, Rich writes, "Art is both tough and fragile. It speaks of what we long to hear and what we dread to find. Its source and native impulse, the imagination, may be shackled in early life, yet may find release in conditions offering little else to the spirit."

In her poem, "Twenty-One Love Poems," Rich celebrates a love affair that has brought joy late in life:

No one has imagined us. We want to live like
   trees,
sycamores blazing through the sulfuric air,
dappled with scars, still exuberantly budding,
our animal passion rooted in the city.

Rich has used her work to explore both feminist and American ideals: freedom of expression and the pursuit of happiness.

Like Rich, Gloria Naylor also celebrates the colorful spirit of the women who inhabit a neighborhood, and although the neighborhood seems somewhat exiled, Naylor portrays seven women of Brewster Place as triumphant, tenacious, and alive. At the end of the novel, Naylor writes,

The colored daughters of Brewster...still wake up with their dreams misted on the edge of a yawn. They get up and pin those dreams to wet laundry hung out to dry, they're mixed with a pinch of salt and thrown into pots of soup, and they're diapered around babies. They ebb and flow, but never disappear.

In the same way, Alice Walker champions the independence and tenacity of an African American woman named Celie in the novel *The Color Purple*. Well into the novel, Celie's husband, the emotionally and physically abusive Mr. _____, confronts her. She records the conversation in one of her letters to God, letters which comprise the novel's entire narrative: "Who you think you is? he say. You can't curse nobody. Look at you. You black, you pore, you ugly, you a woman . . . you nothing at all." Later, Celie acknowledges his claims, yet finds power in her identity and existence: "I'm pore, I'm black, I may be ugly and can't cook. . . . But I'm here."

## Conclusion: The Future of Feminist Dream

In her preface to *The Feminine Mystique*, Betty Friedan introduces her ground-breaking treatise as one of simple humanism:

My answers may disturb the experts and women alike for they imply social change. But there would be no sense in my writing this book at all if I did not believe that women can affect society as well as be affected by it; that, in the end, a woman, as a man, has the power to choose, and to make her own heaven or hell.

Four decades later, American women stand on the shoulders of the giants that came before them—the Abigail Adamses, the Fanny Ferns, the Sojourner Truths, the Angela Davises—and dream of new heavens, to see new horizons, and to claim new triumphs than their foremothers dared imagine. Today's feminist American dream does not hinge on the dreamer's gender, race, wealth, beauty, or even nationality; it is rooted in the past, facing toward the future,

I THINK THAT 'TWIXT THE NEGROES OF THE
SOUTH AND THE WOMEN AT THE NORTH, ALL TALKING
ABOUT RIGHTS, THE WHITE MEN WILL BE IN A FIX
PRETTY SOON."

**Source:** Sojourner Truth, "Ain't I a Woman?"

and propelled by each dreamer's belief in her own worth.

## SOURCES

Adams, Abigail, *Adams Family Papers: Braintree March 31, 1776, Massachusetts Historical Society*, www.masshist.org/digitaladams/aea/cfm/doc.cfm?id = L17760331aa(August 29, 2006).

Angelou, Maya, "Phenomenal Woman," *And Still I Rise*, Random House, 1978.

Chopin, Kate, *The Awakening*, Herbert S. Stone, 1899; reprint, Bantam Classics, 1985, p. 152.

Friedan, Betty, *The Feminine Mystique*, W. W. Norton, 1963; reprint, 2001, pp. 12, 19.

Fuller, Margaret, "Woman in the Nineteenth Century", *The Essential Margaret Fuller*, Rutgers University Press, 1992, p. 260; originally published in 1845.

Hurston, Zora Neale, *Their Eyes Were Watching God*, J. B. Lippincott, 1937; reprint, Harper Collins, 1999, pp. 16, 75.

Naylor, Gloria, *The Women of Brewster Place*, Viking, 1987, p. 192.

Rich, Adrienne, "Letter to Jane Alexander, National Endowment for the Arts," www.barclayagency.com/richwhy.html (October 6, 2006).

———, "Twenty-One Love Poems," www.wwnorton.com/trade/external/nortonpoets/ex/richadream.htm (October 6, 2006); originally published in *Dream of a Common Language*, Norton, 1978.

Truth, Sojourner, "Ain't I a Woman?" in the *Modern History Sourcebook*, www.fordham.edu/halsall/mod/sojruth-woman.html (October 16, 2006); originally delivered at the Women's Convention in Akron, Ohio, 1851.

Walker, Alice, *The Color Purple*, Pocket Books, 1982, pp. 213, 214.

# The American Political Dream

### Introduction

The revolutionary documents, essays, and speeches that make up the literature of the American political dream have, over the centuries, defined not only American laws, but the nation's very identity. Americans are united by a dream of freedom and self-sufficiency, which is, in essence, a political dream; because Americans come from every religion, ethnicity, and race, it is political ideals that bind them. The American political dream is a constant work in progress, a fact made evident after reviewing the literature that spans the centuries beginning with the country's birth. From Patrick Henry's "Give Me Liberty or Give Me Death" speech to the 1775 Virginia Convention to Barbara Jordan's 1976 Democratic Convention Keynote Address, the ever-changing American political dream is consistently written by persuasive leaders intent on building, inspiring, and growing a nation of like-minded yet very independent individuals.

### The Dream of a New Government

Before the American Revolution began, American colonists were devising ways of escaping British rule. After winning the American Revolution, the founding fathers set about creating a government that would serve the new nation's present as well as its future. The speeches and documents that led to the construction of the Declaration of Independence and the U.S. Constitution are more than the building blocks of the country's

*Elizabeth Cady Stanton* AP Images

system of laws—they illustrate its character as a nation.

In 1775, a series of political meetings called the Virginia Conventions were instrumental in guiding the American colonies toward independence from British rule. Patrick Henry, one of the most radical and influential American Revolution advocates, delivered a speech during the second of five Virginia Conventions that persuaded his fellow conventioneers to arm the state's militia, which essentially set the Revolution in motion. Henry's "Give Me Liberty or Give Me Death" is memorable for its eloquence, force, and guiding philosophy. This powerful speech, delivered on March 20, 1775, ended with these words:

> Gentlemen may cry, Peace, Peace but there is no peace. The war is actually begun! The next gale that sweeps from the north will bring to our ears the clash of resounding arms! Our brethren are already in the field! Why stand we here idle? What is it that gentlemen wish? What would they have? Is life so dear, or peace so sweet, as to be purchased at the price of chains and slavery? Forbid it, Almighty God! I know not what course others may take; but as for me, give me liberty or give me death!

Twelve years later, the American Revolution had been fought and won. In 1787, the hard work of creating a system of government for the new nation was under way. Instead of one rousing speech, Alexander Hamilton, James Madison, and John Jay wrote a series of eighty-five persuasive essays between 1787 and 1788. These *Federalist Papers*, as they came to be known, both outlined future interpretations of the U.S. Constitution and urged its ratification. Today, the *Federalist Papers* are viewed as a guide to understanding the motivation and philosophy behind a system of government that was, at the time, merely a proposition. In the general introduction of the *Federalist Papers*, Alexander Hamilton writes,

> After an unequivocal experience of the inefficiency of the subsisting federal government, you are called upon to deliberate on a new Constitution for the United States of America. The subject speaks its own importance; comprehending in its consequences nothing less than the existence of the UNION, the safety and welfare of the parts of which it is composed, the fate of an empire in many respects the most interesting in the world.

One of the more interesting essays included in the *Federalist Papers*, "Federalist No. 84," finds Hamilton opposing the inclusion of a Bill of Rights that enumerates various protections of the rights of the American people. Hamilton's opposition was based on his belief that those rights not enumerated would not be honored. On September 25, 1789, though, twelve amendments to the Constitution were brought before the First Federal Congress. Only ten of these were ratified, which became the first ten amendments to the Constitution. They were called the Bill of Rights because they outlined the liberties and essential rights of Americans that were omitted in the original draft of one the nation's most important legal documents. The First Amendment to the Constitution, in its entirety, reads,

> Congress shall make no law respecting an establishment of religion, or prohibiting the free exercise thereof; or abridging the freedom of speech, or of the press; or the right of the people peaceably to assemble, and to petition the government for a redress of grievances.

The rights promised in the first ten amendments to the Constitution, along with those "unalienable rights" outlined in the Declaration of Independence, form the basis of the political American dream. Included among the remaining nine are the rights to bear arms and to be protected against unreasonable search and seizure, cruel and unusual punishment, and self-incrimination, as well as the guarantee of due process of law and the right to a speedy trial before an impartial jury. The rights promised in these amendments are referred to in countless political documents and continue to define the American character as well as its moral center.

### The Dream of Self-Reliance

In 1849, Henry David Thoreau wrote "Civil Disobedience," an essay that explores the role of man's conscience in a legislative society and continues to inform both American and international political thought to this day. He writes,

> Yet this government never of itself furthered any enterprise, but by the alacrity with which it got out of its way. *It* does not keep the country free. *It* does not settle the West. *It* does not educate. The character inherent in the American people has done all that has been accomplished; and it would have done somewhat more, if the government had not sometimes got in its way.

Thoreau's philosophy of individualism and self-reliance as described in "Civil Disobedience" has become a cornerstone of both the American identity and nonviolent resistance movements worldwide.

### The Dream of Equality for All Americans

In Philadelphia, on July 4, 1776, the Declaration of Independence was signed by the leaders of the original thirteen colonies of the United States of America. Among the foremost tenets of the Declaration is the belief that all men are created equal:

> We hold these Truths to be self-evident, that all Men are created equal, that they are endowed by their Creator with certain unalienable Rights, that among these are Life, Liberty and the Pursuit of Happiness—That to secure these Rights, Governments are instituted among Men, deriving their just Powers from the Consent of the Governed, that whenever any Form of Government becomes destructive to these Ends, it is the Right of the People to alter or to abolish it, and to institute new Government, laying its Foundation on such Principles and organizing its Powers in such Form, as to them shall seem most likely to effect their Safety and Happiness.

Despite the clarity with which the ideal of equality is spelled out in the Declaration, it continues to be one of the country's most rankling issues. African Americans, for instance, have fought for their "inalienable" right to equality since the eighteenth century. Women began

*Daniel Chester French and Henry Bacon in front of French's Lincoln Statue in the Lincoln Memorial* © Corbis

asserting their desire for equal rights in the early nineteenth century. Today, these two groups and countless others—including gay and lesbian Americans and American immigrants—are still fighting for what the Declaration claimed was an inherent human right back in 1776. Because of this, political American dream literature is filled with powerful demands for freedom and equality for all Americans. One of the first came from Elizabeth Cady Stanton in the form of her 1848 *Seneca Falls Declaration of Sentiments*. Using the Declaration of Independence as her guide, Stanton asserted that "all men and women had been created equal" and followed this assertion with a list of eighteen "injuries and usurpations" suffered by women at the hands of men—just as the Declaration of Independence had listed eighteen injuries suffered by the colonies at the hand of the King of England. The first three of those usurpations of women by men are these:

> He has never permitted her to exercise her inalienable right to the elective franchise. He has compelled her to submit to laws, in the

formation of which she had no voice. He has withheld from her rights which are given to the most ignorant and degraded men—both natives and foreigners.

Little came from the *Seneca Falls Declaration*, primarily because the issue of women's suffrage was overshadowed in the storm around slavery and its abolition. Women had to wait until the ratification of the Nineteenth Amendment to the Constitution in 1920 for the right to vote. Stanton's document, though, served as the goal of the women's suffrage movement and remains a powerful reminder of their struggle.

On November 19, 1863, Abraham Lincoln delivered one of American history's most stirring speeches. His "Gettysburg Address," a consecration of the Soldiers' National Cemetery, was a powerful and memorable message about human equality as defined by the Declaration of Independence. Standing on what had been the grounds of the Battle of Gettysburg less than five months earlier, Lincoln framed the Civil War as more than a struggle for the Union, but a struggle to bring true equality to every American citizen:

Four score and seven years ago our fathers brought forth on this continent, a new nation, conceived in Liberty, and dedicated to the proposition that all men are created equal.... [W]e here highly resolve that these dead shall not have died in vain—that this nation, under God, shall have a new birth of freedom—and that government of the people, by the people, for the people, shall not perish from the earth.

Unfortunately, progress in the area of equality and freedom for all—especially for African Americans and other citizens of color—has been slow in coming. One hundred years after Lincoln's famous call for equality, on August 28, 1963, Martin Luther King Jr. stood on the steps of the Lincoln Memorial and delivered his "I Have a Dream" speech. King had led equal rights advocates through nonviolent protests and marches throughout the 1950s and early 1960s and was considered the most prominent leader of the U.S. Civil Rights Movement. His "I Have a Dream" speech was the climax of the March on Washington for Jobs and Freedom. His speech that day, about the dream of all people of every race, religion, and background to live free in a truly democratic nation, became the statement of civil rights in America. Referencing Lincoln's famous "Gettysburg Address," King begins his speech, "Five score years ago, a great American, in whose symbolic shadow we stand today, signed

the Emancipation Proclamation." After acknowledging the "great beacon light of hope" this was "to millions of Negro slaves," King declares that, one hundred years later, "the Negro is still not free." He continues:

I say to you today, my friends, so even though we face the difficulties of today and tomorrow, I still have a dream. It is a dream deeply rooted in the American dream. I have a dream that one day this nation will rise up and live out the true meaning of its creed: "We hold these truths to be self-evident: that all men are created equal."

Malcolm X, another African American civil rights leader of the 1950s and 1960s, took an entirely different approach to the struggle for equal rights. He espoused Black Nationalism, in his words "a political, economic, and social philosophy" based on the idea that black Americans could only achieve the American dream by investing in themselves and their black communities and divesting themselves from the rest of the country. He explained Black Nationalism in his 1964 "The Ballot or the Bullet" speech, which echoed Frederick Douglass's 1859 essay, "The Ballot and the Bullet," which echoed the radical thinking put forth by American colonists like Patrick Henry who called for a war against Great Britain. Malcolm X proclaimed,

No, I'm not an American. I'm one of the 22 million black people who are the victims of Americanism. One of the 22 million black people who are the victims of democracy, nothing but disguised hypocrisy. So, I'm not standing here speaking to you as an American, or a patriot, or a flag-saluter, or a flag-waver—no, not I. I'm speaking as a victim of this American system. And I see America through the eyes of the victim. I don't see any American dream; I see an American nightmare.

### *The American Dream in Troubled Times*

The same year that Malcolm X delivered his "The Ballot or the Bullet" speech and inspired a movement of Black Nationalism, Lyndon Johnson outlined his plan to enact a wide swath of social reform measures. Johnson's "The Great Society" speech, delivered during a particularly tumultuous period of American history, was reminiscent of Franklin Roosevelt's first inaugural address, in which he addressed the dire situation America found itself in at the height of the Great Depression. In 1976, Barbara Jordan, the first woman and first African American to do so, gave the keynote address at

*Dr. Martin Luther King, Jr. delivering the "I Have a Dream" speech* © *Corbis*

that year's Democratic National Convention. Roosevelt, Johnson, and Jordan were all elected government officials who possessed the power and support they needed to enforce the changes they proposed. Their interest in shaping American society inspired them to become public servants, and their speeches express their commitment to the American dream, even during the country's darkest days.

America had reached the depth of the Great Depression by the time President Franklin Delano Roosevelt gave his first inaugural address on March 4, 1933. In the speech, Roosevelt's usual light-hearted, paternalistic approach was traded for a solemn tone, one that more honestly reflected the dire straits the country was in at the moment. He began,

> This is preeminently the time to speak the truth, the whole truth, frankly and boldly. Nor need we shrink from honestly facing conditions in our country today. This great Nation will endure as

it has endured, will revive and will prosper. So, first of all, let me assert my firm belief that the only thing we have to fear is fear itself—nameless, unreasoning, unjustified terror which paralyzes needed efforts to convert retreat into advance. In every dark hour of our national life a leadership of frankness and vigor has met with that understanding and support of the people themselves which is essential to victory. I am convinced that you will again give that support to leadership in these critical days.

By tempering the reality of the truth with the now-famous words, "the only thing we have to fear is fear itself," Roosevelt tapped into the foundation of the American dream and the strength and hope that define Americans as a people.

President Lyndon Baines Johnson first used the phrase "The Great Society" in a speech delivered at the University of Michigan in 1964. Years later, after ratification of the Civil Rights Act, the Medicare Act, and the Immigration Act, Johnson's administration is rightly remembered for the "Great Society" changes that were enacted during his presidency. The speech that started it all focused on preventing war, decreasing poverty, and improving education. The newly elected president described his vision of "The Great Society" to his Ann Arbor audience this way:

> The Great Society rests on abundance and liberty for all. It demands an end to poverty and racial injustice, to which we are totally committed in our time. But that is just the beginning. ... the Great Society is not a safe harbor, a resting place, a final objective, a finished work. It is a challenge constantly renewed, beckoning us toward a destiny where the meaning of our lives matches the marvelous products of our labor.

Like Roosevelt, Johnson encourages his listeners to engage themselves in the ongoing experiment that was—and is—the American dream.

Like Roosevelt and Johnson before her, Barbara Jordan acknowledged the problems facing American society in her 1976 Democratic Convention Keynote Address. She also looked to Americans' "common destiny" as a motivating force to overcome those problems as a nation. She uses the fact that she, an African American woman, was chosen to deliver the keynote address of Democratic National Convention as proof of the strides made as a motivated nation. "I feel that notwithstanding the past that my presence here is one additional bit of evidence that the American dream need not forever be deferred." She goes on:

> Many seek only to satisfy their private work wants. To satisfy private interests. But this is the great danger America faces. That we will cease to be one nation and become instead a collection of interest groups: city against suburb, region against region, individual against individual. Each seeking to satisfy private wants. If that happens, who then will speak for America? Who then will speak for the common good?

## *Conclusion*

With the ever-changing nature of the political American dream and the legislation that both guides and informs it, the body of literature devoted to the subject is sure to continue growing. Americans are united by their dream of freedom and equality, which means that the nation can expect a future that resembles our past in some ways. Because Americans have always been a nation of self-reliant, individualistic optimists, their political landscape, both past and future, will continue to be supported by the foundation of the American dream, which is, of course, inherently political.

I HEARTILY ACCEPT THE MOTTO,—"THAT GOVERNMENT IS BEST WHICH GOVERNS LEAST"; AND I SHOULD LIKE TO SEE IT ACTED UP TO MORE RAPIDLY AND SYSTEMATICALLY."

**Source:** Henry David Thoreau, *Civil Disobedience*

## SOURCES

Hamilton, Alexander, *The Federalist Papers*, 1787–1788, www.foundingfathers.info/federalistpapers/fedindex.htm (December 16, 2006).

Henry, Patrick, "Give Me Liberty or Give Me Death," March 1775, www.history.org/Almanack/life/politics/giveme.cfm (December 16, 2006).

Johnson, Lyndon B., "The Great Society," May 22, 1964, www.lbjlib.utexas.edu/johnson/archives.hom/speeches.hom/640522.asp (December 16, 2006).

Jordan, Barbara, "1976 Democratic Convention Keynote Address: Who Then Will Speak for the Common Good?," July 12, 1976, www.elf.net/bjordan/keynote.html (December16, 2006).

King, Martin Luther, Jr., "I Have a Dream," August 28, 1963, www.usconstitution.net/dream.html (December 16, 2006).

Lincoln, Abraham, "The Gettysburg Address," November 19, 1863, showcase.netins.net/web/creative/lincoln/speeches/gettysburg.htm (December 16, 2006).

Madison, James, *The Bill of Rights*, 1789, usinfo.state.gov/usa/infousa/facts/funddocs/billeng.htm (December 16, 2006).

Roosevelt, Franklin Delano, "The Inaugural Speech of Franklin Delano Roosevelt," March 4, 1933, www.hpol.org/fdr/inaug (December 16, 2006).

Stanton, Elizabeth Cady, *Seneca Falls Declaration of Sentiments*, 1848, usinfo.state.gov/usa/infousa/facts/democrac/17.htm (December 16, 2006).

"Declaration of Independence," on *NARA: The National Archives Experience*, www.archives.gov/national-archives-experience/charters/declaration_transcript.html (January 8, 2007).

Thoreau, Henry David, "Civil Disobedience," in *Walden and Civil Disobedience*, Harper & Row, 1965, pp. 251–52; originally published in 1849.

X, Malcolm, "The Ballot or the Bullet," April 3, 1964, www.edchange.org/multicultural/speeches/malcolm_x_ballot.html (December 27, 2006).

# The Asian American Dream

### Introduction

Although the first Asian immigrants to the United States were eighteenth-century Filipino sailors making port in undeveloped territory now belonging to Louisiana, the steady migration of Asians from their home countries did not begin until a century later with the gold rush, the transcontinental railroad, and the western land boom. The Asian American dream mirrored the traditional American dream: the overwhelming desire both to escape economic, social, and political hardship and to achieve a level of prosperity and success impossible in their homeland. Asian immigrants, like other immigrants, saw America as the land of opportunity and fortune. However, for them the American dream was divided into two distinct promises for the future. Some saw America as a place where they could earn money to support a family and future back in their home country, while others saw America as a place to secure a new, prosperous identity, both personal and national. Both of these promises were difficult to realize.

In the mid-nineteenth century, the Chinese immigrant population became a vital force in the development of the western United States. By 1870, Chinese workers comprised 20 percent of California's labor force and occupied a variety of positions in mining, farming, fishing, factory work, and railroad construction. Though contract laborers from southern China had been recruited as a cheap way to ensure American

*Adults who as children were evacuated from Vietnam as part of Operation Babylift* AP Images

progress, their strong work ethic and willingness to take even the lowest-paying jobs quickly inspired anti-Chinese sentiment. Many Americans, particularly those affected by the depression of 1876, accused the Chinese workers of taking away their jobs and, subsequently, their livelihoods. This negative and often violent opinion eventually inspired Congress to pass the Chinese Exclusion Act of 1882, a law making immigration and naturalization difficult for the Chinese for the next sixty years.

Despite the Chinese Exclusion Act and the volatile relationship between Chinese laborers and their American employers, the Asian American dream was not lost. Americans still wanted a discount on progress and, in the late nineteenth century, replaced the Chinese with hopeful immigrants from Japan, Korea, and India. But, as happened with the Chinese, anti-Asian sentiment soon arose. The U.S. Civil Rights Movement in the 1960s pushed for restrictions to be lifted and annual quotas dramatically increased. Around this time, the United States government, eager to lead the race in technological advancement, created legislation that encouraged foreign-born engineers, doctors, and scientists to immigrate to America. Opportunity invited young and old, and success came in the form of education, a more liberated society, and the promise of a stable future as an American.

## American Opportunity

The Asian immigrants sought the traditional American dream: With a little hard work, certain success would soon follow. Ruthanne Lum McCunn's children's book *Pie-Biter* (1983) tells the story of Hoi, a young Chinese boy whose ingenuity, determination, and love of pies help him triumph over adversity as he works on the transcontinental railroad. To reflect the hero's journey to success, McCunn writes Hoi's tale as a combination of the American tall tale and the quintessential American success story. As Hoi grows from hopeful adolescent to strong young man, McCunn allows Hoi to be a true American hero without sacrificing his culture. Framed in the folk tradition, *Pie-Biter* is an obvious example of how immigrants saw America as the "Land of the Golden Mountain," as is Lawrence Yep's *Dragon's Gate* (1993), part of the author's Golden Mountain Chronicles. In Yep's young adult novel, Otter moves to America when he experiences racial discrimination in his home country, China. Otter, like Hoi, works on the transcontinental railroad, but when Otter arrives in America, he no longer sees the fields of gold he once imagined. In contrast to Hoi, who wants to make something of himself in his new homeland, Otter wishes to take what he learns in America back to China where he will free his people from the invading Manchus. Both *Pie-Biter* and *Dragon's Gate*, though fictional, clearly illustrate the two opposing dreams: reaping the opportunity America has to offer either to improve life back home or to make a fresh start in a young, developing nation.

## American Outcasts

Those immigrants who decided to establish their futures by settling in the United States and becoming American frequently found themselves alienated, punished, and exiled for their Asian heritage. In *Farewell to Manzanar* (1972), Jeanne Houston writes an autobiographical account of her family's experience when the U.S. government sends them, along with 10,000 other Japanese Americans, to an internment camp in Manzanar, California, as a reaction to Japanese involvement in World War II. Houston recounts her father's desperate need to cover up their Japanese roots after Pearl Harbor was bombed: "That night Papa burned the flag he had brought with him from Hiroshima thirty-five years earlier.... He burned a lot of papers too, documents, anything that might suggest he still had some connection with Japan." However, her father's rush to secrecy is not enough, and the family is soon deported to the camp, identified as "Japanese," despite their hard-fought struggle to claim a place in American society.

Monica Itoi Sone tells a similar story in her autobiography, *Nisei Daughter* (1953). With chapters titled "We Meet Real Japanese" and "We Are Outcasts," Sone discusses the personal humiliation and indignities her family suffered as they were sent to a World War II internment camp in Idaho. Sone also talks about the day she first understood her ethnic heritage. She says simply: "One day when I was a happy six-year-old, I made the shocking discovery that I had Japanese blood. I was a Japanese." She was a "Nisei," or American-born child of Japanese immigrants to the United States. As learned from society, Sone believed Japanese was something foreign, something that did not belong, an outsider. Yet Sone quickly realizes she is exactly what she thought she was not; Japanese American is no different from Japanese, as local politician Mr. Sakaguchi declares:

> A future here! Bah! Words, words! How many sons of ours with a beautiful bachelor's degree are accepted into American life? Name me one young man who is now working in an American firm on equal terms with his white colleagues. Our Nisei engineers push lawn mowers. Men with degrees in chemistry and physics do research in the fruit stands of the public market. And they all rot away inside.

Both Houston and Sone show how racial discrimination robbed the Asian American community of their American, not to mention human, rights. For Houston and Sone, the American fairy tale was a tall tale.

## American Pride

Yet for families like Houston's and Sone's, assimilation into the American culture was imagined to be the key to success. They wanted to become part of the mainstream, to be treated as equals in a land that had a Constitution guaranteeing that right. C. Y. Lee's *Flower Drum Song* (1957), as well as the film adaptation of the novel by Rodgers and Hammerstein, focuses on the Wang family. Wang Ta, a second-generation Chinese American living in San Francisco's Chinatown, longs for a successful career and romance, while his brother Wang San tries to become a typical American teenager.

*Chinese laborers on a hand car on the Northwest Pacific Railway in the 1880s* © *Bettmann/Corbis*

The difference between Wang Ta, Wang San, and their father, Wang Chi-yang, is obvious:

> [Wang Chi-yang] lived comfortably in a two-story house three blocks away from Grant Avenue that he had bought four years ago, a house decorated with Chinese paintings and couplet scrolls, furnished with uncomfortable but expensive teakwood tables and chairs, and staffed with two servants and a cook whom he had brought from Hunan Province. The only "impure" elements in his household were his two sons, Wang Ta and Wang San, especially the latter, who had in four years learned to act like a cowboy and talk like the characters in a Spillane movie.

To achieve his father's level of success, Wang Ta "adopted many American ideas" in "four years of American education." As an immigrant himself, Lee wrote *Flower Drum Song* to portray his own experiences and observations as a young man growing up in the United States during the late 1940s. The novel illustrates the complex struggle of a younger generation to adapt to a new culture, much to the dismay and disapproval of an older generation that is desperately trying to keep the traditional ways alive.

### American Identity

As shown in *Flower Drum Song* through Wang San's character, the younger generation struggled to claim a new identity, despite the disapproval of their elders. Maxine Hong Kingston's *Tripmaster Monkey* (1989) focuses on Wittman Ah Sing, a fifth-generation Chinese American artist whose spiritual journey in the 1960s forces him to evaluate who he really is and what he really wants from life. His name points ironically to the tenuous balance between his American culture and his Chinese roots, both playing to the American poet Walt Whitman and his famous line in *Leaves of Grass*, "I sing the body electric," and echoing the aural tones of a traditional Chinese moniker. Like Whitman, Sing explores his identity through his art; Sing's alter ego and the protagonist of his play, the Chinese Monkey King, is a rebellious trickster with the ability to adapt and change. In creating his art, Sing can live in a world of his own making, rather than a world of stereotypes. The use of the trickster monkey also operates on many cultural levels, not only inviting comparison to the Chinese folktale, but also acting as a reminder of the racial epithets of the time. During the Spanish-American War in the Philippines, Filipinos were dubbed monkeys by American soldiers, a name that unfortunately caught on when Filipinos immigrated to the United States.

Philip Kan Gotanda's 2004 play *The Wind Cries Mary* explores ambivalence about one's own cultural ideal. Inspired by *Hedda Gabler*, Heinrik Ibsen's 1890 study of middle-class dissatisfaction, Gotanda presents Eiko, a young Japanese American wife in San Francisco in the late 1960s stifled by societal expectations. Eiko's jealousy, self-loathing, and resentment spring from her own success at becoming what her culture told her she should be: a subservient wife. Her unhappiness leaves a wide swath of destruction in its wake. Eiko exists in a time of great societal change in the United States; if she had channeled the momentum of the era, she may have redefined herself and survived.

Redefining oneself is a theme running through Jean Okimoto's *Molly by Any Other Name* (1990) and Aimee Phan's *We Should Never Meet* (2004). In Okimoto's novel, seventeen-year-old Asian American Molly Fletcher, adopted as an infant by a white couple, longs to discover her birth parents and uncover her national heritage. Molly is a young woman in limbo, uncertain who she is and who she might be. In writing *We Shall Never Meet*, Aimee Phan followed this same type of quest, inspired by her mother, aunt, and uncle, who were all refugee children evacuated from Saigon in 1975 through Operation Babylift. In addition, Phan drew on her mother's social work experiences with Vietnamese foster children, as well as her own research trip to Vietnam. Phan's collection of short stories addresses the limbo of identity and displaced lives created by Operation Babylift, spanning time from 1975 to the present day. The painful loss of and subsequent search for origins, the uncertain future in America, and assimilation of a new culture make forging a new life in the States exceedingly difficult for Phan's characters. In an interview on curledup.com, Phan comments on the way Kim, Huan, Mai, and Vinh handle their experiences:

*Photo of an anti-Japanese WWII propaganda poster* © *Swim Ink 2, LLC/Corbis*

While Kim and Huan were both on the Babylift, Huan's adoption worked out and Kim's didn't. Because of this, Kim's life followed a very different path that was difficult and painful for her. Mai and Vinh were also affected by their foster care upbringings: Mai thrived under her supportive parents, while Vinh dropped out of school because his foster parents didn't care. . . . They think America is to blame for their unhappiness and their only means of action is to return the injustice against people that represent America and assimilation.

Amy Tan also takes on the complicated questions of American assimilation in *The Joy Luck Club* (1989). Suyuan Woo, Lindo Jong, An-Mei Hsu, and Ying-ying St. Clair, four Chinese women who immigrated to the United States after World War II, blame the negative experiences in their lives on the restrictive social codes and traditions of their Chinese heritage, as illustrated by An-Mei's commentary, "I was raised the Chinese way: I was taught to desire nothing, to swallow other people's misery, to eat my own bitterness." But the women also believe their daughters should not completely eschew all traces of their heritage. "I wanted my children to have the best combination: American circumstances and Chinese character," Lindo says. "How could I know these two things do not mix?" This philosophy is also held by Katie Takeshima's mother in Cynthia Kadohata's young adult novel, *Kira-Kira* (2005). Early in the book, Katie reports, "[My mother] was dismayed over how un-Japanese [my sister and I] were and vowed to send us to Japan one day." Despite working in an American poultry processing plant alongside her husband, Mrs. Takeshima tries to instill Japanese values in Katie, shown in this incident prior to her daughter's first day at school: "Right then my mother came in with scissors to chop off my long straight hair. This was a ritual all the local Japanese mothers performed the day before they sent their daughters off to school for the first time." The challenge for the daughters in both *The Joy Luck Club* and *Kira-Kira*, as for many Asian Americans, was difficult: How could people retain the traditions of their homeland and still succeed as Americans?

## Conclusion

Asian Americans are still often asked, "Where are you from?" proving the complex issues surrounding a truly American identity remain. Today, the stereotype of the Asian American has developed from the "yellow peril" into the model minority. Asian Americans work hard to dispel the cardboard image of the hard-working, overachieving, studious researcher/scholar/scientist/math whiz, fighting to achieve the American dream while portraying a real picture

WE HAD EXPLORED THE EXOTIC ISLAND OF THE JAPANESE. I HAD FELT THE CHARM OF ITS PEOPLE. I HAD BEEN IMPRESSED BY ITS MODERN CITIES AS WELL AS BY ITS HISTORIC BEAUTY, BUT I HAD FELT I WAS AN ALIEN AMONG THEM."

**Source:** Monica Sone, *Nisei Daughter*

of what it means to have a rich cultural heritage that is both American and Asian.

## SOURCES

Gaines, Luan, "An Interview with Aimee Phan," *Curledup.com*, www.curledup.com/intaphan.htm (August 21, 2006).

Houston, Jeanne, *Farewell to Manzanar*, Dell Laurel-Leaf, 1983, p. 6.

Kadohata, Cynthia, *Kira-Kira*, Atheneum Books for Young Readers, 2004, p. 51.

Lee, C. Y., *Flower Drum Song*, Dell, 1966, p. 4.

Okimoto, Jean Davies, *Molly by Any Other Name*, Backinprint.com, 2000.

Phan, Aimee, *We Should Never Meet*, St. Martin's Press, 2004.

Sone, Monica Itoi, *Nisei Daughter*, University of Washington Press, 1979, p. 121.

Tan, Amy, *The Joy Luck Club*, G. P. Putnam's Sons, 1989, pp. 215, 254.

# The Colonial American Dream

### Introduction

The roots of the American dream can be traced all the way back to the first colonists to settle the New World. The Puritans who fled religious persecution in England became self-made successes throughout New England largely on the strength of their spiritual beliefs that it was preordained. For them, life on earth was a constant battle between the forces of good and the forces of evil, and the only way to battle evil was to be ambitious, work hard, and always strive for success. Their religion taught them that prosperity on earth would eventually lead to spiritual peace and eternal life. They sought wealth and status, but only to reap the rewards of heaven.

Colonial literature is rife with Puritanical and religious themes, but slavery, the American Revolution, and political and cultural change also appear as topics of special interest in the novels, poetry, short stories, essays, and letters from and about this very unique moment in American history—the moment the American dream was born.

### Religion

Puritanical colonial literature reveals the Pilgrims' belief that they were God's chosen people—the new Israelites—whom God protected on their way to the promised land. Because they were chosen, they felt a special responsibility to God and God's divine plan, which demanded they live according to God's Word.

Bible scripture, then, is often quoted in the works of Puritan writers, as are references to sins against God and punishment for offenses made against God. Religious literature from colonial times also reveals the Puritanical belief that America was the result of God's providential design, that the American experience was reliant on Puritan beliefs and codes of behavior.

William Bradford's *Of Plymouth Plantation* describes the trials experienced by Pilgrims in England, Holland, and North America from 1620 to 1647. In it, Bradford regards his fellow Pilgrims as chosen people destined to fulfill God's divine plan who are, in essence, repeating the biblical history of the Israelites. The most widely recognized section of the book is chapter 9, the part of Bradford's story that tells "Of their Voyage, and how they Passed the Sea; and of their Safe Arrival at Cape Cod." The premise of the chapter is that God provided divine guardianship over the Puritans as they made their way to North America, just as he did for the wandering Israelites before finding the promised land of Canaan.

Once the Pilgrims arrive at Cape Cod, though, Bradford shifts his biblical reference and compares their landing to Acts 28.2, which describes how Paul's shipwrecked company was treated by the inhabitants of Malta. Unlike Paul's hosts who protected them against the cold and fed and sheltered them for three months, the Pilgrims found little welcome in their arrival to the New World:

> Being thus passed the vast ocean, and a sea of troubles before in their preparation (as may be remembered by that which went before), they had now no friends to welcome them nor inns to entertain or refresh their weatherbeaten bodies; no houses or much less town to repair to, to seek for succour.

The adversity the Pilgrims faced at Cape Cod only fuels the fire of Bradford's belief that he and his fellow settlers had made it to the promised land and would continue to be protected by God's divine grace. He concludes chapter 9 with these words:

> Yea, let them which have been redeemed of the Lord, show how he hath delivered them from the hand of the oppressor. When they wandered in the desert wilderness out of the way, and found no city to dwell in, both hungry, and thirsty, their soul was overwhelmed in them. Let them confess before the Lord his loving

kindness, and his wonderful works before the sons of men.

Mary Rowlandson's *Captivity Narrative of a Colonial Woman, February, 1675*, regarded by many historians as the first American bestseller, echoes the same religious sentiments found in Bradford's book. In her autobiographical account of being taken captive by Indians in 1675, she liberally quotes scripture and credits her faith in the providence of God for her eventual reunion with the surviving members of her family.

Rowlandson's belief that God had orchestrated her capture and release only strengthened her faith. Her experience caused her to strive even harder to live according to Scripture and fulfill the covenant God had ordained for her and her fellow Pilgrims. This covenant, among other Puritanical beliefs, is described in Cotton Mather's 1702 *Magnalia Christi Americana*, but with far greater literary opulence and grandeur.

Mather, a Puritanical intellectual, minister, and author, attempted in his seven-book, two-volume collection to detail the religious development of the New England colonies from 1620 to 1698. The Latin title, usually translated *The Ecclesiastical History of New England*, hints at the many Latin, Hebrew, and Greek quotes found within the pages of Mather's analysis of the American experiment.

A portion of the *Magnalia* offers Mather's description of the Salem Witch Trials, the infamous moment in the history of Puritan America of which the minister played a vital role. The trials took place over the course of several months during 1692 in Salem, Massachusetts. During that time, men and women accused and convicted of practicing witchcraft were hanged. The trials inspired a widespread witch-hunting hysteria that died out almost as quickly as it started. The witch-hunt has since become synonymous with a particularly American experience, a warning to learn from the mistakes of history lest they be repeated.

Nathaniel Hawthorne reminds readers of this event in *The Scarlet Letter* (1850). Hawthorne was especially interested in the history of Salem, Massachusetts, where he was born and raised, and—not coincidentally—where his ancestor, John Hathorne, had participated in the trials. Having inherited the guilt of his ancestors for their part in the shameful trials, the writer sought to expose the obsessiveness and spiritual

*Salem Witch Trial scene by Howard Pyle*
© Bettmann/Corbis

intolerance of the Puritans by revealing it in historical fiction. *The Scarlet Letter* focuses on the societal effects of guilt and anxiety in a sin-obsessed Puritan colony. In the story, Hester Prynne is condemned to wear a letter "A" for "adulteress" on her clothing as a sign of shame after giving birth to a daughter while her husband was apparently lost at sea. Prynne refuses to divulge the name of the child's father, bears the letter on her breast with dignity, and eventually becomes an important mother figure to the women in her community. In the final chapter of the book, the author writes,

> But there was a more real life for Hester Prynne, here, in New England, that in that unknown region where Pearl had found a home. Here had been her sin; here, her sorrow; and here was yet to be her penitence. She had returned, therefore, and resumed,—of her own free will, for not the sternest magistrate of that iron period would have imposed it,—resumed the symbol of which we have related so dark a tale. Never afterwards did it quit her bosom. But, in the lapse of the toilsome, thoughtful, and self-devoted years that made up Hester's

life, the scarlet letter ceased to be a stigma which attracted the world's scorn and bitterness, and became a type of something to be sorrowed over, and looked upon with awe, yet with reverence too.

Seen through the lens of the Puritanical world Hawthorne sought to criticize, one can see the dark side of the American dream, its good intentions gone wrong, and the paths it would have to take to become something that was no longer "sorrowed over."

## Education

One of those paths was led by Benjamin Franklin whose *Poor Richard's Almanack*, an entertaining and instructive annual magazine published from the 1730s to the 1750s, encouraged American colonists to procure wealth through frugality and hard work. Franklin used wit, humor, and common sense—not religion—to inspire *Almanack* readers to achieve the American dream of success through industry. Franklin was interested in bettering American society in every way and knew, from his own experience with reading and books, that educating the masses was a fundamental step to their improvement. He also recognized the accessibility of periodicals over books.

Franklin wrote the aphorisms that filled *Poor Richard's Almanack* to educate the common folk who rarely, if ever, bought books. Although Franklin was an accomplished printer, author, inventor, statesman, scientist, and diplomat, he used the homey, folksy language of the people in his *Almanack* to ensure that his lessons would be read and remembered. A testament to his foresight is the fact that many, such as "Eat to live, and not live to eat" and "A penny saved is a penny earned" are still respected as wisdom today.

## Opportunity

Slavery in America began around 1619 when twenty enslaved Africans were brought by a Dutch ship to the Virginia colony of Jamestown. Almost 250 years later, the Thirteenth Amendment to the Constitution abolished legal slavery in the United States in 1865.

Phillis Wheatley—thought to have been born in West Africa—was purchased by the wife of a wealthy Boston businessman when she was just seven or eight years old. When the frail, demure child showed signs of unusual intelligence, her owners decided to educate her rather than train her to be a house servant. Wheatley published her first poem in 1767, which led to other publications that brought the young African American woman widespread acclaim. Her *Poems on Various Subjects, Religious and Moral* was widely regarded as a work of genius when it was published in 1773. Because she received a largely religious education, most of her poems focus on Christian themes with classic elegies dominating the collection. She rarely wrote about her own situation. One of the few poems that mention slavery, "On Being Brought From Africa to America," is hardly an indictment of the practice:

> 'Twas mercy brought me from my Pagan land,
> Taught my benighted soul to understand
> That there's a God, that there's a Saviour too:
> Once I redemption neither sought nor knew.
> Some view our sable race with scornful eye,
> "Their colour is a diabolic die."
> Remember, Christians, Negroes, black as Cain,
> May be refin'd, and join th' angelic train.

While Wheatley was denied most of the opportunities treasured by so many of her fellow free colonials, she presents the controversial view that her life was improved as a slave. The poem has drawn criticism from modern African American literary scholars for its implicit endorsement of slavery. Nonetheless, Wheatley is regarded as one of the more gifted poets of her time and an important American literary figure.

A contemporary of Wheatley's, a French immigrant and New York citizen, also wrote glowing accounts about America while glossing over the issue of slavery. J. Hector St. John de Crèvecoeur was born in Normandy in 1735, educated in Bourbon, then moved to New York where he became a naturalized citizen in 1765. His *Letters from an American Farmer*, published in 1782, is a collection of twelve letters written from the point of view of a farmer named James who records his travels from Martha's Vineyard to Nantucket to Charlestown. The letters were responsible for shaping many Europeans' perceptions of America as well as some of the ideas later adopted by the Romantics. Letter 3, titled, "What is an American?", is a celebration of the fledgling country, a place where oppressed Europeans are given the chance to become independent, self-interested landowners. Some historians go so far as to trace the concept of the American dream to de Crèvecoeur, who wrote in letter 3,

> Here individuals of all nations are melted into a new race of men, whose labours and posterity will one day cause great changes in the world. Americans are the western pilgrims, who are carrying along with them that great mass of arts, sciences, vigour, and industry which began long since in the east; they will finish the great circle.... Here the rewards of his industry follow with equal steps the progress of his labour; his labour is founded on the basis of nature, *self-interest*; can it want a stronger allurement?

## *Change*

John and Abigail Adams exchanged over a thousand letters between 1762 and 1801. These treasured American documents chronicle a wealth of social, cultural, and political change that occurred while John Adams served in the Continental Congress, on various diplomatic assignments, as vice president for two terms under George Washington, and then as the second U.S. president. The letters reflect the temper of the times before, during, and after the American Revolution and cover important moments in American history including the drafting of the Declaration of Independence and the resulting emergence of American democracy. According to Gordon S. Wood's 2004 review of *The Letters of John and Abigail Adams*,

> Indeed, as early as 1774 Abigail reminded John that slavery had "always appeared a most iniquitous scheme to me—to fight ourselves for what we are daily robbing and plundering from those who have as good a right to freedom as we have. You know my mind on this subject." It is Abigail's outspokenness on subjects such as slavery that most distinguishes the Adamses' marriage from those of the other Founders, and indeed from those of most eighteenth-century couples.... Every generation of Americans has read into the Adamses' marriage, and into Abigail's role in it, whatever the times seemed to require. During the past generation the times required a marriage of equals and a spokeswoman for feminism and women's rights, and the Adamses' marriage and Abigail seemed ideally to fit the bill.

Changes in American culture were not always determined by politics. Washington Irving's "Rip Van Winkle" (1819) paints a picture of the vast cultural change brought about by the American Revolution. In Irving's story, Rip Van Winkle, an idler who appreciates leisure and is content with his country life, falls asleep for twenty years only to wake and find his slow and happy life challenged by industry and materialism. The story is an indictment of the ethic of hard work and thrift promoted by Benjamin Franklin's *Poor Richard's*

*Engraving of the Battle of Lexington* © *Bettmann/Corbis*

*Almanack*, whose aphorisms helped shape the American consciousness in the years following the Revolution. Irving's story, in both style and content, reflects a burgeoning discomfort with the rapid changes experienced by Americans at a difficult time in their history.

### Inspiration

The changes that shaped the American consciousness after the Revolution were indelible enough to impact writers over a century later. Curiosity about the historic events leading up to the Revolution led one such writer, Robert W. Chambers, to publish a young adult novel, *War Paint and Rouge*, in 1931. Hoping his own interest in the French and Indian War might intrigue young readers, he wrote a romantic adventure story about the French capture of Fort William Henry and their loss of Louisburg.

Thirteen years later, Esther Forbes published *Johnny Tremain* (1943), another young adult novel set in the early years of the republic. Forbes's book focuses on young Johnny Tremain,

an American patriot and revolutionary soldier, who matures throughout the course of the book. Forbes originally wrote *Johnny Tremain* because she wanted to show children of the twentieth century how hard life was for early American children. Then, after the book was published, America found itself in yet another revolutionary struggle: World War II. In 1944, the year of D-Day and the invasion of Normandy, *Johnny Tremain* won the Newbery Medal, largely due to the book's realistic depiction of the Revolutionary era, a time that found the American dream's focus slightly shifted but firmly rooted in the concept of independence and hard-won success.

### Conclusion

Literature of and about the colonial history of the United States provides as much insight into that past era as it does into our present day. The ideals that inspired the earliest Americans to build their country from the ground up remain the ideals that continue to power modern

> WHAT THEN IS THE AMERICAN, THIS NEW MAN?...HE IS AN AMERICAN, WHO, LEAVING BEHIND HIM ALL HIS ANCIENT PREJUDICES AND MANNERS, RECEIVES NEW ONES FROM THE NEW MODE OF LIFE HE HAS EMBRACED, THE NEW GOVERNMENT HE OBEYS, AND THE NEW RANK HE HOLDS. HE HAS BECOME AN AMERICAN BY BEING RECEIVED IN THE BROAD LAP OF OUR GREAT ALMA MATER. HERE INDIVIDUALS OF ALL RACES ARE MELTED INTO A NEW RACE OF MAN, WHOSE LABOURS AND POSTERITY WILL ONE DAY CAUSE GREAT CHANGES IN THE WORLD. AMERICANS ARE THE WESTERN PILGRIMS."

**Source:** Hector St. John J. de Crévecoeur, *Letters from an American Farmer*

American dreams. Belief in religious freedom, the power of education, opportunities to be seized, and the possibility of positive change inspired the first wave of American settlers, just as they have inspired Americans—whether by birth or by choice—for centuries.

## SOURCES

Bradford, William, *Of Plymouth Plantation: 1620–1647*, Modern Library, 1981; reprint, *The Plymouth Colony Archive*, etext.virginia.edu/users/deetz/Plymouth/bradford.html (December 26, 2006).

de Crévecoeur, J. Hector St. John, "Letter 3" of *Letters from an American Farmer*, reprinted from the original ed. by W. P. Trent, The University of Virginia, 1904, xroads.virginia.edu/~hyper/CREV/letter03.html (December 7, 2006).

Franklin, Benjamin, *Poor Richard's Almanack*, 1773, usinfo.state.gov/usa/infousa/facts/loa/bf1733.htm (December 7, 2006).

Hawthorne, Nathaniel, *The Scarlet Letter*, Ticknor, Reed & Fields, 1850; reprint, Bartleby.com, 1999, www.bartleby.com/83 (December 26, 2006).

Wheatley, Phyllis, "On Being Brought from Africa to America," in *Concise Anthology of American Literature 5th Ed.*, edited by George McMichael, et al., Prentice Hall, 2001, p. 379; originally published in *Poems on Various Subjects*, 1773.

Wood, Gordon S., "Pursuit of Happiness: A Review of The Letters of John and Abigail Adams," in the *New Republic Online*, April 8, 2004, (December 7, 2006).

# The Frontier American Dream

### Introduction: The Frontier Opens

In *The Epic of America*, published in 1931, James Truslow Adams notes the early days of the American dream, as created by the wild frontier:

> Two of the strongest influences in our life, religion and the frontier, made in our formative periods for a limited and intolerant spiritual life.... Because the frontiersmen had developed the right combination of qualities to conquer the wilderness, they began to believe quite naturally that they knew best, so to say, how to conquer the world, to solve its problems, and that their own qualities were the only ones worth a man's having.... The American doctrine had developed, through the long training of the common man in local politics, that anyone could do anything.

The frontier became symbolic of the can-do spirit, as well as of the limitless amount of space where a person could put that spirit to good use. The "American Way" also grew from the freedom to act, and the notion that America was a place where everyone could be and do what they wanted, where they wanted, and how they wanted, was born. Unfortunately, this unbridled access to boundless resources and a self-serving attitude led to fierce competition, greed, and territorial consumption. The frontier went from wide open space for plenty to first-come-first-served. As a result, many novels depicting the period are often considered morality tales because the villainous characters have lost their true American values.

## Trailblazing the Legend of the American Dream

The story of Daniel Boone represents the legend of a true American hero. A pioneer who made a home in the wilderness, Boone wrote his own story in the early 1800s, detailing his life from 1769 to 1784. The second section of the book, written by Francis Lister Hawks, is an account of Boone's life from his childhood to his death in 1818. Boone's experiences with Native Americans and his tales of survival in the frontier establish Boone as the epitome of a free, confident, and independent American man.

A contemporary of Boone, Robert Montgomery Bird wrote *Nick of the Woods, Or Adventures of Prairie Life* in 1837; however, though the story deals with the settlement of Kentucky in the 1780s, an effort with which Boone was actively involved, Bird's novel is not based on biographical or autographical experiences. Instead, *Nick of the Woods* is considered romantic historical fiction, in the style of Sir Walter Scott and James Fenimore Cooper, but Bird and Cooper had different views of the frontiersmen and his Native American counterparts. While Cooper saw Native Americans as "noble savages," Bird believed the opposite, as suggested by the preface to his novel:

> The purposes of the author, in his book, confined him to real Indians. He drew them as, in his judgment, they existed—and as, according to all observation, they still exist wherever not softened by cultivation,—ignorant, violent, debased, brutal; he drew them, too, as they appeared, and still appear, in war—or the scalp-hunt—when all the worst deformities of the savage temperament receive their strongest and fiercest development.

In terms of the white frontiersmen, Bird wanted to show the men also as they were, writing a story that illustrated how the frontier could change a man:

> The whole object was here to portray the peculiar characteristics of a class of men, very limited, of course, in number, but found, in the old Indian days, scattered, at intervals, along the extreme frontier of every State, from New York to Georgia; men in whom the terrible barbarities of the savages, suffered through their families, or their friends and neighbours, had wrought a change of temper as strange as fearful.... No one conversant with the history of border affairs can fail to recollect some one or more instances of solitary men, bereaved fathers or orphaned sons, the sole survivors, sometimes, of exterminated households, who remained only to devote themselves to lives of vengeance; and "Indian-hating."

*Daniel Boone* The Library of Congress

Despite the efforts of Bird and other authors to expose the harsh realities of frontier life, the romantic poetic image of the frontiersman continued to flourish. In 1906, Joseph Altsheler wrote *Kentucky Frontiersman: The Adventures of Henry Ware*, a novel that emphasized the excitement of pioneering across the mountains and into unknown territory. Like Boone, young Henry Ware embodies the true American spirit. He learns the skills to become a man of the forest, gains the respect of Chief Black Cloud when he is captured by an Indian hunting party, and ultimately heads the charge to save the new pioneer settlement from hostile Shawnee. Ware defines American manhood as he proves himself in the wilderness and grows the myth of American adventure.

Forty years after the Henry Ware story, A. B. Guthrie Jr. wrote the first of six books in an epic series, *The Big Sky*. Boone Caudill, Jim Deakins, and Dick Summers travel the Missouri River from St. Louis to the Rockies, living the frontier dream as trappers, traders, guides, and explorers. Like Ware, main character Caudill is a Kentuckian looking for a new life and exciting adventure and becomes an untamed mountain man. But Guthrie did not romanticize the West as did Altsheler; in fact, more like Bird, Guthrie dug deeper, to the heart of the frontier desire. Sherry Jones, in an article describing Guthrie as one of "The 100 Most Influential Montanans of the Century," praises the novel as an

> unflinching account not only of the hardships and dangers of the 1830–1845 mountain man era, but also a glimpse into the meaning of our own existence here—the reasons why we come, the reasons why we stay. True to Guthrie's bid for honesty, the answers aren't always pretty.

Jones also crowns Caudill as a "quintessential anti-hero, a mean moody misanthrope who heads West to escape his troubled past as well as to seek adventure and freedom. . . . [But] the one thing he can't run away from is himself."

## The Good, The Bad, and the Moral

As territories and states were established in western America, the definition of the unexplored, untamed frontier gradually grew to incorporate the definition of the unexplored, untamed Wild West. Along the way, the tough, courageous woodsman transformed into an adventurer of another kind: the cowboy. Walter Van Tilburg Clark published *The Ox-Bow Incident* (1940), a gritty, realistic story of mob violence in the western frontier. Set in 1885, the novel deals with the lynching of three innocent men, but is not an ordinary melodramatic Western. Clark places a universal story about good and evil in the frame of the typical Western genre, as noted by Wallace Stegner in his introduction to the novel. Stegner considers civilization Clark's theme and claims "the West is only his raw material." Clark, Stegner writes, "wanted the West to become a true civilization, not a ruthless occupation disguised as a romantic myth." By thoroughly examining the moral question of the lynching, *The Ox-Bow Incident* demonstrates that good characters cannot be determined by the color of their hats, and those people you assume are evil may not be. In this way, the novel reveals, as Stegner remarks, "an essentially false, excessively masculine society" and "the way in which individuals, out of personal inadequacy, out of mistaken loyalties and priorities, out of a fear of seeming to be womanish, or out of plain cowardice, let themselves be pushed into murder."

Clark's moral questions about the law of the western frontier continue in Cormac MacCarthy's *Blood Meridian* (1985). Set in the 1850s, the violent story follows bounty hunters on their quest for Indian scalps near the Texas-Mexico border. The Kid, a young runaway, joins this murderous posse, and as the bounty hunters become savages who leave a trail of blood across the prairie, the Kid submits to the senseless violence because he has no higher purpose than to help play out this nightmare. Both *Blood Meridian* and *The Ox-Bow Incident* use the conventions of the frontier genre to interrogate and challenge the once clear-cut definition of right and wrong, as defined by the Western stereotype. In these games, the cowboys are not always the correct side to play for, and their motives are not always upstanding.

Pete Dexter's *Deadwood* (1986) also denies the romanticism of the West, despite the reputation of its main characters, Charley Utter and Wild Bill Hickok, two historic figures of the wild frontier. After the Civil War, Utter and Hickok head for Deadwood, a Black Hills gold mining town, where they gamble and reflect on their varied and rough life experiences. Hickok, an old, ailing gunfighter, goes to Deadwood for solitude, drink, and card games. But in this town where unsuccessful miners, bounty hunters, and immigrants settled as a last resort, Hickok leads anything but a peaceful life and is murdered; thus, the legend of the West, the American myth, has been shot cold and left for dead.

## American Women of the West

Zane Grey's *Riders of the Purple Sage* (1912) focuses on a woman's frontier dream. Set in Utah in the late nineteenth century, the plot revolves around Jane Withersteen, a young Mormon woman who, as her father's sole heir, now owns his ranch. The Mormon elders want to control her headstrong ways by marrying her off to a polygamist. Jane does not want to become one of the man's many wives, knowing she will be robbed of both her freedom and the community position that her father's land gives her. As Tull, her potential suitor and a church elder, chides, "Jane Withersteen, your father left you with wealth and power. It has turned your head. You haven't yet come to see the place of Mormon women." Even though Lassiter, heroic gunslinger in black, rides into town and saves the day, the story, at its core, still shows an independent woman solving her own problems and dealing with her own struggles.

Unlike *Riders of the Purple Sage*, Miriam Davis Colt's *Went to Kansas* (1862) is a true account of a woman's experience in the frontier. Published by the Laura Ingalls Wilder Publishing Company, this autobiography does resemble Grey's novel in its portrayal of female strength and perseverance in the Wild West, as Colt describes the harrowing journey her family made from New York to Kansas in the 1850s. This story of overcoming daily hardships shows how women had to keep the family together and provide for basic survival needs, often sacrificing comfort for others, as shown by her May 16, 1856, entry:

> Still rainy, damp and cold. My husband has brought in the two side-boards that fill the vacancy between the "wagon bed" and the white cover, has laid them side by side in the loft above, and says, "Miriam, you may make your bed on the smooth surface of these two boards." I say to him, "No; as you have to work hard, you shall have the boards, and with one pillow and your blanket, you will have an even bed, though it is hard. I will take the other pillow, the comfortable [*sic*] and blankets, and with the children will couch close by, endeavoring to suit myself to the warpings, rough edges and lappings of our 'shaky' floor."

While the strong frontier male was often solitary and self-motivating, the strong frontier woman was inspired by community. Her sense of adventure was tempered by duty and by the need to make a home in an unfamiliar land.

Conrad Richter's *The Town*, published in 1950 as the final chapter in his "Awakening Land" trilogy, places pioneer woman Sayward Wheeler in the middle of Ohio's flourishing growth from wilderness to city. Like Miriam Colt, Wheeler represents the heart and backbone of her family and community. In the first two books of the series, Wheeler struggles, like Colt, to make a home in territory unknown, while *The Town* shows her slowly adjusting to progress. Wheeler is not keen on the changes and, like Jane Withersteen, does not hesitate to express her opinions. Richter won the 1951 Pulitzer Prize for *The Town*.

In 1972, Wallace Stegner wrote *Angle of Repose*, which won the Pulitzer Prize for fiction. Combining Colt's autobiographical flavor and Richter's storytelling style, Stegner, through the character of a retired history professor investigating his grandparents' life, used the personal correspondence of unknown nineteenth-century writer Mary Hallock Foote to make the story of Susan Ward and her husband come to life. Elegant, educated, and independent, Susan provides an interesting contrast to her husband,

*Billy the Kid* Getty Images

Oliver, a charming adventurer lacking manners. With Oliver, Susan endures her first journey across America, and as an easterner, she is mortified by what she finds. Eventually, despite the dismal culture, dirt, and heat, Susan grows to appreciate her new home, though her East Coast background forces her to question Oliver's worth as well as her decision to sacrifice everything for the promise of adventure. In this way, *Angle of Repose* shows America struggling to grow, yet trapped between east and west, risk and comfort, refinement and roughness, dreams and reality.

> "KENTUCKY WAS BECOMING EVERY DAY A MORE SETTLED AND CIVILIZED REGION, AND BOONE'S HEART GREW SICK. HE HAD SOUGHT THE WILDERNESS, AND MEN WERE FAST TAKING IT AWAY FROM HIM. HE BEGAN TO THINK OF MOVING."

**Source:** Daniel Boone, *Daniel Boone: His Own Story*

## Conclusion: The Frontier Closes

Edna Ferber's *Giant* (1952) offers a contrast to the early days of the frontier by framing the story in the years of the Texas oil boom. Gone are the days of exploring mountains and building homes and towns with bare hands. This frontier is a rich one, one in which money is made from exploiting both natural and human resources. This view of Texas is a microcosm for America, as shown when Leslie Lynnton, a Virginian who eventually marries Texan Jordan "Bick" Benedict, accidentally disrespects Texas and must clarify her opinion: "It's another world, it sounds so big and new and different," she says. "I love it. The cactus and the cowboys and the Alamo and the sky and the horses and the Mexicans and the freedom. It's really America, isn't it." Leslie lumps Mexicans in with flora, fauna, and freedom, viewing them as intertwined, inseparable, and there for the taking. In *Giant*, the frontier has become a grab-bag for cattle barons and oil men, where hardtack and hard beds have given way to luxury, and staking a claim on American soil has complex ties to Mexican immigration, rather than wagon trains west. By the end of the epic, transportation and communication are closing the frontier, and the last generation of frontierspeople find themselves vestiges of a passing era.

## SOURCES

Bird, Robert Montgomery, and Curtis Dahl, "Preface," in *Nick of the Woods, Or Adventures of Prairie Life*, Carey, Lea & Blanchard, 1837; reprint, Project Gutenberg eBook, November 2004, www.gutenberg.org/etext/13970 (December 15, 2006).

Boone, Daniel, *Daniel Boone: His Own Story*, Applewood Books, 1844; reprint, 1996, p. 117.

Colt, Miriam D., *Went to Kansas*, Laura Ingalls Wilder Publishing Company, 1862, www.kancoll.org/books/colt/c_chap03.htm (December 30, 2006).

Ferber, Edna, *Giant*, Doubleday, 1952; reprint, Harper Perennial Classics, 2000, p. 75.

Grey, Zane, *Riders of the Purple Sage*, Harper & Brothers, 1912; reprint, Modern Library Classics, 2002, p. 7.

"History of the U.S. Dream (Review of *The Epic of America*)," *Time Magazine*, October 5, 1931, www.time.com/time/magazine/article/0,9171,753061-1,00.html (December 30, 2006).

Jones, Sherry, "A. B. Guthrie: The 100 Most Influential Montanans of the Century," in the *Missoulian Online*, www.missoulian.com/specials/100montanans/list/004.html (December 15, 2006).

Stegner, Wallace, "Introduction: Walter Clark's Frontier," in *The Ox-Bow Incident*, Modern Library Classics, 2001, pp. ix–xix.

# *The Hispanic American Dream*

## *Introduction*

The term "Hispanic American" is a deceptively simplistic one. Hispanic Americans—Americans from a Spanish-speaking background—may be from many different ethnic and cultural groups that hail from dozens of countries. Some were already living on land that now makes up California, Arizona, and New Mexico long before the United States laid claim to it; some came to the United States as political refugees; some came seeking economic opportunities. As such, their American dreams reflect familiar themes across American literature, but with unique perspectives. In the late twentieth century, literature reflecting the rich history of the Hispanic American dream began to flourish, giving modern readers a chance to understand just how varied the experiences that comprise it can be.

## *America Dreams of Mexico*

Jeff Shaara's historical novel *Gone for Soldiers* (2000) creates a portrait of soldiers and commanders who fought in the Mexican-American War, but it focuses mainly on white Americans such as General Winfield Scott and Lieutenant Robert E. Lee. Shaara accurately asserts that this war is greatly overshadowed in the American consciousness by the Civil War, which followed less than fifteen years later, but the Mexican-American War played a crucial role in expanding American cultural heritage while at the same time creating a rift between white

*American troops attacking the Fortress of Chapultec, near Mexico City, during the Mexican-American war* MPI/Getty Images

Americans and Hispanics both in and out of the United States.

Although Shaara centers his novel on a handful of American military commanders who fought in the war (and later in the Civil War), he provides glimpses of the Mexican perspective on the conflict. In one instance, a Mexican reporter asks Scott whether or not he thinks the Americans have waged "a bully's war" against Mexico, which was still weak from fighting for its own independence against Spain. Scott avoids answering the complaint directly but draws comparisons between the soldiers on both sides of the conflict:

> Men on both sides were ordered to march into the guns of the enemy, and they obeyed, they stood tall, and most of the time they did not run. The Mexican soldier who stood up to us at San Cosme gate is as much a hero as the man who finally pushed him back.

### Chicano American Dreams

As a result of the Mexican-American War, the United States gained the territory that would become some or all of the states of California,

Nevada, Utah, Arizona, Wyoming, Colorado, and New Mexico. The fact that Mexicans inhabited that land before it transferred to the United States did not make matters any easier for Mexican Americans to come. Louis Valdez's play *Zoot Suit* (1979) tells of an important event in relations between white and Hispanic Americans: the "Sleepy Lagoon" murder trial, in which more than twenty Hispanic youths were tried for the murder of José Díaz at a Los Angeles reservoir frequented by gang members. In the play, the "zoot suit"—with its baggy trousers and long watch chain—is a symbol of a uniquely Hispanic American subculture that thrives in southern California at the dawn of World War II. The character of El Pachuco is the embodiment of this subculture; he encourages protagonist Henry Leyva to recognize the hostile environment in which Hispanic Americans must live, and to fight back. When Henry tells El Pachuco he wants to join the Navy and fight for his country, El Pachuco tries to dissuade him: "Because this ain't your country. Look what's happening all around you...the Mayor has declared all-out war on Chicanos. On you!" Henry is ultimately arrested, tried, and convicted of murder thanks to an overzealous police force and reporters who sensationalize the story. Though his conviction is later overturned, his life is never the same. The same is true for the Chicano community as a whole: After the murder and trial, Hispanic men in zoot suits are routinely beaten and stripped by American soldiers on leave. While *Zoot Suit* is in many ways a chronicle of the failure of the Hispanic American dream, it also represents a unique story of success for Chicano artists: It was the first play written by a Chicano to be performed on Broadway.

Rudolfo Anaya's *Bless Me, Ultima* (1972) tells of yet another unique branch of Chicano American culture: descendants of the original Spanish settlers of New Mexico. In the novel, a young boy named Antonio witnesses events that bring an end to the peace of the small town where he lives. The two halves of Antonio's family represent dual identities within his Hispanic American heritage: His mother wants Antonio to become a farmer and priest, while his father would like him to become a vaquero (cowboy). Antonio's family takes in an old woman, Ultima, who leads Antonio to question his beliefs about God and the nature of good and evil. The woman is also involved in a mystical battle with three daughters of a man named Tenorio whom she believes are witches. At the same time, the townspeople feel the repercussions of World War II as young men leave to fight overseas; many do not return, and those that do are mentally or spiritually broken. Ultima and the war both represent a loss of innocence to Antonio and the town, with Ultima herself being killed in the end.

### Cuban American Dreams

Of course, all Hispanic Americans are not of Mexican heritage. *Anna in the Tropics* (2003) is a play by Nilo Cruz that offers a glimpse of life in the Cuban communities of Florida just prior to the Great Depression. The play centers on a lector named Juan Julian, who reads news and literature to cigar factory workers as they work in exchange for a small amount of their pay. The newly arrived lector decides to read the Tolstoy novel *Anna Karenina* to the workers, who all become swept up in the story as he progresses. The lector himself becomes a sort of voice for the factory workers when one of the owners tries to introduce new machinery into the plant and is voted down after an impassioned speech by Julian. As a parallel to the plot of the Tolstoy novel, one of the

*Desi Arnaz leading the studio band as they play*
Leonard Mccombe/Time Life Pictures/Getty Images

women at the factory, Conchita, has an affair with the charming lector. Ultimately, the lector— a symbol of the traditional ways and, according to some, a barrier to progress—is shot dead by one of the factory owners. The death of the lector is a symbol for the workers' loss of their connection to their Cuban roots.

Oscar Hijuelos paints a portrait of a different group of Cuban Americans striving to achieve their dreams in post–World War II prosperity in *The Mambo Kings Play Songs of Love* (1989). In this novel, Hijuelos tells the story of Nestor and Cesar Castillo, two immigrant Cuban brothers who gain fame playing Latin music in New York in the early 1950s. For the brothers, their heritage is not an obstacle to be overcome; on the contrary, it is their experience growing up in a rich musical tradition that earns them fame and respect. Nestor dreams of realizing success in America, as an inspiring book he reads promises:

> In today's America one must think about
> the future. Ally yourself with progress and

tomorrow! The confident, self-assured man looks to the future and never backward to the past. The heart of every success is a plan that takes you forward.

The brothers even appear on the legendary television sitcom *I Love Lucy* with the Cuban American icon of success, Desi Arnaz. However, after Nestor is killed in a car accident, Cesar can no longer bear to play the music his brother wrote. The mambo itself serves as a metaphor for the Cuban American identity: After becoming wildly popular for a brief time, the musical style is incorporated into more mainstream American music and ultimately loses its unique cultural distinction.

## Puerto Rican American Dreams

Tales of the experiences of Puerto Rican Americans often take place in New York City, which has several large Puerto Rican communities. Nicholasa Mohr's young adult novel *Nilda* (1974) focuses on a girl growing up in a community of Puerto Rican immigrants during World War II. For Nilda and her neighbors, New York is much less hospitable than it would be for the *Mambo Kings*'s Castillo brothers. Mohr's characters live in poverty and face daily persecution. Nilda, the main character, must come to terms with her mother's death while she is still a young girl.

*Almost a Woman* (1998) by Esmeralda Santiago offers a similar tale, though without the conceit of fiction. Santiago's book, a memoir, chronicles her own life as an adolescent and young adult living with her Puerto Rican immigrant family in New York during the 1960s. As a child old enough to remember her homeland, Santiago recognizes the opportunity America represents, and she wants to become an actress. As the oldest of ten children, however, she must also help support the family. Her two responsibilities—to herself, to become a successful American, and to her family, to honor her Puerto Rican heritage—are often at odds. Just being in the United States, she finds that her cultural identity is to some extent a foregone conclusion. Soon after arriving in New York, she tries to clarify to another girl that she is Puerto Rican, not Hispanic. The girl responds, "Same thing. Puerto Rican, Hispanic. That's what we are here." In other words, white Americans see them as if they were all the same.

## Dominican American Dreams

*How the García Girls Lost Their Accents* by Julia Alvarez (1992) tells of yet another group of Hispanic American immigrants who sought refuge in New York: Dominicans fleeing the iron rule of dictator Rafael Trujillo during the 1950s. Like many other Hispanic American authors, Alvarez bases her novel on her own family experiences. However, the García family is different from most other Hispanic immigrant families discussed here. They are far wealthier, living on an estate in the Dominican Republic until their father's outspoken political views cause them to fear for their safety. The title suggests a story of loss; in addition to losing their accents, the García girls lose their home and at least some of their cultural identity. When Yolanda visits her family on the island as an adult after a five-year absence, she tells them about life in the United States:

> In halting Spanish, Yolanda reports on her sisters. When she reverts to English, she is scolded, *"¡En español!"* The more she practices, the sooner she'll be back into her native tongue, the aunts insist. Yes, when she returns to the States, she'll find herself suddenly going blank over some word in English.

However, the story is told in reverse chronological order, ending with the girls as youngsters on their Dominican estate, which serves to emphasize the conflict between the cultures, as well as those elements of their heritage that they carried with them throughout their lives.

## Chicana American Dreams

Mexican American women in particular have developed a body of literature that reveals the breadth of experiences even within a cultural and gender population segment. Ana Castillo's *So Far From God* (1993) is also set in New Mexico, and, like *Bless Me, Ultima*, the novel features mystical events that draw upon Catholic religion as well as traditional folklore and myth. In the book, a woman named Sofi witnesses the lives and deaths of her four daughters: Esperanza (Hope), Fe (Faith), Caridad (Charity), and Loca (Crazy). Loca even dies twice—the first time, when she is three, she is miraculously resurrected during her funeral. The three oldest daughters, whose names indicate the elements of Catholicism they embody, find that their lives cannot be saved by the qualities after which they are named. Loca, who experiences what seems to be an immaculate contraction of

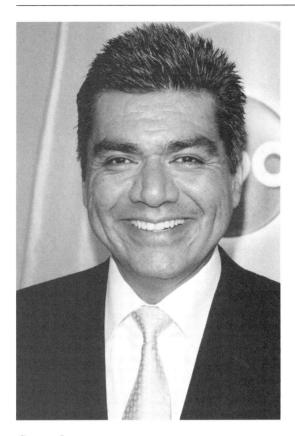

*George Lopez* *Evan Agostini/Getty Images*

HIV—having never engaged in behavior that would expose her to the virus—is sainted after her second death. The novel represents a radical departure from traditional Hispanic American views on Catholicism.

In her work *Borderlands/La Frontera: The New Mestiza* (1987), Gloria Anzaldúa mixes poetry and prose just as she mixes up to eight dialects of English and Spanish to illustrate the existence of people who must live between cultures, not wholly belonging to any single heritage. The "borderlands" to which Anzaldúa refers are both real and symbolic: Having grown up near the Mexico–United States border, and possessing a mixed ancestry, Anzaldúa speaks of transforming landscapes both geographic and emotional. The author discusses the hardships faced by those who are not allowed to be fully integrated into society. At the same time, she points to the strength of a rich cultural heritage as a fundamental source of endurance for those who are kept from the mainstream. Of her faith and philosophy, she writes:

" HELL, ANDY, ... WE CAN'T BUILD OUR LIVES ON THEIR DREAMS. WE'RE MEN, ANDY, WE'RE NOT BOYS ANY LONGER. WE CAN'T BE TIED DOWN TO OLD DREAMS."

**Source:** Rudolfo Anaya, *Bless Me, Ultima*

My spirituality I call spiritual mestizaje, so I think my philosophy is like philosophical mestizaje where I take from all different cultures— for instance, from the cultures of Latin America, the people of color and also the Europeans.

*Real Women Have Curves* (1996) is a play by Josefina Lopez that offers a decidedly different look at cultural heritage. In the play, Ana, a first-generation Mexican American woman who shows great academic promise, is pressured by her mother to forego college and work with her sister in a clothing factory in their East Los Angeles neighborhood. While Ana's mother and sister believe she should dedicate herself to helping the family, Ana believes that they are holding her back from achieving her dreams. Her vision of success is in direct conflict with the sense of duty and traditional values she has inherited from her family. As is the case for so many young Americans as they mature, Ana must balance her parents' dreams for her with her own.

## Conclusion

The Hispanic American dream is best viewed not as a single interwoven tapestry of cultural heritage, but as a mosaic of many different traditions and cultures grouped together solely because they can all be traced in some way back to Spanish explorers and colonists. Though many of these cultures appear only subtly different to outside observers, they are indeed rich and distinct in their views on the promises and opportunities that America represents.

## SOURCES

Alvarez, Julia, *How the García Girls Lost Their Accents*, Plume, 1992, p. 7.

Anaya, Rudolfo, *Bless Me, Ultima*, Warner Books, 1972; reprint, 1994, p. 68.

Anzaldúa, Gloria, *Borderlands/La Frontera: The New Mestiza*, Spinsters/Aunt Lute, 1987, p. 238.

Hijuelos, Oscar, *The Mambo Kings Play Songs of Love*, Farrar, Straus, and Giroux, 1989; reprint, Harper Perennial, 2000, p. 162.

Santiago, Esmeralda, *Almost a Woman*, Perseus Books, 1998, p. 4.

Shaara, Jeff, *Gone for Soldiers*, Ballantine Books, 2000, p. 377.

Valdez, Luis, *Zoot Suit and OtherPlays*, Arte Publico Press, 1992, p. 30.

# *The Immigrant American Dream*

### *Introduction*

For centuries, citizens of the world have arrived on American shores with little more than a suitcase and a dream of a better life. The promise of freedom and opportunity continues to lure foreigners to the United States, even though stories of hardship and isolation comprise the bulk of American immigrant literature. Having reached the promised land, immigrants find themselves faced with unimaginable obstacles. Even Americans who have had a chance to adapt and become "successful"—according to the traditional definition of material success as defined by the American dream—experience feelings of cultural isolation and otherness. Refugees, those who come to America seeking protection from war or political or religious persecution, face entirely different problems. Many of these people long for home and do not necessarily crave the rewards promised by the American dream. Despite the myriad reasons that brought them, American immigrants share a sense of isolation that, in some ways, defines their life experiences.

### *The Jewish American Experience*

The Jewish identity is a complex mélange of religious belief, ethnicity, and culture. This fact is reflected in the rich variety of subjects and styles found in Jewish American literature. The common denominator that ties this body of work together is a sense of otherness expressed by Jewish writers living in a predominately

*The Statue of Liberty* © Corbis

A mighty woman with a torch, whose flame
Is the imprisoned lightning, and her name
Mother of Exiles. From her beacon-hand
Glows world-wide welcome; her mild eyes
    command
The air-bridged harbor that twin cities frame.
"Keep, ancient lands, your storied pomp!" cries
    she
With silent lips. "Give me your tired, your
    poor,
Your huddled masses yearning to breathe free,
The wretched refuse of your teeming shore.
Send these, the homeless, tempest-tost to me,
I lift my lamp beside the golden door!

In Saul Bellow's *Mr. Sammler's Planet* (1970), the Holocaust and the 1960s moon voyages serve as metaphors for distance and detachment. The title character of the novel, Artur Sammler, is a Polish Jew and survivor of World War II. Sammler, an intellectual, philosopher, and occasional Columbia University lecturer, struggles to balance the events of his past and the chaos of contemporary life in 1960s America:

> The persistence, the maniacal push of certain ideas, themselves originally stupid, stupid ideas that had lasted for centuries, this is what drew the most curious reactions from him. The stupid sultanism of a Louis Quatorze reproduced in General de Gaulle—Neo-Charlemagne, someone said. Or the imperial ambition of the Czars in the Mediterranean. They wanted to be the dominant naval power in the Mediterranean, a stupid craving of two centuries, and this, under the "revolutionary" auspices of the Kremlin.

While the United States looks to the future by exploring the frontiers of space, Sammler is caught in the past, unable to distract his consciousness from the horror of the Holocaust. By using the broad context of history, *Mr. Sammler's Planet* illustrates the distance between the myth and the reality of the American dream.

Michael Chabon's Pulitzer Prize–winning novel, *The Amazing Adventures of Kavalier and Clay* (2000), features two Jewish cousins—Joe Kavalier and Sammy Clay—who create a comic-book superhero with Houdini-like powers: the Escapist. The boys, based in part on real-life Superman creators, Joe Shuster and Jerry Siegel, attempt to escape their troubles through the pages of their splashy comic book. Kavalier's family was left behind in Nazi-occupied Prague while Clay, a Brooklyn kid, struggles with secret homosexual urges and an absent father. Set against the backdrop of golden era 1940s adventure comics,

Christian society. Emma Lazarus, who is best known for her poem, "The New Colossus," said, "The truth is that every Jew has to crack for himself this nut of his peculiar position in a non-Jewish country." Although she had an ambivalent relationship with her own Jewishness, Lazarus championed the Jewish cause in her poetry, writing about medieval Christian anti-Semitism from an early age. In 1883, during the rise of American Nativism, she created a society to support the resettlement of exiled East European Jews to Palestine. "The New Colossus" was written specifically for those Jewish exiles but offers a warm welcome to all immigrants. The poem is enshrined on a plaque at the base of the Statue of Liberty, the first glimpse generations of European immigrants saw of their new home as they arrived in New York Harbor:

> Not like the brazen giant of Greek fame,
> With conquering limbs astride from land to
>     land;
> Here at our sea-washed, sunset gates shall
>     stand

swing music, and pulp novels, *The Amazing Adventures of Kavalier and Clay* is an optimistic tragicomedy about escape, transformation, and liberation in post-Depression, pre-war New York. Chabon captures the fantastic struggle between good and evil, both in comics and in American life:

> The Steel Gauntlet, Kapitan Evil, the Panzer, Siegfried, Swastika Man, the Four Horsemen, and Wotan the Wicked all confine their nefarious operations, by and large, to the battlefields of Europe and North Africa, but the Saboteur, King of Infiltration, Vandal Supreme, lives right in Empire City—in a secret redoubt, disguised as a crumbling tenement, in Hell's Kitchen. That is what makes him so effective and feared. He is an American citizen, an ordinary man from a farm in small-town America.

Chabon's story was inspired by the mostly Jewish cartoonists that created comic book heroes like Batman and Superman from the late 1930s through the early 1950s. They created worlds where anything was possible—worlds to which readers could escape. This made them heroes in a sense. In the novel, Clay muses, "Superman, you don't think he's Jewish? Coming over from the old country, changing his name like that. Clark Kent, only a Jew would pick a name like that for himself."

### Outsiders in a New World

Part of the experience of being an immigrant is learning to adapt to American culture. This transition is especially hard for immigrants or descendents of immigrants with existing identity issues. Immigrant literature is rife with stories of minorities within minorities—people whose religious beliefs or sexual identities contrasted with those held by their families or communities. In Gay Talese's *Unto the Sons*, the author describes growing up an outsider on the small island of Ocean City, New Jersey, the son of a southern Italian tailor who immigrated to the United States in 1922. Published in 1992, *Unto the Sons* tells of Talese's family history, written in the author's well-known elegant, exhaustively researched style. His was a Protestant community; he was Catholic. The community was predominantly Irish; Talese was Italian. In chapter 1, Talese writes,

> I was olive-skinned in a freckle-faced town, and I felt unrelated even to my parents, especially my father, who was indeed a foreigner—an unusual man in dress and manner, to whom I bore no physical resemblance and with whom I could never identify. Trim and elegant, with

*Modern apartment building behind slum tenement in Chicago, 1955* © *Bettmann/Corbis*

wavy dark hair and a small rust-colored moustache, he spoke English with an accent and received letters bearing strange-looking stamps.

Like Talese, Frank McCourt was a bookish boy who grew up to write richly detailed narratives about his immigrant experiences. But that is where the similarities end. McCourt, author of the Pulitzer Prize–winning memoir *Angela's Ashes* (1996), about the almost unimaginable poverty he endured as a child in Ireland, followed that best-selling memoir with *'Tis* (1999), a history that focuses on the author's adjustment to the United States as a young man. Born in Brooklyn, New York, in 1930 to Irish parents, McCourt and his family returned to Limerick, Ireland, when he was a small boy. When he was nineteen, McCourt moved back to New York City, served in the army during the Korean War, and then worked a string of jobs before becoming a high school English teacher. It was only after McCourt retired that he pursued his dream of writing. *'Tis* is filled with the language of the exiled. It is rich in despair and anger over having to work so hard to attain the dream—he refers to the American dream as the "tormenting dream" in the book's prologue—that seemed to come so easy to the Ivy League crowd he cleaned up after while working in the Biltmore Hotel's Palm Court. The book begins where *Angela's Ashes* leaves off: with McCourt sailing to America.

There was a book in the ship's library, *Crime and Punishment*, and I thought it might be a good murder mystery even if it was filled with confusing Russian names. I tried to read it in a deck chair but the story made me feel strange, a story about a Russian student, Raskolnikov, who kills an old woman, a moneylender, and then tries to convince himself he's entitled to the money because she's useless to the world and her money would pay for his university expenses so that he could become a lawyer and go round defending people like himself who kill old women for their money. It made me feel strange because of the time in Limerick when I had a job writing threatening letters for an old woman moneylender, Mrs. Finucane, and when she died in a chair I took some of her money to help me pay my fare to America.

It was McCourt's poverty and awkwardness that made him invisible to the brisk, self-assured college students he envied as a nineteen-year-old. Achy Obejas, another immigrant outsider, is the author of the 1994 short story collection, *We Came All the Way From Cuba So You Could Dress Like This?* Obejas, who was born in Havana in 1956 and came to the United States as a child, is dually marginalized as both a Cuban refugee and a lesbian. She plumbs the depths of her complex immigrant identity in her stories, several of which are narrated by lesbians trying to understand the confusing world of love relationships. Refugee outsiders of all kinds—people with AIDS, Cuban boat people, junkies—populate her stories. Unlike immigrants seeking wealth and freedom as promised by the American dream, refugees long, instead, for the comforts of home. It is this distinction that brings the notion of family and cultural history into the discussion of the immigrant American dream.

### The East Indian American Experience

Like the father in the story "We Came All the Way From Cuba So You Could Dress Like This?" the protagonist of Chitra Banerjee Divakaruni's story, "The Unknown Errors of Our Lives," longs for her homeland. More specifically, she longs for her grandmother whom she loves "more than anyone else":

> She had struggled through the Bengali alphabet, submitting to years of classes at that horrible weekend school run by bulge-eyed Mrs. Duttagupta, just so she would be able to read her grandmother's letters and reply to them without asking her parents to intervene. When a letter arrived from India, she slept with it for nights, a faint crackling under her pillow.

When she had trouble making up her mind about something, she asked herself, What would Thakuma do? Ah, the flawed logic of loving! Surprisingly, it helped her, although she was continents and generations apart, in a world whose values must have been unimaginable to a woman who had been married at sixteen and widowed at twenty-four, and who had only left Calcutta once in her entire life for a pilgrimage to Badrinath with the members of her Geeta group.

Divakaruni, born in Calcutta, India, on July 29, 1956, came to the United States when she was nineteen years old. The protagonists that narrate the nine stories of her 2001 collection, *The Unknown Errors of Our Lives*, share Divakaruni's sense of hovering between two worlds: one comprised of her family heritage and traditional Indian beliefs, the other made up of new, American ideas. Divakaruni's hybrid identity is the fodder for her sometimes autobiographical work, which deals mostly with the East Indian American immigrant experience.

The final story in Jhumpa Lahiri's 2000 Pulitzer Prize–winning short story collection, *Interpreter of Maladies*, "The Third and Final Continent," offers another example of East Indian Americans caught between two worlds. This time the protagonist is a male newlywed living in Boston, striving to make the American dream come true for himself and his new, homesick wife. While living and working in America, he finds himself complacently obeying the centuries-old traditions of his homeland:

> My wife's name was Mala. The marriage had been arranged by my older brother and his wife. I regarded the proposition with neither objection nor enthusiasm. It was a duty expected of me, as it was expected of every man. She was the daughter of a school-teacher in Beleghata. I was told that she could cook, knit, embroider, sketch landscapes, and recite poems by Tagore, but these talents could not make up for the fact that she did not possess a fair complexion, and so a string of men had rejected her to her face. She was twenty-seven, an age when her parents had begun to fear that she would never marry, and so they were willing to ship their only child halfway across the world in order to save her from spinsterhood.

Although Lahiri was born in London in 1967 and raised in South Kingstown, Rhode Island, she was steeped in Indian culture from a young age. Her parents followed Indian traditions and took their daughter to Calcutta every two years to visit her grandparents. While abroad, Lahiri spoke Bengali, dressed in Indian clothing, and ate Indian food. These experiences contribute to her understanding of both integration and loss of culture, two predominant themes found in "The Third and Final Continent." Although the narrator is amazed and grateful for his very American achievements of owning a house and sending a son to Harvard, he feels pangs of loss over the culture he has left behind.

### The American Dream Come True

Elia Kazan, Academy Award–winning director of such films as *On the Waterfront*, *Death of a Salesman*, and *A Streetcar Named Desire*, was born Elia Kazanjoglous in Constantinople, Turkey, in 1909. In 1912, his father, a rug merchant, moved the family to the Greek section of Harlem in New York before settling in the suburb of New Rochelle. In 1962, Kazan wrote his first novel, *America, America*, the tale of his uncle's odyssey from poverty-stricken, persecuted Turkey to America and the setbacks that accompanied it. After it became a best seller, Kazan translated it into film. The movie version was named one of the best films of 1963.

One of the more striking moments in the film occurs when the protagonist, twenty-seven-year-old Stavros, falls to his knees and kisses the ground once he reaches America. In *A Life*, Kazan's 1988 autobiography, he relates a disagreement over the scene between he and his production advisors. They thought the gesture cliché and suggested it be cut. Kazan kept the scene because, as he says in the book, "I doubt that anyone born in the United States has or can have a true appreciation of what America is." Clearly, Kazan, despite his outsider status and immigrant background, achieved the American dream and was able to successfully share at least a fictionalized version of it with the world.

### Immigrant Working Conditions

One of the least-discussed aspects of the immigrant experience relates to the working conditions foreign-born citizens and illegal immigrants are often forced to endure. The dark side of the American dream has, from the country's beginnings to present day, involved immigrants working menial jobs for long hours at poverty wages. One of the first writers to explore the world of exploited immigrant labor was Upton Sinclair. While writing for the socialist political journal *Appeal to Reason*, Sinclair employed his particular brand of undercover journalism to reveal the

*Salma Hayek* AP Images

hideous working conditions and unsafe food practices found in Chicago slaughterhouses in the late nineteenth century. Sinclair's story of a family of Lithuanian immigrants employed by Chicago's Union Stock Yards is called *The Jungle*, which describes the dark horror found in the slaughterhouses. When the novel was published in 1906 it became an instant bestseller and spurred the passage of the 1906 Pure Food and Drug Act as well as the Meat Inspection Act. The novel remains one of American literature's more scathing critique's of capitalism.

More recently, Jimmy Breslin, Pulitzer Prize–winning journalist, sportswriter, columnist, novelist, and would-be politician, wrote about the particularly sad life and gruesome death of an eighteen-year-old illegal immigrant named Eduardo Gutierrez. *The Short Sweet Dream of Eduardo Gutierrez* (2002) follows Gutierrez's path along the illegal immigration underground from San Matias, Mexico, to New York, where he gets a job working for a mob-run construction company whose bureaucratic practices made his death a tragic inevitability. He explains the origin of his short, sweet dream:

"

HERE WAS A POPULATION, LOW-CLASS AND MOSTLY FOREIGN, HANGING ALWAYS ON THE VERGE OF STARVATION, AND DEPENDENT FOR ITS OPPORTUNITIES OF LIFE UPON THE WHIM OF MEN EVERY BIT AS BRUTAL AND UNSCRUPULOUS AS THE OLD-TIME SLAVE DRIVERS; UNDER SUCH CIRCUMSTANCES IMMORALITY WAS EXACTLY AS INEVITABLE, AND AS PREVALENT, AS IT WAS UNDER THE SYSTEM OF CHATTEL SLAVERY. THINGS THAT WERE QUITE UNSPEAKABLE WENT ON THERE IN THE PACKING HOUSES ALL THE TIME, AND WERE TAKEN FOR GRANTED BY EVERYBODY; ONLY THEY DID NOT SHOW, AS IN THE OLD SLAVERY TIMES, BECAUSE THERE WAS NO DIFFERENCE IN COLOR BETWEEN MASTER AND SLAVE."

**Source:** Upton Sinclair, *The Jungle*

---

Gustavo, who lived behind him and had gone to America earlier, had called several times from Brooklyn and said he had a construction job and that the boss, Ostreicher, could use more workers. The pay was immense: Gustavo said he was making seven dollars an hour. Seven dollars in one hour! Eduardo carried bricks all day for the equivalent of five dollars a day and talked about the money Gustavo was making in America. Hearing this, his father knew that he was about to lose a son. Eduardo's father had only one thought for him: that liberty is not the country you are in, but the job you have. "If you do not like the job, then you quit and go to another," he said to Eduardo. "It is your only liberty."

## Conclusion

The American dream continues to tempt world citizens with its promise of financial security and freedom, but many who arrive, sometimes risking their lives to get here, find the actuality rarely matches the dream. For most immigrants, legal or otherwise, if they are not working dangerous, low-paying jobs just to make ends meet, they are suffering from cultural detachment and isolation—sometimes both. Of course, there are exceptions, which accounts for the fact that the American immigrant population continues to grow.

## SOURCES

Bellow, Saul, *Mr. Sammler's Planet*, Viking Press, 1970; reprint, Penguin Classics, 1996, p. 143.

Breslin, Jimmy, *The Short Sweet Dream of Eduardo Gutierrez*, Crown, 2002, p. 57.

Chabon, Michael, *The Amazing Adventures of Kavalier and Clay*, Picador, 2001, pp. 328, 585.

Divakaruni, Chitra Banerjee, "The Unknown Errors of Our Lives," in *The Unknown Errors of Our Lives*, Doubleday, 2001; reprint, 2002, pp. 211–36.

Kazan, Elia, *A Life*, Da Capo Press, 1997, p. 444.

Lahiri, Jhumpa, *Interpreter of Maladies*, Mariner Books, 1999, p. 181.

Lazarus, Emma, *The Poems of Emma Lazarus*, Vol. 1, 1889; reprinted at www.libertystatepark.com/emma.htm (December 27, 2006).

McCourt, Frank, *'Tis: A Memoir*, Scribner, First Touchstone ed., 2000, p. 5.

Talese, Gay, *Unto the Sons*, Random House Trade Paperbacks, reprint ed., 2006, p. 2.

Young, Bette Roth, "Emma Lazarus and Her Jewish Problem," in *American Jewish History*, Vol. 84, No. 4, December 1996, pp. 291–313.

# The Native American Dream

## Introduction

What is often depicted in mainstream society as American Indian culture is, in fact, a multitude of unique native cultures that once spanned the thousands of miles that make up the continental United States. For this reason, the notion of a single Native American dream is simplistic and hardly applicable to all Native Americans in any given time or place. However, the role of Native Americans in American society has long been determined by the ruling white majority. In this regard, the Native American dream can be seen as a reflection of how whites viewed American Indians throughout the history of the United States.

## Europeans Arrive

The earliest depictions of the Native American dream are not derived directly from Native Americans, but they are recorded by early white explorers and settlers. Thomas Hariot was one such explorer; his "A Brief and True Report of the New Found Land of Virginia" (1588) was instrumental in shaping European settlers' views of the native people they encountered in the New World. Though Hariot spends the bulk of his report itemizing every natural resource in Virginia that might be used or exploited, he devotes a section at the end of his report to the native people and their customs and beliefs. Hariot's vision of Native American life relates almost entirely to the way the natives

respond to the white settlers in Hariot's group, or in how their beliefs differ from his own Christian perspective. Though he learns the Algonquian language and studies their customs with more care and interest than other European explorers, Hariot never appears to view the native people as equals in any way, calling their religion "far from the truth." He writes, "I rather believe that they will have cause both to fear and to love us," and notes that many of the natives look upon the white settlers as gods. This occurs after many natives mysteriously die after the settlers have passed through their town. While modern readers might view this as an example of indigenous people being devastated by foreign diseases to which they have no immunity, Hariot simply refers to it as a "marvelous accident." He offers this fateful observation of the native people he has encountered:

> Compared with us, the natives are poor. They lack skill and judgment in using the materials we have and esteem trifles above things of greater value. But if we consider that they lack our means, they are certainly very ingenious. Although they do not possess any of our tools, or crafts, or sciences, or art, yet in their own way they show excellent sense. In time they will find that our kinds of knowledge and crafts accomplish everything with more speed and perfection than do theirs. Therefore, when they realize this, they will most probably desire our friendship and love, and, respecting our achievements, they will try to please and obey us. Whereby, if we govern them well, they will in a short time become civilized and embrace the true religion.

### White Men: Friend or Foe?

Shawnee leader Tecumseh would be one of the first Native Americans to have his words and views recorded for historical posterity. In his 1810 speech to Governor William Henry Harrison at Vincennes (in what is now Indiana), Tecumseh protested the "sale" of large areas of tribe-controlled lands to the American government. Because the land was jointly owned by all native people in the region, he argued, any sale of land had to be approved by all who used it—and not just approved by a handful of Native Americans who did not have the legal right to speak for all the others. In the short speech, Tecumseh notes that his people were "once a happy race, since made miserable by the white people who are never contented but always encroaching." Tecumseh was unsuccessful in stopping the encroachment of whites, though he

fought until his death alongside British troops in an attempt to drive back American settlement during the War of 1812. Tecumseh's simple, clear argument about communal ownership of native lands—and his argument that native peoples had first right to ownership, because they were the first to live there—would be used time and again by hundreds of different tribes, though such arguments met with little or no success when it came to preserving tribal lands from the encroachment of white Americans. The idea would become an overarching theme of the Native American dream, which existed above all tribe distinctions and served to unite many different native populations.

### Cultural Conversion

Not all Native Americans resisted the encroachment of white American society entirely. William Apess, a Pequot Indian from Massachusetts, grew up in indentured servitude to many different white families over the course of his youth. His autobiography, *A Son of the Forest* (1829), is the first full-length work to be published by a Native American author. In the book, Apess tells of his conversion to Christianity and his experiences living among white Americans. Even as he accepts many aspects of white culture, Apess strives to serve as an example of the potential of Native Americans to shatter the prejudices held by many white Americans at the time. Apess's dream of a country in which Native Americans would be treated fairly and respectably by whites, and would likewise be free to adopt the beliefs and customs of whites as they wished, was as short-lived as Apess himself; after losing faith in the notion that whites and native tribes could coexist peacefully, Apess descended into alcoholism and obscurity, and died in his early forties.

### The Plight in Print

As the Plains and Pacific Coast Indians were forcibly cleared from their ancestral lands throughout the middle of the nineteenth century, very few Native Americans memorialized the tragic events in writing. Many relied on oral tradition, but such accounts often disappeared as members of the tribe died in battle or perished from the harsh conditions of the reservations. The task of capturing the tragic events was often undertaken by white Americans sympathetic to the Native Americans' plight; Helen Hunt Jackson was one such woman. Although her novel *Ramona* (1884) is a fictional account of

*The Crazy Horse monument in the Black Hills near Rapid City, South Dakota* Francis Temman/AFP/Getty Images

a half-Indian girl and her struggles with the encroachment of white settlers, it incorporates many real-world events in an attempt to appeal directly to the hearts of readers. At the end of the novel, Ramona, having been repeatedly forced off the lands of her ancestors, decides that the only solution is to take her child and leave for Mexico. For her, there is no fulfillment of the American dream.

Though Jackson had hoped to bring awareness of the Native American plight to the American public—much as Harriet Beecher Stowe had done for African Americans in *Uncle Tom's Cabin*—many white Americans had already been conditioned to view Native Americans as hostile outsiders who stood in the way of the natural development of the nation. This view is expressed with brutal simplicity in Robert Frost's poem "The Vanishing Red" (1920), in which an Indian named John is killed by a miller who shows no reason or remorse for his actions. The meaning of the title is twofold: Although John himself vanishes down the wheel-pit of the mill, the "Vanishing Red" also refers to

Native Americans in general, who were quickly disappearing from the American consciousness through death and through government-imposed abandonment of their cultural heritage.

### Rewriting History

Indeed, Native American culture had almost vanished from the American landscape by the 1960s, when the civil rights movement brought renewed interest in the struggle of indigenous American tribes. At around this time, historian Dee Brown was scouring rare and obscure nineteenth-century historical documents in an attempt to create a comprehensive history of the American West from a Native American perspective. His groundbreaking book, *Bury My Heart at Wounded Knee: An Indian History of the American West* (1970), was the first such account to penetrate mainstream American culture. Many of the facts Brown revealed about events such as the Sand Creek massacre and Custer's Last Stand were nothing less than shocking to most Americans, who had been led to believe that Indians had been the aggressors in such incidents. Although Brown meant to document the circumstances surrounding actual events of the American West as accurately as possible, the author clearly attempts to understand and value the traditions and views of the Native American tribes he discusses. He succinctly captures the philosophy of both sides of the struggle with this exchange:

> In 1855 Governor Isaac Stevens of Washington Territory invited the Nez Percés to a peace council. He said there were a great many white people in the country, and many more would come; that he wanted the land marked out so that the Indians and white men could be separated. If they were to live in peace it was necessary, he said, that the Indians should have a country set apart for them, and in that country they must stay.
>
> Tuekakas, a chief known as Old Joseph by the white men, told Governor Stevens that no man owned any part of the earth, and a man could not sell what he did not own.

### Native Voices

In the 1970s, Leslie Marmon Silko was one of a handful of Native American writers who began to achieve a certain degree of literary success. Her 1977 novel *Ceremony*, about a Pueblo Indian named Tayo who returns to his tribe's reservation after fighting against the Japanese in World War II, is widely considered to be one of the greatest accomplishments in Native American literature. Tayo, who fights for the ideals of the American dream in a war against foreign enemies, comes home to find himself unable to participate in the American dream himself. Silko's novel is notable for being one of the first modern expressions of the Native American experience from an insider's perspective; at the same time, Tayo's experiences in *Ceremony* paralleled the experiences of many American soldiers who had recently returned home from the Vietnam War, and the book appealed to many readers for reasons unrelated to its cultural significance.

In addition to Silko, the 1970s and 1980s saw increasing success for other Native American writers such as George Boyce, who wrote *Some People Are Indians* (1974), a noted short story collection about the challenges faced by modern Navajos; and Del Barton, whose *A Good Day to Die* (1980), tells the story of her great-grandfather, the last Dakota chieftain.

In his poetry collection *A Good Journey* (1977), Simon Ortiz, a member of the Acoma Pueblo tribe from New Mexico, combines elements from traditional Native American myths with the gritty reality of life as experienced by his people in modern times. Several of the poems feature Coyote, a mythical trickster found in many Native American cultures. At the same time, poems such as "Grants to Gallup, New Mexico" reveal a keen eye for realistic detail as well as an understanding of the Native American search for a place in American society. As the narrator travels from Grants, Oklahoma, home to New Mexico, he meets an Indian hitchhiker who tells his story:

> Once, I been to California.
> Got lost in L.A., got laid
> in Fresno, got jailed in Oakland,
> got fired in Barstow,
> and came home.

The New Mexico home to which the narrator returns is not much more hospitable than California, though he calls it "The Indian Capital of the World." In the end, he confesses that he sometimes feels like leaving behind the world that no longer seems to have a place for him.

In another Ortiz poem, "Canyon de Chelly," the narrator tries to share his understanding of the eternal spirit of the natural world with his young son. This is significant in two ways. First, it keeps alive the traditional notion of the natural world as something to respect and behold, and something that is a fundamental part of human existence. The narrator finds that a rock fits his body perfectly as he lies gazing at the sky; his son places a rock in his own mouth, symbolically making the earth a part of himself. Second, it upholds the custom of passing this understanding down from generation to generation. At a time when Native American cultures are rapidly vanishing, a father and son keep one small piece of tradition alive.

Throughout the 1980s and 1990s, Native American authors continued to explore the notion of identity and the Indian place in American society. None was more commercially successful than Louise Erdrich, an author of Anishinaabe (Chippewa) descent who grew up on a reservation in North Dakota. Her 1988 novel *Tracks*, like many of her novels, is set on the same reservation where she grew up; the book takes place at the beginning of the twentieth century, when members of the tribe face the possibility of losing their identity to both the dominant white culture around them and the indifference of younger tribe members. The

YOU CAN'T GET BACK AND SEE IT AS HE SAW IT.

IT'S TOO LONG A STORY TO GO INTO NOW.

YOU'D HAVE TO HAVE BEEN THERE AND LIVED IT.

THEN YOU WOULDN'T HAVE LOOKED ON IT AS JUST A

MATTER

OF WHO BEGAN IT BETWEEN THE TWO RACES."

**Source:** Robert Frost, "The Vanishing Red"

---

character of Pauline in particular represents the struggle for identity faced by many people of mixed ancestry, who are too often not fully accepted by whites or by Native Americans. Erdrich's use of traditional Native American character types, such as the trickster who resides within Nanapush, provides a unique way of viewing the world in which the characters live.

In *Indian Killer* (1996), author Sherman Alexie depicts modern race relations in Seattle in the context of a series of murders committed by what appears to be a psychotic Native American. The killer, a full-blooded Indian named John Smith, was raised by white parents and has spent his life completely disconnected from his true heritage. Another Native American, Marie, rejects life on the reservation in an effort to help homeless Indians and educate whites in mainstream society. Another character, a white mystery author named Jack Wilson, openly embraces his Native American heritage—which, in reality, does not exist.

## Conclusion

Throughout American history, the Native American dream has been less a single unified vision than a reaction to the American dream of the white majority in American society. Only in recent decades have Native American writers begun to make significant contributions to American literature. This, coupled with a continued resurgence in the interest to preserve the many Native American cultures that still exist in some form, might someday lead to a clearer understanding of the many rich pieces that make up the tapestry of the Native American dream.

## SOURCES

Brown, Dee, *Bury My Heart at Wounded Knee: An Indian History of the American West*, Holt, Rinehart & Winston, 1971; reprint, Owl Books, 2001, p. 317.

Frost, Robert, "The Vanishing Red," in *Mountain Interval*, Henry Holt, 1920; reprint, Bartelby.com, 1999, www.bartleby.com/119 (November 29, 2006).

Hariot, Thomas, "A Brief and True Reportof the New Found Land of Virginia," in *Roanoke Revisited Heritage Education Program*, www.nps.gov/archive/fora/hariot part3.htm (November 29, 2006); originally published in 1588.

Ortiz, Simon, "Grants to Gallup, New Mexico," from *A Good Journey (Sun Tracks, An American Indian Literary Series, Volume 12)*, University of Arizona Press, 1977, www.hanksville.org/voyage/poems/I40_1.html (November 26, 2006).

Tecumseh, "Tecumseh to Governor Harrison at Vincennes," in *World's Famous Orations*, edited by William Jennings Bryan, Funk and Wagnalls, 1906; reprint; Bartelby.com, 2003, www.bartleby.com/268/8/4.html (November 29, 2006).

# The Southern American Dream

### Introduction

The southern United States are differentiated from the northern United States by far more than geographic location. Unlike other regions of the country, the South is defined by a distinct historic and cultural heritage that goes back to the surveying of the Mason-Dixon line. Originally intended to resolve a border dispute between Pennsylvania and Delaware, the boundary took on greater political and cultural significance when it became the dividing line between free and slave states. The cultural debate led to eleven Confederate states seceding from the Union, triggering the Civil War and the subsequent period of "Reconstruction" in the South. Racial and economic problems got much worse before they got better, but the region emerged to lead the civil rights movement and reinvent its economy and culture.

Much of what defines the South comes from its Confederate history, but southern culture is more than its racial legacies. Writers have long been fascinated by the South, plumbing its depths to establish a unique literary genre. Southern literature addresses a surprising range of themes that reflect the region's rich physical, cultural, and historical tradition.

### Old South versus New South

Native southerner and social critic H. L. Mencken wrote a scathing critique of his homeland in 1917's "The Sahara of the Bozart." The author

*Flannery O'Connor* AP Images

writes about the unfortunate distinctions he sees between the culture of the South before to the Civil War and Reconstruction, and afterward:

> [Prior to the war] there were men of delicate fancy, urbane instinct and aristocratic manner—in brief, superior men, gentry. . . . A certain noble spaciousness was in the ancient southern scheme of things. . . . He liked to toy with ideas. He was hospitable and tolerant. He had the vague thing that we called culture.

This "Old Confederacy" was destroyed, according to Mencken, after Reconstruction. "First the carpetbaggers ravaged the land, and then it fell into the hands of the native white trash, already so poor that war and Reconstruction could not make them any poorer." "The Sahara of the Bozart," then, is a lament over the loss of a civilization. Of the post-Reconstruction South, Mencken writes,

> And yet, for all its size and all its wealth and all the "progress" it babbles of, it is almost as sterile, artistically, intellectually, culturally, as the Sahara Desert. There are single acres in Europe that house more first-rate men than all the states south of the Potomac; there are probably single square miles in America. . . . It would be impossible in all history to match so complete a drying-up of a civilization.

In 1929, W. J. Cash was prompted to write *The Mind of the South* when he realized that the new, post-Reconstruction South, the industrialized South, was not so different from the old, antebellum South. He notes:

> One hears much in these days of the New South. The land of the storied rebel becomes industrialized . . . But I question that it is much more. For the mind of that heroic region, I opine, is still basically and essentially the mind of the Old South. It is a mind, that is to say, of the soil rather than of the mills—a mind, indeed, which, as yet, is almost wholly unadjusted to the new industry.

So what, exactly, constitutes the Old South, other than a reliance on the land? According to Cash, "Its salient characteristic is a magnificent incapacity for the real, a Brobdingnagian talent for the fantastic." He goes on, "Every farmhouse became a Big House, every farm a baronial estate. . . . Their pride and their legend, handed down to their descendants, are today the basis of all social life in the South." Cash argues that the romantic, largely fantastic Old South remains unchanged by industrialization and progress.

Yet another "New South" came into being during the civil rights movement. Flannery O'Connor's "Everything That Rises Must Converge" is a wonderful illustration of what happens when the Old South and the New South clash. Set in the early 1960s, the story focuses on Julian, a white liberal, and his mother, a descendant of a formerly privileged Southern family, on a bus ride to Julian's mother's weekly reducing class at the "Y." Julian feels superior to his mother and finds the purple hat she wears to her class both ugly and bourgeois:

> A purple velvet flap came down on one side of it and stood up on the other; the rest of it was green and looked like a cushion with the stuffing out. He decided it was less comical than jaunty and pathetic. Everything that gave her pleasure was small and depressed him.

Describing the people in her reducing class, she says, "Most of them in it are not our kind of people, but I can be gracious to anybody. I know who I am." Julian replies, "They don't give a damn for your graciousness. Knowing who you are is good for one generation only. You haven't the foggiest idea where you stand now or who you are."

His retort reflects his generation's belief that the Old South and its old ways are on the way out. Integration, one of the new ways, becomes the divisive issue of the story when a black woman boards the bus wearing the same hat as

Julian's mother. Julian relishes the irony: "He could not believe that Fate had thrust upon his mother such a lesson. He gave a loud chuckle so that she would look at him and see that he saw." Only momentarily uncomfortable, his mother soon begins playing with the woman's little boy. Julian thinks, "The lesson had rolled off her like rain on a roof." When Julian's mother tries to offer the little boy a penny, something Julian begs her not to do, the boy's mother turns violent:

> Julian saw the black fist swing out with the red pocketbook. He shut his eyes and cringed as he heard the woman shout, "He don't take nobody's pennies!" When he opened his eyes, the woman was disappearing down the street with the little boy staring wide-eyed over her shoulder. Julian's mother was sitting on the sidewalk.

Although the act of offering the child money was "as natural to her as breathing," Julian's mother is shown just how offensive the gesture is, how outmoded her behavior has become.

### Individualism

Harper Lee's *To Kill a Mockingbird* (1960) packs several themes common to great works of Southern literature into one powerful package. Race, class, caste, history, the New South versus the Old South are all examined in Lee's Pulitzer Prize–winning novel, but individualism is the theme that truly drives the novel. According to W. J. Cash in his *The Mind of the South*, the Southerner's individualistic spirit harkens back "to the Old South, to the soil." In *To Kill a Mockingbird*, that Old South soil-driven individualism has evolved into a nonconformist way of thinking that propels the culture forward.

Atticus Finch, the story's hero, is the widowed father of Scout and Jem. A prominent Depression-era lawyer in the fictional small town of Maycomb, Alabama, Finch agrees to defend a black man, Tom Robinson, accused of raping a white woman. His decision angers Maycomb's racist white community. When Scout gets into a fight at school over the trial and her father's role in it, Finch explains,

> If I didn't [defend Tom Robinson] I couldn't hold up my head in town, I couldn't represent this county in the legislature, I couldn't even tell you or Jem not to do something again. . . . Scout, simply by the nature of the work, every lawyer gets at least one case in his lifetime that affects him personally. This one's mine, I guess.

By heeding both his conscience and his principles, Finch sets himself apart from the rest of his community. When Scout tells her father about others' opinions about the trial, he replies,

> They're certainly entitled to think that, and they're entitled to full respect for their opinions . . . but before I can live with other folks I've got to live with myself. The one thing that doesn't abide by majority rule is a person's conscience.

Much like *To Kill a Mockingbird*, Margaret Mitchell's *Gone With the Wind* (1936) is a treasure trove of Southern themes. The story spans the Civil War and Reconstruction, features the romance and history of the South, but the independent spirit of anti-heroine Scarlett O'Hara is the predominant theme that drives the novel. Unlike Atticus Finch, O'Hara's individualism is not used to promote the good of society, but rather as a survival mechanism used to promote herself and her own happiness.

As a young woman of means, the willful O'Hara constrains her rebellious temperament and learns to behave like the proper young Southern lady her elders expect her to be. As she gets older, though, she is less willing to perform as directed. "I'm tired of everlastingly being unnatural and never doing anything I want to do," she says. After the war, after her mother dies, and her father suffers a mental collapse, and her sisters fall ill, O'Hara is left to take care of Tara, the family home. Her selfish independence drives her to marry a man for money. She secures the financial future of the family home and becomes a successful businesswoman at the same time. As a way of explaining what could be construed as masculine behavior, O'Hara reasons, "You can't be a lady without money."

The Georgian Mitchell and the Alabamian Lee wrote to inspire their fellow Southerners (and countrymen). They both understood the southern need to uphold tradition and reluctance to break precedent. Both used the device of the romantic past to appeal to readers in their present day and crafted alternate, authentic-feeling and ennobling versions of history that their readers could be proud of. Mitchell wanted Depression-era Southerners to be proud of their heritage, so she portrayed it as noble, dignified, and blameless. If a reader in the 1930s ever thought her Confederate ancestors were the skeletons in the family closet, *Gone With the Wind* gave her license to whistle "Dixie" with her head held high. Lee wanted her Civil

*Govenor George Wallace blocking the entrance to the University of Alabama* AP Images

Rights–era readers to reject the racial status quo, so she presented them with a mythic figure of the recent past to show them the way. If a reader in the 1960s thought, "I wish I could question segregation, but that simply isn't *done*," *To Kill a Mockingbird* offered a blueprint of the way it might be done, if one were brave enough.

### Nature

*I'll Take My Stand: The South and the Agrarian Tradition* (1930) is a collection of twelve essays written by twelve different Southerners addressing the premise that with industrialization comes the sure and steady erosion of Southern culture. The introduction of *I'll Take My Stand* begins, "The authors contributing to this book are Southerners, well acquainted with one another and of similar tastes." These tastes include a longing for a way of life nearly gone by the time the book was published. They see growing industrialization as a first step toward man's losing "his sense of vocation." They also agree that industrialization would lead to a disinterest in religion and art, an acceleration in the speed of life that would lead to general instability, and the much-feared advance of a consumer-based society. The introduction goes on to ask,

> How far shall the South surrender its moral, social, and economic autonomy to the victorious principle of the Union? That question remains open. The South is a minority section that has hitherto been jealous of its minority right to live its own kind of life…. Of late, however, there is the melancholy fact that the South itself has wavered a little and shown signs of wanting to join up behind the common or American industrial ideal. It is against that tendency that this book is written.

Rather than specifics about how to shift a rapidly growing industrialized society back to an agrarian one, the book provides a philosophical

*Vivien Leigh and Butterfly McQueen in a scene from* Gone With the Wind *John Kobal Foundation/Getty Images*

argument for retaining the traditions and institutions inherent to the South. "The Agrarians," as the writers would come to be known, feel that industrialization made good, honest, hard work monotonous, which dehumanized the endeavor, turning purposeful labor into servile monotony.

The work of Nobel laureate William Faulkner epitomizes Southern literature, myth, and tradition. A native of Mississippi, Faulkner chose as his primary subject the land he came from. His story, "The Bear," first published in 1935, was later published among a collection entitled, *Go Down, Moses* (1942). Like much of his work, the narrative is complex and its meaning is difficult to discern without multiple readings. One easily comprehensible aspect of the story, though, is the important role nature plays in the action. The hunt for Old Ben, the eponymous bear, represents the ancient ritual of hunting for food and protection, a ritual shared and passed down by Southern families for generations. Ike McCaslin,

the main character, undergoes a traditional rite of passage when he is taught as a ten-year-old boy how to navigate the wilderness and stalk and kill his quarry. The successive hunting seasons throughout "The Bear" may be interpreted as a symbol of man's tendency to destroy the wilderness in an attempt to sustain the culture's values and traditions.

## Class

Pulitzer Prize–winning journalist Rick Bragg's moving memoir, *All Over But the Shoutin'* (1997), wrenchingly illustrates the critical role of class in Southern culture. Bragg was born in 1959 in Possum Trot, Alabama, into a poor, disadvantaged, "white trash" family. He was raised by a loving mother while his abusive father was largely absent.

Bragg remembers his mother dragging him along on a gunny sack while she picked cotton:

The tall woman is wearing a man's britches and a man's old straw hat, and now and then she looks back over her shoulder to smile at the three-year-old boy whose hair is almost as purely white as the bolls she picks, who rides the back of the six-foot-long sack like a magic carpet.

Many of the episodes in *All Over But the Shoutin'* exemplify the pain Bragg felt as a lower-class citizen. He describes the wealthy as "the old-money white Southerners who ran things, who treated the rest of the South like beggars with muddy feet who were about to track up their white shag carpeting." Bragg describes how the common experience of poverty was, at the time, not enough to bridge the gulf between the races in the South. He writes that a black neighbor boy once brought food from his mother to help the Braggs in a particularly rough time, and Bragg recalls:

> In the few contacts we had with them as children, we had thrown rocks at them. . . . I would like to say that we came together after the little boy brought us that food, that we learned about and from each other, but that would be a lie.

## Politics

A seminal work of Southern literature and winner of the Pulitzer Prize for fiction, Robert Penn Warren's *All the King's Men* (1946) is among America's best political novels. Fashioned after the life and political career of Louisiana Governor Huey P. Long, the Depression-era novel tells the story of the rise and fall of political giant Willy Stark. Stark, a blackmailer and bully, raised in poverty, becomes the unnamed Southern state's most powerful political figure. The story also features Stark's right-hand man, the cynical Jack Burden. Burden relinquishes his genteel, Southern upbringing and abandons his dissertation in American history, choosing instead to use his talent for historical research to dig up unsavory secrets about Stark's enemies. Stark threatens and blackmails his way into instituting liberal reforms designed to assist the state's poor farmers, but becoming champion of the people does not come without costs. The tale of Stark's downward spiral illustrates the consequences of every human act and the role politics plays in contemporary society.

But the truth of Southern politics may be stranger than the fiction. Alabama Governor George C. Wallace's 1963 Inaugural Address, delivered in Montgomery, Alabama, at the height of the civil rights movement, is an important artifact of Southern political thought. In 1958, when Wallace decided to run for governor, he denounced the Ku Klux Klan and was supported by the NAACP. His stand lost him the primary. Four years later, determined to win the white vote and the governorship, Wallace drastically reassessed his platform and ran as a pro-segregationist. He won the 1962 election by a landslide. Wallace hired white supremacist and Ku Klux Klansman Asa Carter to write his inaugural address, which is largely remembered for the following lines:

> Let us rise to the call of freedom-loving blood that is in us and send our answer to the tyranny that clanks its chains upon the South. In the name of the greatest people that have ever trod this earth, I draw the line in the dust and toss the gauntlet before the feet of tyranny . . . and I say . . . segregation today . . . segregation tomorrow . . . segregation forever.

The inaugural address outlines Wallace's understanding of segregation and why he felt it was valid:

> The true brotherhood of America, of respecting the separateness of others . . . and uniting in effort . . . has been so twisted and distorted from its original concept that there is small wonder that communism is winning the world.

## Religion

George C. Wallace's 1963 Inaugural Address also touches on the importance of religion in Southern literature. Wallace's personal religious beliefs served as the foundation for his political views, views that Alabamians heartily and repeatedly supported. In his 1963 inaugural address, Wallace said,

> We are faced with an idea that if a centralized government assumes enough authority, enough power over its people, that it can provide a utopian life. . . . It is an idea of government that encourages our fears and destroys our faith. . . . We find we have become a government-fearing people . . . not a God-fearing people. . . . We find we have replaced faith with fear . . . and though we may give lip service to the Almighty . . . in reality, government has become our god.

His emphasis on a faith-based form of government, embraced by the founding fathers, was perceived to stand in opposition to the system called for by the "so-called 'progressives.'" Wallace argues, the "'progressives' tell us that our Constitution was written for 'horse and buggy' days . . . so were the Ten Commandments."

"

PROPER LIVING IS A MATTER OF THE

INTELLIGENCE AND THE WILL, DOES NOT DEPEND ON

THE LOCAL CLIMATE OR GEOGRAPHY, AND IS CAPABLE

OF A DEFINITION WHICH IS GENERAL AND NOT

SOUTHERN AT ALL. SOUTHERNERS HAVE A FILIAL DUTY

TO DISCHARGE TO THEIR OWN SECTION. BUT THEIR

CAUSE IS PRECARIOUS AND THEY MUST SEEK

ALLIANCES WITH SYMPATHETIC COMMUNITIES

EVERYWHERE."

**Source:** The Twelve Southerners, *I'll Take My Stand*

Wallace's views are in sharp contrast to those W. J. Cash set forth more than thirty years earlier in his scathing critique, *The Mind of the South*. Cash blames much of the problems he finds with the South and its people on its emphasis on religion: "The mind of the South begins and ends with God, John Calvin's God— the anthropomorphic Jehovah of the Old Testament." Cash believes this strain of religious devotion keeps Southerners from achieving their greatest potential:

> Whatever exists is ordered. . . . Under this view of things, it plainly becomes blasphemy for the mill-billy to complain. Did God desire him to live in a house with plumbing, did He wish him to have better wages, it is quite clear that He would have arranged it. With that doctrine, the peon is in thorough accord. . . . The peon is always a Christian.

## Conclusion

Southern literature attempts to describe, define, challenge, and celebrate the region's rich and varied culture, sometimes all at the same time. The many themes that run through Southern essays, speeches, memoirs, and novels do more than illustrate a region, they define a people. Mitchell's O'Hara, Lee's Finch, and Bragg's mother are characters shaped by both history and culture. The deep scars left by the Civil War and Reconstruction are felt in integration stories told by Flannery O'Connor in the early 1960s and the declaration of "segregation today, segregation tomorrow, segregation forever" in George Wallace's speech. As critical as they are of southern culture, "Sahara of the Bozart," *The Mind of the South*, and *To Kill a Mockingbird* have at their heart a real love for the South and a true desire to right its wrongs. These authors have shown that learning history's lessons begins by reading and writing authentically about the painful truths of the past.

## SOURCES

Cash, W. J., "The Mind of the South," in *American Monthly*, Vol. 18, No. 70, October 1929, pp. 185–192; reprinted on *W. J. Cash: The Mind of the South*, www.wjcash.org/WJCash1/WJCash/WJCash/mindofthe south.htm (September 1, 2006).

Lee, Harper, *To Kill a Mockingbird*, Lippincott, 1960; reprint, Warner Books, 1982, pp. 75, 105.

Mencken, H. L., "Sahara of the Bozart," in *The American Scene: A Reader*, Knopf, 1977, pp. 157–68; originally published in 1917.

Mitchell, Margaret, *Gone With the Wind*, Macmillan, 1936; reprint, Warner Books, 1993, pp. 81, 600.

O'Connor, Flannery, *The Complete Stories*, Farrar, Straus and Giroux, 1965; reprint, 1984, pp. 405, 407, 418.

The Twelve Southerners, "Introduction: A Statement of Principles," in *I'll Take My Stand: The South and the Agrarian Tradition*, Harper, 1930, reprinted on *Anthology of Thirties prose*, xroads.virginia.edu/~MA01/White/ anthology/agrarian.html (September 1, 2006).

Wallace, George C., "The 1963 Inaugural Address of Governor George C. Wallace," January 14, 1963, www.archives.state.al.us/govs_list/inauguralspeech.html (September 1, 2006).

# What Do I
# Read Next?

# The American Dream: What Do I Read Next?

## The Colonial American Dream

*The Journal of John Winthrop, 1630–1649* (1996) is a collection of the governor's illuminating writings about the establishment of the Massachusetts Bay Colony. A keen observer and thorough documentarian, Winthrop vividly recreates the daily life and struggles of the Puritans as they seek to prosper in the New World.

*Mayflower: A Story of Courage, Community and War* (2006), by Nathaniel Philbrick, tells the true tale of one of the earliest and best-known Puritan settlements in the New World: the Plymouth Colony. Philbrick, winner of the National Book Award, separates fact from myth as he paints a fascinating picture of these early settlers and their interactions with the native peoples of the area, which ultimately—after decades of successful relations—led to war.

Nathaniel Hawthorne's short story "Young Goodman Brown" (1835) is set in seventeenth-century New England, in Salem, Massachusetts. The newly married Puritan Brown takes a dream-like journey into the dark forest where he meets a man who symbolizes the devil. In contrast to the orderly Salem of his home, he finds something like a Black Mass being held by members of his community, including his wife, in the dark forest. While they are upright and faultless by day, Brown sees them give into sin at night. Many critics interpret the story as a condemnation of the intolerance of Puritans.

Nathaniel Hawthorne's *The Scarlet Letter, A Romance* (1850) informs many Americans' concept of life in colonial times, even though it was written centuries later. Set in 1642 in Puritan-era Boston, the story focuses on Hester Prynne. She has been found guilty of adultery and must wear the letter "A" in scarlet on her dress as part of her punishment. Through Hester's experiences, Hawthorne explores the ideas of guilt and redemption as well as social and political forces that were prevalent in early colonial American society.

*Puritans among the Indians: Accounts of Captivity and Redemption, 1676–1724* (2006) offers eight fascinating stories about Puritan settlers who lived among Native American tribes as captives. These accounts offer a unique view of early relations between settlers of European descent and Native American cultures.

Many Americans remained committed Loyalists—often referred to as Tories—an element of the Revolution largely unfamiliar to people today. The most popular recent book is *1776* (2005), a best-selling study of the most crucial year of the Revolution written by David McCullough. One of the leading contemporary historians, McCullough analyzes both American and British attitudes toward Independence and points out how on several occasions simple twists of fate, such as fortuitous weather conditions, made the difference between American victory or defeat.

*Founding Mothers: The Women Who Raised Our Nation* (2004), by Cokie Roberts, spotlights the wives, sisters, and mothers of well-known male revolutionary heroes. Celebrity news analyst Roberts explores the influence dozens of women—from before the Revolution to after the signing of the Constitution—had on shaping the United States.

*His Excellency: George Washington* (2004), by Joseph J. Ellis, is a recent biography of the enigmatic first president. Ellis explores Washington's passions and motivations in his military and political leadership, and offers new insight into both the man and the young country he stewarded.

One of the most useful methods to understand greater thinkers is to read the works they completed themselves. The collection of selected writings *The Portable Thomas Jefferson* (1975) includes such key Jefferson essays as "Notes on the State of Virginia," essentially a historical and geographical study of his native state, and "A Summary View of the Rights of British America," which lists Colonial grievances with the British Crown and foreshadows the Declaration of Independence.

## The American Dream in the Nineteenth Century

*Born Losers: A History of Failure in America* (2005) is Scott A. Sandage's exploration of how failure has marked American society for two centuries and every generation. He primarily focuses on looking at failures in the nineteenth century. An account of the dark side of the American dream, the author describes the changing definition of failure for Americans, how the system creates them, and the many Americans who were failures yet still significant to the country.

"The American Scholar" is Ralph Waldo Emerson's speech delivered for the 1837 Harvard Phi Beta Kappa ceremony. In it, the philosopher rails against an entirely book-based education and promotes instead an education of life experience. In 1993, Dover Publications issued *Self-Reliance and Other Essays*. This volume provides six essays from Emerson, including "History," "Friendship," and his well-known Harvard address.

Henry David Thoreau's essay, "Civil Disobedience," published in 1849, addresses the individual's responsibility to resist unfair governmental practices. Thoreau's philosophy continues to inspire followers, with Martin Luther King Jr. remaining one of its most famous adherents.

Edwin Haviland Miller's *Salem is My Dwelling Place* (1992) is a biography of author Nathaniel Hawthorne. Miller explores the life of the elusive author of "My Kinsman, Major Molineux" and *The Scarlet Letter*, providing much detail about life in America in the early to mid-nineteenth century.

In *March* (2005), Geraldine Brooks imagines the Civil War experiences of the patriarch of the March clan—those "Little Women" left at home without a father in Louisa May Alcott's classic. He becomes a teacher to freed slaves and witnesses the harsh racism of both southern and northern whites.

A collection of poetry published in 1998, *101 Great American Poems*, includes selections from the quintessential American poets: Edgar Allan Poe, Walt Whitman, Robert Frost, Langston Hughes, Emily Dickinson, T. S. Eliot, and Marianne Moore.

An example of symbolic realism, *The Damnation of Theron Ware or Illumination* (1896), by Harold Frederic, explores the spiritual collapse of a young minister in the face of his rural townspeople's progressive ideas. The author shows how the rise of science affected innocence and created collective desolation as the United States reached modernity.

*Life on the Mississippi* (1883), by Mark Twain, is a nonfiction account of his years working on steamboats on the Mississippi River, including the time he worked as a cub pilot on the steamer piloted by Horace Bixby. Based partially on a series of magazine articles about his youthful experiences, the book also includes Twain's return to these places of his past, including another trip with Bixby, to explore larger issues of changes in the American landscape. Twain also explores the lives of those who traveled and worked on the river while emphasizing the mysterious power of the river itself.

J. California Cooper's *Some People Some Other Place*, published in 2004, follows the citizens of Dream Street during the late nineteenth century. It is a story of the race and class struggle in America.

In Mark Twain's *A Connecticut Yankee in King Arthur's Court* (1889), the master satirist explores what might happen when nineteenth century American technology and know-how are brought to sixth-century England by an American to help the more primitive English society. The novel shows the sometimes dire consequences of the transference of the American dream.

### The American Dream in the Twentieth Century

*Spoon River Anthology* (1916), by Edgar Lee Masters, is a collection of autobiographical poems by 244 deceased residents of the fictional city of Spoon River, Illinois. They reveal much about their lives in their individual epitaph-like statements. The author used experiences from his own childhood in two Illinois towns in some of the poems.

Sherwood Anderson's *Winesburg, Ohio* (1919) is a collection of short stories about the residents of this small town. Each character tries to find his place in the community while struggling with a secret life inside themselves. Some of the lives of these Americans are lonely and alienated, others feel joy, while a few are just strange. Anderson shows that life in such small towns is less than idyllic.

Sinclair Lewis's *Babbitt* (1922) is the author's second successful novel, a masterwork satire attack on American middle-class mediocrity. Focusing on George F. Babbitt, Lewis explores his daily life as a man living in urban America in the early 1920s through a plot-less fantasy, if not surreal, writing style. Lewis follows Babbitt as he becomes discontent with conformity and rebels but ends up assimilating into his environment again. Despite Babbitt's many poor qualities, including questionable morals, he remains loveable to many readers.

*Chin Music: A Novel of the Jazz Age* ( 2001), set in the Roaring Twenties, is Paul M. Levitt's novel about plucky young Henrietta Fine. Stylistically, the book contains poetic allusions to W. B. Yeats and Walt Whitman, as well as echoes of *The Great Gatsby* and *Huckleberry Finn*.

In *Sometimes Madness is Wisdom: Zelda and Scott Fitzgerald: A Marriage* (2001), Fulbright scholar and historian Kendall Taylor chronicles the dysfunctional, decadent, and daring marriage of the couple that was the epitome of the Jazz Age: Zelda and Scott.

*The Harvest Gypsies: On the Road to "The Grapes of Wrath"* (1996) is a collection of the seven newspaper articles John Steinbeck wrote for the *San Francisco News* that inspired him to write *The Grapes of Wrath*. Twenty-two photographs shot by Dorothea Lange, many of which accompanied the original newspaper articles, are included.

*All My Sons* (1947), a play by Arthur Miller, is a drama about the manufacturer of American plane parts and his family in which he indicts those who built their American dream by war profiteering. The story focuses on Joe Keller, who owns the Midwestern factory. He knowingly sold defective airplane parts to the armed forces during World War II, causing twenty-one deaths. Keller has denied his part in the manufacture and deception, blaming the matter on his former partner who has been jailed for three years. The cover-up has benefited Keller economically, but it has torn apart his family.

John O'Hara's novel *Ten North Frederick* (1955) is one of several books by the author that explores the emptiness of the lives of seemingly privileged, American dream–living people. The book focuses on the life, ambitions, and death of superficial Joe Chapin, who dreams of leaving $1 million to each of his children.

*The Dharma Bums* (1958) is one of Jack Kerouac's popular autobiographical novels. The book tells the story of two young men in search of spiritual truth. The men engage in both the practice of Buddhism and a wild San Francisco lifestyle reminiscent of that of Sal and Dean in *On the Road*.

*Travels with Charley: In Search of America* (1962), by John Steinbeck, is a travelogue. In 1960, the esteemed author took a three-month tour of the country with his standard poodle, Charley, as his companion. Steinbeck is fascinated by the people and places that make up America, and this fascination is conveyed to the reader through amusing and colorful vignettes. Even while entertaining the reader, the author still manages to touch on serious issues such as racism and pollution.

*Robert Frost: The People, Places, and Stories Behind His New England Poetry* (2000), edited by Lea Newman, puts Frost's well-known poetry in context by providing personal and historical background, literary criticism, and informative essays.

Rachel F. Moran's *Interracial Intimacy: The Regulation of Race and Romance* (2003) explores the history of anti-miscegenation laws, the seminal 1967 *Loving v. Commonwealth of Virginia* Supreme Court decision that made interracial marriages legal in all states, and the continuing complex social issue of intimate mixed-race relationships.

Theodore Roszak's *The Making of a Counter Culture: Reflections on the Technocratic Society and Its Youthful Opposition* (1969) explores the reasons for the rise of the American counterculture movement, its intellectual origins, and its history, focusing on the political and social issues at its core.

## The American Dream Today

Donald Trump's *How to Get Rich* (2004) demonstrates that the real estate magnate is as much a symbol of the dreams of the twenty-first century as he was the excess of the 1980s. In this, his fifth book, Trump continues to inspire the classic American dream of wealth and power.

In *Against All Enemies: Inside America's War on Terror* (2004), former Bush counterterrorism director Richard Clarke contends that the twenty-first century American dream of stability and security at home and abroad has been both misunderstood and undermined by the very government that launched the War on Terror.

*Nickel and Dimed* (2001) is Barbara Ehrenreich's eye-opening look into the modern American dream. It recounts her undercover experiment as she tried to work and live as a minimum-wage earner in American society.

"Twilight of the Superheroes" is the title story in the 2006 collection by Deborah Eisenberg. It tells the story of Nathaniel and his friends who share a loft in Manhattan, which happens to have a perfect view of the World Trade Center. It takes the friends years to recover after they witness the events of 9/11.

*New York Times* journalist Thomas L. Friedman offers a nonfiction look at the defining moment of the twenty-first century in *Longitudes and Attitudes: Exploring the World After September 11* (2002). The book contains his public news columns from the year after the attack, but it also includes his diary entries and personal viewpoint as a reporter in the Middle East and a father in the United States as he grapples with what it means for American society and Americans in the world.

## The African American Dream

Daniel Panger's novel *Black Ulysses* (1982) is a novel inspired by Alvar Núñez Cabeza de Vaca's *Chronicle of the Narváez Expedition*, but it takes the point of view of another of the four survivors, the black slave Estevanico, a Moor from Africa.

Claude McKay's *Harlem Shadows* (1922) is a volume of poetry that is a significant work in the Harlem Renaissance. McKay's collection explores racial prejudice with an angry, bold edge. He also describes poor blacks with compassion and respect. Other poems touch on life in the city, nature, loneliness, and homesickness.

*The Birth of Bebop: A Social and Musical History* (1996), by Scott DeVeaux, examines the roots of bebop music and explores the shifting social landscape in which it thrived. This comprehensive volume includes detailed historical context as well as firsthand accounts of musical history as it was made by masters of the jazz genre.

*The Big Sea: An Autobiography* (1940) was published when Langston Hughes was only thirty-eight, and is therefore not a comprehensive narrative of the author's life. However, Hughes describes his childhood and early professional life in his own unique and engaging style and provides a window into the life of one of the most prestigious African American artists during the Harlem Renaissance.

Ralph Ellison's novel *Invisible Man* (1952) explores how one young African American man experiences ugly racism and cultural intolerance by whites in the post–World War II United States. The author depicts a journey for truth while showing how this exclusion deeply affects him. This book was an instant classic upon its original publication, showing readers a truth about life in the United States.

Lorraine Hansberry's play *A Raisin in the Sun* (1959) takes its title from a line in Langston Hughes's *Montage of a Dream Deferred*. The play centers on the Youngers, a black family living in Chicago; when the family patriarch dies, Mama Younger decides to use the insurance money to put a down payment on a house in a more upscale, predominantly white neighborhood. *A Raisin in the Sun* offers a view of the African American dream from multiple perspectives, across two very different generations.

*Now Is Your Time! The African-American Struggle for Freedom* (1991), by Walter Dean Myers, is nonfiction book that combines biography and history. In the text, Myers explores the lives of black Americans, both famous and not so well known, and links them with their place and time in American history. Myers emphasizes the courage of many of his subjects as they looked to define themselves in American society.

*Here in Harlem: Poems in Many Voices* (2004) is a collection of poetry for young adult readers by Walter Dean Myers. Each poem in the collection is in the voice of a different fictional person who lives in Harlem. Through the poems, Myers offers the perspective of people of different ages and backgrounds as well as in different time periods. Myers shows the diversity of life in Harlem in his text.

Stanley E. Banks's *Blue Beat Syncopation Selected Poems 1977–2002* (2004) is a collection of poetry by a poet often compared to Langston Hughes. In this collection, Banks explores facets of and characters in his hometown, Kansas City, Missouri, by using a blues rhythm.

## The Asian American Dream

*No-No Boy* (1957), by John Okada, tells of Ichiro, a young Japanese American man during World War II and the difficulty he faces in both Japanese American and white American cultures after he opts to remain in the internment camp rather than to enlist and fight the war.

Maxine Hong Kingston's *China Men* (1980) won the 1981 National Book Award. It explores the lives of generations of men in her family and their experiences as Chinese men in various times and places in the United States.

*Songs My Mother Taught Me: Stories, Plays, and Memoir* (1994), by Wakako Yamauchi, offers another look at the struggles of Japanese Americans during the Great Depression, World War II, and beyond, inspired by the author's personal history as a child of Japanese immigrants to the United States.

*Returning a Borrowed Tongue: An Anthology of Filipino and Filipino American Poetry* (1995), edited by noted Filipino poet Nick Carbo, is a well-regarded collection that represents both contemporary poets of note in the Philippines as well as the Filipino American poets they have inspired.

*Mona in the Promised Land* (1996) is a novel by Gish Jen about a Chinese American girl growing up in a Jewish suburb in the 1970s. Jen presents the contrast and conflict between the old ways and the new to great comedic effect without mocking or sacrificing empathy for her characters and their situation.

*The Night My Mother Met Bruce Lee: Observations on Not Fitting In* (2000) is a collection of essays by Taiwanese American poet Paisley Rekdal. The "observations" span past and present, and reach from Mississippi to Taiwan, as the author grapples with her sense of identity.

*Book of My Nights* (2001), by Li-Young Lee, is a poetry collection from an American immigrant, born in Indonesia to Chinese parents. In it, the poet meditates on questions of identity, culture, and family.

*Yellow: Race in America Beyond Black and White* (2002), by Frank H. Wu, investigates the debate about racial identity in the United States, the damaging effects of stereotyping (even when it seems positive), and the difficult balancing act between assimilation and multiculturalism.

## The Native American Dream

*Brutal Journey: The Epic Story of the First Crossing of North America* (2006), by Paul Schneider, is essentially a retelling of Alvar Núñez Cabeza de Vaca's *Chronicle of the Narváez Expedition* with additional secondary research to flesh out the details of the difficult journey by Cabeza de Vaca and his companions. The text also includes more information about the Indian tribes the Spaniards encountered.

Dee Brown's *Bury My Heart at Wounded Knee* (1970) is a comprehensive look at the history of the Old West through the eyes of different American Indian tribes. Like *Black Elk Speaks*, it includes many first-person accounts of different historical events. Instead of focusing on just the Oglala Sioux, however, Brown covers tribes from all across America and provides a sweeping look at American Indian relations throughout the nineteenth century.

*Plenty-Coups: Chief of the Crows* (1935) is an autobiography of the Crow leader written with the assistance of Frank Bird Linderman. It serves as an interesting and unique companion piece to *Black Elk Speaks*, because the Crow were longtime enemies of the Sioux and Cheyenne tribes; Crow often assisted Army soldiers as scouts in their campaigns against the Sioux.

John Neihardt's mammoth poetic work *A Cycle of the West: The Song of Three Friends, the Song of Hugh Glass, the Song of Jed Smith, the Song of the Indian Wars, the Song of the Messiah* (1952) brings together five thematically linked epic poems written over the course of several decades. In these poems, Neihardt tells the story of American Indian relations on the Great Plains, from the time of the first white settlers to the forced relocation of Plains Indians to reservations.

*The Return to Rainy Mountain* (1969), by N. Scott Momaday, is a poetic re-working of Kiowa Indian folktales and mythology interspersed with the author's own childhood stories. The text begins with the emergence of the Kiowa people in Oklahoma, includes their migration from the Yellowstone to the Black Hills, and ends with their modern decline. Momaday comments on this journey, including elements of his own heritage and search for identity.

Michael Dorris's novel *A Yellow Raft in Blue Water* (1987) explores forty years in the lives of three generations of women living together in a house on a reservation in Montana. Dorris highlights the reality of their impoverished lives, loss of culture, and close family ties.

## The Hispanic American Dream

Willa Cather's *Death Comes for the Archbishop* was published in 1927 and is set in the desert of the American southwest. Based on the life of Bishop Jean Baptiste L'Amy, a French-born Ohio clergyman sent by the Catholic church to reform the diocese of New Mexico after being annexed by the United States in 1831, the book is widely regarded as Cather's most straightforward and least dramatic novel.

*Daughter of Fortune* (1999), by Chilean author Isabel Allende, centers on the confluence of four cultures—English, Chilean, Chinese, and American—during the 1849 California gold rush. Its main protagonist is a young Chilean woman, sometimes disguised as a man, searching for her lover on the American frontier.

*The Migrant Earth* (1987), by Rolando Hinojosa-Smith, is a novel based on the classic Chicano fiction . . . *y no se lo tragó la tierra* (. . . *And the Earth Did Not Devour Him*) by Tomás Rivera. Written in English, *The Migrant Earth* adapts the stories and vignettes of the original and puts them in a different order. Hinojosa-Smith also creates a different tone and voice while retaining the powerful stories of living the poor migrant life of the 1940s and 1950s.

*The Fight in the Fields: Cesar Chavez and the Farmworkers Movement* (1997), by Susan Ferriss, Ricardo Sandoval, and Diana Hembree, provides biographical information on the leader and organizer of the United Farm Workers union as well as his many accomplishments. The authors also describe the events that led to the founding of the union, the people who were helped by its founding, and its impact on greater society.

Reinaldo Arenas's memoir *Before Night Falls* (1993) describes his life as a Cuban peasant, rising literati, dissident writer, oppressed homosexual, political prisoner, political exile, and AIDS sufferer in 1980s New York. It is a personal and political account, published shortly after Arenas's suicide at the age of forty-seven.

*La frontera/Borderlands* (1999), by Gloria Anzaldúa, is collection of prose and poetry that explores life as a Chicana from Texas caught between cultures. She also touches on issues of language, being a woman in Spanish-speaking cultures, and the plight of illegal aliens who survive as migrant workers. Angry at those who oppress those who are different, Anzaldúa provides insight into the mentality of a marginalized person.

*Bodega Dreams* (2000), by Ernesto Quiñonez, is a novel about Willie Bodega, a magnanimous drug lord in East Harlem with grand dreams about using drug money to make his Puerto Rican American neighborhood respectable. Quiñonez's debut novel is critically acclaimed for its realistic ear for language and its riveting story.

### The American Immigrant Dream

*Pears on a Willow Tree* (1998), by Leslie Pietrzyk, follows four generations of Polish American women in twentieth-century America. The matriarch, Rose, immigrates to Detroit in 1919; the saga follows her daughter, granddaughter, and great-granddaughter as they struggle to maintain their closeness and traditions, just as they struggle to discover their own identities.

Jhumpa Lahiri explores the significance of names, traditions, and culture in her novel *The Namesake* (2003). When an Indian immigrant couple in Massachusetts has their first child, tradition holds that the maternal grandmother should name him. When the letter bearing that name from India is lost, an unusual nickname sticks. The novel follows mother, father, and son as they adjust—with varying degrees of success—to the alien culture of the United States.

Ruben Martinez's nonfiction *Crossing Over: A Mexican Family on the Migrant Trail* (2001) starts with one family's tragedy as they lose three sons crossing the U.S.–Mexico border, and follows the surviving members of the Chavéz family as they settle in the four corners of the United States and struggle to survive.

Dave Eggers's novel *What is the What* (2006) is a fictionalized memoir of real-life Sudanese refugee Valentino Achak Deng. Deng is just seven years old when he becomes an orphan war refugee in northern Africa, where he survives hunger, disease, neglect, violence, and nature for a decade before facing a whole new set of dangers as an African immigrant in Atlanta, Georgia.

In *Digging to America* (2006), popular novelist Anne Tyler looks at two families—one white Americans, the other Iranian Americans—and their different approaches to culture in the common experience of adopting Korean baby girls.

### The Frontier American Dream

A work of historical fiction for children, *Caddie Woodlawn* (1935), by Carol Ryrie Brink, explores the pioneer life of the title character, a tomboy who lived with her family in Wisconsin in the mid-1860s. As an eleven-year-old, she lives her American dream by freely exploring the frontier landscape with her brothers. She resists becoming a civilized young lady but allows her father to encourage her to accept becoming a wise woman who eventually pioneers westward.

John E. Miller's *Becoming Laura Ingalls Wilder: The Woman Behind the Legend* (1998) is a biography of the author of *Little House on the Prairie*. Miller explores the pioneering life of Wilder, including details and truths, some harsh, not found in the "Little House" series of children's books.

Allan W. Eckert's *The Frontiersmen* (1967) centers on Simon Kenton, a historical figure and contemporary of Shawnee Chief Tecumseh and the legendary Daniel Boone. Kenton leads a cast of remarkable eighteenth-century characters as they navigate the white man's push west from the original colonies into wilderness.

*My Ántonia*, Willa Cather's third frontier novel, was published in 1918. In it, Cather returns to the Nebraska of her youth and writes about the daughter of an immigrant settler family from Bohemia attempting to tame the plains. Jim Burden, an orphan who lives with his grandparents on a neighboring farm, tells the story of Ántonia Shimerda's life. Ántonia is, of course, a tough, independent survivor.

### The Southern American Dream

William Faulkner's Southern gothic classic *The Sound and the Fury* (1929) is a masterwork novel by the Nobel laureate. Using a stream-of-conscious writing style, Faulkner explores the corruption and decomposition of the Compson family as a metaphor for the genteel South in post–Civil War America.

Erskine Caldwell's *Tobacco Road* (1932) explores the lives of sharecroppers in Georgia during the Great Depression. Focusing on a family of poor white cotton farmers, the Lesters, Caldwell explores sex and violence among the limited Lesters and their compatriots. Despite their problems, Jeeter Lester finds solace in the soil he works.

Flannery O'Connor's short story "Everything that Rises Must Converge" (1965) explores the clash between traditional conservatism and emerging intellectual liberalism between two generations of genteel white southerners in the U.S. civil rights era. A mother clings to her superior, condescending, if outwardly polite attitude to African Americans, as her college-educated son revels in her discomfort with the changing times.

*Midnight in the Garden of Good and Evil* (1994) is a nonfiction account of a murder in Savannah, Georgia, that is stranger than any fiction. Focusing less on the tragic event and more on the real-life oddball characters peripheral to it, author John Berendt shows a charming, surreal slice of the American dream that community outsiders could never have imagined.

In *Big Fish* (1998), Daniel Wallace captures the southern flair for storytelling, history, and myth in the creation of one ordinary man's life's legacy. An estranged son comes home to face his father's death and gets a chance to understand the larger-than-life figure and one person's power to craft the meaning of his own life.

*A Killing in This Town* (2006), the second novel by Olympia Vernon, explores racial tensions in a small Mississippi town. The community is dominated by the Ku Klux Klan, whose members have instituted a coming-of-age ritual for its sons as they turn thirteen:lynching a black man. The novel explores this violence from all points of view.

## The Feminist American Dream

Margaret Fuller, a close friend and contemporary of Ralph Waldo Emerson, published *Woman in the Nineteenth Century* in 1845. Fuller discusses a wide range of issues in her treatise of the state of women in culture, analyzing the ways in which history has favored men.

In the novel *The Bostonians* (1886), Henry James explores political themes such as feminism and the role of women in society. Verena Tarrant is a feminist whose ideals are supported by Olive Chancellor. Olive's cousin Basil Ransom convinces Verena to give up her feminist ways and elope with him before she is due to make a major speech, but she does not do so without sorrow.

Mabel Collins Donnelly's *The American Victorian Woman: The Myth and the Reality* (1986) explores the lives of women of the middle and lower classes in the late nineteenth and early twentieth centuries. While some female reformers began questioning women's place in society, the beginning of their realizing their American dream, many women's lives were a daily struggle.

Kate Chopin's *The Awakening* (1899) tells of Enda Pontellier's rejection of marriage and traditional women's roles in turn-of-the-century New Orleans, her discovery of her sense of self, and her death because of her refusal to acquiesce to society's expectations of her. The novel's publication caused a scandal, and its author was largely forgotten until feminist scholars rediscovered her in the 1960s.

Willa Cather's *The Song of the Lark*, published in 1915, is the author's second frontier novel. It is widely considered to be her most autobiographical novel, as it tells the story of Thea Kronborg, an aspiring singer desperate to trade the confines of a small Colorado town for the Metropolitan Opera House. Kronborg is a misunderstood artist, a loner—much like Cather was in her youth.

*Women of the Beat Generation: The Writers, Artists and Muses at the Heart of a Revolution* (2000), by Brenda Knight, is a long-overdue look at the female influences of the Beat Generation. This book not only collects information on these artists, but also features photos and examples of their creative works.

*Women, Race, and Class* (1981), by Angela Y. Davis, frames the struggles for gender equality in the context of the struggle for racial equality, and worker's rights in the context of civil rights. Davis gained notoriety in the 1970s over a crime of which she was later acquitted; she remains a prominent activist for social causes.

*The Handmaid's Tale* (1985), by Margaret Atwood, is a startling look at a possible future in which women have no reproductive rights. Women in this society, the "Republic of Gilead," are either wives, housekeepers, or handmaids. The handmaids bear society's children, which are raised by the wives of the men who control all the women.

## The American Dream Abroad

In *The American* (1877), Henry James explores the American dream of Christopher Newman. This self-made millionaire is on his first tour of Europe looking for new experiences outside of his life as a businessman. He shows his American nature in the first half of the book when he tries to marry the daughter of French aristocrats but cannot please them.

In *French Connections: Hemingway and Fitzgerald Abroad* (1999) J. Gerald Kennedy presents a collection of essays about the Americans most identified with the "Lost Generation" abroad after World War I: Ernest Hemingway and F. Scott Fitzgerald. The essays look at the pair's friendship, particularly during their "Paris years" in the late 1920s.

*The Mosquito Coast* (1981), by Paul Theroux, starts with an American inventor following his dream of creating a utopia for his family. The patriarch, Allie Fox, is disillusioned with life in modern America, but he creates a dangerous hell for his family in Central America as he becomes deluded and obsessed.

In *My Year of Meats* (1998) Ruth L. Ozeki, a Japanese American documentary filmmaker, presents a protagonist like herself, also a Japanese American documentary filmmaker. Assigned to create a series of television shows in the United States promoting American beef to Japanese housewives, the novel's heroine discovers and plots to expose unethical practices in the beef industry. *My Year of Meats* gives an outsider's perspective on a most American institution.

French journalist Bernard-Henri Lévy searches for the true American culture and identity in *American Vertigo: Traveling America in the Footsteps of Tocqueville* (2006). Lévy visits the rich and the poor, the powerful and the disenfranchised, churches, malls, prisons, and everything in between to understand the American conundrum.

## The American Political Dream

*The Rights of Man*, 1791–1792, was published while author Thomas Paine lived in England. The text was popular as it argued against hereditary monarchies, but it brought Paine a governmental charge of sedition on account of which he fled to France. *The Age of Reason* is Paine's critical analysis of religion. Published in 1795, this text helped create an American backlash against the man who helped the colonies gain their independence.

In *Neo-conservatism: The Autobiography of an Idea* (1995) Irving Kristol attempts to define the political philosophy he helped define, one that would so strongly influence American political life in the late twentieth and early twenty-first centuries. The book includes dozens of articles and essays dating to the 1950s.

The loud, opinionated, primarily conservative commentators that Stephen Colbert on *The Colbert Report* mocks have written many successful books that promote their views. Colbert's character is primarily inspired by Fox News Network's Bill O'Reilly, the often aggressive host of the popular show *The O'Reilly Factor*. O'Reilly's most recent tome, *Culture Warrior*, appeared in 2006.

Ann Coulter is an attorney and conservative writer and commentator whose extreme anti-liberal remarks have been frequently criticized for being excessively venomous. Her books include *Treason: Liberal Treachery From the Cold War to the War on Terrorism* (2003) and *Godless: The Church of Liberalism* (2006).

Al Franken, a former writer and performer on the long-running TV show *Saturday Night Live*, has reinvented himself as the liberal counterpart to right-wing radio and TV hosts such as Rush Limbaugh and Bill O'Reilly and has hosted his own left-leaning radio program. In *Lies and the Lying Liars Who Tell Them: A Fair and Balanced Look at the Right* (2003), Franken skewers right-wing pundits with wit and careful research.

Another symbol of America's political left is Michael Moore. The rumpled, bespectacled Moore gained prominence as a documentary filmmaker, most notably with *Fahrenheit 9/11* (2004). Among Moore's best-selling books is *Dude, Where's My Country?* (2003). Although Moore is not a talk-show host, he regularly appears on talk programs as a "talking head" for the left.

Andrew Heywood's *Political Ideologies: An Introduction*, the third edition of which appeared in 2003, is an excellent tool for understanding the fundamental principles at the root of both liberal and conservative thought.

# Media
# Adaptations

# The American Dream: Media Adaptations

## The Colonial American Dream

Arthur Miller's stage play *The Crucible* (1952) offers a dark view of Puritan culture—specifically, the Salem witch trials. Although Miller draws parallels between the witch trials and the anti-Communist paranoia of McCarthyism in 1950s America, he based the play on actual historical documents that reveal a Puritan society in which strict religious doctrines lead many to their unwarranted deaths.

*Squanto: A Warrior's Tale* (1994) tells the tale of a young Patuxet Indian who helped the Pilgrims at Plymouth colony survive their first years in America. Though the film, directed by Xavier Koller, has been criticized for its historical inaccuracies, it remains one of the few cinematic examples of early colonial settlement from a Native American point of view. It is available on DVD from Walt Disney Home Entertainment.

*The Last of Mohicans* (1992) is a film adaptation of the novel by James Fenimore Cooper. Directed by Michael Mann and starring Daniel Day-Lewis, the film is set during the French and Indian War and shows the ravages of the early conflict. British and French forces fight in colonial America with the help of various Indian tribes. An American settler raised as a Mohawk, Hawkeye acts as a guide for the British, pursues his own path in the conflict, and also becomes involved in a romance with the daughter of a British officer. The film is available on Twentieth Century-Fox DVD.

*The Patriot* (2000) is a film directed by Roland Emmerich and starring Mel Gibson and Heath Ledger. Set in South Carolina in 1776, the film follows the fortune of Benjamin Martin, a farmer and a hero of the French and Indian War played by Gibson, who does not want to be part of the Revolutionary War. He is compelled to return to military service and head a militia force to help the colonial cause when one of his eldest sons is killed by a British officer. It is available on Sony Pictures DVD.

*The Crossing* is a 2000 production by A&E, with Jeff Daniels playing George Washington. The movie depicts the desperate conditions the colonial army faced early in the Revolutionary War.

Nick Nolte headlines the feature film *Jefferson in Paris* (1995), which covers Jefferson's time as American ambassador to France. Much of this film is concerned with Jefferson's affair with his slave, Sally Hemings, a matter further investigated in the 2000 TV movie *Sally Hemings: An American Scandal*. Although neither production emphasizes the Declaration itself, both investigate the complex ideas about race, slavery, and freedom that dominated Jefferson's philosophy of government and democracy.

### The American Dream in the Nineteenth Century

The expedition that opened the United States west of the Mississippi River is the focus of National Geographic's *Lewis and Clark: The Great Journey West* (2002). In 1802, Meriweather Lewis, William Clark, Sacagawea, and the Corps of Discovery set off into the Louisiana territory to find a water route across North America to the pacific Ocean. Jeff Bridges narrates this documentary about their journey. It is available on DVD from National Geographic Video.

*Small-Town America: Stereoscopic Views from the Robert Dennis Collection 1850–1920* is a collection of 2,000 photographs of the Mid-Atlantic states housed at the New York Public Library. The collection includes pictures of street scenes in communities large and small, homes, businesses, and natural landscapes. The website for this collection is digital.nypl.org/dennis/stereoviews—the collection can be viewed there.

*The Adventures of Mark Twain* (1944) is a film adaptation of the colorful life of the author of the *Adventures of Huckleberry Finn* and the *Adventures of Tom Sawyer*. Directed by Irving Rapper, the film stars Frederic March as Twain and Alexis Smith as his wife, Olivia Langdon Clemens. It is available on VHS from Metro-Goldwyn-Mayer.

The American dream of Newland Archer changes in *The Age of Innocence* (1993), based on the novel by Edith Wharton. A rich New Yorker in the late nineteenth century, Archer's tidy life becomes upended when he meets the cousin of his fiancée, Countess Olenska. Socially scandalous because she has left her abusive husband, Archer chooses to become involved with the countess and the pair eventually find love. The film stars Daniel Day-Lewis, Michelle Pfeiffer, and Winona Ryder. It is available on DVD from Sony.

Ken Burns's *The Civil War* (1990) is a highly acclaimed eleven-hour miniseries that examines the war from its earliest causes through Lincoln's assassination. Burns uses the participants' own words, through letters and diaries read by actors such as Jason Robards and Morgan Freeman to tell the story, and supplements with comments from modern historians as well as pictures and music from the era. The series is available on five DVDs from PBS Paramount.

### The American Dream in the Twentieth Century

*The Magnificent Ambersons* (1942), directed by Orson Welles, is an adaptation of the 1918, Pulitzer Prize–winning novel by Booth Tarkington. The story focuses the lives of three generations of an American family that made a fortune in the 1870s and became leaders of their Midwestern town but ends up working-class and irrelevant by the third generation. It is available on VHS and DVD. *The Magnificent Ambersons* was remade in 2002 with Madeline Stowe, Jonathan Rhys Myers, and Jennifer Tilly. The 2002 version is available on DVD from A&E Home Video.

Dorothea Lange (1895–1965) was a documentary photographer who captured the plight of those devastated during the Great Depression and Dust Bowl era. She was hired by the Farm Security Administration (FSA) to document the struggles of displaced migrant farm families. The complete catalog of Lange's FSA photographs is online at the Library of Congress website at memory.loc.gov/ammem/fsahtml/fahome.html.

*On the Waterfront* (1954) is a film starring Marlon Brando as a dissatisfied man who has no direction and is unable to state or understand why he is troubled. Directed by Elia Kazan and co-starring Karl Malden, the film is a classic. Brando plays Terry Malloy, a wannabe prize fighter who works as a longshoreman and gets caught up in a union/mob drama. Malloy becomes a physically abused outcast for informing on the mob but tries to become a hero. It is available on DVD from Sony Pictures.

Allen Ginsberg's 1955 poem "Howl" is available on the audio CD *Howl and Other Poems* (1998) as read by the author. "Howl" is a radical, stream-of-consciousness work that defies many of the accepted rules of formal poetry. The poem also exhibits many of the philosophies supported by the Beat Generation artists, including a distrust of authority and government, open sexuality, and experimental drug use. Hearing the poem aloud as the author intended adds a new layer of resonance to the work.

The television series *Leave it to Beaver* epitomizes the white middle-class mainstream American dream in the mid-twentieth century. It ran from 1957 to 1963, first on CBS and then on ABC, and centered on the family life of the Cleavers: parents Ward and June and sons Wally and Theodore, better known as "Beaver." The first two seasons are available on DVD from Universal Studios.

Neil Simon's *Barefoot in the Park* (1967) is the film adaptation of his 1963 comedic stage play. It centers on young newlyweds struggling to adapt to their life together and reconcile their very different takes on the American dream. Robert Redford stars as Paul, the conservative lawyer husband, with Jane Fonda as Corie, the free-spirited wife. It is available on DVD from Paramount.

*Guess Who's Coming to Dinner?* (1967) is the first Hollywood film to depict an interracial relationship with an optimistic ending. Directed by Stanley Kramer and written by William Rose, who won an Academy Award for the script, the film focuses on the romantic relationship between an African American man, Dr. Prentice (played by Sidney Poitier) and a wealthy white woman, Joanna Drayton (Katharine Houghton). Drayton has taken her new fiancé home to meet her parents in California, and the couple deals with the reaction of their families and friends. It is the last film in which Katherine Hepburn and Spencer Tracy, who play Joanna's parents, appear

together. It is available on DVD from Columbia TriStar.

*Glengarry Glen Ross* (1992) is a film adaptation of the 1984 winner of the Pulitzer Prize for drama. The play was written by David Mamet and explores the pressure-filled lives of real estate salesman competing in a career-determining sales contest. Coming in third means losing one's job. The men sell because it is their lifeblood and do everything they can to win, including steal. The film stars Alec Baldwin, Ed Harris, Alan Arkin, Al Pacino, Kevin Spacey, and Jack Lemmon. It was directed by James Foley and is available on DVD from Lions Gate.

### The American Dream Today

*The Colbert Report* airs on the Comedy Central network on weeknights and is often rerun during the day. Stephen Colbert's TV show is probably the best introduction to his humor and his on-air persona. To fully understand the "talking heads" he mocks, watch episodes of *The O'Reilly Factor* or *Hannity & Colmes* on the Fox News Network.

*Crash*, the 2005 Academy Award–winning film starring Don Cheadle, Thandie Newton, Terrence Howard, Sandra Bullock, Brendan Fraser, and Matt Dillon, among many others, examines race, gender, and class roles and prejudices from every angle. Good cops, bad cops, thugs, the privileged, their servants, and working-class families trying to move their dreams forward are all featured. It is available on DVD from Lions Gate.

*Super Size Me*, directed by and starring Morgan Spurlock, is a 2004 documentary analyzing the over-consumption associated with contemporary American culture, as represented by the popularity of McDonalds fast-food restaurants. It depicts an experiment Spurlock performed in 2003 in which he ate nothing but McDonalds fast food three times a day for thirty days. The results and the publicity from the experiment prompted the fast-food giant to drop its "super size" options from its menu. The film is available on DVD from Hart Sharp Video.

*American Beauty* (1999) spotlights the cracks in the American dream as the outwardly perfect suburban Burnham family falls apart in this tragicomedy. It won five Academy Awards including Best Picture, Best Original Screenplay, Best Director (Sam Mendes), and Best Actor

(Kevin Spacey as Lester Burnham). Annette Bening was also nominated for her role as Lester's tightly wound, ambitious, unfaithful wife, Carolyn. The Burnhams' daughter Jane (Thora Birch) is as disillusioned as her parents and explores her understanding of the dream with her cheerleader–best friend and enigmatic, oddball neighbor. It is available on DVD from Dreamworks Video.

*When the Levees Broke: A Requiem in Four Acts* (2006) is Spike Lee's four-hour HBO documentary about Hurricane Katrina's devastation of New Orleans in 2005. It features news footage and firsthand accounts of the disaster, and includes interviews with famous local musicians, politicians, academics, and private citizens. The film focuses on how the tragedy might have been avoided, as well as the city's spirit to survive. It is available on three DVDs from HBO Home Video.

### The African American Dream

The audio recording *Town Hall, New York City, August 22, 1945* (2005) is a treasure of early bebop history. In this recording—which was not even known by music historians to exist for six decades after it was made—two young artists destined to become legends are captured together in one of the first live bebop performances ever preserved. Charlie Parker and Dizzy Gillespie perform forty minutes of a new style of music that was still mostly unknown to their audience but would soon change the face of jazz. It is available on compact disc from Uptown Jazz.

*A Great Day in Harlem* (1995) examines the summer day in 1958 when fledgling photographer Art Kane brought together over fifty legendary jazz musicians for a photo shoot that resulted in an iconic image of American music history. The Academy Award–nominated documentary, directed by Jean Bach and narrated by Quincy Jones, is currently available on DVD from Homevision.

*Boyz N the Hood* (1991) is a film directed and written by African American filmmaker John Singleton. Set in inner-city Los Angeles, *Boys N the Hood* looks at the lives of three teenage boys growing up while dealing with a violent environment. While Ricky Baker hopes a football scholarship from the University of Southern California will lead to a better life outside of the streets, his half-brother Doughboy chooses to

become a victim of his environment. Their friend Tre is guided by his father, who helps him make positive choices in life. *Boyz N the Hood* is available on DVD from Sony Pictures.

The television show *Everybody Hates Chris* (UPN, 2005–2006, The CW, 2006—) is a nontraditional situation comedy based on the life and comedy of comedian Chris Rock. Set in Brooklyn in the early 1980s, the show focuses on Rock's young teenage years, his younger siblings, and his loving but firm parents. Rock also provides the narration for each episode as his younger "self" has to deal with experiences growing up in a sometimes difficult environment. The first season of *Everybody Hates Chris* is available on DVD from Paramount Home Video.

*Ralph Ellison: An American Journey* (2002) is a biographical documentary about the influential African American author directed by Avon Kirkland. Narrated by Andre Braugher, the film follows Ellison from his childhood, attending college at Tuskegee University, and living in New York City. Though he only completed one novel, the powerful *Invisible Man*, he also wrote short stories and essays and mentored other writers, such as James Alan McPherson. This documentary was screened at several film festivals and aired as part of PBS's *American Masters* series.

Jacob Lawrence's *The Great Migration* (1940–1941) is a series of four paintings that express aspects of the African American migration from the South to the North. The paintings emphasize the difficulties faced as blacks pursued the American dream. They are housed at The Museum of Modern Art in New York City and can be seen online at www.columbia.edu/itc/history/odonnell/w1010/edit/migration/migration.html.

*Dave Chappelle's Block Party* (2006) features the subversive celebrity comedian on a mission of goodwill, community, pride, and merriment as he throws a free block party in September 2004 in Brooklyn's Bedford-Stuyvesant neighborhood. The event featured music from Kayne West, the Fugees, and Mos Def, among others, and plenty of comedy. It is available on DVD from Universal Studios.

### The Asian American Dream

"Asian-American Art: California Confluences and Crosscurrents" (shl.stanford.edu/research/

asianamericanart.html) is a comprehensive study of visual art by Asian Americans from the mid-nineteenth to the mid-twentieth century. A touring exhibition based on the research will be launched in 2007, jointly organized by Stanford University, the Fine Arts Museums of San Francisco, and the Los Angeles County Museum of Art.

*The Killing Fields* (1984) tells the true story of Pulitzer Prize–winning *New York Times* journalist Sydney Schanberg (Sam Waterston), who reported from Cambodia at the time of the Khmer Rouge's mass extermination—responsible for the deaths of more than a million people—of those sympathetic to Cambodia's former regime in the late 1970s. Haing S. Ngor won an Academy Award for his supporting role as Schanberg's assistant. This film is available on DVD from Warner Home Video.

*Miss Saigon* (1989) is a stage musical retelling of Puccini's opera *Madame Butterfly*. While the original story is set in Japan, *Miss Saigon* takes place during and after the Vietnam War and looks at not just the heroine's dilemma, but also the fate of the thousands of children born to Vietnamese mothers from American fathers in the 1960s and 1970s. The original London cast recording is available on CD from Decca.

Ang Lee's *The Wedding Banquet* (1993) features a Taiwanese man in a gay relationship with a white man who asks his female Chinese friend to pose as his fiancée when his parents visit. Under pressure from his tradition-minded parents, the two actually marry, and the three (the protagonist, his wife, and his lover) form an unconventional domestic arrangement. It is available on VHS and DVD from MGM.

Short-lived television sitcom *All American Girl* (ABC, 1994–1995) centered on the Korean American Kim family: the immigrant traditional parents, the subversive grandmother, and children in various stages of assimilation. The series, groundbreaking with its presentation of an Asian American family, is itself an example of how the American dream may not live up to its promise, as producers worried that the American-born child of immigrants, Margaret Cho, may not be "Asian" enough to play an Asian American and may not be beautiful enough by western standards to attract an American audience. The complete first (and only) season is available on DVD from Shout! Factory/Sony BMG Music Entertainment.

## The Native American Dream

*Into the West* (2005) is a miniseries about two fictional families—one white, one Native American—who bear witness to many of the most famous and infamous historical moments of the Old West. The miniseries, produced by Steven Spielberg and boasting an all-star cast that includes Beau Bridges, Matthew Modine, Graham Greene, Sean Astin, and Keri Russell, is available on DVD from Dreamworks Video.

*The Outsider* (1961) is a film about Ira Hayes, a Native American who helped raise the American flag on Iwo Jima during World War II. A Marine and member of the Pima tribe, Hayes returned to the United States a hero, but faced difficulties readjusting to life on the reservation. He died of exposure while intoxicated. The film stars Tony Curtis as Hayes and is available on VHS from Nostalgia Home Video.

Allan Houser (1914–1994) is one of the best-known Native American painters and sculptors. Born to members of the Chiricahua Apache tribe who had been prisoners for decades after Chief Geronimo's 1886 surrender to the U.S. Army, Houser studied art in the 1930s and was soon being commissioned to paint memorial murals in government buildings. By the 1960s, he turned his attention to sculpture, and in 1992 he won the National Medal for the Arts. His works can be seen in collections all over the world, including at the National Museum of American Art, the National Portrait Gallery, the Oklahoma State Capitol, and at the United Nations. The artist's official website is www.allanhouser.com/intro.html.

*Running Brave* (1983) is a film about Billy Mills, an Oglala Sioux Indian born and raised on the Pine Ridge Indian Reservation in South Dakota where Black Elk lived. Mills shocked the world in 1964 by upsetting world record holder Ron Clarke to win the 10,000-meter race at the Tokyo Olympics. The film stars Robby Benson as Mills and is available on DVD from Trinity Home Entertainment.

*Pow Wow Highway* (1989) explores the harsh lives of Native Americans living on a reservation, contrasting a close friendship between an Indian who embraces social activism with one who believes in tradition and is on a spiritual quest. It was directed by Jonathan Wacks and stars A. Martinez and Gary Farmer. It is available on DVD from Anchor Bay.

*Smoke Signals* (1998) is a film directed by Chris Eyre and starring Adam Beach and Evan Adams. Based on stories by Sherman Alexie, the film explores life on a reservation in Idaho through the relationship of Thomas, a story-telling, myth-making nerd, and Victor, the hardened son of Arnold Joseph, the man who saved Thomas's life when he was an infant. Victor and Thomas go on a road trip to claim the estranged Arnold's remains after his death in the Southwest. It is available on DVD from Miramax.

The music collection *Native American Music: The Rough Guide* (1998) is a sampling of eighteen songs from tribes across North America: Navajo, Ute, Mohican, Cree, Blackfeet, Zuni, Cherokee, Oneida, Lakota, Comanche, and Kiowa are among the cultures featured, in both traditional and contemporary songs and chants. The collection is available on CD from World Music Network.

### The Hispanic American Dream

*Viva la Causa, 500 Years of Chicano History* (1995) is a documentary directed by Doug Norberg. This film provides an overview of Mexican American history beginning in pre-Columbian America and through over two centuries of American history. Information about the struggles of migrant workers, "Zoot Suit" riots, and Chicano art is included. It is available on VHS.

*My Family* (1995) is a film directed by Gregory Nava and starring Jimmy Smits and Edward James Olmos. It follows three generations of a Latino immigrant family from the 1930s, when Maria and Jose meet, marry, and settle in East Los Angeles. While trying to follow the American dream, their children and grand-children continue to face challenges related to their race and life circumstances through the 1950s and 1960s. Culture and family are emphasized despite trying circumstances. It is available on DVD from New Line Home Video.

Susan Kelk Cervantes has painted many outdoor murals in San Francisco's predominately Latino Mission neighborhood. She is the founder and director of the PrecitaEyes Mural Arts and Visitors Center (www.precitaeyes.org), which works to preserve existing murals and promote new ones, as well as offering walking tours for visitors and information and opportunities to get involved online.

*Maria Full of Grace* (2004) is a movie about a pregnant Colombian teen who tries to make a better life for herself by acting as a "mule" smuggling capsules of heroin in her stomach into the United States. Catalina Sandrino Moreno was nominated for an Academy Award for her performance as the title character. The Spanish-language film is available on DVD from HBO Home Video.

*Ugly Betty* (ABC, 2006—) was the breakout television hit of 2006. Produced by Salma Hayek and based on a Colombian telenovela, the comedy-drama series focuses on Betty (America Ferrera), an "ugly ducking" in the beautiful world of fashion publishing, and a "fish out of water" as the child of an illegal immigrant from Queens in society-minded Manhattan.

### The American Immigrant Dream

*New York* (2004), an eight-episode documentary created by Ric Burns, provides an exhaustive chronology of the city and the people who were instrumental in shaping its identity. The series covers everything from the creation of New York's engineering marvels like the Brooklyn Bridge to its rich immigrant heritage. The final episode even includes material related to the 9/11 tragedy. The series is currently available on DVD from PBS Paramount.

On December 26, 2006, NBC aired a look into one of the year's hottest topics in the United States—illegal immigration—focusing on the human side of the story rather than relying on statistics and sound bites from policy makers. A transcript of the report is available at www.msnbc.msn.com/id/16353653.

The movie *Avalon* (1990) follows a Polish American family, beginning as the first arrives in Baltimore in 1914. He works to earn money to bring the next family member, and the American family grows as more emigrate and new generations are born. It focuses on the tri-generational family's life in the 1950s. It stars Armin Mueller-Stahl, Adian Quinn, and Elijah Wood, as father, son, and grandson, respectively, and is available on DVD from Sony Pictures.

Based on a novel by Amy Tan, *The Joy Luck Club* (1993) tells the stories of four women who immigrated to the United States from China, and of their four first-generation American daughters. Gathered at the occasion of one of the immigrant women's funerals, the mothers and daughters try to understand each other and their experiences, as well as their current paths in the United States. It stars Ming-Na Wen and is available on DVD from Buena Vista Home Entertainment.

*Out of Ireland: Story of Emigration to America* (1995) is a PBS documentary about the history of Irish migration to the United States, highlighting in particular the impact of the uprising of 1798, the famine of the 1840s, the U.S. Civil War, and twentieth-century politics. Actors including Liam Neeson, Kelly McGillis, Adian Quinn, and Gabriel Byrne read excerpts from emigrants' letters and diaries, balancing and humanizing the historical approach to the story. It is available on DVD from Shanachie Entertainment.

## The Frontier American Dream

*The Alamo* (2004) dramatizes the famous siege and battle at the Texas mission in 1836. This movie version, directed by John Lee Hancock, is more historically faithful to the events depicted than the 1960 John Wayne version, but it was less popular than its more romantic predecessor. It stars Billy Bob Thornton as David Crockett, Jason Patric as James Bowie, and Dennis Quaid as Sam Houston, and is available from Buena Vista Home Entertainment.

The classic John Ford film *The Searchers* shares many similarities with *Lonesome Dove*: it is set in Texas in 1868, and features the Texas Rangers battling Comanches. In the film, John Wayne plays a middle-aged horseman named Ethan Edwards whose two nieces are abducted by Comanches during a raid on their home. Ethan and his half-Indian, half-white adopted nephew Martin embark on a years-long search to find the girls and bring them home. The film is often considered to be John Ford's masterpiece, and ranks high on many lists as one of the greatest films of all time.

Charles Marion Russell (1864–1926), also known as C. M. Russell, was a prolific painter of the American West. Though born in Missouri, he worked as a cattle hand in Montana in his teens, where his passion for painting rustic subject matter—cowboys, Indians, landscapes, animals—emerged. His mural, "Lewis and Clark Meeting the Flathead Indians," hangs in the state capitol building in Helena, Montana. The artist's official website is www.cmrussell.org.

The epic film *How the West Was Won* (1962) follows one family's migration westward over several generations. Notable more for its scope than its impact, it was shot using a three-camera panorama technique and features five segments by five star directors and dozens of A-list stars (including Henry Fonda, Karl Malden, Gregory Peck, Debbie Reynolds, James Stewart, Spencer Tracy, and John Wayne). The movie presents the outdated, one-sided, white man's manifest destiny view of the Old West. It is available on DVD from Warner Home Video.

To amuse themselves on long, lonely trail rides, American cowboys developed a style of folk ballad known as "cowboy songs." Warner Brothers released a CD of them in 1998, called *Greatest Cowboy Songs Ever*. The collection features "Home On the Range," "Buffalo Gals/Polly Wolly Doodle," "Cattle Call," "The Yellow Rose of Texas," "The Streets of Laredo," "Tumblin' Tumbleweeds," "(Ghost) Riders in the Sky," "San Antonio Rose," "Don't Fence Me In," and "Happy Trails."

## The Southern American Dream

An American classic of one person's struggle to overcome the worst of circumstances, *Gone with the Wind* (1939) is the Academy Award–winning film adaptation of the 1936 novel by Margaret Mitchell. It was produced by David O. Selznick and directed by Victory Fleming. Starring Clark Cable and Vivien Leigh, the film explores the complicated life of southern belle Scarlett O'Hara in Georgia in the time of the Civil War.

In *Miss Firecracker* (1989), Holly Hunter plays Carnelle, an unhappy Mississippi woman who dreams of winning a beauty title to expand her life's prospects beyond her small hometown. Alfre Woodard, Mary Steenburgen, and Tim Robbins also star in this comic, poignant film, based on Beth Henley's 1984 play *The Miss Firecracker Contest*. It is available on DVD from First Look Pictures.

*Mississippi Masala* (1991) is an interracial and intercultural romance, starring Denzel Washington as a rural Mississippi rug cleaner falling in love with the daughter of Indian immigrants, played by Sarita Choudhury. Racism, dislocation, and the expectations of family all play parts in the drama. It is available on DVD from Sony Pictures.

Southern attempts to right old wrongs are at the heart of *Ghosts of Mississippi* (1996). It is the real-life story of the 1994 trial over the 1963 murder of civil rights–leader Medgar Evers. James Woods plays Byron De La Beckwith, the man finally convicted of the murder after two all-white juries had been unable to reach a verdict thirty years earlier. Alec Baldwin plays the district attorney who wins the conviction in the face of much resistance from his community and family. Whoopi Goldberg plays Myrlie Evers, the widow of the slain man who had all but given up on justice. It is available on DVD from Turner Home Entertainment.

*Junebug* (2005) examines the dichotomy of finding oneself either by rejecting or embracing one's roots. A sophisticated, urban man brings his new wife, a worldly art dealer, from their home in Chicago to meet his family in rural North Carolina in this intriguing, ambiguous, charming story of family and identity. It is available on DVD from Sony Pictures.

### The Feminist American Dream

*Iron Jawed Angels* (2004) depicts the U.S. women's suffrage movement in the 1910s. Led by Alice Paul (Hilary Swank) and Lucy Burns (Frances O'Connor), suffragists demonstrate, protest, and eventually go on hunger strikes to draw attention to their cause. It is available on DVD from HBO Home Video.

Mary Cassatt (1844–1926) was an American-born painter who worked in France. She painted scenes of domesticity and maternity and was among the first artists to explore the mundane details of women's daily lives. Many of her paintings are in the collection held at the National Gallery of Art, in Washington, D.C. (www.nga.gov).

*The Mary Tyler Moore Show* (1970–1977) was a pioneering character-driven situation comedy starring Mary Tyler Moore as Mary Richards, a single career woman making it "on her own," without the help of a husband. The show focuses on Mary's workplace, a Minneapolis newsroom, and her relationships with friends and coworkers, portrayed by Ed Asner, Ted Knight, Cloris Leachman, and Betty White, among others. The first four seasons are available on DVD from Twentieth Century Fox.

Based on the book Class Action: The Story of Lois Jenson and the Landmark Case That Changed Sexual Harassment Law, *North Country* (2005) dramatizes one woman's fight for fair work opportunities in a Minnesota a coal mine. Charlize Theron and Frances McDormand both received Academy Award nominations for their performances. It is available on DVD from Warner Home Video.

Born in 1970, Ani Difranco is a prolific songwriter, singer, and guitarist, whom some consider a folk artist, some consider a punk rocker, and some think of as a women's musician. In 2006, she won the National Organization for Women's Woman of Courage Award for contributions to the feminist movement. Her breakout album was 1990's *Not a Pretty Girl*, which is available on CD from Righteous Babe.

### The American Dream Abroad

A film adaptation of a novel by Henry James, *The Golden Bowl* (2000) explores the complicated love life of a young American woman abroad, Maggie Verver, the daughter of a rich American father. She is married to an Italian, Prince Amerigo, though he is secretly involved with his close friend, Charlotte Stuart. Maggie's life grows complicated as she encourages her father to become involved with Charlotte and the tensions in her life play out. It is available on DVD from Lions Gate.

*The Razor's Edge* (1984) is the second film adaptation of the 1942 W. Somerset Maugham novel about an American war veteran who rejects the traditional American dream of "upward mobility" after World War I and travels the world to find himself. Comedy legend Bill Murray co-wrote and stars in this dramatic role, one of the earliest of his career. It is available on DVD from Sony Pictures.

In one of the greatest accomplishments of American cinema, *Casablanca* (1942), Humphrey Bogart plays Rick, an American nightclub owner in Morocco in World War II. Set prior to the United States' entry into the war, Rick first cynically refuses to take sides between the Nazi-sympathizing Vichy French government of Morocco and the anti-Nazi underground. What starts as a bitter love story becomes the epitome of sacrifice in the name of doing the right thing. The film is available on DVD from Warner Home Video and on VHS from MGM/UA Home Video.

Nominated for the Academy Award for best animated feature in 2004, *The Triplets of Belleville* (2003) offers a perspective on how the American dream is imagined overseas. The movie centers on the French enthusiasm for professional cycling, but when a cyclist is kidnapped and brought to the United States, Americans are portrayed as exaggerations of the worst cultural stereotypes. The film is available on DVD from Sony Pictures.

One of 2006's most talked-about movies, *Borat: Cultural Learnings of America for Make Benefit Glorious Nation of Kazakhstan* is a satire "mock-umentary" about a backward, foreign journalist's quest to understand Americans, their country, and their culture so he can take those lessons home to improve his own country. British comedian Sacha Baron Cohen stars as Borat, the enthusiastic, socially clueless, Kazakh journalist. He is an actor, but most of the Americans he encounters on his cross-country trip are not in on the joke, and their reactions range from outrage to strained politeness to good-natured helpfulness to transparent prejudice.

## The American Political Dream

*The History Channel Presents The Revolution* is a ten-hour documentary series about the Revolution that includes discussion of Jefferson, the Declaration, and other people and issues of interest. Popular actors such as Kelsey Grammer read the words of the historical figures, and recreations of major battles give interested viewers a good idea of the issues and events of the Revolution. It is available in a four-DVD set from A&E Home Video.

In 1997, famed documentary filmmaker Ken Burns directed a three-part series called *Thomas Jefferson*. Featuring the voice of actor Sam Waterston as Jefferson and other performers such as Gwyneth Paltrow contributing vocal performances, the Burns documentary is probably the most informative, accurate, and entertaining of the many Jefferson-inspired nonfiction films.

*Mr. Smith Goes to Washington* (1939) was directed by Frank Capra and stars James Stewart as the title character. It is a classic tale of the corrupt political insider and the common sense of the common man, one that is as appealing and relevant today as it ever was. It is available on DVD from Sony Pictures.

A film version of Robert Penn Warren's classic novel of American political corruption *All the King's Men* (1947) in 2006. It centers on the career of Willie Stark, a character loosely based on Louisiana Governor Huey P. Long. The film stars Sean Penn, Jude Law, Anthony Hopkins, and Kate Winslet. It is available on DVD from Sony Pictures.

*JFK—A Presidency Revealed* is a two-DVD box set that examines the Kennedy administration, using vintage black-and-white and color footage. The set includes two bonus episodes of cable network A&E's *Biography: JFK: A Personal Story* and *Biography: Joseph Kennedy Sr.: Father of an American Dynasty*. The DVD box set was released on November 25, 2003, by A&E Home Video.

A generation of Americans learned their civics lessons (and lessons in grammar and math) from a Saturday-morning cartoon with catchy songs called *Schoolhouse Rock*. The segments aired on ABC television starting in the early 1970s. Eleven of the songs about history and government have been released as *Schoolhouse Rock: America Rock* on CD or audiocassette from Rhino, or on VHS from Walt Disney. The collection includes the classics "No More Kings," "The Preamble," "Elbow Room," "Sufferin' till Suffrage," "I'm Just a Bill," and "Three-Ring Government."

# *Glossary*

## A

**abstract:** as an adjective applied to writing or literary works, abstract refers to words or phrases that name things not knowable through the five senses. Examples of abstracts include the *Cliffs Notes* summaries of major literary works. Examples of abstract terms or concepts include "idea," "guilt," "honesty," and "loyalty."

**aestheticism:** a literary and artistic movement of the nineteenth century. Followers of the movement believed that art should not be mixed with social, political, or moral teaching. The statement "art for art's sake" is a good summary of aestheticism. The movement had its roots in France, but it gained widespread importance in England in the last half of the nineteenth century, where it helped change the Victorian practice of including moral lessons in literature.

**Age of Johnson:** the period in English literature between 1750 and 1798, named after the most prominent literary figure of the age, Samuel Johnson. Works written during this time are noted for their emphasis on "sensibility," or emotional quality. These works formed a transition between the rational works of the Age of Reason, or Neoclassical period, and the emphasis on individual feelings and responses of the Romantic period. Significant writers during the Age of Johnson included the novelists Ann Radcliffe and Henry Mackenzie, dramatists Richard Sheridan and Oliver Goldsmith, and poets William Collins and Thomas Gray.

**Age of Reason:** see *neoclassicism*

**Age of Sensibility:** see *Age of Johnson*

**agrarians:** a group of Southern American writers of the 1930s and 1940s who fostered an economic and cultural program for the South based on agriculture, in opposition to the industrial society of the North. The term can refer to any group that promotes the value of farm life and agricultural society. Members of the original Agrarians included John Crowe Ransom, Allen Tate, and Robert Penn Warren.

**allegory:** a narrative technique in which characters representing things or abstract ideas are used to convey a message or teach a lesson. Allegory is typically used to teach moral, ethical, or religious lessons but is sometimes used for satiric or political purposes. Examples of allegorical works include Edmund Spenser's *The Faerie Queene* and John Bunyan's *The Pilgrim's Progress*.

**allusion:** a reference to a familiar literary or historical person or event, used to make an idea more easily understood. For example, describing someone as a "Romeo" makes an allusion to William Shakespeare's famous young lover in *Romeo and Juliet*.

**amerind literature:** the writing and oral traditions of Native Americans. Native American literature was originally passed on by word of mouth, so it consisted largely of stories and events that were easily memorized. Amerind prose is often rhythmic like poetry because it was recited to the beat of a ceremonial drum. Examples of Amerind literature include the autobiographical *Black Elk Speaks,* the works of N. Scott Momaday, James Welch, and Craig Lee Strete, and the poetry of Luci Tapahonso.

**analogy:** a comparison of two things made to explain something unfamiliar through its similarities to something familiar, or to prove one point based on the acceptedness of another. Similes and metaphors are types of analogies. Analogies often take the form of an extended simile, as in William Blake's aphorism: "As the caterpillar chooses the fairest leaves to lay her eggs on, so the priest lays his curse on the fairest joys."

**angry young men:** a group of British writers of the 1950s whose work expressed bitterness and disillusionment with society. Common to their work is an anti-hero who rebels against a corrupt social order and strives for personal integrity. The term has been used to describe Kingsley Amis, John Osborne, Colin Wilson, John Wain, and others.

**antagonist:** the major character in a narrative or drama who works against the hero or protagonist. An example of an evil antagonist is Richard Lovelace in Samuel Richardson's *Clarissa,* while a virtuous antagonist is Macduff in William Shakespeare's *Macbeth.*

**anthropomorphism:** the presentation of animals or objects in human shape or with human characteristics. The term is derived from the Greek word for "human form." The fables of Aesop, the animated films of Walt Disney, and Richard Adams's *Watership Down* feature anthropomorphic characters.

**anti-hero:** a central character in a work of literature who lacks traditional heroic qualities such as courage, physical prowess, and fortitude. Anti-heros typically distrust conventional values and are unable to commit themselves to any ideals. They generally feel helpless in a world over which they have no control. Anti-heroes usually accept, and often celebrate, their positions as social outcasts. A well-known anti-hero is Yossarian in Joseph Heller's novel *Catch-22.*

**anti-novel:** a term coined by French critic Jean-Paul Sartre. It refers to any experimental work of fiction that avoids the familiar conventions of the novel. The anti-novel usually fragments and distorts the experience of its characters, forcing the reader to construct the reality of the story from a disordered narrative. The best-known anti-novelist is Alain Robbe-Grillet, author of *Le voyeur.*

**antithesis:** the antithesis of something is its direct opposite. In literature, the use of antithesis as a figure of speech results in two statements that show a contrast through the balancing of two opposite ideas. Technically, it is the second portion of the statement that is defined as the "antithesis"; the first portion is the "thesis." An example of antithesis is found in the following portion of Abraham Lincoln's "Gettysburg Address"; notice the opposition between the verbs "remember" and "forget" and the phrases "what we say" and "what they did": "The world will little note nor long remember what we say here, but it can never forget what they did here."

**apocrypha:** writings tentatively attributed to an author but not proven or universally accepted to be their works. The term was originally applied to certain books of the Bible that were not considered inspired and so were not included in the "sacred canon." Geoffrey Chaucer, William Shakespeare, Thomas Kyd, Thomas Middleton, and John Marston all have apocrypha. Apocryphal books of the Bible include the Old Testament's Book of Enoch and New Testament's Gospel of Peter.

**apprenticeship novel:** see *bildungsroman*

**archetype:** the word archetype is commonly used to describe an original pattern or model from which all other things of the same kind are made. This term was introduced to literary criticism from the psychology of Carl Jung. It expresses Jung's theory that behind every person's "unconscious," or repressed memories of the past, lies the "collective unconscious" of the human race: memories of the countless typical experiences of our ancestors. These memories are said to prompt illogical associations that trigger powerful emotions in the reader. Often, the emotional process is primitive, even primordial. Archetypes are the literary images that grow out of the "collective unconscious." They appear in literature as incidents and plots that repeat basic patterns of life. They may also appear as stereotyped characters. Examples of literary archetypes include themes such as birth and death and characters such as the Earth Mother.

**argument:** the argument of a work is the author's subject matter or principal idea. Examples of defined "argument" portions of works include John Milton's *Arguments* to each of the books of *Paradise Lost* and the "Argument" to Robert Herrick's *Hesperides.*

**art for art's sake:** see *aestheticism*

**audience:** the people for whom a piece of literature is written. Authors usually write with a certain audience in mind, for example, children, members of a religious or ethnic group, or colleagues in a professional field. The term "audience" also applies to the people who gather to see or hear any performance, including plays, poetry readings, speeches, and concerts. Jane Austen's parody of the gothic novel, *Northanger Abbey,* was originally intended for (and also pokes fun at) an audience of young and avid female gothic novel readers.

**autobiography:** a connected narrative in which an individual tells his or her life story. Examples include Benjamin Franklin's *Autobiography* and Henry Adams's *The Education of Henry Adams.*

**automatic writing:** writing carried out without a preconceived plan in an effort to capture every random thought. Authors who engage in automatic writing typically do not revise their work, preferring instead to preserve the revealed truth and beauty of spontaneous expression. Automatic writing was employed by many of the Surrealist writers, notably the French poet Robert Desnos.

*avant-garde*: French term meaning "vanguard." It is used in literary criticism to describe new writing that rejects traditional approaches to literature in favor of innovations in style or content. Twentieth-century examples of the literary *avant-garde* include the Black Mountain School of poets, the Bloomsbury Group, and the Beat Movement.

# B

**baroque:** a term used in literary criticism to describe literature that is complex or ornate in style or diction. Baroque works typically express tension, anxiety, and violent emotion. The term "Baroque Age" designates a period in Western European literature beginning in the late sixteenth century and ending about one hundred years later. Works of this period often mirror the qualities of works more generally associated with the label "baroque" and sometimes feature elaborate conceits. Examples of Baroque works include John Lyly's *Euphues: The Anatomy of Wit,* Luis de Gongora's *Soledads,* and William Shakespeare's *As You Like It.*

**baroque age:** see *baroque*

**baroque period:** see *baroque*

**beat generation:** see *beat movement*

**beat movement:** a period featuring a group of American poets and novelists of the 1950s and 1960s—including Jack Kerouac, Allen Ginsberg, Gregory Corso, William S. Burroughs, and Lawrence Ferlinghetti—who rejected established social and literary values. Using such techniques as stream of consciousness writing and jazz-influenced free verse and focusing on unusual or abnormal states of mind—generated by religious ecstasy or the use of drugs—the Beat writers aimed to create works that were unconventional in both form and subject matter. Kerouac's *On the Road* is perhaps the best-known example of a Beat Generation novel, and Ginsberg's *Howl* is a famous collection of Beat poetry.

**beats, the:** see *beat movement*

*belles-lettres*: a French term meaning "fine letters" or "beautiful writing." It is often used as a synonym for literature, typically referring to imaginative and artistic rather than scientific or expository writing. Current usage sometimes restricts the meaning to light or humorous writing and appreciative essays about literature. Lewis Carroll's *Alice in Wonderland* epitomizes the realm of *belles-lettres.*

*bildungsroman*: a German word meaning "novel of development." The *bildungsroman* is a study of the maturation of a youthful character, typically brought about through a series of social or sexual encounters that lead to self-awareness. *Bildungsroman* is used interchangeably with *erziehungsroman,* a novel of initiation and education. When a *bildungsroman* is concerned with the development of an artist (as in James Joyce's *A Portrait of the Artist as a Young Man*), it is often termed a *kunstlerroman.* Well-known *bildungsroman* include J. D. Salinger's *The Catcher in the Rye,* Robert Newton Peck's *A Day No Pigs Would Die,* and S. E. Hinton's *The Outsiders.*

**biography:** a connected narrative that tells a person's life story. Biographies typically aim to be objective and closely detailed. James Boswell's *The Life of Samuel Johnson,* LL.D is a famous example of the form.

**black aesthetic movement:** a period of artistic and literary development among African Americans in the 1960s and early 1970s. This was the first major African-American artistic movement since the Harlem Renaissance and was closely paralleled by the civil rights and black power movements. The black aesthetic writers attempted to produce works of art that would be meaningful to the black masses. Key figures in black aesthetics included one of its founders, poet and playwright Amiri Baraka, formerly known as LeRoi Jones; poet and essayist Haki R. Madhubuti, formerly Don L. Lee; poet and playwright Sonia Sanchez; and dramatist Ed Bullins. Works representative of the Black Aesthetic Movement include Amiri Baraka's play *Dutchman,* a 1964 Obie award-winner; *Black Fire: An Anthology of Afro-American Writing,* edited by Baraka and playwright Larry Neal and published in 1968; and Sonia Sanchez's poetry collection *We a BaddDDD People,* published in 1970.

**black arts movement:** see *black aesthetic movement*

**black comedy:** see *black humor*

**black humor:** writing that places grotesque elements side by side with humorous ones in an attempt to shock the reader, forcing him or her to laugh at the horrifying reality of a disordered world. Joseph Heller's novel *Catch-22* is considered a superb example of the use of black humor. Other well-known authors who use black humor include Kurt Vonnegut, Edward Albee, Eugene Ionesco, and Harold Pinter.

**bloomsbury group:** a group of English writers, artists, and intellectuals who held informal artistic and philosophical discussions in Bloomsbury, a district of London, from around 1907 to the early 1930s. The Bloomsbury Group held no uniform philosophical beliefs but did commonly express an aversion to moral prudery and a desire for greater social tolerance. At various times the circle included Virginia Woolf, E. M. Forster, Clive Bell, Lytton Strachey, and John Maynard Keynes.

***bon mot:*** a French term meaning "good word." A *bon mot* is a witty remark or clever observation. Charles Lamb and Oscar Wilde are celebrated for their witty *bon mots.* Two examples by Oscar Wilde stand out: (1) "All women become their mothers. That is their tragedy. No man does. That's his." (2) "A man cannot be too careful in the choice of his enemies."

**burlesque:** any literary work that uses exaggeration to make its subject appear ridiculous, either by treating a trivial subject with profound seriousness or by treating a dignified subject frivolously. The word "burlesque" may also be used as an adjective, as in "burlesque show," to mean "striptease act." Examples of literary burlesque include the comedies of Aristophanes, Miguel de Cervantes's *Don Quixote,* Samuel Butler's poem "Hudibras," and John Gay's play *The Beggar's Opera.*

## C

**Celtic renaissance:** a period of Irish literary and cultural history at the end of the nineteenth century. Followers of the movement aimed to create a romantic vision of Celtic myth and legend. The most significant works of the Celtic Renaissance typically present a dreamy, unreal world, usually in reaction against the reality of contemporary problems. William Butler Yeats's *The Wanderings of Oisin* is among the most significant works of the Celtic Renaissance.

**Celtic twilight:** see *Celtic renaissance*

**character:** broadly speaking, a person in a literary work. The actions of characters are what constitute the plot of a story, novel, or poem. There are numerous types of characters, ranging from simple, stereotypical figures to intricate, multifaceted ones. In the techniques of anthropomorphism and personification, animals—and even places or things—can assume aspects of character. "Characterization" is the process by which an author creates vivid, believable characters in a work of art. This may be done in a variety of ways, including (1) direct description of the character by the narrator; (2) the direct presentation of the speech, thoughts, or actions of the character; and (3) the responses of other characters to the character. The term "character" also refers to a form originated by the ancient Greek writer Theophrastus that later became popular in the seventeenth and eighteenth centuries. It is a short essay or sketch of a person who prominently displays a specific attribute or quality, such as miserliness or ambition. Notable characters in literature include Oedipus Rex, Don Quixote de la Mancha, Macbeth, Candide, Hester Prynne, Ebenezer Scrooge, Huckleberry Finn, Jay Gatsby, Scarlett O'Hara, James Bond, and Kunta Kinte.

**characterization:** see *character*

**chronicle:** a record of events presented in chronological order. Although the scope and level of detail provided varies greatly among the chronicles surviving from ancient times, some, such as the *Anglo-Saxon Chronicle,* feature vivid descriptions and a lively recounting of events. During the Elizabethan Age, many dramas—appropriately called "chronicle plays"—were based on material from chronicles. Many of William Shakespeare's dramas of English history as well as Christopher Marlowe's *Edward II* are based in part on Raphael Holinshead's *Chronicles of England, Scotland, and Ireland.*

**classical:** in its strictest definition in literary criticism, classicism refers to works of ancient Greek or Roman literature. The term may also be used to describe a literary work of recognized importance (a "classic") from any time period or literature that exhibits the traits of classicism. Classical authors from ancient Greek and Roman times include Juvenal and Homer. Examples of later works and authors now described as classical include French literature of the seventeenth century, Western novels of the nineteenth century, and American fiction of the mid-nineteenth century such as that written by James Fenimore Cooper and Mark Twain.

**classicism:** a term used in literary criticism to describe critical doctrines that have their roots in ancient Greek and Roman literature, philosophy, and art. Works associated with classicism typically exhibit restraint on the part of the author, unity of design and purpose, clarity, simplicity, logical organization, and respect for tradition. Examples of literary classicism include Cicero's prose, the dramas of Pierre Corneille and Jean Racine, the poetry of John Dryden and Alexander Pope, and the writings of J. W. von Goethe, G. E. Lessing, and T. S. Eliot.

**climax:** the turning point in a narrative, the moment when the conflict is at its most intense. Typically, the structure of stories, novels, and plays is one of rising action, in which tension builds to the climax, followed by falling action, in which tension lessens as the story moves to its conclusion. The climax in James Fenimore Cooper's *The Last of the Mohicans* occurs when Magua and his captive Cora are pursued to the edge of a cliff by Uncas. Magua kills Uncas but is subsequently killed by Hawkeye.

**colloquialism:** a word, phrase, or form of pronunciation that is acceptable in casual conversation but not in formal, written communication. It is considered more acceptable than slang. An example of colloquialism can be found in Rudyard Kipling's *Barrack-room Ballads:* "When 'Omer smote 'is bloomin' lyre//He'd 'eard men sing by land and sea;// An' what he thought 'e might require//'E went an' took—the same as me!"

**coming of age novel:** see *bildungsroman*

**concrete:** concrete is the opposite of abstract, and refers to a thing that actually exists or a description that allows the reader to experience an object or concept with the senses. Henry David Thoreau's *Walden* contains much concrete description of nature and wildlife.

**connotation:** the impression that a word gives beyond its defined meaning. Connotations may be universally understood or may be significant only to a certain group. Both "horse" and "steed" denote the same animal, but "steed" has a different connotation, deriving from the chivalrous or romantic narratives in which the word was once often used.

**convention:** any widely accepted literary device, style, or form. A soliloquy, in which a character reveals to the audience his or her private thoughts, is an example of a dramatic convention.

**crime literature:** a genre of fiction that focuses on the environment, behavior, and psychology of criminals. Prominent writers of crime novels include John Wainwright, Colin Watson, Nicolas Freeling, Ruth Rendell, Jessica Mann, Mickey Spillane, and Patricia Highsmith.

# D

**dadaism:** a protest movement in art and literature founded by Tristan Tzara in 1916. Followers of the movement expressed their outrage at the destruction brought about by World War I by revolting against numerous forms of social convention. The Dadaists presented works marked by calculated madness and flamboyant nonsense. They stressed total freedom of expression, commonly through primitive displays of emotion and illogical, often senseless, poetry. The movement ended shortly after the war, when it was replaced by surrealism. Proponents of Dadaism include Andre Breton, Louis Aragon, Philippe Soupault, and Paul Eluard.

**decadent:** see *decadents*

**decadents:** the followers of a nineteenth-century literary movement that had its beginnings in French aestheticism. Decadent literature displays a fascination with perverse and morbid states; a search for novelty and sensation—the "new thrill"; a preoccupation with mysticism; and a belief in the senselessness of human existence. The movement is closely associated with the doctrine Art for Art's Sake. The term "decadence" is sometimes used to denote a decline in the quality of art or literature following a period of greatness. Major French decadents are Charles Baudelaire and Arthur Rimbaud. English decadents include Oscar Wilde, Ernest Dowson, and Frank Harris.

**deduction:** the process of reaching a conclusion through reasoning from general premises to a specific premise. An example of deduction is present in the following syllogism: Premise: All mammals are animals. Premise: All whales are mammals. Conclusion: Therefore, all whales are animals.

**denotation:** the definition of a word, apart from the impressions or feelings it creates in the reader. The word "apartheid" denotes a political and economic policy of segregation by race, but its connotations—oppression, slavery, inequality—are numerous.

*denouement*: a French word meaning "the unknotting." In literary criticism, it denotes the resolution of conflict in fiction or drama. The *denouement* follows the climax and provides an outcome to the primary plot situation as well as an explanation of secondary plot complications. The *denouement* often involves a character's recognition of his or her state of mind or moral condition. A well-known example of *denouement* is the last scene of the play *As You Like It* by William Shakespeare, in which couples are married, an evildoer repents, the identities of two disguised characters are revealed, and a ruler is restored to power.

**description:** descriptive writing is intended to allow a reader to picture the scene or setting in which the action of a story takes place. The form this description takes often evokes an intended emotional response—a dark, spooky graveyard will evoke fear, and a peaceful, sunny meadow will evoke calmness. An example of a descriptive story is Edgar Allan Poe's *Landor's Cottage*, which offers a detailed depiction of a New York country estate.

**detective story:** a narrative about the solution of a mystery or the identification of a criminal. The conventions of the detective story include the detective's scrupulous use of logic in solving the mystery; incompetent or ineffectual police; a suspect who appears guilty at first but is later proved innocent; and the detective's friend or confidant—often the narrator—whose slowness in interpreting clues emphasizes by contrast the detective's brilliance. Edgar Allan Poe's "Murders in the Rue Morgue" is commonly regarded as the earliest example of this type of story. With this work, Poe established many of the conventions of the detective story genre, which are still in practice. Other practitioners of this vast and extremely popular genre include Arthur Conan Doyle, Dashiell Hammett, and Agatha Christie.

**dialogue:** in its widest sense, dialogue is simply conversation between people in a literary work; in its most restricted sense, it refers specifically to the speech of characters in a drama. As a specific literary genre, a "dialogue" is a composition in which characters debate an issue or idea. The Greek philosopher Plato frequently expounded his theories in the form of dialogues.

**diary:** a personal written record of daily events and thoughts. As private documents, diaries are supposedly not intended for an audience, but some, such as those of Samuel Pepys and Anais Nin, are known for their high literary quality. *The Diary of Anne Frank* is an example of a well-known diary discovered and published after the author's death. Many writers have used the diary form as a deliberate literary device, as in Nikolai Gogol's story "Diary of a Madman."

**diction:** the selection and arrangement of words in a literary work. Either or both may vary depending on the desired effect. There are four general types of diction: "formal," used in scholarly or lofty writing; "informal," used in relaxed but educated conversation; "colloquial," used in everyday speech; and "slang," containing newly coined words and other terms not accepted in formal usage.

**didactic:** a term used to describe works of literature that aim to teach some moral, religious, political, or practical lesson. Although didactic elements are often found in artistically pleasing works, the term "didactic" usually refers to literature in which the message is more important than the form. The term may also be used to criticize a work that the critic finds "overly didactic," that is, heavy-handed in its delivery of a lesson. Examples of didactic literature include John Bunyan's *Pilgrim's Progress,* Alexander Pope's *Essay on Criticism,* Jean-Jacques Rousseau's *Emile,* and Elizabeth Inchbald's *Simple Story.*

**doppelganger:** a literary technique by which a character is duplicated (usually in the form of an alter ego, though sometimes as a ghostly counterpart) or divided into two distinct, usually opposite personalities. The use of this character device is widespread in nineteenth- and twentieth- century literature, and indicates a growing awareness among authors that the "self" is really a composite of many "selves." A well-known story containing a *doppelganger* character is Robert Louis Stevenson's *Dr. Jekyll and Mr. Hyde,* which dramatizes an internal struggle between good and evil.

***double entendre***: a corruption of a French phrase meaning "double meaning." The term is used to indicate a word or phrase that is deliberately ambiguous, especially when one of the meanings is risque or improper. An example of a *double entendre* is the Elizabethan usage of the verb "die," which refers both to death and to orgasm.

**double, the:** see *doppelganger*

**draft:** any preliminary version of a written work. An author may write dozens of drafts which are revised to form the final work, or he or she may write only one, with few or no revisions. Dorothy Parker's observation that "I can't write five words but that I change seven" humorously indicates the purpose of the draft.

**dramatic irony:** occurs when the audience of a play or the reader of a work of literature knows something that a character in the work itself does not know. The irony is in the contrast between the intended meaning of the statements or actions of a character and the additional information understood by the audience. A celebrated example of dramatic irony is in Act V of William Shakespeare's *Romeo and Juliet,* where two young lovers meet their end as a result of a tragic misunderstanding. Here, the audience has full knowledge that Juliet's apparent "death" is merely temporary; she will regain her senses when the mysterious "sleeping potion" she has taken wears off. But Romeo, mistaking Juliet's drug-induced trance for true death, kills himself in grief. Upon awakening, Juliet discovers Romeo's corpse and, in despair, slays herself.

***dramatis personae***: the characters in a work of literature, particularly a drama. The list of characters printed before the main text of a play or in the program is the *dramatis personae.*

**dream allegory:** see *dream vision*

**dream vision:** a literary convention, chiefly of the Middle Ages. In a dream vision a story is presented as a literal dream of the narrator. This device was commonly used to teach moral and religious lessons. Important works of this type are *The Divine Comedy* by Dante Alighieri, *Piers Plowman* by William Langland, and *The Pilgrim's Progress* by John Bunyan.

**dystopia:** an imaginary place in a work of fiction where the characters lead dehumanized, fearful lives. Jack London's *The Iron Heel,* Yevgeny Zamyatin's *My,* Aldous Huxley's *Brave New World,* George Orwell's *Nineteen Eighty-four,* and Margaret Atwood's *Handmaid's Tale* portray versions of dystopia.

# E

**Edwardian:** describes cultural conventions identified with the period of the reign of Edward VII of England (1901–1910). Writers of the Edwardian Age typically displayed a strong reaction against the propriety and conservatism of the Victorian Age. Their work often exhibits distrust of authority in religion, politics, and art and expresses strong doubts about the soundness of conventional values. Writers of this era include George Bernard Shaw, H. G. Wells, and Joseph Conrad.

**Edwardian age:** see *Edwardian*

**electra complex:** a daughter's amorous obsession with her father. The term Electra complex comes from the plays of Euripides and Sophocles entitled *Electra,* in which the character Electra drives her brother Orestes to kill their mother and her lover in revenge for the murder of their father.

**Elizabethan age:** a period of great economic growth, religious controversy, and nationalism closely associated with the reign of Elizabeth I of England (1558–1603). The Elizabethan Age is considered a part of the general renaissance—that is, the flowering of arts and literature—that took place in Europe during the fourteenth through sixteenth centuries. The era is considered the golden age of English literature. The most important dramas in English and a great deal of lyric poetry were produced during this period, and modern English criticism began around this time. The notable authors of the period—Philip Sidney, Edmund Spenser, Christopher Marlowe, William Shakespeare, Ben Jonson, Francis Bacon, and John Donne—are among the best in all of English literature.

**empathy:** a sense of shared experience, including emotional and physical feelings, with someone or something other than oneself. Empathy is often used to describe the response of a reader to a literary character. An example of an empathic passage is William Shakespeare's description in his narrative poem *Venus and Adonis* of: "the snail, whose tender horns being hit, Shrinks backward in his shelly cave with pain." Readers of Gerard Manley Hopkins's *The Windhover* may experience some of the physical sensations evoked in the description of the movement of the falcon.

**enlightenment, the:** an eighteenth-century philosophical movement. It began in France but had a wide impact throughout Europe and America. Thinkers of the Enlightenment valued reason and believed that both the individual and society could achieve a state of perfection. Corresponding to this essentially humanist vision was a resistance to religious authority. Important figures of the Enlightenment were Denis Diderot and Voltaire in France, Edward Gibbon and David Hume in England, and Thomas Paine and Thomas Jefferson in the United States.

**epigram:** a saying that makes the speaker's point quickly and concisely. Samuel Taylor Coleridge wrote an epigram that neatly sums up the form: "What is an Epigram? A Dwarfish whole,//Its body brevity, and wit its soul."

**epilogue:** a concluding statement or section of a literary work. In dramas, particularly those of the seventeenth and eighteenth centuries, the epilogue is a closing speech, often in verse, delivered by an actor at the end of a play and spoken directly to the audience. A famous epilogue is Puck's speech at the end of William Shakespeare's *A Midsummer Night's Dream.*

**epiphany:** a sudden revelation of truth inspired by a seemingly trivial incident. The term was widely used by James Joyce in his critical writings, and the stories in Joyce's *Dubliners* are commonly called "epiphanies."

**episode:** an incident that forms part of a story and is significantly related to it. Episodes may be either self-contained narratives or events that depend on a larger context for their sense and importance. Examples of episodes include the founding of Wilmington, Delaware in Charles Reade's *The Disinherited Heir* and the individual events comprising the picaresque novels and medieval romances.

**episodic plot:** see *plot*

**epistolary novel:** a novel in the form of letters. The form was particularly popular in the eighteenth century. Samuel Richardson's *Pamela* is considered the first fully developed English epistolary novel.

**epitaph:** an inscription on a tomb or tombstone, or a verse written on the occasion of a person's death. Epitaphs may be serious or humorous. Dorothy Parker's epitaph reads, "I told you I was sick."

**epithet:** a word or phrase, often disparaging or abusive, that expresses a character trait of someone or something. "The Napoleon of crime" is an epithet applied to Professor Moriarty, arch-rival of Sherlock Holmes in Arthur Conan Doyle's series of detective stories.

*erziehungsroman:* see *bildungsroman*

**essay:** a prose composition with a focused subject of discussion. The term was coined by Michel de Montaigne to describe his 1580 collection of brief, informal reflections on himself and on various topics relating to human nature. An essay can also be a long, systematic discourse. An example of a longer essay is John Locke's An Essay Concerning Human Understanding.

*exempla:* see *exemplum*

*exemplum:* a tale with a moral message. This form of literary sermonizing flourished during the Middle Ages, when *exempla* appeared in collections known as "example-books." The works of Geoffrey Chaucer are full of *exempla.*

**existentialism:** a predominantly twentieth-century philosophy concerned with the nature and perception of human existence. There are two major strains of existentialist thought: atheistic and Christian. Followers of atheistic existentialism believe that the individual is alone in a godless universe and that the basic human condition is one of suffering and loneliness. Nevertheless, because there are no fixed values, individuals can create their own characters—indeed, they can shape themselves—through the exercise of free will. The atheistic strain culminates in and is popularly associated with the works of Jean-Paul Sartre. The Christian existentialists, on the other hand, believe that only in God may people find freedom from life's anguish. The two strains hold certain beliefs in common: that existence cannot be fully understood or described through empirical effort; that anguish is a universal element of life; that individuals must bear responsibility for their actions; and that there is no common standard of behavior or perception for religious and ethical matters. Existentialist thought figures prominently in the works of such authors as Eugene Ionesco, Franz Kafka, Fyodor Dostoyevsky, Simone de Beauvoir, Samuel Beckett, and Albert Camus.

**expatriates:** see *expatriatism*

**expatriatism:** the practice of leaving one's country to live for an extended period in another country. Literary expatriates include English poets Percy Bysshe Shelley and John Keats in Italy, Polish novelist Joseph Conrad in England, American writers Richard Wright, James Baldwin, Gertrude Stein, and Ernest Hemingway in France, and Trinidadian author Neil Bissondath in Canada.

**exposition:** writing intended to explain the nature of an idea, thing, or theme. Expository writing is often combined with description, narration, or argument. In dramatic writing, the exposition is the introductory material which presents the characters, setting, and tone of the play. An example of dramatic exposition occurs in many nineteenth-century drawing-room comedies in which the butler and the maid open the play with relevant talk about their master and mistress; in composition, exposition relays factual information, as in encyclopedia entries.

**expressionism:** an indistinct literary term, originally used to describe an early twentieth-century school of German painting. The term applies to almost any mode of unconventional, highly subjective writing that distorts reality in some way. Advocates of Expressionism include dramatists George Kaiser, Ernst Toller, Luigi Pirandello, Federico Garcia Lorca, Eugene O'Neill, and Elmer Rice; poets George Heym, Ernst Stadler, August Stramm, Gottfried Benn, and Georg Trakl; and novelists Franz Kafka and James Joyce.

# F

**fable:** a prose or verse narrative intended to convey a moral. Animals or inanimate objects with human characteristics often serve as characters in fables. A famous fable is Aesop's "The Tortoise and the Hare."

**fairy tales:** short narratives featuring mythical beings such as fairies, elves, and sprites. These tales originally belonged to the folklore of a particular nation or region, such as those collected in Germany by Jacob and Wilhelm Grimm. Two other celebrated writers of fairy tales are Hans Christian Andersen and Rudyard Kipling.

**falling action:** see *denouement*

**fantasy:** a literary form related to mythology and folklore. Fantasy literature is typically set in non-existent realms and features supernatural beings. Notable examples of fantasy literature are *The Lord of the Rings* by J. R. R. Tolkien and the Gormenghast trilogy by Mervyn Peake.

**farce:** a type of comedy characterized by broad humor, outlandish incidents, and often vulgar subject matter. Much of the "comedy" in film and television could more accurately be described as farce.

***femme fatale*:** a French phrase with the literal translation "fatal woman." A *femme fatale* is a sensuous, alluring woman who often leads men into danger or trouble. A classic example of the *femme fatale* is the nameless character in Billy Wilder's *The Seven Year Itch*, portrayed by Marilyn Monroe in the film adaptation.

***festschrift*:** a collection of essays written in honor of a distinguished scholar and presented to him or her to mark some special occasion. Examples of *festschriften* are *Worlds of Jewish Prayer: A Festschrift in Honour of Rabbi Zalman M. Schachter-Shalomi* and *The Organist as Scholar: Essays in Memory of Russell Saunders.*

**fiction:** any story that is the product of imagination rather than a documentation of fact. characters and events in such narratives may be based in real life but their ultimate form and configuration is a creation of the author. Geoffrey Chaucer's *The Canterbury Tales,* Laurence Sterne's *Tristram Shandy,* and Margaret Mitchell's *Gone with the Wind* are examples of fiction.

**figurative language:** a technique in writing in which the author temporarily interrupts the order, construction, or meaning of the writing for a particular effect. This interruption takes the form of one or more figures of speech such as hyperbole, irony, or simile.

Figurative language is the opposite of literal language, in which every word is truthful, accurate, and free of exaggeration or embellishment. Examples of figurative language are tropes such as metaphor and rhetorical figures such as apostrophe.

**figures of speech:** writing that differs from customary conventions for construction, meaning, order, or significance for the purpose of a special meaning or effect. There are two major types of figures of speech: rhetorical figures, which do not make changes in the meaning of the words, and tropes, which do. Types of figures of speech include simile, hyperbole, alliteration, and pun, among many others.

***fin de siecle*:** a French term meaning "end of the century." The term is used to denote the last decade of the nineteenth century, a transition period when writers and other artists abandoned old conventions and looked for new techniques and objectives. Two writers commonly associated with the *fin de siecle* mindset are Oscar Wilde and George Bernard Shaw.

**first person:** see *point of view*

**flashback:** a device used in literature to present action that occurred before the beginning of the story. Flashbacks are often introduced as the dreams or recollections of one or more characters. Flashback techniques are often used in films, where they are typically set off by a gradual changing of one picture to another.

**foil:** a character in a work of literature whose physical or psychological qualities contrast strongly with, and therefore highlight, the corresponding qualities of another character. In his Sherlock Holmes stories, Arthur Conan Doyle portrayed Dr. Watson as a man of normal habits and intelligence, making him a foil for the eccentric and wonderfully perceptive Sherlock Holmes.

**folklore:** traditions and myths preserved in a culture or group of people. Typically, these are passed on by word of mouth in various forms—such as legends, songs, and proverbs—or preserved in customs and ceremonies. This term was first used by W. J. Thoms in 1846. Sir James Frazer's *The Golden Bough* is the record of English folklore; myths about the frontier and the Old South exemplify American folklore.

**folktale:** a story originating in oral tradition. Folktales fall into a variety of categories, including legends, ghost stories, fairy tales, fables, and anecdotes based on historical figures and events. Examples of folktales include Giambattista Basile's *The Pentamerone,* which contains the tales of Puss in Boots, Rapunzel, Cinderella, and Beauty and the Beast, and Joel Chandler Harris's Uncle Remus stories, which represent transplanted African folktales and American tales about the characters Mike Fink, Johnny Appleseed, Paul Bunyan, and Pecos Bill.

**foreshadowing:** a device used in literature to create expectation or to set up an explanation of later developments. In Charles Dickens's *Great Expectations,* the graveyard encounter at the beginning of the novel between Pip and the escaped convict Magwitch foreshadows the baleful atmosphere and events that comprise much of the narrative.

**form:** the pattern or construction of a work which identifies its genre and distinguishes it from other genres. Examples of forms include the different genres, such as the lyric form or the short story form, and various patterns for poetry, such as the verse form or the stanza form.

**futurism:** a flamboyant literary and artistic movement that developed in France, Italy, and Russia from 1908 through the 1920s. Futurist theater and poetry abandoned traditional literary forms. In their place, followers of the movement attempted to achieve total freedom of expression through bizarre imagery and deformed or newly invented words. The Futurists were self-consciously modern artists who attempted to incorporate the appearances and sounds of modern life into their work. Futurist writers include Filippo Tommaso Marinetti, Wyndham Lewis, Guillaume Apollinaire, Velimir Khlebnikov, and Vladimir Mayakovsky.

# G

**genre:** a category of literary work. In critical theory, genre may refer to both the content of a given work—tragedy, comedy, pastoral— and to its form, such as poetry, novel, or drama. This term also refers to types of popular literature, as in the genres of science fiction or the detective story.

**genteel tradition:** a term coined by critic George Santayana to describe the literary practice of certain late nineteenth-century American writers, especially New Englanders. Followers of the Genteel Tradition emphasized conventionality in social, religious, moral, and literary standards. Some of the best-known writers of the Genteel Tradition are R. H. Stoddard and Bayard Taylor.

**gilded age:** a period in American history during the 1870s characterized by political corruption and materialism. A number of important novels of social and political criticism were written during this time. Examples of Gilded Age literature include Henry Adams's *Democracy* and F. Marion Crawford's *An American Politician.*

**gothic:** see *gothicism*

**gothicism:** in literary criticism, works characterized by a taste for the medieval or morbidly attractive. A gothic novel prominently features elements of horror, the supernatural, gloom, and violence: clanking chains, terror, charnel houses, ghosts, medieval castles, and mysteriously slamming doors. The term "gothic novel" is also applied to novels that lack elements of the traditional Gothic setting but that create a similar atmosphere of terror or dread. Mary Shelley's *Frankenstein* is perhaps the best-known English work of this kind.

**gothic novel:** see *gothicism*

**great chain of being:** the belief that all things and creatures in nature are organized in a hierarchy from inanimate objects at the bottom to God at the top. This system of belief was popular in the seventeenth and eighteenth centuries. A summary of the concept of the great chain of being can be found in the first epistle of Alexander Pope's *An Essay on Man,* and more recently in Arthur O. Lovejoy's *The Great Chain of Being: A Study of the History of an Idea.*

**grotesque:** in literary criticism, the subject matter of a work or a style of expression characterized by exaggeration, deformity, freakishness, and disorder. The grotesque often includes an element of comic absurdity. Early examples of literary grotesque include Francois

Rabelais's *Pantagruel* and *Gargantua* and Thomas Nashe's *The Unfortunate Traveller,* while more recent examples can be found in the works of Edgar Allan Poe, Evelyn Waugh, Eudora Welty, Flannery O'Connor, Eugene Ionesco, Gunter Grass, Thomas Mann, Mervyn Peake, and Joseph Heller, among many others.

# H

**hamartia:** in tragedy, the event or act that leads to the hero's or heroine's downfall. This term is often incorrectly used as a synonym for tragic flaw. In Richard Wright's *Native Son,* the act that seals Bigger Thomas's fate is his first impulsive murder.

**Harlem renaissance:** the Harlem Renaissance of the 1920s is generally considered the first significant movement of black writers and artists in the United States. During this period, new and established black writers published more fiction and poetry than ever before, the first influential black literary journals were established, and black authors and artists received their first widespread recognition and serious critical appraisal. Among the major writers associated with this period are Claude McKay, Jean Toomer, Countee Cullen, Langston Hughes, Arna Bontemps, Nella Larsen, and Zora Neale Hurston. Works representative of the Harlem Renaissance include Arna Bontemps's poems "The Return" and "Golgotha Is a Mountain," Claude McKay's novel *Home to Harlem,* Nella Larsen's novel *Passing,* Langston Hughes's poem "The Negro Speaks of Rivers," and the journals *Crisis* and *Opportunity,* both founded during this period.

**Hellenism:** imitation of ancient Greek thought or styles. Also, an approach to life that focuses on the growth and development of the intellect. "Hellenism" is sometimes used to refer to the belief that reason can be applied to examine all human experience. A cogent discussion of Hellenism can be found in Matthew Arnold's *Culture and Anarchy.*

**hero/heroine:** the principal sympathetic character (male or female) in a literary work. Heroes and heroines typically exhibit admirable traits: idealism, courage, and integrity, for example. Famous heroes and heroines include Pip in Charles Dickens's *Great Expectations,* the anonymous narrator in

Ralph Ellison's *Invisible Man,* and Sethe in Toni Morrison's *Beloved.*

**heroine:** see *hero/heroine*

**historical criticism:** the study of a work based on its impact on the world of the time period in which it was written. Examples of postmodern historical criticism can be found in the work of Michel Foucault, Hayden White, Stephen Greenblatt, and Jonathan Goldberg.

**holocaust:** see *holocaust literature*

**holocaust literature:** literature influenced by or written about the Holocaust of World War II. Such literature includes true stories of survival in concentration camps, escape, and life after the war, as well as fictional works and poetry. Representative works of Holocaust literature include Saul Bellow's *Mr. Sammler's Planet,* Anne Frank's *The Diary of a Young Girl,* Jerzy Kosinski's *The Painted Bird,* Arthur Miller's *Incident at Vichy,* Czeslaw Milosz's *Collected Poems,* William Styron's *Sophie's Choice,* and Art Spiegelman's *Maus.*

**horatian satire:** see *satire*

**humanism:** a philosophy that places faith in the dignity of humankind and rejects the medieval perception of the individual as a weak, fallen creature. "Humanists" typically believe in the perfectibility of human nature and view reason and education as the means to that end. Humanist thought is represented in the works of Marsilio Ficino, Ludovico Castelvetro, Edmund Spenser, John Milton, Dean John Colet, Desiderius Erasmus, John Dryden, Alexander Pope, Matthew Arnold, and Irving Babbitt.

**humors:** mentions of the humors refer to the ancient Greek theory that a person's health and personality were determined by the balance of four basic fluids in the body: blood, phlegm, yellow bile, and black bile. A dominance of any fluid would cause extremes in behavior. An excess of blood created a sanguine person who was joyful, aggressive, and passionate; a phlegmatic person was shy, fearful, and sluggish; too much yellow bile led to a choleric temperament characterized by impatience, anger, bitterness, and stubbornness; and excessive black bile created melancholy, a state of laziness, gluttony, and lack of motivation. Literary treatment of the humors is exemplified by several characters in Ben Jonson's plays *Every Man in His Humour* and *Every Man out of His Humour.*

**humours:** see *humors*

**hyperbole:** in literary criticism, deliberate exaggeration used to achieve an effect. In William Shakespeare's *Macbeth,* Lady Macbeth hyperbolizes when she says, "All the perfumes of Arabia could not sweeten this little hand."

# I

**idiom:** a word construction or verbal expression closely associated with a given language. For example, in colloquial English the construction "how come" can be used instead of "why" to introduce a question. Similarly, "a piece of cake" is sometimes used to describe a task that is easily done.

**image:** a concrete representation of an object or sensory experience. Typically, such a representation helps evoke the feelings associated with the object or experience itself. Images are either "literal" or "figurative." Literal images are especially concrete and involve little or no extension of the obvious meaning of the words used to express them. Figurative images do not follow the literal meaning of the words exactly. Images in literature are usually visual, but the term "image" can also refer to the representation of any sensory experience. In his poem "The Shepherd's Hour," Paul Verlaine presents the following image: "The Moon is red through horizon's fog;/ In a dancing mist the hazy meadow sleeps." The first line is broadly literal, while the second line involves turns of meaning associated with dancing and sleeping.

**imagery:** the array of images in a literary work. Also, figurative language. William Butler Yeats's "The Second Coming" offers a powerful image of encroaching anarchy: "Turning and turning in the widening gyre The falcon cannot hear the falconer; Things fall apart...."

**in medias res:** a Latin term meaning "in the middle of things." It refers to the technique of beginning a story at its midpoint and then using various flashback devices to reveal previous action. This technique originated in such epics as Virgil's *Aeneid.*

**induction:** the process of reaching a conclusion by reasoning from specific premises to form a general premise. Also, an introductory portion of a work of literature, especially a play. Geoffrey Chaucer's "Prologue" to the *Canterbury Tales,* Thomas Sackville's "Induction" to *The Mirror of Magistrates,* and the opening scene in William Shakespeare's *The Taming of the Shrew* are examples of inductions to literary works.

**intentional fallacy:** the belief that judgments of a literary work based solely on an author's stated or implied intentions are false and misleading. Critics who believe in the concept of the intentional fallacy typically argue that the work itself is sufficient matter for interpretation, even though they may concede that an author's statement of purpose can be useful. Analysis of William Wordsworth's *Lyrical Ballads* based on the observations about poetry he makes in his "Preface" to the second edition of that work is an example of the intentional fallacy.

**interior monologue:** a narrative technique in which characters' thoughts are revealed in a way that appears to be uncontrolled by the author. The interior monologue typically aims to reveal the inner self of a character. It portrays emotional experiences as they occur at both a conscious and unconscious level. images are often used to represent sensations or emotions. One of the best-known interior monologues in English is the Molly Bloom section at the close of James Joyce's *Ulysses.* The interior monologue is also common in the works of Virginia Woolf.

**Irish literary renaissance:** a late nineteenth- and early twentieth-century movement in Irish literature. Members of the movement aimed to reduce the influence of British culture in Ireland and create an Irish national literature. William Butler Yeats, George Moore, and Sean O'Casey are three of the best-known figures of the movement.

**irony:** in literary criticism, the effect of language in which the intended meaning is the opposite of what is stated. The title of Jonathan Swift's "A Modest Proposal" is ironic because what Swift proposes in this essay is cannibalism—hardly "modest."

# J

**Jacobean age:** the period of the reign of James I of England (1603-1625). The early literature of this period reflected the worldview of the Elizabethan Age, but a darker, more cynical attitude steadily grew in the art and literature of the Jacobean Age. This was an important time for English drama and poetry. Milestones include William Shakespeare's tragedies, tragi-comedies, and sonnets; Ben Jonson's various dramas; and John Donne's metaphysical poetry.

**jargon:** language that is used or understood only by a select group of people. Jargon may refer to terminology used in a certain profession, such as computer jargon, or it may refer to any nonsensical language that is not understood by most people. Literary examples of jargon are Francois Villon's *Ballades en jargon,* which is composed in the secret language of the *coquillards,* and Anthony Burgess's *A Clockwork Orange,* narrated in the fictional characters' language of "Nadsat."

**journalism:** writing intended for publication in a newspaper or magazine, or for broadcast on a radio or television program featuring news, sports, entertainment, or other timely material. The essays and reviews written by H. L. Mencken for the *Baltimore Morning Herald* and collected in his *Prejudices* are an example of journalism.

**juvenalian satire:** see *satire*

### K

**knickerbocker group:** a somewhat indistinct group of New York writers of the first half of the nineteenth century. Members of the group were linked only by location and a common theme: New York life. Two famous members of the Knickerbocker Group were Washington Irving and William Cullen Bryant. The group's name derives from Irving's *Knickerbocker's History of New York.*

***kunstlerroman:*** see *bildungsroman*

### L

***leitmotiv:*** see *motif*

**literal language:** an author uses literal language when he or she writes without exaggerating or embellishing the subject matter and without any tools of figurative language. To say "He ran very quickly down the street" is to use literal language, whereas to say "He ran like a hare down the street" would be using figurative language.

**literature:** literature is broadly defined as any written or spoken material, but the term most often refers to creative works. Literature includes poetry, drama, fiction, and many kinds of nonfiction writing, as well as oral, dramatic, and broadcast compositions not necessarily preserved in a written format, such as films and television programs.

**lost generation:** a term first used by Gertrude Stein to describe the post-World War I generation of American writers: men and women haunted by a sense of betrayal and emptiness brought about by the destructiveness of the war. The term is commonly applied to Hart Crane, Ernest Hemingway, F. Scott Fitzgerald, and others.

### M

**mannerism:** exaggerated, artificial adherence to a literary manner or style. Also, a popular style of the visual arts of late sixteenth-century Europe that was marked by elongation of the human form and by intentional spatial distortion. Literary works that are self-consciously high-toned and artistic are often said to be "mannered." Authors of such works include Henry James and Gertrude Stein.

**memoirs:** an autobiographical form of writing in which the author gives his or her personal impressions of significant figures or events. This form is different from the autobiography because it does not center around the author's own life and experiences. Early examples of memoirs include the Viscount de Chateaubriand's *The Memoirs of Chateaubriand* and Giacomo Casanova's *History of My Life,* while modern memoirs include reminiscences of World War II by Dwight Eisenhower, Viscount Montgomery, and Charles de Gaulle.

**metaphor:** a figure of speech that expresses an idea through the image of another object. Metaphors suggest the essence of the first object by identifying it with certain qualities of the second object. An example is "But soft, what light through yonder window breaks? / It is the east, and Juliet is the sun" in William Shakespeare's *Romeo and Juliet.* Here, Juliet, the first object, is identified with qualities of the second object, the sun.

**modernism:** modern literary practices. Also, the principles of a literary school that lasted from roughly the beginning of the twentieth century until the end of World War II. Modernism is defined by its rejection of the literary conventions of the nineteenth century and by its opposition to conventional morality, taste, traditions, and economic values. Many writers are associated with the concepts of Modernism, including Albert Camus, Marcel Proust, D. H. Lawrence, W. H. Auden, Ernest Hemingway, William Faulkner, William Butler Yeats, Thomas Mann, Tennessee Williams, Eugene O'Neill, and James Joyce.

**mood:** the prevailing emotions of a work or of the author in his or her creation of the work. The mood of a work is not always what might be expected based on its subject matter. The poem "Dover Beach" by Matthew Arnold offers examples of two different moods originating from the same experience: watching the ocean at night. The mood of the first three lines—"The sea is calm tonight//The tide is full, the moon lies fair//Upon the straights...." is in sharp contrast to the mood of the last three lines— "And we are here as on a darkling plain// Swept with confused alarms of struggle and flight,//Where ignorant armies clash by night."

*motif:* a theme, character type, image, metaphor, or other verbal element that recurs throughout a single work of literature or occurs in a number of different works over a period of time. For example, the various manifestations of the color white in Herman Melville's *Moby Dick* is a "specific" *motif,* while the trials of star-crossed lovers is a "conventional" *motif* from the literature of all periods.

*motiv:* see *motif*

**muckrakers:** an early twentieth-century group of American writers. Typically, their works exposed the wrongdoings of big business and government in the United States. Upton Sinclair's *The Jungle* exemplifies the muckraking novel.

**muses:** nine Greek mythological goddesses, the daughters of Zeus and Mnemosyne (Memory). Each muse patronized a specific area of the liberal arts and sciences. Calliope presided over epic poetry, Clio over history, Erato over love poetry, Euterpe over music or lyric poetry, Melpomene over tragedy, Polyhymnia over hymns to the gods, Terpsichore over dance, Thalia over comedy, and Urania over astronomy. Poets and writers traditionally made appeals to the Muses for inspiration in their work. John Milton invokes the aid of a muse at the beginning of the first book of his *Paradise Lost:* "Of Man's First disobedience, and the Fruit of the Forbidden Tree,//whose mortal taste Brought Death into the World, and all our woe, With loss of Eden, till one greater Man//Restore us, and regain the blissful Seat,//Sing Heav'nly Muse, that on the secret top of Oreb, or of Sinai, didst inspire// That Shepherd, who first taught the chosen Seed,//In the Beginning how the Heav'ns and Earth//Rose out of Chaos...."

**mystery:** see *suspense*

**myth:** an anonymous tale emerging from the traditional beliefs of a culture or social unit. Myths use supernatural explanations for natural phenomena. They may also explain cosmic issues like creation and death. Collections of myths, known as mythologies, are common to all cultures and nations, but the best-known myths belong to the Norse, Roman, and Greek mythologies. A famous myth is the story of Arachne, an arrogant young girl who challenged a goddess, Athena, to a weaving contest; when the girl won, Athena was enraged and turned Arachne into a spider, thus explaining the existence of spiders.

## N

**narration:** the telling of a series of events, real or invented. A narration may be either a simple narrative, in which the events are recounted chronologically, or a narrative with a plot, in which the account is given in a style reflecting the author's artistic concept of the story. Narration is sometimes used as a synonym for "storyline." The recounting of scary stories around a campfire is a form of narration.

**narrative:** a verse or prose accounting of an event or sequence of events, real or invented. The term is also used as an adjective in the sense "method of narration." For example, in literary criticism, the expression "narrative technique" usually refers to the way the author structures and presents his or her story. Narratives range from the shortest accounts of events, as in Julius Caesar's remark, "I came, I saw, I conquered," to the longest historical or biographical works, as in Edward Gibbon's *The Decline and Fall of the Roman Empire,* as well as diaries, travelogues, novels, ballads, epics, short stories, and other fictional forms.

**narrator:** the teller of a story. The narrator may be the author or a character in the story through whom the author speaks. Huckleberry Finn is the narrator of Mark Twain's *The Adventures of Huckleberry Finn.*

**naturalism:** a literary movement of the late nineteenth and early twentieth centuries. The movement's major theorist, French novelist Emile Zola, envisioned a type of fiction that would examine human life with the objectivity of scientific inquiry. The Naturalists typically viewed human beings as either the products of "biological determinism," ruled by hereditary instincts and engaged in an endless struggle for survival, or as the products of "socioeconomic determinism," ruled by social and economic forces beyond their control. In their works, the Naturalists generally ignored the highest levels of society and focused on degradation: poverty, alcoholism, prostitution, insanity, and disease. Naturalism influenced authors throughout the world, including Henrik Ibsen and Thomas Hardy. In the United States, in particular, Naturalism had a profound impact. Among the authors who embraced its principles are Theodore Dreiser, Eugene O'Neill, Stephen Crane, Jack London, and Frank Norris.

**negritude:** a literary movement based on the concept of a shared cultural bond on the part of black Africans, wherever they may be in the world. It traces its origins to the former French colonies of Africa and the Caribbean. Negritude poets, novelists, and essayists generally stress four points in their writings: One, black alienation from traditional African culture can lead to feelings of inferiority. Two, European colonialism and Western education should be resisted. Three, black Africans should seek to affirm and define their own identity. Four, African culture can and should be reclaimed. Many Negritude writers also claim that blacks can make unique contributions to the world, based on a heightened appreciation of nature, rhythm, and human emotions—aspects of life they say are not so highly valued in the materialistic and rationalistic West. Examples of Negritude literature include the poetry of both Senegalese Leopold Senghor in *Hosties noires* and Martiniquais Aime-Fernand Cesaire in *Return to My Native Land.*

**negro renaissance:** see *Harlem renaissance*

**neoclassical period:** see *neoclassicism*

**neoclassicism:** in literary criticism, this term refers to the revival of the attitudes and styles of expression of classical literature. It is generally used to describe a period in European history beginning in the late seventeenth century and lasting until about 1800. In its purest form, Neoclassicism marked a return to order, proportion, restraint, logic, accuracy, and decorum. In England, where Neoclassicism perhaps was most popular, it reflected the influence of seventeenth- century French writers, especially dramatists. Neoclassical writers typically reacted against the intensity and enthusiasm of the Renaissance period. They wrote works that appealed to the intellect, using elevated language and classical literary forms such as satire and the ode. Neoclassical works were often governed by the classical goal of instruction. English neoclassicists included Alexander Pope, Jonathan Swift, Joseph Addison, Sir Richard Steele, John Gay, and Matthew Prior; French neoclassicists included Pierre Corneille and Jean-Baptiste Moliere.

**neoclassicists:** see *neoclassicism*

**new criticism:** a movement in literary criticism, dating from the late 1920s, that stressed close textual analysis in the interpretation of works of literature. The New Critics saw little merit in historical and biographical analysis. Rather, they aimed to examine the text alone, free from the question of how external events—biographical or otherwise—may have helped shape it. This predominantly American school was named "New Criticism" by one of its practitioners, John Crowe Ransom. Other important New Critics included Allen Tate, R. P. Blackmur, Robert Penn Warren, and Cleanth Brooks.

**new journalism:** a type of writing in which the journalist presents factual information in a form usually used in fiction. New journalism emphasizes description, narration, and character development to bring readers closer to the human element of the story, and is often used in personality profiles and in-depth feature articles. It is not compatible with "straight" or "hard" newswriting, which is generally composed in a brief, fact-based style. Hunter S. Thompson, Gay Talese, Thomas Wolfe, Joan Didion, and John McPhee are well-known New Journalists.

**new journalists:** see *new journalism*

**new negro movement:** see *Harlem renaissance*

**noble savage:** the idea that primitive man is noble and good but becomes evil and corrupted as he becomes civilized. The concept of the noble savage originated in the Renaissance period but is more closely identified with such later writers as Jean-Jacques Rousseau and Aphra Behn. First described in John Dryden's play *The Conquest of Granada,* the noble savage is portrayed by the various Native Americans in James Fenimore Cooper's "Leatherstocking Tales," by Queequeg, Daggoo, and Tashtego in Herman Melville's *Moby Dick,* and by John the Savage in Aldous Huxley's *Brave New World.*

**novel:** a long fictional narrative written in prose, which developed from the novella and other early forms of narrative. A novel is usually organized under a plot or theme with a focus on character development and action. The novel emerged as a fully evolved literary form in the mid-eighteenth century in Samuel Richardson's *Pamela; or, Virtue Rewarded.*

**novella:** an Italian term meaning "story." This term has been especially used to describe fourteenth-century Italian tales, but it also refers to modern short novels. The tales comprising Giovanni Boccaccio's *Decameron* are examples of the novella. Modern novellas include Leo Tolstoy's *The Death of Ivan Ilich,* Fyodor Dostoyevsky's *Notes from the Underground,* Joseph Conrad's *Heart of Darkness,* and Henry James's "The Aspern Papers."

**novel of ideas:** a novel in which the examination of intellectual issues and concepts takes precedence over characterization or a traditional storyline. Examples of novels of ideas include Aldous Huxley's *Crome Yellow, Point Counter Point,* and *After Many a Summer.*

**novel of manners:** a novel that examines the customs and mores of a cultural group. The novels of Jane Austen and Edith Wharton are widely considered novels of manners.

# O

**objective correlative:** an outward set of objects, a situation, or a chain of events corresponding to an inward experience and evoking this experience in the reader. The term frequently appears in modern criticism in discussions of authors' intended effects on the emotional responses of readers. This term was originally used by T. S. Eliot in his 1919 essay "Hamlet."

**objectivity:** a quality in writing characterized by the absence of the author's opinion or feeling about the subject matter. Objectivity is an important factor in criticism. The novels of Henry James and, to a certain extent, the poems of John Larkin demonstrate objectivity, and it is central to John Keats's concept of "negative capability." Critical and journalistic writing usually are or attempt to be objective.

**Oedipus complex:** a son's amorous obsession with his mother. The phrase is derived from the story of the ancient Theban hero Oedipus, who unknowingly killed his father and married his mother. Literary occurrences of the Oedipus complex include Andre Gide's *Oedipe* and Jean Cocteau's *La Machine infernale,* as well as the most famous, Sophocles' *Oedipus Rex.*

**omniscience:** see *point of view*

**onomatopoeia:** the use of words whose sounds express or suggest their meaning. In its simplest sense, onomatopoeia may be represented by words that mimic the sounds they denote such as "hiss" or "meow." At a more subtle level, the pattern and rhythm of sounds and rhymes of a line or poem may be onomatopoeic. A celebrated example of onomatopoeia is the repetition of the word "bells" in Edgar Allan Poe's poem "The Bells."

**oxymoron:** a phrase combining two contradictory terms. Oxymorons may be intentional or unintentional. The following speech from William Shakespeare's *Romeo and Juliet* uses several oxymorons: "Why, then, O brawling love! O loving hate!//O anything, of nothing first create!//O heavy lightness! serious vanity! //Mis-shapen chaos of well-seeming forms!//

Feather of lead, bright smoke, cold fire, sick health!//This love feel I, that feel no love in// this."

## P

**pantheism:** the idea that all things are both a manifestation or revelation of God and a part of God at the same time. Pantheism was a common attitude in the early societies of Egypt, India, and Greece—the term derives from the Greek *pan* meaning "all" and *theos* meaning "deity." It later became a significant part of the Christian faith. William Wordsworth and Ralph Waldo Emerson are among the many writers who have expressed the pantheistic attitude in their works.

**parable:** a story intended to teach a moral lesson or answer an ethical question. In the West, the best examples of parables are those of Jesus Christ in the New Testament, notably "The Prodigal Son," but parables also are used in Sufism, rabbinic literature, Hasidism, and Zen Buddhism.

**paradox:** a statement that appears illogical or contradictory at first, but may actually point to an underlying truth. "Less is more" is an example of a paradox. Literary examples include Francis Bacon's statement, "The most corrected copies are commonly the least correct," and "All animals are equal, but some animals are more equal than others" from George Orwell's *Animal Farm*.

**parallelism:** a method of comparison of two ideas in which each is developed in the same grammatical structure. Ralph Waldo Emerson's "Civilization" contains this example of parallelism: "Raphael paints wisdom; Handel sings it, Phidias carves it, Shakespeare writes it, Wren builds it, Columbus sails it, Luther preaches it, Washington arms it, Watt mechanizes it."

**parnassianism:** a mid nineteenth-century movement in French literature. Followers of the movement stressed adherence to well-defined artistic forms as a reaction against the often chaotic expression of the artist's ego that dominated the work of the Romantics. The Parnassians also rejected the moral, ethical, and social themes exhibited in the works of French Romantics such as Victor Hugo. The aesthetic doctrines of the Parnassians strongly influenced the later symbolist and decadent movements. Members of the Parnassian school include Leconte de Lisle, Sully Prudhomme, Albert Glatigny, Francois Coppee, and Theodore de Banville.

**parody:** in literary criticism, this term refers to an imitation of a serious literary work or the signature style of a particular author in a ridiculous manner. A typical parody adopts the style of the original and applies it to an inappropriate subject for humorous effect. Parody is a form of satire and could be considered the literary equivalent of a caricature or cartoon. Henry Fielding's *Shamela* is a parody of Samuel Richardson's *Pamela*.

**pastoral:** a term derived from the Latin word "pastor," meaning shepherd. A pastoral is a literary composition on a rural theme. The conventions of the pastoral were originated by the third-century Greek poet Theocritus, who wrote about the experiences, love affairs, and pastimes of Sicilian shepherds. In a pastoral, characters and language of a courtly nature are often placed in a simple setting. The term pastoral is also used to classify dramas, elegies, and lyrics that exhibit the use of country settings and shepherd characters. Percy Bysshe Shelley's "Adonais" and John Milton's "Lycidas" are two famous examples of pastorals.

*pelado*: literally the "skinned one" or shirtless one, he was the stock underdog, sharp-witted picaresque character of Mexican vaudeville and tent shows. The *pelado* is found in such works as Don Catarino's *Los effectos de la crisis* and *Regreso a mi tierra*.

**pen name:** see *pseudonym*

*persona*: a Latin term meaning "mask." *Personae* are the characters in a fictional work of literature. The *persona* generally functions as a mask through which the author tells a story in a voice other than his or her own. A *persona* is usually either a character in a story who acts as a narrator or an "implied author," a voice created by the author to act as the narrator for himself or herself. *Personae* include the narrator of Geoffrey Chaucer's *Canterbury Tales* and Marlow in Joseph Conrad's *Heart of Darkness*.

*personae*: see *persona*

**personal point of view:** see *point of view*

**personification:** a figure of speech that gives human qualities to abstract ideas, animals, and inanimate objects. William Shakespeare used personification in *Romeo and Juliet* in the lines "Arise, fair sun, and kill the envious moon, / Who is already sick and pale with grief." Here, the moon is portrayed as being envious, sick, and pale with grief—all markedly human qualities.

**phenomenology:** a method of literary criticism based on the belief that things have no existence outside of human consciousness or awareness. Proponents of this theory believe that art is a process that takes place in the mind of the observer as he or she contemplates an object rather than a quality of the object itself. Among phenomenological critics are Edmund Husserl, George Poulet, Marcel Raymond, and Roman Ingarden.

**picaresque novel:** episodic fiction depicting the adventures of a roguish central character ("picaro" is Spanish for "rogue"). The picaresque hero is commonly a low-born but clever individual who wanders into and out of various affairs of love, danger, and farcical intrigue. These involvements may take place at all social levels and typically present a humorous and wide-ranging satire of a given society. Prominent examples of the picaresque novel are *Don Quixote* by Miguel de Cervantes, *Tom Jones* by Henry Fielding, and *Moll Flanders* by Daniel Defoe.

**plagiarism:** claiming another person's written material as one's own. Plagiarism can take the form of direct, word-for-word copying or the theft of the substance or idea of the work. A student who copies an encyclopedia entry and turns it in as a report for school is guilty of plagiarism.

**Platonic criticism:** a form of criticism that stresses an artistic work's usefulness as an agent of social engineering rather than any quality or value of the work itself. Platonic criticism takes as its starting point the ancient Greek philosopher Plato's comments on art in his *Republic*.

**Platonism:** the embracing of the doctrines of the philosopher Plato, popular among the poets of the Renaissance and the Romantic period. Platonism is more flexible than Aristotelian Criticism and places more emphasis on the supernatural and unknown aspects of life. Platonism is expressed in the love poetry of the Renaissance, the fourth

book of Baldassare Castiglione's *The Book of the Courtier,* and the poetry of William Blake, William Wordsworth, Percy Bysshe Shelley, Friedrich Holderlin, William Butler Yeats, and Wallace Stevens.

**plot:** in literary criticism, this term refers to the pattern of events in a narrative or drama. In its simplest sense, the plot guides the author in composing the work and helps the reader follow the work. Typically, plots exhibit causality and unity and have a beginning, a middle, and an end. Sometimes, however, a plot may consist of a series of disconnected events, in which case it is known as an "episodic plot." In his *Aspects of the Novel,* E. M. Forster distinguishes between a story, defined as a "narrative of events arranged in their time- sequence," and plot, which organizes the events to a "sense of causality." This definition closely mirrors Aristotle's discussion of plot in his *Poetics.*

**poetic justice:** an outcome in a literary work, not necessarily a poem, in which the good are rewarded and the evil are punished, especially in ways that particularly fit their virtues or crimes. For example, a murderer may himself be murdered, or a thief will find himself penniless.

**poetic license:** distortions of fact and literary convention made by a writer—not always a poet—for the sake of the effect gained. Poetic license is closely related to the concept of "artistic freedom." An author exercises poetic license by saying that a pile of money "reaches as high as a mountain" when the pile is actually only a foot or two high.

**poetics:** this term has two closely related meanings. It denotes (1) an aesthetic theory in literary criticism about the essence of poetry or (2) rules prescribing the proper methods, content, style, or diction of poetry. The term poetics may also refer to theories about literature in general, not just poetry.

**point of view:** the narrative perspective from which a literary work is presented to the reader. There are four traditional points of view. The "third person omniscient" gives the reader a "godlike" perspective, unrestricted by time or place, from which to see actions and look into the minds of characters. This allows the author to comment openly on characters and events in the work. The "third person" point of view presents the events of the story from outside of any single character's perception, much like the omniscient point of view, but the reader must understand the action as it takes place and without any special insight into characters' minds or motivations. The "first person" or "personal" point of view relates events as they are perceived by a single character. The main character "tells" the story and may offer opinions about the action and characters which differ from those of the author. Much less common than omniscient, third person, and first person is the "second person" point of view, wherein the author tells the story as if it is happening to the reader. James Thurber employs the omniscient point of view in his short story "The Secret Life of Walter Mitty." Ernest Hemingway's "A Clean, Well-Lighted Place" is a short story told from the third person point of view. Mark Twain's novel *Huck Finn* is presented from the first person viewpoint. Jay McInerney's *Bright Lights, Big City* is an example of a novel which uses the second person point of view.

**polemic:** a work in which the author takes a stand on a controversial subject, such as abortion or religion. Such works are often extremely argumentative or provocative. Classic examples of polemics include John Milton's *Aeropagitica* and Thomas Paine's *The American Crisis.*

**pornography:** writing intended to provoke feelings of lust in the reader. Such works are often condemned by critics and teachers, but those which can be shown to have literary value are viewed less harshly. Literary works that have been described as pornographic include Ovid's *The Art of Love,* Margaret of Angouleme's *Heptameron,* John Cleland's *Memoirs of a Woman of Pleasure; or, the Life of Fanny Hill,* the anonymous *My Secret Life,* D. H. Lawrence's *Lady Chatterley's Lover,* and Vladimir Nabokov's *Lolita.*

**post-aesthetic movement:** an artistic response made by African Americans to the black aesthetic movement of the 1960s and early '70s. Writers since that time have adopted a somewhat different tone in their work, with less emphasis placed on the disparity between black and white in the United States. In the words of post-aesthetic authors such as Toni

Morrison, John Edgar Wideman, and Kristin Hunter, African Americans are portrayed as looking inward for answers to their own questions, rather than always looking to the outside world. Two well-known examples of works produced as part of the post-aesthetic movement are the Pulitzer Prize-winning novels *The Color Purple* by Alice Walker and *Beloved* by Toni Morrison.

**postmodernism:** writing from the 1960s forward characterized by experimentation and continuing to apply some of the fundamentals of modernism, which included existentialism and alienation. Postmodernists have gone a step further in the rejection of tradition begun with the modernists by also rejecting traditional forms, preferring the anti-novel over the novel and the anti-hero over the hero. Postmodern writers include Alain Robbe-Grillet, Thomas Pynchon, Margaret Drabble, John Fowles, Adolfo Bioy-Casares, and Gabriel Garcia Marquez.

**pre-Raphaelites:** a circle of writers and artists in mid nineteenth-century England. Valuing the pre-Renaissance artistic qualities of religious symbolism, lavish pictorialism, and natural sensuousness, the Pre-Raphaelites cultivated a sense of mystery and melancholy that influenced later writers associated with the Symbolist and Decadent movements. The major members of the group include Dante Gabriel Rossetti, Christina Rossetti, Algernon Swinburne, and Walter Pater.

**primitivism:** the belief that primitive peoples were nobler and less flawed than civilized peoples because they had not been subjected to the tainting influence of society. Examples of literature espousing primitivism include Aphra Behn's *Oroonoko: Or, The History of the Royal Slave,* Jean-Jacques Rousseau's *Julie ou la Nouvelle Heloise,* Oliver Goldsmith's *The Deserted Village,* the poems of Robert Burns, Herman Melville's stories *Typee, Omoo,* and *Mardi,* many poems of William Butler Yeats and Robert Frost, and William Golding's novel *Lord of the Flies.*

**prologue:** an introductory section of a literary work. It often contains information establishing the situation of the characters or presents information about the setting, time period, or action. In drama, the prologue is spoken by a chorus or by one of the principal characters.

In the "General Prologue" of *The Canterbury Tales,* Geoffrey Chaucer describes the main characters and establishes the setting and purpose of the work.

**prose:** a literary medium that attempts to mirror the language of everyday speech. It is distinguished from poetry by its use of unmetered, unrhymed language consisting of logically related sentences. Prose is usually grouped into paragraphs that form a cohesive whole such as an essay or a novel. Recognized masters of English prose writing include Sir Thomas Malory, William Caxton, Raphael Holinshed, Joseph Addison, Mark Twain, and Ernest Hemingway.

*prosopopoeia:* see *personification*

**protagonist:** the central character of a story who serves as a focus for its themes and incidents and as the principal rationale for its development. The protagonist is sometimes referred to in discussions of modern literature as the hero or anti-hero. Well-known protagonists are Hamlet in William Shakespeare's *Hamlet* and Jay Gatsby in F. Scott Fitzgerald's *The Great Gatsby.*

**protest fiction:** protest fiction has as its primary purpose the protesting of some social injustice, such as racism or discrimination. One example of protest fiction is a series of five novels by Chester Himes, beginning in 1945 with *If He Hollers Let Him Go* and ending in 1955 with *The Primitive.* These works depict the destructive effects of race and gender stereotyping in the context of interracial relationships. Another African American author whose works often revolve around themes of social protest is John Oliver Killens. James Baldwin's essay "Everybody's Protest Novel" generated controversy by attacking the authors of protest fiction.

**proverb:** a brief, sage saying that expresses a truth about life in a striking manner. "They are not all cooks who carry long knives" is an example of a proverb.

**pseudonym:** a name assumed by a writer, most often intended to prevent his or her identification as the author of a work. Two or more authors may work together under one pseudonym, or an author may use a different name for each genre he or she publishes in. Some publishing companies maintain "house pseudonyms," under which any number of authors may write installations in a series. Some authors also choose a pseudonym over their real names the way an actor may use a stage name. Examples of pseudonyms (with the author's real name in parentheses) include Voltaire (Francois-Marie Arouet), Novalis (Friedrich von Hardenberg), Currer Bell (Charlotte Bronte), Ellis Bell (Emily Bronte), George Eliot (Maryann Evans), Honorio Bustos Donmecq (Adolfo Bioy-Casares and Jorge Luis Borges), and Richard Bachman (Stephen King).

**pun:** a play on words that have similar sounds but different meanings. A serious example of the pun is from John Donne's "A Hymne to God the Father": "Sweare by thyself, that at my death thy sonne//Shall shine as he shines now, and hereto fore;//And, having done that, Thou haste done;//I fear no more."

# R

**realism:** a nineteenth-century European literary movement that sought to portray familiar characters, situations, and settings in a realistic manner. This was done primarily by using an objective narrative point of view and through the buildup of accurate detail. The standard for success of any realistic work depends on how faithfully it transfers common experience into fictional forms. The realistic method may be altered or extended, as in stream of consciousness writing, to record highly subjective experience. Seminal authors in the tradition of Realism include Honore de Balzac, Gustave Flaubert, and Henry James.

**renaissance:** the period in European history that marked the end of the Middle Ages. It began in Italy in the late fourteenth century. In broad terms, it is usually seen as spanning the fourteenth, fifteenth, and sixteenth centuries, although it did not reach Great Britain, for example, until the 1480s or so. The Renaissance saw an awakening in almost every sphere of human activity, especially science, philosophy, and the arts. The period is best defined by the emergence of a general philosophy that emphasized the importance of the intellect, the individual, and world affairs. It contrasts strongly with the medieval worldview, characterized by the dominant concerns of faith, the social collective, and spiritual salvation. Prominent writers during the Renaissance include Niccolo Machiavelli and Baldassare Castiglione in Italy, Miguel de Cervantes and Lope de Vega in Spain, Jean Froissart and Francois Rabelais in France, Sir Thomas More and Sir Philip Sidney in England, and Desiderius Erasmus in Holland.

*repartee*: conversation featuring snappy retorts and witticisms. Masters of *repartee* include Sydney Smith, Charles Lamb, and Oscar Wilde. An example is recorded in the meeting of "Beau" Nash and John Wesley: Nash said, "I never make way for a fool," to which Wesley responded, "Don't you? I always do," and stepped aside.

resolution: the portion of a story following the climax, in which the conflict is resolved. The resolution of Jane Austen's *Northanger Abbey* is neatly summed up in the following sentence: "Henry and Catherine were married, the bells rang and every body smiled."

restoration: see *restoration age*

restoration age: a period in English literature beginning with the crowning of Charles II in 1660 and running to about 1700. The era, which was characterized by a reaction against Puritanism, was the first great age of the comedy of manners. The finest literature of the era is typically witty and urbane, and often lewd. Prominent Restoration Age writers include William Congreve, Samuel Pepys, John Dryden, and John Milton.

rhetoric: in literary criticism, this term denotes the art of ethical persuasion. In its strictest sense, rhetoric adheres to various principles developed since classical times for arranging facts and ideas in a clear, persuasive, appealing manner. The term is also used to refer to effective prose in general and theories of or methods for composing effective prose. Classical examples of rhetorics include *The Rhetoric of Aristotle,* Quintillian's *Institutio Oratoria,* and Cicero's *Ad Herennium.*

rhetorical question: a question intended to provoke thought, but not an expressed answer, in the reader. It is most commonly used in oratory and other persuasive genres. The following lines from Thomas Gray's "Elegy Written in a Country Churchyard" ask rhetorical questions: "Can storied urn or animated bust//Back to its mansion call the fleeting breath?//Can Honour's voice provoke the silent dust,//Or Flattery soothe the dull cold ear of//Death?"

rising action: the part of a drama where the plot becomes increasingly complicated. Rising action leads up to the climax, or turning point, of a drama. The final "chase scene" of an action film is generally the rising action which culminates in the film's climax.

*rococo*: a style of European architecture that flourished in the eighteenth century, especially in France. The most notable features of *rococo* are its extensive use of ornamentation and its themes of lightness, gaiety, and intimacy. In literary criticism, the term is often used disparagingly to refer to a decadent or over-ornamental style. Alexander Pope's "The Rape of the Lock" is an example of literary *rococo*.

***Roman a clef***: a French phrase meaning "novel with a key." It refers to a narrative in which real persons are portrayed under fictitious names. Jack Kerouac, for example, portrayed various real-life beat generation figures under fictitious names in his *On the Road*.

romance: a broad term, usually denoting a narrative with exotic, exaggerated, often idealized characters, scenes, and themes. Nathaniel Hawthorne called his *The House of the Seven Gables* and *The Marble Faun* romances in order to distinguish them from clearly realistic works.

romantic age: see *romanticism*

romanticism: this term has two widely accepted meanings. In historical criticism, it refers to a European intellectual and artistic movement of the late eighteenth and early nineteenth centuries that sought greater freedom of personal expression than that allowed by the strict rules of literary form and logic of the eighteenth-century neoclassicists. The Romantics preferred emotional and imaginative expression to rational analysis. They considered the individual to be at the center of all experience and so placed him or her at the center of their art. The Romantics believed that the creative imagination reveals nobler truths—unique feelings and attitudes—than those that could be discovered by logic or by scientific examination. Both the natural world and the state of childhood were important sources for revelations of "eternal truths." "Romanticism" is also used as a general term to refer to a type of sensibility found in all periods of literary history and usually considered to be in opposition to the principles of classicism. In this sense, Romanticism signifies any work or philosophy in which the exotic or dreamlike figure strongly, or that is devoted to individualistic expression, self-analysis, or a pursuit of a higher realm of knowledge than can be discovered by human reason. Prominent Romantics include Jean-Jacques Rousseau, William Wordsworth, John Keats, Lord Byron, and Johann Wolfgang von Goethe.

**romantics:** see *romanticism*

**Russian symbolism:** a Russian poetic movement, derived from French symbolism, that flourished between 1894 and 1910. While some Russian Symbolists continued in the French tradition, stressing aestheticism and the importance of suggestion above didactic intent, others saw their craft as a form of mystical worship, and themselves as mediators between the supernatural and the mundane. Russian symbolists include Aleksandr Blok, Vyacheslav Ivanovich Ivanov, Fyodor Sologub, Andrey Bely, Nikolay Gumilyov, and Vladimir Sergeyevich Solovyov.

# S

**satire:** a work that uses ridicule, humor, and wit to criticize and provoke change in human nature and institutions. There are two major types of satire: "formal" or "direct" satire speaks directly to the reader or to a character in the work; "indirect" satire relies upon the ridiculous behavior of its characters to make its point. Formal satire is further divided into two manners: the "Horatian," which ridicules gently, and the "Juvenalian," which derides its subjects harshly and bitterly. Voltaire's novella *Candide* is an indirect satire. Jonathan Swift's essay "A Modest Proposal" is a Juvenalian satire.

**science fiction:** a type of narrative about or based upon real or imagined scientific theories and technology. Science fiction is often peopled with alien creatures and set on other planets or in different dimensions. Karel Capek's *R.U.R.* is a major work of science fiction.

**second person:** see *point of view*

**semiotics:** the study of how literary forms and conventions affect the meaning of language. Semioticians include Ferdinand de Saussure, Charles Sanders Pierce, Claude Levi-Strauss, Jacques Lacan, Michel Foucault, Jacques Derrida, Roland Barthes, and Julia Kristeva.

**setting:** the time, place, and culture in which the action of a narrative takes place. The elements of setting may include geographic location, characters' physical and mental environments, prevailing cultural attitudes, or the historical time in which the action takes place. Examples of settings include the romanticized Scotland in Sir Walter Scott's "Waverley" novels, the French provincial setting in Gustave Flaubert's *Madame Bovary,* the fictional Wessex country of Thomas Hardy's novels, and the small towns of southern Ontario in Alice Munro's short stories.

**short story:** a fictional prose narrative shorter and more focused than a novella. The short story usually deals with a single episode and often a single character. The "tone," the author's attitude toward his or her subject and audience, is uniform throughout. The short story frequently also lacks *denouement*, ending instead at its climax. Well-known short stories include Ernest Hemingway's "Hills Like White Elephants," Katherine Mansfield's "The Fly," Jorge Luis Borge's "Tlon, Uqbar, Orbis Tertius," Eudora Welty's "Death of a Travelling Salesman," Yukio Mishima's "Three Million Men," and Milan Kundera's "The Hitchhiking Game."

**signifying monkey:** a popular trickster figure in black folklore, with hundreds of tales about this character documented since the 19th century. Henry Louis Gates Jr. examines the history of the signifying monkey in *The Signifying Monkey: Towards a Theory of Afro-American Literary Criticism,* published in 1988.

**simile:** a comparison, usually using "like" or "as", of two essentially dissimilar things, as in "coffee as cold as ice" or "He sounded like a broken record." The title of Ernest Hemingway's "Hills Like White Elephants" contains a simile.

**slang:** a type of informal verbal communication that is generally unacceptable for formal writing. Slang words and phrases are often colorful exaggerations used to emphasize the speaker's point; they may also be shortened versions of an often-used word or phrase. Examples of American slang from the 1990s include "yuppie" (an acronym for Young Urban Professional), "awesome" (for "excellent"), wired (for "nervous" or "excited"), and "chill out" (for relax).

**slave narrative:** autobiographical accounts of American slave life as told by escaped slaves. These works first appeared during the abolition movement of the 1830s through the 1850s. Olaudah Equiano's *The Interesting Narrative of Olaudah Equiano, or Gustavus Vassa, The African* and Harriet Ann Jacobs's *Incidents in the Life of a Slave Girl* are examples of the slave narrative.

**social realism:** see *socialist realism*

**socialist realism:** the Socialist Realism school of literary theory was proposed by Maxim Gorky and established as a dogma by the first Soviet Congress of Writers. It demanded adherence to a communist worldview in works of literature. Its doctrines required an objective viewpoint comprehensible to the working classes and themes of social struggle featuring strong proletarian heroes. A successful work of socialist realism is Nikolay Ostrovsky's *Kak zakalyalas stal* (*How the Steel Was Tempered*).

**stereotype:** a stereotype was originally the name for a duplication made during the printing process; this led to its modern definition as a person or thing that is (or is assumed to be) the same as all others of its type. Common stereotypical characters include the absent-minded professor, the nagging wife, the troublemaking teenager, and the kindhearted grandmother.

**stream of consciousness:** a narrative technique for rendering the inward experience of a character. This technique is designed to give the impression of an ever-changing series of thoughts, emotions, images, and memories in the spontaneous and seemingly illogical order that they occur in life. The textbook example of stream of consciousness is the last section of James Joyce's *Ulysses*.

**structuralism:** a twentieth-century movement in literary criticism that examines how literary texts arrive at their meanings, rather than the meanings themselves. There are two major types of structuralist analysis: one examines the way patterns of linguistic structures unify a specific text and emphasize certain elements of that text, and the other interprets the way literary forms and conventions affect the meaning of language itself. Prominent structuralists include Michel Foucault, Roman Jakobson, and Roland Barthes.

**structure:** the form taken by a piece of literature. The structure may be made obvious for ease of understanding, as in nonfiction works, or may obscured for artistic purposes, as in some poetry or seemingly "unstructured" prose. Examples of common literary structures include the plot of a narrative, the acts and scenes of a drama, and such poetic forms as the Shakespearean sonnet and the Pindaric ode.

***sturm und drang*:** a German term meaning "storm and stress." It refers to a German literary movement of the 1770s and 1780s that reacted against the order and rationalism of the enlightenment, focusing instead on the intense experience of extraordinary individuals. Highly romantic, works of this movement, such as Johann Wolfgang von Goethe's *Gotz von Berlichingen,* are typified by realism, rebelliousness, and intense emotionalism.

**style:** a writer's distinctive manner of arranging words to suit his or her ideas and purpose in writing. The unique imprint of the author's personality upon his or her writing, style is the product of an author's way of arranging ideas and his or her use of diction, different sentence structures, rhythm, figures of speech, rhetorical principles, and other elements of composition. Styles may be classified according to period (Metaphysical, Augustan, Georgian), individual authors (Chaucerian, Miltonic, Jamesian), level (grand, middle, low, plain), or language (scientific, expository, poetic, journalistic).

**subject:** the person, event, or theme at the center of a work of literature. A work may have one or more subjects of each type, with shorter works tending to have fewer and longer works tending to have more. The subjects of James Baldwin's novel *Go Tell It on the Mountain* include the themes of father-son relationships, religious conversion, black life, and sexuality. The subjects of Anne Frank's *Diary of a Young Girl* include Anne and her family members as well as World War II, the Holocaust, and the themes of war, isolation, injustice, and racism.

**subjectivity:** writing that expresses the author's personal feelings about his subject, and which may or may not include factual information about the subject. Subjectivity is demonstrated in James Joyce's *Portrait of the Artist as a Young Man,* Samuel Butler's *The Way of All Flesh,* and Thomas Wolfe's *Look Homeward, Angel.*

**subplot:** a secondary story in a narrative. A subplot may serve as a motivating or complicating force for the main plot of the work, or it may provide emphasis for, or relief from, the main plot. The conflict between the Capulets and the Montagues in William Shakespeare's *Romeo and Juliet* is an example of a subplot.

**surrealism:** a term introduced to criticism by Guillaume Apollinaire and later adopted by Andre Breton. It refers to a French literary and artistic movement founded in the 1920s. The Surrealists sought to express unconscious thoughts and feelings in their works. The best-known technique used for achieving this aim was automatic writing—transcriptions of spontaneous outpourings from the unconscious. The Surrealists proposed to unify the contrary levels of conscious and unconscious, dream and reality, objectivity and subjectivity into a new level of "super-realism." Surrealism can be found in the poetry of Paul Eluard, Pierre Reverdy, and Louis Aragon, among others.

**suspense:** a literary device in which the author maintains the audience's attention through the buildup of events, the outcome of which will soon be revealed. Suspense in William Shakespeare's *Hamlet* is sustained throughout by the question of whether or not the Prince will achieve what he has been instructed to do and of what he intends to do.

**syllogism:** a method of presenting a logical argument. In its most basic form, the syllogism consists of a major premise, a minor premise, and a conclusion. An example of a syllogism is: Major premise: When it snows, the streets get wet. Minor premise: It is snowing. Conclusion: The streets are wet.

**symbol:** something that suggests or stands for something else without losing its original identity. In literature, symbols combine their literal meaning with the suggestion of an abstract concept. Literary symbols are of two types: those that carry complex associations of meaning no matter what their contexts, and those that derive their suggestive meaning from their functions in specific literary works. Examples of symbols are sunshine suggesting happiness, rain suggesting sorrow, and storm clouds suggesting despair.

**symbolism:** this term has two widely accepted meanings. In historical criticism, it denotes an early modernist literary movement initiated in France during the nineteenth century that reacted against the prevailing standards of realism. Writers in this movement aimed to evoke, indirectly and symbolically, an order of being beyond the material world of the five senses. Poetic expression of personal emotion figured strongly in the movement, typically by means of a private set of symbols uniquely identifiable with the individual poet. The principal aim of the Symbolists was to express in words the highly complex feelings that grew out of everyday contact with the world. In a broader sense, the term "symbolism" refers to the use of one object to represent another. Early members of the Symbolist movement included the French authors Charles Baudelaire and Arthur Rimbaud; William Butler Yeats, James Joyce, and T. S. Eliot were influenced as the movement moved to Ireland, England, and the United States. Examples of the concept of symbolism include a flag that stands for a nation or movement, or an empty cupboard used to suggest hopelessness, poverty, and despair.

**symbolist:** see *symbolism*

**symbolist movement:** see *symbolism*

## T

**tale:** a story told by a narrator with a simple plot and little character development. Tales are usually relatively short and often carry a simple message. Examples of tales can be found in the work of Rudyard Kipling, Somerset Maugham, Saki, Anton Chekhov, Guy de Maupassant, and Armistead Maupin.

**tall tale:** a humorous tale told in a straightforward, credible tone but relating absolutely impossible events or feats of the characters.

Such tales were commonly told of frontier adventures during the settlement of the west in the United States. Tall tales have been spun around such legendary heroes as Mike Fink, Paul Bunyan, Davy Crockett, Johnny Appleseed, and Captain Stormalong as well as the real-life William F. Cody and Annie Oakley. Literary use of tall tales can be found in Washington Irving's *History of New York,* Mark Twain's *Life on the Mississippi,* and in the German R. F. Raspe's *Baron Munchausen's Narratives of His Marvellous Travels and Campaigns in Russia.*

**textual criticism:** a branch of literary criticism that seeks to establish the authoritative text of a literary work. Textual critics typically compare all known manuscripts or printings of a single work in order to assess the meanings of differences and revisions. This procedure allows them to arrive at a definitive version that (supposedly) corresponds to the author's original intention. Textual criticism was applied during the Renaissance to salvage the classical texts of Greece and Rome, and modern works have been studied, for instance, to undo deliberate correction or censorship, as in the case of novels by Stephen Crane and Theodore Dreiser.

**theme:** the main point of a work of literature. The term is used interchangeably with thesis. The theme of William Shakespeare's *Othello*—jealousy—is a common one.

**thesis:** a thesis is both an essay and the point argued in the essay. Thesis novels and thesis plays share the quality of containing a thesis which is supported through the action of the story. A master's thesis and a doctoral dissertation are two theses required of graduate students.

**thesis novel:** see *thesis*

**third person:** see *point of view*

**tone:** the author's attitude toward his or her audience may be deduced from the tone of the work. A formal tone may create distance or convey politeness, while an informal tone may encourage a friendly, intimate, or intrusive feeling in the reader. The author's attitude toward his or her subject matter may also be deduced from the tone of the words he or she uses in discussing it. The tone of John F. Kennedy's speech which included the appeal to "ask not what your country

can do for you" was intended to instill feelings of camaraderie and national pride in listeners.

**transcendentalism:** an American philosophical and religious movement, based in New England from around 1835 until the Civil War. Transcendentalism was a form of American romanticism that had its roots abroad in the works of Thomas Carlyle, Samuel Coleridge, and Johann Wolfgang von Goethe. The Transcendentalists stressed the importance of intuition and subjective experience in communication with God. They rejected religious dogma and texts in favor of mysticism and scientific naturalism. They pursued truths that lie beyond the "colorless" realms perceived by reason and the senses and were active social reformers in public education, women's rights, and the abolition of slavery. Prominent members of the group include Ralph Waldo Emerson and Henry David Thoreau.

**trickster:** a character or figure common in Native American and African literature who uses his ingenuity to defeat enemies and escape difficult situations. Tricksters are most often animals, such as the spider, hare, or coyote, although they may take the form of humans as well. Examples of trickster tales include Thomas King's *A Coyote Columbus Story,* Ashley F. Bryan's *The Dancing Granny* and Ishmael Reed's *The Last Days of Louisiana Red.*

# U

**understatement:** see *irony*

**urban realism:** a branch of realist writing that attempts to accurately reflect the often harsh facts of modern urban existence. Some works by Stephen Crane, Theodore Dreiser, Charles Dickens, Fyodor Dostoyevsky, Emile Zola, Abraham Cahan, and Henry Fuller feature urban realism. Modern examples include Claude Brown's *Manchild in the Promised Land* and Ron Milner's *What the Wine Sellers Buy.*

**utopia:** a fictional perfect place, such as "paradise" or "heaven." Early literary utopias were included in Plato's *Republic* and Sir Thomas More's *Utopia,* while more modern utopias can be found in Samuel Butler's *Erewhon,* Theodor Herzka's *A Visit to Freeland,* and H. G. Wells' *A Modern Utopia.*

**utopian:** see *utopia*

**utopianism:** see *utopia*

## V

**verisimilitude:** literally, the appearance of truth. In literary criticism, the term refers to aspects of a work of literature that seem true to the reader. Verisimilitude is achieved in the work of Honore de Balzac, Gustave Flaubert, and Henry James, among other late nineteenth-century realist writers.

**Victorian:** refers broadly to the reign of Queen Victoria of England (1837-1901) and to anything with qualities typical of that era. For example, the qualities of smug narrowmindedness, bourgeois materialism, faith in social progress, and priggish morality are often considered Victorian. This stereotype is contradicted by such dramatic intellectual developments as the theories of Charles Darwin, Karl Marx, and Sigmund Freud (which stirred strong debates in England) and the critical attitudes of serious Victorian writers like Charles Dickens and George Eliot. In literature, the Victorian Period was the great age of the English novel, and the latter part of the era saw the rise of movements such as decadence and symbolism. Works of Victorian literature include the poetry of Robert Browning and Alfred, Lord Tennyson, the criticism of Matthew Arnold and John Ruskin, and the novels of Emily Bronte, William Makepeace Thackeray, and Thomas Hardy.

**Victorian age:** see *Victorian*

**Victorian period:** see *Victorian*

## W

**weltanschauung:** a German term referring to a person's worldview or philosophy. Examples of *weltanschauung* include Thomas Hardy's view of the human being as the victim of fate, destiny, or impersonal forces and circumstances, and the disillusioned and laconic cynicism expressed by such poets of the 1930s as W. H. Auden, Sir Stephen Spender, and Sir William Empson.

**weltschmerz:** a German term meaning "world pain." It describes a sense of anguish about the nature of existence, usually associated with a melancholy, pessimistic attitude. *Weltschmerz* was expressed in England by George Gordon, Lord Byron in his *Manfred* and *Childe Harold's Pilgrimage,* in France by Viscount de Chateaubriand, Alfred de Vigny, and Alfred de Musset, in Russia by Aleksandr Pushkin and Mikhail Lermontov, in Poland by Juliusz Slowacki, and in America by Nathaniel Hawthorne.

## Z

**zeitgeist:** a German term meaning "spirit of the time." It refers to the moral and intellectual trends of a given era. Examples of *zeitgeist* include the preoccupation with the more morbid aspects of dying and death in some Jacobean literature, especially in the works of dramatists Cyril Tourneur and John Webster, and the decadence of the French Symbolists.

# Author/Title Index

# Nationality/Ethnicity Index

## Native American

Momoday, N., Scott
  *House Made of Dawn,* 1: 277–290
Neihardt, John G.
  *Black Elk Speaks,* 1: 110–124

## Spanish

de Vaca, Alvar Núñez Cabeza
  *Chronicle of the Narvãez*
  *Expedition,* 1: 153–167